My Prayer Book

His Holiness (Pope Pius XI) wishes that these volumes, which assuredly will promote the spiritual life, may receive an ever-increasing welcome in all the Christian families of your great country.

(From letter to Father Lasance written at the Pope's direction, May 10, 1927.)

This is one of Father Lasance's books to which His Holiness refers in the above letter.

Jesus, Mary, and Joseph, I give you my heart
and my soul.--100 days' indulgence.   Pius VII.

My Prayer=Book

Happiness in Goodness

Reflections, Counsels, Prayers, and Devotions

BY

Rev. F. X. Lasance

"Thou shalt love the Lord thy God with thy whole heart, and with thy whole soul, and with thy whole mind, and with thy whole strength. This is the first commandment. And the second is like to it, thou shalt love thy neighbor as thyself. There is no other commandment greater than these."— MARK xii. 30, 31.

NEW YORK, CINCINNATI, CHICAGO

Benziger Brothers

Printers to the Holy Apostolic See

Nihil Obstat.

REMY LAFORT,

Censor Librorum.

Imprimatur.

✠ JOHN M. FARLEY,

Archbishop of New York.

NEW YORK, September 19, 1908.

Joy in the Lord

"REJOICE in the Lord always: again, I say, rejoice" (*Philipp.* iv. 4).

"My peace I give unto you. Let not your heart be troubled, nor let it be afraid. You believe in God, believe also in Me. These things I have spoken to you, that My joy may be in you. In the world you shall have distress: but have confidence, I have overcome the world." — *St. John:* Christ's Discourse at the Last Supper.

"Have a good heart, it is I, fear ye not" (Our Lord — *Mark* vi. 50).

Self-Conquest — Self-Control

"THE patient man is better than the valiant: and he that ruleth his spirit than he that taketh cities" (*Prov.* xvi. 32).

"And He (Christ) said to all: If any man will come after Me, let him deny himself, and take up his cross daily, and follow Me" (*Luke* ix. 23).

"There is no peace to the wicked, saith the Lord" (*Is.* xlviii. 22).

"Their feet run to evil; . . . they have not known the way of peace" (*Is.* lix. 7–8).

3

"The work of justice shall be peace" (*Is.* xxxii. 17).

"Glory and honor and peace to every one that worketh good" (*Rom.* ii. 10).

"If you live according to the flesh, you shall die: but if by the Spirit you mortify the deeds of the flesh, you shall live" (*Rom.* viii. 13).

"The fruit of the Spirit is charity, joy, peace, patience, benignity, goodness, longanimity, mildness, faith, modesty, continency, chastity. They that are Christ's have crucified their flesh with the vices and concupiscences. If we live in the Spirit, let us also walk in the Spirit" (*Gal.* vi. 22, 25).

"He who reigns within himself and rules passions, desires, and fears, is more than a king." — MILTON.

"There never did and never will exist anything permanently noble and excellent in a character which was a stranger to the exercise of resolute self-denial." — SIR WALTER SCOTT.

"He is most powerful who has himself in his power." — SENECA.

———◆———

"ENTBEHREN sollst du! sollst entbehren!
      Das ist der ewige Gesang
   Der jedem an die Ohren klingt,
      Den unser ganzes Leben lang
   Uns heiser jede Stunde singt." — GOETHE.

The Beatitudes

1. "**B**LESSED are the poor in spirit; for theirs is the kingdom of heaven."

2. "Blessed are the meek; for they shall possess the land."

3. "Blessed are they that mourn; for they shall be comforted."

4. "Blessed are they that hunger and thirst after justice; for they shall have their fill."

5. "Blessed are the merciful; for they shall obtain mercy."

6. "Blessed are the clean of heart; for they shall see God."

7. "Blessed are the peacemakers; for they shall be called the children of God."

8. "Blessed are they that suffer persecution for justice sake; for theirs is the kingdom of heaven."

"Blessed are ye when they shall revile you, and persecute you, and speak all that is evil against you, untruly, for My sake:

"Be glad and rejoice; for your reward is very great in heaven" (*Matt.* v. 3–12).

5

Introduction

MY PRAYER-BOOK is more than a book of *prayers* and *devotions;* the sub-title, *Happiness in Goodness,* indicates that it is also a book of *counsels* and *reflections* on the pursuit of happiness, not only with a view to the eternal life, but also with regard to our present existence *"in hac lacrymarum valle."*

"All desire peace," says "The Following of Christ," "but all care not for those things which appertain to true peace."

We may say the same thing with regard to happiness. All desire it, but many do not attain to it because they seek it where it can not be found. The one thing necessary to true and lasting happiness is the state of sanctifying grace — the love of God — union with God, in whom alone man's heart can find rest. *"Rejoice in the Lord, always!"* Seek happiness in goodness, in virtue; in loving God above all things and in loving all things in God; in loving your neighbor; in doing good to others for the love of Jesus Christ — that is the key-note — the dominant note of this book. It is an exponent of the greatest thing in the world.

6

Charity; it is a preacher, an advocate of *Christian* philanthropy, of *true* altruism, of which a well-known writer says:[1]

"We hear a great deal of altruism, as it is called, nowadays — the doctrine, in other words, of living entirely for others. This is man's true happiness and peace, his only good — making others happy. And we at once ask, what is this happiness which we are to secure for others — the same kind as our own, or a different kind? Surely the same kind, for we are all men of like nature, more or less. It seems, then, as far as we can catch the idea, that I am to seek true happiness in making others seek their true happiness, making yet others seek their true happiness, and so on without end; and we never learn what that happiness, personal and independent, consists in. We are told that our modern moralists have improved very much on Christianity; that they have interpreted it to itself; that they have discovered the unknown, or at least only half-known, secret of unselfishness, of true benevolence and philanthropy, which Christ was only groping after according to old-world lights. They would take, as an extreme embodiment of a certain egoistic spirit which they deplore in Christianity, St. Simon Stylites, standing year after year on his pillar in the desert, isolated almost ostentatiously (if it be not a contradiction) from all intercourse with his fellow men; intent wholly on his own interior spiritual perfection and on

[1] Vide: Another Handful of Myrrh.

communion with God; living, it would seem, purely and entirely for himself, hoping for nothing but his own future reward, fearing nothing but his own future hurt.

"What is the true meaning of these words, 'Charity,' or Love, 'seeketh not her own'?

"When we examine a tree or a flower, we see that the root seems to be subservient to the stalk or trunk, the trunk and branches to be for the sake of the leaves, the leaves for the sake of the flower, the flower for the sake of the fruit, the fruit for the sake of the seed, the seed for the sake of the future plant, and so on; and we wonder which is the principal part, if there be any, that exists for its own sake, and not for the sake of something else. The truth is, no doubt, that each exists for its own sake *and* for the sake of the whole and of its fellow parts. It struggles for and seeks its own advantage directly and before all, and, by following this tendency of its own nature, it eventually *profits the rest*, whereas the greatest injury it could inflict on the other parts would be to suffer itself to decay and perish. We, collectively, are the Body of Christ and members in particular, and this fact is the basis of the doctrine of Christian charity. '*Lie not one to another,*' '*defraud not one another,*' says St. Paul, '*because we are fellow members of one body.*' Each member exists for its own sake *and also* for the sake of the whole body, the head and the fellow members. Each member tends directly to its own well-being and advantage, *and thereby* to the profit of all the rest, each by being what it should be, by doing what it should do — in a word, by its own perfection, perfects the whole. So, too, by being and acting otherwise than it should, it injures itself and it injures the whole. Where brain or eye is diseased it ceases to live for the whole body, to be serviceable and helpful; it lives for itself, nay rather, it lives at the expense of the rest, *seeking its own.* It begins to seek its own exclusively, it ceases to co-operate with the rest, to bear their burdens, to sympathize with their joys and sorrows — it becomes selfish.

"Here, then, is the true altruism, the Christian conception of charity — to seek ourselves, our own things, for the sake of others; to seek others by seeking ourselves after His pattern who said: *Propter eos sanctifico meipsum* — 'For their sakes I sanctify Myself.' If we ourselves are what we ought to be, we shall be to others what we ought to be. And as the higher and more complex structures of the body are more widely and eminently useful to the rest, so those who are themselves nearer to the perfection of our blessed Lord, the Head and Saviour of the Body, are so far nearer to Him in the depth and extent of their utility toward others. He, as the Head and Soul of the Body, is most intimate in His relation to the very least of the subject members; and the measure of His love for them is the measure of His own perfection and dignity — the measure, moreover, of that most just love which He bears toward Himself. For, quibble about it as we will, we only love others so far as we can recognize them as ours, as belonging to or connected with us in some way. Thus it follows that our love for others is only an extension or overflow of our laudable self-love. Who then is the selfish man? He whose self-love is perverted and feeble, and does not overflow, reach out, extend itself, and draw all things into itself; whose first thought thenceforth is to sacrifice others to himself, and who corrects it only as an afterthought. Who is the unselfish man? He who does not, as the other, view himself falsely as an isolated unit, but sees how all others pertain to him, are *his* in some sense, are fellow members of greater or less import, and who therefore finds his own happiness in the happiness of others; whose first thought is to sacrifice himself, and who corrects it, if necessary, only on an afterthought. He whose self-love is true and strong, and rises up high and overflows and diffuses itself to whatever in any way pertains to him; who, like God, loves all things both great and small, just because all things belong to Him, and because He loves Himself with an infinite and everlasting love.

"True altruism or charity circles out from self, first, to our God, and then to His creatures, who, through Him, are variously bound to us, in due order. And the greater we are in ourselves, the more godlike, the intenser our rightful self-love, so much the farther shall we stretch out beyond ourselves with an all-enfolding charity. For

God's love has well been described as a sphere whose center is everywhere, whose circumference is at infinity or nowhere. The same truth is aptly illustrated by Our Lord's metaphor for divine charity, which compares it to a fire: 'I came to send fire upon the earth, and what will I but that it be kindled;' 'Let your light shine before men;' 'Let your lamps be burning in your hands.'

"It is by keeping alive and fostering in our own hearts the fire of God's love, the light of God's truth, that we shall most effectually diffuse light and warmth to others. Spontaneously, and without conscious effort on our part, the light will shine from us, and the warmth radiate from us; we shall make ourselves felt without knowing it; *'Let not thy left hand know what thy right hand doth.'*

"St. Paul knows nothing of the altruism which saves others and cares not to save itself; which seeks for others a vague, undefined happiness, unknown, unsought for, unvalued by itself; which throws itself into labors involving patience, self-conquest, prudence, fortitude, temperance, and all virtues, before these virtues have been rooted, grown, and matured in itself.

"*Seeketh not her own.*" To seek the good of others is therefore the outcome, the fruit, the proof, the manifestation of charity, but it is not the substance. Charity is the personal love of God, our Lord, the wedding-garment of the soul, the treasure of great price which each must seek long and diligently for himself, and finds and heaps up more and more, that he may give to others, of his abundance abundantly, the fire of divine love, which kindles and enlightens the hearts of others the more brightly it burns in our own. 'Now this I pray,' says St. Paul, 'that your charity may abound more and more in all knowledge and discernment, so that you may approve the things which are excellent;' for to love God is an art — the one work of our lives. It is only God's Holy Spirit 'who diffuses the charity of Christ in our hearts,' who can teach us and train us. *Da nobis in eodem Spiritu recta sapere* — 'Grant us by that same Spirit to have a refined taste and relish for what is right.' This is our direct work, to perfect ourselves in the love of God; the rest will follow."

Baxter, in his "Meditations," commenting on the words, "*You are the light of the world*" (*Matt.* v. 14) says:

"It is a property of light to warm and enlighten. Examine yourself how you perform your duty, and seize every opportunity of being beneficial to your neighbors, particularly by 'letting the light of your example shine before them.' All instruction is cold, unless it be accompanied and enforced by example.

"Christ 'was the true light, which enlighteneth every man, that cometh into this world' (*John* i. 9). He communicated a divine system of doctrine to mankind, illustrated and enforced it by His example, and gives His followers grace to profit by it, to glorify Him, and secure the end of their creation. When light passes through loathsome or infected places, it emerges as pure and uncontaminated as it entered; thus Christ and His apostolic followers, although they converse and treat with sinners, do not partake of their uncleanness. Hence, no one whose duty it is to reclaim sinners ought to fear the danger of corruption, if he act in obedience to God, and follow the example of Christ and His apostles.

"Christ says, that no one puts a light under a bushel. Thus He reprehends those who do not employ the talents which they have received in enlightening their neighbors, but hide their light from pusillanimity or sloth. They ought to imitate the stars at their creation, of which Baruch speaks in the sublimest strains. 'They were called by the Almighty,' says the prophet, 'and they said, here we are, and with cheerfulness they have shined forth to Him, that made them'" (*Bar.* iii. 25).

And again in reference to the words: "*You are the salt of the earth*" (*Matt.* v. 13), the same writer says:

"As salt preserves from corruption and putrefaction, so is it the part of all apostolical men to preserve souls from the corruption of sin, and to render the exercise of virtue palatable and agreeable to them. These men, then, ought to be pure and refined from all the dross and alloy of earthly passion by the influence of divine charity, in order that they may be such themselves as they wish to make others."

In thought and tendency, MY PRAYER-BOOK purposes to be the embodiment of Christian optimism and altruism; the exponent of all that is helpful and invigorating in the Christian life — of whatever is calculated to promote man's temporal and eternal welfare; it lays stress upon the fact that while the short cut to happiness is by way of self-renunciation, self-denial, self-conquest, self-control, in the following of Christ, nevertheless good cheer, heartfelt joy, and genuine happiness, far from being incompatible with the practice of religion, and of the Catholic faith in particular, are really the concomitant or rather the outgrowth and efflorescence of a virtuous Christian life.

"Virtue only makes our bliss below." — POPE.

" 'Tis virtue makes the bliss where'er we dwell."
— COLLINS.

If Christianity sends men to learn the solemn lessons of the grave and asks them to keep in view their eternal destiny and the salvation of their priceless immortal souls, this need not make them gloomy and morose, this should not and does not make them sad and depressed; it tends, in fact, to keep them in that state in which they will be able to "*rejoice in the Lord always,*" to be glad and cheerful and hopeful and helpful also to others, no matter what may be their outward circumstances. The peace of God is with them always; interior joy is theirs both in adversity and prosperity.

Religion does not take the sunshine out of a man's life. The true follower of Christ has a blessing on his lips, a song in his mouth, amid sorrows and trials. Faith — Christianity — does, indeed, make a man serious and thoughtful, but it does not rob him of the real pleasures of life, nor does it paralyze his energies, but it directs them aright. No more joyous hearts can be found anywhere in the world than the hearts of *Religious* — the hearts that beat behind the grilles of the cloister. Religious not only lead good Christian lives, but also practise heroic penance, austere mortification, complete self-renunciation; yet their hearts overflow with joy, they abound with mirth and innocent glee such as is quite unknown to the butterflies of "society," to those who seek their happiness in the gratification of self in the treasures and pleasures of the world.

A devout Christian life certainly implies self-denial and self-control.

Good is never done except at the expense of those who do it. — CARDINAL NEWMAN.

It seldom happens that one can do good without any trouble. — ST. VINCENT DE PAUL.

> "Life is all a void,
> On selfish thoughts alone employed."
> — JANE TAYLOR.

> "Self-reverence, self-knowledge, self-control, —
> These three alone lead life to sovereign power."
> — TENNYSON.

To be a Christian means to follow Christ. And Christ Himself has said: "If any man will come after Me, let him deny himself, take up his cross, and follow Me."

Spiritual joy — joy in the Lord — is the portion of those who are living in the state of grace, who love God and are faithful in the observances of His commandments. Fidelity in this respect, however, implies self-restraint and self-denial.

Alexander conquered the world, but he did not conquer himself. In a fit of intemperance he slew his best friend.

Napoleon made himself master of all Europe and played with its kingdoms; but he failed to master himself. Yielding to violent anger, he acted at times like a madman, who knows not what he does. "*The patient man is better than the valiant, and he that ruleth his spirit better than he that taketh cities*" (*Prov.* xvi. 32).

MY PRAYER-BOOK aims to emphasize the fact that while being good we can enjoy in many ways this beautiful world which God has made for us, and which is truly a mirror of His own beauty and perfections; it aims to inculcate the lessons of nature; how all its beauties reflect the greatness and loving kindness of the Creator and should draw us to love our good God with a grateful heart.

"*The heavens show forth the glory of God, and the firmament declareth the work of His hands*" (*Ps.* xviii. 1).

"And this our life, exempt from public haunt,
  Finds tongues in trees, books in the running brooks,
  Sermons in stones, and good in everything."
                    — *As You Like It.*

The Royal Psalmist says: "I remembered the days of old, I meditated on all Thy works: I mused upon the works of Thy hands. Cause me to hear Thy mercy in the morning; for in Thee have I hoped. Make the way known to me wherein I should walk; for I have lifted up my soul to Thee" (*Ps.* cxlii. 5, 8).

As we read in "The Crown of Jesus": "We can meditate when we sit in the house; when we walk on the way; when we lie down; when we rise up. We can meditate by considering all earthly things as types of holy truths. In trees, the wood of the cross, our Redemption; in dust, our origin. In the sky, heaven, our reward. In the stars, the heavenly mansions of those who by their glorious deeds have brought many to justice. In the moon, the Queen of heaven. In the sun, the Son of justice. In the sea, the ocean of eternity. In the waves, the progress of time. In the seashore covered with the waters, our mortality. In the footmarks on the sand erased, fame. In the sudden darkness, mortal sin. In the bright light, God's grace. In the gentle wind, the breath of the Holy Ghost the Comforter. In bread, the Blessed Sacrament, the true Bread of life. In water, the cleansing grace of Baptism. In oil, the anointing of the young and of the sick. In the sound of the clock, the irrevocable progress of time.

"We can meditate by adoring the presence of God all around us, as we walk in the midst of Him, or as causing by His presence in each object we behold, its continued existence and its qualities of good."

St. Francis of Sales says: "As they that are enamored with human and natural love have almost always their thoughts fixed on the person beloved, their heart full of affection toward her, their mouth filled with her praise, and when their beloved is absent they lose no occasion to testify their passion by letters, and on every tree they meet they engrave the name of their beloved; — even so, such as love God can never cease to think upon Him, they breathe only for Him, they aspire only to Him, and speak only of Him, and, if it were possible, they would grave the sacred name of Our Lord Jesus on the breasts of all men in the world."

And all creatures invite them to this, each one in its kind declaring to them the praises of their Beloved; and, as St. Augustine says, "all things in this world speak to us in a kind of dumb language, yet intelligible enough, in praise of our Love; all things provoke us to good thoughts, from whence afterward arise many motions and aspirations of our soul to God."

St. Francis of Assisi, for instance, seeing a sheep all alone amidst a herd of goats, remarked to his companions: "Observe the poor little sheep, how mild it is among the goats; our blessed Lord walked as meekly and humbly among the *Pharisees*." At another time, seeing a lambkin devoured by a hog, he said: "Ah! little lamb, how lively dost thou represent my Saviour's death." St. Basil the Great says of the rose among its thorns: "The most pleasant things in this world are mingled with sorrow. The rose is a fair flower, but it puts me in mind of sin, for which the earth has been condemned to bring forth thorns."

My Prayer-Book aims to point out the brighter side of life — the silver lining to the cloud o'erhead — the sunshine that follows the rain — the sweet little wildflowers that grow by the wayside amid thorns and briers.

"Sweet are the uses of adversity
Which like the toad, ugly and venomous,
Wears yet a precious jewel in his head."
— *As You Like It.*

"The good are better made by ill,
As odors crushed are sweeter still."
— Rogers, *Jacquelin.*

"As aromatic plants bestow
No spicy fragrance while they grow,
But crushed or trodden to the ground
Diffuse their balmy sweets around."
— Goldsmith, *The Captivity.*

The Royal Psalmist voices the sentiments of a deeply religious soul in many expressions of grateful praise to God, of joy in the Lord, and of absolute confidence in Divine Providence. Religion gladdens the heart by inspiring trust in the goodness and mercy of God.

"Thou, O Lord, art my protector and the lifter up of my head" (*Ps.* iii. 4).

"Thou hast given gladness in my heart" (*Ps.* iv. 7).

"Let all them be glad that hope in Thee; they shall rejoice forever, and Thou shalt dwell in them" (*Ps.* v. 12).

"I will be glad and rejoice in Thee; I will sing to Thy name, O Thou Most High" (*Ps.* ix. 3).

"Thou hast made known to me the ways of life; Thou shalt fill me with joys with Thy countenance; at Thy right hand are delights even to the end" (*Ps.* xv. 11). "I will love Thee, O Lord, my strength. The Lord is my refuge and my deliverer. My God is my helper and in Him will I put my trust" (*Ps.* xvii. 3).

"Though I should walk in the midst of the shadow of death, I will fear no evils, for Thou art with me. Thy rod and Thy staff they have comforted me" (*Ps.* xxii. 4).

"Rejoice to God our Helper" (*Ps.* lxxx. 2). "He will overshadow Thee with His shoulders, and under His wings thou shalt trust" (*Ps.* xc. 4).

MY PRAYER-BOOK aims to lay stress upon the advantages of being sweet-spirited and sunny-tempered, of diffusing around us an atmosphere of good cheer, of being ever ready in a generous way, in an unselfish manner, to hasten to the relief or comfort of others in the hour of their sorrow and trial, mindful of the Apostle's admonition: "Bear ye one another's burdens and so you shall fulfil the law of Christ" (*Gal.* vi. 2), and in imitation of the divine Master Himself, who said to His disciples: "You call Me Master, and Lord, and you say well; for so I am. If, then, I being your Lord and Master have washed your feet, you also ought to wash one another's feet; for I have given you an example, that as I have done, so you do also" (*John* xiii. 13–15); and again: "He that is the greatest among you shall be your servant; he that shall humble himself shall be exalted" (*Matt.* xxiii. 11, 12). As Christians it behooves us to follow Christ, who "did all things well," who had "compassion on the multitude," who "went about doing good to all," who "hath borne our infirmities" and "carried our sorrows," who sacrificed Himself for all, even to the death of the Cross, thus manifesting the greatest love; for "greater love than this no man hath, that a man lay down his life for his friends" (*John* xv. 13).

Our thought in compiling MY PRAYER-BOOK was this: We will try by means of this little work to send forth some notes of gladness into the world amid the sounds of discord, the cries of pain, the sobbings of sorrow and the wailings of overburdened hearts; we will try to be helpful to our brethren in the pursuit and attainment of real and lasting happiness, and in these our humble efforts we shall hope and pray for a blessing from *Him*, whose "*goodness and kindness hath appeared to all men,*" whose "*lips are as lilies dropping choice myrrh,*" whose ministry of mercy and good cheer extended to the greatest sinners, and of whom Isaias the Prophet foretold: "*The bruised reed He shall not break and smoking flax He shall not extinguish.*"

One word more, with regard to the various *Methods of Assisting at Mass.* We call the reader's particular attention to the explanatory *Note* which precedes the first set of *Prayers for Mass.* Our purpose in the arrangement of these *Mass Devotions* was to lead pious souls to the use of meditation while assisting at the Holy Sacrifice, that is, to combine mental prayer with vocal prayer. Another object was, to popularize the habit of making use of *indulgenced* ejaculations, especially for the benefit of the poor souls in purgatory. All the indulgenced prayers in this book are found in the "New Raccolta," except those of recent date, which have not yet been incorporated in that work.

With the most profound sentiments of love and devotion to the Holy Family, we humbly and reverently dedicate this little volume to Jesus, Mary, and Joseph, to the end that it may, under their patronage, be a means of glorifying God and sanctifying souls.

F. X. LASANCE.

CINCINNATI, OHIO,
  May 24, 1908.

Contents

PART I

Reflections

PART II

Prayers and Devotions

Morning Prayer

Evening Prayer

Prayers During the Day

The Holy Sacrifice of the Mass

𝔇𝔢𝔟𝔬𝔱𝔦𝔬𝔫𝔰 𝔣𝔬𝔯 ℭ𝔬𝔫𝔣𝔢𝔰𝔰𝔦𝔬𝔫

𝔇𝔢𝔟𝔬𝔱𝔦𝔬𝔫𝔰 𝔣𝔬𝔯 ℭ𝔬𝔪𝔪𝔲𝔫𝔦𝔬𝔫

𝔅𝔢𝔫𝔢𝔡𝔦𝔠𝔱𝔦𝔬𝔫 𝔬𝔣 𝔱𝔥𝔢 𝔅𝔩𝔢𝔰𝔰𝔢𝔡 𝔖𝔞𝔠𝔯𝔞𝔪𝔢𝔫𝔱

𝔗𝔥𝔢 𝔖𝔱𝔞𝔱𝔦𝔬𝔫𝔰 𝔬𝔣 𝔱𝔥𝔢 ℭ𝔯𝔬𝔰𝔰

Litanies

General Devotions

Table of Movable Feasts

Year of Our Lord.	Ash-Wednesday.	Easter Sunday.	Ascension Day.	Whit-sunday.	Corpus Christi.	First Sunday of Advent.
1923	Feb. 14	Apr. 1	May 10	May 20	May 31	Dec. 2
1924	Mar. 5	Apr. 20	May 29	June 8	June 19	Nov. 30
1925	Feb. 25	Apr. 12	May 21	May 31	June 11	Nov. 29
1926	Feb. 17	Apr. 4	May 13	May 23	June 3	Nov. 28
1927	Mar. 2	Apr. 17	May 26	June 5	June 16	Nov. 27
1928	Feb. 22	Apr. 8	May 17	May 27	June 7	Dec. 2
1929	Feb. 13	Mar. 31	May 9	May 19	May 30	Dec. 1
1930	Mar. 5	Apr. 20	May 29	June 8	June 19	Nov. 30
1931	Feb. 18	Apr. 5	May 14	May 24	June 4	Nov. 29
1932	Feb. 10	Mar. 27	May 5	May 15	May 26	Nov. 27
1933	Mar. 1	Apr. 16	May 25	June 4	June 15	Dec. 3
1934	Feb. 14	Apr. 1	May 10	May 20	May 31	Dec. 2
1935	Mar. 6	Apr. 21	May 30	June 9	June 20	Dec. 1
1936	Feb. 26	Apr. 12	May 21	May 31	June 11	Nov. 29
1937	Feb. 10	Mar. 28	May 6	May 16	May 27	Nov. 28
1938	Mar. 2	Apr. 17	May 26	June 5	June 16	Nov. 27
1939	Feb. 22	Apr. 9	May 18	May 28	June 8	Dec. 3
1940	Feb. 7	Mar. 24	May 2	May 12	May 23	Dec. 1
1941	Feb. 26	Apr. 13	May 22	June 1	June 12	Nov. 30
1942	Feb. 18	Apr. 5	May 14	May 24	June 4	Nov. 29
1943	Mar. 10	Apr. 25	June 3	June 13	June 24	Nov. 28
1944	Feb. 23	Apr. 9	May 18	May 28	June 8	Dec. 3
1945	Feb. 14	Apr. 1	May 10	May 20	May 31	Dec. 2
1946	Mar. 6	Apr. 21	May 30	June 9	June 20	Dec. 1
1947	Feb. 19	Apr. 6	May 15	May 25	June 5	Nov. 30

Holy-Days of Obligation

On which the Faithful are Bound to Hear Mass and to Abstain from Servile Work

Holy-Days of Obligation in United States

All the Sundays of the year.

Jan. 1. The Circumcision.

Ascension Day.

Aug. 15. The Assumption.

Nov. 1. All Saints.

Dec. 8. The Immaculate Conception.

Dec. 25. Christmas Day.

The solemnity of Sts. Peter and Paul is kept on the Sunday next following the feast (June 29).

Holy-Days of Obligation in Canada

All the Sundays of the year.

Jan. 1. The Circumcision.

Jan. 6. The Epiphany.

Ascension Day.

Nov. 1. All Saints.

Dec. 8. The Immaculate Conception.

Dec. 25. Christmas Day.

The Church Law of Abstinence and Fast

1. The Law of Abstinence forbids the use of flesh meat and of the juice thereof (soup, etc.). Eggs, cheese, butter and seasonings of food are permitted. The Law of Fasting forbids more than one full meal a

37

day, but does not forbid a small amount of food in the morning and in the evening.

2. All Catholics seven years old and over are obliged to abstain. All Catholics from the completion of their twenty-first to the beginning of their sixtieth year, unless lawfully excused, are bound to fast.

3. Abstinence alone is prescribed every Friday, unless a holy-day falls thereon. Fasting and abstinence are prescribed in the United States on the Wednesdays and Fridays of Lent and Holy Saturday forenoon (on all other days of Lent fasting alone is prescribed and meat is allowed once a day), the Ember days, viz.: the Wednesday, Friday and Saturday following the first Sunday of Lent, Pentecost or Whitsunday, the 14th of September, and the third Sunday of Advent; the vigils of Pentecost, Assumption, All Saints and Christmas. There is no fast or abstinence if a vigil falls on a Sunday. Whenever meat is permitted, fish may be taken at the same meal. A dispensation is granted to the laboring classes and their families on all days of fast and abstinence except Fridays, Ash Wednesday, Wednesday in Holy Week, Holy Saturday forenoon, and the vigil of Christmas. When any member of such a family lawfully uses this privilege all the other members may avail themselves of it also; but those who fast may not eat meat more than once a day.

PART ONE

REFLECTIONS

1.—The Quest of Happiness

"Thou Shalt Love the Lord Thy God with Thy Whole Heart"

THE human heart craves and seeks unceasingly for happiness. Many find but a small measure of happiness in this life because they lose sight of their eternal destiny — the object of their creation — which is to know God, to love Him, to serve Him, and to be happy with Him. "Thou shalt love the Lord thy God with thy whole heart and thou shalt love thy neighbor as thyself" (*Matt.* xxii. 37, 39). The whole law depends on these two commandments; so Our Lord Himself assures us. The fullest measure of happiness even here on earth is attained by harmonizing one's conduct with the commandments of God, by doing well one's duties to God and man; for this means the possession of a peaceful conscience, a clean heart, a sinless soul; and this is essential to happiness; hence, St. Ignatius prays: "Give me, Lord, only Thy love and Thy grace; with these I shall be rich enough; there is nothing more that I desire." To be in the state of grace — to have God's love — that is essentially necessary to true happiness. "*Si Deus pro nobis, quis contra nos?*" "If God be for us, who is against us?" (*Rom.* viii. 31.) The end of man's creation is to glorify God. But in promoting God's glory we are at the same time promoting our own happiness. Ergo, let our watchword be: *"Omnia ad majorem Dei gloriam!"* "All for the greater glory of God!"

"Know then this truth — enough for man to know:
  Virtue alone is happiness below." — POPE.

"Happiness and virtue are the same." — FRANCIS.

"There can be no harmony in our being except our happiness coincides with our duty." — WHEWELL.

"Chain down some passion; do some generous deed;
  Teach ignorance to see; or grief to smile;
  Correct thy friend; befriend thy greatest foe;
  With warm heart and confidence divine,
  Spring up and lay strong hold on Him who made thee."
                                        — YOUNG.

"All who joy would win
Must share it — happiness was born a twin."
                                        — BYRON.

2. — Charity the Greatest Thing in the World

"IF I should have all faith, so that I could remove mountains, and have not charity, I am nothing" (1 *Cor.* xiii. 2).
  "Now there remain faith, hope, and charity — these three: but *the greatest of these is charity*" (1 *Cor.* xiii. 2).

"God is charity. By this hath the charity of God appeared toward us, because God hath sent His only begotten Son into the world, that we may live by Him. . . .

"My dearest, if God hath so loved us, we also ought to love one another. . . . Let us love God because God first hath loved us. And this commandment we have from God, that he, who loveth God, love also his brother" (1 *John* iv).

"And this is charity, that we walk according to His commandments" (2 *John* vi).

"Before all things have a constant mutual charity among yourselves: for charity covereth a multitude of sins" (1 *Peter* iv. 8).

"*Love is the fulfilling of the law*" (*Rom.* xiii. 10).

"All the law and the prophets depend upon the law of love" (*Matt.* xxii. 40).

A rightly ordered love moves us to the observance of every law. A loving soul is most obedient to the law. Love is the spring of its actions. Its love impels it to obey. St. Augustine understood this so well, that he hesitated not to say: "*Dilige et fac quod vis*": "*Love, and do what you will.*" — St. Augustine, *Tract. vii, in Epis.*

"The end of the commandment is charity from a pure heart, and a good conscience, and an unfeigned faith" (1 *Tim.* i. 5).

And this is the "game of love": "By how much the more a man dies to himself, by so much more he lives to God." — St. Catherine Sien., *Dialogue on Perfection.*

All good things, all great things, in the world, have been accomplished through self-denial and self-control.

St. Teresa says: "Love spurs us on to do great

things, and makes all that is bitter sweet and savory."
— ST. TERESA, *Foundat.* c. v.

The perfection of charity is attained by self-renunciation, by entire mortification, by purity of heart, and total abandonment to God.

Our Lord says: "Learn of Me"; "He that followeth Me walketh not in darkness"; "If any man will come after Me, let him deny himself, and take up his cross and follow Me" (*Matt.* viii. 34).

Father Buckler, speaking of charity, the essence of perfection, asks: "How are we to follow Christ?" And he replies: "The answer is, that Our Lord's way is the way of perfect love. He is the divine Lover of God and of men. For the love of God and of men He became incarnate, lived on earth, taught the law of love and the life of love, suffered for love and died for love; sent down the Spirit of His love upon the Church, to be the ruling power of our lives and actions, by *the charity of God poured forth into our hearts* (*Rom.* v. 5), and left us the marvelous gift of Himself, to the end of the world, in the mystery of love on the altar, wherein He dwells as the divine Lover in the midst of those He loves — working with us, nourishing and perfecting His life of love in the souls of men. 'Be ye followers of God,' says St. Paul, 'and walk in love, as most dear children' (*Eph.* v. 2)."

It is by charity that we follow Our Lord in the way of perfection.

3. — Fraternal Charity

OUR *happiness depends to a great extent on our observance of the law of fraternal charity:* "Thou shalt love thy neighbor as thyself," and of the golden rule announced by our blessed Saviour: "As you would that men should do to you, do you also to them in like manner" (*Luke* vi. 31). In doing good to others we become like to Christ, of whom we read in the Gospel that "He went about doing good to all."

"This commandment we have from God," says the disciple, whom Jesus loved, "that he, who loveth God, love also his brother" (1 *John* iv. 21). And St. Paul observes: "He, who loveth his neighbor, hath fulfilled the law" (*Rom.* xiii. 8).

What Shakespeare says of mercy, pertains also to charity and kindness: "It droppeth as the gentle rain from heaven; it is twice blessed; it blesseth him that gives and him that takes." We reap what we sow. Kindness begets kindness. Man can scarcely enjoy a sweeter satisfaction than that which results from good deed generously performed or a kind word un-selfishly spoken. "Happy is he, who has charity for every one," says the Blessed Egidius of Assisi; "happy is he, who performs great services for his neighbor, yet does not trouble about receiving anything in return."

Our deeds of disinterested charity are recorded in the Book of Life. On the great day of recompense, our blessed Saviour will say: "Come, ye blessed of My Father, possess the kingdom prepared for you from the foundation of the world; for I was hungry and you gave Me to eat; I was thirsty and you gave Me to drink; I was a stranger and you took Me in; naked, and you covered Me; sick, and you visited Me; I was in prison, and you came to Me; . . . As long as you did it to one of these little children you did it to Me" (*Matt.* xxv. 34–36).

"In charity," says St. Mary Magdalen of Pazzi, "we must be cheerful and prompt, knowing that by serving our fellow-creatures, we serve God in His members, and that He regards a service done to our neighbor as done to Himself."

4. — The Spectrum of Charity

ST. PAUL, writing to the Corinthians, ascribes to charity all the virtues that make a perfect man: "Charity is patient, is kind; charity envieth not, dealeth not perversely; is not puffed up, is not ambitious; seeketh not her own; is not provoked to anger; thinketh no evil; rejoiceth not in iniquity, but rejoiceth with the truth; beareth all things, believeth all things, endureth all things" (1 *Cor.* xiii. 4–7). And writing to the Colossians he says: "Above all things have charity, which is the bond of perfection" (*Col.* iii. 14). "Let each one love his brother"; says St. Alphonsus Liguori. "We have each our faults. He, who has to put up with his brother's fault to-day, will have to be borne with himself to-morrow."

"Bear ye one another's burdens," writes the Apostle to the Galatians, "and so you shall fulfil the law of Christ; for if any man think himself to be something, whereas he is nothing, he deceiveth himself" (*Gal.* vi. 2, 3). The following homely lines contain a beautiful truth: —

"There is so much bad in the best of us,
  There is so much good in the worst of us,
  That it ill behooves any of us
  To rail at the faults of the rest of us."

5. — Be Indulgent

THERE is a word which can not be said too often to every Christian whom God has destined to live, converse, and labor in the society of his fellow-creatures: *Be indulgent.* Yes, be indulgent; it is necessary for others, and it is necessary for your own sake. Forget the little troubles that others may cause you; keep up no resentment for the inconsiderate or unfavorable words that may have been said about you; excuse the mistakes and awkward blunders of which you are the victim; always make out good intentions for those who have done you any wrong by imprudent acts or speeches; in a word, smile at everything, show a pleasant face on all occasions, maintain an inexhaustible fund of goodness, patience, and gentleness. Thus you will be at peace with all your brethren; your love for them will suffer no alteration, and their love for you will increase day by day. But above all, you will practise in an excellent manner Christian charity, which is impossible without this toleration and indulgence at every instant.

— RUSSELL, *The Art of Being Happy.*

*

LET us take heed of the habits, tastes, and even the little hobbies of those around us, in order not to cross them in anything, especially our superiors and our kinsfolk. There are a thousand minute details of manner and conduct, insignificant in themselves no doubt, but to which some, especially old people and nervous people, attach so much importance that a slight negligence with regard to one of these little points puts them in bad humor for a whole day. There is question, for instance, of shutting a door, of making a little too much noise going upstairs, of being punctual to some appointment, of playing one game rather than another, of listening to a story that we have heard a hundred times before. A thoughtless or overbearing person will despise such petty matters as mere trifles, and, in despising them, will spoil all the comfort of some one perhaps to whom he owes gratitude and respect. A more pliant and more amiable Christian will for virtue's sake submit to what is required of him, and thus he will please God and make himself loved by his fellow-creatures; and he will himself enjoy that sweet satisfaction which charity secures for us when it is joined to humility. — *Ibid.*

6. — Be of Good Cheer!

"Be of good cheer!" "Be of good heart!" "Have confidence!" "Fear ye not!" So said Our Lord on various occasions.

And the Apostle admonishes us not to be anxious about our affairs, but to trust in the loving kindness of God, "casting all your care upon Him; for He hath care of you" (1 *Peter* v. 7).

Don't brood over what is past; forget it!

Be not too eager and anxious in the present.

Do your best; leave the rest to God, your good Father in heaven; keep your peace.

Don't worry about the future. What is the use of doing so? When you see trouble, blessings may really be in store for you. Hope for the best. Accept what happens philosophically. Always act with a pure intention and with deliberation.

The author of "The Art of Being Happy" says:

"A great secret for preserving peace of heart is to do nothing with overeagerness, but to act always calmly, without trouble or disquiet. We are not asked to do much, but to do well. At the Last Day God will not examine if we have performed a multitude of works but if we have sanctified our souls in doing them. Now the means of sanctifying ourselves is to do everything for God and to do perfectly whatever we have to do. The works that have as their motive vanity or selfishness make us neither better nor happier, and we shall receive no reward for them."

Cultivate a cheerful temper. Says the Wise Man in the Book of Proverbs: "A joyful mind maketh age flourishing: a sorrowful spirit drieth up the bones" (*Prov.* xvii. 22).

Look at the bright side of things.

> "Two men looked out through their prison bars;
> The one saw mud, and the other stars."
> — STEVENSON.

"A poet," writes Father Russell, "was gazing one day at a beautiful rose-tree. 'What a pity,' said he 'that these roses have thorns!' A man who was passing by said to him: 'Let us rather thank our good God for having allowed these thorns to have roses.' Ah! how ought we also to thank Him for so many joys that He grants to us in spite of our sins, instead of complaining about the slight troubles that He sends us!"

7.—Don't Worry

Nowadays we hear and read frequently about "Don't-Worry Clubs." Membership in one of these clubs of optimists may be a desideratum, but it is not a necessity to a practical Catholic; for there can be no doubt that the best "don't-worry club" in the world is the Catholic Church, because she directs her members to lead a pure and holy life, to do their duty, *to rejoice in the Lord always,* and to preserve their peace of soul by a simple, childlike confidence in the providence of Our Father in heaven, in accordance with the words of St. Paul: *"We know that to them that love God all things work together unto good"* (*Rom.* viii. 28).

"Happy is the man," says the dear St. Francis of Assisi, "who does not worry, nor grieve himself, about anything in this world, but leads a holy life, without any inordinate attachment, and abandons himself cheerfully to the will of God."

St. Francis of Sales, knowing that all the accidents of life, without exception, happen by the order of Providence, reposed in Him with the greatest tranquillity, like a child on the bosom of its mother. This gentle saint was filled with so great a confidence in God that in the midst of the greatest disasters nothing could disturb the peace of his soul. "I can not but be persuaded," he often said, "that he who believes in an infinite Providence, which extends even to the lowest worm, must expect good from all that happens to him."

In the same spirit, St. Vincent de Paul exhorts us:

"Let us place our confidence in God and establish ourselves in an entire dependence on Him. Then fear not what men may say or do against us, all will turn to our advantage. Yes, if all the earth should rise up against us, nothing will happen but as God pleases, in whom we have established our hopes."

Says the author of the "Spiritual Combat": "Nothing is impossible to God, since His power is infinite.

Nothing is difficult to God, since His wisdom is equally infinite. God desires our good with an infinite desire, since His goodness is without limit. What can be more capable of inspiring us with great confidence in Him?"

"*Have confidence*" (*Mark* vi. 50). Let your care be to possess your soul in peace and tranquillity; let no accident be to you a cause of ill humor.

8. — One Little Secret of a Happy Life

ONE secret of a sweet and happy Christian life is learning to live by the day. It is the long stretches that tire us. We think of life as a whole, running on for us. We can not carry this load until we are three score and ten. We can not fight this battle continually for half a century. But really there are no long stretches. Life does not come to us all at one time; it comes only a day at a time. Even to-morrow is never ours until it becomes to-day, and we have nothing whatever to do with it but to pass down to it a fair and good inheritance in to-day's work well done, and to-day's life well lived.

It is a blessed secret this, of living by the day. Any one can carry his burden, however heavy, till nightfall. Any one can do his work, however hard, for one day. Any one can live sweetly, patiently, lovingly, purely, until the sun goes down. And this is all life ever means to us — just one little day. "Do to-day's duty; fight to-day's temptations, and do not weaken or distract yourself by looking forward to things you can not see, and could not understand if you saw them." God gives us nights to shut down upon our little days. We can not see beyond. Short horizons make life easier

and give us one of the blessed secrets of brave, true
holy living.

9. — Abandonment

Two principles form the unalterable basis of the
virtue of *abandonment or absolute surrender to
divine providence.*

First Principle: Nothing is done, nothing happens,
either in the material or in the moral world, which God
has not foreseen from all eternity, and which He has
not willed, or at least permitted.

Second Principle: God can will nothing, He can
permit nothing, but in view of the end He proposed to
Himself in creating the world; *i.e.*, in view of His glory
and the glory of the Man-God, Jesus Christ, His only
Son.

To these two principles we shall add a third, which
will complete the elucidation of this whole subject,
viz.: As long as man lives upon earth, God desires to
be glorified through the happiness of this privileged
creature; and consequently in God's designs the interest of man's sanctification and happiness is inseparable from the interest of the divine glory.

If we do not lose sight of these principles, which no
Christian can question, we shall understand that our
confidence in the providence of Our Father in heaven
can not be too great, too absolute, too childlike. If
nothing but what He permits happens, and if He can
permit nothing but what is for our happiness, then we
have nothing to fear, except not being sufficiently submissive to God. As long as we keep ourselves united
with Him and we walk after His designs, were all
creatures to turn against us they could not harm us.

He, who relies upon God, becomes by this very reliance as powerful and as invincible as God, and created powers can no more prevail against him than against God Himself. This confidence in the fatherly providence of God can not, evidently, dispense us from doing all that is in our power to accomplish His designs; but, after having done all that depends upon our efforts, we will abandon ourselves completely to God for the rest. — FR. RAMIERE, S. J., in *Abandonment.*

*

"WHEN we will what God wills," says St. Alphonsus, "it is our own greatest good that we will; for God desires what is for our greatest advantage. Let your constant practice be to offer yourself to God, that He may do with you what He pleases." God can not be deceived and we may rest assured that what He determines will be best for us. Can there be a better prayer than this: *"Fiat Voluntas Tua!"* *"Thy Will be done!"* *"My Lord, My God, and My All!"*

10. — Holy Indifference: Self-Immolation

To BE "in tune with the Infinite" means, in a truly Christian sense, to live in perfect conformity with the will of God; it means, in its perfect sense, not only submission or resignation to the divine will, but thorough self-abandonment, prompted by the pure love of God; it means the cultivation of that peaceable state — "the peace of expectant love" — which St. Francis of Sales calls "holy indifference" — "a word we now understand to mean," as we read in his "Life" by De Margerie, "not the coldness, the torpor of a heart, that does not feel, but the supreme effort of a supremely loving heart, the term of self-immolation, — the immolation of self-will and the heart of flesh, to replace them by the will, the heart, the mind of God Himself."

"The sovereign love of God teaches the soul to have the same utter confidence in God's holy will that a little child has in its father; — here we have harmony, detachment, trust; in a word, the natural atmosphere of holy peace."

"Some," says the Imitation, "are at peace with themselves and others; some are at peace neither with themselves nor others; some, being themselves established in peace, strive to establish it among their brethren."

"Him, who belongs to this last category, the 'Imitation' calls the *Bonus Homo Pacificus*, the *good pacific man*. This exactly describes what St. Francis of Sales was. He recommended peace to all the souls he governed and he worked zealously to impart it to every one he could. The number of lawsuits he prevented and the disputes he calmed were almost infinite. This contagious peace sprang from the same fixed principle that has given all his writings, and every recorded act of his life, a grace of ineffable serenity; a frank gentle gaiety that is grave as well as gay, a depth of calm joy which neither tribulation nor press of toil ever troubled, and which, to use one of his own symbols, is like the "nightingale pouring out her song from the middle of a thorn-bush."

"When we are truly abandoned to God's will," says Bossuet, "we are ready for all that may come to us; we suppose the worst that can be supposed, and we cast ourselves blindly on the bosom of God. We forget ourselves, we lose ourselves; and this entire forgetfulness of self is the most perfect penance we can perform, for all conversion consists only in truly renouncing and forgetting ourselves, to be occupied with God and filled with Him. This forgetfulness of self is the martyrdom of self-love; it is its death, and an annihilation which leaves it without resources; then the heart dilates and is enlarged. We are relieved by casting from us the dangerous weight of self which formerly overwhelmed us. We look upon God as a good Father who leads us, as it were, by the hand in the present moment; and all our rest is in humble and firm confidence in His fatherly goodness.

"If anything is capable of making a heart free and unrestrained, it is perfect abandonment to God and His holy will; this abandonment fills the heart with a divine peace more abundant than the fullest floods. If anything can render a mind serene, dissipate the keenest anxieties, soften the bitterest pains, it is assuredly this perfect simplicity and liberty of a heart wholly abandoned to the hands of God."

EJACULATION

MAY *the most just, most high, and most amiable will of God be done in all things, be praised and magnified forever.*

100 days' indulgence once a day. — Pius VII, May 19, 1818.

11. — The Saved and Lost

A CERTAIN man said to our blessed Saviour, as we read in the Gospel of St. Luke (xiii. 23): "Lord, are they few that are saved?" Jesus simply replied: "Strive to enter by the narrow gate."

"It is a question," says Father Walsh, S.J., in his admirable and consoling study, "The Comparative Number of the Saved and Lost," "about which there is no authoritative decision of the Church, nor unanimous opinion of her Fathers or theologians.

"Many, notably Suarez, hold — as Father Faber does — that the great majority of adult Catholics will be saved. Some, amongst whom we are glad to count the illustrious Dominican, Father Lacordaire, hold or incline to the opinion that the *majority of mankind*, including heathens and heretics, will be saved.

"Pere Monsabrè, O.P., Father Castelein, S.J., and Rev. Joseph Rickaby, S.J., advocate this mildest opinion. Father Rickaby says in his Conference, 'The Extension of Salvation': 'As to what proportion of men die in sanctifying grace, and what proportion in mortal sin, nothing is revealed, nothing is of faith, and nothing is really known to theologians. If ever you find a theologian confidently consigning the mass of human souls to eternal flames, be sure he is venturing beyond the bounds of Christian faith and of theological science. You are quite free to disbelieve his word. I do not believe it myself.

"'The rigor of the older theologians culminated in Jansenism. To the Jansenist the elect were *the few grapes left upon the vine after a careful vintage* (*Is.* xxiv. 13). Since the extirpation of Jansenism, the pendulum of theological speculation has swung the other way, and theologians generally hope more of the mercy of God, or, at least, speak with less assurance of the range of His rigorous justice.'

"The reasons," continues Father Walsh, "which

have induced me to think the mildest opinion, namely, that the majority — and I scarcely fear to add, the *great majority* — of mankind will be saved, are: First, because the study of God's character urges, if not forces, me to do so. Second, because this opinion appears to make most for His greater honor and glory, and for the *merits of Christ.* Third, because the belief in it is better calculated to make us love God, and to serve Him the more from love.

" Cardinal Bellarmine, in one of his expositions of the Psalms, writes: 'David records God's providence in regard of the beasts and the birds in order to let man see that he will never be forsaken by God in His providence. God, who so bounteously feeds beasts and ravens, will never desert those who are made to His own image and likeness.' Is not such Our Lord's reasoning and conclusions as we have them in His Sermon on the Mount: 'Behold the birds of the air; for they neither sow nor do they reap, nor gather into barns, and your heavenly Father feedeth them. Are you not of much more value than they?' The most learned theologians lay down and prove the following proposition: That God really and sincerely wishes the salvation of all men, *because He is the Creator of all men.* In the words of St. Ambrose: 'God wishes all whom He creates to be saved; would to God, O men, that you would not fly and hide yourselves from Him; but even if you do He seeks you, and does not wish you to perish.' It is more probable that though many can and will fight God to the end and be lost, they will be fewer far than those whom He will tenderly, and in His own way, bring home to Himself. God is not only the *Creator* but the *Father* of all men without any exception. He has commanded us to address Him by this title: 'Our Father, who art

in heaven.' All Christians do so; and a preacher, in
his opening instructions, would teach and exhort the un-
tutored savage to believe in and speak to Him as such.

"God is the Father of all men and eminently a perfect Father. We could not imagine such a father casting out, expelling from his home forever a child, until
he had tried the proper means to keep him with himself—
until the child deserts him, or, by wilful, obstinate,
persistent disobedience to his father's will, necessitates
his own expulsion. Such a father will do all he well
can for the welfare of his children — do everything
short of violence to enable his children to succeed in
all that is for his own and their good. The dominant
desire — wish — will — of such a father must be to
make his children happy; his dominant dread and
horror, that one of them should be unhappy.

"Our Lord tells us how easy and swift true repentance
can be in the case of the *publican* — the notorious and
typical sinner — who by making an act of sorrow for
his sins, in seven words, went home to his house justified. God is far more ready and generous in forgiving
the worst than men — even good men — are in forgiving each other, and bad would it be for the best of
us if He were not.

"By way of showing the effect which can be produced
by the very thought of God *Our Father*, and belief in
Him as such, I may give a fact told to me by the person
concerned — now dead for some years. He fell into
a state akin to despair about his salvation. A confessor,
to whom he opened his mind, told him to go, take his
Bible, and write out all the texts in which God calls
Himself his Father. He did so, and was blessed with
calm and peace before he had written twenty." — FR.
NICHOLAS WALSH, S.J.

"Say to them: As I live, saith the Lord God: I desire not the death of the wicked, but that the wicked turn from his way, and live" (*Ezech.* xxxiii. 11).

"The Son of Man is come to seek and to save that which was lost" (*Luke* xix. 10).

"Behold what manner of charity the Father hath bestowed upon us, that we should be called, and should be the sons of God" (1 *John* iii. 1).

"But I say to you: Love your enemies, do good to them that hate you, and pray for them that persecute and calumniate you; that you may be the children of your Father who is in heaven, who maketh the sun to rise upon the good and bad, and raineth upon the just and unjust. . . . Be you perfect as also your heavenly Father is perfect." — *Words of our blessed Saviour; Matt.* v. 44, 45, 48.

"Yea, I have loved thee with an everlasting love; therefore have I drawn thee, taking pity on thee" (*Jer.* xxxi. 3).

"The Lord is gracious and merciful; patient and plenteous in mercy."

"The Lord is sweet to all, and His tender mercies are over all His works."

"Every day will I bless Thee, and I will praise Thy Name forever" (*Ps.* cxliv. 8, 9, 2).

Let us give the good God, our Father in heaven, a service of *Love*, in the spirit of St. Francis Xavier, who said: "O God! I love Thee, not for the sake of winning heaven, or of escaping hell, not for the hope of gaining aught, but solely because Thou art my God."

"Not with the hope of gaining aught,
Not seeking a reward;
But as Thyself hast loved me,
O ever-loving Lord.

> E'en so I love Thee, and will live,
>   And in Thy praise will sing;
> Solely because Thou art my God
>   And my eternal King."

12.—Lord, Are There Few Saved?

OUR LORD was journeying through the towns and
villages on the way to Jerusalem, there to suffer
death for us, when some one came up and asked Him
exactly the question that we should have liked to put:
Lord, are there few saved? What was He to reply?
Suppose He had answered: "Oh, no, nearly all men
will be saved, very few will be lost." What easy going,
what laxity would have followed upon such a declaration!
He answered, therefore, not to the gratification of our
curiosity but to the profit of our souls: *Strive ye to enter
in at the narrow gate: for many, I say unto you, shall
seek to enter in, and shall not be able* (*Luke* xiii. 24).
They *shall not be able*, because they have not *striven:*
they have sought the Kingdom of God after a fashion,
but not with sufficient earnestness; and, Our Lord
warns us, there shall be *many* such. How many?
Shall there be many more saved? Shall the lost be
comparatively few? Our Lord has left His Church
no revelation upon this subject: consequently no answer returnable to these inquiries carries the certainty
of faith. On such an open question preachers have
said strong things, and theologians have divided on this
side and on that, with more or less of probability.
Father Faber in his *Creator and Creature* argues that
"the great mass of believers" are saved. But there is
one class of people who are all saved. Who? All
priests? No. All Religious? No. Who then? All

wh。 pray. Prayer is knocking at the gate of heaven; and we have Our Lord's assurance, *Knock, and it shall be opened to you* (*Luke* xi. 9).

"*Ask, seek, knock*" (*Matt.* vii. 7): that denotes earnestness of petition. Ask, and fear not to ask, for temporal favors, as health and victory, yet so that they make for the salvation of your soul. "*Seek ye first the Kingdom of God and His justice, and all these things shall be added unto you*" (*Matt.* vi. 33).

No one, I persuade myself, enters heaven, who has not either prayed much or been prayed much for. But my salvation is too precious to me for me to leave it to the charity of others. I will help myself and pray for myself. — *Ye are Christ's.*

13. — Forgive Us Our Trespasses as We Forgive Those Who Trespass Against Us

"IF a man finds it very hard to forgive injuries, let him look at a crucifix, and think that Christ shed all His blood for him, and not only forgave His enemies, but even prayed His heavenly Father to forgive them also. Let him remember that when he says the "*Our Father*" every day, instead of asking pardon for his sins, he is calling down vengeance on himself." — ST. PHILIP NERI.

"If you will forgive men their offences," says Our Lord, "your heavenly Father will forgive you also your offences" (*Matt.* vi. 14).

"Dismiss all anger," says St. Thomas of Villanova, "and look a little into yourself. Remember that he of whom you are speaking is your *brother*, and as he is in the way of salvation, God can make him a saint, notwithstanding his present weakness. You may fall into the same faults or perhaps into a worse fault. But supposing you remain upright, to whom are you indebted for it, if not to the pure mercy of God? "— *Readings with the Saints.*

One day St. Peter said to our Saviour, as we read in the Gospel of St. Matthew (xviii. 21): "Lord, how often shall my brother offend against me, and I forgive him? till seven times?" Jesus replied: "I say not to thee, till seven times; but till seventy times seven times;" — *i.e.*, not only frequently, but innumerable times, in fact always.

The apostle St. Paul admonishes us: "Be ye kind one to another, merciful, forgiving one another, even as God hath forgiven you in Christ" (*Eph.* iv. 32).

"How patiently Christ, the king of heaven, bore with the apostles, enduring at their hands many incivilities, for they were but poor, rough, and illiterate fishermen. How much more ought we to bear with our neighbor. if he treats us with unkindness." — St. Philip.

14. — Kindness

"LET us be kind if we would promote the interests of the Sacred Heart, of which kindness was the special characteristic. Let it not be in isolated acts — 'few and far between'; no, it must be like prayer — an *habitual disposition* of heart, which is ready to manifest itself without any effort, at all seasons and in all circumstances, and thus it will be with hearts which are united to that Heart of love. Kindness will flow from them, as it were, naturally, just as the flowers give forth their perfume, the birds their song, and as the sun shines down alike on good and bad as it goes on its daily circuit — because all this is of their very nature. In the most trivial things of daily life the spirit of kindness should render itself evident." . . .

"Kindness is as the bloom upon the fruits — it renders charity and religion attractive and beautiful. Without it, even charitable works lose their power of winning souls; for, without kindness, the idea of love, the idea of anything supernatural — in a word, of Jesus, is not conveyed to the mind by the works performed, even though they be done from a right motive. There is such a thing as doing certain exterior actions, which are intended to be charitable, ungraciously. Now, actions thus performed, do not manifest the kindness of the heart of Jesus, nor will they be efficacious in extending the empire of His love, or in winning souls to His kingdom. The fruit may be sound, but the bloom is not on it; hence it is uninviting. . . .

"How many a noble work has been nipped in the bud by the blast of an unkind judgment; how many a generous heart has been crushed in its brightest hopes by a jealous criticism; how many a holy aspiration, destined to bear abundant fruit for God and souls, has been forced back into the poor heart from whence it had ascended, there to be stifled utterly and forever, leaving that heart, as the poet so graphically represents it, 'like a deserted bird's nest filled with snow,' because unkindness had robbed it of that for which, perhaps, alone it cared to live. How much, then, we may believe has been lost to the world of all that is good and great and beautiful through the instrumentality of unkindness; and if it be thus, what developments, on the other hand, may we not expect, in the order of grace as well as of nature, in the hearts and minds of men beneath the genial sun of kindness.

"Even in the common things of life, and in the natural order, how striking are the results of the passage of this Heaven-sent missioner, this angel of light and consolation.

"If we reflect upon it, kindness is but the outcome and exemplar of the divine precept: *Thou shalt love thy neighbor as thyself.* There is nothing we personally so much appreciate as kindness. We like others to think of us kindly, to speak to us kindly, and to render us kindly actions and in a kindly manner. Now, we should know how to put ourselves in the place of others, and thus we should testify to them that kindliness that we value so much ourselves.

"When our divine Lord came down upon earth, He came not only to save us by shedding His blood for us, but to teach us by His example how to co-operate with Him in extending the Kingdom of His Father. And one of the most powerful means which He employed for this purpose was kindness, gentleness, and forbearance. 'The goodness and kindness of God our Saviour appeared' (*Titus* iii. 4), by which words we learn that kindness is not altogether synonymous with goodness, but, as it were, a luster, a bloom, an attraction superadded to it.

"We might regard this sweet reflection from the Heart of Jesus from many points of view, but it is especially under one aspect that we have been considering it; namely, as a powerful weapon in our hands for the efficacious exercise of our apostolate. Kindly thoughts of others will be productive of prayer in their regard, at once fervent and affectionate — prayer such as the loving Heart of Jesus willingly listens to; kindly words and deeds will draw souls to the love of Him whose spirit they behold so attractively reproduced in His members. As the wood-violets give forth their perfume from beneath the brushwood that conceals them from view, telling us of their unseen nearness, so kindness reveals to us the nearness of Jesus, the sweetness of whose Spirit is thus breathed forth.

"Such is the kindness which is that great missioner sent by the Heart of Jesus to exercise an apostolate of love upon earth, and so to promote the glory of God and the salvation of souls." — *The Voice of the Sacred Heart.*

"I pass through this world but once. If, therefore, there is any good that I can do, any kindness that I can show to any human being, let me do it now; let me not defer nor neglect it, for I shall not pass this way again."

15. — Thoughts from Father Faber on Kindness

THE worst kinds of unhappiness, as well as the greatest amount of it, come from our conduct to each other. If our conduct, therefore, were under the control of kindness, it would be nearly the opposite of what it is, and so the state of the world would be almost reversed.

*

KINDNESS is the overflowing of self upon others. We put others in the place of self. We treat them as we would wish to be treated ourselves. We change places with them. For the time self is another, and others are self. Our self-love takes the shape of complacence in unselfishness.

*

KINDNESS adds sweetness to everything.

OF GREAT consequence is the immense power of kindness in bringing out the good points of the characters of others.

*

A KIND act has picked up many a fallen man who has afterward slain his tens of thousands for his Lord, and has entered the Heavenly City at last as a conqueror amidst the acclamations of the saints, and with the welcome of its Sovereign.

*

KINDNESS has converted more sinners than either zeal, eloquence, or learning; and these three last have never converted any one unless they were kind also. In short, kindness makes us as Gods to each other. Yet while it lifts us so high, it sweetly keeps us low. For the continual sense which a kind heart has of its own need of kindness keeps it humble.

*

KINDNESS is infectious. One kind action leads to another. Our example is followed. This is the greatest work which kindness does to others — that it makes them kind themselves.

*

A PROUD man is seldom a kind man. Humility makes us kind, and kindness makes us humble.

*

A KIND man is a man who is never self-occupied. He is genial, he is sympathetic, he is brave.

*

IF A MAN *habitually* has *kind thoughts* of others, and that on supernatural motives, he is not far from being a saint.

THERE is one class of kind thoughts which must be dwelt upon apart. I allude to *kind interpretations*. The habit of not judging others is one which it is very difficult to acquire, and which is generally not acquired till late on in the spiritual life.

*

Now, the standard of the *Last Judgment* is absolute. It is this — the measure which we have meted to others. Our present humor in judging others reveals to us what our sentence would be if we died·now. Are we content to abide that issue? But, as it is impossible all ·at once to stop judging, and as it is also impossible to go on judging uncharitably, we must pass through the intermediate stage of kind interpretations. Few men have passed beyond this to a habit of perfect charity, which has blessedly stripped them of their judicial ermine and their deeply-rooted judicial habits of mind. We ought, therefore, to cultivate most sedulously the habit of kind interpretations.

Men's actions are very difficult to judge. Their real character depends in a·great measure on the motives which prompt them, and those motives are invisible to us. Appearances are often against ·what we afterward discover to·have been deeds of virtue.

*

WHAT mistakes have we not made in judging others! Have we not always found in our past experience that on the whole our kind interpretations were truer than our harsh ones?

How many times in·life have we been wrong when we put a kind construction on the conduct of others? We shall not need our fingers to count those mistakes upon.

BUT while common sense convinces us of the truth of kind interpretations, common selfishness ought to open our eyes to their wisdom and their policy. We must have passed through life unobservantly if we have never perceived that a man is very much himself what he thinks of others. Of course his own faults may be the cause of his unfavorable judgments of others; but they are also, and in a very marked way, effects of those same judgments. A man who was on a higher eminence before will soon by harsh judgments of others sink to the level of his own judgments. When you hear a man attribute meanness to another, you may be sure not only that the critic is an ill-natured man, but that he has got a similar element of meanness in himself, or is fast sinking to it. A man is always capable himself of a sin which he thinks another is capable of, or which he himself is capable of imputing to another.

*

KIND words are the music of the world.

*

KIND words produce happiness. How often have we ourselves been made happy by kind words, in a manner and to an extent which we are quite unable to explain? No analysis enables us to detect the secret of the power of kind words; even self-love is found inadequate as a cause. Now, as I have said before, happiness is a great power of holiness. Thus, kind words, by their power of producing happiness, have also a power of producing holiness, and so winning men to God.

*

KIND words cost us nothing, yet how often do we grudge them? On the few occasions when they do imply some degree of self-sacrifice, they almost instantly repay us a hundredfold. The opportunities are frequent, but we show no eagerness either in looking out for them, or in embracing them. What inference are we to draw from all this? Surely this: That it is next to impossible to be habitually kind, except by the help of divine grace and upon supernatural motives. Take life all through, its adversity as well as its prosperity, its sickness as well as its health, its loss of its rights as well as its enjoyment of them, and we shall find that no natural sweetness of temper, much less any acquired philosophical equanimity, is equal to the support of a uniform habit of kindness. Nevertheless, with the help of grace, the habit of saying kind words is very quickly formed, and when once formed it is not speedily lost.

*

IT IS natural to pass from the facility of kind words to its reward. I find myself always talking about happiness when I am treating of kindness. The fact is the two things go together; the double reward of kind words is in the happiness they cause in others and the happiness they cause in ourselves. The very process of uttering them is a happiness in itself. Even the imagining of them fills our minds with sweetness, and makes our hearts glow pleasurably. Is there any happiness in the world like the happiness of a disposition made happy by the happiness of others? There is no joy to be compared with it. The luxuries which wealth can buy, the rewards which ambition can attain, the pleasures of art and scenery, the abounding sense of health, and the exquisite enjoyment of mental creations, are nothing to this pure and heavenly happiness, where self is drowned in the blessedness of others. Yet this happiness follows close upon kind words, and is their legitimate result. But, independently of this, kind words make us happy in ourselves. They soothe our own irritation, they charm our cares away, they draw us nearer to God, they raise the temperature of our love. They produce in us a sense of quiet restfulness like that which accompanies the consciousness of forgiven sin. They shed abroad the peace of God within our hearts.

*

THERE is always one bright thought in our minds when all the rest is dark. There is one thought out of which a moderately cheerful man can always make some satisfactory sunshine, if not a sufficiency of it. It is the thought of the bright populous heaven. There is a joy there at least, if there is a joy nowhere else. There is true service of God there, however poor and interested the love of Him may be on earth. Multitudes are abounding in the golden light there, even if they that rejoice on earth be few. At this hour it is all going on so near us that we can not be hopelessly unhappy with so much happiness so near. Yet its nearness makes us wistful. Then let us think that there are multitudes in heaven to-day who are there because of *kind actions;* many are there for doing them, many for having had them done to them.

*

WE MUST say something about *kind suffering.* Kind suffering is, in fact, a form of kind action. With the Christian, kind suffering must be almost wholly supernatural. There is a harmonious fusion of suffering and gentleness effected by grace, which is one of the most attractive features of holiness. What is more beautiful than considerateness for others when we our-selves are unhappy?

*

To BE subject to low spirits is a sad liability. Yet, to a vigorous, manly heart, it may be a very com-plete sanctification. What can be more unkind than to communicate our low spirits to others, to go about the world like demons, poisoning the fountains of joy? Have I more light because I have managed to involve those I love in the same gloom as myself? Is it not pleasant to see the sun shining on the mountains, even though we have none of it down in our valley? Oh, the littleness and the meanness of that sickly appetite for sympathy which will not let us keep our tiny Lilli-putian sorrows to ourselves! Why must we go sneak-ing about, like some dishonorable insect, and feed our darkness on other people's light? We hardly know in all this whether to be more disgusted with the mean-ness, or more indignant at the selfishness, or more sor-rowful at the sin. The thoughts of the dying mother are all concentrated on her new-born child. It is a beautiful emblem of unselfish holiness. So also let us hide our pains and sorrows. But while we hide them, let them also be spurs within us to urge us on to all manner of overflowing kindness and sunny humor to those around us. When the very darkness within us creates a sunshine around us, then has the spirit of Jesus taken possession of our souls.

*

KINDNESS is the turf of the spiritual world whereon the sheep of Christ feed quietly beneath the Shep-herd's eye.

RIGHTLY considered, kindness is the grand cause of God in the world. Where it is natural, it must forthwith be supernaturalized. Where it is not natural, it must be supernaturally planted. What is our life? It is a mission to go into every corner it can reach, and reconquer for God's beatitude His unhappy world back to Him. It is a devotion of ourselves to the bliss of the Divine Life by the beautiful apostolate of kindness.

*

LET us conclude. We have been speaking of kindness. Perhaps we might better have called it the spirit of Jesus. What an amulet we should find it in our passage through life if we would say to ourselves two or three times a day these soft words of Scripture: "My spirit is sweet above honey, and my inheritance above honey and the honeycomb" (*Ecclus*. xxiv. 27).

16.—Seek the Things Above

*

"Seek the things that are above"

AN IDEAL life would be so to live as to be "an *inspiration, strength,* and *blessing* to those whose lives are touched by ours." Such was our dear Lady's life task. To lead others onward, upward, heavenward, was her earnest joy and endeavor. Such should be also the noble aim of her true children.

How can we accomplish this superhuman task? By living for *the things above*. If we endeavor to see God's hand in all that happens, and to live as "pilgrims and strangers" that seek a country, then our lives, though exteriorly *simple* and *commonplace*, will be as beacon lights guiding souls to that blessed region we call "Home," where, with all we love on earth and in heaven, we hope to pass our eternity. For each of us, soon *"time shall be no longer"*; meanwhile *"Sursum Corda."* — *Mater Mea.*

17. — What Is It that Secures Happiness in a Home

BEFORE everything religion. Let all love well our good God; let all observe the commandments of God and the Church; let all say their prayers morning and night, let all put their trust in divine Providence. In the next place, union: let the members of the household be affectionate toward one another, having only one heart and one soul, not saying or doing anything that can pain any one of them. Then again, the spirit of sacrifice; we must be ready to do without something in order to make another member of the family enjoy it, we must give up our own personal tastes to conform to the tastes of others. Finally, pliancy of character; not to be hard to deal with, touchy, sour, proud; not to be obstinately rooted in one's ideas, not to grow impatient about mere nothings, but to have a large mind and a generous heart. The home of a family whose members possess these qualities is a paradise on earth.
— RUSSELL, *The Art of Being Happy.*

*

THERE are other things than merely food and clothing, which make up a good home. Love and kindness are essential to a happy home; — not the mistaken love and the foolish kindness which give way to every selfish whim of childhood, but the patient, far-seeing virtues that look beyond the present to the child's future life here and hereafter.

Children, particularly boys, need to be studied and understood. They need to be treated justly, but kindly. The tolerant father and mother who try to understand their children are too few. They want to drive the boys, whereas they should rather try to lead them. It is of very little use for parents to preach the virtues to children while they themselves disregard them. If you would have children just and kind, well-mannered and truthful, be all these things yourself first. These virtues practised by the parents, and insisted upon kindly and firmly from the children, are what go to make up that which truly deserves to be called "a good home." — *The Sentinel of the Blessed Sacrament.*

18. — The Power of a Smile

AN EXCELLENT remedy for "*the blues*" and preventive of dumpishness will be found in this suggestion, "Keep the corners of your mouth turned up;" in other words, keep a smile upon your lips, even when you are alone. Try it. It acts like a charm. It keeps one in good spirits, and it drives the frown from other faces too. It acts like sunshine. It warms and brightens all it falls upon. A smile will suppress the angry retort that is dancing on the quivering lips. Smiling faces make a peaceful, happy home. — *Anonymous.*

19. — A New Virtue

THERE is a virtue, which may be new to the hearing of many of us. It was discovered and named by Aristotle; and he called it by the pretty Greek name of *eutrapelia*. *Eutrapelia* may be defined "playfulness in good taste." Aristotle himself defines it: "a chastened

love of putting out one's strength upon others."
There is in every ordinary boy a disposition to romp,
to play the fool, and to destroy property; a disposition
which ought to be sternly repressed, subdued, and kept
under by those responsible for the boy's education, beginning with himself. Otherwise the boy can have no
place in civilized society: he will turn out a young
savage. But though repressed, the disposition should
not be killed within him and extirpated altogether.
It is a defect of character to have no playfulness, no
drollery, no love of witnessing or even creating a ridicu-
lous situation. *Eutrapelia* knows exactly when and
how to be funny, and where and when to stop. *All
things have their season*, says Ecclesiastes (iii. 1, 4);
*a time to weep, and a time to laugh; a time to mourn, and
a time to dance.* A proud and quarrelsome man is never
a funny man. Many a difficulty, many an incipient
quarrel, many a dark temptation, is dissipated, the moment one catches sight of some humorous side to the
matter. A humble man makes merry over his own
misadventures; and when he is inclined to storm and
rage listens to a good angel whispering in his ear:
"John, don't make a fool of yourself." A merry boy
is seldom a bad boy.

Life is not all play: indeed it is a very serious thing;
but on account of its very seriousness we require some
play to set it off. That is why you find excellent men
and great doers of good with an extraordinary faculty,
which they use at times, of talking nonsense and playing
the fool. *Eutrapelia* is a blend of playfulness and earnestness. Without earnestness, playfulness degenerates
into frivolity. "O Lord, give me not over to an irrev-
erent and frivolous mind" (*Ecclus.* xxiii. 6). We generally wear our lighter clothing underneath, and our

heavier clothing above it; and perhaps that is the best
way for a man, to veil his *eutrapelia* under a serious
exterior. But for a boy the other way about is the
better fashion; he should be playful and mirthful to
the eye, but have seriousness and earnestness underneath, known only to those who know him well. In the
earliest days of the Society of Jesus, there was a novice
much given to laughing. One day he met Father
Ignatius, and thought that he was in for a scolding.
But St. Ignatius said to him: "Child, I want you to
laugh and be joyful in the Lord. A Religious has no
cause for sadness, but many reasons for rejoicing, and
that you may always be glad and joyful, be humble
always and always obedient." — FR. JOSEPH RICKABY,
S. J., in *Ye are Christ's.*

20. — Faith and Humor

NOT long ago, in the course of a conversation, a
person remarked to me: "But you Catholics are
such gloomy persons!" I tried to refute the charge
by smiling largely — *probatur ridendo.* But my companion subsumed: "O! I don't mean universally and
in every individual case. But your religion — you
know — your attitude, your temper, is severe and for-
bidding and all that."

This saying seems typical. The days have gone by
when Protestants believed that Catholic priests had
horns and cloven feet; but the days will hardly come
when Protestants will give up their notion that Catholi-
cism and gloom are synonymous, and that the outward
badge of our religion is an abiding frown. Stripping
the idea of all that is exaggerated in it, it does us honor,
perhaps more honor than Catholics individually can

in conscience accept; being a testimony to the serious and wise character of our lives. For obviously life is no jest to a man who believes in its purpose and its eternal duration; who reads its value in the blood of Christ, as our Catholic faith teaches us to do. Indeed there is none of us but can wish sincerely that we merited a little better the title to somberness in the sense of Catholic seriousness and determination.

But what we are charged with is not, of course, this right sincerity and purposefulness, but an excess of seriousness, a depressing solemnity and heaviness — in a word, a lack of humor. Moreover, the charge is distinctively put against us, not as men, but as Catholics. We are said to be gloomy by a necessity flowing from our worship, from our belief. It would further seem that not Protestants only, but even Catholics themselves occasionally entertain this notion of the harshness and narrowness and cheerless rigorism of our faith. It may not be easy to show such as these that in truth our religion is in reality instinct with the subtlest, deepest, richest humor possible to men. Indeed so essential is great humor to Catholic faith that the practical presence or absence of this humor is not a bad test of a man's vigor or weakness in faith.

Humor is the just appreciation of the incongruous things of life. That is a part definition, at least; for humor is an elusive quality, existing in the concrete, dealing with the concrete, surrounding living things and entering into them, as the oxygen of the air enters into and vivifies our blood. Men feel its presence and recognize it and honor it and delight in it; but can no more analyze it than one can analyze life, which departs at the touch of the dissecting instrument. One takes up "Henry IV," or "Alice in Wonderland," or "The Frogs," or "Three Men in a Boat," or "Hudibras," or "Mr. Dooley's Philosophy," — and grows mellow with them, and wise, and says: "What humor may be in the categories, I know not; but they who wrote these things are humorists, children of comprehension and of wisdom." They compel us, not to laugh, but to smile. They widen our horizon and draw out our sympathies. In gentleness and with great pity and love, we look from end to end of the earth and are filled with kindly merriment at the misfits we see.

But we know this, that humor is built on truth and knowledge. A man who knows only a fraction of himself and others can not have that plenitude of humor of one who knows the whole. The humor that is bounded by this world is feeble beside that humor which draws from earth and heaven, from time and eternity.

Faith is the olution and interpretation of life, the bestower of knowledge and of wisdom more than knowledge. Faith widens our limited days here into endless days, and lays bare men's souls and the secrets of God, and gives us that mastery of life which is needed to laugh at life, and shows us the relation of all things and their harmony, and what preserves that harmony and is admirable, and what jars with that harmony and is laughable. Knowledge and power, wisdom and love, these are at the roots of all right humor and ring in every laugh that befits the soul of a man. *"Credo"* — *"I believe in God the Father Almighty"* — can bring smiles where tears were, and light where darkness was, and courage and saneness of view where all was gloomy and distorted by sadness.

"The fashion of this world passeth away" — and we alone who know this are the truly light-hearted of the world. *"You shall take none of these things with you,"*

says St. Paul, and I have seen a man smile through his tears beside the grave of his son, because he knew that afterward he himself would leave in another grave the heartache begun at this one.

No, our faith does not lack humor. It abounds in humor; it is humor — the tenderest, most cheery, most lasting humor. St. Lawrence, directing the roasting of his own body with the nicety of a cook; our Irish peasant who says: "Thanks be to God, my rheumatism is much worse to-day," our nuns who can be merry in the abode of death; — these are some instances of the humor of faith. In its fulness, perhaps only the saints have it — those serene, large beings, beneath whose awe-inspiring calmness runs an unbroken ripple of laughter at the follies and pettinesses that surround them; whom no adversity disheartens and no sufferings sour; whose eyes are bright with eternal merriment looking on the fashion of this world which passeth away.

I have before me, while writing, the picture of a young man clad in cassock and surplice; a man of lean ascetic face; who holds in his hand a crucifix, and stands by a table on which rest a discarded coronet and a penitential scourge. Beneath the picture are the words, *"Quid hoc ad æternitatem?"* The picture is familiar to all of us, and represents that great saint and universal patron of Catholic youth, Aloysius Gonzaga. The legend under it is a pet saying of Aloysius, a pertinent question applied by him to the thousand and one minutiæ of daily life — "How does this look in the light of eternity?" We can imagine this boy saint, as he passed through the streets of Rome on his way to or from school, or to some hospital or church. An unbeliever would be chilled at his constraint and austerity.

"Another example of monkish, Catholic gloom — a zealot, a fanatic; a man bereft of all sanity or humaneness, looking at life in warped, crabbed manner!" Yet the unbeliever would be the fanatic, the narrow-minded man; and Aloysius the humorist. For if the gorge of our spectator friend rose; if he gave expression to his scorn in words; if even he spat upon this Jesuit bigot, Aloysius would have said to himself "*Quid hoc ad æternitatem?*" and would have gone on his way with a smile, making merry in his heart.

Fancy a man who all day long, in every varying circumstance, was asking himself, "*Quid hoc ad æternitatem?*" What an infinity of laughable things he would see! What a wide, kindly, smiling view of life he would acquire! Think of the countless occurrences that fret and annoy, that drive a man into himself and shut up his outlook over the world which the good God has given him, that make him petty and irritable and sour — how they would go down before such a question, as rank weeds before a scythe; how they would be lost sight of, as a swarm of gnats becomes invisible under the full light of an unclouded noon!

Whatever be the definition of humor — and it matters exactly nothing what it be — the essence of it is saneness, balance, breadth; and complete saneness, undisturbed balance, infinite breadth, are the gifts of faith and of faith only. Knowledge stops at the edge of the earth. Faith goes on beyond the stars, illimitable, calm, all-comprehending. The wisdom of the world is a surface wisdom and breeds only a surface humor. The wisdom of faith reaches from heaven to hell, into the heart of all living; and when it smiles the angels of God smile with it. The humor of men may be on the lips and in the mind only. The humor of faith must come from the heart, from the "understanding heart."

St. Paul bids us "rejoice in the Lord always: again, I say, rejoice." For ours is the heritage of joy; since it is given us to know what God knows, and to love all that He loves, to feel the presence of His angels round about us, to consider life in its completeness, and to look forward unavertedly, beholding the brightness of eternal peace and the sea which is about the throne of God, where the world looks out upon only chaos and the night. Our faith has a higher purpose than merely to make us wise and patient and kindly. The humor of life is not its object, but it is its true and certain concomitant; growing as it grows, waning as it wanes. If it can with truth be said of us that we lack humor, we must blame the lack of it not upon our religion, our faith, but upon our unfaith, and our irreligion. — WILL-IAM T. KANE, S.J., in *The American Ecclesiastical Review*.

Apropos of this subject, the following item is interesting and instructive:

" Dr. A. B. Richardson, for many years in charge of institutions for the insane — among others, the United States Hospital at Washington — was recently asked about the amount of insanity in his institutions that could fairly be attributed to religion. His answer is interesting:

" You have asked me a very easy question. I have tested that matter thoroughly. There are only two patients in this hospital whose insanity has any relation to religion; and I think, from their predisposition to insanity, that they would probably have become insane on some other subject, if they had not on religion. Now, if you had asked me how many people in Ohio

are kept by religion from insanity and out of these
hospitals, you would have given me a question hard
to answer; for they are a multitude.   The good cheer,
bright hopes, rich consolations, good tempers, regular
habits, and glad songs of religion are such an antidote
for the causes of insanity that thousands of people in
Ohio are preserved from insanity by them.   But for
the beneficent influence of religion, the State would
have to double the capacity of her hospitals in order
to accommodate her insane patients."

The most recent psychological researches are in
agreement with Dr. Richardson's views; and it is
practically certain that religion has been bearing for
years past one source of odium for which it is in no
way responsible. — *Ave Maria*.

21. — Peace Is Happiness

ALL desire happiness.   But peace brings happiness.
It is a threefold peace, that is accompanied by
heavenly happiness; *peace with God, peace with one's
neighbor*, and *peace with oneself*.

Peace with God means union with God, perfect conformity of one's own will with the divine will, the state
of grace, the joy of a good conscience, which surpasses
every joy on earth.

Peace with one's neighbor means the exercise of
fraternal charity, the observance of the golden rule,
"do unto others as you would that they should do unto
you," the avoidance of contention, the patient endurance
of others' faults, the forgiveness of injuries, the joy of
unselfish, disinterested well-doing.

Peace with oneself means the victory over self, the
mastery of one's passions and emotions, self-poise,

self-control, and the sweet joy of the consciousness of duty well done — done with the best motive and the purest intention.

We read in the Book of Proverbs (xvi. 32): "The patient man is better than the valiant; and he that ruleth his spirit than he that taketh cities." Perfect self-mastery is the grand achievement of the humble follower of Christ.

"Peace is what all desire," we read in the "Imitation," "but all care not for those things which appertain to true peace. My peace is with the humble and meek of heart. Thy peace shall be in much patience. He who knows how to suffer will enjoy much peace. Such a one is a conqueror of himself and lord of the world, a friend of Christ and an heir of heaven." The majestic power of self-control keeps the heart quiet in danger, calm in trial, and undisturbed in suffering. Much more, however, does our peace depend upon our trust in God, submission to His holy will, and perfect confidence in His providence. "Blessed be the Lord, my God," sings the Royal Psalmist, " my mercy and my refuge: my support and my deliverer: my protector; and I have hoped in him" (*Ps.* cxliii. 1, 2). "He that dwelleth in the aid of the most High shall abide under the protection of the God of Jacob: my God, in Him will I trust. He will overshadow thee with His shoulders; and under His wings thou shalt trust. . . . He hath given His angels charge over thee: to keep thee in all thy ways. In their hands they shall bear thee up; lest thou dash thy foot against a stone" (*Ps.* xc. 1, 4, 11, 12).

The "Imitation" says:

" MAKE no great account who is for thee or against thee, but let it be thy business and thy care that

God may be with thee in everything thou dost (*Rom.*
viii. 31).

"Have a good conscience, and God will sufficiently
defend thee.

"For he whom God will help no man's malice can
hurt.

"If thou canst but hold thy peace and suffer, thou
shalt see, without doubt, that the Lord will help thee.

"He knows the time and manner of delivering thee
and therefore thou must resign thyself to Him.

"It belongs to God to help and to deliver us from all
confusion.

"When a man humbles himself for his defects he
then easily appeases others, and quickly satisfies those
that are angry with him.

"The humble man God protects and delivers; the
humble He loves and comforts; to the humble He in-
clines Himself; to the humble He gives grace (*Prov.*
xxix. 23), and after he has been depressed. raises him
to glory."

You desire happiness; well, then, here is a good
resolution for you in the words of Bishop Challoner:

"I am resolved therefore, to live in peace with God,
by obeying Him in all things; in peace with my neighbor, by not censuring his conduct or interfering with his
affairs; and in peace with myself, by combating and
subduing, on all occasions, the emotions and repug-
nances of my heart."

22. —Ibappiness in Suffering

"BLESSED are they that mourn, for they shall be com
forted. Blessed are they that suffer persecution for justice' sake; for theirs is the kingdom of

heaven. Blessed are ye when they shall revile you
and persecute you, and speak all that is evil against you,
untruly, for My sake: be glad and rejoice, for your
reward is very great in heaven" (*Matt.* v. 5, 10–12).

By sufferings we become like to Christ and His
blessed Mother, Our Lady of Sorrows. Suffering was
the lot of all the saints. Suffering is very meritorious.
Suffering intensifies our love of God. Suffering has
a refining influence upon our character. Suffering
tends to free us from selfish motives and purifies our
aspirations. Suffering elevates the mind and chastens
the heart and its affections. Suffering braces the will
and gives it tone. Suffering develops manliness and
tries earnestness of purpose. Suffering is a test of
virtue.

Suffering is conducive to sanctity, for every sorrow,
every trial, can be turned into a blessing by the will of
the Christian sufferer. St. Ignatius Loyola says: "If
the Lord send you great tribulations, it is an evidence
that He has great designs upon you, and that He wills
that you become a saint. There is no wood more
proper to enkindle and feed the fire of divine love than
the wood of the Cross."

Sufferings and afflictions are a token of God's love;
"for," as St. Paul tells us, "whom the Lord loveth He
chastiseth. God dealeth with you as with His sons;
for what son is there, whom the father doth not correct?"
(*Heb.* xii. 6, 7.)

"Now all chastisement for the present indeed seemeth
not to bring with it joy, but sorrow; but afterward it
will yield to them that are exercised by it the most
peaceable fruit of justice" (*Heb.* xii. 11).

"Know ye not," writes the Apostle again to the
Romans, "that to them that love God all things work

together unto good — to such as are called to be saints"
(*Rom.* viii. 28).

"The sufferings of this life are not worthy to be compared with the glory to come, that shall be revealed
in us " (*Rom.* viii. 18).

God is good, He loves us as a Father; and our sorrows are blessings in disguise.

Sufferings afford opportunities for the practice of
many virtues — of patience, repentance, fortitude,
compassion, kindness, humility, courage, generosity —
virtues which develop greatness and nobility of soul.

Suffering is undoubtedly a source of great merit and
happiness, when the sufferer is animated by a supernatural motive — and especially the motive of love.
The grandest music of the human heart breaks forth in
the day of trial; the sweetest songs are sung in sorrow;
the best things in character are developed in the time of
affliction.

"Our sincerest laughter with some pain is fraught;
Our sweetest songs are those that tell of saddest thought."
— SHELLEY.

Jesus said to His disciples: *"My chalice indeed
you shall drink"* (*Matt.* xx. 23). Commenting on
these words, Father Gallwey writes in "The Watches
of the Passion": "To His chosen ones, to those to
whom He afterward said: '*I will not now call you servants, but I have called you friends,*' the grand and
special promise that He makes is this, 'You shall, I
promise you, before you die, drink of My chalice.' To
His own blessed Mother, as they conversed together in
Nazareth, this, doubtless, was the assurance that He
often repeated in order to console her, that she should
be with Him to the end, and share His bitter chalice to

the dregs. His golden promise afterward to St. Paul was, '*I will show him what great things he must suffer for My name's sake*' (*Acts* ix. 16).

"How blind then are we if we believe that every suffering is a calamity and a proof of God's wrath; and that prosperity, and nothing but prosperity, is a sure sign of His favor!

"(*a*) He sends suffering in His mercy to *atone* here for past sin, to do here quickly the slow work of purgatory.

"(*b*) He sends suffering also to *prevent* sin; and to *draw* us out of sin, as suffering brought the prodigal home to Him.

"(*c*) Lastly He sends suffering to His *chosen* ones, as to St. Paul; and these chosen ones then become, like Himself, Saviour unto many."

Sorrow and suffering are especially blessed and sanctified by the sacred passion of Jesus, and ought to help us powerfully to greater union with Him.

St. Francis Xavier, while at Lisbon, was afflicted to see that everything prospered with him. He was afraid that God was not pleased with him when He favored him with no cross. And when sufferings were sent him, he would exclaim: "Still more, my God, still more!"

The Apostle plainly tells us that those who would live piously in Jesus Christ must suffer persecution.

Our Lord Himself says: "He that taketh not up his cross and followeth Me is not worthy of Me" (*Matt.* x. 38). "If any man will come after Me, let him deny himself and take up his cross and follow Me" (*Matt.* xvi. 24).

"The Son of God," says St. Teresa, "has accomplished our salvation by the means of sufferings; He would by this teach us that there is no means more proper to glorify God and to sanctify our souls than to suffer."

"If we knew," writes St. Vincent de Paul, "the precious treasure which is hidden in our infirmities, we would receive them with the same joy that we receive the greatest benefits, and we would bear them without complaining."

Each year brings its trials; let us learn from the saints to receive all that happens as from the hand of God and appointed for our sanctification and salvation. "Patience is necessary for you, that doing the will of God you may receive the promise" (*Heb.* x. 36).

23. — The Practice of Charity [1]

SEEK occasions to please the Heart of Jesus by the practice of holy charity, in always thinking and speaking well of your neighbor, assisting the poor according to your ability, spiritually and corporally, considering Jesus Christ in their person, and doing nothing to them which you would not wish to be done to yourself. Be patient toward all, in order to give confidence to each one, and above all to the poor who come to you in their need. Be a friend to every one and an enemy to no one; then you will become like unto God.

Charles IX, King of France, once asked the poet Tasso who, in his estimation, was happiest. Tasso replied without hesitation: "God." "Everybody knows that," continued the king; "but who is next?"

---

[1] With the exception of a few slight alterations and additions paragraphs 23–44 are extracts from The Sentinel of the Blessed Sacrament.

And Tasso answered: "He who becomes most like to God."

24. — The Highest Pleasures

THE highest, the best, the most permanent pleasures are those which are not sought, but which come from the faithful fulfilment of life's duties and obligations. Indeed, eager search after pleasure in any direction is always fruitless, because it implies a condition of mind to which enduring happiness is a stranger. Selfishness and enjoyment may dwell together for a brief season, but the latter will soon wither away under the absorbing influence of the former.

25. — Don't Go To Heaven Alone

DON'T go to Heaven alone! Take somebody with you. Mothers, take your children with you. Pray as long as you have breath in your body — never despair and never give up the hope that your loved ones, no matter how far their footsteps have wandered, will one day stand with you before the Great White Throne.

26. — Let Us Go About Doing Good

IF WE are educated, let us, in the Master's name, instruct the ignorant; if we possess wealth, let us use it as God intended; if we have health, let us cheer some drooping soul; if we enjoy any singular opportunities, consider them prayerfully, and in so doing we shall find that the moments that really shine out in our lives are those in which we have buried self and gone out into this busy and sinful world, and have endeavored, by prayer and effort, to do the will of Him, whose one great mission was to go about doing good.

27. — The Love of God

IF YOU love God, you will keep His commandments. That is the visible proof of charity. Love can not rest in words — it must go out into action. If you love God, you will do something for Him. Love is ingenious at finding ways in which to show itself. It manifests itself in acts of praise, in acts of self-denial, in acts of kindness to God's other creatures. Love without works is dead.

28. — Character

CHARACTER is the product of daily, hourly actions, and words, and thoughts; daily kindnesses, sacrifices for the good of others, struggles against temptation, submissiveness under trial. Oh! it is these, like the blending colors in a picture, or the blending notes of music, which constitute the man.

Saints are men of character. A man has character, when he is conscientious; when he is not moved by every passing impulse or feeling but by a fixed will to do always what is right and good; when he does not go where it is easiest to go, but where it is his duty to go; when he controls his passions; when he has the moral courage to stand up for his religious convictions.

29. — A Young Man and his Beads

IN ONE of the largest military colleges of France, a pair of beads was picked up from the ground by one of the oldest students, who thought he would have some fun at the next recreation. Accordingly, after dinner he suspended the beads on a branch of a tree and called out publicly: "Who has lost his beads?" No one expected an answer; but suddenly a young student went toward the tree and with his sword gently caused the beads to drop into his hand. "They are mine, sir," said he, "I have lost them, and now I thank you for the favor." "Bravo, young man," said a grave voice from behind. They all turned in surprise; it was the general himself, for whom they made room, until he reached his young hero, whose hand he seized warmly, saying: "Continue, my child; you have done a noble action. Never fear; you will make your way." From that day the young man was esteemed and loved by all his comrades.

30. — What Flowers Indicate

I HAVE always noticed that wherever you find flowers, no matter whether in a garret or in a palace, it is a pretty sure sign that there is an inner refinement of which the world is not cognizant. I have seen flowers cultivated and cherished by some of the lowest and poorest of our people. Where these emblems of purity are found, you may rest assured that they represent a hope, and speak of a goodness of heart not to be found where they are absent.

31. — Pictures in a Home

A ROOM with good Catholic pictures in it and a room without such pictures differ as much as a room with windows and one without these necessities. Pic-

tures, and I mean only good, pure pictures, are consolers of loneliness, and a relief to the troubled mind.
They are windows to the imprisoned heart, books, his-
tories, sermons which we can read without the trouble
of turning over the leaves or straining the eyes. They
make up for the want of many other enjoyments to
those whose life is mostly passed amid the smoke and
din, the bustle and noise of a large city. Pictures of
Our Lord and His saints inspire us, give us courage,
and induce us to bear our cross with Christian resignation.

32. — Be at Peace

DO NOT look forward to what may happen to-morrow;
the same everlasting Father who cares for you
to-day will take care of you to-morrow and every day.
Either He will shield you from suffering or He will give
you unfailing strength to bear it. Be at peace, then,
and put aside all anxious thought and imaginations.

33. — Trust in God

IT IS true there are times of trial and days of darkness, when the best of us are apt to mistrust the
providence of God over us, and are tempted to lose
heart and hope altogether; but if we are seeking first
the kingdom of heaven we shall understand that it is
God who gives and God who takes away; and that He
gives and takes away for our soul's sake, that we are of
much more value in His sight than the birds of the air.
We shall put our trust in His providence and suffer not
the wants of the body, the things of sense, and the trials
of this life to fill our souls with bitterness; we shall be

trustful in the hour of need, patient in the hour of disappointment, tranquil in the hour of trial, and when the hour of deliverance shall come we shall count as nothing the anxiety and sorrows through which we have passed for "the sufferings of this present time are not worthy to be compared with the glory to come that shall be revealed in us."

34. — Be Affable Always

THERE are some who are affable and gracious to every one as long as things go according to their wishes; but if they meet with a contradiction, if an accident, a reproach or even less should trouble the serenity of their soul, all around them must suffer the consequences. They grow dark and cross; very far from keeping up the conversation by their good humor, they answer only monosyllables to those who speak to them. Is this conduct reasonable? Is it Christian? — *The Art of Being Happy.*

*

IT is to be regretted that so many people who are very pious are very censorious in their comments upon their neighbors. Piety ought to find expression in kindness to our neighbors as well as in devotion to God. We should remember that the Christ whom we serve was kind.

35. — Enthusiasm

IT is faith in something, and enthusiasm for something, that makes a life worth looking at.
— OLIVER WENDELL HOLMES.

KEEP a hobby and ride it with enthusiasm. It will keep you out of mischief, to say the least; it will keep you cheerful. Here as in all things you can apply the *Ad Majorem Dei Gloriam.*

36. — In the Home

HOME is the place where a man should appear at his best. He who is bearish at home and polite only abroad is no true gentleman; indeed, he who can not be considerate to those of his own household will never be really courteous to strangers. There is no better training for healthy and pleasant intercourse with the outer world than a bright and cheerful demeanor at home. It is in a man's home that his real character is seen; as he appears there, so he is really elsewhere, however skilfully he may for the time conceal his true nature.

37. — Promote Happiness in Your Homes

IT WOULD do much to promote happiness in the home if all the members of the family were to be as kind and courteous to one another as they are to guests. The visitor receives bright smiles, pleasant words, constant attention, and the fruits of efforts to please. But the home folks are often cross, rude, selfish, and faultfinding toward one another. Are not our own as worthy of our love and care as is the stranger temporarily within our gates?

38. — A Sunshiny Disposition

THERE is a charm which compensates so much for the lack of good looks that they are never missed, and when combined with good looks it doubly enhances them. The name of this charm is *a sunshiny disposition*. If things go wrong, as they will go once in a while, does it mend matters to cry over them? Sensible women will say "no," but women who do not know how to control themselves will say: "Yes, it does me good to cry; I feel better after it." There are times when tears must come, but these are beautiful, holy tears. Quite the contrary are the tears shed over selfish, petty annoyances "to relieve nerves." The grandest quality of the human mind is self-control.

39. — The Blessing of Pain and Grief

PAIN and grief clear the mind and help man to know himself Trouble sweeps away as a mist all deceits and false living, and leaves man to see himself just as he is. Hence he can study his motives, his tendencies, his character honestly. Temporary pleasures, momentary delights, the glare of sunlight, are all taken away, and just as the eyes can often see farther on a cloudy day than in the full sunlight, so the man sees more exactly his life and all that touches his life. Thank God that sometimes all the fancy touches and adornments of existence are removed, and we see plainly. For God looks at the heart of us, not at the dress; and to master life is to see it with His eyes. So, when trouble comes, when loneliness or grief approaches, when a dark day dawns, be glad that there is a chance

for self-study, for stock-taking, for a clearing up, for a
moral and spiritual housecleaning.

40. — The Path of Sorrow

DO AWAY with penance, humility, obedience, and
self-denial, and you abolish the crucifix.   But so
long as we retain that symbol, constantly preaching to
us the story of God's sufferings; so long as we believe
that He suffered not merely to make atonement for
our sins, but to teach us to "fill up those things that are
wanting of the sufferings of Christ" in our flesh (*Col.
i.* 24); so long must the spirit of self-denial remain in
practice in the Church that He has founded.

> *The path of sorrow, and that path alone,*
> *Leads to the land where sorrow is unknown.*

41. — Job's Comforters

MANY, like the comforters of Job, look upon all
calamity and suffering as the direct result of sin
and say: "Sin, and you suffer; sin not, and you suffer
not."   But Christ seems to point to a higher harmony
and a more profound reason, and indeed to a solution
of the problem which, though it may leave something
to be desired by human reason, is all satisfactory to
reason illumined by faith.   "Neither this man hath
sinned nor his parents, but that the works of God may
be made manifest in him."   Out of suffering comes
all good, and in the providence of God it is the means
of lifting man to the very pinnacle of greatness here
below and to eternal beatitude hereafter.

42. — Peace

WHEN our divine Lord sent His disciples out to preach, one of His instructions was: "Into whatsoever house you enter, first say: Peace be to this house." Peace is a good word. It is more than a salutation; falling from the Master's lips, it is a divine benediction as well. Peace, too, is a fruit of grace, which includes all that is sweetest and divine in Christian culture. Christ's peace is a blessing which comes out of struggle and discipline. Well, therefore, does the salutation "Peace!" befit a Catholic home, which ought to be the abode of peace.

43. — Heart and Face

A GOOD heart makes a good face — perhaps not beautiful or classic, but refined, sincere, and noble. The face will shine with God behind it. There are some faces even to-day that at times seem to have a glow upon them. There are faces that are quiet and uninteresting in repose, that light up amazingly with the animation of talking. There are some who can never get a good photograph, because the camera can not catch the subtle sparkle of the eye in which the whole individuality lies. There are some whom you would not at first call handsome, whose faces grow on you with constant acquaintance until they become beautiful to you. For you see the soul shining through, you see the splendor of a noble character glorifying every feature. True beauty in the soul will come out in the sweetness, the brightness, the quiet glory of the face.

44.—Reading, a Molder of Character

THE inspiration of a single book has made teachers, preachers, philosophers, authors, and statesmen. The first good book read by one has often appeared before him through life as a beacon which has saved him from many a danger. On the other hand, the demoralizing effects of one book have made profligates and criminals. Many youths and adults now in prison trace the beginning of their downfall to the reading of a bad book.

*

A MAN'S character is shown by the books he reads.

*

GOOD books add to the happiness of a home. The true university of these days is a collection of books. — CARLYLE.

*

THE Bible, "The Lives of the Saints," and "The Imitation of Christ" ought to be well thumbed.

*

IT IS quite reasonable to look for a Catholic magazine and a Catholic newspaper on the library table of a Catholic home.

The Catholic press ought to be supported by every Catholic family. It is a mighty apostolate; the good it does is incalculable.

*

A HOUSE is no home unless it contains food and fire for the mind as well as for the body. — OSSOLI

PEOPLE are not usually better than the books they read. — *Anon.*

*

THERE is no friend so faithful as a good book. There is no worse robber than a bad book.
— *Italian Proverb.*

*

THE books which help you most are those which make you think the most. — THEODORE PARKER.

*

A HABIT all should cultivate
Is oft to read and ruminate.

*

'TIS not how much but how well we read. — *Anon.*

*

BOOKS should to one of these four ends conduce:
For wisdom, piety, delight, or use. — DENHAM.

45. — Faults of Those We Love

WHO does not know, alas, the touching charm with which death envelops all memories? The faults of those who are gone are forgotten, for we have ceased to suffer from them. We feel only the void which our loved ones have left, and however wayward their course, we can recall a time in their lives that was good, sentiments that were noble and touching. This period and these sentiments are our most vivid memories, and suffice to make us regret them.

Ah, why should we only discover the virtues of those who love us when it is too late to appreciate them, to enjoy them, and to let our loved ones see that we appreciate them! — *Golden Sands.*

46. — Little Kindnesses

NO SINGLE great deed is comparable to the multitude of little kindnesses performed by those unselfish souls who forget their own sorrows and as true followers of Christ scatter happiness on every side, and strew all life with hope and good cheer.

47. — The Power of Silence

WHAT a strange power there is in silence! How many resolutions are formed — how many sublime conquests effected during that pause when the lips are closed and the soul secretly feels the eye of her Maker upon her. When some of these cutting, sharp, blighting words have been spoken, which send the hot indignant blood to the face and head, if those to whom they are addressed keep silent, look on with awe, for a mighty work is going on within them, and the spirit of evil or their guardian angel is very near to them in that hour. During that pause they have made a step toward heaven or toward hell, and an item has been scored in the book which the Day of Judgment shall see opened. They are the strong ones of the earth, the mighty forces for good or evil, those who know how to keep silence when it is a pain or grief to them. — *Anon.*

48. — The Title of Our Lady

THE title of "Our Lady" first came into general use in the days of chivalry; for she was the Lady "of all hearts," whose colors all were proud to wear. Hundreds upon hundreds had enrolled themselves in brotherhoods vowed to her especial service, or devoted to acts of charity to be performed in her name.

GO TO Our Lady, whose love is as the sea; pray her to help you to overcome your faults, to obtain for you never to commit a deliberate fault, never to offend God. She will not only make you very good but very happy. — FATHER DIGNAM, S.J.

*

BEAR this in mind: it was *because of his mother*, "being moved with mercy toward her" (*Luke* vii. 13) that Jesus raised the dead man at the gate of Naim. Be careful, when you desire any great favor, to implore the intercession of *your Mother*, of Mary. Ask for great favors and for all graces in the name of Christ's Mother, remind Our Lord of her agony, when, her soul pierced with a sword of sorrow, she stood at the foot of the cross. Have the most unbounded confidence in Mary's intercession. — *Ibid.*

*

O LADY, thou art the Mother of Him who pardons and of those who are pardoned; of Him who justifies and of those who are justified; of Him who saves and of those who are saved. O blessed confidence! O safe refuge! The Mother of God is our Mother; the Mother of Him in whom alone we hope, and whom alone we fear, is our Mother; the Mother of Him who alone can save or destroy is our Mother. — ST. ANSELM.

When we have handled something fragrant, our hands perfume whatever they touch; let our prayers pass through the Blessed Virgin's hands, and she will give them fragrance. — THE BLESSED CURÉ D'ARS.

49. — The Gentle Saint

AS FOR gentle St. Joseph, he has a place in the affections of all Catholics. They learned to love him in the first Bible stories heard at their mother's knee, in their school days, when they learned his hymns, and "honored" him one special day during his month, by placing a plant before his statue, and wearing his badge throughout the day; and when, school days over, they go out into the world, he is still their cherished and favorite protector, as he was the faithful guardian of the Blessed Mother and Child. He will be honored then, in this his month — the month of March — and on his especial feast-day, Wednesday. Every Wednesday in the year is consecrated to St. Joseph, and his clients practise especial devotions in his honor on that day. — *Anon.*

ACT OF CONSECRATION TO ST. JOSEPH

O BLESSED Joseph, faithful guardian of my Redeemer, Jesus Christ, protector of thy chaste spouse, the virgin Mother of God, I choose thee this day to be my special patron and advocate, and I firmly resolve to honor thee all the days of my life. Therefore I humbly beseech thee to receive me as thy client, to instruct me in every doubt, to comfort me in every affliction, to obtain for me and for all the knowledge and love of the Heart of Jesus, and finally to defend and protect me at the hour of my death. Amen.

Ejaculation

ST. JOSEPH, model and patron of those who love the Sacred Heart of Jesus, pray for us. — (100 days' indulgence once a day. Leo XIII, Dec. 19, 1891.)

50. — St. Joseph the Patron of Those Who Love the Sacred Heart of Jesus

DEVOUT clients of the foster-father of Our Saviour welcome each year the return of the month set aside especially to honor him, and the month in which his feast is celebrated. There is no devotion so wide-spread or so popular as that to the gentle saint whom all revere, and the world over devout Catholics unite to show their fealty and affection for one so particularly blessed. As he was close to the Heart of the Saviour in this life, so is he close to the hearts of those who follow that heart, no matter how haltingly and weakly; and it is safe to assume that in the realms of eternal happiness St. Joseph is still the chosen one of Jesus and Mary. Ask for his intercession, then, in this his particular month, and the gentle saint will lay your petitions at the foot of the Great White Throne. — *The Sentinel of the Blessed Sacrament.*

*

"I KNOW by experience," says St. Teresa, "that the glorious St. Joseph assists us generally in *all* necessities. I never asked him for anything which he did not obtain for me."

51. — The Guardian Angels

"HE HATH given His angels charge over thee, to keep thee in all thy ways" (*Ps. xc. 11*).

St. Francis of Sales had a particular devotion to his guardian angel; he celebrated the feast with special care and piety; in spirit he received his blessing in the most important actions of his life; and not only was he devout to his good angel, but also to the angels of his friends. He had even a devotion to those of the heretics, his enemies; for he said that in disputing with the Huguenots he exorcised the demons who possessed and obsessed them, and afterward invoked their angels. When he was absent from his diocese, he recommended it in an especial manner to the care of his holy angel. He never failed to salute the angels of the kingdoms, provinces, or parishes which he entered. In the confessional he frequently invoked the guardian angel of his penitent, and we may read in his letters how much he recommended to his pious friends devotion to their guardian angel. He said that in this world the angels attend to almost everything, as they are the messengers of God, and invisible; and that to accomplish much for His divine service and not wish to appear was to serve God in an angelic manner. — *New Month of the Holy Angels.*

52. — Exercise Your Charity in Behalf of the Poor Souls in Purgatory

ST. THOMAS declares that prayer for the dead is the most excellent of all kinds of intercessory prayer.

The holy Curé d'Ars once said: "Oh, my friends, let us pray much, and let us obtain many prayers from others, for the poor dead; the good God will render us back the good we do to them a hundredfold. Ah! if every one knew how useful this devotion to the holy souls in purgatory is to those who practise it, they would not be forgotten so often; the good God regards all that we do for them as if it were done to Himself."

53. — By Prayer and Almsdeeds

"**D**o you wish to honor the dead?" asks St. Chrysostom. "Give alms for them! For what will weeping alone avail? What good can a pompous funeral and vain display achieve? Rather be intent with all your might to assist the departed soul by alms, deeds, prayer, and holy Masses. Let mourners weep and show their grief; let them find consolation in tears: but let them not forget to come, with still greater zeal, to the aid of the departed, by the Holy Sacrifice, by prayer and almsdeeds."

54. — It Is Sure To Come

Look at your fellow human beings; what befalls them. Some of them fall dead on the streets; some are found dead in their beds; some have their lives suddenly crushed out; some are cut off in their occupations; some die in agonizing pains; some go forth in the morning and return not in the evening; some die in the midst of mirth and laughter; some meet violent death at the hands of others; some die at their meals, away from home, separated from friends, and many die in their sins. Nearly all are called when they least expect it. Consider these stern facts and you will not easily sin. "It is appointed unto men once to die, and after this the judgment" (*Heb.* ix. 27). *Death is sure to come.*

*

One tear of the heart over the passion of our blessed Lord! How much fire of purgatory has it the power to quench. — Faber.

55. — Keep Your Eye on Heaven

IF THE sun is going down, look up at the stars; if the earth is dark, keep your eye on heaven. With God's presence and God's promises, any one may be cheerful.

56. — Use Your Gentlest Voice at Home

I WOULD say to all: Use your gentlest voice at home. Watch it day by day as a pearl of great price; for it will be worth more to you in days to come than the best pearl hid in the sea. A kind voice is joy, like a lark's song, to a hearth at home. Train it to sweet tones now, and it will keep in tune through life. — ELIHU BURRITT.

*

ST. FRANCIS OF SALES says: "Accustom yourself in all that you do to act and speak gently and quietly, and you will see that in a short time you will completely control that abrupt impulsiveness."

*

"COURAGE! Let us keep on in the low valleys of the little virtues. I love these three little virtues: *gentleness of heart, firmness of mind,* and *simplicity of life.*"

*

"DO NOT be quick to speak. Say much by a modest and judicious silence."

*

"GREAT evenness of temper, continual gentleness, and suavity of heart are more rare than perfect charity, yet very desirable."

"DISPOSE your soul to tranquillity in the morning and be careful during the day to recall it frequently to that state. Be on your guard and keep your soul within your control."

57. — Do It Now

THIS short sentence is often seen inscribed upon calendars. It is a constant injunction to attend promptly to present duties.

The motto is a good one for the new year. There is a great fascination about the unknown future and the distant past. "Distance lends enchantment to the view." Some are occupied with vain regrets for the "good old times," now gone forever. Others are looking eagerly forward to the days that are to come. There is danger lest the value and meaning of to-day be entirely forgotten. We need the sharp reminder "Do it now." Do not put off till to-morrow what can be and ought to be done to-day.

"Ever keep in mind thy end," says Thomas à Kempis, "and that time lost returneth no more." Take to heart the following admonition from "The Little Treasury of Leaflets":

" At the falling of another,
   Be it friend or be it brother,
Never sneer, and ne'er deride,
   Help the weak and conquer pride.

"Let no good by thee be marred,
   Let no duty seem too hard,
In all things bravely do your best,
   And then to God we'll leave the rest."

" If we sit down at set of sun,
And count the things that we have done,
One self-denying act, one word
That eased the heart of him who heard,
One glance most kind,
That fell like sunshine where it went,
Then we may count the day well spent."

*

WE CAN easily manage our affairs, if we only take each day the burden appointed for it. But the load will be too heavy for us if we add to its weight the burden of to-morrow before we are called to bear it.

58. — Frankness; Prudence; Simplicity

THERE is a *frankness* which is brutal, and I detest it; a frankness which is indiscreet, and I fear it; a foolish frankness, and I pity it. There is also a frankness which is opportune, delicate and good; honor to it! — ABBÉ ROUX.

"Be ye, therefore, wise as serpents and simple as doves" (*Matt.* x. 16).

"*Prudence*," says St. Vincent de Paul, "prompts us to speak with due caution, so as to suit our discourse to the time, place, and subject. It causes us to abstain from such remarks as offend God or our neighbor, as well as those which tend to our own praise, or other evil consequences.

" In regard to *simplicity*, the companion of prudence, we should be simple in our affections, intentions, actions, and words; we should do what we find to do without artifice or guile, making our exterior conformable to our interior; we should have no other object but God in our actions and seek to please Him alone in all things."

59. — By Trying We Learn

O ONE knows what he can do until he tries. The germs of success are in every nature, but hard work is required in order to mature them. It has been said that genius is infinite patience. He who fixes his eyes on a certain goal, be it ever so high, and makes for it with all his strength, is pretty sure to rise above the difficulties that beset his path. This is true in the moral as well as in the intellectual world.

*

OU can be a saint, and indeed a great saint; it depends on your own will what shall be your lot in eternity; God gives abundant grace in response to prayer. With the Apostle you can say: "I can do all things in Him, who strengtheneth me" (*Philipp.* iv. 13).

"To be saints," says the Blessed Antony Grassi, "we need not work miracles, but we must faithfully observe the Christian faith." If you are in the state of grace and firmly resolved not to offend God, you are a saint. Aim high; strive to become ever more perfect. "Be you perfect," says Our Lord, "as also your heavenly Father is perfect."

Let "Excelsior" be your watchword.

What does Longfellow tell us in his "Psalm of Life":

"Life is real! Life is earnest!
And the grave is not its goal;
Dust thou art, to dust returnest,
Was not spoken of the soul.

"Not enjoyment, and not sorrow,
Is our destined end or way;
But to act that each to-morrow
Find us farther than to-day."

A GOOD motto is, *Altiora peto:* "I seek the higher things," or, *Ad astra per ardua:* "Through difficulties to the stars." St. Teresa was willing to bear any pain or hardship, for any length of time, for the sake of one little degree of extra glory in heaven. "For star differeth from star in glory" (1 *Cor.* xv. 41).

60. — For His Glory

WHAT a subject of humiliation it is to think how few actions we do solely and entirely from the love of God; with what mixed motives we do even our good actions! Let us beg for a great purity of heart; then will come purity of thought, purity of action; then indeed all things will be done purely for God's glory and His love. Then shall we be on the road to become saints.

*

TEMPTATIONS are overcome by the three words. *Credo! Spero! Amo!* I believe, I hope, I love.
— BLESSED ANTONY GRASSI.

61. — Guard of Chastity

MEDITATION on the sufferings of Our Lord has a special power in overcoming temptations against purity. By the very fact that the vivid scenes of the sufferings of Christ imprint themselves on our imagination, the evil thought is immediately expelled. Love for Christ at the sight of His agony makes us reject the temptation promptly and incites also to works of mortification.

*

AVOID the occasions of sin and shun evil associations.

*

LET us keep ourselves in the presence of God. In all our ways, let us ever have before us the example of Our Lord, and how He thought, spoke, and acted; and in every circumstance of life let us copy His example.

62. — Holy Communion [1]

1. FREQUENT and daily communion, as a thing most earnestly desired by Christ our Lord and by the Catholic Church, should be open to all the faithful, of whatever rank and condition of life; so that no one who is in the state of grace, and who approaches the holy table with a right and devout intention, can lawfully be hindered therefrom.

2. A right intention consists in this: that he who approaches the holy table should do so, not out of routine, or vainglory, or human respect, but for the purpose of pleasing God, or being more closely united with Him by charity, and of seeking this divine remedy for his weaknesses and defects.

3. Although it is more expedient that those who communicate frequently or daily should be free from venial sins, especially from such as are fully deliberate, and from any affection thereto, nevertheless it is suf-

[1] Extract from the Pontifical Decree on Daily Communion. — Pius X, 1905.

ficient that they be free from mortal sin, with the purpose of never sinning mortally in future; and, if they have this sincere purpose, it is impossible but that daily communicants should gradually emancipate themselves from even venial sins, and from all affection thereto.

4. But whereas the sacraments of the New Law, though they take effect *ex opere operato*, nevertheless produce a greater effect in proportion as the dispositions of the recipient are better; therefore, care is to be taken that holy communion be preceded by serious preparation, and followed by a suitable thanksgiving according to each one's strength, circumstances, and duties.

5. That the practice of frequent and daily communion may be carried out with greater prudence and more abundant merit, the confessor's advice should be asked. Confessors, however, are to be careful not to dissuade any one (*ne quemquam avertant*) from frequent and daily communion, provided that he is in a state of grace and approaches with a right intention.

*

IF THE world asks you why you communicate so often, say you do so in order to learn how to love God; to purify yourself from your imperfection, to deliver yourself from your miseries, to seek for consolations in your trials, and to strengthen yourself in your weakness. — ST. FRANCIS OF SALES.

*

THIS sacrament is the gift of gifts and the grace of graces. When the almighty and eternal God comes to us, with all the perfections of His thrice-holy humanity and His divinity, He surely does not come empty-handed. Provided that you have proved yourself, as

the Apostle enjoins, He remits your temporal punishment, strengthens you against temptation, weakens
the power of your enemies, and increases your merits.
— ST. ANGELA OF FOLIGNO.

*

THE Eucharist heals the maladies of the soul. It
strengthens it against temptation. It deadens
the ardor of concupiscence. It incorporates us with
Jesus Christ. — ST. CYRIL OF ALEXANDRIA.

*

DO YOU wish to love God sincerely, . . . to maintain
in your heart the divine and eternal life of Jesus
Christ? Communicate *often* and regularly.
— DE SÉGUR.

*

ONE of the most admirable effects of holy communion is to preserve souls from falling, and to help
those who fall from weakness to rise again; therefore
it is much more profitable frequently to approach this
divine sacrament with love, respect, and confidence
than to keep back from an excess of fear and cowardice.
— ST. IGNATIUS.

*

TO COMMUNICATE every day, and partake of the
sacred body and blood of Christ is a most beautiful and profitable practice, for He has clearly said:
"He who eateth My flesh and drinketh My blood,
hath everlasting life." — ST. BASIL.

*

O SACRED banquet, in which Christ is received, the
memory of His passion is renewed, the mind is filled
with grace, and a pledge of future glory is given to us.
— ST. THOMAS, *Office of the Blessed Sacrament.*

THE fruit we ought to derive from holy communion consists in being transformed into the likeness of Jesus Christ. We must endeavor to render ourselves like Him throughout the whole course of our lives; to be as He was, chaste, meek, humble, patient, obedient.

— RODRIGUEZ.

*

THE body of the Lord is eaten, and the blood of the Lord is received in memory of Our Lord's obedience unto death, that they who live may live no longer to themselves, but to Him who died and rose again for them. — ST. BASIL THE GREAT.

63. — Christ in the Eucharist

JESUS knowing that His hour was come, that He should pass out of this world to the Father, having loved His own who were in the world, He loved them to the end. And so at the end, came the Last Supper and the First Communion; for this jealous Lover could not bear to leave us without a keepsake, a love token, a perpetual remembrancer, such as only God could imagine it, as only God could give it.

— REV. M. RUSSELL, S.J.

*

IT IS no strain of music, no tinsel of vestment, no pomp of ceremonial which attracts us to our churches, which holds us captive in them. No! For us Jesus in the Blessed Sacrament offers the same attractions, commands the same reverent attention, elicits the same humble adoration, whether we assist at His worship amid the poverty and simplicity of an Indian chapel, or assist at it amid the wealth and grandeur of a stately cathedral; it is Christ in the

Eucharist who holds us captive. It matters not to us whether He is worshiped amid the squalor of a stable, as at Bethlehem, by the lowly and illiterate, or as afterward when offered gold and incense He is adored by the high-born and learned, by kings and wise men.

*

LET us do all in our power, however, to beautify the house of God; let us endeavor to render to Our Lord in the Sacrament of the Altar an external worship worthy of His majesty and goodness; let us in particular aid the tabernacle society, whose aim is to furnish gratuitously to poor churches and foreign missions the requisites for divine service.

*

LOVE keeps Jesus in our midst; love shall engage me to pay Him frequent visits, and to prolong them as much as possible; and this same love shall cause my thoughts and desires to remain with the God of the tabernacle when I am forced to quit His presence.

— PÈRE HUBY.

64. — Salute Your Lord in the Blessed Sacrament

WHILE passing a church, manifest your devotion to the Blessed Sacrament by some sign of reverence. Lift your hat and incline your head, when you pass your divine *Friend*, and say in your heart that you love Him and will be faithful to Him. Say, for instance, "*All for Thee, O Jesus!*" or "*Jesus my Love!*" or "*My God and my All!*" or "*Praised be Jesus Christ!*" or "*Jesus, bless me; I thank Thee for all Thy blessings!*"

or "*O Sacrament most holy, O Sacrament divine; All praise and all thanksgiving be every moment Thine!*"

If you have time (perhaps you can "make time") step in and visit Our Lord for a few moments. You are busy, — yes; but remember, there is but one *real* business in life, but "*one thing necessary.*" Keep that in mind all the time. Save your soul! "*Seek ye first the Kingdom of God, and all these things shall be added unto you*" (*Matt.* vi. 33). Your business will not suffer if you spend a few moments with your *best Friend* — the same who will one day be your *Judge.* Keep Him as your Friend. And if you think of Him and His interests, He will think of you and prosper your affairs.

At the hour of luncheon — at midday — it would be worth while to go out of your way to visit the Blessed Sacrament, to have a few moments' conversation with the *divine Lover of souls*, who abides with us "all days" for our good. It would refresh you, soul and body; it would certainly make you feel better; it would help you to forget your disappointments, and to take up your burden again with a light heart. Our Lord did not say in vain: "Come to Me all you that labor and are burdened, and I will refresh you" (*Matt.* xi. 28).

65. — What Mass Is

NON-CATHOLICS who are present at Mass, not understanding the ceremony, wonder why we should be so diligent in assisting at it. To them the idea of church and public worship is associated with preaching and hymn singing. They are surprised at a function in which a clergyman takes no notice of the people and at which often there is no sermon.

What, then, is the Mass that so attracts Catholics and attendance at which is made obligatory on them, at least once a week, under pain of deadly sin?

The Mass is the Last Supper over again. In it the priest takes bread and wine, and pronounces over them the sacred words of consecration used by the Lord in the upper chamber wherein He instituted the Eucharist and where first the elements were changed into His body and blood. So the memory of that supper and of the sacrament that was then instituted is perpetuated.

But the Mass is more than the Last Supper. It is the Sacrifice of Calvary all over again. In it Jesus Christ is really and personally offered to the eternal Godhead for the Almighty's honor and glory, in thanksgiving for all His benefits and blessings, in satisfaction for the sins of mankind, and in supplication for the spiritual and temporal needs of His people. He is there on the altar and He is sacrificed. He is offered up to the Father as He was offered upon Golgotha, only that now the oblation is unbloody. But the same victim is presented, the same sacrifice takes place.

— Anon.

66. — Benediction of the Blessed Sacrament

I

"SUFFER the little children to come unto Me, and forbid them not" (*Mark* x. 14). Thus spoke Our Lord when He blessed the little ones who flocked around Him and whom the disciples tried to keep back, because they feared that their Master would be fatigued.

II

WHAT a memorable day that must have been for those children and their happy mothers! These mothers pressed forward eagerly and were most anxious that their dear little ones should see and touch the divine Master and be blessed by Him.

III

THE same good Lord and Master, the same mighty God is on our altars and bids us come to Him that He may impart His blessing and His gifts to us. We deeply prize the blessings of priests and saintly people; we travel a great distance to secure the benediction of the Holy Father. How is it we are so utterly indifferent about God's blessing in the Benediction of the Blessed Sacrament? A living, fervent faith should make us realize and appreciate the value of Benediction.

*

WE READ of another benediction which Our Lord Jesus Christ will pronounce in these words: "Come ye blessed of My Father; possess you the kingdom prepared for you from the foundation of the world" (*Matt.* xxv. 34). Mindful of this benediction at the Last Judgment, we can pray to God that we may be numbered among the elect; we can ask of Jesus the grace of final perseverance, the most precious of His gifts, which will secure for us the crown of immortal glory. Some there are who, in the multiplicity of their necessities and under the weight of their sorrows and perplexities, express at Benediction their faith and confidence in the goodness of God, whilst they submit their hearts and bow their heads in perfect resignation to the divine will; they strike their breasts when the sacred Host is held over them at the moment of Benediction, while they whisper: "Jesus, I believe in Thee; Jesus, I place all my confidence in Thee; Jesus, I love Thee with my whole heart. Thy will be done. Bless me, my Lord, my God, and my All!" Yes; great moments of grace, indeed, are the short moments of Benediction. The place itself is holy, we are in the presence of God, we kneel at His sacred feet. The angels of heaven surround the beautifully decorated and illuminated altar, as on the holy night they hovered about the manger in the stable of Bethlehem, chanting the joyful tidings of man's redemption and salvation. The hour, the flowers, the lighted candles, the scent of incense, the sweet and mellow tones of the organ, the sacramental hymns — all attune the heart and excite the mind to pious acts, serious reflections, consoling thoughts, and holy aspirations. Earth vanishes in these blessed moments; we feel as if transported to heaven, uniting our prayers with the supplications of the saints, and our praises with the music of angelic choirs. Here is found a balm for every wound — a solace in every sorrow. Here the high and the low, the learned and the ignorant, the sick and the weary, the anxious and the unhappy, can find sympathy with Jesus, who opens His heart and His hand, and cries out to us from His throne of grace: "Come to Me, all ye that are weary and heavy laden, and I will refresh you." Great and manifold are the graces that come to us from the hands of our blessed Saviour at Benediction. The light and warmth of divine grace flow upon us to illumine the dark spots of our soul, to strengthen us in our weakness, to enlighten us in our doubts, to enliven us in our faith, to fill us with consolation in our misfortunes, to drive away the

evil spirits that tempt us, and to inspire our guardian
angels with the best means for our guidance and protection.   At Benediction a peace comes over us that is
not of earth, a calm resignation which comes from
intimate union with God, who alone is immutable,
and without whom all is vanity and affliction of spirit.
We leave the church strong and willing to fight the
battle of life; we leave with an abiding faith and confidence in God; and as the scent of incense lingers
about the sanctuary long after Benediction, so do the
graces of this devotion accompany and sweeten our
actions long after we have left the house of God to
mingle again with-the busy throngs and to engage in
the distracting scenes of life.

Oh! Let us ponder well these things and resolve
to take advantage of every opportunity of being blessed
by God; for if the blessings of holy people are so fruitful
of good, how much more so will be that of Him, who
is the source of "all good" — the all-holy and all-
powerful God!

Surely we shall be amply repaid for our efforts,
when we kneel before the Master's throne and know,
that besides gaining incalculable good for ourselves,
we are giving pleasure to Him, whose "delight" is to
"be with the children of men."

Adoremus in æternum Sanctissimum Sacramentum.
— *Anon.*

67.—Visits to Jesus in the Tabernacle

ONE of our duties to Our Lord in the Blessed Sacrament is, evidently, to visit Him; for it is not for nothing that He deigns to remain in permanent residence

among us; and the hearing of Mass on Sundays and holydays, in which He comes and goes, can hardly be called a visit to our neighbor of the Eucharist.

We ought to visit Him more frequently, and our visits ought to be made not only from a sense of duty, but also from motives of love and delight. Yet sometimes the Tenant of the Tabernacle would seem to be the only neighbor with whom we are hardly on visiting terms, or, at least, the house of God would seem to be the only house in the parish where we pay none but duty calls.

If we remembered and realized that the Blessed Sacrament is a person and not a thing, our duty in this respect would stand out more clearly in our minds.

Often enough we have an unpleasant experience on our visits to our common acquaintances, but never on our visits to Jesus in His sacrament of love.

> In sorrows, Lord, I'll try to see
>   Thy loving hand,
> With wisdom guiding me unto
>   A better land.
>
> Through the veiled future, Lord, be this
>   My prayer, my plea,
> That it may bring me nearer still,
>   Dear Lord, to Thee. — *Anon.*

*

IN THE same way as a friend doth often visit his friend, so do thou often visit Jesus in the holy Sacrament of the Altar; and, as often as thou dost so visit Him, offer again and again His most precious blood to the eternal Father. If thou wilt do this thou wilt find that the love of God will wonderfully increase in thy heart, and that thou wilt become truly devout and spiritual. — ST. MARY MAGDALEN OF PAZZI.

*

PRAYER FOR UNION WITH JESUS CHRIST

O MY JESUS! grant that Thou mayest be the object of my thoughts and affections, the subject of my conversations, the end of my actions, the companion of my life, the companion of my death, and my reward eternally in Thy heavenly kingdom. Amen.
— REV. ALOYSIUS STURZO, S.J.

68. — Daily Attendance at Mass

ALL Catholics, unfortunately, do not regard this Great Act, as we call it, with the same awe or attention — and yet it should be approached much as some of the old writers have put it. "If the sacrifice," they tell us, "were to be celebrated but once since the death of Our Saviour, it would be an event of such tremendous significance as to excite the awe and reverence of the whole world." And indeed we might conceive for ourselves what would be our feelings if it were announced for the first time that Our Saviour would descend from heaven upon an altar, and that there and then the sacrifice of Calvary would be renewed! Beside such an event all historical events would become tame and insignificant. It would be next in interest only to the original coming of Our Lord. Yet most Catholics, from habit and familiarity, "*Go to Mass,*" as it is called, in a languid, irresponsible fashion, for the most part once in the week. How many look on it as some airy function or formula — a qualification, as it were, for

Sunday, much as university students "put in" their "chapels." In foreign countries how often do we see the bottom of the church crowded with men standing for the necessary twenty minutes, and then hurrying away with impatience, almost before it is concluded. How few make it a practice of attending on week-days, on the ground of there being "no obligation" — a curious delusion! It surely ought to be a wonderful feeling for the Catholic to think, during the day, that he has actually witnessed this great act, the change of bread and wine into the Lord's body, and His descent upon the altar of men! The day that follows may be considered hallowed, or even, in a lower sense, a "lucky one." Indeed, those who have gained the long habit of hearing Mass *every day*, will own that when they have been hindered by some casualty, there has been a sense of incompleteness and discomfort, as though the whole day had been thrown out of gear. St. Augustine is indeed said to have declared authoritatively that whoever hears Mass devoutly shall never die a sudden death. — PERCY FITZGERALD in *The Jewels of the Mass.*

*

DOUBTLESS there are many devout Christians who would go to Mass *daily* if they could. Let them assist at the Mass in spirit. Let them make the *morning offering* of the League of the Sacred Heart or the "*Apostleship of Prayer*," and thus present their prayers, works, and sufferings, *each day*, to God, in union with the Sacred Heart of Jesus and for the *intentions* for which *He* pleads and offers Himself in the *holy sacrifice of the Mass.*

69. — Practical Suggestions for Fostering Devotion to the Most Blessed Sacrament

1. LIVE habitually in close union with Jesus in the Blessed Sacrament. "My Beloved to me and I to Him." Consider this union as your highest good. Join devotion to the Sacred Heart to that of the Blessed Sacrament. Seek out and adore the Heart of Jesus present, living, and loving you in the Blessed Eucharist.

2. Frequently use ejaculations expressive of your desire and love for the Blessed Sacrament. *Adoremus in æternum Sanctissimum Sacramentum:* "Let us adore forever the most holy Sacrament!" *O Salutaris Hostia, da robur, fer auxilium:* "O Saving Host, give me strength, help me!" *O Sacrum Convivium in quo Christus Sumitur:* "O Sacred Banquet, in which Christ is received!" *Bone Pastor Panis vere, Jesu nostri miserere:* "O Good Shepherd, true Bread, O Jesus, have mercy on us!" *Adoro te devote latens Deitas:* "O hidden God, I adore Thee devoutly!" *Tu in me et ego in Te, et sic nos pariter in unum concede:* "Thou in me and I in Thee, and so grant that we may be one!" One of these might be taken each morning, or words like them, as a watchword for the day; *e.g.,* "All for Jesus!" "Jesus, mercy!" "Jesus, I love Thee!" "Jesus, my God, I love Thee above all things!" "Jesus, I will be kind to others, and suffer patiently for love of Thee!" "O Sacrament most holy, O Sacrament divine; all praise and all thanksgiving be every moment thine!"

3. Ever bear in mind that the fervent adorer of Jesus in the tabernacle is bound to pay honor and veneration

to His blessed Mother. In your daily visits to Our Lord in the Eucharist, give expression to your devotion to our blessed Lady. You might say: "Our Lady of the most blessed Sacrament, pray for us."

4. St. Joseph, the foster-father of Our Lord, stands very close to Jesus and Mary. How good and how great he must have been in the eyes of God, to have deserved the honor and the prerogative of being chosen as the foster-father of Jesus and the guardian and protector of His blessed Mother! Honor him especially in your visits to Jesus, and say: "St. Joseph, pray for me, that like thee I may die in the arms of Jesus and Mary!" St. Joseph, having always watched with paternal solicitude over the interests of the Holy Family at Nazareth, must love the poor tabernacles where Jesus Christ dwells, and will protect those who work to render them less unworthy of the divine Host.

5. When possible, make your meditation in the church before the Blessed Sacrament. If you can not be present in the church, then, at your exercises of devotion, turn toward the nearest tabernacle.

6. Make frequent visits to the church where the Blessed Sacrament is solemnly exposed. If Jesus delights to come out of the tabernacle to be surrounded with lights and flowers on His altar-throne, it is that He may be visited, adored, and loved by souls. Do not pass a church without going in, if only for a moment, to salute your Lord. If you can not enter, then before the door, offer up a little prayer to Jesus: "My God and my all!" Greet Him in the sacrament of His love with some external sign of reverence. Give Him your heart: say that you love Him.

7. Examine yourself every week as to your devotion to the Blessed Eucharist; whether you love Him more

and live in closer union with Jesus in this sacrament of His love; whether you are becoming more like to Him in meekness, humility, and all other virtues.

8. Keep all the feasts of the Blessed Sacrament with special fervor — Corpus Christi, Holy Thursday, the Forty Hours, first communion of the children, the anniversary of your own first communion. "And this day shall be for a memorial to you, and you shall keep it a feast to the Lord with an everlasting observance."

9. Keep the Hour of Adoration at least once a month. Join the *Eucharistic League,* or *The Tabernacle Society,* or *The League of the Sacred Heart.*

*

Oh, see upon the altar placed
　The Victim of the greatest love!
Let all the earth below adore,
　And join the choirs of heaven above.
Sweet Sacrament, we thee adore;
Oh! make us love thee more and more.

*

SWEET is Our Lord in thought, sweet in the pages of the holy Gospel, sweet in the shadowy symbol or the devout picture, and yet more in the holy crucifix; but sweeter beyond comparison in the adorable sacrament of His love. Wherefore the Church sings in the words of her saint.

"O Jesus! the very thought of Thee
　With sweetness fills my breast;
But sweeter far Thy face to see
　And in Thy presence rest."

70. — The Sacred Heart

IF YOU want to know the true devotion to the Sacred Heart, you must study the Passion. See the agony in the garden, the keen cutting pain at the kiss of Judas, the cold shiver at the denial of Peter, the dragging with cords, the blow on the sacred face, the spitting, the shame, the foul words, yet all this was nothing, it was little to the longing pain of God seeking man's love. The scourging, the crowning with thorns, the heavy cross placed on those poor, torn, bleeding shoulders, yet even this is little, and why? Because there is still a greater proof of love. "Greater love hath no man than this, that he lay down his life for his friend." Study the Crucifixion; see there what God rejoiced to suffer, if so He only might give us proofs which we might believe of this longing for our love. He chose gladly, nay even willingly, to suffer all this; it was even less pain to Him than the coldness of our hearts. The devotion to the Sacred Heart is simply this: Devotion to a Heart that loves and is not loved, that is lavishing favors on His loved ones, and is in return treated with coldness, ingratitude, and outrage. So the two special objects of this devotion are love and reparation. And now how are we to do this? It is easy enough. Do what your own heart dictates. Do what you think would please this dear Lord, and avoid what would cause Him pain. The dictates of a loving heart are sure to be unerring in this respect to the Prisoner of Love in the Tabernacle. We know that He is there whole and entire, that His Heart is there, loving, praying, and suffering. That every drop of His precious Blood, and every fiber of His sacred Heart are there. Oh! how He longs for love and sympathy; let us try to be filled with this thought, so that it may become part of our very life, and thus render our every thought, word, and deed, a message of love and reparation to that loving, outraged Heart. Let us try to think how He loves us, and let us ever remember that it is on those hearts on which He has lavished the greatest gifts and graces, that He inflicts the deepest wounds. It may be only a simple aspiration of love we can offer Him, a simple thought of Him in His loving abjection, a little flower laid at His feet, but whatever it is it speaks to Him in language He understands, and which He will not forget. Let us try to make others realize this love, and remember the great secret of influence over souls is — to make them know and feel that Jesus loves them, before we try to make them love Him, and in our work when we have to deal with souls who perhaps have very little intellect, but often a great deal of heart, this is the only means of doing real good. Let us then when we come before Jesus in the Tabernacle bring a lively faith in His presence, and in His loving suffering Heart. — *Leaflets,* FATHER DIGNAM, S.J.

71. — A Good Old Custom of the Servants of God

IT IS an old custom with the servants of God always to have some little prayers ready and to be darting them up to heaven frequently during the day, lifting their minds to God out of the filth of this world. He who adopts this plan will get great fruit with little pains.

— ST. PHILIP NERI.

72.—The habit of Prayer

THE habit of prayer is no burden to any one, for we can pray worthily at any time, in any place, and in any posture. Even the motion of the lips is not necessary; the mind and heart can be engaged in it while we read or converse or go about our daily work. Moreover, prayer produces a delicious feeling of hope and rest in God; and this feeling is worth more than all the happiness that wealth can purchase or the world can give.

God respects not the arithmetic of our prayers, how many they are; nor the rhetoric of our prayers, how elegant they are; nor the music of our prayers, how melodious they are; nor the logic of our prayers, how methodical they are; but the sincerity of our prayers, how heart-sprung they are. — *Anon.*

73.—Morning Prayer

THERE is a freshness about the early morning which belongs to no other period of the day. The sun has a more kindly brightness and the air a fresh crispness which are lost largely as the day grows older. Upon awakening we throw open the window wide and let in the buoyant atmosphere of the new-born day. It fills our lungs and brightens our eye and makes us feel how good it is to live.

What the new-born day is to our physical nature the morning prayer is to the life of the soul. It is opening the windows of the heart that the clear air of heaven may flow in. It reinvigorates the life within us and turns our thoughts toward the One we love the most. It is a source of renewed strength, and gives a buoyancy to the spiritual step and a clearness to the inner vision. It floods the heart with the breath of life and bathes it in the sunshine of God's smile.

To begin the day without imploring God's grace and thanking Him for benefits received, is certainly wrong and exposes us to great danger. St. Francis Xavier says: "When you wake in the morning, raise your thoughts at once to heaven, and while you are putting on your clothes and washing your hands and face, call to mind the faults into which you fell the day before, and ask your Lord grace to avoid them this day."

The faithful Christian, before giving himself up to the occupations of the day, will meditate a certain space of time on the commandments of God and the example of Christ.

"*I will meditate on Thee in the morning*" (*Ps.* lxii. 7).

"*The wise man will give his heart to resort early to the Lord that made him, and he will pray in the sight of the Most High*" (*Ecclus.* xxxix. 6).

"*With desolation is all the land made desolate because there is none that considereth in the heart*" (*Jer.* xii).

"*O how I have loved Thy law, O Lord! it is my meditation all the day*" (*Ps.* cxviii. 97).

74. — Evening Prayer

IF IT be a duty of the greatest importance to begin the day well, it is one of no less consequence to conclude it properly. The graces conferred on us during the course of the day, and the protection we stand in need of against the dangers of the night, are urgent reasons why we should address ourselves to God, and pray to Him with the utmost gratitude and fervor.

A daily examination of conscience in general, with

regard to our whole conduct throughout the day, and in particular with regard to our predominant vice, passion, or evil custom; and the virtue we want most to acquire is strongly recommended by all spiritual writers as one of the most important duties of Christian life, and the most profitable exercise we can apply ourselves to, for avoiding sin and acquiring virtue. It is a looking-glass in which we see ourselves in our true colors, and come to the knowledge of our sins and evil inclinations. It is a sponge by which we wipe away guilt from our souls, and become the more pure before God the more diligently we practise it. If we do not daily weed the garden of our souls by this holy exercise, the corrupt ground of the heart will naturally produce vices and imperfections in abundance.

The examination of conscience and act of contrition form the most important part of your evening exercise.

The many signal blessings which God has bestowed, and does bestow, on those families where prayers are regularly said in common, should be a sufficient inducement to establish this practice everywhere; and chiefly at night, when all may be assembled with greater convenience. *"Where two or three persons shall be assembled in my name, there,"* saith Christ, *"shall I be in the midst of them."* — *Crown of Jesus.*

St. Francis Xavier says: "At night, before you go to sleep, you must examine your conscience, inquiring into your thoughts, words, and deeds of the whole day, and also whether you have left out anything of what you ought to have done."

Sleep is the likeness of death. Meditate on death and eternity. Retire not without being prepared for death.

"Compose yourself to rest in such a way that sleep

may steal upon you with your thoughts fixed on divine things, and your mind preparing itself to spend the next day in greater holiness. Always keep in mind that saying of our heavenly Master: "What shall it profit a man if he gain the whole world, and suffer the loss of his soul?" (*St. Mark* viii. 36.)

75. — Mental Prayer [1]

"In my meditation a fire shall flame out" (*Ps.* xxxviii. 4).

MAKE at least a short *meditation* every day. *Mental prayer* is a more appropriate and comprehensive term for that spiritual exercise which is so highly praised and commended by the saints and so conducive to holiness and perfection.

Mental prayer is within the reach of all who earnestly desire their salvation. In order to pray with fruit and without distraction it is most useful and almost necessary to spend some time in *meditation* or pious reflection on some supernatural truth, and from this fact the whole exercise is often called meditation instead of mental prayer.

In mental prayer, meditation (the exercise of the intellect) is only a means to the end, which is the elevation of the soul to God — *conversation with God.* When thinking and reflecting the soul speaks to itself, reasons with itself; in prayer that follows it speaks to God. It is plain that mental prayer or meditation is something more than mere spiritual reading.

But we can easily turn our spiritual reading into a meditation, as, for instance, when we read only a few

[1] Adapted from the Leaflet: Is Mental Prayer Easy?

lines at a time from "The Following of Christ"; then meditate, reflect, consider our own conduct in connection with the subject treated, make devout acts and pious resolutions, and finally pray to God for His grace that we may conquer our wicked inclinations, practise some particular virtue, and lead a holy life. After this we can read a few more lines; then meditate again.

Bishop Challoner in his translation of "The Following of Christ" or "The Imitation of Christ," as this golden book is sometimes called, has added some excellent *practical reflections* at the end of each chapter.

"Meditation," as Madame Cecilia says in her admirable work, "At the Feet of Jesus,"—"consists in occupying ourselves mentally and prayerfully with some mystery of the Faith. We call to mind the chief facts, ponder over them, and then stir up our will to regulate our conduct in consequence. Hence meditation is an exercise of the faculties of our soul — *memory, understanding,* and *will.*"

"Meditation, as a part of *mental prayer,*" says St. Francis of Sales, "is an attentive thought voluntarily repeated or entertained in the mind *to excite the will to holy and salutary affections and resolutions.*" It differs from mere *study* in its object. We study to improve our *minds* and to store up information; we meditate to move the *will* to pray and to embrace what is good. We study that we may know; we meditate that we may pray.

"In mental prayer," says St. Alphonsus, "meditation is the needle, which only passes through that it may draw after it the golden thread, which is composed of affections, resolutions, and petitions."

As soon as you feel an impulse to pray while meditating, give way to it at once in the best way you can, by devout acts and petitions; in other words, begin your conversation with God on the subject about which you have been thinking.

In order to help the mind in this pious exercise we must have some definite subject of thought upon which it is well to read either a text of *Holy Scripture* or a few lines out of some other holy book, for instance: "The Spiritual Exercises of St. Ignatius"; "The Following of Christ"; "The Spiritual Combat"; Challoner's "Think Well On't"; St. Alphonsus Liguori's "Devout Reflections," "The Way of Salvation," "The Love of Christ," and "The Blessed Eucharist"; St. Frances of Sales' "Introduction to a Devout Life," "Meditations for Retreats," and other works; Bishop Hedley's "Retreat"; Cochem's "Meditations on the Four Last Things"; Baxter's "Meditations for Every Day in the Year"; or any one of the popular books of meditation used by Religious, such as Hamon's, De Brandt's, Segneri's, Vercruysse's, and Ilg's "Meditations on the Life and Passion of Our Lord." Father Gallwey's "Watches of the Passion," and Da Bergamo's "Thoughts and Affections on the Passion" are worthy of the highest commendation.

St. Alphonsus says: "It is good to meditate upon the last things — death, judgment, eternity — but let us above all meditate upon the passion of Christ." This saint, the great *Doctor of Prayer*, has given us a beautiful work on "The Passion."

St. Teresa tells us that in her meditations she helped herself with a book for seventeen years. By reading the points of a meditation from a book, the mind is rendered attentive and is set on a train of thought. Further to help the mind you can ask yourself some such questions as the following: What does this mean?

What lesson does it teach me? What has been my conduct regarding this matter? What have I done, what shall I do, and how shall I do it? What particular virtue must I practise? But do not forget to pray.

Do not imagine, moreover, that it is necessary to wait for a great fire to burn up in your soul, but cherish the little spark that you have got. Above all, never give way to the mistaken notion that you must restrain yourself from prayer in order to go through all the thoughts suggested by your book, or because your prayer does not appear to have a close connection with the subject of your meditation. This would simply be to turn from God to your own thoughts or to those of some other man.

To meditate means in general nothing else than to reflect seriously on some subject. Meditation, as mental prayer, is a serious reflection on some religious truth or event, united with reference and application to ourselves, in order thereby to excite in us certain pious sentiments, such as contrition, humility, faith, hope, charity, etc., and to move our will to form good resolutions conformable to these pious sentiments. Such an exercise has naturally a beneficial influence on our soul and greatly conduces to enlighten our mind and to move our will to practise virtue.

Meditation is a great means to salvation. It aids us powerfully in the pursuit of our destiny, to know God, to love Him, to serve Him, that we may be happy with Him forever; it helps us to know ourselves and to discover the means of avoiding and correcting our vices, our faults, and weaknesses; it reveals to us the dangers to which our salvation is exposed and leads us to pray with a contrite and humble heart for the necessary graces to cope with temptations, to control our passions, and to lead a holy life. Mental prayer inflames our hearts with the love of God and strengthens us to do His holy will with zeal and perseverance.

As regards the *place of meditation*, St. Alphonsus says:

"We can meditate in every place, at home or elsewhere, even in walking and at our work. How many are there who, not having any better opportunity, raise their hearts to God and apply their minds to mental prayer, without leaving their occupations, their work, or who meditate even while traveling. He who seeks God will find Him, everywhere and at all times. The most appropriate place for meditation, however, is the church, in the presence of Jesus Christ in the Blessed Sacrament."

"Not a few pious persons," says Father Girardey in his "Popular Instructions on Prayer," "before setting out for their daily occupations, go to Mass in the early hours of the morning, make their meditation during the Holy Sacrifice, and thus draw on themselves the divine blessing for the whole day.

"As regards the *time of meditation*, it would be well if we were to make a meditation both in the morning and in the evening. If this is not feasible, we should, if convenient, prefer the morning to any other part of the day. The reason is because in the morning we are fresh in mind and have as yet hardly any cause for distractions, while later in the day we are apt to be more or less absorbed by our occupations and other worldly matters. Moreover, by a good meditation in the morning we begin the day well, drawing down God's blessing on us, and deriving grace and strength to avoid sin and fulfil our obligations. When we make our meditation in the morning, we ought to prepare its subject on the eve before retiring to rest, and make thereon some brief reflections before falling asleep, and also after rising in the morning. We ought, more-over, to recall our meditation to mind from time to time during the day, recommending our resolution to the Blessed Virgin by a *Hail Mary*.

"We should endeavor to spend at least a quarter of an hour daily in mental prayer. The saints used daily to spend many hours therein; and when they had much to do they would subtract some hours from the time allotted to their sleep, in order to devote them to this holy exercise. If we can not spend in it half an hour every day, let us at least devote to it a quarter of an hour. The longer and the more fervent our mental prayer, the more we shall like it, and we shall learn by our own experience the truth of the saying of the Royal Prophet: 'Taste and see that the Lord is sweet' (*Ps.* xxxiii. 9).

"Pope Benedict XIV grants to all the faithful making mental prayer devoutly for a whole month for half an hour, or at least a quarter of an hour every day, a plenary indulgence, if, truly penitent, after confession and holy communion, they devoutly pray for the intentions of the Church. This indulgence is applicable to the souls in purgatory."

As to our *petitions* and *resolutions*, Father Girardey says:

"In mental prayer it is very profitable, and perhaps more useful than any other act, to address repeated petitions to God, asking with great humility and un-bounded confidence for His graces — such as His light, resignation in adversity, patience, perseverance, etc., but, above all, for the inestimable gift of His holy love.

'By obtaining divine love,' says St. Francis of Sales, 'we obtain all graces'; 'For,' says St. Alphonsus, 'he who truly loves God with all his heart will, of himself, abstain from causing Him the least displeasure, and will strive to please Him to the best of his ability.' If we feel dry or despondent and unable to meditate or pray well, let us repeat many times as earnestly as possible: 'My Jesus, mercy! Lord, for Thy mercy's sake, assist me.'

"Let us offer all our petitions for grace in the name and through the merits of Jesus Christ, and we shall surely obtain all that we ask. 'Mental prayer,' said a holy soul, 'is the breathing of the soul, as in corporal breathing the air is first inhaled and then exhaled, so in mental prayer the soul first receives light and other graces from God, and then by acts of self-offering and love, it gives itself wholly to Him.'

"Before concluding the meditation, we should make some specified good resolution, appropriate, as far as possible, to the subject of our meditation. This resolution should be directed to the shunning of some sin, of some occasion of sin, to the correction of some defect, or to the practice of some act of virtue during the day. It would now be well to renew our baptismal vows, or the promises we made during our retreat, during the mission, or at our confessions.

"The preparation of our meditation consists of (1) an act of *faith* in the presence of God, and of *adoration;* (2) an act of *humility* and of *contrition*, and (3) an act of *petition for light*. We should then recommend ourselves to the Blessed Virgin Mary by reciting a *Hail Mary*, and also to St. Joseph, to our Guardian Angel, and to our holy patrons. These acts should be brief but very earnest and fervent.

"The conclusion of our meditation consists of these three acts: (1) thanksgiving to God for the light He imparted to us; (2) purposing to fulfil our good resolutions at once; and (3) beseeching the eternal Father, for the love of Jesus and Mary, to grant us the grace and strength to put them into practice. Before finishing our meditation let us never omit to recommend to God the souls in purgatory and poor sinners. In concluding our mental prayer let us, after the advice of St. Francis of Sales, pick out a thought or an affection from our mental prayer, in order to reflect on it or repeat it from time to time during the day."

76.—Prayers for Meditation

FROM

MADAME CECILIA'S "RETREAT MANUAL"

Preparatory Prayer

ACT OF THE DIVINE PRESENCE

MY GOD, I firmly believe that Thou art everywhere present and seest all things. Thou seest my nothingness, my inconstancy, my sinfulness. Thou seest me in all my actions; Thou seest me in this my meditation. I bow down before Thee, and worship Thy divine majesty with my whole being. Cleanse my heart from all vain, wicked, and distracting thoughts. Enlighten my understanding, and inflame my will, that I may pray with reverence, attention, and devotion.

PRAYER

O GOD, my Lord and my Creator, look graciously on Thy child, the work of Thy hands, and mercifully grant me the help of Thy grace, that all my intentions and acts during this meditation may be directed purely to the service and praise of Thy divine majesty, through Christ our Lord.

OFFERING OF THE RESOLUTIONS

MY GOD, I offer Thee these resolutions; unless Thou deignest to bless them, I can not be faithful to them. From Thy goodness, then, I hope to obtain this blessing which I ask of Thee in the name and through the merits of Jesus, my divine Saviour.

Holy Virgin, Mother of my God, who art also my Mother, my good angel, and my holy patron saints, obtain for me the grace to keep these resolutions with perfect fidelity.

ASPIRATIONS

Anima Christi, sanctifica me.

Soul of Christ, sanctify me.

Corpus Christi, salva me.

Body of Christ, save me.

Sanguis Christi, inebria me.

Blood of Christ, inebriate me.

Aqua lateris Christi, lava me.

Water from the side of Christ, wash me.

Passio Christi, comforta me.

Passion of Christ, strengthen me.

O bone Jesu, exaudi me.

O good Jesus, hear me.

Intra tua vulnera absconde me.

Within Thy wounds hide me.

Ne permittas me separari a te.

Permit me not to be separated from Thee.

Ab hoste maligno defende me.

From the malignant enemy defend me.

In hora mortis meæ voca me,

In the hour of my death call me,

Et jube me venire ad te,

And bid me come to Thee,

Ut cum sanctis tuis laudem te.

That, with Thy saints, I may praise Thee.

In sæcula sæculorum. Amen.

For ever and ever. Amen.

Indulgence of 300 days, every time. — Pius IX, Jan. 9, 1854.

Prayer of St. Ignatius Loyola

MEDITATE on the following prayer of St. Ignatius, till the lessons it teaches, like good seed, sink deeply into your soul and ripen into convictions.

Suscipe, Domine, universam meam libertatem. Accipe memoriam, intellectum atque voluntatem omnem. Quidquid habeo, vel possideo, mihi largitus es: id tibi totum restituo, ac tuæ prorsus voluntati trado gubernandum. Amorem tui solum cum gratia tua mihi dones, et dives sum satis nec aliud quidquam ultra posco.

Take, O Lord, and receive my entire liberty, my memory, my understanding, and my whole will. All that I am, all that I have, Thou hast given me, and I give it back again to Thee, to be disposed of according to Thy good pleasure. Give .me only Thy love and Thy grace; with these I am rich enough, nor do I ask for aught besides.

77. — Vocal Prayer

VOCAL prayer is prayer recited with the lips, and usually according to some certain formula. Al-

though in itself vocal prayer is not so excellent as menta
prayer, we should, nevertheless, beware of underrating
its usefulness or necessity. All true Christians frequently recite vocal prayers, such as the Our Father,
the Hail Mary, the Apostles' Creed, the acts of faith,
hope, charity, and contrition. The Church prescribes
vocal prayer very strictly to her priests and her Religious,
in the Mass, in the liturgy, and in the divine office.
She has enriched many vocal prayers with numerous
indulgences, and has approved of many prayer-books
filled with prayers suited to every want and devotion.
Vocal prayer, then, is both useful and necessary for
all men without exception — even for those who are
soaring in the heights of contemplation. In reciting
vocal prayers, we should strive to attend to the meaning
of the words, appropriating it to ourselves with all
possible fervor and earnestness. A few short vocal
prayers well said are far more acceptable to God than
a great many long ones recited without attention or
fervor.

One of the best forms of vocal prayer is the frequent
recitation during the day of some favorite aspiration or
ejaculatory prayer, especially if we do so in time of
trial and temptation. This commendable practice
gradually imparts a habit of recollection, and renders
all other prayers comparatively easy and free from
distraction. We should, as far as practicable, prefer
reciting those vocal prayers which the Church has enriched with indulgences, for we thereby gain a twofold
advantage — the benefit of the beautiful and devout
prayers themselves, and the indulgences, which help
us to acquit ourselves of the great temporal debt which
we have contracted toward the divine justice on account of our numerous sins. Or we may also apply

said indulgences, when so applicable, to the souls in purgatory, who will be relieved thereby and will not fail to intercede for us in our wants.

It would be well to join, to a certain extent, mental prayer with our vocal prayers, for the merit of the latter would be thereby greatly increased. We may do so in this wise. During the recitation of our vocal prayers we pause at short intervals to reflect either on their meaning or on some supernatural truth; or, without at all pausing, we reflect thereon while actually pronouncing the prayers with our lips. The Rosary is the most common and readily understood example of this manner of praying. While we are reciting the Our Father and the Hail Marys of each decade of the rosary, we meditate or reflect on some mystery connected with the life of Jesus Christ or of His blessed Mother.

It is also useful, in using the prayers of our prayerbook, to read them slowly and deliberately, making in the meantime practical reflections on their contents, or pausing from time to time to meditate a little and apply the words of the prayers to our own wants. If we accustom ourselves to recite our vocal prayers in this way, we shall not only make them our own and pray well, but we shall also gradually acquire the habit of making mental prayer, which tends to unite us more closely to God, and, through the practical imitation of our divine Saviour's virtues, to render us conformable to Him.

"The Lord," says the Royal Prophet, "is nigh to all them that call upon Him in truth; He will do the will of them that fear Him; He will hear their prayer, and will save them" (*Ps.* cxliv. 18, 19).

We have the formal and solemn promise of Our Lord Jesus Christ that God will hear our prayers and grant us all we ask, for He says expressly: "Amen, amen, I say unto you, if you ask the Father anything in My name, He will give it to you. . . . Ask, and you shall receive" (*John* xvi. 23, 24). "You shall ask whatever you will, and it shall be done unto you" (*John* xv. 7). God is faithful and just, and will, therefore, surely keep His promise to grant us all we pray for. Moreover, He is bound to grant us the graces we need, because we have a claim to them. They are the price of the blood and merits of Jesus Christ, for He died to save us. His merits are, then, ours; and, when we claim by our prayers a share in them or in their fruits, God can not refuse to grant us what we ask.

The Holy Scriptures are full of examples of the efficacy of prayer as a means of obtaining whatever we need to secure our salvation. It was by his prayer that the publican was justified, by her prayer that the Samaritan woman was converted; it was by his prayer that David obtained the forgiveness of his sin, and that the good thief on the cross was converted and received the promise of paradise. We find in Holy Writ also many examples of prayer as an efficacious means of obtaining even temporal favors. It was by prayer that Moses obtained the victory over the Amalekites; Elias obtained rain after a three years' drought; Manassas, his deliverance from prison and his restoration to his kingdom; Ezechias, the prolongation of his life; Solomon, wisdom; Susanna, the proof of her innocence; Daniel, his deliverance from the lions; the blind man, his sight; and the Church, St. Peter's deliverance from prison and death.

"He who prays," says St. Alphonsus, "is certainly saved; he who prays not is certainly lost. All the blessed (except infants) have been saved by prayer.

All the damned have been lost by not praying; had they prayed, they would not have been lost. And this is and will be their greatest torment in hell, to think how easily they might have been saved, had they only prayed to God for His grace; but the time of prayer is now over for them." St. Augustine is, then, right in calling prayer "the key of heaven."

Since prayer is the sufficient grace for salvation, it is evident that our prayers should have reference, either directly or indirectly, to our salvation. If their object is directly connected with it, they will surely be heard, for our divine Saviour, as we have seen, has solemnly promised that His Father would grant us whatsoever we should ask in His name, because He, as Our Redeemer, purchased for us all the graces of salvation with His most precious blood. St. Alphonsus repeatedly insists that in all our prayers, at all the Masses we hear, at all our holy communions, and in all our visits to the Blessed Sacrament, we should pray for these four graces, *viz.*, the forgiveness of our sins, the love of God, the love of prayer, and final perseverance. If we obtain these, our salvation will be assured.

When our prayers for temporal favors, either for ourselves or in behalf of others, are not granted, we should consider God's refusal a real benefit rather than a misfortune. In beseeching God for temporals we should be indifferent as to the result of our prayers, being equally ready to accept a refusal as a favorable hearing from Him. If such should be our dispositions, God, when refusing our request, will not fail to compensate us by bestowing on us more excellent favors which we do not think of asking. We have no reason to hope that God will hear our prayers for those temporal favors that may prove hurtful to our salvation, or that He will exempt us from certain corporal pains and trials, if such an exemption would lead us to sin or endanger our salvation. The granting of such prayers would be, not a favor, but a terrible punishment. We should, then, ask for temporal favors conditionally — that is, under the condition that they may promote our salvation, or at least not hinder it. We ought never to lose sight of this saying of our loving Redeemer: "What doth it profit a man, if he gain the whole world, and suffer the loss of his own soul?" (*Matt.* xvi. 26.) — FATHER GIRARDEY, C.SS.R., in *Popular Instructions on Prayer*.

*

COUNTLESS numbers are deceived in multiplying prayers. I would rather say five words devoutly with my heart, than five thousand which my soul does not relish with affection and understanding. "Sing to the Lord wisely," says the Royal Psalmist. What a man repeats by his mouth, that let him feel in his soul. — ST. EDMUND, B.C.

*

GOD will grant all that thou askest for in prayer, provided it be expedient; if it be not expedient, He will bestow something more conducive to thy welfare. He best knows how and when to supply thy wants. When, through ignorance, thou askest for what is not beneficial, it is better thy petition should not be granted.
— VEN. BLOSIUS.

78.—Ejaculatory Prayers

IT WOULD be well if every breath could be a loving sigh, and every moment be filled with the thought of God. If this can not be, form a habit of recollecting yourself from time to time; the more frequently the better. Let the striking of the hour be a signal for recalling the presence of God. Accustom yourself to the easy and frequent use of ejaculatory prayers. We need but to love in order to pray and to sigh for God. These outpourings of the heart proceed from the Holy Spirit; they are a language of love readily understood by this God of love. We naturally think of what we love; hence we can not say we love God if we rarely or never think of Him.

"Aspire to God," says St. Francis of Sales, "with short but frequent outpourings of the heart.

"As those who are influenced by human and natural love have their minds and hearts constantly fixed on the objects of their affections; as they speak often in their praise, and when absent lose no opportunity of expressing by letters this affection for them, and can not even pass a tree without inscribing on the bark the name of their beloved; so those who are possessed of divine love have their minds and hearts constantly turned toward the divine object of their love, they are ever thinking of Him, they long after Him; they aspire to Him, and frequently speak of Him; and were it possible, would engrave in the hearts of all mankind the name of their beloved Jesus."

You will find many *Short Indulgenced Prayers* in this book. Ejaculations approved by the Church are certainly most commendable.

79. — The Apostleship of Prayer

CONTINUAL PRAYER

"We must always pray, and not faint" (*Luke* xviii. 1).
"Pray without ceasing" (1 *Thess.* v. 17).

THE LEAGUE OF THE SACRED HEART is the proper name of the "Apostleship of Prayer" as an association. Its associates league together in certain easy but strong devotions to the Sacred Heart of Jesus, to obtain His *Intentions*, and their own, thus practising an "Apostleship of Prayer," with mutual share in merits. It numbers 30,000,000 associates in all parts of the world, including nearly all Religious Orders. Its motto is *Thy Kingdom Come*.

Its devotions are the *Three Degrees*.

First Degree: Every morning offer your prayers, works, and sufferings to the Sacred Heart. It may be done in your own words. Nothing more is required of the members.

Those whose zeal prompts them to do more may also practise the devotions of the second and third degrees, and gain thereby many indulgences.

Practice of the Second Degree: Members join Rosary Bands, and say daily one decade of the Rosary, *viz.:* one Our Father, ten Hail Marys, and one Glory be to the Father, etc.

Practice of the Third Degree: Members offer a monthly or weekly Communion of Reparation for sins against Our Lord in the holy Sacrament of the Altar.

I. Each associate's name must be registered at a local center. Apply to any Jesuit or Franciscan Father or to your parish priests.

II. Each associate receives a certificate of admission.

Morning Offering

OF

The Apostleship of Prayer

O MY God, I offer Thee my prayers, works, and sufferings this day in union with the Sacred Heart of Jesus, for the intentions for which He pleads and offers Himself in Holy Mass, in thanksgiving for Thy favors, in reparation for our offenses, and for the petitions of all our associates; especially this month for the particular intention of the Apostleship of Prayer.

or:

O JESUS, through the Immaculate Heart of Mary, I offer Thee my prayers, works, and sufferings of this day for all the intentions of Thy sacred Heart, in union with the holy sacrifice of the Mass throughout the world, for the intentions of all our associates and in particular for . . .

*

YOU know now that as members of the League of the Sacred Heart only one duty is imposed on us, *viz.*, to make the morning offering. This may be done whilst you are walking from one room into another. It takes none of your time, it costs no money, it gives no pain. It requires only an act of your will. But you share every day in the prayers and good works of 30,000,000 associates, and of nearly all the Religious Orders in the world. You gain numerous indulgences, thereby satisfying for temporal punishments that may be due on account of your sins and omissions, and saving yourself from a longer purgatory. By these indulgences you may also help your friends and other poor souls who have gone before you into the next world, and who will in gratitude become your intercessors forever. You may keep away afflictions and trials that may be now in store for you on account of your lukewarmness. You will surely receive from God more abundant spiritual and temporal blessings.

Says Father Rickaby, S.J., in "Ye Are Christ's":

"This devotion of the *morning offering* rests on the main and essential principles of Christianity; namely, that in *Christ we have access to the Father* (*Eph*. ii. 18): that *there is no salvation in any other, no other name under heaven given to man, whereby we are to be saved* (*Acts* iv. 12); that this salvation was wrought out by the death of Christ on the cross, who *made peace through the blood of His cross, blotted out the handwriting that was against us, and took it away, nailing it to the cross* (*Col*. i. 20; ii. 14); that this redeeming sacrifice and death of our Saviour is continually *shown forth* and re-enacted in His own very body and blood, made present at the consecration in Holy Mass (1 *Cor*. xi. 24; *Luke* xxii. 19).

Many things Our Lord intends and wills only conditionally, if men co-operate with Him. Thus He does not intend to convert the Chinese, unless missionaries go to China. Prayers are a sort of missionaries. Many souls will be converted if they are well prayed for, and not otherwise. But the most efficacious prayer is that which goes up in closest union with Christ crucified, pleading in sacrifice for us. Christ crucified thus pleads in every Mass. In every Mass, as the Church says, "the memory of His passion is celebrated anew." I can not spend my day in hearing Mass, traveling from altar to altar. It is not God's purpose that I should do that. But the Morning

Offering of the Apostleship of Prayer, as sanctioned by the Holy See, puts me in relation with every Mass that is said that day, and lays upon every Christian altar my work and my play, my words and thoughts, my pains and sorrows, my delights and joys, and every conscious action of my will, — always excepting that which is sinful, and so unacceptable, incapable of entering into holy union with the oblation of the body and blood of 'my Saviour. When I lie down to rest at night, I may ask myself: "Of all that I have done to-day, of all my goings and comings, what shall endure to my eternal good? What have I laid up in the form of treasure for heaven?" And, provided I have spent the day in the state of grace, I may answer: "All and every one of my deliberate acts of will that were right in themselves, and, very signally and specially, all that has received the consecration of my Morning Offering." Of my strivings after the good things of this life, some will succeed, others will fail: but alike in success and failure, practising the Apostleship of Prayer, I may take to myself the Apostle's consoling words: *Be ye steadfast and immovable, always abounding in the work of the Lord, knowing that your labor is not vain in the Lord* (1 *Cor.* xv. 58).

*

IN connection with this subject another good work may be commended, *viz.*, the Society for the Propagation of the Faith.

*

THERE are in the world over 1000 millions of men and women in pagan and non-Catholic countries who do not love the Sacred Heart of Jesus, because *they do not know Him!*

They are laboring in darkness and the shadow of

death, because the invitation of our gentle Saviour: "Come to me, all you that labor and are burdened and I will refresh you" *has not reached them* as yet!

For love of the Sacred Heart help and interest others in the work of Catholic Missions. Join the "Society for the Propagation of the Faith" (central direction) 627 Lexington Avenue, New York, N.Y.

80. — Continual Prayer

APROPOS of the *Apostleship of Prayer*, a few words on *continual* prayer will not be out of place. The Gospel says: "*We must always pray and not faint,*" and St. Paul exhorts us "*to pray without ceasing.*" What does this mean? The Gospel seems to enjoin *continual* p.ayer. How can we pray *without ceasing?* We can not be *always* engaged in either *vocal* or *mental* prayer. Father Grou, S.J., has a chapter on this subject in his book "How To Pray." He says:

"The words of the Gospel ought to have opened our eyes to see the necessity of another kind of prayer, which is of such a nature that every Christian can apply himself to it continually. And what is this prayer? It is the essential, the most absolutely necessary part of prayer, that which alone draws God's attention on us, that which gives value to all the rest; in one word, it is the prayer of the heart. This can be made without any interruption. No other can. So it is evidently this that is of precept, and there is no need of making any restriction of which the words do not seem to admit. It is the prayer of the heart, unknown to the Jews, for which Jesus Christ upbraids them, and that God through His prophet foretold should be the privilege of the New Law: '*In that day,*' says He, '*I will pour out upon the house of David, and upon the inhabitants of Jerusalem the spirit of grace and of prayer*' (*Zach.* xii. 10), a spirit of grace that will urge them to pray without ceasing, and a spirit of prayer that will incessantly draw down on them fresh graces; a double spirit that will keep up a constant communication between our heavenly Father and His children. It is this prayer of the heart to which the apostle St. Paul alludes when he exhorts the faithful to '*pray without ceasing*' (1 *Thess.* v. 17), and when he assures them that he continually remembered them in his prayers.

"It is just as easy and quite as natural to the heart to pray without ceasing, as to love always. We can always love God, though we are not always thinking of Him nor always telling Him we love Him. It suffices that we should be resolved at all times, not only never to do anything contrary to this love, but ready to give to God, on every occasion, proof of this by actions inspired by grace. Is it not thus that a mother loves her children, a wife her husband, a friend his friend? The cherished object never comes to our mind without calling forth a feeling of love; we would like never to lose sight of it, and if the mind is at times drawn off by other objects, the heart never is. Just so is it with prayer. We have the merit to be always praying when we wish so to be, when at every moment we are ready to follow the movements of grace. It would be quite a mistake to imagine that the avocations of life are an obstacle to this prayer. On the contrary, they are, or at least may be, an exercise of it, and there is a prayer that is correctly called the prayer of action. Every action done for God, as being His will, and in the way in which God wills, is a prayer, better even than an actual prayer that might be made at this time. **It** is not even necessary that the action be good and holy in itself; an indifferent act is no less a prayer in virtue of the intention with which we do it. Thus the Apostle virtually enjoins the faithful to pray always when he says: '*All whatsoever you do in word or in work, all things do you in the name of the Lord Jesus Christ, giving thanks to God and the Father by Him*' (*Col.* iii. 17). And again: '*Whether you eat or drink, or whatsoever else you do, do all to the glory of God*' (*Cor.* x. 31). We are always praying, if we are doing our duty, and are doing it to please God.

"As there is a prayer of action, so is there also a prayer of suffering, and this is the most excellent and pleasing to God. It is a very common thing for us to complain of not being able to pray because we are ill, we are suffering acute pain, or we are in a state of weakness or languor. Did not our blessed Lord pray on the cross, and the martyrs on the scaffold? Actual prayer at such a time is impossible, unless it be at intervals, and by short aspirations; neither is it expected. But suffer for God; suffer with submission and patience; suffer in union with Jesus Christ, and you will be praying exceedingly well.

"Thus it is that a truly Christian heart can and ought to pray unceasingly, partly by consecrating a fixed time for prayer, partly by acting, and partly also by suffering."

81. — Presence of God

I F YOU wish to find a short and compendious method, which contains in itself all other means, and is most efficacious for overcoming every temptation and difficulty, and for acquiring perfection, it is the exercise of the presence of God. — St. Basil.

*

IN THE midst of our employments, we ought to have God present to our minds, in imitation of the holy angels who, when they are sent to attend on us, so acquit themselves of the functions of this exterior ministry, as never to be drawn from their interior attention to God. — St. Bonaventure.

*

GOD sees thee; go in where thou wilt, He sees thee; light thy lamp, He sees thee; quench its light, He sees thee. Fear Him who ever beholds thee. If thou wilt sin, seek a place where He can not see thee, and then do what thou wilt. — St. Augustine.

WHO shall dare, in presence of his prince, to do what displeases that prince? — St. Basil.

82. — Happiness in Goodness

SHALL I be happy, if I am good? I know I shall be happy in heaven, but that seems a long way off. Shall I be happy on earth? I ask the question in some anxiety, because I hear a great deal about carrying the cross; and I can not conceive how any one can carry the cross and be happy. Carrying the cross means, I suppose, making oneself miserable. Now, though I should like to be good, I have no mind to make myself miserable. What am I to do? I am to put out of my head forever the notion that carrying the cross means making oneself miserable. There is one indeed who, if I try to be good, will do everything in his power to

make me miserable. That is my enemy, the devil.
whom St. Peter bids me to *resist, strong in faith* (1 *Pet.*
v. 9). St. Chrysostom says that as a Christian resists
thoughts of impurity, so he should resist thoughts of
sadness: indeed the one often leads to the other. And
St. Ignatius: "It is proper to the evil spirit to sting,
to sadden, to put obstacles in the way, making the soul
restless by false reasonings to prevent its getting on.
And it is proper to the Good Spirit to give courage and
strength, consolation and rest of soul, making things
easy and removing all obstacles, that the soul may go
on further in doing good." And St. John Chrysostom
again: "It is proper to the devil to create trouble
and excitement and to shroud the mind in darkness:
whereas it belongs to God to shed light, and with understanding to teach us what we need to know." In
short, there are two crosses, Our Lord's cross and the
devil's cross. Our Lord's cross consists of the labors
of my state, and the pain and sorrow that go with
labor, of whatever sort it be, as God said in the beginning
to Adam: *in the sweat of thy brow thou shalt eat thy
bread: thorns and briers shall the earth bear to thee*
(*Gen.* iii. 18, 19). This cross I must submit to be
nailed to, and never come down till death releases
me, never abdicate, never resign. The devil's cross
consists of feelings of wretchedness, black discontent,
irritation, complainings, downheartedness, and misery, — as it were whiffs from the cloud that envelopes
Satan in eternal despair. This cross I must fling far
from me.

There is no virtue in long faces, even when pious
people pull them. To carry Christ's cross manfully,
one should be reluctant to avow that one has got any
great weight of it on one's shoulder. Let me take an

example: the case of a young man or of a young woman at college.

A frequent cross with youth is the cross of examinations. I was going to add "in uncongenial matter"; but somehow nearly everything that one is examined in, and has to plod through during months of preparation, comes to be felt as uncongenial matter. Here are two wrong things to do, and one right thing. The first wrong thing is to refuse the examination, get oneself let off, or let oneself off by ceasing to study. That is like resigning a burdensome office in later life, usually a mistake. It is flinging Christ's cross away. The second wrong thing is to go on studying, making oneself miserable all the while with lamentations about the disagreeableness of the task and the prospects of failure. That is adding to Christ's cross Satan's cross, and may likely enough end in casting off both, — *quod erat faciendum*, in Satan's plan. The one right thing is to work hard, serenely and faithfully, day by day, doing all one can, and committing results to God. The moral is this: the cross of sadness should always be got rid of by a Christian, so far as ever he is able to shake it off: but the cross of arduous and at times disagreeable employment should be held on to and cheerfully borne. — *Ye Are Christ's.*

83. — 𝕾uccess

"IN ALL thy works be excellent" (*Ecclus.* xxxiii. 23). If success does not come, it shall not be for want of effort on my part. A good Catholic standing high in his profession (or business) is a great support to the Church. His example shows that the life of the world to come does not mean the wrecking of the life that now is. But is there not danger of vainglory in the pursuit of success? To this question St. Ignatius makes answer as follows: "When a good soul thinks of doing something that may turn to the glory of God within the area of activity that the Church allows, and thereupon encounters some temptation not to do it, the tempter alleging specious pretexts of vainglory, then the soul should raise its gaze to its Creator and Lord, and if it sees that the thing is not contrary to God's service, it ought to take the very opposite course to the course suggested by the tempter, and say with St. Bernard: *I did not begin for you, and I will not leave off for you.*" Besides, success in any profession is not attained except by hard work, and hard work is a wonderful cure for vainglory. Hard work crowds out thoughts of vanity. Work is hard, because we are weak. Hard work reveals our weakness, and humbles us. Real hard work is not work done with facility and zest, as when a healthy lad runs his mile. Real hard work is gone through in spite of reluctance and pain, and occasional inability to proceed: it is as the limping, hobbling gait of a lame man. The advantages that men are born with, or come in for without labor, or possess henceforth in comfortable security without further need of effort, such are the advantages most likely to turn a man's head with vainglory. Still, labor as we may, some of us will never attain success in this world. God has His own way of treating every soul. Some He leads to heaven by the road of temporal success, but many by the way of failure, poverty, and humiliation, the same by which Himself, as Man, mounted to His heavenly throne. Never was there to human eyes such an utterly hopeless failure as Christ crucified.

Accused, found guilty, and condemned, dying the death
of a felon and of a slave, deserted by His friends,
mocked by His enemies, apparently forsaken by God,
and His wonder-working powers taken away from
Him — would He not have come down from the cross,
if He could? — in this plight our blessed Saviour
closed His eyes, beholding with His last glance what
appeared to be the ruin of His work and the failure of
His mission. After such an example, no Christian
need be surprised at disaster. There must be other
avenues to heaven than the way of the "prosperous
gentleman." I will work hard to succeed in my profession; and if, with all my hard work, I fail and die
a ruined man, still *this hope is stored up in my breast*
(*Job* xix. 27), that my Saviour will love me the better
for my failure, and that I shall be the nearer Him in
that account in paradise. — FR. JOSEPH RICKABY, S.J.,
in *Ye Are Christ's*.

84. — Why Deny Yourself? — Worth While Now

I MUST deny myself, because many of the things that
I desire can not go together: to have one is to give
up another. No great end in life is gained without an
active and watchful resistance, now to one distracting
impulse, now to another. The name for that repres-
sive vigilance is *self-denial*. Self-denial is continually
practised in view of mere worldly success. A good
oarsman is made by self-denial, a good marksman,
a good musician, and a good scholar. It takes self-
denial to write even a novel of any merit. Self-denial,
then, is needful because of the variety of our desires;
and that variety arises out of the composition of our

nature. Some things we desire inasmuch as we are animals, as food and warmth and rest; some things as we are reasonable beings, as honor, knowledge, friendship; other things as we are Christians, as holiness, sacraments, heaven. All these desires can be accommodated and harmonized; but not without a watchful effort; they will not fall into harmony of themselves. The desire of food and drink carries some persons to such lengths that they become incapable of the pursuit of knowledge; their study hours are turned into revels. In others the curiosity of knowledge is gratified to the neglect of prayer and the endangering of faith. Thus self-denial in me is called upon to do the function of the policeman, to keep order in the crowd of my jostling and conflicting desires.

Then there is the desire of ease, the sheer, pure, undiluted love of doing nothing and vegetating quietly. *Otium, Grosphe*, and the rest, as Horace sings. There are those in whom this desire does not wait the hour of enfeebled old age to attain its majority. The indulgence of that do-nothing desire will not make my fortune in this life; and for the world to come, when they pray over my dead body: "Eternal rest give to him, O Lord!" may not the angels reply: "Why, this creature entered into his rest long ago, and has slept throughout life like a dormouse; what claim has he to rest for eternity, who has not labored in time." I need self-denial to overcome my laziness.

What Is Worth While Now?

IT is always worth while doing the good that just at this moment lies within my power to do. St. Francis of Sales, when a student at the University of Paris, suf-

fered long and cruelly from a horrible thought, that he
was sure to be damned. At length he flung the temptation from him and conquered it quite, in this way.
He said manfully: "Well, if I am not to see and love
God for eternity, at least I will love Him with all my
heart this hour while I may." It is worth while
now for me, — now while the brief occasion lasts — to
overcome one temptation, to do one small kindness,
to improve my mind by one half-hour of study, to
wait in patience when there is nothing else to be done,
to bear a headache, or sleeplessness, or some small
pain. Life can not be filled with great deeds, nor deeds
of manifest profit and advantage to oneself and mankind. There must be margins and leavings in the
web of human existence: there must be pieces over,
the use of which is not apparent; and these leavings,
as they seem void of good, are readily turned to evil
use. We shall find, if we think, that many of our sins
are committed in these loose and unoccupied times;
whereas our hours of active and successful work, or
keen sport and play, are usually innocent. The
author of the "Imitation of Christ" has a chapter
(iii. 51), "that we must apply ourselves to humble
works when we are not up to our best." We must
be content at certain times to do anything that is innocent and lawful; and console ourselves with the reflection that all lawful works are works of grace in him
who is in the state of grace. On the other hand, I
must be jealous of the hours in which my faculties are
bright and available for work. Even in my worldly
interest I must be jealous of them. Those are precious
hours. — *Ye Are Christ's.*

*

Keep your eyes fixed upon your heavenly home,

upon the long, long, everlasting vacation, upon the eternal rest of the just. "*Blessed are the dead who die in the Lord; from henceforth now, saith the Spirit, that they may rest from their labors; for their works follow them*" (*Apoc.* xiv. 13).

85. — Sanctify the Day

1. **B**y *mental* and *vocal* prayer, especially at morning and at night.

2. By means of the *Good Intention* or *Morning Offering*, by praying with the heart all day long in doing all things and bearing all sufferings in union with the Sacred Heart of Jesus and for the greater glory of God.

3. By means of *Ejaculatory Prayers*, and especially short indulgenced prayers.

4. By the practice of the *Presence of God*.

5. By a *Spiritual Reading*, for instance, from "The Imitation of Christ," or "The Lives of the Saints"; by the *Particular Examen* and by the practice of a *particular virtue* in honor of your patron saint.

N.B. Father Bowden's "Miniature Lives of the Saints for Every Day in the Year" is a very beautiful and practical work that we recommend to all classes. This precious little book contains just one leaf for each day. "The face of each leaf," the preface tells us, "contains a simple outline of the saint's life, in which great care has been taken to insure historical accuracy. The reverse bears as its title a *virtue* characteristic of the saint, and comprises an exhortation, a maxim of the saint or of some spiritual writer; an illustrative anecdote; and finally a text from Scripture.

"Each section is intended to enforce the lesson taught by the life, much as the lections, chapter, hymn, and antiphon of the breviary narrate the history, extol the virtues, and implore the suffrages of the saint, to whose Office they belong."

Butler's "Lives of the Saints" and Benziger Brothers' "Pictorial Lives of the Saints" are also recommended.

Let us cultivate the devotion, which consists in venerating, imitating, and invoking a particular saint for each day and with this end in view read daily from the "Lives of the Saints." The saints are our models in the following of Christ; they teach us the way of salvation; let us honor them, imitate their virtues, and invoke their intercession that we also may become saints.

86. — Sanctify the Week

"THE WEEK SANCTIFIED" is a popular term applied to the custom in vogue among religious people, whereby each day of the week is consecrated to a particular devotion, thus:

Sunday..............To the Holy Trinity.
Monday.............To the Holy Ghost and to the Holy Souls in Purgatory.
Tuesday.............To the Holy Angels.
Wednesday...........To St. Joseph.
Thursday............To the Blessed Sacrament.
Friday...............To the Passion of Our Lord and also to the Sacred Heart of Jesus.
Saturday.............To the Blessed Virgin Mary.

During the week prayers are said and devotions are practised in accordance with this classification. As "The Crown of Jesus" suggests,

"It would also be well to devote particular days to meditation on particular subjects, for instance:

"Sunday — *the Holy Trinity* — faith, hope, and charity — love of God — conformity to the will of God — desire of heaven.

"Monday — the Holy Ghost — the duties of your state of life — the sanctification of your actions — fidelity to the inspiration of the Holy Spirit.

"Tuesday — the Holy Angels — your ruling passion — the virtues — venial sin — mortal sin.

"Wednesday — St. Joseph — the example of patron saints — the Childhood of Our Lord — the works of mercy.

"Thursday — the Blessed Sacrament — virtues taught by Our Lord in the Blessed Sacrament (*i.e.*, humility, silence, forbearance) — the Holy Mass.

"Friday — the Passion of Our Lord — the virtues specially taught by the Passion, *i.e.*, penances, resignation, fraternal charity, mortification — the Sacred Heart of Jesus.

"Saturday — *the Blessed Virgin Mary* — her purity, humility, obedience, gentleness — her love to Jesus Christ — also death — judgment — eternity — purgatory — hell."

87. — Sanctify the Month

MANY devout souls choose a patron saint for each month, in whose honor they cultivate a certain virtue. They also practise each month a particular devotion. The monthly devotions are usually arranged in the following order:

January............The Holy Infancy.
February............The Holy Trinity (also the Holy Family).
March........:......St. Joseph.
April...............The Holy Ghost (also the Passion for Lent).
May.............:....The Blessed Virgin Mary.
June...............The Blessed Sacrament and the Sacred Heart of Jesus.
July.............,...The Precious Blood of Jesus.
August.............The Most Pure Heart of Mary.
September.......,....The Holy Cross.
October......,......The Holy Angels and the Holy Rosary.
November...........The Holy Souls in Purgatory.
December (Advent)....The Immaculate Conception.

A particular virtue may be assigned to each month as follows:

January — Love of Jesus Christ.
February — Humility.
March — Mortification.
April — Patience.
May — Meekness — purity — the spirit of poverty.
June — Obedience — piety — dutifulness.
July — Simplicity — faith — liberty of spirit — cheerfulness.
August — the sanctification of our actions — diligence — edification — fidelity in little things.
September — Piety — fervor in the performance of sacred duties — the spirit of prayer.

October — Confidence.
November — Charity — kindness.
December — Conformity to the will of God — divine
love.

88. — Gems of the Months with Their Significance[1]

ACCORDING to ancient tradition assigning certain
stones to certain months.

January......Garnet.......Perseverance; Constancy.
February.....Pearl.........Faith and Innocence.
March........Hyacinth.....Moral Beauty — Moral
Goodness.
April.........Diamond.....Purity and Fortitude.
May..........Emerald......Faith in God and Faith-
fulness in Friendship.
June.........Amethyst.....Peace of Mind; also
Sincerity.
July..........Ruby.........Success; Devotedness to
Duty.
August.......Sardonyx.....Felicity; Conformity to
the Will of God.
September....Sapphire......Divine Love and Mercy.
Love and Repentance in
Man.
October.......Opal.........Happiness of a Pure Life;
also Hope.
November....Topaz.......Divine Providence; Res-
ignation; Fidelity.
December.....Turquoise....Piety; Fervor in God's
Service; Prosperity.

[1] Consult The Floral Apostles, Rev. A. Ambauen.

89. — Reflections on the Gems of the Months and Their Significance

January

GARNET

PERSEVERANCE

"HE THAT shall persevere unto the end, he shall be saved" (*Matt.* x. 22). — "Step by step one gets to Rome." — "Little strokes fell great oaks." — " Through difficulties to the stars."

February

PEARL

FAITH AND INNOCENCE — THE GRACE AND THE LOVE OF GOD

"THE kingdom of heaven is like to a merchant seeking good pearls: who, when he had found *one pearl of great price*, went his way, and sold all that he had, and bought it" (*Matt.* xiii. 45, 46).

The one pearl without price is the true faith and the state of grace. Guard this treasure carefully. Sacrifice everything to preserve your faith and the grace and love of God.

March

HYACINTH

MORAL BEAUTY — MORAL GOODNESS

"**B**EAUTY without virtue is a rose without fragrance." — *French Proverb*.

"How goodness heightens beauty." — HANNAH MORE.

Goodness is beauty and real happiness is found in goodness.

April

DIAMOND

PURITY AND FORTITUDE — STRENGTH OF CHARACTER

PERFORM your actions with a pure intention, not out of human respect, but for the love of God. Do what is right because it is right. Have the moral courage to stand up for your convictions. If you are conscientious, you cannot but have some character.

May

EMERALD

FAITH IN GOD AND FAITHFULNESS IN FRIENDSHIP

" *An emerald of light!*" — COLERIDGE.

AITH in God is our beacon light in the storms of life; our strength and consolation in the greatest trials.

> "A friend in need
> Is a friend indeed."

"Adversity is the touchstone of friendship." — *Anon.*

June

AMETHYST

PEACE OF MIND — SINCERITY

BE SINCERE, truthful, honest, and fair to all; be the master of your passions and emotions; be intent on doing God's will; preserve a clear conscience; then you will have peace with God and man.

> "I feel within me
> A peace above all earthly dignities,
> A still and quiet conscience."
> — SHAKESPEARE.

"He who reigns within himself, and rules passions, desires, and fears, is more than a king." — MILTON.

July

RUBY

SUCCESS — DEVOTEDNESS TO DUTY

"WHAT things a man shall sow, those also shall he reap. In doing good, let us not fail; for in due time we shall reap, not failing" (*Gal.* vi. 8, 9).

"Brethren, be not weary in well-doing" (2 *Thess.* iii. 13).

Success is ordinarily the reward of merit. Our *eternal* reward, however, will be most assuredly in proportion to our deserts. We can all become saints with the assistance of God's grace. Whatever we shall enjoy in heaven we are earning now; and if in eternity we shall not be numbered among the saints, the fault will be our own. Do well whatever you do, and do it all to please God.

"Think of heaven with hearty purposes and peremptory designs to get thither." — JEREMY TAYLOR.

August

SARDONYX

FELICITY — CONFORMITY TO THE DIVINE WILL

ONE who loves finds it sweet to do the will of the person loved.

"Make up your mind," says Fénelon, "always to conform your will to the most holy will of God; then shall you 'taste and see that the Lord is sweet.'"

"He that hath my commandments and keepeth them, he it is that loveth Me. And he that loveth Me shall be loved of My Father; and I will love him; and will manifest Myself to him" (*John* xiv. 21).

"Thou hast made us for Thyself, O Lord! And our heart is restless until it rests in Thee." — ST. AUGUSTINE.

September

SAPPHIRE

DIVINE LOVE AND MERCY — LOVE AND REPENTANCE IN MAN

GOD *is love,* as St. John tells us: *God is our Father.* *"The Lord is sweet; His mercy endureth forever"* (*Ps.* xcix. 5).

"A contrite and humbled heart, O God, Thou wilt not despise" (*Ps.* l. 19).

"I say to you, that even so there shall be joy in heaven upon one sinner that doth penance, more than upon ninety-nine just who need not penance" (*Luke* xv. 7).

October

OPAL

HAPPINESS OF A PURE LIFE; HOPE

"OH, HOW beautiful is the chaste generation with glory, for the memory thereof is immortal; because it is known both with God and with men" (*Wis.* iv. 1).

A pure life insures happiness here below and gives a man the right to entertain the hope of eternal blessedness.

"Who shall ascend into the mountain of the Lord; or who shall stand in his holy place? The innocent in hands and clean of heart" (*Ps.* xxiii. 3, 4).

"The chaste generation triumpheth forever" (*Wis.* iv. 2).

> " Never say die !
> Up, man, and try ! "
> —*Anon.*

> " Cease, every joy, to glimmer on my mind,
> But leave — oh ! leave the light of Hope behind."
> — CAMPBELL.

November

TOPAZ

DIVINE PROVIDENCE — RESIGNATION — FIDELITY

BE FAITHFUL to your duty and abandon yourself to Divine Providence.

"We know that to them that love God, all things work together unto good" (*Rom.* viii. 28).

Divine Providence watches over every creature. "The very hairs of your head are all numbered," says Our Lord (*Luke* xii. 7).

"To preserve peace in time of trouble our will must remain firm in God, and be ever directed toward Him, that is, we should be disposed to receive all things from the hand of God, from His justice, and from His bounty, with humble submission to His blessed will. Good and evil, health and sickness, prosperity and adversity, consolation and dryness, temptation and tranquillity, interior sweetness, trials, and chastisements, all should be received by the soul with humility, patience, and resignation, as coming to us by the appointment of God. This is the only means of finding peace in the midst of great troubles and adversities." — BISHOP CHALLONER.

December

TURQUOISE

PIETY — FERVOR IN GOD'S SERVICE — PROSPERITY

Motto: All in God; all with God; all for God!
Deus meus et omnia! My God and my all!
 — St. Francis of Assisi.

"WITH two wings a man is lifted up above earthly things," says Thomas à Kempis; "that is, with *simplicity* and *purity*. Simplicity must be in the intention, purity in the affection. Simplicity aims at God. Purity takes hold of Him and tastes Him."

"Religiousness shall keep and justify thy heart; it shall give joy and gladness" (*Ecclus.* i. 18).

"*Piety is profitable to all things*" (*Tim.* iv. 8).

"The just shall flourish like the palm-tree: he shall grow up like the cedar of Libanus. They that are planted in the house of the Lord shall flourish in the courts of the house of our God" (*Ps.* xci. 13, 14).

"To be faithful in little things is a *great* thing," says St. Augustine; and, "to maintain *fervor*," says Father Petit, S.J., "it is a good plan to choose *one* exercise, however small, and to perform it every day in the best manner possible." Let us perform some pious exercise, or say a little prayer, for instance, the *Memorare*, every day, with great fervor, to obtain the grace of perseverance and a happy death.

"Only serve Jesus out of love, and while your eyes are yet unclosed, before the whiteness of death is yet upon your face, or those around you are sure that that gentle breathing is your last, what an unspeakable surprise will you have had at the judgment seat of your dearest love!" — FABER.

"Let us pray, and, like sowers sowing their seed, let us not faint; the time when we shall reap is not far distant." — ST. AUGUSTINE.

One day we shall look up into the face of our dear Lord; may He then say to us: "Well done, good and faithful servant; because thou hast been faithful over a few things, I will place thee over many things; enter thou into the joy of thy Lord" (*Matt.* xxv. 23).

90. — Self-Restraint

He Is Most Powerful Who Has Himself in His Power.
— SENECA.

A TONE of pride or petulance repressed,
 A selfish inclination firmly fought,
  A shadow of annoyance set at nought,
A murmur of disquietùde suppressed,
A peace in importunity possessed,
 A reconcilement generously sought,
  A purpose put aside — a banished thought,
A word of self-explaining unexpressed, —
 Trifles they seem, these petty soul restraints,
Yet he who proves them such must needs possess
  A constancy and courage grand and bold.
 They are the trifles that have made the saints;
Give me to practise them in humbleness,
  And nobler power than mine doth no man hold.
— *Leaflets.*

91. — A Good Scrap-book

MANY men of literary taste, and many professional writers, have the practice of gathering the justest and most striking thoughts they meet with in the course of their reading, they thus form a repertory which grows richer day by day, and becomes in the end an invaluable treasure. Here is an excellent device which we ought to make use of in the spiritual life. We read the Gospel, the writings of the saints, certain ascetic works; let us faithfully note down the thoughts which make the most impression upon us, and even the personal reflections which these thoughts suggest to us. In a few years we shall possess a collection more precious than all our books of piety, and one which we may read again and again with great profit, especially in moments of *ennui* and sadness. Each phrase of our little note-book will become like a ray of light to dissipate the darkness of our soul, or a drop of balm to calm our sorrows. — REV. MATTHEW RUSSELL, S.J., *The Art of Being Happy.*

92. — Read the Lives of the Saints

LET us often read the "Lives of the Saints," specially those inner lives in which the details are given in abundance. There we shall learn how we ought to behave toward God, toward others, and toward ourselves, in order to possess true happiness. Nothing is more instructive or more profitable as regards piety and even as regards our temporal interests, properly understood, than the attentive and meditative reading of the "Lives of the Saints." — *Ibid.*

93. — Be Careful in the Choice of Your Books and Magazines

EVERYTHING we read makes us better or worse, and, by a necessary consequence, increases or lessens our happiness. Be scrupulous in the choice of your books; often ask yourself what influence your reading exercises upon your conduct. If after having read such and such a work that pleases you — philosophy, history, fiction — or else such and such a review, or magazine, or newspaper in which you take delight — if you then find yourself more slothful about discharging your duties, more dry and cross toward your equals, harder toward your inferiors, with more disrelish for your state of life, more greedy for pleasures, enjoyments, honors, riches — do not hesitate about giving up such readings: they would poison your life and endanger your eternal happiness. — *Ibid.*

On the inestimable value of good literature, Father Morgan M. Sheedy writes in "Benziger's Magazine":

"Apart from the influence of our holy religion there is no one thing which enters more deeply into the warp and woof of our character than the books we read. One of the greatest blessings that can come to any life is the love of books. The practice of keeping, especially before the young, growing mind, beautiful and uplifting images and bright, cheerful, healthy thoughts from books, is of inestimable value. Next to the actual society of a noble, high-minded author is the benefit to be gained by reading his books. The mind is brought into harmony with the hopes, the aspirations, the ideals of the writer, so that it is impossible afterward to be satisfied with low or ignoble things. The horizon of the reader broadens, his point of view changes, his ideals are higher and nobler, his outlook on life is more elevated.

"The importance of having great models, high ideals, held constantly before the mind when it is in a plastic condition cannot be overestimated. The books we read in youth make or mar our lives. Many a man has attributed his first start and all his after success in life to the books read in his youth. They opened up to him his possibilities, indicated his tastes, and helped him to find his place in life.

> "Seekest thou for bliss?
> Lo! here it is —
> In quiet nook,
> With well-loved book."

" Good books are not only our friends; they are also our best teachers. But bad books are a curse and do a world of harm. Evil men, evil lives, evil examples spread a moral pestilence openly and powerfully; but nothing spreads falsehood and evil more surely and deeply than a bad book.

"But what of the novel? Fulfilling its proper end and aim at elevating the reader and enlarging his knowledge of man and of nature and its mysteries, captivating the wayward fancy, arraying salutary knowledge with true wisdom in pleasing garb, arousing the soul to strive after ideals worthy of man's mind and heart, the novel would play a most desirable part in the betterment of man. We cannot deny its immense power, the greater because it reaches many unwilling to read more serious books. Indeed, many master-pieces of fiction are worthy of all the encomiums which the greatest admirer of the novel could bestow on them.

"But the tendency of to-day, reflected in the popular novel, is to remove all thought of the claims of almighty God, to substitute humanity and philanthropy for religion and Christian charity, and science for revealed truth.

"The other day I was reading the pastoral letter of one of our bishops on 'Christian Instruction.' This is what he wrote: 'Every doctrine of our holy faith, from the existence of God down to the least Catholic practice of devotion, is denied or assailed. Sometimes it is attacked by open hostility, but more often by a chilling indifference, or by a bitter ridicule of all the claims of religion.'

"Now if this be the actual state of things, let me ask: Are we Catholics fully alive to the very grave dangers that beset us from the literature of all kinds that is being daily and hourly issued in such enormous quantities by the publishing houses of America?

"Too many of us seem to have a positive distaste for the best, what has been written by Catholics. In fact, many of us are utter strangers to our own authors, outside of a few great names. We know little or nothing of our greatest writers. Their writings are a sealed book to many. The very name of a Catholic publishing house on the title-page of a book seems to repel rather than attract the purchaser. That is the present situation; it is one to be deplored and must be entirely changed before we Catholics come into the full possession of the literary treasures that are our rightful inheritance."

Says Bishop Hedley in his pastoral letter, "On Reading":

"There ought undoubtedly to be a great advance on the part of Catholics in the knowledge of religion by means of print. And, happily, it can not be pretended that there is nothing to read. If we consider, for example, the list of the publications of the Catholic Truth Society, we find among them instructions of every kind: exposition of doctrine, controversy, history, biography, devotion, moral and social papers, besides tales and verse.

"No one is too poor to be able to afford the half-penny or the penny which is the price of most of these brochures and leaflets; whilst there are books and larger pamphlets for those who look for something more extended, and the bound volumes of the series form a small library of the handiest and the most useful kind. For readers of greater education and leisure there are materials in abundance which it is unnecessary to specify at this moment. A catalogue of any of our Catholic publishers will suggest to every one how many subjects there are on which it would be useful to be well-informed, and how much there is to be known in the grand and wide kingdom of the holy Catholic faith. No one can love Our Lord who does not know about Him, and no one can be truly loyal to the Church who does not take the trouble to study her.

"If instruction is so deeply important, devotion and piety are not less so. With most of us prayer is very short and very slight. There is one means which will both make us more regular in our daily prayers and deepen our earnestness in that sacred duty. This is, *spiritual reading*.

"No one should be without a book about Our Lord, His sacred Heart, His blessed Mother, or the saints. No one should be without a book on the Mass. Besides one's prayer-book, one should have manuals of meditation and of instruction on Christian virtues. More extended devotional treatises will keep alive the piety of those for whom they are suitable. But all Catholics, whatever their condition, should make use of spiritual reading. It is impossible to exaggerate the effect on the lives and characters of Christians of the words of holy men, of the heroic acts of the martyrs, of the example of the lovers of Jesus in every age, of the contemplation of our Lady's prerogatives and goodness, and, above all, of the story of Our Lord and Saviour Jesus Christ. The "Following of Christ," and other books of a like nature, are at once a guide to virtue, an encouragement to prayer, and an influence drawing the heart daily nearer to God. The reading of Holy Scripture, of the sermons and conferences of distinguished preachers, and of the penetrating devotional books in which our language is by no means deficient, is adapted to sanctify the house, and to keep out of it, to a greater or less degree, that flood of objectionable printed matter which overflows the land at the present moment.

"Priests and laity can not do more for souls than to encourage by every means in their power good and cheap Catholic literature — *instruction, devotion, tales,* and *periodicals* — and to bring it within the reach of every class of the faithful. All read; they must read, and they will read. Let us strive to check the evils of bad reading by the dissemination of that which is good."

If you wish to keep yourself informed in regard to current Catholic literature, write for the publications of the Catholic Truth Society and for the "Catholic Book News," a monthly review of Catholic publications issued by Benziger Brothers. This same firm solicits correspondence in regard to their plan for disseminating Catholic literature, fiction, etc., by means of their Catholic Circulating Library. This plan makes it very easy and inexpensive to place Catholic literature in every Catholic home in the land.

94. — The Imitation of Christ

"**F**OLLOW *Me!*" — *Words of Our Lord.*
    "*Master, I will follow Thee whithersoever Thou shalt go.*"— *Words of His disciple S. Matthew*, viii. 19.
    "*And I live, now not I; but Christ liveth in me.*" — *St. Paul to the Galatians*, ii. 20.

"Follow Me!" says Our Lord; "I am the way and the truth and the life; no man cometh to the Father but by Me" (*John* xiv. 6). I am the way you ought to follow, the truth you ought to hear, the life you ought to live. In the following of Christ we shall find peace and happiness on earth and eternal beatitude in heaven. The Son of God descended from heaven to earth not only to redeem us, but also to be our model, to teach us the Christian life by His example, as He Himself says: "*I have given you an example that as I have done to you, so you do also*" (*John* xiii. 15).

St. Basil tells us that Christianity is nothing more than the imitation of Jesus Christ; St. Gregory of Nyssa, that he alone deserves the name of Christian, who shows forth in his life the life of Jesus Christ; St. Augustine, that Jesus Christ came upon earth there to be an example of a perfect life; St. Lawrence Justinian that the life of Jesus is the type of a good life and the expression of all the virtues.

"Have we, up to the present time," asks Father Hamon, "understood this fundamental truth, and striven to rule our life according to that of Jesus Christ, or do we live according to the maxims of the world? Jesus led a simple and ordinary life; He ate, slept, labored like us; He suffered, wept, passed through all our trials, in order to serve us as an example in everything. Do we strive to copy so admirable a model, and say to ourselves: 'Is it thus that Jesus Christ would act, would speak, would think? Is this His religion, His charity, His meekness, His modesty, His recollection, His spirit of sacrifice?"

When I shall have been formed upon Jesus Christ, then am I declared by God to be one of His predestined: *for whom He foreknew, He also predestined to be made conformable to the image of His Son.*

If we do not imitate Jesus Christ, we are none of His — "*He who followeth Me not can not be My disciple.*"

Here then is the study, the occupation of our life; — to meditate upon the life of Jesus Christ, to reproduce in *our* lives the life of Jesus Christ. To follow Christ we must be ruled and guided by the *spirit* of Christ. On this subject Father Cuthbert writes in "De Torrente":

"The object of the Christian religion is to produce in each of us the life of Christ, so that in all our thoughts, words, and actions, we shall live as He would have us live, and our whole being move in harmony with His mind and will. The perfect Christian is indeed one in whose life the life of Christ Himself may be said to be reflected; nay more, through whose life the light of Christ's life may be said to shine, so that what you see is not merely the mind or action of the disciple, but of the Master in the disciple. Not that the individual character of the disciple is in any way blurred or destroyed. The disciple does not cease to be himself because of his relationship with his Lord. Nay, in all true discipleship this indwelling of the spirit of Christ develops and accentuates individual character, as we see in the lives of the saints; for nowhere do you get greater individuality of character than amongst the saints. In each personality Christ finds as it were a fresh medium for the manifestation of Himself, and in no two people does the Christ-life appear in quite the same form or with quite the same lineaments. The general lines are the same: there is the meekness, the purity, the unworldliness of Our Lord; there is His pity for the unfortunate, His love of souls, and so on.

"Yet though the general lines are the same in each disciple, the character of each as a whole will be different. There will be subtle distinctions of personality; the meekness of Christ in one will shine forth from a setting of character different in many subtle ways from the setting of character in another. And so with all the other Christian qualities. And this indeed is what we should expect from Our Lord's relation to His human creatures; for He stands in immediate relation not only with humanity as a whole, but with each individual. As our exemplar and teacher He came not to set before us a merely external type of life, but to draw out of us the good already in us, the good which lay dormant in the life our Creator had already given us, and by the breath of His own life to infuse new life — a still higher life — into our being. Our Lord's action on the soul which is His is analogous to that which takes place in the higher forms of friendship. True friends will ever impress themselves on each other, yet in doing so they do not damp down each other's individuality, but rather they quicken and exalt it, so that each is more himself for the influence of the other. So the influence of Christ in our lives does not make us less ourselves, but rather vivifies us, quickens our powers, and brings out our dormant faculties of mind and heart.

"That is an altogether false devotion which devitalizes personal character, and makes of men little more than walking statues — even though they are labelled statues of Christ. But true devotion shows itself in a quickening of our life, in an intensifying of all those faculties of mind and heart which go to make up personal character. True devotion purifies and cleanses, but it also quickens and exalts individual character.

"I make these remarks lest I should be misunderstood, when I say that the object of the Christian religion is to produce in us the life of Christ. It is not the external life of Christ as He lived it in Galilee and Judea during His earthly sojourn that is to be reproduced in us. How could it be? We can not all be carpenters, we can not all be public preachers. That was but a transient phase of Our Lord's human life, rendered necessary by the work He was set to do by His Father's will, during those thirty-three years. We are called to imitate this external life of Our Lord only in so far as we are called to do similar work on earth to His. But many have to do work for God which Our Lord did not have to do, and they can not therefore find in His earthly life any exact model of their own. And yet they are Christian only in so far as their lives are an expression of Our Lord's life.

"No, it is not Our Lord's exterior earthly life, but rather His interior eternal life that we have to reproduce in *our* lives; or I may put it in another way: it is not any particular manifestation of His life, but the living mind and power of Christ itself that must be in us if we would be true disciples. It is the spirit of Christ, in a word, which must be in us; which must guide us and fashion us, and which must find in us — in each one of us — a vehicle to express itself, a jewel through which to convey its sunshine.

"For this reason it is that you might set yourself to imitate the external life of the Gospel to the very letter — dwell in poverty at Nazareth, go about through Galilee practising the Gospel, even raise up the sick, and yet not be a true disciple; yet be nothing more than a window coated with a film to look like stained glass. Such merely external imitation of Christ is nothing; it is but a parody of the Christian life. But our religion consists not in imitating the external acts of Christ, but in letting the spirit of Christ animate us and produce in us what acts He wills.

"Doubtless in every Christian life there is a certain external conformity to the earthly life of Our Lord, since the same spirit will ever tend to manifest itself under similar forms in the same circumstances. Hence we shall ever find some Christian people renouncing home and wealth as Christ did when He set forth upon His public life; so too, whilst there are sick in the world we shall find the spirit of Christ moving people to have compassion on the sick. But in all these cases the external conformity proceeds from the direct guidance of Christ in our souls. We act not so much because He Himself acted in this way when on earth, but because more or less His spirit is leading us to act. He might lead us to a life apparently quite different from the type of His own earthly life, as in the case of those who conscientiously keep possession of much wealth, knowing that such is the will of Christ in their regard; and they are as truly Christ-like in their lives as those who 'obey Christ in poverty. Hence living the life of Christ does not mean always living in Christ's earthly fashion, but it means living in conformity with the mind and will of Our Lord, living in union of thought and affection with Him.

"But then how can this be? How can we enter into this communion with the living Christ? By faith and by love.

"Faith is, as it were, the hand which lifts the veil which hides Him from our carnal minds and shows Him to us that we may gaze and see.

"Love binds us to Him in the bond of understanding and sympathy. By faith we come to gaze upon Him, to find Him; love completes the work begun by faith and makes us one with Him. It is by faith that the spouse exclaims: 'I will seek Him whom my soul loves.' Her faith has passed into perfect love when she is able to say, 'I have found Him, nor will I let Him go.' —*Canticle of Canticles.*

"You have faith, you say, but do you use your faith to find Christ, to see Him? Faith is but a faculty of gaining knowledge, but the knowledge of Christ is to be found in the teaching of the Church, in the lives of the saints, and in prayer. How much attention do you pay to the Church's teaching? How often do you study the lives of the saints? How do you pray?

"If your mind is chiefly, perhaps altogether, wrapt up in things which do not lead to Christ, how can you wonder that with all your faith, you do not know Him? If you prefer to give your attention to the observation of the world and yourself, you naturally fail to observe the things which make Christ known to you. And then there is the love of Christ. It is not enough to know Him; He must be loved, too. We must enter into personal relationship with Him. Again you may say: We wish to love Christ; we do love Him in a way — and yet we are so far off. Yes — because you do not love Him with a whole heart; your heart is divided; and other things come between you and Him, and keep you apart from Him. There is a sense in which they who love Christ must love nothing else but Christ, though in a sense also the love of Christ makes us love all things better.

"It is of the nature of human love that it is both exclusive and inclusive. Loving one truly leads you to love all; and yet in every true love there is an element of exclusiveness which gives the relationship it creates its special character. So in our love of Christ — in its properties it implies a high exclusiveness from all else; a surrender of self which can be made to Him alone. And if any interest or creature tends to break down that exclusiveness, to claim an equal share with Him, to set us apart from Him, then it must go. He must be loved for Himself in the highest degree — all else only as it leads up to Him, or is related to Him.

"It is, then, when the soul is guided by faith and love, that it comes to that true union with Christ which is the perfect Christian life, and which St. Paul sums up in words: 'I live, yet not I, but Christ liveth in me.'"

*

IN His hidden life at Nazareth we have to learn from our divine Master the great lesson of obedience, the love of obscurity, the love of humility, the love of poverty (the spirit of poverty, detachment from creatures), and the love of labor.

In His public life and in His passion we must also consider Jesus Christ as our model and learn from Him the lessons He inculcates both by word and example,

notably, meekness, humility, patience, charity, kind‑
ness, forbearance, forgiveness of injuries, love of prayer,
zeal for souls, self-restraint, self-denial, and conformity
to the will of God.

The Gospel tells us that our blessed Saviour went
about doing good to all, relieving suffering humanity,
healing the sick, comforting the afflicted, blessing and
embracing little children, and, while denouncing the
iniquity of the proud Pharisee, treating the poor despised
sinners with the greatest mercy, gentleness, and compassion.

"The meekness of our divine Saviour," as the Most
Rev. Dr. Moriarty observes [1] "shows itself in a particular manner in His society with His chosen companions. He has told us Himself how He acted among
them. 'You know that the princes of the Gentiles
lord it over them, and they that are the greater, exercise
power over them; it shall not be so among you, but
whosoever shall be the greater among you, let him be
your minister, and he that will be the first among you
shall be your servant. Even as the Son of Man is not
come to be ministered unto, but to minister. I am in
the midst of you as he that serveth' (*Matt.* xx. 25-28;
Luke xxii. 27).

"Look at Him sitting down with them to the last
feast of love, and read His tender, farewell discourse
to them. Look at Him rising up from table and
kneeling to wash their feet. And it was then He said
—'I have given you an example that as I have done
so you do also.'

"History has not left us a description on whose
authority at least we can altogether rely. Certain it

[1] Moriarty, Retreat of Eight Days for Religious.

is that He possessed the charms of modesty and meekness. 'Learn of Me,' He says, 'that I am meek and humble of heart!'

"'Thou art beautiful,' says the Psalmist, 'above the sons of men; grace is poured abroad in thy lips; with thy comeliness and thy beauty, set out, proceed prosperously, and reign.' How lovely must He have been when He was growing up in wisdom and age and grace — which was manifest not only to God, but also to men. When all that heard Him in the Temple were astonished at His wisdom and at His answers, and when as He read in the synagogue all wondered at the words of grace that proceeded from His mouth. Why did His simple words produce this impression?

"Because with the latent power of divine grace, the 'goodness and kindness of God our Saviour hath appeared to all men, instructing us.' His hatred of sin did not make Him gloomy and melancholy, nor did his zeal for justice make Him hasty and disagreeable. The Prophet said of Him that He would not be sad nor troublesome — all His senses are under control, and the placid restraint which is upon His whole manner and person is the reflection of the calm and peace and order that reign within. 'He shall not cry aloud, nor shall His voice be heard abroad — the bruised reed He shall not break, and smoking flax He shall not quench.'

"If we had only the first ten verses of the fifth chapter of St. Matthew left, out of the whole body of revelation, they would suffice to make known to us the modest deportment, the blessed character, the divine conversation of Jesus amongst men.

"When we wish to know the characteristic manner, and the characteristic spirit which Christianity has

sought to create in the world, and which it has created
in all those who have fully submitted themselves to
its divine influence, let us read and meditate on the
eight beatitudes, by which our divine Saviour com-
menced his teaching on earth.

"God, at sundry times and in divers manners, spoke
in times past by the prophets; but in these days He
hath spoken to us through His Son. For the first
time since the fall of man, God becomes immediately
and visibly our instructor. Surely it must interest us
to know and to hear the first words that fell from the
lips of Jesus.

"And opening His mouth, He taught them, saying:

"'1. Blessed are the poor in spirit: for theirs is the
kingdom of heaven;

"'2. Blessed are the meek: for they shall possess
the land;

"'3. Blessed are they that mourn: for they shall
be comforted;

"'4. Blessed are they that hunger and thirst after
justice: for they shall have their fill;

"'5. Blessed are the merciful: for they shall obtain
mercy;

"'6. Blessed are the clean of heart: for they shall
see God;

"'7. Blessed are the peacemakers: for they shall
be called the children of God;

"'8. Blessed are they that suffer persecution for
justice' sake: for theirs is the kingdom of heaven.'

"These words teach me the manner and deportment of Jesus. You will not deny it. Were you to
find that page in a desert, you would say that the man
who spoke it was gentle and modest in manner and
mien, that he was mild, affable, and affectionate in

his character and conversation with his friends, that he was patient, kind, and merciful with all."

In this same Sermon on the Mount Our Lord said:

"Love your enemies: do good to them that hate you: and pray for them that persecute and calumniate you:

"That you may be the children of your Father, who is in heaven, who maketh His sun to rise upon the good and bad, and raineth upon the just and the unjust.

"For if you love them that love you, what reward shall you have? Do not even the publicans this?

"And if you salute your brethren only, what do you more? Do not also the heathens this?

"Be you, therefore, perfect, as also your heavenly Father is perfect" (*Matt.* v. 44-48).

"*Search the Scriptures!*" Our Lord Himself said; "*the same are they that give testimony of Me*" (*John* v. 39).

Read the *New Testament! Read the "Life of Christ"!*

You will find that to the young and the old, to friends and strangers, to the good and the wayward, Jesus was meek and gentle, kind and compassionate, agreeable and respectful. He said truly: *I am in the midst of you as he that serveth*. In this manner He conquered the world. Let us follow Jesus. Let us learn of our blessed Saviour to be meek and humble of heart.

"*Servant of the servants of God*," [1] says Father Rickaby, "has been the Pope's official title ever since the days of Gregory the Great. From the days of Edward III the Prince of Wales has borne for his motto two words, signifying *I serve*."

---

[1] Rev. Joseph Rickaby, S.J., Ye are Christ's.

"That wherein one man excels another man is given him of God that therewith he may serve other men" — says the Angelic Doctor, St. Thomas Aquinas. A principle worthy of consideration.

"There was One whose glory the prophet saw in vision: *thousands of thousands ministered to him, and ten thousand times a hundred thousand stood before him (Dan.* vii. 10). But, coming upon earth, He tells us of Himself: *the Son of man came not to be ministered unto, but to minister (Matt.* xx. 28). Coming a man among men, He subjected Himself to that law of human kind which enacts, not that all are to command all, or that all are to obey all, but that all are to serve all, and he who commands most is most of all to serve his fellow-men. Here is a youth who believes that his birth, his money, his education, his fine clothes, were bestowed on him, not that he might render special service to his country and his people, but that he might strut about and command admiration. That youth's name is written down in an ignoble register, the Book of Snobs.

"To go back to St. Thomas. 'It is to be considered,' says the Holy Doctor, 'that whatever excellence a man has, is given to him by God, to use for the service of his fellow-men: hence the testimony that other men render to his excellence ought so far forth to be matter of complacency to him as it shows the way open to him to make himself of service to others.' So, if I can make a good speech, or sing well, or have money, it shows the way open to me to make myself of service to others. Really this is a new view, and one not generally taken, of ability and wealth and power! But it is taken by the Creator, who has bestowed those gifts, and by the Judge who will call the receiver to account for them. *A certain nobleman went to a far country to take to himself a kingdom and to return. And calling his ten servants, he gave them ten pounds, and said to them, Traffic till I come* (*Luke* xix. 12, 13). What sort of traffic he intended, is evident from another place. To traffic with these pounds was to lay out one's powers and gifts for the service of one's neighbor. *As long as ye did it to one of these my least brethren, ye did it to Me* (*Matt.* xxv. 40). There was one who wrapped up his pound in a napkin. It is not said that he put it to any bad use, but he did no good with it; he made it a means of his own enjoyment; his neighbors were none of them the better for his being rich, noble, talented, and great. And he was met by his Lord with the reproach, *Thou good-for-nothing servant* (*Luke* xix. 21, 22); and his place was with the reprobate on the left hand (*Matt.* xxv. 30; 41–45) and with the rich glutton (*Luke* xvi. 19–23). Whatever advantage I enjoy over my companions, I should count it all the greater call on me to be of service to others. With the heir to the throne, 'I serve.' "

95. — Advantages of a Rule of Life

"Let us serve God in holiness and justice before Him all our days" (*Luke* i. 75).

"ONE of the means," says a spiritual writer, "of acquiring and perfecting in us the interior life, which raises a man above the merely terrestrial and animal life to the height of the divine life in Jesus Christ, consists in adopting and following a *rule of life*, which does not leave the employment of our time to caprice, but assigns to each moment its own proper duty." "*Let all things be done decently and according to order*," says St. Paul (1 *Cor.* xiv. 40).

"Where there is no rule there is no order," says Father Hamon. "We live by caprice and fancies. With a rule of life, on the contrary, all is done in an orderly manner; each duty has its proper time set apart for it; nothing is forgotten; nothing is done in haste or in a careless manner. Thanks to a rule of life, all is done well; and that which is true in regard to order is equally so in regard to practices of piety. With a rule of life they are done with exactitude; without a rule they have no fixed hour; we defer them, then we again defer them, and we finish by omitting them entirely."

We have some good old proverbs on the value of order and method:

"Order is heaven's first law." — POPE.

"To him who does everything in its proper time one day is worth three."

"Method will teach you to win time." — GOETHE.

"There is a time to fish and a time to dry nets."
— *From the Chinese.*

"Set all things in their own peculiar place,
And know that order is the greatest grace."
—DRYDEN.

It is obvious that the same *rule of life* can not be followed by all Christians, but the following regulations from "The Secret of Sanctity" are most commendable and worthy of being adopted by all whose aim is "*to serve God in holiness and justice*," whose desire is "*to live godly in Christ Jesus*."

"Prescribe a certain order for your day. Begin and

end the day with prayer. Regulate the time for your meals, for your work, and for your recreation.

"Order is the law of heaven; begin, therefore, here on earth a life which you will continue throughout eternity, a life which will be more pleasing to God, more agreeable and satisfactory to those about you, and more profitable for your salvation. There is much merit in the self-restraint and mortification resulting from a rule of life."

96. — A Rule of Life

I. HAVE a fixed hour for rising; from seven to eight hours' sleep are usually sufficient. Beware of beginning your day by sacrificing to sloth hours every moment of which may avail you for eternity.

Let your first thought be of God; let it refer as much as possible to the subject of your meditation, and let it be accompanied with the resolution to combat the fault which is the subject of your particular examen.

"There is this difference between the *general* and the *particular* examination," says Father Hamon, "that the first embraces the whole of the sins which we have committed during the day, or the space of time to which the examination is limited, whilst the particular examen has for its aim a special subject, for example, a vice, a virtue, an exercise, above all, the besetting sin, which is the weak side by which we are most exposed to lose our souls. This exercise is of great importance."

It is indeed a very efficacious means of perfection.

"The particular examen is a concentrated struggle of the will, not with all our faults equally, but with one specially chosen as the most important to be overcome. It consists of two parts, the matter and the form. The matter is the fault selected for attack, or the virtue of which a habit is to be acquired; and the aid of a wise counsellor is often necessary for its choice.

"The form is the practice of the exercise three times a day. Of these three times the first is at rising, when the resolution to watch and struggle against the fault chosen should be renewed *for the coming morning;* the second is at noon, when the conscience is examined, and the number of times the fault has been committed is noted in a book; the due acts of self-humiliation, contrition, hope, and the renewal of our resolution *for the rest of that day* are made; the third is before retiring to rest, when the exercise is repeated as at noon." — *Flowers of Nazareth.*

II. Give as much time as possible each day to prayer; determine this time according to your occupation, your attraction, and the advice of your director. Let your heart take much more part in this holy exercise than your mind; and let the mysteries of the life and passion of your Saviour be the usual subject.

III. Do not voluntarily deprive yourself, even for a day, of the inestimable happiness of assisting at the holy sacrifice of the Mass. Unite yourself to Our Lord by means of spiritual communion; offer yourself with Him to God His Father, and ask with perfect confidence, through the merits of His sacrifice, the graces of which you stand in need. Do not fail to pray thus and to offer all your actions of the day in union with the merits of Jesus Christ, for the conversion of infidels, heretics, and sinners, for the progress of the just, and the triumph of our holy mother, the Church.

The *morning offering* of the "Apostleship of Prayer" is most commendable, *viz.:*

"O my God I offer Thee my prayers, works, and sufferings this day in union with the Sacred Heart of Jesus, for the intentions for which He pleads and offers Himself in Holy Mass, in thanksgiving for Thy favors, in reparation for our offenses and for the petitions of all our Associates; especially this month for the *intention* recommended by His Holiness, the Pope."

IV. Give a certain time each day to the reading of a good book, according to the advice of your director. Read it in the presence of God, who speaks to you Himself. Reflect upon what you read; relish it; ask God to give you the grace to carry out the good desires with which He inspires you by means of this reading. Spiritual reading made in this way is a sort of easy meditation, and when we are deprived of a sermon may take its place.

V. Say your rosary every day, either alone or with others, and as you recite it accustom yourself to meditate affectionately on the mysteries of Our Saviour and of His holy Mother. This is the easiest and frequently the most fruitful of all meditations.

VI. Make a daily visit, if possible to the Blessed Sacrament; go to Our Lord with the simplicity of a child; confide to His heart your joys, your sorrows, your temptations, and your faults. Make acts of *adoration, thanksgiving, reparation, supplication,* and *spiritual communion.*

VII. The life of a Christian should be a continual exercise of penance. Mortify yourself in common and ordinary things; nothing is more necessary in order to establish in your soul the empire of grace and destroy that of nature. Here are a few practices to this end:

Resist your inclination to do something which is useless. Keep careful guard over your eyes. Refrain from raillery. Withhold a clever word likely to wound, or intended merely to satisfy self-love. Do not seek what merely flatters sensuality. Regulate innocent pleasures. Refrain sometimes, through a spirit of penance, even from permitted pleasures. Moderate that excessive tenderness we all have for ourselves. Detach your mind from pleasurable sentiments. Speak little and with moderation. Be courteous and kind to persons for whom you feel an antipathy. Be silent under affliction, and bear your cross with resignation.

VIII. Devote yourself to your labor as well as to the fulfilment of all your duties energetically and with a pure intention to please God and make yourself useful to your neighbor. Do not forget that the most indifferent actions acquire, through a fervent intention, inappreciable merit for eternity. Raise your heart to God from time to time by means of fervent ejaculations, that it may not be narrowed and absorbed by earthly occupations.

IX. Let no meal pass without offering a slight mortification to your Saviour, who accepted the bitter draught on the cross for love of you. These little sacrifices will avail you many graces, and will preserve you from the dangers of sensuality.

X. Go to bed as far as possible at a fixed hour, and before doing so carefully make your particular examen as well as a general examination of the day. Let there be, if possible, family prayer, that your petitions thus united may be more efficacious before God, and more advantageous to your children and to your servants.

XI. Go to confession at least every fortnight; prepare yourself for it in the morning during your meditation and the holy sacrifice of the Mass. Give most care to exciting yourself to sincere contrition for your faults.

XII. Receive communion as frequently as your director permits; bring to this great action all the devotion and care of which you are capable; approach the Holy Table with a contrite and humble heart, and an ardent desire to be united with Jesus. Pray that you may love Him more, that you may become more and more like to Him, and be ruled and guided by His spirit.

XIII. In your relations with the members of your family and those about you, be kind and considerate; endeavor to make piety loved through you. Avoid with the greatest care that spirit of criticism, those little jealousies, petty weaknesses, and caprices which many vainly seek to reconcile with true piety.

XIV. When you go out into the world avoid with equal care unseemly levity and repellent austerity, and while the politeness of the old school seems to be disappearing more and more, endeavor to revive it in your social intercourse by that delicate courtesy, thoughtful consideration, and simple, modest bearing which are the natural outcome of humility and Christian charity.

XV. Be inflexible in regard to dangerous books and questionable plays. Let even innocent pleasures be moderate.

XVI. If God has placed you in a position to give yourself to good works, let them be your pleasantest recreation. Remember that in helping the poor and the afflicted you are helping Jesus Christ Himself, and that they, in thus affording you the means of meriting the gratitude of your God and the indulgence of your Judge, confer a greater benefit upon you than you can bestow upon them. Regulate your expenses, moderate your attachment to the things of this world, and remember that you will be judged by a God who for love of you bore poverty, humility, and suffering. If your crucified Saviour wills to give you a small share of His sufferings, do not forget that the cross is the only incontestable mark of real love and the strongest bond by which your soul may be united with God. This conviction will give you strength to overcome the repugnance of nature and to bless God in the midst of the most cruel trials.

XVII. Select a day each month to prepare yourself for death, and on that day perform each duty as faithfully as if it were to be the last of your life. Go to confession and receive communion as viaticum. Examine what might trouble you if this day were the last of your life: unjust possessions, unreconciled quarrels, etc. Repeat the acts made by the dying; acts of resignation, acts accepting the time, the place, the manner of the death God wishes you to die; acts of thanksgiving, of lively faith, of hope, of confidence, of sincere sorrow, of love of God, etc. Invoke Jesus crucified; implore the Blessed Virgin, St. Joseph, your angel guardian, your patron saint, to plead for you, that you may live a holy life and die a happy death.

XVIII. Faithful devotion to the Sacred Heart of Jesus and His blessed Mother is regarded as a certain means of salvation. Unite yourself with confraternities established in their honor. Practices enjoined by these associations are not onerous, do not oblige under pain of sin, and are enriched with numerous indulgences. Nourish also in your soul sincere devotion to St. Joseph, the spouse of our Lady, to the holy angels, and the saint whose name you received in Baptism. Finally pray frequently for the dying and for the souls in purgatory.[1]

97. — Death

"ET MORTUUS *est;*" "*And he died.*" With this record ends every life — even the longest life. One day it shall be said of me: "he is dead," "she is dead."

"See then how matters stand with thee," says the gentle *Thomas à Kempis;* "a man is here to-day and to-morrow he is vanished.

"And when he is taken away from the sight he is quickly also out of mind.

"Oh, the dulness and hardness of man's heart, which only thinks of what is present, and looks not forward to things to come.

"If thou hadst a good conscience thou wouldst not much fear death.

"If thou art not prepared to-day, how shalt thou be to-morrow.

"To-morrow is an uncertain day; how dost thou know that thou shalt be alive to-morrow?

"Blessed is he that has always the hour of death before his eyes and every day disposes himself to die.

"Many die suddenly and when they little think of it: '*Because at what hour you know not the Son of Man will come*' (*Matt.* xxiv. 44).

"How happy and prudent is he, who strives to be during all his life and especially now as he desires to be found at his death.

[1] See, The Secret of Sanctity, According to St. Francis of Sales and Father Crasset, S.J.

"Trust not in thy friends and relations, nor put off the welfare of thy soul to hereafter; for men will sooner forget thee than thou imaginest.

"It is better now to provide in time and send some good before thee, than to trust to the help of others after thy death (*Matt.* vi. 20).

"How many die each day and how many thinking to live long have been deceived and unexpectedly snatched away!

"Strive now so to live that in the hour of thy death thou mayst rather rejoice than fear.

"Learn now to die to the world that then thou mayst begin to live with Christ (*Rom.* vi. 8).

"Chastise thy body now by penance that thou mayst then have an assured confidence (1 *Cor.* ix. 27).

"Make now to thyself friends, by honoring the saints of God, and imitating their actions, that when thou shalt fail in this life they may receive thee into everlasting dwellings (*Luke* xvi. 9).

"Keep thyself as a pilgrim, and a stranger upon earth. Refrain yourselves from carnal desires, which war against the soul (1 *Peter* ii. 11).

"Keep thy heart free and raised upward to God, because thou hast not here a lasting abode.

"Send thither thy daily prayers, with sighs and tears, that after death thy spirit may be worthy to pass happily to Our Lord.   Amen."

98. — Heaven

"EYE hath not seen, nor ear heard, neither hath it entered into the heart of man, what things God hath prepared for them that love Him " (1 *Cor.* ii. 9).

"Heavenly happiness," as Boethius observes, "is a

state made perfect by the concurrence of every good."
This perfect happiness, moreover, will be eternal and
can not be lost.

"Your joy," says Christ, "no man shall take from
you" (*John* xvi. 22).

The oracle of the Royal Prophet will be fulfilled in
heaven: "They (the saints) shall be inebriated with
the plenty of Thy house, and Thou shalt make them
drink of the torrent of pleasure" (*Ps.* xxxv. 9).

"The sufferings of this life," says St. Paul, "are not
worthy to be compared with the glory to come, that
shall be revealed to us" (*Rom.* viii. 18).

"Would you know what heaven is ?" asks St. Bernard; "it is a place where there is nothing that causes
pain, where there is everything which you might desire."
From heaven are banished all evils and all sufferings;
for "God shall wipe away all tears from their eyes, and
death shall be no more, nor mourning, nor crying,
nor sorrow shall be any more" (*Apoc.* xxi. 4).

In heaven shall be found every good and every delight. But the greatest joy of heaven is to behold the
face of God, and in Him to be possessed of every
good.

"*I am thy reward exceeding great*" (*Gen.* xv. 1);
thus spoke the Lord to Abraham. And what can he
lack who possesses God, Who is the source of all that
is good, true, and beautiful? Hence the prophet
says: "*I shall be satisfied when Thy glory shall appear*"
(*Ps.* xv. 15).

"How lovely are Thy tabernacles, O Lord of hosts,
my soul longeth and fainteth for the courts of the
Lord!" (*Ps.* lviii. 2).

In all the trials of life, keep your eyes directed
toward heaven, then you can not lose your peace of

soul; let your heart pant after the imperishable treasures of heaven.

"But we must remember," as Lescoubier observes in his "Monthly Recollection," "that heaven is a reward promised to them that deserve it through their good works. *Labor as a good soldier of Christ Jesus* (2 *Tim*. ii. 3); and if perchance the burden weighs heavy and the labor is hard, encourage yourself by looking up to the reward. . . . Fulfil faithfully all your duties: *be ye steadfast and unmovable, always abounding in the work of the Lord, knowing that your labor is not vain in the Lord* (1 *Cor*. xv. 58).

"Heavenly glory is called a *crown*. Now, *he that striveth for the mastery, is not crowned except he strive lawfully* (2 *Tim*. ii. 5). Fight then the good fight of the Faith, the battles of the Lord; be steadfast and courageous; and soon *you shall receive a never-fading crown of glory* (1 *Pet*. v. 4).

"Heaven is the *kingdom* of God; we are its heirs. But it is the will and the law of God that *through many tribulations we must enter into that kingdom* (*Acts* xiv. 21) as Christ also had to *suffer and so to enter into His glory* (*Luke* xxiv. 26). So that the way to heaven is the way of the cross. Let us then follow our beloved Master on the way of His passion, and *that which is at present momentary and light of our tribulation, shall work for us above measure exceedingly an eternal weight of glory* (2 *Cor*. iv. 17)."

O Mary, conceived without sin, pray for us who have recourse to thee.—100 days' indulgence, once a day. Leo XIII.

PART TWO

PRAYERS AND DEVOTIONS

Morning Prayer

IN THE name of the Father, ✠ and of the Son, and of the Holy Ghost. Amen.

Blessed be the Holy Trinity, One God, now and forever. Amen.

Glory to the Father, Who created me; glory to the Son, Who redeemed me; glory to the Holy Ghost, Who sanctifieth me.

ACT OF ADORATION AND THANKSGIVING

ALMIGHTY and eternal God, I adore Thee, and I *thank* Thee for all the benefits which Thou, in Thy infinite goodness and mercy, hast conferred upon me. I thank Thee especially for having preserved and protected me this night.

ACT OF FAITH

I BELIEVE in Thee, because Thou art Truth itself, and, as Thou hast revealed them to her, I believe all the sacred truths which the holy Catholic Church believes and teaches.

ACT OF HOPE

I HOPE in Thee, because Thou art omnipotent, most merciful, and faithful to Thy promises;

I hope to obtain the pardon of my sins, the grace to live a holy life, to die a happy death, and to obtain life everlasting, through the merits of Jesus Christ, my Lord and Redeemer.

ACT OF LOVE

I LOVE Thee with my whole heart, and above all things, because Thou art infinitely good; and for the love of Thee I love my neighbor as myself.

ACT OF SUPPLICATION

I BESEECH Thee most earnestly to bless me, that I may serve Thee faithfully this day by a perfect devotedness to all my duties and a steadfast adherence to all my promises and good resolutions.

ACT OF CONTRITION

I AM truly sorry for having sinned because Thou art infinitely good and sin displeases Thee. I will avoid the occasions of sin and strive in all things to do Thy holy will.

ACT OF CONSECRATION

I WISH to *consecrate* this day and all the days of my life to Thy honor and glory.

OFFERING

I OFFER Thee all my prayers, works, and sufferings in union with the Sacred Heart of Jesus, for the intentions for which He pleads and offers Himself in the holy sacrifice of the Mass, in thanksgiving for Thy

favors, in reparation for my offenses, and in humble
supplication for my temporal and eternal welfare, for
the wants of our holy Mother the Church, for the conversion of sinners, and for the relief of the poor souls in
purgatory.

I have the intention to gain all the indulgences
attached to the prayers I shall say, and to the good
works I shall perform this day. I resolve to gain all
the indulgences I can in favor of the souls in purgatory.

Our Father, Hail Mary, Apostles' Creed, Glory.

O sweetest Heart of Jesus! I implore
That I may ever love Thee more and more.

Indulgence of 300 days, each time. — Pius IX, Nov.
26, 1876.

Jesus, meek and humble of heart, make my heart
like unto Thine.

Indulgence of 300 days, once a day. — Pius IX, Jan
25, 1868.

Sweet Heart of Jesus, be my love!

Indulgence of 300 days, once a day. — Leo XIII, May
21, 1892.

Sweet Heart of Mary, be my salvation!

Indulgence of 300 days, each time. — Pius IX, Sept.
30, 1852.

O MARY! my Queen! my Mother! I give myself entirely to thee; and to show my devotion
to thee, I consecrate to thee this day my eyes, my
ears, my mouth, my heart, my whole being,
without reserve. Wherefore, good mother, as I am

thine own, keep me, guard me, as thy property and possession.

His Holiness, Pope Pius IX, by a decree of the Sacred Congregation of Indulgences, Aug. 5, 1851, granted to all the faithful who, with fervor and at least contrite heart, shall say, morning and evening, one *Hail Mary*, together with this prayer, to implore of the Blessed Virgin victory over temptations, especially over those against chastity, an *indulgence of one hundred days*, once a day.

St. Joseph, model and patron of those who love the Sacred Heart of Jesus, pray for us!

Indulgence of 100 days, once a day. — Leo XIII, Dec. 19, 1891.

> Angel of God, my guardian dear,
> To whom His love commits me here,
> Ever this day be at my side,
> To light and guard, to rule and guide.
> Amen.

The Sovereign Pontiff, Pius VI, by a brief, Oct. 2, 1795, granted to all the faithful, every time that, with at least contrite heart and devotion, they shall say this prayer, an *indulgence of one hundred days*.

All ye holy angels and saints of God, and especially you, my dear patron saint, pray for me!

May the Lord bless me, preserve me from all evil, and bring me to life everlasting.

May the souls of the faithful departed, through the mercy of God, rest in peace.

V. Eternal rest give to them, O Lord;

R. And let perpetual light shine upon them.

Indulgence of 50 days, each time. — Leo XIII, March 22, 1902.

Morning Offering
of the Apostleship of Prayer

O JESUS, through the immaculate heart of Mary, I offer Thee my prayers, works, and sufferings of this day for all the intentions of Thy sacred Heart, in union with the holy sacrifice of the Mass throughout the world, for the intentions of all our associates, and in particular for the intention recommended this month by the Holy Father.

Evening Prayer

IN THE name of the Father, ✠ and of the Son, and of the Holy Ghost. Amen.

Blessed be the Holy Trinity, One God, now and forever. Amen.

Glory to the Father, Who created me; glory to the Son, Who redeemed me; glory to the Holy Ghost, Who sanctifieth me.

ACT OF ADORATION

ALMIGHTY and eternal God, I adore Thee, and I *thank* Thee for all the benefits I have received this day through Thy infinite goodness and mercy. Give me light to know my faults and grant me grace to be truly sorry for my sins.

Here examine your conscience on the faults of the day; on the offenses against God, against your neighbor, and against yourself; on the commandments of God and of the Church; and particularly as regards your predominant passion, promises, and resolutions.

In the event that you have sinned grievously, resolve to go to confession at the first opportunity. Meditate for a few moments on eternity, death, judgment, heaven, and hell, mindful of the admonition of the Holy Spirit: "*In all thy works, O man, remember thy last end and thou wilt never sin.*" Make an act of contrition.

ACT OF CONTRITION

O MY God, I am truly sorry for having sinned, because Thou art infinitely good and sin displeases

212

Thee. I am firmly resolved, with the help of Thy grace, never more to offend Thee, and I will carefully avoid the occasions of sin.

ACT OF LOVE

I LOVE Thee, my Lord and my God, with my whole heart and above all things, and for the love of Thee I love my neighbor as myself. Grant that I may love Thee more and more and give me the grace of perseverance, that I may live a holy life, die a happy death, and glorify Thee eternally in heaven.

Our Father, Hail Mary, Apostles' Creed, Glory.

O sweetest Heart of Jesus! I implore
That I may ever love Thee more and more.
Indulgence of 300 days, each time. — Pius IX, Nov. 26, 1876.

Sweet Heart of Jesus, be my love!
Indulgence of 300 days, once a day. — Leo XIII, May 21, 1892.

Sweet Heart of Mary, be my salvation!
Indulgence of 300 days, each time. — Pius IX, Sept. 30, 1852.

The Memorare

MEMORARE, O piissima virgo Maria, non esse auditum a sæculo quemquam ad tua currentem præsidia, tua implorantem auxilia, tua petentem suf-

REMEMBER, O most gracious Virgin Mary! that never was it known that any one who fled to thy protection, implored thy help, and sought thy inter-

fragia, esse derelictum. Ego tali animatus confidentia, ad te, virgo virginum, Mater, curro, ad te venio, coram te gemens peccator assisto; noli, mater Verbi, verba mea despicere, sed audi propitia, et exaudi. Amen.

cession, was left unaided. Inspired with this confidence, I fly unto thee, O Virgin of virgins, my mother! To thee I come; before thee I stand, sinful and sorrowful. O mother of the Word incarnate! despise not my petitions, but, in thy mercy, hear and answer me. Amen.

His Holiness, Pope Pius IX, by a rescript of the Sacred Congregation of Indulgences, Dec. 11, 1846, granted to all the faithful every time that, with at least contrite heart and devotion, they shall say this prayer, an *indulgence of three hundred days;* and a *plenary indulgence,* once a month, to all those who, having said it at least once a day for a month, on any day, being truly penitent, after confession and communion, shall visit a church or public oratory, and pray there, for some time, for the intention of His Holiness.

EJACULATIONS

O MARY! my Queen! my Mother! remember I am thine own. Keep me, guard me, as thy property and possession.

Jesus, Mary, and Joseph, I give you my heart and my soul.
Jesus, Mary, and Joseph, assist me in my last agony.
Jesus, Mary, and Joseph, may I breathe forth my soul in peace with you. Amen.

Indulgence of 300 days, each time. — Pius VII, Aug. 26, 1814.

AY the Blessed Virgin Mary, St. Joseph, and all
the saints, pray for us to Our Lord, that we
may be preserved this night from sin and evil.
Amen.

O my good angel, whom God has appointed to be my
guardian, watch over me during this night. ˙

May Our Lord bless us and preserve us from all evil
and bring us to life everlasting.

May the souls of the faithful departed, through the
mercy of God, rest in peace.   Amen.

De Profundis

for the Faithful Departed

Ps. 129

DE PROFUNDIS clamavi
ad te, Domine:
Domine, exaudi vocem
meam.

Fiant aures tuæ inten-
dentes, in vocem depre-
cationis meæ.

Si iniquitates observa-
veris, Domine: Domine,
quis sustinebit?

Quia apud te propitia-
tio est: et propter le-
gem tuam sustinui te, Do-
mine.

Sustinuit anima mea in
verbo ejus: speravit anima
mea in Domino.

A custodia matutina us-
que ad noctem, speret Israel
in Domino.

OUT of the depths
I have cried to Thee,
O Lord! Lord, hear my
voice.

Let Thine ears be atten-
tive to the voice of my supplication.

If Thou, O Lord, shalt
mark our iniquities: O
Lord, who shall stand it?

For with Thee there is
merciful forgiveness: and by
reason of Thy law I have
waited for Thee, O Lord.

My soul hath relied on
His word: my soul hath
hoped in the Lord.

From the morning watch
even unto night, let Israel
hope in the Lord

Quia apud Dominum misericordia, et copiosa apud eum redemptio.	Because with the Lord there is mercy: and with Him plenteous redemption.
Et ipse redimet Israel ex omnibus iniquitatibus ejus.	And He shall redeem Israel from all his iniquities.

The Sovereign Pontiff, Clement XII, by a brief, *Cœleste Ecclesiæ thesauros*, Aug. 11, 1736, granted an *indulgence of one hundred days* to all the faithful who, at the sound of the bell, at the first hour after nightfall, shall say devoutly on their knees the psalm *De profundis*, or the *Our Father*, the *Hail Mary*, and the *Requiem æternam*.

The Sovereign Pontiff, Pius VI, by a rescript of the Sacred Congregation of the Propaganda, March 18, 1781, granted these indulgences to all the faithful who may happen to dwell in a place where no bell for the dead is sounded, provided they shall say the *De profundis*, or the *Our Father*, and the *Hail Mary*, etc., about nightfall.

Have mercy, O Lord, have mercy on the poor souls in purgatory.

V. Eternal rest give unto them, O Lord;

R. And let perpetual light shine upon them!

V. O Lord, hear my prayer;

R. And let my cry come unto Thee!

Let us pray

O GOD! the Creator and Redeemer of all the faithful, grant to the souls of Thy servants departed the remission of all their sins, that through pious supplications they may obtain that pardon which they have always desired, Who livest and reignest now and forever. Amen.

PRAYER

VISIT, we beseech Thee, O Lord, this habitation, and drive far from it all the snares of the enemy: let Thy holy angels dwell herein, to keep us in peace, and may Thy blessing be always upon us. Through Our Lord Jesus Christ, Thy Son, Who liveth and reigneth with Thee, in the unity of the Holy Ghost, one God, world without end. Amen.

Sprinkle your bed with holy water and, blessing yourself, say when you lie down to rest:

Lord, into Thy hands I commend my spirit.

Prayers During the Day

GRACE BEFORE MEALS

BLESS us, O Lord, and these Thy gifts which we are about to receive from Thy bounty: through Christ Our Lord.

R. Amen.

GRACE AFTER MEALS

WE GIVE Thee thanks, almighty God, for all Thy benefits, Who livest and reignest world without end.

R. Amen.

Vouchsafe, O Lord, to reward with eternal life all those who do us good for Thy name's sake.

R. Amen.

V. Let us bless the Lord.

R. Thanks be to God.

V. May the souls of the faithful departed, through the mercy of God, rest in peace.

R. Amen.

ACT OF FAITH

O MY God! I firmly believe all the sacred truths which the Catholic Church believes and teaches, because Thou, Who canst neither deceive nor be deceived, hast revealed them.

ACT OF HOPE

O MY God, trusting in Thy promises and relying on Thy infinite power and goodness I hope to obtain pardon for my sins, the assistance of Thy grace, and life everlasting, through the merits of Jesus Christ, my Lord and Redeemer.

ACT OF LOVE

O MY God, I love Thee with my whole heart and above all things, because Thou art the Supreme Good and worthy of all our love. I am sorry for having displeased Thy infinite goodness by my sins. I desire to do Thy holy will and to love Thee more and more. For the love of Thee I will love my neighbor as myself.

The Sovereign Pontiff, Benedict XIV, considering that it is not only useful, but also truly necessary, for eternal salvation to make frequent acts of the theological virtues of faith, hope, and charity, in order to excite the faithful to make these acts, granted, by a decree of the Sacred Congregation of Indulgences, Jan. 28, 1756, confirming the grant already made by Benedict XIII, Jan. 15, 1728, a *plenary indulgence*, once a month, to all those who shall, daily, devoutly say, and, at the same time, make with their heart these acts. This indulgence may be gained on any day, when, being truly penitent, after confession and communion, they shall pray for peace and union among Christian princes, for the extirpation of heresy, and for the triumph of Holy Church.

He granted in like manner a *plenary indulgence* at the hour of death. Finally, to excite the faithful to a very frequent use of these acts, he extended the *indulgence of seven years and seven quarantines* (which, by the grant of his predecessor, could be gained only once a day) to every time that these acts are said with heartfelt devotion.

The same Sovereign Pontiff further declared that, to gain these indulgences, it is not necessary to make use of any set form of words, but that any one may use any form of words which he pleases, provided it expresses the particular motive of each of the three theological virtues.

—The New Raccolta.

The Angelus

ANGELUS Domini nuntiavit Mariæ. *R.* Et concepit de Spiritu Sancto.

Ave, Maria, etc.

V. Ecce ancilla Domini. *R.* Fiat mihi secundum verbum tuum. Ave, Maria, etc.

V. Et Verbum caro factum est. *R.* Et habitavit in nobis. Ave, Maria, etc.

V. Ora pro nobis, sancta Dei Genitrix. *R.* Ut digni efficiamur promissionibus Christi.

THE Angel of the Lord declared unto Mary. *R.* And she conceived of the Holy Ghost. Hail, Mary.

V. Behold the handmaid of the Lord. *R.* Be it done unto me according to thy word. Hail, Mary, etc.

V. And the Word was made Flesh. *R.* And dwelt among us. Hail, Mary, etc.

V. Pray for us, O Holy Mother of God. *R.* That we may be made worthy of the promises of Christ.

Oremus

GRATIAM tuam, quæsumus, Domine, mentibus nostris infunde, ut qui, Angelo nuntiante, Christi filii tui incarnationem cognovimus, per passionem ejus et crucem ad resurrectionis gloriam

Let us pray

POUR forth, we beseech Thee, O Lord, Thy grace into our hearts; that as we have known the incarnation of Christ Thy Son by the message of an angel, so, by His passion and cross, we may be brought to the glory

perducamur; per eumdem Christum Dominum nostrum. Amen.

of His resurrection; through the same Christ our Lord. Amen.

Regina Cœli

During Eastertide, from Holy Saturday till Trinity Sunday, instead of the *Angelus*, the *Regina Cœli* is recited *standing*.

REGINA cœli, lætare,
    Alleluia.
Quia quem meruisti portare,
    Alleluia.
Resurrexit, sicut dixit,
    Alleluia.
Ora pro nobis Deum,
    Alleluia.
    V. Gaude et lætare, Virgo Maria,
    Alleluia.
    R. Quia surrexit Dominus vere,
    Alleluia.

QUEEN of heaven, rejoice,
    Alleluia.
For He Whom thou didst deserve to bear,
    Alleluia.
Hath risen as He said,
    Alleluia.
Pray for us to God,
    Alleluia.
    V. Rejoice and be glad,
O Virgin Mary!
    Alleluia.
    R. Because Our Lord is truly risen,
    Alleluia.

Oremus

Let us pray

DEUS, qui per 'resurrectionem Filii tui, Domini nostri, Jesu Christi, mundum lætificare dignatus es, præsta, quæsumus, ut per ejus genitricem Virginem Mariam perpetuæ capiamus gaudia vitæ: per eumdem Christum, Dominum nostrum.
    R. Amen.

O GOD, Who by the resurrection of Thy Son, Our Lord Jesus Christ, hast vouchsafed to make glad the whole world, grant, we beseech Thee, that, through the intercession of the Virgin Mary, His mother, we may attain the joys of eternal life. Through the same Christ our Lord. Amen.

The Sovereign Pontiff Benedict XIII, by a brief, *Injunctæ nobis*, Sept. 14, 1724, granted a *plenary indulgence*, once a month, to all the faithful who, every day, at the sound of the bell, in the morning, or at noon, or in the evening at sunset, shall say devoutly, on their knees, the *Angelus Domini*, with the *Hail Mary*, three times, on any day when, being truly penitent, after confession and communion, they shall pray for peace and union among Christian princes, for the extirpation of heresy, and for the triumph of Holy Mother Church; also an *indulgence of one hundred days*, on all the other days in the year, every time that, with contrite heart and devotion, they shall say these prayers.

Salve Regina

In the Morning

SALVE regina, mater misericordiæ, vita dulcedo, et spes nostra salve. Ad te clamamus exules filii Hevæ; ad te suspiramus, gementes et flentes in hac lacrymarum valle. Eja ergo, advocata nostra, illos tuos misericordes oculos ad nos converte; et Jesum benedictum fructum ventris tui nobis post hoc exilium ostende, O clemens, O pia, O dulcis virgo Maria.

V. Dignare me laudare te, virgo sacrata.

R. Da mihi virtutem contra hostes tuos.

HAIL, holy queen, mother of mercy, our life, our sweetness, and our hope; to thee do we cry, poor banished sons of Eve, to thee do we send up our sighs, mourning and weeping in this valley of tears. Turn then, most gracious advocate, thine eyes of mercy toward us, and after this, our exile, show unto us the blessed fruit of thy womb, Jesus, O clement, O loving, O sweet Virgin Mary!

V. Make me worthy to praise thee, holy Virgin.

R. Give me strength against thine enemies.

V. Benedictus Deus in sanctis suis.

R. Amen.

V. Blessed be God in his saints.

R. Amen.

Sub Tuum Praesidium

In the Evening

SUB tuum præsidium confugimus, sancta Dei genitrix; nostras deprecationes ne despicias in necessitatibus nostris; sed a periculis cunctis libera nos, semper virgo gloriosa et benedicta.

V. Dignare me, laudare te, virgo sacrata.

R. Da mihi virtutem contra hostes tuos.

V. Benedictus Deus in sanctis suis.

R. Amen.

WE FLY to thy patronage, O holy mother of God! despise not our petitions in our necessities, but deliver us from all dangers, O ever glorious and blessed Virgin.

V. Make me worthy to praise thee, holy Virgin.

R. Give me strength against thine enemies.

V. Blessed be God in his saints.

R. Amen.

The Sovereign Pontiff, Pius VI, by a decree of the Sacred Congregation of Indulgences, April 5, 1786, granted an *indulgence of one hundred days*, once a day, to all the faithful who, moved by the true spirit of religion to atone in some manner for the insults offered to the most blessed Virgin Mary, mother of God, and to the saints, and to defend and promote the worship and veneration of their holy images, shall say, with at least contrite heart and devotion, the *Salve Regina*, with the versicles, *Dignare me* and *Benedictus Deus*, in the morning, and *Sub tuum præsidium*, with the same versicles, in the evening. Also an *indulgence of seven years and seven quarantines* on all the Sundays of the year

The Lord's Prayer

PATER noster, qui es in cœlis, sanctificetur nomen tuum: adveniat regnum tuum: fiat voluntas tua, sicut in cœlo, et in terra. Panem nostrum quotidianum da nobis hodie: et dimitte nobis debita nostra, sicut et nos dimittimus debitoribus nostris. Et ne nos inducas in tentationem: sed libera nos a malo. Amen.

OUR Father, Who art in heaven, hallowed be Thy name. Thy kingdom come; Thy will be done on earth, as it is in heaven. Give us this day our daily bread; and forgive us our trespasses, as we forgive those who trespass against us. And lead us not into temptation; but deliver us from evil. Amen.

The Hail Mary

AVE, Maria, gratia plena; Dominus tecum; benedicta tu in mulieribus, et benedictus fructus ventris tui, Jesus. Sancta Maria, Mater Dei, ora pro nobis peccatoribus, nunc et in hora mortis nostræ. Amen.

HAIL, Mary, full of grace; the Lord is with thee; blessed art thou among women, and blessed is the fruit of thy womb, Jesus. Holy Mary, Mother of God, pray for us sinners, now and at the hour of our death. Amen.

The Apostles' Creed

CREDO in Deum, Patrem omnipotentem, Creatorem cœli et terræ; et in Jesum Christum, Filium ejus unicum, Dominum nostrum: qui conceptus est de Spiritu Sancto, natus ex Maria Virgine, passus sub Pontio Pilato, crucifixus, mortuus, et sepultus. Descendit ad inferos; tertia die resur-

I BELIEVE in God, the Father Almighty, Creator of heaven and earth; and in Jesus Christ, His only Son, our Lord: Who was conceived by the Holy Ghost, born of the Virgin Mary, suffered under Pontius Pilate, was crucified, died, and was buried. He descended into hell; the third day He

rexit a mortuis; ascendit ad cœlos, sedet ad dexteram Dei Patris omnipotentis; inde venturus est judicare vivos et mortuos. Credo in Spiritum Sanctum, Sanctam Ecclesiam Catholicam, sanctorum communionem, remissionem peccatorum, carnis resurrectionem, vitam æternam. Amen.

rose again from the dead; He ascended into heaven, sitteth at the right hand of God, the Father Almighty; from thence He shall come to judge the living and dead. I believe in the Holy Ghost, the holy Catholic Church, the communion of saints, the forgiveness of sins, the resurrection of the body, and the life everlasting. Amen.

Prayer before Meditation, Study, or Spiritual Reading

MY GOD, I firmly believe that Thou art here present, and I humbly adore Thee in union with the angels and saints. I am sorry for having sinned, because Thou art infinitely good and sin displeases Thee.

I love Thee above all things and with my whole heart. I offer Thee all that I am and all that I have, — my soul with all its faculties, my body with all its senses.

Enlighten my understanding and inflame my will, that I may know and do what is pleasing to Thee. I beseech Thee to direct all the powers of my soul, all my thoughts and affections to Thy service and Thy glory as well as to my own sanctification and salvation.

Prayer to the Holy Ghost

VENI, Sancte Spiritus, reple tuorum corda fidelium, et tui amoris in eis ignem accende.

COME, O Holy Ghost, fill the hearts of Thy faithful, and enkindle in them the fire of Thy love.

V. Emitte Spiritum tuum et creabuntur.

R. Et renovabis faciem terræ.

V. Send forth Thy Spirit and they shall be created.

R. And Thou shalt renew the face of the earth.

Oremus

DEUS, qui corda fidelium sancti Spiritus illustratione docuisti, da nobis in eodem Spiritu recta sapere, et de ejus semper consolatione gaudere. Per Christum Dominum nostrum.

R. Amen.

Let us pray

O GOD, Who hast taught the hearts of the faithful by the light of the Holy Spirit, grant that by the gift of the same Spirit we may be always truly wise, and ever rejoice in His consolations, through Christ our Lord.

R. Amen.

EJACULATION

Our Lady of Good Studies, pray for us !

Indulgence of 300 days. — Pius X, May 22, 1906.

Prayer after Meditation

O MY God, I give Thee heartfelt thanks for all the graces Thou hast conferred on me during this meditation. Pardon me, I beseech Thee, all the negligence and all the distractions of which I have been guilty. Give me strength to carry out the resolutions that I have made. Fortify me, that from henceforth I may diligently practise this virtue . . . avoid this fault . . . perform this action . . . to Thy honor. Help me to keep my good resolutions, O sweet Virgin Mary; and do thou, my good angel, recall them to my memory, if I should ever forget or neglect them. *Omnia ad majorem Dei gloriam !*

"Anima Christi"

SOUL of Christ, sanctify me;
Body of Christ, save me;
Blood of Christ, inebriate me;
Water from the side of Christ, wash me;
Passion of Christ, strengthen me:
O good Jesus, hear me;
Within Thy wounds hide me;
Suffer me not to be separated from Thee;
From the evil enemy defend me;
In the hour of my death call me,
And bid me come unto Thee,
That with all Thy saints I may praise Thee
For all eternity. Amen.

"Suscipe"

PRAYER TAKEN FROM THE BOOK OF "THE SPIRITUAL EXERCISES" OF ST. IGNATIUS OF LOYOLA

SUSCIPE, Domine, universam meam libertatem. Accipe memoriam, intellectum atque voluntatem omnem. Quidquid habeo vel possideo, mihi largitus es; id tibi totum restituo ac tuæ prorsus voluntati trado gubernandum. Amorem tui solum cum gratia tua mihi dones et dives sum satis, nec aliud quidquam ultra posco.

TAKE, O Lord, and receive all my liberty, my memory, my understanding and my whole will. Thou hast given me all that I am and all that I possess; I surrender it all to Thee that Thou mayest dispose of it according to Thy will. Give me only Thy love and Thy grace; with these I will be rich enough, and will have no more to desire.

His Holiness, Pope Leo XIII, by a rescript of the Sacred Congregation of Indulgences, May 26, 1883, granted to all the faithful who, with at least contrite heart and devotion.

shall recite the above prayer, an *indulgence of three hundred days*, once a day.

Prayer of St. Thomas Aquinas

WHICH HE WAS ACCUSTOMED TO RECITE EVERY DAY BEFORE THE IMAGE OF JESUS CHRIST

CONCEDE mihi, misericors Deus, quæ tibi placita sunt ardenter concupiscere, prudenter investigare, veraciter agnoscere et perfecte adimplere, ad laudem et gloriam nominis tui. Amen.

GRANT me grace, O merciful God, to desire ardently all that is pleasing to Thee, to examine it prudently, to acknowledge it truthfully, and to accomplish it perfectly, for the praise and glory of Thy name. Amen.

His Holiness, Pope Leo XIII, by a rescript of the Sacred Congregation of Indulgences, June 21, 1879, granted an *indulgence of three hundred days* to all the faithful who, before studying or reading, shall, with at least contrite heart and devotion, recite this prayer.

Indulgences

FOR READING THE HOLY GOSPEL

His Holiness, Leo XIII, by a rescript of the Sacred Congregation of Indulgences, Dec. 13, 1898, granted to the faithful who spend at least a quarter of an hour in reading the Holy Gospel, an *indulgence of three hundred days*, once a day; also a *plenary indulgence* once a month, on any day of the month, to those who shall have spent a quarter of an hour a day on every day of the month in reading the Holy Gospel, on the usual conditions — confession and communion, and praying for the intention of the Sovereign Pontiff.

FOR MENTAL PRAYER

The Sovereign Pontiff, Benedict XIV, in the brief, *Quemadmodum*, Dec. 16, 1746, granted to all the faithful who shall make mental prayer devoutly for half an hour, or at least for a quarter of an hour, every day, for a month, a *plenary indulgence*, once a month, on the day when, being truly penitent, after confession and communion, they shall pray devoutly for peace and union among Christian princes, for the extirpation of heresy, and for the triumph of Holy Mother Church.

St. Teresa's Book-Mark

LET nothing disturb thee,
Let nothing affright thee.
All things are passing;
God only is changeless.
Patience gains all things.
Who hath God wanteth nothing —
Alone God sufficeth.

I always find almost all the wisdom I need in " St. Teresa's Book-Mark." It is a volume in itself. My great comfort in distressing circumstances is that "all things are passing." — FATHER JOSEPH FARRELL, author of " Lectures by a Certain Professor."

Prayer before any Good Work

BEAR in mind the injunction of the holy Apostle: "Whatsoever you do in word or in work, do all in the name of the Lord Jesus Christ" (*Col.* iii. 17). Resolve to do all things for the glory of God *in the name of Jesus.*

O JESUS, sweet Jesus, O Jesus divine,
My life and my death unto Thee I resign.
Every action of mine shall Thy patronage claim;
For whatever I do shall be done in Thy name.

Renew your good intention frequently during the day and especially at the beginning of any important work or duty by some short ejaculatory prayer; *e.g.*:

"All in the name of Jesus."

"All for the glory of God."

"All for Jesus."

"All for the Sacred Heart of Jesus through the immaculate heart of Mary."

"In the name of the Father, ✠ and of the Son, and of the Holy Ghost. Amen."

"Come Holy Spirit, enlighten my mind and direct my will, that I may do what is pleasing to Thee and conducive to my salvation."

The Holy Sacrifice of the Mass

I. Mass the Sacrifice of the New Law

HOLY Mass is the sacrifice of the true body and blood of Jesus Christ, really present upon the altar, under the appearances of bread and wine, and offered to God by the priest for the living and the dead.

Holy Mass is the same sacrifice as that which was offered up by Our Lord Himself on the cross of Calvary, the manner alone of the offering being different. On the cross, He actually died by the shedding of His blood. On the altar, He renews His death in a mystical manner, without the reshedding of blood. This is done at the Consecration, for by the separate and distinct consecration of the two species, namely of the bread and of the wine, the blood of Christ is exhibited as being once more separate from His body; and thus Jesus Christ is placed on the altar, and offered to heaven, under the appearance of death, as if slain again and immolated.

II. The Four Great Ends of Mass

HOLY Mass is offered to God for four great ends, corresponding to the four great duties we owe to Him; these are:

1. To praise, honor, and adore the infinite majesty of God, Who is infinitely deserving of all the glory that can be given Him by His creatures.

2. To satisfy the infinite justice of God, Who is infinitaly offended by the sins committed against Him.

3. To thank the infinite liberality of God, Who requires an infinite return for all the favors bestowed upon His creatures.

4. To petition the infinite goodness of God, Whom nothing but a pleading of infinite value can move to grant us all needful blessings.

When Jesus Christ by the Holy Ghost offered Himself unspotted to God on Mount Calvary, He paid infinite adoration to the divine majesty, gave infinite satisfaction to the divine justice, made an infinite return to the divine liberality and moved the divine goodness by an appeal of infinite efficacy.

Now in Holy Mass, Jesus places Himself entirely in your hands, that you may offer to God the same great sacrifice of infinite value for the same most excellent ends, in your behalf as well as for others, whether living or dead. For all who devoutly assist at Holy Mass are made one with the priest, and along with him present to heaven the ador‑able sacrifice. What would you, therefore, do without the Holy Mass?

"Holy Mass is the sun of Christianity, the soul of faith, the center of the Catholic religion, the grand object of all her rites, ceremonies, and sacraments, in a word, it is a summary of all that is grand and beautiful in the Church of God."—St. Leonard of Port Maurice.

"When a priest celebrates Holy Mass, he honors God, he rejoices the angels, he edifies the Church, he helps the living, he obtains rest for the departed, and makes himself partaker of all blessings. —*Following of Christ.*

With the view, therefore, that God may receive from His creatures that clean oblation which alone is worthy of Him, and that the faithful be not deprived of the immense benefit of the same adorable sacrifice, Holy Church com‑mands her children under pain of grievous sin to hear Mass on all Sundays and holydays of obligation. But, surely, no Catholic who has any right idea of the importance and value of Holy Mass will remain satisfied with this. He will attend Holy Mass as often as he can on week-days as well.

He will, likewise, have Masses offered up by the priest, both for himself and others, living or dead. — Fr. Fiege, in *The Paraclete*.

Important Comment on the Following Method of Assisting at Mass

THERE is no need of attempting to say *all* the prayers for Mass given in a prayer-book. As regards the following method of assisting at Mass, it combines *vocal prayer* with *meditation*. Our aim has been to lead pious souls to devote some time at Mass to *mental prayer;* hence the reflections on the *Passion of Our Lord* in the Canon and on the *Pater Noster;* hence the *scriptural extracts* and the *thoughts from spiritual writers*, which are found scattered among the prayers. Many of the prayers, it will be observed, are *indulgenced*, and therefore particularly commendable.

All through this book, indeed, our aim has been to insert *indulgenced* prayers and ejaculations, wherever these could find a proper setting. The use of indulgenced prayers for the relief of the holy souls in purgatory is very desirable and advisable.

However, it is not intended that *all* the prayers here given should be invariably used; nor will it be possible always to say them all, especially not at Low Mass. Devotion would at times only be hampered in an attempt to say all the prayers.

Furthermore, our pious readers are not expected to make use of *all* the moral reflections and scriptural quotations every time they assist at Mass; dwell on those that excite special devotion or inflame your heart with pious affections and good resolutions. Any part of the prayers and reflections may be omitted.

If, while reading from your prayer-book at Mass, a good thought should make a strong impression on your mind, pause, meditate upon this point, and evoke spiritual affections and such resolutions as are calculated to help you in overcoming your evil inclinations and in leading a more perfect life.

"*Mental Prayer* or Meditation," says St. Francis of Sales, "is an earnest thought, voluntarily repeated or entertained in the *mind*, to excite the *will* to holy and salutary affections and resolutions."

Salutary acts of the will are acts of faith, hope, charity, humility, contrition, praise, adoration, thanksgiving, reparation, oblation, and petition.

When you intend to receive holy communion, the whole time of Mass may be employed most profitably in making such acts, with or without the use of a prayer-book.

Many acts and prayers contained elsewhere in this book may be substituted occasionally for those given in the following methods of assisting at Mass, especially such as relate to the Passion, the Blessed Sacrament, and the Sacred Heart of Jesus.

You may also very appropriately recite the Rosary during Mass, and in particular the *Eucharistic Rosary*, in which we meditate on the life, passion, and death of Our Lord in connection with the sacred mysteries of the altar. Formulate your own prayers occasionally.

Converse with God in a familiar manner. Prayer is the elevation of the soul to God. Speak to your heavenly Father from your heart with filial piety, simplicity, and confidence.

Prayers at holy Mass

Offering According to the Four Great Ends of Sacrifice

ETERNAL Father, I offer Thee the sacrifice which Thy beloved Son, our blessed Redeemer, made of Himself on the cross and now renews on this altar. I offer it in union with all the Masses which have been said and which shall be said throughout the whole world, for all the intentions and interests of the Sacred Heart of Jesus, in *praise and adoration* of Thy supreme majesty; in *thanksgiving* for the numberless benefits which Thy divine mercy has conferred upon me; in *reparation* for my offences and in atonement for the sins of all mankind; finally, in humble *supplication* for my temporal and eternal welfare, for the wants of our holy Mother the Church, for the conversion of sinners, for the propagation of the Faith, and for relief of the souls in purgatory.

Special Offering of the Mass for the Souls in Purgatory

St. Alphonsus Liguori

O GOD of love, Father of Our Lord Jesus Christ, on this altar behold the unbloody sacrifice of the body and blood of Thy Son, representing that of His most holy death and grievous passion, which He, the great High Priest, offered

Thee on Calvary. In consideration of this holocaust of sweet odor, have mercy on the souls in purgatory; open to them the gates of heaven, that they may love and praise Thee, and enjoy Thee eternally in the abode of the saints. Together with the sufferings of Thy divine Son, I likewise offer Thee the sorrows of His blessed mother, whose soul was crucified at the foot of her Son's cross; for the lance which pierced the side and heart of Jesus, thine adorable Son, also transfixed the soul and heart of Mary, according to Simeon's prophecy, and made her the queen of martyrs. Behold then, O heavenly Father! the disfigured countenance of Thy Son on the cross and the crucified heart of His Mother at the foot of this same cross; and by the merits of all the sufferings of that Son and that Mother, grant eternal repose to the souls in purgatory.

Indulgenced Prayer

By Which All the Masses Celebrated Throughout the World are Daily Offered to God

MY GOD, I offer Thee all the Masses this day celebrated throughout the world, for sinners in their agony, and for those who shall be overtaken by death to-day! May the precious blood of Jesus, our Redeemer, obtain for them mercy!

Indulgence of 300 days. — Pius X, Dec. 18, 1907.

At the Confiteor

Adoration and Contrition

MY LORD and my God! I adore Thee, and acknowledge Thee as the Master of my whole being. All that I am, and all that I have is from Thee. Without Thee I am nothing. Without Thee I can do nothing. Powerless as I am to render worthy homage to Thy majesty, I offer Thee the humiliation and the love of Jesus on the altar. With Him I praise and worship Thee. In His name I appeal to Thy mercy; I pray Thee to accept my prayers in union with the precious blood and merits of Thy divine Son, offered on all the altars of the world. I rejoice, O my God, that I am able by this august sacrifice to glorify Thee as Thou art glorified in heaven. I also join my praises to those of the most blessed Virgin, the angels, and the saints. I adore Thee with all the heavenly host, and love Thee with my whole heart above all things, and will love Thee for ever. Would that by the ardor of my love I could make up for the time in which I loved creatures too much! How I thank Thee for not having wearied of so long an abuse of Thy graces!

I confess, O my God! not only in Thy presence, Who seest the secrets of hearts, but in the presence of all the blessed in Heaven and of all the faithful on earth, that I have often and grievously offended Thee by my thoughts, words, actions, and omissions. Yes, I have sinned, O my God! I have sinned; I acknowledge it to my shame, and with the most bitter regret. I am sorry that I have sinned, because Thou art infinitely good and sin displeases Thee! I am unworthy to appear before Thee. But Thy mercies, O my God! are above all thy works; Thou wilt not despise a contrite and humble heart.

O most holy Virgin! and ye angels and saints of heaven, I humbly beseech you to intercede for me! May God have mercy on me, forgive me my sins, and lead me to eternal life! May He grant me pardon, absolution, and remission of all my sins!

At the Introit

From the Psalms

"COME, let us *praise* the Lord with joy: let us come before His presence with *thanksgiving*."

"Praise the Lord, for He is good: His mercy endureth forever."

"The Lord is just in all His ways, and holy in all His works."

"In Thee, O God, have I hoped: O Lord, let me never be confounded."

"The Lord is the protector of my life: of whom shall I be afraid? If I should walk in the midst of the shadow of death, I will fear no evils: for Thou art with me, O Lord" (*Ps.* xxii).

"Keep me, O Lord, as the apple of Thy eye: protect me under the shadow of Thy wings."

"The Lord is high unto all them that call upon Him: He will do the will of them that fear Him and He will hear their prayers and save them" (*Ps.* cxliv).

"Expect the Lord and do manfully: let thy heart take courage and wait for the Lord."

"Blessed are the undefiled in the way: who walk in the law of the Lord."

At the "Kyrie Eleison"

FATHER in Heaven, my Creator, have mercy on me. Son of God, my Redeemer, save me. Holy Spirit, sanctify me and bring me to life everlasting.

At the "Gloria in Excelsis Deo"

Glory be to God on High, and on Earth Peace to Men of Good Will.

Men of good will are those who give glory to God by loving Him and doing His holy will, by observing His commandments, by faithfully fulfilling the duties of their state of life; thereby they secure for themselves at the same time peace of soul and true happiness.

GLORY be to God by all nations and in all places! Blessed be God now and forever.

Blessed be His holy name.

Blessed be Jesus Christ, true God and true man.

Blessed be the name of Jesus.

Blessed be His most sacred Heart.

Blessed be Jesus in the most holy Sacrament of the Altar.

Peace to Men of Good Will!

PEACE to those who possess the love and grace of God. Peace to those who fight manfully against their predominant passion and gain the mastery over their evil inclinations. Peace to those who forgive their enemies, who love their fellow-men and are kind to them in thought, word, and deed.

My God! I desire to glorify Thee by the purest intention in all my actions. I purpose to do all things to Thy greater glory. Keep me in Thy love and Thy grace. Grant that I may glorify Thee on earth by doing Thy will, by my devotedness to all my duties, so that I may one day see Thee face to face and hear those blessed words: "Enter thou into the joy of Thy Lord."

"The saints shall rejoice in glory: the high praises of God shall be in their mouths" (Ps. cxlix. 5).

"The souls of the just are in the hands of God: they are in peace" (Wis. iii. 1).

At the Collects

ALMIGHTY and eternal God, I beseech Thee, by the passion and death of Thy beloved Son and the sorrows of His holy Mother Mary, grant me grace to be truly sorry for my sins and to amend my life; to love Thee above all things and to do Thy holy will; to be kind and merciful to my neighbor; to conquer my evil passions, to be guided by the spirit of my blessed Saviour and to follow His example; to carry my daily cross with patience and resignation; to be faithful in the performance of every duty; to live a good life, to die a holy death, and thus to attain the everlasting bliss of heaven. Amen.

I unite my prayers with those of Thy minister at the altar, and implore of Thee, O Lord, all the graces for which he prays. Father in heaven, I beseech Thee to bless the Pope, the bishops, the priests, and all Religious, that they may do Thy will and glorify Thee. Bless all the faithful, that they may persevere in Thy grace; convert all sinners and heretics; bring the pagan nations to the knowledge of the true Faith; look with compassion on those who are in their last agony; and have mercy on the poor souls in purgatory.

Bless all my relatives, benefactors, and all those who are in distress and for whom I have promised to pray. Bless me that I may become a saint.

I offer all these prayers to Thee, eternal Father, through Our Lord Jesus Christ. Amen.

At the Epistle

EPISTLE. 1 *Peter* iv. 7–9. *Most dearly beloved:* "Be prudent and watch in prayers. But before all things have a constant mutual charity among yourselves: for charity covereth a multitude of sins. Using hospitality one toward another, without murmuring."

James i. 22, 26, 27. "Be ye doers of the word, and not hearers only. . . . If any man think himself religious, not bridling his tongue, but deceiving his own heart, this man's religion is vain. Religion clean and undefiled before God and the Father is this; to visit the fatherless and the widows in their tribulation; and to keep one's self unspotted from the world."

Rom. xii, xiii. "Let love be without dissimulation. Hating that which is evil, cleaving to that which is good. Loving one another with the charity of brotherhood. Rejoicing in hope. Patient in tribulation. Instant in prayer. Communicating to the necessities of the saints. Bless them that persecute you: bless and curse not. Rejoice with them that rejoice: weep with them that weep. Being of one mind, one toward another. Not minding high things, but consenting to the humble. Be not wise in your own conceits. To no man rendering evil for evil. If it be possible, as much as is in you, have peace with all men. Revenge not yourselves, my dearly beloved, but give place unto wrath, for it is written: '*Revenge is mine, I will repay,*' saith the Lord. Render to all men their dues. Owe no man anything, but to love one another; for he that loveth his neighbor hath fulfilled the law. For thou shalt not commit adultery; thou shalt not kill; thou shalt not steal; thou shalt not bear false witness; thou shalt not covet; and if there be any other commandment, it is comprised in this word, '*thou shalt love thy neighbor as thyself.*' But thou, why judgest thou thy brother? Or thou, why dost thou despise thy brother? For we shall all stand before the judgment seat of Jesus Christ. Every one of us shall render an account to God for himself. Let us not, therefore, judge one another any more. Now the God of patience and of comfort grant you to be of one mind, one toward another, according to Jesus Christ. That with one mind and with one mouth, you may glorify God and the Father of Our Lord Jesus Christ."

At the Gradual

Who shall ascend to the mountain of the Lord, or who shall stand in His holy place? The innocent in hands, and clean of heart (*Ps.* xxiii. 3, 4).

Be glad in the Lord, and rejoice, ye just: and glory, all ye right of heart (*Ps.* xxxi. 11).

A sacrifice to God is an afflicted spirit: a contrite and humble heart, O God, thou wilt not despise (*Ps.* l. 19).

Our God is our refuge and strength: a helper in troubles (*Ps.* xlv. 2).

Blessed is the man, whose trust is in the name of the Lord (*Ps.* xxxix. 5).

For thou, O Lord, art sweet and mild: and plenteous in mercy to all that call upon Thee (*Ps.* lxxxv. 5).

Conduct me, O Lord, in Thy ways and I will walk in Thy truth (*Ps.* lxxxv. 11).

What doth it profit a man, if he gain the whole world and suffer the loss of his own soul? Or what exchange shall a man give for his soul? For the Son of man shall come in the glory of His Father with His angels; and then will He render to every man according to his works (Matt. xvi. 26–27).

At the Gospel

GOSPEL. *Luke* vi. 36–38. *At that time:* Jesus said to His disciples: "Be ye merciful, as your heavenly Father also is merciful. Judge not, and you shall not be judged. Condemn not, and you shall not be condemned. Forgive, and you shall be forgiven. Give, and it shall be given to you; good measure, and pressed down and shaken together and running over, shall be given into your bosom. For with the same measure that you shall mete withal, it shall be measured to you again."

Matt. xxii. 34–40. *At that time:* the Pharisees came to Jesus; and one of them, a doctor of the law, asked Him, tempting Him: "Master, which is the great commandment of the law?" Jesus said to him: "Thou shalt love the Lord thy God with thy whole heart, and with thy whole soul, and with thy whole mind. This is the greatest and the first commandment. And the second is like to this: Thou shalt love thy neighbor as thyself. On these two commandments dependeth the whole law and the prophets."

"Thy words have I hidden in my heart, that I may not sin against Thee. Thy word is a lamp to my feet and a light to my paths. Lead me into the path of Thy commandments, for this same have I desired. I will meditate on Thy commandments, I will not forget Thy words" (*Ps.* cxviii).

At the Credo

Faith — Hope — Love

I BELIEVE in Thee, O my God! For Thou art Truth itself, and canst neither deceive nor be deceived. I believe all that the Catholic Church teaches, because Thou hast promised to preserve her from all error. Gladly would I shed my blood for this faith!

I believe in Thee, O adorable Trinity, Father, Son, and Holy Ghost! I believe in Thee, O only-begotten Son of the Father! I believe that Thou becamest man; that Thou didst suffer and die for my salvation. I believe that Thou art in heaven, and in the most holy Sacrament of the Altar, where Thou intercedest for me. Increase my faith, and deign to enlighten those who are in the darkness of error.

And do Thou, O Holy Ghost, Whom I adore as my true God, receive my heartfelt thanks for the consolation and the strength which come to my soul through the Bread of Life and the Holy Sacrifice. I offer Thee my whole heart, O Holy Spirit, divine Consoler, and thank Thee most heartily for all the benefits that Thou dost unceasingly bestow upon the world. I beseech Thee to bless me with a lively faith in the Holy Eucharist. Keep my soul ever bright for the coming of the Bridegroom. Grant me Thy sevenfold gift, in order that I may with ardent love follow Christ, and with perseverance walk in the way of salvation.

As my *faith* in Thee, my God, is strong and invincible, so my *hope* and my *confidence* in Thee are supreme and impregnable.

I am fully convinced that Thou dost watch over all those who hope in Thee and I am resolved henceforth to live without anxiety and to cast all my care upon Thee. From Thy goodness and mercy, O Lord, I hope to obtain perseverance in grace and eternal happiness.

In peace I will sleep and I will rest: for Thou, O Lord, hast wonderfully established me in hope (*Ps.* iv. 9, 10). And as I believe and hope in Thee, so do I love Thee, my God, with all the strength of my soul, with my whole heart.

I love Thee above all things, because Thou art the highest and most perfect good.

INDULGENCED INVOCATIONS

I. To God

MY GOD, grant that I may love Thee, and be the only reward of my love to love Thee always more and more.

His Holiness, Leo XIII, by a rescript of the Sacred Congregation of Indulgences, March 15, 1890, granted to the faithful who recite the above invocation, an *indulgence of one hundred days*, once a day.

II. *To the Holy Trinity*

OMNIPOTENCE of the Father, help my weakness, and deliver me from the depth of misery.

Wisdom of the Son, direct all my thoughts, words, and actions.

Love of the Holy Ghost, be Thou the source and beginning of all the operations of my soul, whereby they may be always conformable to the divine will.

Indulgence of 200 days, once a day. — Leo XIII, March 15, 1890.

At the Offertory

ACCEPT, O holy Father, almighty, eternal God, this immaculate Host which I, Thy unworthy servant, offer unto Thee by the hands of Thy priest, for my innumerable sins, offences, and negligences; and for all here present, also for all faithful Christians both living and dead, that it may be profitable for my own and for their salvation.

To this oblation of bread and wine, which will shortly be changed into the body and blood of Our Lord Jesus Christ, I unite the offering of myself, and present unto Thee, O heavenly Father, all my thoughts, words, and works. All that I am and all that I have I consecrate to Thy service. Amen.

O Jesus, my divine Master, reign in my soul, rule over me and transform me into the likeness of Thee.

Jesus, meek and humble of heart, make my heart like unto Thine!

Indulgence of 300 days, every time.—Pius X. Sept. 15, 1905.

AN OFFERING TO THE SACRED HEART OF JESUS

MY LOVING Jesus! I (N.N.) give Thee my heart. and I consecrate myself wholly to Thee, out of the grateful love I bear Thee, and as a reparation for all my unfaithfulness; and with Thy aid I purpose never to sin again.

Indulgence of 100 days, once a day, if recited before a picture of the Sacred Heart. — Pius VII, June 9, 1807.

At the Secret

SEC. Receive, O Lord, the gifts we offer in commemoration of the passion and death of Thy Son, and grant that we may be delivered from present dangers and arrive at eternal life.

SEC. Omniscient and merciful God! Who dost permit evil that good may spring from it; listen to the humble prayers by which we ask of Thee the grace of remaining faithful to Thee, even unto death. Grant us also, through the intercession of Mary ever blessed, that we may always conform ourselves to Thy most holy will.

May the Sacred Heart of Jesus be loved everywhere!

Indulgence of 100 days, once a day. — Pius IX, Sept. 23, 1860.

Heart of Jesus, burning with love for us, inflame our hearts with love of Thee!

Indulgence of 100 days, once a day. — Leo XIII, June 16, 1893.

At the Preface

In Commemoration of the Passion and Death of Our Lord

IT IS truly meet and just, right and available to salvation, that we should always and in all places give thanks to Thee, O holy Lord, Father almighty, eternal God, Who hast appointed the salvation of mankind to be wrought on the wood of the cross; that from whence death came, thence life might arise, and that He Who overcame by the tree might also by the tree be overcome. Through Jesus Christ our Lord, through Whom the angels praise Thy majesty, the dominations adore it, the powers tremble before it; the heavens, the heavenly virtues, and blessed·seraphim, with common jubilee, glorify it. Together with whom we beseech Thee that we may be admitted to join our humble voices, saying:

Holy, holy, holy, Lord God of hosts. Heaven and earth are full of Thy glory. Hosanna in the highest. Blessed is He that cometh in the name of the Lord. Hosanna in the highest.

THE ANGELIC TRISAGION

SANCTUS, Sanctus, Sanctus, Dominus Deus exercituum: Plena est terra gloria tua: Gloria Patri, gloria Filio, gloria Spiritui Sancto.

HOLY, holy, holy, Lord God of hosts, the earth is full of thy glory! Glory be to the Father, glory be to the Son, glory be to the Holy Ghost.

The Sovereign Pontiff, Clement XIV, by a decree of the Sacred Congregation of Indulgences, June 6, 1769, granted to the faithful who, with at least contrite heart and devotion, shall say this *Angelic Trisagion*, an *indulgence of one hundred days*, once a day. Also an *indulgence of one hundred days*, three times every Sunday, as well as on the feast of the most holy Trinity, and during its octave.

At the Canon

In Commemoration of the Living

WE HUMBLY pray and earnestly beseech Thee, most merciful Father, through Jesus Christ, Thy Son our Lord, to look with favor upon these gifts, which we present to Thee in union with the priest at the altar, to accept and to bless this sacrifice of praise, thanksgiving, and propitiation, which we offer Thee, in the first place, for Thy holy Catholic Church, to which vouchsafe to grant peace and union throughout the world.

Bless our Holy Father the Pope, our bishops, priests, Religious, and apostolic missionaries, that their labor in the propagation of the Faith and for the salvation of souls may be fruitful.

Lord, through the merits of the Sacred Heart of Jesus, I especially recommend to Thee the intentions for which I am assisting at this Mass; the interests of my relatives, friends, and benefactors; and the wants of all those for whom I have promised to pray and for whom I am bound to pray in justice and charity.

I beseech Thee, also, to bless my enemies, those who are dying, and all the faithful who are in the state of grace; grant us the gift of perseverance in Thy love.

Finally, I recommend to Thy goodness and clemency all infidels, heretics, and sinners. Vouchsafe to enlighten and strengthen them that they may know Thee and love Thee and serve Thee and be happy with Thee forever in heaven.

THOUGHTS AND AFFECTIONS ON THE PASSION OF OUR LORD

GOOD and merciful Jesus, my blessed Saviour! what a world of anguish pierced Thy sacred Heart, what a flood of bitterness deluged Thy soul, what a torrent of humiliation overwhelmed Thee in Thy passion, from Gethsemani to Calvary!

When I contemplate Thee in Thy bitter passion, looking at my crucifix, and reflecting on all Thy sufferings of soul and body — on Thy mental anguish and dereliction; on Thy agony in the garden; Thy betrayal by Judas; the rudeness of the soldiers, dragging and striking Thee and spitting in Thy face; Thy contemptuous treatment at the tribunal of the haughty high priests Annas and Caiphas; Thy shameful mockery and humiliation at the court of Herod, where Thou wert treated as a fool; the cruel scourging and crowning with thorns, which made Thee so pitiable in appearance, as to cause even the Roman governor to exclaim, "*Ecce Homo!*" and the Royal Psalmist to lament in prophetic vision, "I am a worm and no man, the reproach of men and the outcast of the people"; the derisive yells and the brutal cry of the frenzied and bloodthirsty rabble, "Crucify him!"; the carrying of the heavy cross in Thy enfeebled condition; the painful meeting with Thy sorrowful Mother, and at length the dreadful crucifixion between two thieves, and the hours of suffering on Calvary, which ended in Thy death amid the awful gloom and convulsive desolation of nature; — reflecting upon all these pains and torments, insults and outrages, to which Thou wert subjected in Thy passion, I bow my head in shame and sorrow on account of my many sins, and deeply regret my self-indulgence and pride, which have led me so often to abuse Thy graces, to forget Thy love, and to wound Thy sacred Heart.

O King of glory, Jesus, my Saviour! what marvelous virtue Thou dost display in this flood of sorrows, sufferings, and humiliations, which overwhelmed Thy Heart! What meekness, what resignation, what patience, what charity! Thou dost pray for those who outrage Thee. Thou offerest

Thy sufferings for those who persecute and afflict Thee.

How unlike I am to Thee, my divine Model! How great is the change that must be effected in me, if I wish to be Thy true disciple and to bear a resemblance to Thee! In all sincerity, however, I pray: "Jesus, meek and humble of heart, make my heart like unto Thine." How different a rule of life, how great a reform of conduct is required of me before I shall be able to say with the Apostle: "I live, now not I, but Christ liveth in me." How unwilling I am to bear the slightest pain! How I shrink from the lightest cross! How impatient I am in sufferings, disappointments, and contradictions! And yet the Holy Spirit tells us, "Jesus Christ suffered for us, leaving us an example, that we should follow His steps"; and again, "All that will live godly in Christ Jesus shall suffer."

How the apostles, the martyrs, and all the saints have suffered! But they entered with firm tread the grotto of the Agony and stood bravely by the Cross. They rejoiced in suffering and persecution, because they became thereby more like to Christ; they bore in mind that great and abundant merit is attached to patient endurance of trials; they remembered that those who suffer with Christ, those who tread courageously the royal road of the Cross to Calvary, shall also ascend with Him to heaven and reign with Him in immortal glory.

Henceforth I shall look upon pains and sufferings and humiliations as blessings sent me from heaven as a means to make me become more Christlike, to atone for my sins, to wean me from the love of self and the gratification of my passions, to teach me the vanities of the world, to lead me to greater perfection — in a word, to make me a saint. I will remember my Saviour's words: "If any man will come after Me, let him deny himself, take up his cross *daily* and follow Me" (*Luke* ix. 23).

I will accept with resignation and bear with patience every cross that comes to me, mindful of the Apostle's words, "We know that to them that love God all things work together unto good (*Rom.* viii. 28). Every pain may help us to shorten our purgatory; every pain, moreover, is a means of merit and reparation when it is met in the spirit of our blessed Saviour, when it is accepted in union with His sufferings and endured for His sake on behalf of souls for which He died.

O Jesus! I adore Thee carrying with love for us the cross prepared for Thee by Thy Father, and we beg of Thee, through the intercession of Thy holy and sorrowful Mother, patience and resignation in the trials of this life.

Divine Jesus! we adore Thee in the unfathomable debasements of Thy passion and of Thy presence on the altar; we adore Thee, O loving King! overwhelmed with insults both in Thy passion and in the sacred Host, and we beg of Thee, through the intercession of Thy holy and sorrowful Mother, the penitential spirit, the spirit of humility, obedience, and sacrifice, the grace of mortifying our pride and self-love. Heart of Jesus, wounded by my infidelities, forgive me my sins. I am sorry for having offended Thee, because Thou art infinitely good. Sin displeases Thee; I will not sin again. Heart of Jesus, let me drink of Thy chalice.

Sweet Heart of Jesus, be my love! Thy Kingdom come! Mayest Thou reign in all hearts! Be Thou the sole Master of all that I am and have! May I live henceforth only to love Thee, to follow Thee, to serve Thee!

"Master, go on, and I will follow Thee,
To the ast gasp with truth and loyalty."

At the Consecration and Elevation

AFTER the words of consecration have been pronounced, when the priest genuflects, make a profound inclination of the head; then, kneeling erect, *look at* the sacred Host, and say with a strong faith, a firm hope, an ardent love, and a tender devotion:

"My Lord and My God!"

Then again bow the head in humble adoration of the Blessed Sacrament, as the celebrant makes a genuflection.

Pope Pius X, May 18, 1907, granted an indulgence of seven years and seven quarantines to all the faithful, who, at the *Elevation* during Mass, or during Exposition and Benediction of the Blessed Sacrament, *look at* the sacred Host and say: *"My Lord and My God!"* Also a plenary indulgence once a week, provided they receive the sacraments.

Other prayers and especially indulgenced ejaculations may be added in honor of the Precious Blood, the Blessed Sacrament, and the Sacred Heart, at the consecration and for a short time after the elevation of the chalice; such as the following:

ETERNAL Father! I offer Thee the Precious Blood of Jesus in satisfaction for my sins and for the wants of Holy Church.

Indulgence of 100 days, each time. — Pius VII, Sept. 22, 1817.

O SACRAMENT most holy! O Sacrament divine!
All praise and all thanksgiving be every moment Thine!

Indulgence of 100 days, at the elevation. — Pius VII, June 30, 1818.

JESUS, my God, I love Thee above all things! Indulgence of 50 days, each time. — Pius IX, May 7, 1854.

MAY the Heart of Jesus in the Most Blessed Sacrament be praised, adored, and loved with grateful affection, at every moment, in all the tabernacles of the world, even to the end of time. Amen.

Indulgence of 100 days, once a day. — Pius IX, Feb. 29, 1868.

O PRECIOUS Blood of Jesus, cleanse my soul from every stain! Most pure Heart of Jesus, purify me! Most humble Heart of Jesus, teach me Thy humility! Sweetest Heart of Jesus, communicate to me Thy gentleness and patience! Most merciful Heart of Jesus, have mercy on me! Most loving Heart of Jesus, inflame my heart with love of Thee!

> I see upon the altar placed
>> The Victim of the greatest love;
> Let all the earth below adore,
>> And join the heavenly choirs above:
> Sweet Sacrament, we Thee adore,
> Oh! make us love Thee more and more.

> Jesus! dear Pastor of the flock,
>> That crowds in love about Thy feet,
> Our voices yearn to praise Thee, Lord,
>> And joyfully Thy presence greet:
> Sweet Sacrament, we Thee adore,
> Oh! make us love Thee more and more.

Commemoration of the Dead

BE MINDFUL, O Lord, of Thy servants N. and N., who are gone before us with the sign of faith, and rest in the sleep of peace.

Here the priest, with hands joined, prays for such of the dead as he wishes to pray for in particular. Then, extending his hands, he continues:

To these, O Lord, and to all that sleep in Christ, grant, we beseech Thee, a place of refreshment, light, and peace. Through the same Christ our Lord. Amen.

To us also, Thy sinful servants, who hope in the multitude of Thy mercies, vouchsafe to grant that

we may be united in the realms of eternal bliss
with Thy holy apostles and martyrs, and with
all Thy saints, through Jesus Christ our Lord.
Amen.

THE POOR SOULS IN PURGATORY

The holy souls suffering in the prison of purgatory are
incapable of helping themselves.

Out of the depths of torturing flame they call to us
"*Miseremini!*" "*Have pity on us!*"

We have it in our power to help these suffering friends of
God. We can do so by prayer, alms-deeds, works of mercy,
holy communion, the Holy Mass, and *indulgences*, and to
do so is certainly an act of charity. Understanding this
full well, the saints, without exception, have been most
earnest and constant in their efforts to help them. Some
of them have made this devotion one of the strong character-
istics of their sanctity, and we venture to say that no truly
devout or sincere Catholic neglects this spiritual work of
mercy.

Even the very poor, in Ireland for instance, and also in
this country, make many sacrifices in order to secure for their
departed relatives and others the special benefits of the
Holy Mass. May the same enlightened piety ever remain
firmly rooted in the hearts of our people, and may the day
never come when they will cease to follow beyond the grave
with tender solicitude the souls of those they loved in life.

In praying for the dead and gaining indulgences for them,
let us remember that every prayer we say, every sacrifice
we make, every alms we give for the repose of the dear
departed ones, will all return upon ourselves in hundredfold blessings. They are God's friends, dear to His sacred
Heart, living in His grace, and in constant communion with
Him; and though they may not alleviate their own sufferings, their prayers in our behalf always avail. They
can aid us most efficaciously. God will not turn a deaf

ear to their intercession. Being holy souls, they are grateful souls. The friends that aid them, they in turn will also aid. We need not fear praying to them in all faith and confidence. They will obtain for us the graces that we ask for the good of our souls. They will watch over us and protect us in the dangers of life and they will intercede with God for our eternal salvation. — See *Forget-Me-Nots from Many Gardens.*

Prayers for the Dead

According to St. Alphonsus Liguori

MY GOD! I recommend to Thee the souls of my relations, my benefactors, my friends, and my enemies, and of those who are in purgatory on my account.

I recommend to Thee the souls of evangelical laborers, of Religious and priests, and especially of those who had charge of my soul.

I recommend to Thee the souls of those who were most devout to the passion of Our Lord, to the Blessed Sacrament, to the Sacred Heart of Jesus, and to the Blessed Virgin Mary, the souls who are most abandoned, those who suffer most, and those who are nearest to the entrance into paradise.

It is an excellent practice to renew these offerings daily at Mass.

Eternal rest give to them, O Lord; and let perpetual light shine upon them.

May their souls and the souls of all the faithful departed, through the mercy of God, rest in peace.

And may the divine assistance always remain with us and bring us to life everlasting.   Amen.

Short Indulgenced Prayers

For the Holy Souls in Purgatory

N. B.   It is a good practice to say some short indulgenced prayers for the relief of the holy souls in purgatory occasionally during the day and especially at the *memento for the dead* after the elevation in the holy sacrifice of the Mass.

REQUIEM æternam dona eis, Domine; R. Et lux perpetua luceat eis.

ETERNAL rest give to them, O Lord; R. And let perpetual light shine upon them.

Indulgence, applicable to the poor souls alone, 50 days, each time. — Leo XIII, March 22, 1902.

My Jesus, mercy!

Indulgence of 100 days, each time. — Pius IX, Sept. 24, 1846.

My God and my All!

Indulgence of 50 days, each time. — Leo XIII, May 4, 1888.

My sweetest Jesus, be not my Judge, but my Saviour!

Indulgence of 50 days, each time. — Pius IX, Aug. 11, 1851.

May the most just, most high, and most amiable will of God be done in all things; may it be praised and magnified forever.

Indulgence of 100 days, once a day. — Pius VII, May 19, 1818.

Jesus, my God, I love Thee above all things.

Indulgence of 50 days, each time. — Pius IX, May 7, 1854.

Sweetest Jesus, grant me an increase of faith, hope, and charity, a contrite and humble heart.

Indulgence of 100 days, once a day. — Leo XIII, Sept. 13, 1893.

May the Sacred Heart of Jesus be loved everywhere.

Indulgence of 100 days, once a day. — Pius IX, Sept. 23, 1860.

O sweetest Heart of Jesus, I implore, that I may ever love Thee more and more.

Indulgence of 300 days, each time. — Pius IX, Nov. 26, 1876.

Sweet Heart of Jesus, be my love.

Indulgence of 300 days, once a day. — Leo XIII, May 21, 1892.

Heart of Jesus, burning with love for us, inflame our hearts with love of Thee.

Indulgence of 100 days, once a day. — Leo XIII, June 16, 1893.

Mary!

Indulgence of 25 days, each time. — Clement XIII, Sept. 5, 1759.

Sweet heart of Mary, be my salvation!

Indulgence of 300 days, each time. — Pius IX, Sept. 30, 1852.

Jesus, Mary, and Joseph, I give you my heart and my soul.

Jesus, Mary, and Joseph, assist me in my last agony.

Jesus, Mary, and Joseph, may I breathe out my soul in peace with you!

Indulgence of 300 days, each time, for all three. — Pius VII, Aug. 26, 1814.

To thee, O virgin Mother, never touched by stain of sin, actual or venial, I recommend and confide the purity of my heart.

Indulgence of 100 days, once a day. — Pius IX, Nov. 26, 1854.

O Mary, conceived without sin, pray for us who have recourse to thee.

Indulgence of 100 days, once a day. — Leo XIII, March 15, 1884.

Our Lady of Lourdes, pray for us!

Indulgence of 100 days, once a day. — Leo XIII, June 25, 1902.

Mary, our hope, have pity on us!

Indulgence of 300 days. — Pius X, Jan. 8, 1906.

Sacred Heart of Jesus, Thy kingdom come!

Indulgence of 300 days. — Pius X, May 4, 1906.

Jesus, Mary, Joseph!

Indulgence of 7 years and 7 quarantines, each time. — Pius X, June 16, 1906.

Heart of Jesus, I confide in Thee!

Indulgence of 300 days, each time. — Pius X, June 27, 1906.

Mary, most sorrowful Mother of all Christians, pray for us.

Indulgence of 300 days. — Pius X, June 27, 1906.

Divine Heart of Jesus, convert sinners, save the dying, deliver the holy souls from purgatory!

Indulgence of 300 days for each recitation. — Pius X, Nov. 6, 1906.

At the Pater Noster

"OUR *Father, Who art in heaven!*" — O my God! Thou art my Father, and the Father of all, the rock of our salvation. Thou art my protector and my refuge; in Thee will I place my trust. If Thou be with me, who can be against me? I will cast my care upon Thee; for as a Father Thou dost love me and provide for my welfare. "We know that to them that love God all things work together unto good," says the Apostle (*Rom.* viii. 28). And Jesus Himself tells us to place our hope in Thee: "Behold the birds of the air; for neither do they sow, nor do they reap, nor gather into barns; and your heavenly Father feedeth them. Are not you of much more value than they? Be not solicitous for to-morrow. Seek ye first the kingdom of God, and His justice, and all these things will be added unto you" (*Matt.* vi. 23, 33, 34).

Jesus Himself directs us to address Thee as "Our Father," and to pray to Thee in His name with the utmost confidence: "Ask and it shall be given you, for every one that asketh, receiveth; if you being evil know how to give good gifts to your children, how much more will your Father Who is in heaven give good things to them that ask Him" (*Matt.* vii. 7, 11).

Do Thou, then, listen to my prayer. From the summit of heaven, where Thou dost dwell and where Thou art the supreme happiness of the blessed, look down upon me with loving-kindness and guard me as Thy child in all my ways. Keep me in Thy love and grant me perseverance in Thy grace, that I may one day see Thee face to face in my true Fatherland, and bless and glorify Thee forever in the company of the saints.

"*Hallowed be Thy Name.*" — May Thy name be sanctified. Mayest Thou be known and loved, praised, and glorified by all men. May all Thy children please and honor Thee by the sanctification of their lives, by the faithful discharge of every duty, by walking before Thee and striving after perfection. I desire to become a saint and to help others through the "*narrow gate*" and in the "*straight way*" that leadeth to life everlasting.

Thy Kingdom come. — Thou, O Lord, art my King; destroy in my soul the kingdoms of avarice, pride, and sensuality; reign in me now by Thy grace, that I may one day reign with Thee in heaven. May Thy kingdom, the holy Catholic

Church, be triumphant in the world. May the vicar of Christ be delivered from his enemies, and may all the nations be brought to the knowledge and the practice of the one true Faith.

Thy will be done on earth as it is in heaven.— Grant me always to desire and will that which is most acceptable to Thee and which pleaseth Thee best.

Let Thy will be mine, and let my will always follow Thine, and agree perfectly with it.

I desire to do Thy will with the same love and perfection as the angels and saints do it in heaven.

Give us this day our daily bread.— Take my home, myself, my relatives, my friends, and my benefactors under Thy special protection. And may I daily love more and more, and enjoy the sweetness of the Bread of angels, the living Bread that came down from heaven, the Bread that Jesus has given us — His own flesh in the Eucharist for the life of the world.

Forgive us our trespasses as we forgive those who trespass against us.— The Apostle admonishes us: "Let all bitterness and anger be put away from you, with all malice. And be ye kind one to another, merciful, forgiving one another, even as God hath forgiven you in Christ" (*Eph.* iv. 31, 32).

My God, I love, without exception, for the love of Thee, all my enemies, and all for whom I have had any antipathy. Remember, O Lord, that Thou hast said: "Pardon and you shall be pardoned."

Lead us not into temptation. — Protect us against
the wiles and machinations of the evil spirit; let
me not yield to any temptation on the part of the
enemies of my soul; remove from me the occasions
of sin and come to my assistance that I may not
expose myself to them.

Deliver us from evil.—Guard us against evils,
both temporal and spiritual. Sin is the greatest
of all evils. Purify me from all the sins that I
have committed. Suffer me not to offend Thee
again. Preserve me from the pain of hell. Give
me Thy love and Thy grace that I may serve Thee
faithfully on earth and bless and glorify Thee forever in heaven.

Amen. Father in heaven! grant my petitions,
all of which I present to Thee through the merits
of Our Lord and Saviour Jesus Christ.

At Holy Communion

An Act of Spiritual Communion

MY DEAR Lord and Saviour! Though I am
but a sinful servant, I approach Thee with
confidence, for Thou hast said in Thy goodness
and mercy: "Come to Me all you that labor and
are heavy laden, and I will refresh you." Thou
wilt not despise a contrite and humble heart. I
am truly sorry for having offended Thee by my
sins, because Thou art infinitely good. I have
wounded Thy sacred Heart by foolishly resisting

Thy holy will and transgressing Thy commandments; but I love Thee now with my whole heart and above all things. I adore Thee truly present on the altar. I have a great desire, dear Jesus, to receive Thee in holy communion, and since I cannot now approach the Holy Table to be united to Thee in the Blessed Sacrament, I beseech Thee most earnestly to come to me at least spiritually and to refresh my soul with the sweetness of Thy grace.

Come, my Lord my God, and my All! Come to me, and let me never again be separated from Thee by sin. I wish to become like to Thee. Teach me Thy blessed ways; help me with Thy grace to practise meekness, humility, purity, charity, and all the virtues of Thy sacred Heart.

Oh, Thou Lamb of God! Who takest away the sins of the world, take away from me whatever may hurt me and displease Thee. With St. Francis of Assisi I pray: May the fire of Thy love consume my soul, so that I may die to self and the world for the love of Thee, Who hast vouchsafed to die on the cross for the love of me!

Jesus, I consecrate to Thee my heart with all its affections, my soul with all its powers, and my body with all its senses. In union with Thee I will live and labor and suffer to do the heavenly Father's will. I will ever be mindful of the presence of my God and strive to be perfect. Bless me in life and in death that I may praise Thee forever in heaven. Amen.

O JESUS, sweetest Love, come Thou to me;
   Come down in all Thy beauty unto me;
Thou Who didst die for longing love of me;
And never, never more depart from me.

Free me, O beauteous God, from all but Thee;
Sever the chain that holds me back from Thee;
Call me, O tender Love, I cry to Thee;
Thou art my all! O bind me close to Thee.
                                    —SHAPCOTE.

SOUL of Christ, sanctify me.
   Body of Christ, save me.
Blood of Christ, inebriate me.
Water from the side of Christ, wash me.
Passion of Christ, strengthen me.
O good Jesus, hear me.
Within Thy wounds hide me.
Never permit me to be separated from thee.
From the malignant enemy, defend me.
In the hour of my death, call me,
And bid me come to Thee,
That with the saints I may praise Thee
For all eternity. Amen.

Indulgence of 300 days, each time. — Pius IX, Jan. 9, 1854.

"O SACRUM CONVIVIUM"

ANT. Most Holy Sacrament, in which Jesus Christ is received, the memory of His passion is renewed, the mind filled with grace, and the pledge of future glory given to us!
   V. Thou hast given them bread from heaven;
   R. Which containeth in itself all sweetness.

V. Praised, adored, loved, and blessed be the Most Holy Sacrament,

R. By all creatures, everywhere, and forever. Amen.

Let us pray

O GOD, Who in this wonderful sacrament hast left us a memorial of Thy passion; grant us the grace so to venerate the sacred mysteries of Thy body and blood, that we may ever feel within us the fruit of Thy redemption; Who livest and reignest world without end. Amen.

PRAYER TO OVERCOME EVIL PASSIONS AND TO BECOME A SAINT

DEAR Jesus, in the Sacrament of the Altar, be forever thanked and praised. Love, worthy of all celestial and terrestrial love! Who, out of infinite love for me, ungrateful sinner, didst assume our human nature, didst shed Thy most precious blood in the cruel scourging, and didst expire on a shameful cross for our eternal welfare! Now, illumined with lively faith, with the outpouring of my whole soul and the fervor of my heart, I humbly beseech Thee, through the infinite merits of Thy painful sufferings, give me strength and courage to destroy every evil passion which sways my heart, to bless Thee in my greatest afflictions, to glorify Thee by the exact fulfilment of my duties, supremely to hate all sin, and thus to become a saint.

Indulgence of 100 days, once a day. — Pius IX, Jan. 1, 1866.

At the Blessing

ᴹᴬʏ the blessing of God Almighty, ✠ of the Father, and of the Son, and of the Holy Ghost, descend upon us and remain with us forever. Amen.

Blessed be the Sacred Heart of Jesus!

Bless us, O Lord, as Thou didst bless the little children and again Thy disciples at Thy glorious ascension into heaven, so that we may persevere in Thy grace and be numbered on the last day among the elect, whom Thou wilt call the blessed of Thy Father, and invite into Thy eternal kingdom.

PRAYER OF ST. ALPHONSUS DE LIGUORI, TO THE BLESSED VIRGIN MARY

ᴹᴼˢᵀ holy and immaculate Virgin! O my mother! thou who art the mother of my Lord, the queen of the world, the advocate, hope, and refuge of sinners! I, the most wretched among them, now come to thee. I worship thee, great queen, and give thee thanks for the many favors thou hast bestowed on me in the past; most of all, do I thank thee for having saved me from hell, which I had so often deserved. I love thee, lady most worthy of all love, and, by the love which I bear thee, I promise ever in the future to serve thee, and to do what in me lies to win others to thy love. In thee I put all my trust, all my hope of salvation. Receive me as thy servant, and cover me with the mantle of thy protection, thou who art the mother of mercy! And since thou hast so much power with God, deliver me from all temptations, or at least obtain for me the grace ever to overcome them. From thee I ask a true love of Jesus Christ, and the grace of a happy death. O my mother! by thy love for God, I beseech thee to be at all times my helper, but, above all, at the last moment of my life. Leave me not until you see me safe in heaven, there for endless ages to bless thee, and sing thy praises. Amen.

His Holiness, Pope Pius IX, by an autograph rescript, Sept. 7, 1854, granted to all the faithful, every time that, with at least contrite heart and devotion, they shall say this prayer before an image or picture of the Blessed Virgin, an *indulgence of three hundred days.*

PRAYER OF ST. ALOYSIUS GONZAGA TO THE BLESSED VIRGIN

MOST holy Mary, my Lady, to thy faithful care and special keeping and to the bosom of thy mercy, to-day and every day, and particularly at the hour of my death, I commend my soul and my body; all my hope and consolation, all my trials and miseries, my life and the end of my life I commit to thee, that through thy most holy intercession and by thy merits all my actions may be directed and ordered according to thy will and that of thy divine Son. Amen.

His Holiness, Leo XIII, by a rescript of the Sacred Congregation of Indulgences, March 15, 1890, granted to the faithful who recite this prayer an *indulgence of two hundred days,* once a day.

EJACULATION

O MARY, who didst come into this world free from stain! obtain of God for me that I may leave it without sin.

His Holiness, Pope Pius IX, by a rescript from the Office of the Secretary of Briefs, March 27, 1863, granted to all the faithful who, with at least contrite heart and devotion, shall say this ejaculation, an *indulgence of one hundred days* once a day.

Prayers Ordered by Pope Leo XIII to be Said after Every Low Mass in All the Churches of the World

The priest with the people recites the Hail Mary thrice, then the Salve Regina:

HAIL, holy Queen, mother of mercy, our life, our sweetness, and our hope! To thee do we cry, poor banished children of Eve; to thee do we send up our sighs, mourning and weeping in this valley of tears. Turn, then, most gracious advocate, thine eyes of mercy toward us, and after this our exile show unto us the blessed fruit of thy womb, Jesus. O clement, O loving, O sweet Virgin Mary!

V. Pray for us, O holy Mother of God.

R. That we may be made worthy of the promises of Christ.

Let us pray

O GOD, our refuge and our strength, look down in mercy on Thy people who cry to Thee; and by the intercession of the glorious and immaculate Virgin Mary, Mother of God, of St. Joseph her spouse, of Thy blessed apostles Peter and Paul, and of all the saints, in mercy and goodness hear our prayers for the conversion of sinners, and for the liberty and exaltation of our holy Mother the Church. Through the same Christ our Lord. Amen.

Holy Michael Archangel, defend us in the day of battle; be our safeguard against the wickedness and snares of the devil. May God rebuke him, we humbly pray; and do thou, prince of the heavenly host, by the power of God, thrust down to hell Satan and all wicked spirits, who roam through the world seeking the ruin of souls. Amen.

Indulgence of 300 days. — Leo XIII, Sept. 25, 1888.

Add the Invocation

Most sacred Heart of Jesus, have mercy on us! (*Thrice*).

Indulgence of 7 years and 7 quarantines. — Pius X, June 17, 1904.

Mass

In Honor of the Passion of Our Lord and the Sorrows of Our Lady

We repeat the comment made previously, that it is not necessary, nor always possible, nor even desirable, to say *all* the prayers according to the methods of assisting at Mass found in a prayer-book. These prayers at Mass are merely suggested to the pious reader as an aid to devotion. Other prayers may be substituted, especially acts of adoration, thanksgiving, reparation, and petition, such as are found in this book, in honor of the Blessed Sacrament and the Sacred Heart of Jesus. Vary your devotions. The Rosary, and in particular the Eucharistic Rosary, together with a litany, or some other indulgenced prayers and ejaculations, may be recited with profit to oneself as well as to the poor souls in purgatory. Or you may form your own prayers. Speak to God from your heart ; or you may read a little from your prayer-book, and then meditate for a while, thus combining mental and vocal prayer. Dwell on any point that suggests particularly pious thoughts, affections, and good resolutions.

Preparatory Prayer

JESUS, my merciful Saviour ! I present myself before Thy altar for the purpose of assisting at the holy sacrifice of the Mass. I desire to assist at it with the same reverential awe, the same tender compassion with which my heart would have been filled had I beheld Thee in the Garden of Gethsemani, or on Mount Calvary, where Thou didst offer Thyself to Thy heavenly Father for love of me. Give Thy blessing, O Lord, to this my desire, and infuse into my soul those holy dispositions of which I stand in need in order to share in the abundant merits and fruits of Thy Redemption. Mary, most sorrowful Mother, pray for me.

> "Bid me bear, O Mother blessed!
> On my heart the wounds impressed
> Suffered by the Crucified."

At the Commencement of the Mass

IN UNION with the Sacred Heart of Jesus, my Saviour, and in commemoration of that sublime oblation which Thy well-beloved Son offered Thee upon the hallowed cross, I humbly offer Thee, eternal Father, this holy sacrifice: to the honor and glory of Thy holy name; in thanksgiving for all the blessings and benefits I have received from Thee; in satisfaction for my sins; in the hope of obtaining Thy divine assistance in all my necessities and afflictions, and for the succor and solace of the living and the dead. Accept this oblation, O merciful God and Father; let my intention be pleasing in Thy sight; hear and grant my petitions. Through Jesus Christ, our Lord. Amen.

At the Confiteor

CONFITEOR Deo omnipotenti, beatæ Mariæ semper virgini, beato Michaeli Archangelo, beato Joanni Baptistæ, sanctis Apostolis Petro et Paulo, et

I CONFESS to Almighty God, to blessed Mary, ever virgin, to blessed Michael, the archangel, to blessed John the Baptist, to the holy apostles Peter

omnibus sanctis, quia peccavi nimis cogitatione, verbo et opere; mea culpa, mea culpa, mea maxima culpa. Ideo precor beatam Mariam semper virginem, beatum Michaelem archangelum, beatum Joannem Baptistam, sanctos Apostolos Petrum et Paulum, omnes sanctos, orare pro me ad Dominum Deum nostrum.

Misereatur nostri omnipotens Deus, et dimissis peccatis nostris, perducat nos ad vitam æternam. Amen.

Indulgentiam, ✠ absolutionem, et remissionem peccatorum nostrorum, tribuat nobis omnipotens et misericors Dominus. Amen.

and Paul, and to all the saints, that I have sinned exceedingly in thought, word, and deed; through my fault, through my fault, through my most grievous fault. Therefore I beseech the blessed Mary, ever virgin, blessed Michael, the archangel, blessed John the Baptist, the holy apostles Peter and Paul, and all the saints, to pray to the Lord, our God, for me.

May almighty God have mercy upon us, and forgive us our sins, and bring us unto life everlasting. Amen.

May the almighty and merciful Lord grant us pardon, ✠ absolution, and remission of our sins. Amen.

JESU, DOMINE!

FOR me, dear Pelican, Thy bosom bled,
    For me Thy blood was shed.
Stained and polluted though my life has been,
    That blood can make me clean.
That blood whereof one precious drop could win
Abundant pardon for a thousand worlds of sin.
    — From *Confession and Communion*.

At the Introit

Jesus has entered the Garden of Gethsemani. He is kneeling for the last time under the familiar olive trees.

"My soul is sorrowful even unto death," He said to His disciples, whom He asked to watch with Him. Fear, sadness, and a loathing for the sins of which He is the innocent Victim, and of the horrible tortures and death awaiting Him, besides the sorrow of His Heart on account of the ingratitude of men and their insensibility to His love, which He foresaw, have forced a sweat of blood from His sacred veins. Exhausted with the intensity of His anguish, He falls prostrate on His face to the ground. In His agony He prays: "My Father, if it be possible, let this chalice pass from Me; nevertheless, not as I will, but as Thou wilt" (*Matt.* xxvi. 39).

When your heart bleeds, pray as Jesus prayed to His Father in Heaven. Fear not to say: "O my God, remove this chalice; it is too much, I can bear no more!" But also add, as He did: "Nevertheless, O my Father, as Thou wilt; Thy will be done, not mine!" And by virtue of this divine prayer your heart will be consoled, or, at least, it will always be strengthened, as was Jesus, to Whom an angel descended; and this angel, instead of removing the chalice, presented it to His lips.

There is a blessing in the cup of bitter sorrow; there is salvation in the chalice of suffering. Some day this will be revealed to us. Jesus received no sympathy, no comfort from His friends, His disciples, who slept while He was in His agony. He says by His prophet: "I looked for one that would grieve together with Me, but there was none; and for one that would comfort Me, and I found none" (*Ps.* lxviii. 21).

Place your confidence in the Sacred Heart of Jesus, which has experienced every kind of human woe, and which, loving you, is both able and willing to help and comfort you.

Jesus suffered so intensely in the garden on account of the vision He then had of the loss of so many souls, despite His passion, and of the ingratitude with which men would meet His love.

Oh! let us, then, repent sincerely for the past, considering how poorly we have met the countless benefits of Our Lord, and resolve henceforth to make good use of His graces and holy inspirations.

O MY good Jesus, my dear Saviour, I compassionate Thee in Thy sufferings. I fervently bless Thee and thank Thee for all Thou hast done and suffered for me; give me grace to weep over the sins and the ingratitude which caused Thy dreadful agony. Sweet Jesus, mercy! Pardon me, O Lord, for my past indifference to Thy love.

Heart of Jesus, inflamed with love of us, inflame our hearts with love of Thee.

Indulgence of 100 days. — Leo XIII, June 16, 1893.

At the Kyrie Eleison

Think of Jesus taken and bound with cords, and say:

MAY those bonds which confined Thy hands burst the fetters of my sins, and restore me to the sweet liberty of Thy children! I cast myself at Thy sacred feet, O my King and my God; and since Thou hast undergone the humiliation of allowing Thyself to be bound by Thy creatures, may I place my happiness in sharing Thy humiliations, and carrying Thy cross.

At the Collects

COLL. My Lord Jesus Christ, Who didst descend from heaven, from the bosom of the

Father, and didst shed Thy precious blood for the remission of our sins, we humbly beseech Thee that, placed at Thy right hand on the day of judgment, we may be found worthy to hear these words: Come, ye blessed.   Amen.

COLL. O my Jesus, Thou knowest well that I love Thee; but I do not love Thee enough; O grant that I may love Thee more.   O love that burnest ever and never failest, my God, Thou Who art charity itself, enkindle in my heart that divine fire which consumes the saints and transforms them into Thee.   Amen.

His Holiness, Leo XIII, by a rescript of the Sacred Congregation of Indulgences, February 6, 1893, granted to the faithful who recite the above prayer, an *indulgence of fifty days*, twice a day.

EJACULATION OF ST. PHILIP NERI

VIRGIN Mother of God, Mary, pray to Jesus for me.

His Holiness, Leo XIII, by a rescript of the Sacred Congregation of Indulgences, March 29, 1894, granted to the faithful who recite the above ejaculation, an *indulgence of fifty days*, once a day.

At the Epistle

ST. PAUL *to the Galatians*, vi. "God forbid that I should glory, save in the cross of Our Lord Jesus Christ, by Whom the world is crucified to me and I to the world. . . . If a man be overtaken in any fault, you, who are spiritual, instruct such a one in the spirit of *meekness*, considering thyself, lest thou also be tempted. Bear ye one another's burdens and so you shall fulfil the law of Christ. For if any man think himself to be something, whereas he is nothing, he deceiveth himself. Be not deceived; God is not mocked; for what things a man shall sow, those also shall he reap. And in doing good, let us not fail; for in due time we shall reap, not failing."

Philip. ii. "Brethren, let this mind be in you, which was also in Christ Jesus. He humbled Himself, becoming obedient unto death, even the death of the Cross. For which cause God also hath exalted Him, and hath given Him a name which is above all names; that in the name of Jesus every knee shall bow, of those that are in heaven, on earth, and under the earth. And that every tongue should confess that the Lord Jesus Christ is in the glory of the Father.

Jesus, meek and humble of heart, make my heart like unto Thine!

Indulgence of 300 days, every time. — Pius X, Sept. 15, 1905.

Heart of Jesus, I confide in Thee!

Indulgence of 300 days. — Pius X, 1906.

Mary, most sorrowful Mother of all Christians, pray for us.

Indulgence of 300 days. — Pius X, 1906.

At the Gradual

HAIL, Thou, our King: Thou alone hast compassion on our errors: obedient to the Father, Thou wert led to be crucified, like a meek lamb to the slaughter.

"The chastisement of our peace was upon Him; and by His bruises we are healed. . . . He hath borne our infirmities and carried our sorrows. . . . He was wounded for our iniquities, He was bruised for our sins" (*Is.* liii).

"They have pierced my hands and my feet; the have numbered all my bones" (*Ps.* xxi. 17, 18).

Sorrowful and sad art thou, O Virgin Mary, standing by the cross of the Lord Jesus, thy Son, our Redeemer. We bless thee and thank thee for all thou didst suffer for love of us. Pray for us that through the passion of thy divine Son we may attain to life everlasting.

At the Gospel

Reflect on the patience and gentleness of Jesus in allowing Himself to be dragged from tribunal to tribunal, and say:

O SPOTLESS Lamb of God! while Thy judges proclaim Thee an impostor, I rise without fear or shame to declare, in the face of heaven and earth, that Thou art Christ, the Son of the living God, and that I unreservedly assent to all the dogmas and to every article of truth proposed by

Thy holy Church to my belief; but, O divine Lord, give me grace to profess by my *actions* as well as by my words the faith that is in me.

Have mercy on all who are involved in the dreadful night of infidelity; may the light of Thy grace shine upon them, and so penetrate their hearts that they may embrace the truth, and be admitted to the communion of Thy holy Church.

UNSELFISHNESS

"Christ did not please Himself"

THE mainspring of Our Lord's life was to do the will of God. In His all-holy soul there was the greatest singleness of *thought, affection,* and *intention.* By seeing God in all things, Jesus gives us an example of how He would have us live. How many sins have we committed because we were inordinately attached to our own will, our opinions, our pleasures, or our reputation! Christ, the all-holy, "did not please Himself." Shall we sinful creatures allow ourselves full liberty to follow our evil inclinations and disordered passions?

Look out for occasions of practising self-denial. Jesus Christ condescends to call us not servants, but friends; but let us note the condition! "You are My friends *if ye do the things* that I command you."

The Sacred Heart of Jesus desires our perfection:

"Be you perfect as also your heavenly Father is perfect. This is the will of God, your sanctification."

The treasure of holiness lies open to all, and the secret of utilizing these precious treasures consists in turning to our spiritual profit the common routine of every-day duties and the events of Providence. That which happens to us hour by hour, by God's will, is what is best and most profitable for us. Daily we have *active or passive* means of sanctity offered us. Active sanctity consists in fulfilling with purity of intention the duties imposed by God, by the Church, by our state of life. Passive sanctity consists in the loving acceptation of what is painful and repugnant to nature, *without heeding our likes and dislikes.* If only we utilize the means of holiness thus provided, we shall surely become saints sooner or later. — MADAME CECILIA, *Cor Cordium.*

At the Offertory

Represent Jesus bound to the pillar and cruelly scourged

JESUS, in His cruel scourging, shed His blood most painfully and abundantly, offering it to His eternal Father in payment of our impatience and our wantonness. How is it, then, that we do not curb our wrath and self-love? Oh! let us henceforth try to be more patient in our trials, to cultivate self-control, and to bear in peace the injuries men do us.

O Jesus, Thou art the Love and Life of my soul. I find true peace and real happiness only in Thy love, in Thy service, and in the imitation of Thy virtues. I offer myself to Thee; do what Thou willest with me; henceforth my motto shall be, "All for Jesus."

My God and my All!

Indulgence of 50 days, each time. — Leo XIII, May 4, 1888.

Sweet Heart of Jesus, be my love!

Indulgence of 300 days, once a day. — Leo XIII, May 21, 1892.

SELF-SURRENDER

"Into Thy Hands I commend My Spirit"

JESUS came on earth as our Master, and He wills that we should learn from Him the lesson of full and entire submission to the will of God. His life was one uninterrupted act of self-abandonment, beginning with the *"Ecce venio"* of the Incarnation, ' *Lo, I come to do Thy will,"* till the final commendation of His soul on the cross. Like Him, we must yield ourselves as living sacrifices to God, content *as far as our will goes* to accept health or illness, wealth or poverty, interior peace or the conflict with temptation. God knows what is best, and He can and will provide the necessary means of sanctification for each of the souls that are so dear to Him, and this thought should help us to cast all our care on Him. — MADAME CECILIA, *Cor Cordium.*

PRAYER TAKEN FROM "THE SPIRITUAL EXERCISES" OF ST. IGNATIUS LOYOLA

SUSCIPE, Domine, universam meam libertatem. Accipe memoriam, intellectum atque voluntatem omnem. Quidquid habeo vel possideo, mihi largitus es; id tibi totum restituo ac tuæ prorsus voluntati trado gubernandum. Amorem tui solum cum gratia tua mihi dones et dives sum satis, nec aliud quidquam ultra posco.

TAKE, O Lord, and receive all my liberty, my memory, my understanding, and my whole will. Thou hast given me all that I am and all that I possess; I surrender it all to Thee that Thou mayest dispose of it according to Thy will. Give me only Thy love and Thy grace; with these I will be rich enough, and will have no more to desire.

His Holiness, Pope Leo XIII, by a rescript of the Sacred Congregation of Indulgences, May 26, 1883, granted to all the faithful who, with at least contrite heart and devotion, shall recite this prayer, an *indulgence of three hundred days*, once a day.

MAY the most just, most high, and most amiable will of God be done in all things; may it be praised and magnified forever.

Indulgence of 100 days, once a day. — Pius VII, May 19, 1818.

At the Preface and the Sanctus

Contemplate your Saviour crowned with thorns; reflect on the words "Behold the Man!" and say:

BEHOLD me, most merciful Jesus: A poor sinner; I cast myself at Thy sacred feet, penetrated with sorrow for my sins. Oh! let not pride any longer occupy my heart. How vain I am! How sensitive to the least humiliation! How anxious for the praise and esteem of men! How easily influenced by human respect! How many sins against charity I have committed through pride, — unkind words and actions, anger, hatred, jealousy, and revenge! Let not pride any longer dominate and disturb the peace of my soul — that soul, which Thou, my Saviour, hast so tenderly loved and redeemed at so great cost!

Cleanse my poor soul, O Jesus, from all offensive stains, and drown my imperfections in the boundless ocean of Thy mercy.

My Jesus, mercy!

Indulgence of 100 days, each time. — Pius IX, Sept. 24, 1846.

Sweetest Jesus, grant me an increase of faith, hope, and charity; a contrite and humble heart.

Indulgence of 100 days, once a day. — Leo XIII, Sept. 13, 1893.

THANKSGIVING

Cast a rapid glance over the graces with which you have been favored at all periods of your life, and offer to the Lord in exchange the holy Victim of the altar.

MY GOD, I thank Thee for the numberless benefits which I have received from Thy merciful providence; through the gift of my holy faith; through the passion and death of Jesus Christ, Thy divine Son; through the institution of the Blessed Eucharist, and through the operations of the Holy Spirit for my sanctification. I grieve that I have been ungrateful to Thee by not following Thy good inspirations and by not doing Thy holy will on so many occasions. Pardon my offences for the sake of Jesus crucified for love of me. I will henceforth be faithful to Thee and strive to do what is most pleasing to Thee. I consecrate to Thy service my soul and my body, all that I am and all that I have.

Eternal Father! Receive in *thanksgiving* for all Thy graces and blessings the adorable body and the most precious blood of Jesus Christ, Thy well-beloved Son.   This sublime offering which the priest makes to Thee in our name is of infinite value and in every way worthy of Thee.   Blessed be Thy holy name now and forever more.

Pray the angels and saints to join their thanksgiving to yours.

HOLY angels, who surround this altar, my faithful guardian, and all ye heavenly hosts, I entreat you to bless God for the numberless blessings I have received from Him.   Offer Him the Holy Mass, at which I am assisting, to acknowledge His graces, and to obtain for me the gift of perseverance.
Blessed be the Holy Trinity !

HOLY, holy, holy, Lord God of hosts; the earth is full of Thy glory: glory be to the Father, glory be to the Son; glory be to the Holy Ghost.

Indulgence of 100 days, once a day; an indulgence of 100 days, three times every Sunday, as well as on the feast of the Most Holy Trinity, and during its octave. — Clement XIV, June 6, 1769.

At the Canon

RECALL to mind all the sad and sorrowful scenes of the Way of the Cross — all the sufferings of Our Lord, from the crowning with thorns to the crucifixion; then remember that the passion of Jesus Christ, our Redeemer, is a revelation of the heinousness of sin and an evidence of the priceless value of man's immortal soul. Reflect upon the words: "What shall it profit a man, if he gain the whole world, and suffer the loss of his soul?" (*Mark* viii. 36).

EJACULATION

ETERNAL Father! I offer Thee the precious blood of Jesus, in satisfaction for my sins, and for the wants of Holy Church.

Indulgence of 100 days, each time. — Pius VII, Sept. 22, 1817.

PRAYER: DIVINE JESUS!

DIVINE Jesus, incarnate Son of God, Who for our salvation didst vouchsafe to be born in a stable, to pass Thy life in poverty, trials, and misery, and to die amid the sufferings of the cross, I entreat Thee, say to Thy divine Father at the hour of my death, *Father, forgive him;* say to Thy beloved Mother, *Behold thy Son;* say to my soul, *This day thou shalt be with Me in paradise.* My God, my God, forsake me not in that hour. *I thirst;* yes, my God, my soul thirsts after Thee, Who art the fountain of living waters. My life passes like a shadow; yet a little while, and all will be consummated. Wherefore, O my adorable Saviour! from this moment, for all eternity, *into Thy hands I commend my spirit.* Lord Jesus, receive my soul. Amen.

His Holiness, Pope Pius IX, by a decree of the Sacred Congregation of Indulgences, June 10, 1856, confirmed an *indulgence of three hundred days,* to be gained by all the faithful every time that they shall say this prayer with a contrite heart and with devotion.

PRAYER: O MOST COMPASSIONATE JESUS!

O MOST compassionate Jesus! Thou alone art our salvation, our life, and our resurrection. We implore Thee, therefore, do not forsake us in our needs and afflictions, but, by the agony of thy most sacred Heart, and by the sorrows of Thy immaculate Mother, succor Thy servants whom Thou hast redeemed by Thy most precious blood.

Indulgence of 100 days, once a day. — Pius IX, Oct. 6, 1870.

At the Commemoration of the Living

REMEMBER, O Lord, Thy servants and all here present, for whom we offer, or who offer to Thee, this sacrifice of praise for themselves and all pertaining to them, for their temporal welfare and their eternal salvation. Pour Thy blessings on Our holy Father, the Pope, on our bishops, priests, Religious, relatives, friends, and benefactors. Look with pity upon sinners, heretics, and unbelievers, and in particular upon all who are at the point of death. Save them in Thy mercy. Assist all those who have recommended themselves and their interests to my prayers. Grant us an increase of sanctifying grace, the gifts of the Holy Spirit, and final perseverance.

Prayer to The Holy Virgin, Our Lady of Sorrows

MARY most holy, Mother of Sorrows, by that intense martyrdom which thou didst suffer at the foot of the cross during the three hours of Jesus' agony, deign to aid us all, children of thy sorrows, in our last agony, that we may pass from our bed of death to heaven's eternal joys.

EJACULATIONS

Jesus, Mary, and Joseph! I give you my heart and my soul.

Jesus, Mary, and Joseph! assist me in my last agony.

Jesus, Mary, and Joseph! may I breathe forth my soul in peace with you.

Indulgence of 300 days, each time. — Pius VII, Aug. 26, 1814.

The following prayer may be said, in place of the previous form of *Commemoration for the Living*. It includes a remembrance of the holy souls in purgatory.

Prayer During the Canon

O JESUS, dying on the cross for love of poor sinners, by *Thy sacred head* crowned with thorns I beg Thee to have mercy on the Pope, all bishops, priests, and Religious Orders.

Through the wound in *Thy right hand* I recommend to Thee my father, mother, brothers, sisters, relations, friends, and benefactors.

Through the wound in *Thy left hand*, my enemies, all poor sinners, and those who have never been baptized. Help Thy servants who are trying to convert them.

Through the wound in *Thy right foot* I pray for the poor, the sick, and the dying, and for all who are in any kind of pain, temptation, or trouble.

Through the wound in *Thy left foot* I beg of Thee mercifully to grant eternal rest to the souls of the faithful departed, especially N.N.   .

Through *Thy sacred Heart*, O Jesus, I offer myself to do and suffer all things for Thy love. Give me all the graces I stand in need of to do what is most pleasing to Thee, and especially the grace of perseverance. Grant me, in particular, the favor I implore and desire to obtain through Thy clemency by assisting this day at the holy sacrifice of the Mass.

At the Elevation of the Sacred Host

Contemplate Jesus hanging on the cross, and adore the same Jesus here present on the altar; look at the sacred Host and say with strong faith, firm hope, tender love, and earnest devotion:

My Lord and My God!

His Holiness, Pope Pius X, on May 18, 1907, granted an indulgence of seven years and seven quarantines, to all the faithful, who, at the elevation during Mass, or at public exposition of the Blessed Sacrament, look at the sacred Host and say: "*My Lord and my God!*"

At the Elevation of the Sacred Chalice

HAIL, saving Victim, offered on the gibbet of the cross for me and for the whole human race! Hail, precious Blood, flowing from the wounds of our crucified Lord Jesus Christ and washing away the sins of the whole world! Remember, O Lord, Thy creature that Thou hast redeemed by Thy precious blood.

His Holiness, Leo XIII, by a rescript of the Sacred Congregation of Indulgences, June 30, 1893, granted to the faithful who shall recite the above prayer at the Elevation during Holy Mass, an *indulgence of sixty days*, once a day.

EJACULATIONS

ADORAMUS te, sanctissime Domine Jesu Christe, benedicimus tibi; quia per sanctam crucem tuam redemisti mundum.

WE ADORE Thee, O most blessed Lord, Jesus Christ, we bless Thee; because by Thy holy cross Thou hast redeemed the world.

His Holiness, Pope Leo XIII, by a rescript of the Sacred Congregation of Indulgences, March 4, 1882, granted to all the faithful who, with at least contrite heart and devotion, shall recite this ejaculation, an *indulgence of one hundred days*, once a day.

Deus meus et omnia! My God and my all!

His Holiness, Leo XIII, by a rescript of the Sacred Congregation of Indulgences, May 4, 1888, granted to the faithful as often as they recite this ejaculation, an *indulgence of fifty days.*

My God, grant that I may love Thee, and be the only reward of my love to love Thee always more and more.

His Holiness, Leo XIII, by a rescript of the Sacred Congregation of Indulgences, March 15, 1890, granted to the faithful who recite the above invocation, an *indulgence of one hundred days*, once a day.

O Sacrament most holy! O Sacrament divine!
All praise and all thanksgiving be every moment thine.

Indulgence of 100 days, once a day; and once during each Mass to all, who, at the elevation of both species, shall say this ejaculation.

Saviour of the world, have mercy on us!

Indulgence of 50 days, once a day. — Leo XIII, Feb. 21, 1891.

Continuation of the Canon

An Offering

ETERNAL Father, we offer Thee the blood, the passion, and the death of Jesus Christ, the sorrows of Mary most holy, and of St. Joseph, in satisfaction for our sins, in aid of the holy souls in purgatory, for the needs of holy Mother Church, and for the conversion of sinners.

His Holiness, Pope Pius IX, by an autograph rescript April 30, 1860, granted to all the faithful who, with at least contrite heart and devotion, shall say this prayer, an *indulgence of one hundred days*, once a day.

INVOCATIONS

O JESUS, my crucified Saviour, Thou didst die for love of me, let me die to self and to the world for love of Thee! O crucified Love! Most precious blood of Jesus! May all hearts love Thee, may all tongues praise and glorify Thee, now and forever more.

O DIVINE blood of my Jesus, I adore Thee from the depth of my heart! I invoke Thee most fervently, for Thou art my salvation, and by Thee I hope to obtain the joys of paradise.

Most precious blood of Jesus, cry to heaven for mercy on our behalf and deliver us!

By the precious blood of Jesus, I beseech Thee, Father in heaven, have mercy on the poor souls in purgatory.

Adore the five wounds of your crucified Jesus, kissing them in spirit, praying for true and abiding sorrow for your sins, for perfect conformity to the will of God, and for the grace of perseverance.

JESU DULCIS AMOR MEUS

JESUS! as though Thyself wert here
I draw in trembling sorrow near;
And hanging o'er Thy form divine,
Kneel down to kiss these wounds of Thine.

How pitifully Thou art laid!
Bloodstain'd, distended, cold, and dead!
Joy of my soul, my Saviour sweet,
Upon this sacred winding-sheet!

Hail, awful brow! hail, thorny wreath!
Hail, countenance now pale in death!
Whose glance but late so brightly blazed,
That angels trembled as they gazed.

And hail to thee, my Saviour's side;
And hail to thee, thou wound so wide:
Thou wound more ruddy than the rose,
True antidote of all our woes!

Oh, by those sacred hands and feet
For me so mangled! I entreat,
My Jesus, turn me not away,
But let me here forever stay.

PRAYERS FOR THOSE IN THEIR AGONY

O MOST merciful Jesus, lover of souls, I pray Thee by the agony of Thy most sacred Heart, and by the sorrows of Thy immaculate Mother, wash in Thy blood the sinners of the whole world who are now in their agony, and are to die this day. Amen.

V. Heart of Jesus, once in agony, pity the dying.

An indulgence of one hundred days every time the above prayer is said with contrite heart and devotion; granted Feb. 2, 1850, by Pius IX.

Commemoration of the Dead

O FATHER of mercies, in the name of Jesus, Thy beloved Son, in memory of His bitter passion and cruel death, in virtue of the wound of His sacred Heart, and in consideration also of the sorrows of the immaculate heart of Mary, of the heroic deeds of all the saints and of the torments of all the martyrs; I implore Thee to have pity on the souls of the faithful departed now suffering in purgatory.

To thy mercy I recommend especially the souls of my relatives, friends, and benefactors, and of all those for whom I have promised to pray.

V. Eternal rest give to them, O Lord;
R. And let perpetual light shine upon them.

Indulgence of 50 days for each recitation of this versicle and response for the poor souls. — Leo XIII, March 23, 1902.

At the Pater Noster

Recite slowly and devoutly the sublime prayer which Jesus Himself taught His disciples.

OUR Father, Who art in heaven, hallowed be Thy name; Thy kingdom come, Thy will be done on earth as it is in heaven; give us this day our daily bread, and forgive us our trespasses as we forgive those who trespass against us, and lead us not into temptation, but deliver us from evil. Amen.

My God, Thou art the fountain of all grace and the source of all good. Thy beloved Son has commanded me to pray to Thee, and to call Thee by the consoling name of Father. Therefore I prostrate myself with confidence before Thee, and present to Thee my humble supplication through the same Lord Jesus Christ, Who makes intercession for me. Grant me a lively faith, a firm and constant hope, and an ardent charity toward Thee and my neighbor. Save my soul. Give me strength to vanquish my spiritual enemies and to become a saint. Grant me a humble resignation to Thy holy will in the adversities of this life; and, above all, the gift of final perseverance in Thy love and service. Through Christ our Lord. Amen.

WITH OUR KING

"In what place soever Thou shalt be, Lord my King, either in death or in life, there will Thy servant be."

WHICH of us will have the courage to say this as we kneel before our King crowned with thorns? Or at the foot of the cross? Let me look into the heart of my King. What makes Him suffer willingly in spite of the repugnance of nature? The same recognition of the Father's hand in all that befalls Him, to which His word in the Garden testified: "The chalice that My Father hath given Me, shall I not drink it?" The faith that sees the Father's hand in every trial, this it is that holds the secret of meekness. To it alone belongs the strength of endurance, the peacefulness of trust, the *crown of thorns to-day, the crown of glory hereafter.*" — MOTHER MARY LOYOLA.

EJACULATION

FIAT, laudetur atque in æternum superexaltetur justissima, altissima et

MAY the most just, most high, and most amiable will of God be done in amabilissima voluntas Dei all things, be praised and in omnibus.   magnified forever.

Indulgence of 100 days, once a day. — Pius VII, May 19, 1818.

MARY, MY MOTHER!

JESUS, my Redeemer, in Thy agony on the cross, Thou didst not forget me.   Before saying *All is consummated*, Thou didst bequeath to me a tender legacy. Thou didst leave me Thy sorrowful Mother to be my Mother also, in the words, *Behold thy son — behold thy mother!* Thy beloved disciple represented us all while standing beside Thy afflicted Mother in the shadow of the cross.

I return Thee thanks, O my Saviour, for this inestimable favor.   And thou, my tender Mother, thou hast begotten me at the foot of the cross. I am the child of thy sorrow.   Take me under thy protection.   Conduct me to Jesus.   Teach me to love Him, to please Him, to be like to Him. O Mother, O tender Mother! how happy am I in the glorious privilege of being thy child!   O Mary, show that thou art my Mother.   Obtain for me the grace of a holy life and a happy death.

EJACULATION

HOLY Virgin Mary, immaculate Mother of God and our Mother, speak thou for us to the Heart of Jesus, Who is thy Son and our Brother.

Indulgence of 100 days, once a day. — Leo XIII, Dec. 20, 1890.

Sweet Heart of Mary, be my salvation!

Indulgence of 300 days, each time. — Pius IX, Sept. 30, 1852.

At the Agnus Dei and Communion

LAMB of God, Who takest away the sins of the world, have mercy on us.

SPIRITUAL COMMUNION

O JESUS! Thou hast given us in the Hóly Eucharist Thy body and blood to be our spiritual nourishment, through which we may have life everlasting. Would that I were now prepared to approach the Holy Table to be united with Thee in the Blessed Sacrament! I desire, with all my heart, to receive this living Bread which came down from heaven.

O Lord, I am not worthy that Thou shouldst enter under my roof; say but the word, and my soul shall be healed. (*Three times.*) Let me taste, at least, the sweetness of a spiritual communion. Come to me, Jesus, my Lord, my Master. Come and refresh my soul. Strengthen me, that in union with Thee I may do perfectly the heavenly Father's will. Let me never be separated from Thee by sin.

Keep me in Thy love and Thy grace. I will not be lured away from Thee by the deceitful honors and pleasures of the world. I love Thee above all things and with my whole heart. *"Thou art the God of my heart, and the God that is my portion forever."*

Increase my faith, strengthen my hope, kindle my love, that I may die to self and live but for **Thee**.

Omnia ad majorem Dei gloriam!
All for the greater glory of God!

At the Post-Communion

O LORD! how glorious is Thy kingdom, in which Thy saints see and enjoy Thee, and shall forever rejoice with Thee, Lamb of God! *How lovely are Thy tabernacles!*

My heart yearns for those heavenly dwellings, that I may forever praise Thee, with this holy and happy multitude.

Glory, praise, and thanksgiving be to our God forever and ever.

V. O Lord, hear my prayer.

R. And let my cry come unto Thee.

Let us pray

LORD JESUS CHRIST, we thank Thee for all the blessings that have come to us through Thy sacred passion and death, and we beseech Thee by Thy glorious resurrection and ascension into heaven, where Thou art the joy of the martyrs and the saints, who followed Thee in the way of

the cross; grant that after our death we may joyfully enter the gates of paradise.

V. Pray for us, Mary, most sorrowful Virgin!

R. That we may be made worthy of the promises of Christ.

O THOU Mother! fount of love!
 Touch my spirit from above,
 Make my heart with thine accord;
Make me feel as thou hast felt,
Make my soul to glow and melt
 With the love of Christ my Lord.

Holy Mother! pierce me through;
In my heart each wound renew
 Of my Saviour crucified;
Let me share with thee His pain,
Who for all my sins was slain,
 Who for me in torments died.

Christ, when Thou shalt call me hence,
Be thy Mother my defense,
 Be thy cross my victory;
While my body here decays,
May my soul Thy goodness praise,
 Safe in paradise with Thee.

At the Blessing

O ADORABLE Heart of my Saviour, Thou wast
not always in humiliation, suffering, and
sorrow. After so many trials and conflicts, Thou,
my blessed Redeemer, didst ascend into heaven, the
conqueror of Thy enemies. Triumphing over the
world, death, and all the powers of hell, Thou art

exalted in glory, and seated at the right hand of the heavenly Father.

Sacred Heart of Jesus, I rejoice in Thy glory and Thy triumph. Shall I one day share Thy glory and Thy happiness? It is only through Thee and Thy merits that I can hope for and merit this grace. I beseech Thee to give it to me in virtue of the holy sacrifice of the Mass at which I have assisted, and through the intercession of Thy blessed Mother, the queen of heaven, and the prayers of all the saints. Vouchsafe to ratify in heaven the blessing which Thy priest gives us on earth, in the name of the Father, ✠ and of the Son, and of the Holy Ghost.

Bless us, O Lord, as Thou didst bless the little children, and again Thy disciples at Thy glorious ascension into heaven, so that we may persevere in Thy grace, and be numbered on the last day among the elect, whom Thou wilt call the blessed of Thy Father, and invite into Thy eternal kingdom.

At the End of Mass

MY GOOD God! I thank Thee with all my heart for the good inspirations, consolations, and graces, which have come to me through this holy Mass. I leave this place of benedictions, where Thou dost abide for love of us in the Blessed Sacrament, to resume my occupations with a brave heart, a firm confidence in Thy benign providence, perfect submission to Thy holy will, and a determination to subdue my evil inclinations.

to conquer my passions, and to please Thee in all
things. My watchword shall be: *Omnia ad
majorem Dei gloriam! All to the greater glory
of God!*

Do Thou, O my Jesus, establish in my soul Thy
kingdom, that Thy image may be perfectly formed
in me and the virtues of Thy sacred Heart shine
forth in all my actions.

TEACH me, teach me, dearest Jesus,
In Thine own sweet, loving way,
All the lessons of perfection
    I must practise day by day.

Teach me fervor, dearest Jesus,
    To comply with every grace,
So as never to look backward,
    Never slacken in the race.

Teach to me *Thy Heart*, dear Jesus,
    Is my fervent, final prayer,
For all beauties and perfections
    Are in full perfection there.

May the grace and blessing of Thy sacred
Heart be with me in all my ways, that my heart
may become like to Thine in purity, meekness,
humility, and charity, and inflamed with zeal to do
the heavenly Father's will and to perform all my
duties with exactness and perfection; that I may
be kind in thought, word, and deed to my neighbor;
that I may persevere in holiness to the end of my
life and enjoy the Beatific Vision as my eternal
recompense.

The Ordinary of the Mass

With the Proper Parts from the Mass to Beg the Grace of a happy Death [1]

IN NOMINE Patris, ✠ et Filii, et Spiritus Sancti. Amen.

P. Introibo ad altare Dei.

R. Ad Deum qui laetificat juventutem meam.

IN THE name of the Father, ✠ and of the Son, and of the Holy Ghost. Amen.

P. I will go in to the altar of God.

R. To God, Who giveth joy to my youth.

PSALM XLII

(To be omitted in Passion-tide and in Masses for the Dead)

JUDICA me, Deus, et discerne causam meam de gente non sancta: ab homine iniquo et doloso erue me.

R. Quia tu es, Deus, fortitudo mea: quare me repulisti, et quare tristis incedo, dum affligit me inimicus?

P. Emitte lucem tuam, et veritatem tuam: ipsa me deduxerunt, et adduxerunt in montem sanctum tuum, et in tabernacula tua.

R. Et introibo ad altare

JUDGE me, O God, and distinguish my cause from the nation that is not holy; deliver me from the unjust and deceitful man.

R. For Thou art, God, my strength: why hast Thou cast me off? and why do I go sorrowful whilst the enemy afflicteth me?

P. Send forth Thy light and Thy truth: they have conducted me and brought me unto Thy holy hill, and into Thy tabernacles.

R. And I will go in to

---

[1] The Mass to beg the grace of a happy death was inserted in the Roman Missal at the beginning of the eighteenth century. The corresponding devotion of the Bona Mors is now widely spread in the Church.

Dei: ad Deum, qui lætificat juventutem meam.

P. Confitebor tibi in cithara, Deus, Deus meus: quare tristis es, anima mea, et quare conturbas me?

R. Spera in Deo, quoniam adhuc confitebor illi: salutare vultus mei, et Deus meus.

P. Gloria Patri, et Filio, et Spiritui Sancto.

R. Sicut erat in principio, et nunc, et semper: et in sæcula sæculorum. Amen.

P. Introibo ad altare Dei.

R. Ad Deum, qui lætificat juventutem meam.

P. Adjutorium nostrum in nomine Domini.

R. Qui fecit cœlum et terram.

the altar of God: to God Who giveth joy to my youth.

P. To Thee, O God, my God, I will give praise upon the harp: why art thou sad, O my soul, and why dost thou disquiet me?

R. Hope in God, for I will still give praise to Him, the salvation of my countenance and my God.

P. Glory be to the Father, and to the Son, and to the Holy Ghost.

R. As it was in the beginning, is now, and ever shall be, world without end. Amen.

P. I will go in to the altar of God.

R. To God, Who giveth joy to my youth.

P. Our help is in the name of the Lord.

R. Who made heaven and earth.

Humbly bowing down, the priest says:

CONFITEOR Deo omnipotenti, beatæ Mariæ semper virgini, beato Michaeli archangelo, beato Joanni Baptistæ, sanctis apostolis Petro et Paulo, omnibus sanctis et vobis, fratres, quia peccavi nimis cogitatione, verbo, et opere: mea culpa,

I CONFESS to almighty God, to blessed Mary ever virgin, to blessed Michael the archangel, to blessed John the Baptist, to the holy apostles Peter and Paul, to all the saints and to you, brethren, that I have sinned exceedingly

mea culpa, mea maxima culpa. Ideo precor beatam Mariam semper virginem, beatum Michaelem archangelum, beatum Joannem Baptistam, sanctos apostolos Petrum et Paulum, omnes sanctos, et vos, fratres, orare pro me ad Dominum Deum nostrum.

R. Misereatur tui omnipotens Deus, et dimissis peccatis tuis, perducat te ad vitam æternam.

P. Amen.

in thought, word, and deed: through my fault, through my fault, through my most grievous fault. Therefore I beseech the blessed Mary ever virgin, blessed Michael the archangel, blessed John the Baptist, the holy apostles Peter and Paul, all the saints and you, brethren, to pray to the Lord our God for me.

R. May almighty God have mercy on thee and, having forgiven thee thy sins, bring thee to life everlasting.

P. Amen.

The acolytes, bowing down, repeat the words of the Confiteor:

CONFITEOR Deo omnipotenti, beatæ Mariæ semper virgini, beato Michaeli archangelo, beato Joanni Baptistæ, sanctis apostolis Petro et Paulo, omnibus sanctis, et tibi, Pater, quia peccavi nimis cogitatione, verbo, et opere: mea culpa, mea culpa, mea maxima culpa. Ideo precor beatam Mariam semper virginem, beatum Michaelem archangelum, beatum Joannem Baptistam, sanctos apostolos Petrum et Paulum, omnes sanctos, et te, Pater,

I CONFESS to almighty God, to blessed Mary ever virgin, to blessed Michael the archangel, to blessed John the Baptist, to the holy apostles Peter and Paul, to all the saints, and to thee, Father, that I have sinned exceedingly in thought, word, and deed: through my fault, through my fault, through my most grievous fault. Therefore I beseech the blessed Mary ever virgin, blessed Michael the archangel, blessed John the Baptist, the holy apostles

orare pro me ad Dominum Deum nostrum.

Peter and Paul, all the saints, and thee, Father, to pray to the Lord our God for me.

P. Misereatur vestri omnipotens Deus, et dimissis peccatis vestris, perducat vos ad vitam æternam.

R. Amen.

P. Indulgentiam, absolutionem, et remissionem peccatorum nostrorum, tribuat nobis omnipotens et misericors Dominus.

R. Amen.

P. May almighty God have mercy on you and, having forgiven you your sins, bring you to life everlasting.

R. Amen.

P. May the almighty and merciful God grant us pardon, absolution, and remission of our sins.

R. Amen.

Again bowing down the priest goes on:

P. D e u s, tu conversus vivificabis nos.

R. Et plebs tua lætabitur in te.

P. Ostende nobis, Domine, misericordiam tuam.

R. Et salutare tuum da nobis.

P. Domine, exaudi orationem meam.

R. Et clamor meus ad te veniat.

P. Dominus vobiscum.

R. Et cum spiritu tuo.

P. Oremus.

P. Thou wilt turn again, O God, and quicken us.

R. And Thy people will rejoice in Thee.

P. Show us, O Lord, Thy mercy.

R. And grant us Thy salvation.

P. O Lord, hear my prayer.

R. And let my cry come unto Thee.

P. The Lord be with you.

R. And with thy spirit.

P. Let us pray.

Going up to the altar the priest prays silently:

AUFER a nobis, quæsumus, Domine, iniquitates nostras: ut ad

MAKE away from us our iniquities, we beseech Thee, O Lord; that, be-

Sancta Sanctorum puris mereamur mentibus introire. Per Christum Dominum nostrum. Amen.

ing made pure in heart we may be worthy to enter into the Holy of Holies. Through Christ our Lord. Amen.

He bows down over the altar, which he kisses, saying:

ORAMUS te, Domine, per merita sanctorum tuorum, quorum reliquiæ hic sunt, et omnium sanctorum: ut indulgere digneris omnia peccata mea. Amen.

WE BESEECH Thee, O Lord, by the merits of those of Thy saints whose relics are here, and of all the saints, that Thou wouldst vouchsafe to pardon me all my sins. Amen.

The Introit
(*Ps.* xii.)

ILLUMINA oculos meos, ne umquam obdormiam in morte, nequando dicat inimicus meus: Prævalui adversus eum. *Ps. ibid.* Usquequo, Domine, oblivisceris me in finem? Usquequo avertis faciem tuam a me ?

V. Gloria Patri.

ENLIGHTEN mine eyes, that I never sleep in death: lest at any time mine enemy say, I have prevailed against him. *Ps.* How long, O Lord, wilt Thou forget me altogether? How long wilt Thou turn away Thy face from me?

V. Glory, etc.

Kyrie Eleison

S. KYRIE, eleison.
   M. Kyrie, eleison.

S. Kyrie, eleison.
M. Christe, eleison.

S. Christe, eleison.

P. LORD, have mercy on us.
   R. Lord, have mercy on us.

P. Lord, have mercy on us.
R. Christ, have mercy on us.

P. Christ, have mercy on us.

M. Christe, eleison.

S. Kyrie, eleison.
M. Kyrie, eleison.
S. Kyrie, eleison.

R. Christ, have mercy on us.

P. Lord, have mercy on us.
R. Lord, have mercy on us.
P, Lord, have mercy on us.

Gloria in Excelsis

GLORIA in excelsis Deo. Et in terra pax hominibus bonæ voluntatis. Laudamus te. Benedicimus te. Adoramus te. Glorificamus te. Gratias agimus tibi propter magnam gloriam tuam. Domine Deus, rex cœlestis, Deus Pater omnipotens, Domine Fili unigenite Jesu Christe. Domine Deus, Agnus Dei, Filius Patris. Qui tollis peccata mundi, miserere nobis. Qui tollis peccata mundi, suscipe deprecationem nostram. Qui sedes ad dexteram Patris, miserere nobis. Quoniam tu solus sanctus. Tu solus Dominus. Tu solus altissimus, Jesu Christe, cum Sancto Spiritu, in gloria Dei Patris. Amen.

GLORY be to God on high, and on earth peace to men of good will. We praise Thee; we bless Thee; we adore Thee; we glorify Thee. We give Thee thanks for Thy great glory, O Lord God, heavenly king, God the Father almighty, O Lord Jesus Christ, the only-begotten Son. O Lord God, Lamb of God, Son of the Father, Who takest away the sins of the world, have mercy on us. Who takest away the sins of the world, receive our prayer. Who sittest at the right hand of the Father, have mercy on us. For Thou alone art holy; Thou alone art the Lord; Thou alone, O Jesus Christ, together with the Holy Ghost, art most high in the glory of God the Father. Amen.

V. Dominus vobiscum.
R. Et cum spiritu tuo.

V. The Lord be with you.
R. And with thy spirit.

The Prayer

OMNIPOTENS et misericors Deus, qui humano generi et salutis remedia, et vitæ æternæ munera contulisti: respice propitius nos famulos tuos, et animas refove, quas creasti: ut in hora exitus earum absque peccati macula tibi creatori suo per manus sanctorum angelorum repræsentari mereantur. Per Dominum.

ALMIGHTY and merciful God, Who hast bestowed upon mankind both the means of salvation and the blessing of everlasting life: look down with pity upon Thy servants, and cherish the souls which Thou hast created; so that in the hour of their going forth they may be found worthy to be presented without stain of sin, by the hands of Thy holy angels, to Thee, their Creator.

The Epistle

(Lesson from the Epistle of St. Paul to the Romans, xiv. 7-12)

FRATRES: Nemo nostrum sibi vivit, et nemo sibi moritur. Sive enim vivimus, Domino vivimus: sive morimur, Domino morimur. Sive ergo vivimus, sive morimur, Domini sumus. In hoc enim Christus mortuus est, et resurrexit: ut et mortuorum, et vivorum dominetur. Tu autem quid judicas fratrem tuum? aut tu quare spernis fratrem tuum? Omnes enim stabimus ante tribunal Christi. Scriptum est enim: Vivo ego, dicit

BRETHREN, none of us liveth to himself; and no man dieth to himself. For whether we live, we live unto the Lord; or whether we die, we die unto the Lord. Therefore, whether we live or whether we die, we are the Lord's. For to this end Christ died and rose again: that He might be Lord both of the dead and of the living. But thou, why judgest thou thy brother? or thou, why dost thou despise thy brother? For we shall all stand before the

Dominus, quoniam mihi flectetur omne genu: et omnis lingua confitebitur Deo. Itaque unusquisque nostrum pro se rationem reddet Deo.

judgment-seat of Christ. For it is written: As I live, saith the Lord, every knee shall bow to Me; and every tongue shall confess to God. Therefore every one of us shall render account to God for himself.

The Gradual

(*Ps.* xxii)

SI AMBULEM in medio umbræ mortis, non timebo mala: quoniam tu mecum es, Domine. *V.* Virga tua, et baculus tuus, ipsa me consolata sunt. Alleluia, alleluia. *V. Ps.* xxx. In te, Domine, speravi, non confundar in æternum: in justitia tua libera me et eripe me: inclina ad me aurem tuam, accelera, ut e r i p i a s me. Alleluia.

THOUGH I should walk in the midst of the shadow of death, I will fear no evils: for Thou art with me, O Lord. *V.* Thy rod and Thy staff, they have comforted me. Alleluia, alleluia. *Ps.* In Thee, O Lord, have I hoped; let me never be confounded: deliver me in Thy justice and save me: bow down Thy ear to me: make haste to deliver me. Alleluia.

The Tract

(*Ps.* xxiv)

From Septuagesima to Easter, in place of the Alleluias and verse, the following is said, or sung:

DE NECESSITATIBUS meis eripe me, Domine: vide humilitatem meam, et laborem meum et dimitte omnia peccata mea. *V.* Ad te, Domine, levavi animam me-

DELIVER me from my necessities, O Lord; see my abjection and my labor, and forgive me all my sins. *V.* To Thee, O Lord, I have lifted up my soul. In

am: Deus meus, in te confido, non erubescam: neque irrideant me inimici mei. *V.* Etenim universi qui te exspectant, non confundentur: confundantur omnes facientes vana.

Thee, O my God, I put my trust: let me not be ashamed, neither let my enemies laugh at me. *V.* For none of them that wait on Thee shall be confounded: let all those be confounded that seek after vain things.

In Paschal Time, for the Gradual, is said, or sung:

Alleluia, alleluia. *V. Ps.* cxiii. In exitu Israel de Ægypto, domus Jacob de populo barbaro. Alleluia. *V. Ps.* cvii. Paratum cor meum, Deus, paratum cor meum: cantabo, et psallam tibi, gloria mea. Alleluia.

Alleluia, alleluia. *V.* When Israel went out of Egypt, the house of Jacob from a barbarous people. *V.* My heart is ready, O God, my heart is ready: I will sing, I will give praise with my glory. Alleluia.

Munda Cor Meum

MUNDA cor meum, ac labia mea, omnipotens Deus, qui labia Isaiæ prophetæ calculo mundasti ignito: ita me tua grata miseratione dignare mundare, ut sanctum Evangelium tuum digne valeam nuntiare. Per Christum Dominum nostrum. Amen.

CLEANSE my heart and my lips, O almighty God, Who didst cleanse with a burning coal the lips of the prophet Isaias; and vouchsafe in Thy lovingkindness so to purify me that I 'may be enabled worthily to announce Thy holy G o s p e l. Through Christ our Lord. Amen.

Jube, Domine, benedicere.

Vouchsafe, O Lord, to bless me.

Dominus sit in corde meo, et in labiis meis; ut digne

The Lord be in my heart and on my lips, that I may

et competenter annuntiem evangelium suum. Amen.

worthily and becomingly announce His gospel. Amen.

The Gospel

V. Dominus vobiscum.

R. Et cum spiritu tuo.

V. ✠ Sequentia sancti Evangelii secundum Lucam (xxi. 34-36).

R. Gloria tibi, Domine.

IN ILLO tempore: Dixit Jesus discipulis suis: Attendite vobis, ne forte graventur corda vestra in crapula, et ebrietate, et curis hujus vitæ et superveniat in vos repentina dies illa: tamquam laqueus enim superveniet in omnes, qui sedent super faciem omnis terræ. Vigilate itaque, omni tempore orantes, ut digni habeamini fugere ista omnia, quæ futura sunt, et stare ante Filium hominis.

R. Laus tibi, Christe.

P. Per evangelica dicta deleantur nostra delicta.

V. The Lord be with you.

R. And with thy spirit.

V. ✠ The following is taken from the Holy Gospel according to St. Luke (xxi. 34-36).

R. Glory be to Thee, O Lord.

AT THAT time Jesus said to His disciples: Take heed to yourselves lest perhaps your hearts be overcharged with surfeiting and drunkenness and the cares of this life: and that day come upon you suddenly. For as a snare shall it come upon all that sit upon the face of the whole earth. Watch ye, therefore, praying at all times, that you may be accounted worthy to escape all these things that are to come, and to stand before the Son of man.

R. Praise be to Thee, O Christ.

P. May our sins be blotted out by the words of the Gospel.

The Nicene Creed

CREDO in unum Deum, Patrem omnipotentem, factorem cœli et terræ,

I BELIEVE in one God, the Father almighty, maker of heaven and earth,

visibilium omnium, et invisibilium. Et in unum Dominum Jesum Christum, Filium Dei unigenitum. Et ex Patre natum ante omnia sæcula. Deum de Deo, lumen de lumine, Deum verum de Deo vero. Genitum, non factum, consubstantialem Patri: per quem omnia facta sunt. Qui propter nos homines, et propter nostram salutem descendit de cœlis. ET INCARNATUS EST DE SPIRITU SANCTO EX MARIA VIRGINE: ET HOMO FACTUS EST. Crucifixus etiam pro nobis, sub Pontio Pilato passus, et sepultus est. Et resurrexit tertia die, secundum Scripturas. Et ascendit in cœlum: sedet ad dexteram Patris. Et iterum venturus est cum gloria, judicare vivos et mortuos: cujus regni non erit finis. Et in Spiritum Sanctum, Dominum et vivificantem: qui ex Patre Filioque procedit. Qui cum Patre et Filio simul adoratur et conglorificatur: qui locutus est per prophetas. Et unam sanctam catholicam et apostolicam Ecclesiam. Confiteor unum baptisma in remissionem peccatorum. Et

and of all things visible and invisible. And in one Lord Jesus Christ, the only-begotten Son of God, born of the Father before all ages; God of God, light of light, true God of true God; begotten, not made; consubstantial with the Father, by Whom all things were made. Who for us men, and for our salvation, came down from heaven AND WAS INCARNATE BY THE HOLY GHOST OF THE VIRGIN MARY, AND WAS MADE MAN. He was crucified also for us, suffered under Pontius Pilate, and was buried. And the third day He arose again, according to the Scriptures, and ascended into heaven. He sitteth at the right hand of the Father: and He shall come again with glory, to judge the living and the dead: and His kingdom shall have no end. And in the Holy Ghost, the Lord and Giver of life, · Who proceedeth from the Father and the Son, Who, together with the Father and the Son, is adored and glorified: Who spoke by the prophets. And one holy, catholic, and apostolic Church. I confess

exspecto resurrectionem mortuorum. Et vitam venturi sæculi. Amen.

one baptism for the remission of sins. And I expect the resurrection of the dead, and the life of the world to come. Amen.

V. Dominus vobiscum.
R. Et cum spiritu tuo.
S. Oremus.

V. The Lord be with you.
R. And with thy spirit.
P. Let us pray.

The Offertory

(Ps. xxx)

IN TE speravi, Domine; dixi: tu es Deus meus, in manibus tuis tempora mea.

I HAVE put my trust in Thee, O Lord: I said, Thou art my God: my lots are in Thy hands.

OFFERING OF THE HOST

SUSCIPE, sancte Pater, omnipotens æterne Deus, hanc immaculatam hostiam, quam ego indignus famulus tuus offero tibi Deo meo vivo et vero, pro innumerabilibus peccatis, et offensionibus, et negligentiis meis, et pro omnibus circumstantibus, sed et pro omnibus fidelibus Christianis vivis atque defunctis: ut mihi et illis proficiat ad salutem in vitam æternam. Amen.

RECEIVE, O Holy Father, almighty and eternal God, this spotless host, which I, Thine unworthy servant, offer unto Thee, my living and true God, for my countless sins, trespasses, and omissions; likewise for all here present, and for all faithful Christians, whether living or dead, that it may avail both me and them to salvation, unto life everlasting. Amen.

The priest pours wine and water into the chalice

DEUS, qui humanæ substantiæ dignitatem mirabiliter condidisti, et

O GOD, Who in creating man didst exalt his nature very wonderfully

mirabilius reformasti: da nobis per hujus aquæ et vini mysterium, ejus divinitatis esse consortes, qui humanitatis nostræ fieri dignatus est particeps, Jesus Christus Filius tuus Dominus noster: Qui tecum vivit et regnat in unitate Spiritus Sancti Deus: per omnia sæcula sæculorum. Amen.

and yet more wonderfully didst establish it anew: by the mystery signified in the mingling of this water and wine, grant us to have part in the Godhead of Him Who hath vouchsafed to share our manhood, Jesus Christ, Thy Son, Our Lord, Who liveth and reigneth with Thee in the unity of the Holy Ghost; world without end. Amen.

OFFERING OF THE CHALICE

OFFERIMUS tibi, Domine, calicem salutaris, tuam deprecantes clementiam: ut in conspectu divinæ majestatis tuæ, pro nostra et totius mundi salute cum odore suavitatis ascendat. Amen.

WE OFFER unto Thee, O Lord, the chalice of salvation, beseeching Thy clemency that it may ascend as a sweet odor before Thy divine majesty, for our own salvation, and for that of the world. Amen.

IN SPIRITU humilitatis, et in animo contrito suscipiamur a te, Domine: et sic fiat sacrificium nostrum in conspectu tuo hodie, ut placeat tibi, Domine Deus.

HUMBLED in mind, and contrite of heart, may we find favor with Thee, O Lord; and may the sacrifice we this day offer up be well pleasing to Thee, Who art our Lord and our God.

VENI, sanctificator omnipotens æterne Deus, et benedic hoc sacrifi-

COME, Thou, the Sanctifier, God, almighty and everlasting: bless this

cium tuo sancto nomini præparatum.

sacrifice which is prepared for the glory of Thy holy name.

The priest washes his fingers

LAVABO inter innocentes manus meas: et circumdabo altare tuum, Domine.

Ut audiam vocem laudis: et enarrem universa mirabilia tua.

Domine, dilexi decorem domus tuæ: et locum habitationis gloriæ tuæ.

Ne perdas cum impiis, Deus, animam meam: et cum viris sanguinum vitam meam.

In quorum manibus iniquitates sunt: dextera eorum repleta est muneribus.

Ego autem in innocentia mea ingressus sum: redime me, et miserere mei.

Pes meus stetit in directo: in ecclesiis benedicam te, Domine.

Gloria, etc.

SUSCIPE, sancta Trinitas, hanc oblationem, quam tibi offerimus ob memoriam passionis, resurrectionis, et ascensionis Jesu Christi Do-

I WILL wash my hands among the innocent, and will compass Thine altar, O Lord.

That I may hear the voice of praise, and tell of all Thy wondrous works.

I have loved, O Lord, the beauty of Thy house, and the place where Thy glory dwelleth.

Take not away my soul, O God, with the wicked: nor my life with men of blood.

In whose hands are iniquities: their right hand is filled with gifts.

But as for me, I have walked in my innocence; redeem me, and have mercy on me.

My foot hath stood in the right way; in the churches I will bless Thee, O Lord.

Glory, etc.

RECEIVE, O holy Trinity, this oblation offered up by us to Thee, in memory of the passion, resurrection, and ascension

mini nostri: et in honorem beatæ Mariæ semper virginis, et beati Joannis Baptistæ, et sanctorum apostolorum Petri et Pauli, et istorum, et omnium sanctorum: ut illis proficiat ad honorem, nobis autem ad salutem: et illi pro nobis intercedere dignentur in cœlis, quorum memoriam agimus in terris. Per eumdem Christum Dominum nostrum.

of Our Lord Jesus Christ, and in honor of blessed Mary, ever a virgin, of blessed John the Baptist, of the holy apostles Peter and Paul, of these, and of all the saints, that it may be available to their honor and to our salvation; and may they whose memory we celebrate on earth vouchsafe to intercede for us in heaven. Through the same Christ our Lord. Amen.

The Orate Fratres

ORATE, fratres, ut meum ac vestrum sacrificium acceptabile fiat apud Deum Patrem omnipotentem.

BRETHREN, pray that my sacrifice and yours may be well pleasing to God the Father almighty.

R. SUSCIPIAT Dominus sacrificium de manibus tuis, ad laudem et gloriam nominis sui, ad utilitatem quoque nostram, totiusque Ecclesiæ suæ sanctæ.

MAY the Lord receive this sacrifice at thy hands, to the praise and glory of His name, to our own benefit, and to that of all His holy Church.

The Secret Prayer

SUSCIPE, quæsumus, Domine, hostiam, quam tibi offerimus pro extremo vitæ nostræ, et concede: ut per eam universa nostra purgentur delicta: ut, qui

RECEIVE, we b e s e e c h Thee, O Lord, the sacred victim which we offer up in preparation for our last hour, and grant that for its sake all our sins

tuæ dispositionis flagellis in hac vita atterimur, in futura requiem consequamur æternam.

may be blotted out; so that we, who by Thy providence have been scourged in this life, may enjoy rest everlasting in that which is to come.

Per Dominum nostrum Jesum Christum, Filium tuum, qui tecum vivit et regnat, in unitate Spiritus Sancti Deus.

Through Jesus Christ, Thy Son our Lord, who liveth and reigneth with Thee in the unity of the Holy Ghost.

The Preface

V. Per omnia sæcula sæculorum. *R.* Amen.
V. Dominus vobiscum.
R. Et cum spiritu tuo.
V. Sursum corda.
R. Habemus ad Dominum.

V. Gratias agamus Domino Deo nostro.
R. Dignum et justum est.

V. World without end.
R. Amen.
V. The Lord be with you.
R. And with thy spirit.
V. Lift up your hearts.
R. We have them lifted up unto the Lord.

V. Let us give thanks to the Lord our God.
R. It is meet and just.

VERE dignum et justum est, æquum et salutare, nos tibi semper, et ubique, gratias agere: Domine sancte, Pater omnipotens, æterne Deus, per Christum Dominum nostrum. Per quem majestatem tuam laudant angeli, adorant dominationes, tremunt potestates. Cœli cœlorumque virtutes, ac beata seraphim, socia exsultatione concele-

IT IS truly meet and just, right, and profitable for us, at all times, and in all places, to give thanks to Thee, O holy Lord, Father almighty, eternal God, through Christ our Lord. Through Whom the angels praise, the dominations adore, the powers, trembling with awe, worship Thy majesty: which the heavens, and the forces of heaven, together

brant. Cum quibus et nostras voces, ut admitti jubeas deprecamur, supplici confessione dicentes:

with the blessed seraphim, joyfully do magnify. And do Thou command that it be permitted to our lowliness to join with them in confessing Thee and unceasingly to repeat:

Sanctus, sanctus, sanctus, Dominus Deus Sabaoth.
Pleni sunt cœli et terra gloria tua.
Hosanna in excelsis.
Benedictus qui venit in nomine Domini.
Hosanna in excelsis.

Holy, holy, holy, Lord God of hosts.
The heavens and the earth are full of Thy glory. Hosanna in the highest.
Blessed is He Who cometh in the name of the Lord.
Hosanna in the highest.

The Canon of the Mass

TE IGITUR, clementissime Pater, per Jesum Christum, Filium tuum, Dominum nostrum, supplices rogamus ac petimus, uti accepta habeas, et benedicas hæc ✝ dona, hæc ✝ munera, hæc ✝ sancta sacrificia illibata, in primis quæ tibi offerimus pro Ecclesia tua sancta Catholica: quam pacificare, custodire, adunare, et regere digneris toto orbe terrarum: una cum famulo tuo Papa nostro N., et Antistite nostro N., et omnibus orthodoxis, atque catholicæ et apostolicæ fidei cultoribus.

WHEREFORE, we humbly pray and beseech Thee, most merciful Father, through Jesus Christ Thy Son, Our Lord, to receive and to bless these ✝ gifts, these ✝ presents, these ✝ holy unspotted sacrifices, which we offer up to Thee, in the first place, for Thy holy Catholic Church, that it may please Thee to grant her peace, to guard, unite, and guide her, throughout the world; as also for Thy servant N. our Pope, and N. our Bishop, and for all who are orthodox in belief and who profess the catholic and apostolic faith.

Commemoration for the Living

MEMENTO, Domine, famulorum famularumque tuarum, N. et N., et omnium circumstantium, quorum tibi fides cognita est, et nota devotio, pro quibus tibi offerimus, vel qui tibi offerunt hoc sacrificium laudis, pro se suisque omnibus: pro redemptione animarum suarum, pro spe salutis, et incolumitatis suæ: tibique reddunt vota sua æterno Deo, vivo et vero.

BE MINDFUL, O Lord, of Thy servants, N. and N., and of all here present, whose faith and devotion are known to Thee, for whom we offer, or who offer up to Thee, this sacrifice of praise, for themselves, their families, and their friends, for the salvation of their souls and the health and welfare they hope for, and who now pay their vows to Thee, God eternal, living, and true.

COMMUNICANTES, et memoriam venerantes, in primis gloriosæ semper Virginis Mariæ, Genitricis Dei et Domini nostri Jesu Christi: sed et beatorum apostolorum ac martyrum tuorum, Petri et Pauli, Andreæ, Jacobi, Joannis, Thomæ, Jacobi, Philippi, Bartholomæi, Matthæi, Simonis et Thaddæi, Lini, Cleti, Clementis, Xysti, Cornelii, Cypriani, Laurentii, Chrysogoni, Joannis et Pauli, Cosmæ et Damiani, et omnium sanctorum tuorum; quorum meritis, precibusque concedas, ut in omnibus protectionis tuæ muniamur auxilio. Per eumdem Chris-

HAVING communion with and venerating the memory, first, of the glorious Mary, ever a virgin, mother of Jesus Christ, our God and our Lord: likewise of Thy blessed apostles and martyrs, Peter and Paul, Andrew, James, John, Thomas, James, Philip, Bartholomew, Matthew, Simon and Thaddeus; of Linus, Cletus, Clement, Sixtus, Cornelius, Cyprian, Lawrence, Chrysogonus, John and Paul, Cosmas and Damian, and of all Thy saints: for the sake of whose merits and prayers do Thou grant that in all things we may

tum Dominum nostrum. Amen.

ᚻANC igitur oblationem servitutis nostræ, sed et cunctæ familiæ tuæ, quæsumus, Domine, ut placatus accipias: diesque nostros in tua pace disponas, atque ab æterna damnatione nos eripi, et in electorum tuorum jubeas grege numerari. Per Christum Dominum nostrum. Amen.

QUAM oblationem tu, Deus, in omnibus, quæsumus benedictam ✠, adscriptam ✠, ratam ✠, rationabilem, acceptabilemque facere digneris: ut nobis corpus ✠ et sanguis ✠ fiat dilectissimi Filii tui Domini nostri Jesu Christi.

QUI pridie quam pateretur, accepit panem in sanctas ac venerabiles manus suas, et elevatis oculis in cœlum ad te Deum Patrem suum omnipotentem, tibi gratias agens, benedixit ✠, fregit, deditque discipulis suis, dicens: Ac-

be defended by the help of Thy protection. Through the same Christ, our Lord. Amen.

ᚹHEREFORE, we beseech Thee, O Lord, graciously to receive this oblation which we Thy servants, and with us Thy whole family, offer up to Thee: dispose our days in Thy peace; command that we be saved from eternal damnation and numbered among the flock of Thine elect.

ᚪND do Thou, O God, vouchsafe in all respects to bless, ✠ consecrate, ✠ and approve ✠ this our oblation, to perfect it and to render it well-pleasing to Thyself, so that it may become for us the body ✠ and blood ✠ of Thy most beloved Son, Jesus Christ our Lord.

ᚹHO, the day before He suffered, took bread into His holy and venerable hands, and having lifted up His eyes to heaven, to Thee, God, His almighty Father, giving thanks to Thee, blessed it ✠, broke it, and gave it to His dis-

cipite, et manducate ex hoc omnes:

Hoc est enim corpus meum.

SIMILI modo postquam cœnatum est, accipiens et hunc præclarum calicem in sanctas ac venerabiles manus suas: item tibi gratias agens bene✠dixit, deditque discipulis suis, dicens: Accipite, et bibite ex eo omnes:

Hic est enim calix sanguinis mei, novi et æterni testamenti: mysterium fidei, qui pro vobis et pro multis effundetur in remissionem peccatorum.

Hæc quotiescumque feceritis, in mei memoriam facietis.

UNDE et memores, Domine, nos servi tui, sed et plebs tua sancta, ejusdem Christi Filii tui Domini nostri, tam beatæ passionis, necnon et ab inferis resurrectionis, sed et in cœlos gloriosæ ascensionis: offerimus præclaræ majestati tuæ de tuis donis ac datis, hóstiam ✠ puram, hostiam ✠ sanctam, hostiam

ciples, saying: Take ye, and eat ye all of this:

For this is My body.

IN LIKE manner, after He had supped, taking also into His holy and venerable hands this goodly chalice, again giving thanks to Thee, He blessed it ✠, and gave it to His disciples, saying: Take ye, and drink ye all of this:

For this is the chalice of My blood, of the new and everlasting testament, the mystery of faith, which for you and for many shall be shed unto the remission of sins.

As often as ye shall do these things, ye shall do them in memory of Me.

WHEREFORE, O Lord, we, Thy servants, as also Thy holy people, calling to mind the blessed passion of the same Christ, Thy Son, our Lord, His resurrection from the grave, and His glorious ascension into heaven, offer up to Thy most excellent majesty of Thine own gifts bestowed upon us, a victim ✠ which

✚ immaculatam, panem sanctum ✚ vitæ æternæ, et calicem ✚ salutis perpetuæ.

is pure, a victim ✚ which is holy, a victim ✚ which is stainless, the holy bread ✚ of life everlasting, and the chalice ✚ of eternal salvation.

Supra quæ propitio ac sereno vultu respicere digneris, et accepta habere, sicuti accepta habere dignatus es munera pueri tui justi Abel, et sacrificium Patriarchæ nostri Abrahæ: et quod tibi obtulit summus sacerdos tuus Melchisedech, sanctum sacrificium, immaculatam hostiam.

Vouchsafe to look upon them with a gracious and tranquil countenance, and to accept them, even as Thou wast pleased to accept the offerings of Thy just servant Abel, and the sacrifice of Abraham, our patriarch, and that which Melchisedech, Thy high priest, offered up to Thee, a holy sacrifice, a victim without blemish.

Supplices te rogamus, omnipotens Deus, jube hæc perferri per manus sancti angeli tui in sublime altare tuum, in conspectu divinæ majestatis tuæ: ut quotquot, ex hac altaris participatione, sacrosanctum Filii tui corpus ✚ et ✚ sanguinem sumpserimus, omni benedictione cœlesti et gratia repleamur. Per eumdem Christum Dominum nostrum. Amen.

We humbly beseech Thee, almighty God, to command that these our offerings be borne by the hands of Thy holy angel to Thine altar on high in the presence of Thy divine Majesty; that as many of us as shall receive the most sacred ✚ body and ✚ blood of Thy Son by partaking thereof from this altar may be filled with every heavenly blessing and grace: Through the same Christ our Lord. Amen.

Commemoration for the Dead

MEMENTO etiam, Domine, famulorum famularumque tuarum N. et N., qui nos præcesserunt cum signo fidei, et dormiunt in somno pacis.

IPSIS, Domine, et omnibus in Christo quiescentibus, locum refrigerii, lucis et pacis, ut indulgeas, deprecamur. Per eumdem Christum, etc. Amen.

NOBIS quoque peccatoribus famulis tuis, de multitudine miserationum tuarum sperantibus, partem aliquam, et societatem donare digneris, cum tuis sanctis apostolis et martyribus: cum Joanne, Stephano, Matthia, Barnaba, Ignatio, Alexandro, Marcellino, Petro, Felicitate, Perpetua, Agatha, Lucia, Agnete, Cæcilia, Anastasia, et omnibus sanctis tuis: intra quorum nos consortium, non æstimator meriti, sed veniæ, quæsumus, largitor admitte. Per Christum Dominum nostrum.

PER quem hæc omnia, Domine, semper bona creas, sancti✠ficas, vi-

BE MINDFUL also, O Lord, of Thy servants N. and N., who have gone before us with the sign of faith and who sleep the sleep of peace.

TO THESE, O Lord, and to all who rest in Christ, grant, we beseech Thee, a place of refreshment, light, and peace. Through the same Christ our Lord. Amen.

TO US sinners, also, Thy servants, who put our trust in the multitude of Thy mercies, vouchsafe to grant some part and fellowship with Thy holy apostles and martyrs: with John, Stephen, Matthias, Barnabas, Ignatius, Alexander, Marcellinus, Peter, Felicitas, Perpetua, Agatha, Lucy, Agnes, Cecilia, Anastasia, and with all Thy saints. Into their company do Thou, we beseech Thee, admit us, not weighing our merits, but freely pardoning our offences: through Christ our Lord.

BY WHOM, O Lord, Thou dost always create, sanctify ✠, quicken, ✠

vi-✝-ficas, bene-✝-dicis, et præstas nobis.

PER ip-✝-sum, et cum ip-✝-so, et in ip-✝-so, est tibi Deo Patri ✝ omnipotenti, in unitate Spiritus ✝ Sancti, omnis honor et gloria. Per omnia sæcula sæculorum. Amen.

bless, ✝ and bestow upon us all these good things.

THROUGH Him, ✝ and with Him, ✝ and in Him, ✝ is to Thee, God the Father ✝ almighty, in the unity of the Holy ✝ Ghost, all honor and glory. World without end. Amen.

The Pater Noster

PRÆCEPTIS salutaribus moniti, et divina institutione formati, audemus dicere:

ADMONISHED by salutary precepts, and following divine directions, we presume to say:

PATER noster, qui es in cœlis: sanctificetur nomen tuum: adveniat regnum tuum: fiat voluntas tua, sicut in cœlo, et in terra. Panem nostrum quotidianum da nobis hodie: et dimitte nobis debita nostra, sicut et nos dimittimus debitoribus nostris. Et ne nos inducas in tentationem.

R. Sed libera nos a malo.

V. Amen.

OUR Father, Who art in heaven, hallowed be Thy name; Thy kingdom come; Thy will be done on earth as it is in heaven; give us this day our daily bread; and forgive us our trespasses, as we forgive those who trespass against us; and lead us not into temptation.

R. But deliver us from evil.

V. Amen.

LIBERA nos, quæsumus, Domine, ab omnibus malis præteritis, præsentibus, et futuris: et intercedente beata et gloriosa semper virgine Dei genitrice Maria, cum beatis apostolis tuis Petro

DELIVER us, we beseech Thee, O Lord, from all evils, past, present, and to come: and by the intercession of the blessed and glorious Mary, ever a virgin, Mother of God, and of Thy holy apos-

et Paulo, atque Andrea, et omnibus sanctis ✛; da propitius pacem in diebus nostris: ut ✛ ope misericordiæ tuæ adjuti, et a peccato simus semper liberi, et ab omni perturbatione securi. Per eumdem Dominum nostrum Jesum Christum Filium tuum, qui tecum vivit et regnat in unitate Spiritus Sancti Deus. Per omnia sæcula sæculorum.

R. Amen.
V. Pax ✛ Domini sit ✛ semper vobis✛cum.
R. Et cum spiritu tuo.

Ħæc commixtio et consecratio corporis et sanguinis Domini nostri Jesu Christi, fiat accipientibus nobis in vitam æternam. Amen.

tles Peter and Paul, of Andrew, and of all the saints, ✛ graciously grant peace in our days, that through the help of Thy bountiful mercy we may always be free from sin and secure from all disturbance. Through the same Jesus Christ, Thy Son, our Lord, Who liveth and reigneth with Thee in the unity of the Holy Ghost, world without end.

R. Amen.
V. May the peace ✛ of the Lord ✛ be always ✛ with you.
R. And with Thy spirit.

May this commingling and consecrating of the body and blood of Our Lord Jesus Christ avail us who receive it unto life everlasting. Amen.

The Agnus Dei

Agnus Dei, qui tollis peccata mundi: miserere nobis.

Agnus Dei, qui tollis peccata mundi: miserere nobis.

Agnus Dei, qui tollis peccata mundi: dona nobis pacem.

Lamb of God, Who takest away the sins of the world: have mercy on us.

Lamb of God, Who takest away the sins of the world: have mercy on us.

Lamb of God, Who takest away the sins of the world: grant us peace.

DOMINE Jesu Christe, qui dixisti apostolis tuis: Pacem relinquo vobis,, pacem meam do vobis: ne respicias peccata mea, sed fidem Ecclesiæ tuæ: eamque secundum voluntatem tuam, pacificare et coadunare digneris: Qui vivis et regnas Deus, per omnia sæcula sæculorum. Amen.

DOMINE Jesu Christe, Fili Dei vivi, qui ex voluntate Patris, co-operante Spiritu Sancto, per mortem tuam mundum vivificasti: libera me per hoc sacrosanctum corpus et sanguinem tuum, ab omnibus iniquitatibus meis, et universis malis: et fac me tuis semper inhærere mandatis, et a te nunquam separari permittas: Qui cum eodem Deo Patre et Spiritu Sancto vivis et regnas Deus in sæcula sæculorum. Amen.

PERCEPTIO corporis tui, Domine Jesu Christe, quod ego indignus sumere præsumo, non mihi proveniat in judicium et condemnationem: sed pro tua pietate prosit mihi ad tutamentum

O LORD Jesus Christ, Who didst say to Thine apostles: Peace I leave you, My peace I give you: look not upon my sins, but upon the faith of Thy Church, and vouchsafe to grant her peace and unity according to Thy will: Who livest and reignest God, world without end. Amen.

O LORD Jesus Christ, Son of the living God, Who, according to the will of the Father, through the co-operation of the Holy Ghost, hast by Thy death given life to the world: deliver me by this Thy most sacred body and blood from all my iniquities, and from every evil; make me always cleave to Thy commandments, and never suffer me to be separated from Thee, Who with the same God, the Father and the Holy Ghost, livest and reignest God, world without end. Amen.

LET not the partaking of Thy body, O Lord Jesus Christ, which I, all unworthy, presume to receive, turn to my judgment and condemnation; but through Thy loving-kindness

mentis et corporis, et ad medelam percipiendam: qui vivis et regnas cum Deo Patre in unitate Spiritus Sancti Deus, per omnia sæcula sæculorum. Amen.

may it be to me a safeguard and remedy for soul and body; Who, with God the Father, in the unity of the Holy Ghost, livest and reignest, God: world without end. Amen.

At the Communion

PANEM cœlestem accipiam, et nomen Domini invocabo.

I WILL take the bread of heaven, and will call upon the name of the Lord.

DOMINE, non sum dignus, ut intres sub tectum meum: sed tantum dic verbo, et sanabitur anima mea.

LORD, I am not worthy that Thou shouldst enter under my roof; but only say the word, and my soul shall be healed.

CORPUS Domini nostri Jesu Christi custodiat animam meam in vitam æternam. Amen.

MAY the body of Our Lord Jesus Christ keep my soul unto life everlasting. Amen.

QUID retribuam Domino pro omnibus quæ retribuit mihi? Calicem salutaris accipiam, et nomen Domini invocabo. Laudans invocabo Dominum, et ab inimicis meis salvus ero.

WHAT shall I render unto the Lord for all the things that He hath rendered unto me? I will take the chalice of salvation and will call upon the name of the Lord. With high praises will I call upon the Lord, and I shall be saved from all mine enemies.

SANGUIS Domini nostri Jesu Christi custodiat animam meam in vitam æternam. Amen.

MAY the blood of Our Lord Jesus Christ keep my soul unto life everlasting. Amen.

QUOD ore sumpsimus, Domine, pura mente capiamus: et de munere temporali fiat nobis remedium sempiternum.

INTO a pure heart, O Lord, may we receive the heavenly food which has passed our lips; bestowed upon us in time, may it be the healing of our souls for eternity.

CORPUS tuum, Domine, quod sumpsi, et sanguis, quem potavi, adhæreat visceribus meis: et præsta, ut in me non remaneat scelerum macula, quem pura et sancta refecerunt sacramenta: Qui vivis et regnas in sæcula sæculorum. Amen.

MAY Thy body, O Lord, which I have received, and Thy blood which I have drunk, cleave to mine inmost parts: and do Thou grant that no stain of sin remain in me, whom pure and holy mysteries have refreshed: Who livest and reignest, world without end. Amen.

The Communion
(*Ps.* lxx)

DOMINE, memorabor justitiæ tuæ solius: Deus, docuisti me a juventute mea: et usque in senectam, et senium, Deus, ne derelinquas me.
V. Dominus vobiscum.
R. Et cum spiritu tuo.
S. Oremus.

O LORD, I will be mindful of Thy justice alone: Thou hast taught me, O God, from my youth, and unto old age and gray hairs, O God, forsake me not.
V. The Lord be with you.
R. And with thy spirit.
P. Let us pray.

The Post-Communion

QUÆSUMUS clementiam tuam, omnipotens Deus: ut per hujus virtutem sacramenti nos famulos tuos gratia tua confirmare digneris: ut in hora mortis no-

WE IMPLORE of Thy mercy, almighty God, that in virtue of this sacrament Thou wouldst vouchsafe to strengthen us, Thy servants, with Thy grace;

stræ non prævaleat contra nos adversarius; sed cum angelis tuis transitum habere mereamur ad vitam. Per.

so that at the hour of our death the enemy may not prevail against us, but we may be found worthy, in company with Thy holy angels, to enter into life everlasting.

V. Dominus vobiscum.
R. Et cum spiritu tuo.
V. Ite, missa est.
R. Deo gratias.

P. The Lord be with you.
R. And with thy spirit.
P. Go, the Mass is ended.
R. Thanks be to God.

PLACEAT tibi, Sancta Trinitas, obsequium servitutis meæ: et præsta ut sacrificium quód oculis tuæ majestatis indignus obtuli, tibi sit acceptabile, mihique, et omnibus, pro quibus illud obtuli, sit, te miserante, propitiabile. Per Christum Dominum nostrum. Amen.

MAY the lowly homage of my service be pleasing to Thee, O most holy Trinity: and do Thou grant that the sacrifice which I, all unworthy, have offered up in the sight of Thy majesty may be acceptable to Thee, and, because of Thy loving-kindness, may avail to atone to Thee for myself and for all those for whom I have offered it up. Through Christ our Lord. Amen.

The Blessing

BENEDICAT vos omnipotens Deus, Pater ✠, et Filius, et Spiritus Sanctus.
R. Amen.
S. Dominus vobiscum.
R. Et cum spiritu tuo.
S. Initium sancti Evangelii secundum Joannem.
R. Gloria tibi, Domine.

MAY almighty God, the Father ✠, and the Son, and the Holy Ghost, bless you.
R. Amen.
P. The Lord be with you.
R. And with thy spirit.
P. The beginning of the Gospel, according to St. John.
R. Glory be to Thee, O Lord.

The Last Gospel

IN PRINCIPIO erat Verbum, et Verbum erat apud Deum, et Deus erat Verbum. Hoc erat in principio apud Deum. Omnia per ipsum facta sunt, et sine ipso factum est nihil quod factum est. In ipso vita erat, et vita erat lux hominum; et lux in tenebris lucet, et tenebræ eam non comprehenderunt. Fuit homo missus a Deo, cui nomen erat Joannes. Hic venit in testimonium, ut testimonium perhiberet de lumine, ut omnes crederent per illum. Non erat ille lux, sed ut testimonium perhiberet de lumine. Erat lux vera, quæ illuminat omnem hominem venientem in hunc mundum. In mundo erat, et mundus per ipsum factus est, et mundus eum non cognovit. In propria venit, et sui eum non receperunt. Quotquot autem receperunt eum, dedit eis potestatem filios Dei fieri, his qui credunt in nomine ejus, qui non ex sanguinibus, neque ex voluntate carnis, neque ex voluntate viri, sed ex Deo nati sunt.

IN THE beginning was the Word, and the Word was with God, and the Word was God. The same was in the beginning with God. All things were made by Him, and without Him was made nothing that was made. In Him was life, and the life was the light of men: and the light shineth in darkness, and the darkness did not comprehend it. There was a man sent from God, whose name was John. This man came for a witness to give testimony of the light, that all men might believe through him. He was not the light, but was to give testimony of the light. That was the true light which enlighteneth every man that cometh into this world. He was in the world, and the world was made by Him, and the world knew Him not. He came unto His own, and His own received Him not. But as many as received Him, to them He gave power to become the sons of God: to them that believe in His name: who are born, not of blood, nor of the will of the flesh, nor of the will of man, but of God.

ET VERBUM CARO FACTUM EST, et habitavit in nobis: et vidimus gloriam ejus, gloriam quasi unigeniti a Patre, plenum gratiæ et veritatis.

R. Deo gratias.

AND THE WORD WAS MADE FLESH, and dwelt among us, and we saw His glory, the glory as of the only-begotten of the Father, full of grace and truth.

R. Thanks be to God.

Prayers after Low Mass

After the celebration of Low Mass the priest, kneeling at the altar steps, says with the people the prayers which follow. "Hail Mary," three times. Then

SALVE REGINA

HAIL, holy Queen, Mother of mercy, hail, our life, our sweetness, and our hope! To thee do we cry, poor banished children of Eve, to thee do we send up our sighs, mourning and weeping in this valley of tears. Turn then, most gracious advocate, thine eyes of mercy towards us; and after this our exile show unto us the blessed fruit of thy womb, Jesus. O clement, O loving, O sweet virgin Mary.

V. Pray for us, O holy mother of God.

R. That we may be made worthy of the promises of Christ.

Let us Pray

O GOD, our refuge and our strength, look down with favor upon Thy people who cry to Thee; and through the intercession of the glorious and immaculate Virgin Mary, Mother of God, of her spouse, blessed Joseph, of Thy holy apostles, Peter and Paul, and all the saints, mercifully and graciously hear the prayers which we pour forth to Thee for the conversion of sinners and for the liberty and exaltation of holy mother Church. Through the same Christ our Lord. Amen.

St. Michael, the archangel, defend us in battle, be our protection against the malice and snares of the devil. We humbly beseech God to command him, and do thou, O prince of the heavenly host, by the divine power thrust into hell Satan and the other evil spirits who roam through the world seeking the ruin of souls.   Amen.

Indulgence of 300 days.—Leo XIII, Sept. 25, 1888.

EJACULATION AFTER MASS

MOST sacred Heart of Jesus, have mercy on us! (Three times.)

Indulgence of seven years and seven quarantines.—Pius X, June 17, 1904. This indulgence holds good if the prayer is said alternately with the priest. (*The Raccolta.*)

The Eucharistic Rosary

A Devotion that is suitable at Holy Mass and at the Hour of Adoration

THE Holy Rosary, on account of the meditations on the mysteries in the life of Our Lord and the Blessed Virgin, which we make while reciting it, is one of the most useful devotions while assisting at Mass, or, in connection with our visits to the Blessed Sacrament and the Hour of Adoration.

The Eucharistic Rosary is especially recommended for this purpose, as it unites meditation on the sacred mysteries of the rosary with reflections on the life of Our Lord in the Holy Eucharist. The rosary is one of the most admirable and beneficial devotions practised in the Catholic Church.   Its method and design are stated to have been revealed to St. Dominic by the Blessed Virgin Mary, who admonished him to preach it with all the fervor of his soul as a singularly efficacious remedy for the over-throw of heresy and the extirpation of vice. And she said to him: "Thou shalt inform my people that it is a devotion most acceptable to my Son and to me." It is adapted alike to the learned and ignorant, to the cloister and the world, and to every capacity, the words being so easy that the most illiterate may learn them, and the mysteries so sublime as to afford matter of contemplation and entertainment to the highest intellects. No Christian could slight it without irreverence or neglect its frequent use without serious detriment to piety. The numerous indulgences attached to the recitation of the rosary make this form of devotion a powerful instrument for the relief of the poor souls in purgatory.

The whole rosary is composed of fifteen decades (the chaplet or ordinary beads containing five decades); each of the fifteen decades is recited in honor of a mystery of Our Lord's life and that of His blessed Mother, beginning with the *Annunciation*, or Christ's Incarnation, and ending with Mary's *Coronation* in Heaven.

A decade consists of one *Our Father*, ten *Hail Marys*, and a *Glory be to the Father*. While reciting a decade, let faith place before your mind the mystery honored, and pray that the virtue it particularly teaches may be impressed on your heart. It is a pious custom to recite a chaplet, that is, five decades of the beads, every day. If you persevere in this pious practice you will increase daily in love to Jesus Christ, and in imitation of the virtues of the Holy Family, Jesus, Mary and Joseph.

The Mysteries of the Holy Rosary

THE FRUIT OF EACH MYSTERY

Joyful Mysteries — Spirit of Holy Joy

1. — Annunciation	Humility.
2. — Visitation	Fraternal charity.

3. — Nativity	Spirit of poverty; or **detachment** from temporal goods.
4. — Presentation	Obedience and purity.
5. — Jesus with the Doctors in the Temple.	Love of Jesus and of His holy services; or fidelity and devotedness to one's duties.

Sorrowful Mysteries — Spirit of Compassion, Contrition, and Reparation

1. — Agony	Fervor in prayer and sorrow for sin.
2. — Scourging	Penance, and especially mortification of the senses.
3. — Crowning with Thorns	Moral courage, and love of humiliations.
4. — Carriage of the Cross	Patience.
5. — Crucifixion	Self-sacrifice for God and our neighbor, forgiveness of injuries.

Glorious Mysteries — Spirit of Adoration and Faith

1. — Resurrection	Faith, hope, and charity.
2. — Ascension	Confidence in God and desire of heaven.
3. — Descent of the Holy Ghost	The gifts of the Holy Spirit; love of God and zeal for souls.
4. — Assumption	Filial devotion to Mary.
5. — Coronation of the B. V. M.	Perseverance in holiness unto a happy death will merit a crown of eternal glory.

The Mysteries of the Rosary
as applied to
THE MYSTERIES OF THE ALTAR
IN
The Eucharistic Rosary
OR
The Recitation of the Holy Rosary in the Presence of the Blessed Sacrament

THE JOYFUL MYSTERIES

THE FIRST JOYFUL MYSTERY

The Annunciation

O JESUS, born of Thy Father from all eternity; filled with an incomprehensible love for men, Thou didst become man in the womb of the Blessed Virgin Mary through the operation of the Holy Ghost, humbling Thyself to such a degree as to take the form of a servant. The same charity hath prompted Thee to perpetuate, in the Eucharist, this mystery of annihilation and love, even to improve on it by becoming the food of our souls.

Divine Jesus, we adore Thee in these unfathomable debasements, and we beg of Thee, through the intercession of Thy holy Mother, a deep and heartfelt humility.

THE SECOND JOYFUL MYSTERY

The Visitation

DIVINE Saviour, from the womb of Mary, wherein Thou didst become incarnate, Thou breathest forth sanctity into John the Baptist and upon the whole house of Elizabeth. From the Host wherein Thou dwellest, Thou spreadest all over the world the influence of Thy grace and Thy love throughout the whole Church.

O divine Jesus, full of love and kindness, we adore Thee, and we beg of Thee, through the intercession of Thy holy Mother, perfect charity toward our neighbors.

THE THIRD JOYFUL MYSTERY

The Nativity of Our Lord

O KING of kings! poor indeed, yet most lovely in the crib of Bethlehem, Thou callest the simple and the poor to be Thy first adorers: poorer and no less amiable to the eyes of faith in the sacrament of Thy love, Thou art still delighted to see around Thy person the humble and the little.

O Jesus, in Thy destitution we adore Thee, to Whom belong all the treasures of the Godhead, and we beg of Thee, through the intercession of Thy holy Mother, detachment from the goods of this world.

THE FOURTH JOYFUL MYSTERY

The Presentation of Our Lord in the Temple

LAMB of God, Who takest away the sins of the world, Thou offerest Thyself with perfect obedience and love to Thy Father, through the hands of the high-priest, as the Victim that is to be immolated on the cross; every day also Thou offerest Thyself upon the altar by the hands of the priest, with the same obedience and love as our Victim always sacrificed and always living.

O sweet Victim, we adore Thee and we beg of Thee, through the intercession of Thy holy Mother, the spirit of obedience and sacrifice.

THE FIFTH JOYFUL MYSTERY

The Finding of Our Lord in the Temple

O JESUS, Thou withdrawest and leavest Mary and Joseph in tears to do the work of Thy Father; but Thou fillest them with joy when they find Thee in the midst of the Doctors amazed at Thy knowledge and wisdom. Veiled in the Eucharist, Thou impartest there divine teachings, and Thou fillest with joy those who seek Thee with their whole heart.

O hidden God! we adore Thee, and we beg of Thee, through the intercession of Thy holy Mother, the grace of seeking Thee with a lively and persevering faith in the sacrament of Thy love.

THE SORROWFUL MYSTERIES

THE FIRST SORROWFUL MYSTERY

The Agony of Our Lord in the Garden of Olives

DIVINE Saviour, under the weight of sorrow and sadness caused by our sins, Thou fallest, bathed in a sweat of blood, and Thou endurest a mortal agony. In the Blessed Sacrament, also, Thou art still more humbled and annihilated on account of our sins.

We adore Thee and we compassionate Thy agony of suffering in the Garden of Gethsemani, as well as Thy agony of humiliation in the Eucharist, and we beg of Thee, through the intercession of Thy holy Mother, a heartfelt sorrow for our sins.

THE SECOND SORROWFUL MYSTERY

The Flagellation

O GOOD Jesus! scourged and covered with wounds, the sins committed by men against the holy virtue of purity thus torture Thy innocent flesh; and in the Blessed Sacrament impure hearts insult Thee by their sacrilegious communions.

O Thou bloody Victim, scourged at the pillar, patient Victim abused in the sacrament, we adore Thee and we beg of Thee, through the intercession of Thy holy Mother, the grace of mortifying our senses.

THE THIRD SORROWFUL MYSTERY

The Crowning with Thorns

O KING of glory! crowned with thorns and proclaimed in derision king of the Jews by brutal soldiers who ignominiously spit upon Thy adorable face, Thou fallest a victim to the sins committed by pride; in the Blessed Sacrament also Thou bearest a crown of ignominy made up of the many acts of irreverence, contempt, hypocrisy, and vanity committed by Christians in Thy sanctuary.

O loving King! overwhelmed with insults both in Thy passion and in the sacred Host, we adore Thee and we beg of Thee, through the intercession of Thy holy Mother, the grace of mortifying our self-love.

THE FOURTH SORROWFUL MYSTERY

The Carrying of the Cross

CURSES, outrages, ill-treatments, anguish of heart, sufferings of all kinds, nothing can, O dear Redeemer, alter the mildness and patience with which Thou carriest Thy heavy cross; with like sweetness and patience dost Thou bear in the long course of ages, doubts, want of confidence, murmurs, insults, discouragement on the part of Thy children

O Jesus! we adore Thee carrying with love the cross prepared for Thee by Thy Father, and we beg of Thee, through the intercession of Thy holy Mother, patience in the trials of this life.

THE FIFTH SORROWFUL MYSTERY

The Crucifixion and Death of Our Lord

O GOOD and merciful Saviour! Thy love, more than iron nails, keeps Thee riveted to the cross whereon Thou atonest for our sins in the midst of unspeakable torments; we find Thee also riveted by the same love in the Sacrament of the Altar, continuing Thy sacrifice to the end of ages in order to apply to us the fruits thereof.

Sweet Lamb, perpetually immolated for us, we adore Thee, and we beg of Thee, through the intercession of Thy holy Mother, such a hatred of sin as will make us prefer the death of the body to the staining of the soul.

THE GLORIOUS MYSTERIES

THE FIRST GLORIOUS MYSTERY

The Resurrection of Our Lord

O CHRIST Jesus! Thou comest forth glorious from the tomb, victorious over all infernal powers; henceforth sufferings and death have lost their empire over Thy glorious humanity. What a consolation for us to know that, though confined to the humble condition of Thy sacrament, Thou art in full possession of the life, joy, and glory of Thy resurrection!

We adore Thee, O immortal King of ages, and we beg of Thee, through the intercession of Thy holy Mother, a lively and loving faith in Thy real and lifegiving presence in the Blessed Sacrament.

THE SECOND GLORIOUS MYSTERY

The Ascension

O DIVINE Saviour! ·Thy triumph in this mystery has reached its perfection! By raising Thyself up to heaven through Thy own power, Thou hast taken possession of Thy Kingdom, and Thou art seated at the right hand of Thy Father to be forever the joy of the angels and saints. Every day also without quitting Thy throne Thou comest upon our altars, under the form of bread, to bring us a foretaste of the heavenly beatitude.

O Thou, the delight of pure souls, we adore Thee and we beg of Thee, through the intercession of Thy holy Mother, an ardent desire of possessing Thee here below under the eucharistic veils, and to possess Thee in heaven in the splendor of Thy glory.

THE THIRD GLORIOUS MYSTERY

The Coming Down of the Holy Ghost upon the Apostles

O JESUS, scarcely hadst Thou entered into Thy glory at the right hand of Thy Father, when Thou didst show Thy munificence by sending forth the Holy Spirit with His many and various gifts to Thy growing Church. From the Eucharist, as if from another heaven, wherein Thou hast set up Thy throne of love, Thou impartest to souls the spirit of life and strength, and Thou kindlest in them the fire of Thy divine charity.

O Jesus, King in heaven, King also in the Eucharist, we adore Thee and we beg of Thee, through the intercession of Thy holy Mother, fidelity to grace in order to reap all the fruits produced in the souls of men by the gifts of the Holy Ghost.

THE FOURTH GLORIOUS MYSTERY

The Death and Assumption of Mary

O JESUS, no longer canst Thou leave here below Thy blessed Mother; already she heareth Thy voice calling her, and amid the transports of an ineffable communion, love taketh away her soul from the land of exile. But her virginal body, like that of her divine Son, must not know corruption; Thou raisest her from the dead, and, brilliant as the sun, she soars on angels' wings to the seat of eternal glory.

O Jesus, our resurrection and our life, we adore Thee and we pray that, through the intercession of Thy holy Mother, we may die in the arms of her who is also our own Mother, after having received in a fervent communion the pledge of our glorious resurrection.

THE FIFTH GLORIOUS MYSTERY

The Crowning of Mary in Heaven

DIVINE Son of Mary, to make Thy holy Mother partaker of Thy own glory, Thou hast crowned her queen of heaven and earth and appointed her our advocate and the living channel of Thy graces. From the Eucharist not less than from heaven, Thou willest that every grace shall reach us through her maternal hands.

O Jesus, we adore Thee in Thy unspeakable glory, of which Thou hast made Thy Mother partake with Thee, and we beg of Thee, through her intercession, a great confidence in her powerful protection and great earnestness in imitating her virtues; in particular her purity, humility, and fidelity to grace.

Devotions for Confession

Before Confession

CALL to mind that this confession may be the last of your life. Therefore, prepare yourself for it as if you were lying sick upon your deathbed, and already at the brink of the grave. Ask God to give you the grace to make a good examination of conscience, the light to see your sins clearly, and the strength to make a sincere confession and to amend your life.

Prayer

MOST merciful God, Father in heaven, relying on Thy goodness and mercy, I come to Thee with filial confidence to confess my sins and to implore Thy forgiveness. Thou wilt not despise a contrite and humble heart. Bless me and receive me again into Thy favor; I acknowledge that I have been most ungrateful to Thee, but I sincerely repent and detest the wrong I have done, and I desire henceforth to walk in the way of perfection in accordance with Thy holy will.

O Jesus, my Saviour, my good Shepherd, I have strayed far from the path that Thou hast marked out for me; I did not follow in Thy footsteps; I wandered into forbidden places. Repentant and sorrowful, I beg to be admitted again into the fold of Thy faithful followers. I want to confess my sins with the same sincerity as I should wish to do at the moment of my death. My Jesus, I look to Thee with confidence for the grace to examine my conscience well.

O Holy Spirit come in Thy mercy; enlighten my mind and strengthen my will that I may know my sins, humbly confess them, and sincerely amend my life.

Mary, my Mother, immaculate Spouse of the Holy Ghost, refuge of sinners, assist me by thy intercession.

Holy angels and saints of God, pray for me. Amen.

Examination of Conscience

BEGIN by examining yourself on your last confession: Whether a grievous sin was forgotten through want of proper examination, or concealed or disguised through shame. Whether you confessed without a true sorrow and a firm purpose of amendment. Whether you have repaired evil done to your neighbor. Whether the penance was performed without voluntary distractions. Whether you have neglected your confessor's counsel, and fallen at once into habitual sins.

Then examine yourself on the Ten Commandments; the Commandments of the Church; the Seven Capital Sins; the duties of your state of life; and your ruling passion. Calmly recall the different occasions of sin which have fallen in your way, or to which your state and condition in life expose you; the places you have frequented; the persons with whom you have associated. Do not neglect to consider the circumstances which alter the grievousness of the sin, nor the various ways in which we become accessory to the sins of others.

THE TEN COMMANDMENTS OF GOD

1. I AM the Lord thy God, Who brought thee out of the land of Egypt, and out of the house of bondage. Thou shalt not have strange gods before Me. Thou shalt not make to thyself a graven thing, nor the likeness of any thing that is in heaven above, or in the earth beneath, nor of those things that are in the waters under the earth. Thou shalt not adore them, nor serve them.

2. Thou shalt not take the name of the Lord thy God in vain; for the Lord will not hold him guiltless that shall take the name of the Lord his God in vain.

3. Remember that thou keep holy the Sabbath day.

4. Honor thy father and thy mother, that thou mayest be long-lived upon the land which the Lord thy God will give thee.

5. Thou shalt not kill.

6. Thou shalt not commit adultery.

7. Thou shalt not steal.

8. Thou shalt not bear false witness against thy neighbor.

9. Thou shalt not covet thy neighbor's wife.

10. Thou shalt not covet thy neighbor's goods.

THE SIX COMMANDMENTS OF THE CHURCH

1. To hear Mass on Sundays, and holydays of obligation.

2. To fast and abstain on the days appointed.

3. To confess at least once a year.

4. To receive Holy Eucharist during the Easter time.

5. To contribute to the support of our pastors.

6. Not to marry persons who are not Catholics, or who are related to us within the third degree of kindred, nor privately without witnesses, nor to solemnize marriage at forbidden times.

THE SEVEN DEADLY SINS, AND THE OPPOSITE VIRTUES

1. Pride.......................... Humility.
2. Covetousness................... Liberality.
3. Lust........................... Chastity.
4. Anger.......,................... Meekness.
5. Gluttony....................... Temperance.
6. Envy........................... Brotherly love.
7. Sloth.......................... Diligence.

THE FOUR SINS WHICH CRY TO HEAVEN FOR VENGEANCE

1. Wilful murder. 2. The sin of Sodom. 3. Oppression of the poor. 4. Defrauding the laborer of his wages.

NINE WAYS OF BEING ACCESSARY TO ANOTHER'S SIN

1. By counsel. 2. By command. 3. By consent. 4. By provocation. 5. By praise or flattery. 6. By concealment. 7. By partaking. 8. By silence. 9. By defense of the ill done.

THE SEVEN SPIRITUAL WORKS OF MERCY

1. To admonish sinners. 2. To instruct the ignorant. 3. To counsel the doubtful. 4. To comfort the sorrowful. 5. To bear wrongs patiently. 6. To forgive all injuries. 7. To pray for the living and the dead.

THE SEVEN CORPORAL WORKS OF MERCY

1. To feed the hungry. 2. To give drink to the thirsty. 3. To clothe the naked. 4. To visit and ransom the captives. 5. To harbor the harborless. 6. To visit the sick. 7. To bury the dead.

PRELIMINARY EXAMINATION

WHEN did you make your last confession? Did you take sufficient pains to awaken contrition?

Did you omit to confess a mortal sin, either intentionally or through forgetfulness?

Did you intentionally neglect to say the penance which was imposed on you, or were you so careless as to forget it?

Have you carried out the resolutions you made at your last confession or have you paid no heed at all to them?

EXAMINATION ON THE TEN COMMANDMENTS OF GOD

I. HAVE you doubted in matters of faith? Murmured against God at your adversity or at the prosperity of others? Despaired of His mercy?

Have you believed in fortune-tellers or consulted them?

Have you gone to places of worship belonging to other denominations?

Have you recommended yourself daily to God? Neglected your morning or night prayers? Omitted religious duties or practices through motives of human respect?

Have you rashly presumed upon God's forbearance in order to commit sin?

Have you read books, papers, and periodicals of anti-Catholic or atheistic tendency? Made use of superstitious practices? Spoken with levity or irreverence of priests, Religious, or sacred objects?

II. Have you taken the name of God in vain? Profaned anything relating to religion?

Have you sworn falsely, rashly, or in slight and trivial matters? Cursed yourself or others, or any creature? Angered others so as to make them swear, or blaspheme God?

III. Have you kept holy the Lord's Day, and all other days commanded to be kept holy? Bought or sold things, not of necessity, on that day? Done or commanded some servile work not of necessity? Missed Mass or been wilfully distracted during Mass? Talked, gazed, or laughed in the church? Profaned the day by dancing, drinking, gambling, or in other ways?

IV. Have you honored your parents, superiors, and masters, according to your just duty? Deceived them? Disobeyed them?

Have you failed in due reverence to aged persons?

V. Have you procured, desired, or hastened the death of any one? Borne hatred? Oppressed any one? Desired revenge? Not forgiven injuries? Refused to speak

to others? Used provoking language? Injured others?
Caused enmity between others?

VI and IX. Have you been guilty of lascivious dressing?
Been in lewd company? Read immodest books? Been
guilty of unchaste songs, discourses, words, or actions?
Wilfully entertained impure thoughts or desires?

VII. Have you been guilty of stealing, or of deceit in
buying, or selling, in regard to wares, prices, weights,
or measures? Have you wilfully damaged another man's
goods, or negligently spoiled them?

VIII. Have you borne false witness? Called injurious
names? Disclosed another's sins? Flattered others?
Judged rashly?

X. Have you coveted unjustly anything that belongs to
another?

EXAMINATION ON THE PRECEPTS OF THE CHURCH

HAVE you gone to confession at least once a year?
Received holy communion during Easter-time?

Have you violated the fasts of the Church, or eaten
flesh-meat on prohibited days?

Have you sinned against any other commandment of
the Church?

Examine yourself also in regard to the Seven Capital
Sins and the nine ways of being accessary to another's
sin.

After the Examination

HAVING discovered the sins of which you have been
guilty, together with their number, enormity, or such
circumstances as may change their nature, you should endeavor to excite in yourself a *heartfelt sorrow* for having
committed them, and a sincere detestation of them. This
being the most essential of all the dispositions requisite
for a good confession, with what humility, fervor, and
perseverance should you not importune Him Who holds
the hearts of men in His hands to grant it to you!

CONSIDERATIONS TO EXCITE IN OUR HEART TRUE CONTRITION FOR OUR SINS

CONSIDER Who He is, and how good and gracious He is to you, Whom you have so often and so deeply offended by these sins. He made you — He made you for Himself, to know, love, and serve Him, and to be happy with Him forever. He redeemed you by His blood. He has borne with you and waited for you so long. He it is Who has called you and moved you to repentance. Why have you thus sinned against Him? Why have you been so ungrateful? What more could He do for you? Oh, be ashamed, and mourn, and despise yourself, because you have sinned against your Maker and your Redeemer, Whom you ought to love above all things!

Consider the consequences of even one mortal sin. By it you lose the grace of God. You destroy peace of conscience; you forfeit the felicity of heaven, for which you were created and redeemed; and you prepare for yourself eternal punishment. If we grieve for the loss of temporal and earthly things, how much more should we grieve for having deliberately exposed ourselves to the loss of those which are eternal and heavenly!

Consider how great is the love of God for you, if only from this, that He hath so long waited for you, and spared you, when He might have so justly cast you into hell. Behold Him fastened to the cross for love of you! Behold Him pouring forth His precious blood as a fountain to cleanse you from your sins! Hear Him saying, "I thirst," — "I thirst with an ardent desire for your salvation!" Behold Him stretching out His arms to embrace you, and waiting until you should come to yourself and turn unto Him, and throw yourself before Him, and say, "Father, I have sinned against heaven and before Thee, and am no more worthy to be called Thy son." Let these considerations touch your heart with love for Him Who so loves you, and love will beget true contrition, most acceptable to God.

Say an *Our Father*, a *Hail Mary*, and a *Glory* to obtain true contrition.   Then add the

INVOCATIONS

IN THY Conception, O Virgin Mary, thou wast immaculate!   Pray for us to the Father, Whose Son Jesus, conceived in Thy womb by the Holy Ghost, thou didst bring forth!

Indulgence of 100 days, each time. — Pius VI, Nov. 21, 1793.

Holy Virgin, Mary immaculate, Mother of God and our Mother, speak thou for us to the Heart of Jesus, Who is thy Son and our Brother!

Indulgence of 100 days, once a day. — Leo XIII, Dec. 20, 1890.

An Act of Contrition

Recite very attentively one of the following acts.

I

ETERNAL Father!   I am heartily sorry for having offended Thee, and I detest all my sins, because I dread the loss of heaven and the pains of hell, but most of all because they displease Thee, my God, Who art all-good and deserving of all my love.   I firmly resolve, with the help of Thy grace, to confess my sins, to do penance, and to amend my life.

II

O MY God, I am truly sorry that I have sinned, because Thou art infinitely good and sin displeases Thee. I promise not to offend Thee again. I love Thee above all things with my whole heart and soul, and I will endeavor to please Thee in everything.

III

O GOD! infinitely worthy of all love, my Creator, my Saviour, my Benefactor, why did I ever offend Thee? Lord, have mercy on me. How ungrateful I have been to Thee, Who art infinitely good! Father, forgive me. I love Thee, my God, with my whole heart and above all things; I hate sin because it is offensive to Thy goodness. I am truly sorry for having offended Thee, and with Thy help I will shun the occasions of sin and seek to please Thee in all things.

IV

HEAVENLY Father! I am heartily sorry for having offended Thee, and I detest my sins above every other evil, because they displease Thee, my God, Who for Thy infinite goodness art so deserving of all my love; and I firmly resolve, with the aid of Thy holy grace, never more to offend Thee, and to amend my life.

V

O MY God! confessing my guilt and with a contrite heart I kneel before Thee and implore Thee to look upon me according to the multitude of Thy mercies. I detest and am heartily sorry for all my sins, not only because I dread the loss of heaven and the pain of hell, but also and principally because by them I have offended Thee, Who art infinitely good and deserving of all my love. I firmly resolve, with the help of Thy grace, to confess my sins and to amend my life. I acknowledge Thee, O God, to be the Supreme Good, and I love Thee with all my heart. Be merciful to me, a poor sinner. I beseech Thee, by the passion and death of Jesus Christ, Thy Son, to forgive me my sins. Amen.

APPROACH the confessional with the same recollectedness and reverence as would fill your heart if Christ our Lord were seated there in person ready to hear your confession. The priest is really the representative of Christ.

When you kneel down, say: *Bless me, Father, for I have sinned*, and then begin the *Confiteor*, proceeding as far as *Through my fault*, etc.

THE CONFITEOR

I CONFESS to Almighty God, to Blessed Mary, ever Virgin, to blessed Michael the archangel, to blessed John the Baptist, to the holy apostles Peter and Paul, and to all the saints, that I have sinned exceedingly in thought, word, and deed, through my fault, through my fault, through my most grievous fault. . . .

Then tell when you made your last confession and begin the avowal of your sins. Confess all your sins with a contrite and humble heart, and conclude thus.

For these and all the sins of my past life, especially my sins of (*naming some grievous sin*), I am heartily sorry, beg pardon of God, and absolution of you, my Father; *then finish the Confiteor.*

. . . Therefore, I beseech the blessed Mary, ever Virgin, blessed Michael the archangel, blessed John the Baptist, the holy apostles Peter and Paul, and all the saints, to pray to the Lord our God for me.

Listen then with humility and docility to the instruction of your confessor, and during this time avoid all recurrence as to the confession itself; remembering that sins forgotten after a serious examination are really comprised in the absolution. Accept with submission the penance imposed, and if any obstacle that you foresee will prevent your accomplishing it, state this respectfully.

While the priest pronounces the words of absolution, endeavor to excite an act of perfect contrition. Should your spiritual Father deem it proper to defer absolution, acknowledge your unworthiness, and do not murmur. Leave the confessional resolved to use every effort, by an amendment of life and sincere repentance, to obtain God's pardon, which His minister will ratify.

Thanksgiving after Confession

Eternal Father! I thank Thee, I bless Thee, for Thy goodness and mercy. Thou hast had compassion on me, although in my folly I had wandered far away from Thee and offended Thee most grievously. With fatherly love Thou hast received me anew after so many relapses into sin and forgiven me my offenses through the holy sacrament of penance. Blessed forever, O my God, be Thy loving-kindness, Thy in-

·finite mercy! Never again will I grieve Thee by ingratitude, by disobedience to Thy holy will. All that I am, all that I have, all that I do shall be consecrated to Thy service and Thy glory.

"Heart of Jesus, I confide in Thee."
Indulgence of 300 days. — Pius X, June 27, 1906.

"Jesus, my God, I love Thee above all things."
Indulgence of 50 days, each time. — Pius IX, May 7, 1854.

O DIVINE Spirit! penetrate my soul with true horror and loathing of sin. Grant that I may be more exact in the fulfilment of all my duties, and strengthen me by Thy grace, that I may not again yield to temptation.

"Sweet heart of Mary, be my salvation."
Indulgence of 300 days, each time. — Pius IX, Sept. 30, 1852.

"O Mary, conceived without sin, pray for us, who have recourse to Thee."
Indulgence of 100 days, once a day. — Leo XIII, March 15, 1884.

"My Queen! My Mother! Remember I am thine own; keep me, guard me, as thy property and possession."
Indulgence of 40 days, each time, when tempted. — Pius IX, Aug, 5, 1851.

"Mary, our hope, have pity on us!"
Indulgence of 300 days. — Pius X, Jan. 8, 1906.

In conclusion, reflect on the following verses from the. Psalms:

"**B**LESSED are they whose iniquities are forgiven, and whose sins are covered."

"Blessed are the undefiled in the way, who walk in the law of the Lord."

"I cried with my whole heart, hear me, O Lord. I will seek Thy justifications."

"I cried unto Thee, save me: that I may keep Thy commandments."

"I will praise Thee, because Thou hast heard me, and art become my salvation."

"O praise the Lord, for He is good and His mercy endureth forever."

"The Lord is my helper; I will not fear what man can do unto me."

"I will please the Lord in the land of the living."

"The perils of hell have found me: O Lord, deliver my soul."

"I have acknowledged my sin unto Thee, and mine iniquity I have not concealed."

"I said, I will confess against myself mine iniquity with the Lord, and Thou hast forgiven the wickedness of my sin."

"Thou art my refuge from the trouble which hath encompassed me; my joy. Deliver me from them that surround me."

"**B**LESS the Lord, O my soul, and let all that is within me, bless His holy name. Bless the Lord, O my soul, and never forget all He hath done for thee."

"Who forgiveth all thy iniquities; Who healeth all thy diseases."

"Who redeemeth thy life from destruction; Who crowneth thee with mercy and compassion."

"The Lord is compassionate and merciful; long suffering and plenteous in mercy."

"He will not always be angry; nor will He threaten forever."

"He hath not dealt with us according to our sins; nor rewarded us according to our iniquities."

"AS FAR as the east is from the west, so far hath He removed our iniquities from us."

"As a father hath compassion on his children, so hath the Lord compassion on them that fear Him."

"For He knoweth our frame; He remembereth that we are dust."

"Bless the Lord, all ye His angels; bless the Lord all ye His hosts."

"Bless the Lord all His works; in every place of His dominion, O my soul, bless thou the Lord."

Holy Communion

Holy Mass for Communion Days

In Honor of the Blessed Sacrament

Preparation for and Thanksgiving after Holy Communion

THE following prayers are so arranged as to occupy your time usefully whenever you assist at Mass in preparation for holy communion. Remember, however, that you are not in any way bound to say all these prayers; nor, indeed, any of them. In place of them, you may choose other prayers from this book, or substitute such acts of faith, hope, charity, adoration, contrition, reparation, thanksgiving, and supplication, as are found under the section *Devotions for Holy Communion* immediately following this *Method of Hearing Mass for Communion Days.* If you can occupy a part or the whole of the time in meditating or reflecting on the Holy Eucharist in connection with the passion and death of Our Lord; on the Last Supper and the wonderful love and kindness of Jesus, our Saviour, in instituting this marvelous sacrament; and in exciting in your heart holy desires and pious affections together with good resolutions, so much the better. Otherwise you will find suitable occupation of mind in the following prayers. Do not aim at too great accuracy in saying the prayers at the time marked in the Mass, as this might tend only to disturb and distract you. When you feel inspired to do so, discard the book, speak to God from your heart, converse with Him freely and familiarly with the simplicity and confidence with which a child addresses a good and kind father.

358

Offering of Intentions for Mass and Communion

Preparatory Prayer

O HOLY Tabernacle! Thou dost enclose the precious Bread of heaven, the food of angels, the eucharistic manna of the soul. My heart longs and sighs for Thee, O good and gentle Jesus, Who art hidden in the Blessed Sacrament! Thou art my Lord, my God, and my all, and Thou wilt deign to come to me this day in holy communion. I adore Thee profoundly, with the angels who surround Thy altar-throne of mercy and compassion; I bless Thee; I thank Thee for all the graces I have received through the Holy Eucharist; I am sorry for having offended Thee; I love Thee now with all my heart. I wish to offer this holy communion in reparation for all the offenses that have been committed against Thee in the sacrament of Thy love, and especially in atonement for my own sins and negligences. I have also some other particular intentions and petitions which I now recommend to Thy sacred Heart (mention them), and I shall approach the Holy Table to-day with the greatest confidence that Thou, O Lord, wilt grant me all my requests.

EJACULATIONS

MAY the Heart of Jesus in the Most Blessed Sacrament be praised, adored, and loved with grateful affection, at every moment, in all the tabernacles of the world, even to the end of time.   Amen.

Indulgence of 100 days, once a day. — Pius IX, Feb. 29, 1868.

HEART of Jesus, burning with love for us, inflame our hearts with love of Thee!

Indulgence of 100 days, once a day. — Leo XIII, June 16, 1893.

HOLY Mary, Mother of God, St. John, evangelist and beloved disciple of Our Lord, St. Thomas Aquinas, St. Alphonsus Liguori, St. Paschal Baylon, St. Francis Xavier, St. Aloysius, St. Juliana, St. Margaret Mary Alacoque, St. Clara, St. Gertrude, St. Mechtildis!   Ye great saints and lovers of Jesus in the sacrament of His love, pray for me that I may receive the Lord most worthily in holy communion; that I may love Him more and more; that I may follow His example in the practice of every virtue and in the faithful discharge of all my duties; that I may persevere in holiness to the end of my life and attain to eternal salvation.

At the Beginning of Mass

I BELIEVE in Thee, O Lord Jesus Christ, because Thou art Truth itself, and Thou hast said: "My flesh is meat indeed; and My blood is drink indeed."   I hope in Thee, O infinite Mercy, because in Thy goodness toward us Thou hast promised that "whosoever shall eat of this bread shall live forever." I love Thee, O eternal Goodness, above all things, with that love "which is diffused in our hearts by the Holy Spirit, Who is given to us;" and therefore I grieve with my whole heart for the sins I have committed, and I detest them, with the resolution of not sinning again. "A contrite and humble heart, O God, Thou wilt not despise."

O my God, I wish to assist at the holy sacrifice of the Mass which is about to begin, with all possible attention and devotion, for I believe it is the very same sacrifice, offered now in an unbloody manner, which was once offered for us on Calvary. In union with the intention of the priest at the altar, I offer this holy sacrifice to Thee as an act of *adoration, thanksgiving, reparation,* and *prayer;* particularly to obtain the grace of a good communion, and a complete transformation of myself into the likeness of Jesus Christ.

At the Confiteor and Kyrie

O MY God, give me the purity and holiness necessary to approach the Holy Table in a most worthy and profitable manner. Lord, I am a poor sinner. I am heartily sorry for all the sins of my life, because by them I have offended Thee, Who art infinitely good and worthy of all love. *Kyrie eleison!* Have mercy on me, and, according to the multitude of Thy mercies, blot out my iniquities.

At the Gloria in Excelsis

GLORY and thanks be to Thee, O God, for having worked such wonders for us, Thy creatures, born in sin. I praise, O Lord, Thy goodness; I bless Thy holy name; I adore Thy greatness and power; I beg of Thee to infuse into my heart that peace and joy which Thou didst come on earth to spread amongst men. Give me strength of will against my evil tendencies; destroy my bad habits; help me to do Thy will and thus to become a saint.

At the Collects

O GOD, Who, under a wonderful sacrament, hast left us a memorial of Thy passion, grant us Thy grace, we beseech Thee, so to venerate the sacred mysteries of Thy body and blood, that we may ever feel within us the fruit of Thy redemption. Who livest and reignest world without end. Amen.

Give me daily more and more, O my God, Thy grace and Thy love, that I may keep my eyes fixed upon eternal things and persevere in Thy service, until with the saints and angels I may praise and glorify Thee forever in heaven. Amen.

At the Epistle

THE saints and prophets of the Old Law desired to see the things that I see, and did not see them. How ardently Abraham and Moses, and David and Daniel and Elias, desired the coming of

the world's redeemer. They saw the types and
figures; I see the reality. Moses saw the manna
and the paschal lamb; I see the Bread from
heaven and the Lamb of God Who takes away
the sins of the world. The heart of David panted
for Thee, my God, as the hart for the water-
brooks, and Daniel was called "a man of desires."
Oh, that I could desire Thee as they did! What
a shame it would be if their desires were more
fervent than my thanksgiving now for the favors
and graces that I have received through the incarnation and passion of Jesus, and especially
through the Holy Eucharist. I offer Thee all
their desires, and with David I cry out: "What
have I in heaven but Thee? And, besides Thee,
what do I desire upon earth? Thou art the God
of my heart, and my portion forever."

At the Gospel

Promise God that you will always listen with great reverence to His word, saying:

MAY Thy word, O my God, be always as sweet
music to my ears, and as honey to my lips.
To whom shall I listen but to Thee, Who hast the
words of eternal life. The words of men are as
chaff scattered by the wind, but Thy words endure
forever. These are Thy words, O Lord: "Labor
not for the meat that perisheth, but for that which
endureth unto life everlasting." "The bread of
God is that which cometh down from heaven."

"I am the Bread of life; he that cometh to Me shall not hunger, and he that believeth in Me shall not thirst forever." "He that eateth My flesh and drinketh My blood hath everlasting life, and I will raise him up at the Last Day."

O Sacrament most holy! O Sacrament divine,
All praise and all thanksgiving be every moment thine!

Indulgence of 100 days, once a day. — Pius VI, May 24, 1776.

At the Credo

An Act of Faith, Adoration, Hope, and Love

O MY God, I firmly believe that Thou art really, truly, and substantially present, as God and man, with soul and body, with flesh and blood, in the most holy Sacrament of the Altar. I adore Thee beneath the sacramental veil, which Thou hast mercifully chosen in order to approach us. I *believe* that Thou dwellest on our altars to be the food of our souls, our sacrifice to the infinite majesty of the heavenly Father, our light in darkness, our strength in temptation, our consolation in affliction, our master and model in the school of perfection, our friend in every need. Thou art our hope and our salvation. O Sacred Heart of Jesus, I trust in Thee. I *hope* in that boundless love, which keeps Thee a prisoner in the tabernacle. "No one hath hoped in the Lord and been put to shame." By thy goodness and mercy I hope to be eternally happy.

My dear Lord Jesus in the Holy Eucharist, I *love* Thee with my whole heart and wish to love Thee more and more.

Forgive my past indifference, my coldness toward Thee in the sacrament of Thy love.

My Jesus, mercy!

Indulgence of 100 days, each time. — Pius IX, Sept. 24, 1846.

MAY Thy sacred Heart be loved everywhere! Grant that I may love Thee ever more generously, and be ever ready to sacrifice all to Thy love. I wish by my presence at this Mass to honor especially the wound in Thy sacred Heart, in order that through it Thou mayest pour Thy blessings, according to Thy good pleasure, on Thy friends and mine. Pardon my sins; establish Thy kingdom in my heart; reign therein supremely. Raise a barrier against the spirit of the world. Teach me to transform my actions into as many acts of love, so that after having known and loved Thee here below, by the light of faith, I may behold Thee face to face in all Thy glory, and love Thee in heaven for all eternity.

At the Offertory

Present yourself to God, begging of Him to effect an entire change in your heart.

O JESUS, Thou art all-powerful, and it is this power, which, through the words of Thy priest, changes bread into Thy body, and wine into,

Thy precious blood. O my good God, do Thou work a like change in me, that no longer of this world as I have hitherto been, I may become truly spiritual; that I may seek after and relish only the things of God; that grace, virtue, and heaven may be in my eyes the only true and solid goods; that, animated with Thy sentiments, O my Jesus, I may be transformed into Thee, and that in my conduct toward my neighbor I may be ruled by Thy spirit. In union with this holy sacrifice I consecrate my heart to Thee, O my God; I place it in Thy hands; transform it completely, so that in the future it may follow only the sweet impulse of Thy grace, which shall make it love virtue. I consecrate to Thee my mind and my body, my whole self, to be employed in Thy service and to Thy glory, so that by Thy grace I may be able to say with the Apostle: "I live, now not I, but Christ liveth in me."

At the Secret Prayers

GRACIOUSLY hear us, O God, that, by virtue of this sacrament, Thou mayest defend us from all enemies both of body and soul, and give us grace in this life and glory in the next, through Jesus Christ our Lord. Amen.

At the Preface and the Sanctus

LET us give thanks to the Lord our God; for it is meet and just. I give Thee thanks, my

divine Saviour, for the institution of this most wonderful sacrament, in which Thou hast bequeathed
to us the fountain of all graces, as a perpetual
remembrance of Thy boundless love and bitter
sufferings. I give Thee thanks for the numerous
graces that I have received through this sacrament
at Mass, holy communion, benediction, and in my
visits to Thy sanctuary.

I love Thee, my Lord, and because I love Thee, I
give myself entirely to Thee. I long to receive
Thee this day; however, while longing for Thee,
dear Jesus, to come into my heart, and to unite
Thyself to me as the best of all friends, I must not
forget Thy might and majesty. How great and
glorious, how wise and beautiful art Thou, O my
God! How presumptuous it would be to entertain
the desire to come so near to Thee, hadst not Thou
Thyself invited me. I am a sinner; yet I love Thee,
and because Thou art infinitely good, I am sorry
for having offended Thee. And though I believe
that Thou, the great God, art coming into my
heart, I do not lose my awe and reverence for
Thee, but can only wonder at Thy marvelous
goodness and condescension. Let me, then, join
my feeble voice to that of the thousands of angels
who surround Thy throne, singing before Thee in
unceasing chorus: Holy, Holy, Holy, Lord God of
hosts! The heavens and the earth are full of Thy
glory. Hosanna in the highest! Blessed is He
that cometh in the name of the Lord. Hosanna
in the highest!

At the Canon

Memento for the Living

IN THIS holy sacrifice, O Lord and Saviour, Jesus Christ, Thou art the mediator between the heavenly Father and sinful man; Thou art the High Priest appointed for man to present his petitions to his God. Therefore I implore Thee to hearken to my prayer, not only for myself but also for all for whom I am in charity bound to pray. Obtain for us through this holy sacrifice the remission of our sins, mercy, and reconciliation with the heavenly Father; imbue us with strength and valor in the warfare against the enemies of our soul; give us fortitude and fidelity in the pursuit of virtues; aid us in the practice of all good works, and bless us with the grace of final perseverance. Permit me to offer my supplications for the peace and prosperity of Thy holy Church; bless and protect the Holy Father, Thy vicar on earth; have mercy on the bishops, priests, Religious, and all who labor in Thy vineyard; animate them with zeal for the sanctification and salvation of souls. Inflame their hearts with divine charity; render their lives as holy as the law they inculcate; make them all according to Thine own divine Heart, and let their light so shine before men that they, seeing their good works, may glorify the Father Who is in heaven. Pardon the sinners and convert all to the true faith. O ye holy apostles, martyrs, and virgins, whom the Church remembers in the Canon of the Mass, intercede for us, for all our friends, relatives, benefactors, and for all those to whom we have promised our prayers, that the good God may give them that grace which will most help them to save their souls, to lead a holy and peaceful life in this world, and to be happy forever in heaven. And do Thou, O divine Saviour, graciously condescend to come now upon our altar, to bless Thy servants who are assisting at this Mass, and especially those who are longing to be united to Thee in holy communion.

At the Consecration and Elevation

When the priest genuflects immediately after the consecration, make a profound inclination of the head; then, kneeling erect, *look at* the sacred Host when raised above the head of the priest, and say devoutly:

My Lord and My God!

Indulgence of seven years and seven quarantines granted to all the faithful who, whilst directing their eyes toward the Blessed Sacrament at the elevation during Mass, devoutly recite the ejaculation "*My Lord and My God!*" — Pius X, May 18, 1907.

Then bend the head again and adore the Blessed Sacrament while the priest genuflects.

At the elevation of the chalice, adore the precious blood of Jesus Christ and say an ejaculatory indulgenced prayer.

ETERNAL Father, I offer Thee the precious blood of Jesus in satisfaction for my sins and for the wants of Holy Church!

Indulgence of 100 days, each time. — Pius VII, Sept. 22, 1817.

Another Indulgenced Prayer at the Elevation During Mass

SALVE, salutaris Victima, pro me et omni humano genere in patibulo crucis oblata.

Salve, pretiose sanguis, de vulneribus crucifixi Domini nostri Jesu Christi profluens, et peccata totius mundi abluens.

Recordare, Domine, creaturæ tuæ, quam tuo pretioso sanguine redemisti.

HAIL, saving Victim, offered on the gibbet of the cross for me and for the whole human race. Hail, precious blood, flowing from the wounds of our crucified Lord Jesus Christ and washing away the sins of the whole world.

Remember, O Lord, Thy creature that Thou hast redeemed by Thy precious blood.

Indulgence of 60 days, once a day, at the elevation during Mass. — Leo XIII, June 30, 1893.

EJACULATION

O SACRAMENT most holy! O Sacrament divine! All praise and all thanksgiving be every moment Thine!

Indulgence of 100 days, once during each Mass, when said at the elevation of both species. — Pius VII, Dec. 7, 1819.

After the Elevation

Memento for the Dead

Reflect on the happiness you are about to receive at holy communion. Make acts of love, desire, contrition, and reparation. Pray for the faithful departed.

O LORD Jesus Christ, on Whose glory the angels and saints in heaven gaze with rapturous delight, Thou hast deigned out of love for us to veil Thy beauty under the appearances of bread and wine, that we might approach Thee more confidently; Thou art even now ready to come into our hearts. Would that my soul were adorned with all those virtues which my good Jesus desires to find at His coming. In my poverty, I must appeal to Thyself, my Lord, and I therefore beseech Thee, when Thou comest into my heart, to plant there the seed of every flower of virtue that is pleasing to Thee. I promise Thee to water and nourish them all by prayer and self-denial, so that every time Thou comest into my heart Thou mayest find them growing and flourishing more and more. I know, O my God, the work of keeping them alive will be difficult to flesh and blood, but I am willing to make any sacrifice to please Thee, and I trust also in Thee to water them plentifully with dew from heaven — the precious dew of Thy grace.

Merciful God! I beseech Thee, have pity on the poor holy souls in purgatory, who are longing to be admitted into the heavenly paradise — longing more to see Thy face than to be freed from the fierce flames in which Thy justice is obliged to keep them, till their debt is paid. I offer Thee the precious blood of Jesus; I offer Thee the sacred Heart of Jesus to pay their debt. Eternal rest give unto them, O Lord, and let perpetual light shine upon them.

At the Pater Noster

Say the " Our Father" slowly and devoutly.

At the Agnus Dei

Beg of God once more to forgive your sins and negligences, saying:

O GOOD and gentle Jesus, Who wast "led like a lamb to the slaughter without opening Thy mouth;" O Thou, Whose blood was shed to wash away the sins of the world, cleanse my soul once more in that saving bath, that it may be pure and bright and altogether spotless when Thou comest to take up Thy abode within me. May Thy coming bring joy and peace to my soul, that peace which the world can not give, because it does not possess it. May this holy communion not be to my judgment and condemnation, but to my pardon and salvation.

At the "Domine, non Sum Dignus"

Give expression to your unworthiness and at the same time to your vehement desire to receive Our Lord in the Holy Eucharist.

LORD, I am not worthy that Thou shouldst come to me; for what am I, or what have I ever done to merit this wonderful favor? I have been ungrateful; I have often displeased Thee; yet, though I am not worthy of Thy love and condescension, I am truly sorry for having offended

Thee, and I will approach Thee with hope and confidence, because Thou Thyself dost invite me in Thy goodness and mercy. I desire most earnestly to receive Thee, my dear Lord, in holy communion.

COMFORT my poor soul distressed,
Come and dwell within my breast.
Oh, how oft I sigh for Thee!
Jesus, Jesus, come to me!
My Saviour, Jesus, come to me;
With all my heart I long for Thee!
Most firmly I believe in Thee,
Most trustfully I hope in Thee,
Most ardently I love Thee,
Then come, O Jesus, come to me.

After Communion

Make acts of adoration, thanksgiving, reparation, and prayer, according to the directions of Père Eymard (page 377), after you have spent a few moments in holy recollection.

MY JESUS, sweet Spouse of my soul, my King, my God! I *adore* Thee. With Magdalen I kiss Thy sacred feet. With John, the beloved disciple, let me rest upon Thy sacred Heart. I love Thee and desire to love Thee more and more. Speak to me and tell me what Thou wishest me to do. I am Thy servant ready to execute Thy will. Establish Thy kingdom firmly in my heart; crush out its self-love and pride. I give Thee *thanks*, O Lord, for condescending in Thy goodness and love to give Thyself to me — to me, so poor and miserable, so imperfect and unfaithful.

Mary, my Queen, my Mother, and all ye angels and saints of heaven, thank the Lord for me; praise Him for His goodness; bless Him for His mercy.

I am truly *sorry* for having offended Thee, my God, so often and so grievously. I will endeavor to make *reparation* to Thee for my past ingratitude by my fidelity to Thy grace, by my devotedness to my duties, by seeking to please Thee perfectly in all my actions, and by honoring Thee especially in the Holy Eucharist. I am resolved to overcome my predominant passion and to resist every evil inclination of my heart. For love of Thee, I will also be kind to others in thought, word, and deed.

I *pray* Thee to bless me; keep me in Thy love; grant me the grace of perseverance.

Sweet Heart of Jesus, I implore that I may love Thee more and more. Jesus, meek and humble of heart, make my heart like unto Thine. May Thy holy will, O God, be done in me and through me now and forever.

Suscipe

TAKE, O Lord, and receive all my liberty, my memory, my understanding, and whole will. Thou hast given me all that I am, and all that I possess. I surrender it all to Thee, that Thou mayest dispose of it according to Thy will. Give me only Thy love and Thy grace; with these I will

be rich enough, and will have no more to desire.
—St. Ignatius Loyola.

Soul of Christ, sanctify me.
   Body of Christ, save me.
Blood of Christ, inebriate me.
Water from the side of Christ, wash me.
Passion of Christ, strengthen me:
O good Jesus, hear me.
Within Thy wounds hide me.
Permit me not to be separated from Thee.
From the malignant enemy defend me.
In the hour of my death call me,
And bid me come to Thee,
That, with Thy saints, I may praise Thee for all
   eternity.   Amen.

At the Blessing

May Thy blessing, O Lord, descend upon us all, that we may love Thee and love one another for Thy sake. In the name of the Father, and of the Son, and of the Holy Ghost. Amen.

At the Last Gospel

What a wonderful invention of Thy love it was, O my God, to become man like one of us, to redeem us, and to teach us how to live in a manner worthy of our high calling and destination, instead of living as the brutes that perish. Left to ourselves what would have become of us? We should have taken pleasure only in what gratifies the body and pleases the senses. But Thou hast enlightened us, O Thou true light, that shineth in the darkness of the world; Thou hast taught us the value of our immortal soul by Thy death upon the cross; Thou hast taught us to detach our hearts from the things of earth, to raise up our thoughts to Thee and to journey onward and upward through weariness and toil to our true and lasting country in heaven. There, Thou hast assured us, if we persevere in Thy service and love, we shall find peace after the conflict, rest from our trouble, and perfect happiness.

O God, may my soul become a perpetual sacrifice in Thy honor; grant that it may always seek Thy greater glory here on earth in order that it may one day come to enjoy the beauty and the glory of Thy infinite perfections in heaven. Amen.

Indulgenced Prayer before a Crucifix

LOOK down upon me, good and gentle Jesus, while before Thy face I humbly kneel, and with burning soul pray and beseech Thee to fix deep in my heart lively sentiments of faith, hope, and charity, true contrition for my sins, and a firm purpose of amendment; and while I contemplate with great love and tender pity Thy five wounds, pondering over them within me, and calling to mind the words which David, Thy prophet, said of Thee, my Jesus: "They have pierced

My hands and my feet; they have numbered all
My bones" (*Ps.* xxi. 17, 18).

Say five times the *Our Father* and *Hail Mary* and *Glory*
for the Catholic Church and the intentions of the Holy
Father. His Holiness Pope Pius IX, July 31, 1858, con-
firmed anew the plenary indulgence granted by Clement
VIII and Benedict XIV, and confirmed by Pius VII and
Leo XII, to those who shall say this prayer with devotion
before an image or picture of our crucified Redeemer.
To gain this plenary indulgence, some time must be spent
in prayer after communion for the intention of the Holy
Father.

Père Eymard on Holy Communion

HAVING received Jesus into your heart at holy communion, spend some time in simple recollection, without
vocal prayers. Adore Him in silence; sit like Magdalen
in humble, adoring love at His feet; gaze upon Him
like Zaccheus, love Him in mute worship, like Mary, His
Mother.

Call Him your King, the Spouse of your soul. Say
to Him: "Speak, Lord, for Thy servant heareth." Offer
yourself to Him as His servant, ready to execute His will.
Bind your heart to His footstool, that it may wander no
more, or rather, put it under His feet, that He may crush
out its self-love and pride.

While your soul remains in recollection, in the hushed
calm of His holy presence, do not seek to disturb it. It
is the sleep of the soul upon the breast of Jesus, and this
grace, which strengthens and unites it to Our Lord, will be
more profitable than any other exercise.

The first state having passed, we may then proceed to
acts of thanksgiving, and the exercise of the Four Ends of
Sacrifice may prove useful, *viz.*:

Adoration, Thanksgiving, Reparation, and Prayer

I. ADORE Jesus upon the throne of your heart, and kiss His sacred feet and wounded hands. Rest upon that Heart which is burning with love for you. Offer Him the keys of your home, like St. Catherine of Genoa, "with full power to do all."

II. Thank Jesus for having so honored and loved you, as to give you this communion; to you, so poor and miserable, so imperfect and unfaithful. Call upon Mary and all the saints and angels to thank and praise Jesus for His wonderful love and excessive goodness.

III. Make reparation to Jesus by expressing your intense sorrow for your sins, and by protestations of love at His feet with Magdalen. Give Him some proof of your fidelity and gratitude by the sacrifice of some unregulated affection or the definite resolution to overcome some particular passion with more persistent energy and perseverance. Beg of Him the grace never to offend Him more, and desire to die rather than offend Him by mortal sin.

IV. Petition: Ask what you will; these are the precious moments of grace. The Lord is passing; cry out to Him for mercy and help. He lingers under your roof. Jesus is ready to listen to your complaints, and to give you all that you ask. Beg Him not so much for temporal favors, but rather that you may become a saint — that you may be more holy, more spiritual, more perfect, more and more pleasing to Him. Pray that His kingdom may be extended and that He may rule all hearts.

Pray for your daily needs.

Pray for your relations, your pastors, for the Holy Father, for the triumph of faith, and the exaltation of the Church.

For peace upon earth.

For vocations to the priesthood and the perfection and sanctification of those who have already embraced it.

For the fervor and perseverance of Religious.

For fervid and persevering adorers among the laity.

For the spread of the eucharistic kingdom of Christ.

For the conversion of sinners, especially those in whom you are most interested, or those recommended to your prayers.

Pray that Jesus may be known, loved, and served by all men.

Conclude by offering some little flower to Our Lord, by a practical resolution, or the promise of a particular sacrifice during the day.

Then say a few vocal prayers for the intentions of the Holy Father, *e.g.*, five *Our Fathers* and five *Hail Marys* in union with the prayer which is to be recited before a crucifix: "*Look down upon me, good and gentle Jesus*," in order to obtain a plenary indulgence.

There are many indulgences that we can gain very easily, and we are too often forgetful of these riches that are so profitable when applied to the wants of the suffering souls. The holy souls will thus join in your thanksgiving. During the day do not forget the royal visit of Jesus, the King of kings; preserve a remembrance of the morning's grace, like a vase that has gathered up some precious perfume, like a soul that has spent one hour of the busy day in the courts of paradise.

Devotions for Holy Communion

VARIOUS EXERCISES

NOTE. For the purpose of varying your devotions at communion the following exercises may be found helpful. These acts and prayers may be substituted at times in place of those which are found in the Mass for communion days. We should not adhere slavishly to one form of prayers. Learn to converse with God familiarly. Speak to Him from your heart with the simplicity of a child, humbly, contritely, respectfully, lovingly, hopefully, confidently. Jesus, our dear Lord, loves us with the love of a Father, Friend, and Brother.

He is, moreover, our God, all-powerful, able, and willing to help us in all our needs; let us approach Him with confidence, with faith, hope, and love, and let us pray with perseverance.

Before receiving holy communion, direct your intention, that is, offer to God your Mass and communion for the glory of His holy name, in thanksgiving for benefits received, in reparation to the Sacred Heart of Jesus for the outrages committed against the Blessed Sacrament, in satisfaction for your own sins, and in humble supplication that you may obtain new graces and blessings, above all the gift of final perseverance. Offer to God also some special intention, *e.g.*, the conversion of a friend, the welfare of your family, the relief of the souls in purgatory. Remember also the needs of the Holy Father and of the Church. Resolve to struggle earnestly against your ruling passion and pray that the spirit of Christ may dominate all your actions.

SHORT ACTS AND PRAYERS FOR HOLY COMMUNION

Before Holy Communion

Act of Faith

DEAR Jesus, I believe that Thou art present in the Blessed Sacrament as truly as Thou art in heaven. Relying on Thy infallible word, I believe most firmly that under the appearance of bread I shall receive in holy communion Thy sacred body and Thy precious blood. In this Most Holy Sacrament I adore Thee as my Lord and my God.

Act of Hope

MY JESUS, I hope in Thee because Thou art infinitely good, almighty, and faithful to Thy promises. Through Thy mercy, through Thy passion and death, I hope to obtain the pardon of my sins, the grace of final perseverance, and a happy eternity.

Act of Charity

JESUS, my God, I love Thee with my whole heart and above all things because Thou art the one supremely good and infinitely perfect Being. My desire is to love Thee more, and my endeavor shall be in all things to please Thee.

Act of Contrition

JESUS, my Saviour, I appear before Thee as a poor, miserable sinner. But Thou wilt not despise a contrite and humble heart. I am truly sorry for having sinned because Thou art infinitely good and sin displeases Thee.

Act of Desire

JESUS, my King, my God, and my All, my soul longs for Thee, my heart yearns to receive Thee in holy communion. Come, Thou Bread of heaven, come, Thou Food of angels, to nourish my soul and to rejoice my heart. Come, most amiable Spouse of my soul, to inflame me with such love of Thee that I may never again displease Thee, never again be separated from Thee by sin. "My soul hath thirsted after the strong living God; when shall I come and appear before the face of God?" (*Ps.* xli. 2). "Thou art the God of my heart and the God that is my portion forever" (*Ps.* lxxii. 26).

Act of Humility

O LORD of glory, O God of infinite sanctity, who am I that Thou shouldst deign to come to me! "The heavens are not pure in Thy sight," and wilt Thou dwell in my heart? "Lord! I am not worthy that Thou shouldst enter under my roof." The consciousness of my unworthiness would prompt me to exclaim, "Depart from me, O Lord, for I am a sinner," but Thy pressing invitation to approach Thy Holy Table encourages me and dispels all my fears. "Here I am, for Thou didst call me." Come, then, O Jesus, take possession of a heart that wishes to belong to Thee. "Create a clean heart in me, O God, and renew a right spirit within me." "Have mercy on me, O God, and according to the multitude of Thy tender mercies, blot out my iniquity" (*Ps.* l. 3).

"Lord, I am not worthy that Thou shouldst enter under my roof; say but the word, and my soul shall be healed."

When the moment comes to approach the railing, excite in your heart a new act of contrition while the *Confiteor* is recited and the priest pronounces the absolution, in order to merit more and more the remission of your sins, and obtain a perfect purity to receive the spotless Lamb.

At the *Ecce Agnus Dei* and *Domine non sum dignus*, pour forth your heart in sentiments of humility, love, joy, adoration, and self-immolation. Having received the sacred Host, that pledge of your salvation, retire with respectful modesty, and remain some time in simple recollection, in silent contemplation. Sit like Magdalen in humble, adoring love at the feet of Jesus, gaze upon Him like Zaccheus, love Him in mute worship like Mary, His blessed Mother. Consecrate your heart to Jesus and make good resolutions. Then you may continue your devotions with the help of your prayer-book.

After Holy Communion

Act of Faith and Adoration

JESUS, my Lord and my God, I bless Thee because Thou hast come to visit me. I bow down before Thee, now really present in my heart with Thy body and blood, soul and divinity. Thou art the same Jesus Who was born in Bethlehem and dwelt in Nazareth; Who suffered and died for my salvation; Who ascended into heaven and sitteth at the right hand of God the Father. I believe in Thee, and with all the powers of my soul I adore Thee, in union with the angels and saints. Thou art my King; reign Thou alone over my heart and my whole being. Let me never be separated from Thee by sin. I wish to serve Thee faithfully on earth that I may love and adore Thee, praise and glorify Thee forever in heaven.

Act of Hope

MY JESUS, I trust in Thee, I place all my hope in Thee, because Thou alone art my salvation, my strength, my refuge, and the foundation of all my happiness. "The light of Thy countenance, O Lord, is signed upon us: Thou hast given gladness in my heart. . . . O taste and see that the Lord is sweet: blessed is the man that hopeth in Him. . . . In peace, in the selfsame, I will sleep and I will rest: for Thou, O Lord, singularly hast settled me in hope" (*Ps.* xxxiii).

"In the shadow of Thy wings will I hope, until iniquity pass away" (*Ps.* lvi. 2).

Act of Love

GOOD Jesus, I love Thee. I love Thee with my whole heart and above all things. Thou knowest that I love Thee, but I wish to love Thee daily more and more, and to do what is most pleasing to Thee.

"My heart and my flesh have rejoiced in the living God. . . . For the sparrow hath found herself a house and the turtle a nest for herself. . . . Thy altars, O Lord of hosts, my King and my God" (*Ps.* lxxxiii. 3, 4).

"What have I in heaven? And besides Thee what do I desire upon earth? . . . Thou art the God of my heart, and the God that is my portion forever" (*Ps.* lxxii. 25, 26).

Act of Thanksgiving

MY DEAR Jesus, I thank Thee with all my heart for coming to me and nourishing my soul with Thy sacred body and most precious blood. I thank Thee for all the graces and blessings I have ever received through the merits of Thy sacred passion and through the institution of the most holy Sacrament of the Altar. With the help of Thy grace I will endeavor to manifest my gratitude to Thee by greater devotion to Thee in the sacrament of Thy love, by obedience to Thy holy commandments, by fidelity to my duties, by kindness to my neighbor, and by an earnest endeavor to become more like to Thee in my daily conduct. Blessed be Thy holy name!

"O Sacrament most holy, O Sacrament divine,
All praise and all thanksgiving be every moment Thine!"

Indulgence of 100 days. — Pius VI, May 24, 1776.

Act of Reparation and Consecration

MOST adorable Saviour, in Thy wondrous love for us Thou hast instituted the blessed Sacrament of the Altar as a memorial of Thy passion, and therein Thou dost remain with us in order to be the life-giving Manna of our souls, the propitiatory Victim for our sins, our Mediator with Thy heavenly Father, our Teacher, and our Friend.

I am sorry that I have so often offended Thee, O God of infinite love and mercy, by my ingratitude, by my resistance to Thy holy will, and in particular by my indifference toward Thee in the sacrament of Thy love. In atonement for my own sins, and in reparation for all the offenses committed against Thee in the Holy Eucharist by others, I offer Thee my poor heart filled with sentiments of sorrow, sincere repentance, and deepest affection, and I consecrate to Thee all my works and sufferings in union with Thy own bitter passion, the sorrows of Thy blessed Mother, and the merits of the martyrs and of all the saints. I place myself entirely in Thy hands: do with me according to Thy pleasure. With St. Ignatius I pray: "Give me but Thy love and Thy grace; more than this I do not ask;" and with the seraphic St. Francis I cry to Thee: "My Lord and my God, may the sweet flame of Thy love destroy in me all that does not please Thee; Thou didst yield Thyself to death for love of me, let me also die to self for love of Thee!"

"May the Heart of Jesus in the Most Blessed Sacrament be praised, adored, and loved, with grateful affection at every moment, in all the tabernacles of the world, even to the end of time."

Indulgence of 100 days. — Pius IX, Feb. 29, 1868.

Petitions

JESUS, my Lord, since Thou hast come to me to grant me graces, bidding me to ask with confidence, I now pray Thee not for earthly riches, honors, and transitory pleasures, but for the greatest spiritual treasures, namely, a supernatural horror of sin, and intense sorrow for past offenses, freedom from inordinate affections, a meek and humble heart like Thine, the most perfect submission and even abandonment to Thy will, a holy life, and a happy death. Help me to live daily more perfectly in accordance with Thy spirit and with the teachings of the holy Catholic Church.

Permit me also to ask for some special favors (*mention them*). O heavenly Father! Since our dear Lord and Saviour Himself has said: "Amen, amen, I say to you, if you ask the Father anything in My name, He will give it you," I beseech Thee, for the love of Thy Son, Jesus Christ, Who now dwells within me, and Whose infinite merits I offer up to Thee, do Thou graciously hear my prayers and grant all my petitions.

Memento of the Living

O LORD, my God! I recommend to Thee: 1. the Sovereign Pontiff, and all prelates, bishops, priests, and Religious; grant them, O Lord, zeal and the spirit of their state, that they may sacrifice themselves to the salvation of souls.

2. My relatives, benefactors, friends, and enemies; the sick, especially those who are in the agony of death! and all the faithful who are in Thy grace; give them, O Lord, perseverance and fervor in Thy love.

3. All infidels, heretics, and sinners; give them light and strength that they may all know and love Thee.

Memento of the Dead

I RECOMMEND to Thee: 1. the souls of my parents, benefactors, friends, and enemies; and of those who are in purgatory through my fault.

2. The souls of priests and those who labored for souls. Especially . . .

3. The souls of those who were most devout to the passion of Jesus Christ, to the Most Holy Sacrament, to the Sacred Heart of Jesus, and to His blessed Mother; the souls who are the most neglected and forgotten; those who are suffering the most; and those who are nearest to the gates of paradise.

Jesus, Master, Teach Me

TEACH me, teach me, dearest Jesus,
In Thine own sweet loving way,
All the lessons of perfection
I must practise day by day.

Teach me *Meekness*, dearest Jesus,
Of Thine own the counterpart;
Not in words and actions only,
But the meekness of the heart.

Teach *Humility*, sweet Jesus,
  To this poor, proud heart of mine,
Which yet wishes, O my Jesus,
  To be modeled after Thine.

Teach me *Fervor*, dearest Jesus,
  To comply with every grace,
So as never to look backward,
  Never slacken in the race.

Teach me *Poverty*, sweet Jesus,
  That my heart may never cling,
To whate'er its love might sever,
  From my Saviour, Spouse, and King.

Teach me *Chastity*, sweet Jesus,
  That my every day may see
Something added to the likeness
  That my soul should bear to Thee.

Teach *Obedience*, dearest Jesus,
  Such as was Thy daily food
In Thy toilsome earthly journey
  From the cradle to the rood.

Teach *Thy Heart*, to me, dear Jesus,
  Is my fervent, final prayer;
For all beauties and perfections
  Are in full perfection there.
                                        — *Leaflets.*

MY SAVIOUR! I cheerfully accept all the painful dispositions, in which it is Thy pleasure to place me. My wish is in all things to conform myself to Thy holy will. Whenever I kiss Thy cross, it is to show that I submit perfectly to mine. — BLESSED MARGARET MARY.

Final Prayers, Reflections, and Resolutions after Communion

I MUST now beg once more for Thy blessing, dear Jesus, before my departure from this holy place, where I have been blessed so abundantly this morning.

How delicious is the sweetness of this heavenly Bread, which I have received in holy communion! How delightful the peace, how perfect the tranquillity of a soul that receives Thee after having deplored and sincerely confessed her offenses! Be blessed a thousand times, O my Jesus! When I was a sinner I was miserable; but now not only do I enjoy the sweetest tranquillity of soul, but it seems to me that I experience a foretaste of the peace and bliss of paradise! It is, indeed, most certain that my heart has been made for Thee, my beloved Lord, and finds no joy but when it reposes in Thee. I therefore give Thee thanks; I firmly resolve to avoid sin and the occasions of sin; I will dwell permanently in Thy divine Heart, whence I expect the grace of loving Thee unto death.

WHAT strength hast Thou not imparted to my soul, good Lord, by means of this holy communion! Oh! how much I need it. The road I have to traverse is so difficult, that without Thee I should fear to venture upon it. In a short time I shall return to my daily occupations; I shall continue my life of yesterday; I shall be exposed to the same temptations, I shall find myself with my usual faults. But Jesus, Thou Who didst help the saints, Thou hast come to me. Stay, oh, stay with me, and do Thou by Thy grace, help me to preserve in all my words and actions, modesty, meekness, and humility. Help me to make Thy presence within me visible to all; let others see in me the sweetness of Thy charity, generosity, and kindness.

Prayer of Father Olier

O JESUS, living in Mary,
Come and live in Thy servants,
In the spirit of Thy holiness,
In the fulness of Thy might,
In the truth of Thy virtues,
In the perfection of Thy ways,
In the communion of Thy mysteries.
Subdue every hostile power,
In Thy Spirit, for the glory of the Father.
Amen.

Indulgence of 300 days, once a day. — Pius IX, Oct. 14, 1859.

N.B. — Say before a crucifix the prayer, "*Look down upon me, good and gentle Jesus!*" (p. 376) and the *Our Father, Hail Mary,* and *Glory* five times for the holy Catholic Church and the intentions of the Holy Father in order to gain a plenary indulgence.

Prayer: Memorare to the Blessed Virgin Mary

MEMORARE, O piissima virgo Maria, non esse auditum a sæculo quemquam ad tua currentem præsidia, tua implorantem auxilia, tua petentem suffragia, esse derelictum. Ego tali animatus confidentia, ad te, virgo virginum, Mater, curro, ad te venio, coram te gemens peccator assisto; noli, mater Verbi,

REMEMBER, O most gracious Virgin Mary! that never was it known that any one who fled to thy protection, implored thy help, and sought thy intercession, was left unaided. Inspired with this confidence, I fly unto thee, O Virgin of virgins, my Mother! To thee I come; before thee I stand, sinful and sorrowful.

verba mea despicere, sed
audi propitia, et exaudi.
Amen.

O mother of the Word in-
carnate! despise not my
petitions, but, in thy mercy,
hear and answer me. Amen.

His Holiness, Pope Pius IX, by a rescript of the Sacred
Congregation of Indulgences, Dec. 11, 1846, granted to
all the faithful every time that, with at least contrite heart
and devotion, they shall say this prayer, an *indulgence
of three hundred days;* also a *plenary indulgence*, once a
month, to all those who, having said it at least once a day
for a month, on any day, being truly penitent, after confession and communion, shall visit a church or public
oratory, and pray there, for some time, for the intention of
His Holiness.

Ejaculation

O Domina mea! O
mater mea! memento
me esse tuum.

My Queen! my Mother!
remember I am thine
own.

Serva me, defende me,
ut rem et possessionem
tuam.

Keep me, guard me, as
thy property and posses-
sion.

Indulgence of 40 days, each time. — Pius IX, Aug.
5, 1851.

Litany for Holy Communion

(Before or After)

This litany from Mother Loyola's *Confession and Communion* is intended for private devotion. The approved
and indulgenced Litanies of the *Holy Name of Jesus* and
of the *Sacred Heart of Jesus*, when recited *slowly* after holy
communion, are apt to excite happy inspirations and
devout reflections.

Lord, have mercy on us.
Christ, have mercy on us.

Lord, have mercy on us.
Christ, hear us.
Christ, graciously hear us.
God the Father of Heaven,
God, the Son, Redeemer of the world,
God the Holy Ghost,
Holy Trinity one God,
Jesus, living Bread which came down from Heaven,[1]
Jesus, Bread from Heaven giving life to the world,[2]
Hidden God and Saviour,[3]
My Lord and my God,[4]
Who hast loved us with an everlasting love,[5]
Whose delights are to be with the children of men,[6]
Who hast given Thy flesh for the life of the world,[7]
Who dost invite all to come to Thee,[8]
Who dost promise eternal life to those who receive Thee,[9]
Who with desire dost desire to eat this Pasch with us,[10]
Who art ever ready to receive and welcome us,
Who dost stand at our door knocking,[11]
Who hast said that if we will open to Thee the door,
    Thou wilt come in and sup with us,[12]
Who dost receive us into Thy arms and bless us with the
    little children,
Who dost suffer us to sit at Thy feet with Magdalen,
Who dost invite us to lean on Thy bosom with the be-
    loved disciple,
Who hast not left us orphans,[13]
Most dear Sacrament,
Sacrament of love,
Sacrament of sweetness,
Life-giving Sacrament,

Have mercy on us

---

[1] John vi. [2] John vi. [3] Is. xlv. [4] John xx. [5] Jer. xxxi.
[6] Prov. viii. [7] John vi. [8] Matt. xi. [9] John vi.
[10] Luke xxii. [11] Apoc. iii. [12] Apoc. iii. [13] John xiv.

Sacrament of strength, Have mercy on us.

My God and my all, Have mercy on us.

That our hearts may pant after Thee as the hart after the fountains of water,[1]

That Thou wouldst manifest Thyself to us as to the two disciples in the breaking of bread,[2]

That we may know Thy voice like Magdalen,

That with a lively faith we may confess with the beloved disciple — "It is the Lord," [3]

That Thou wouldst bless us who have not seen and have believed,[4]

That we may love Thee in the Blessed Sacrament with our whole heart, with our whole soul, with all our mind, and with all our strength,[5]

That the fruit of each communion may be fresh love,

That our one desire may be to love Thee and to do Thy will,

That we may ever remain in Thy love,[6]

That Thou wouldst teach us how to receive and welcome Thee,

That Thou wouldst teach us to pray, and Thyself pray within us,[7]

That with Thee every virtue may come into our souls,

That through this day Thou wouldst keep us closely united to Thee,

That Thou wouldst give us grace to persevere to the end,[8]

That Thou wouldst then be our support and Viaticum,

That with Thee and leaning on Thee we may safely pass through all dangers,

That our last act may be one of perfect love, and our last breath a long deep sigh to be in Our Father's house,

[1] Ps. xli.   [2] Luke xxiv.   [3] John xxi.   [4] John xx.
[5] Mark xii.   [6] John xv.   [7] Luke xi.   [8] Matt. x.

That Thy sweet face may smile upon us when we appear before Thee, We beseech Thee, hear us.

That our banishment from Thee, dearest Lord, may not be very long, We beseech Thee, hear us.

That when the time is come, we may fly up from our prison to Thee and in Thy sacred Heart find our rest forever, We beseech Thee, hear us.

Lamb of God, Who takest away the sins of the world, spare us, O Lord.

Lamb of God, Who takest away the sins of the world, graciously hear us.

Lamb of God, Who takest away the sins of the world, have mercy on us.

V. Stay with us, Lord, because it is toward evening.

R. And the day is now far spent.

Let us pray

WE COME to Thee, dear Lord, with the apostles, saying, *Increase our faith.*[1] Give us a strong and lively faith in the mystery of Thy real presence in the midst of us. Give us the splendid faith of the centurion, which drew from Thee such praise. Give us the faith of the beloved disciple to know Thee in the dark and say, *It is the Lord!*[2] Give us the faith of Martha to confess, *Thou art Christ the Son of the living God.*[3] Give us the faith of Magdalen to fall at Thy feet crying, *Rabboni, Master.*[4] Give us the faith of all Thy saints, to whom the Blessed Sacrament has been heaven begun on earth. In every communion increase our faith; for with faith, love and humility, and reverence and all good, will come into our souls.

Dearest Lord, *increase our faith.*

[1] Luke xvii.   [2] John xxi.   [3] John xi.   [4] John xx.

Another Exercise of Devotion for Holy Communion

METHOD OF PREPARATION

Before receiving, endeavor to excite in yourself the proper dispositions

LIVELY *Faith.* — Ask yourself, Whom am I going to receive? The divine Master answers: "This is My body, My blood." It is Our Lord Jesus Christ, immolated on the cross, triumphant in heaven. . . . It is the eternal Word, the sovereign Lord and Creator, my supreme Judge. Continue repeating: "Yes, my God, it is Thou indeed, it is Thou; I believe it more firmly on Thy word, Thy infallible word, than if, with my own eyes, I beheld Thy resplendent Majesty."

Adoration. — Acknowledge Him with all your heart to be your absolute Master, from Whom you hold everything and to Whom you entirely belong.

Humble compunction. — "Who am I that am about to receive Him?" . . . Lord, Thou art the Holy of holies, infinitely good, infinitely perfect, and I am the last of sinners. . . .

My heart has been defiled with many and many a sin, . . . it has been so ungrateful. I am so tepid and inclined to fall again. Lord, I am not worthy. . . . And yet Thou desirest me to come to Thee with filial confidence, as to my kind Saviour, my charitable Physician!

Thou callest Thyself *the Good Shepherd*, Who seeks lovingly the sheep that have gone astray.

Thou art the divine Lover of souls. Thou willest not the death of the sinner, but that he may be converted and live. "Behold, I stand at the gate and knock. If any man shall hear My voice, and open to Me the door, I will come in to him, and will sup with him, and he with Me" (*Apoc.* iii. 20).

Confidently, then, O Lord, yet humbly and contritely will I approach Thy Holy Table to be refreshed and strengthened by the Food of angels, the Bread of heaven, which Thou givest us.

Endeavor to strengthen your soul more and more by exciting yourself to hearty contrition at the sight of so much goodness and love. — "Forgive me, O my good Master! I detest all my sins . . . for they have wounded Thy loving Heart. Never again will I offend Thee. Lord, I am truly sorry that I have sinned, because Thou art infinitely good and sin displeases Thee."

Generous love. — Like that of Jesus — He gives you all . . . all . . . in an ineffable union . . . His flesh to purify yours, His soul to impregnate yours with His spirit of abnegation and contempt of the world . . . His Heart to inflame yours with His generous devotedness . . . His divinity to transform you . . . His treasures of merit to enrich you . . . and His graces to strengthen you. Love Him then in return *generously, nobly, practically*, that is to say, give yourself to Him without reserve, by the flight of all sin, the fulfilment of every duty, the struggle against pride, sensuality, cowardice. . . . What sacrifice did Jesus refuse to make for you? Can you then deny Him anything? . . . Desire Him earnestly. . . . Call upon Him ardently: "Come, Lord Jesus, come!"

PRAYERS BEFORE COMMUNION

Acts of Faith and Adoration

MY GOOD Jesus, I believe with a firm and lively faith, that in this adorable sacrament are Thy body and blood, soul and divinity. I believe that in this consecrated Host I shall receive that same body which was born of the most pure Virgin Mary in Bethlehem, which suffered so many pains and torments for love of me on the Way of the Cross and on Calvary, and which rose gloriously the third day from the dead. I believe that I shall receive that most holy soul which is enriched with all the treasures of the Divinity; I believe that I shall receive God Himself.

I adore Thee, O my God, as my Creator, my Preserver, my Redeemer, and my Judge, truly present in the Holy Eucharist.

Divine Host, I adore Thee with the angels who fill the sanctuary and hover over the tabernacle as they hovered over the cave of Bethlehem in the Holy Night; I adore Thee, my God, with the Blessed Virgin, and in union with all the saints.

Lord and Master of the universe, Who hast fixed Thy dwelling amongst men, I adore Thee with profound gratitude. O my Jesus, bless this temple wherein Thou residest, but still more the heart that I offer Thee as a living abode and place of rest. Deign ever to inhabit it by Thy grace and Thy love, and may my sins never banish Thee from it! Lord, I have a firm faith, but do Thou strengthen my faith, and animate it so that it may produce in my soul deeper sentiments of adoration and love.

Good Lord, increase my faith that I may love Thee more, and be more generous in my sacrifices for the love of Thee and for the love of my neighbors.

Who Comes?

The Word made flesh for me,
The Lord Who died for me,
The Love made food for me,
　　He comes!

To Whom Does He Come?

To one redeemed by Him,
To one allied with Him,
To one who longs for Him,
　　He comes!

Why Does He Come?

To reign upon His throne,
To reign *supreme alone*,
To make me all His own,
　　He comes!

Oh, I am glad to come to Thee,
　　My only rest;
To lay my weary head awhile,
　　Upon Thy breast;
To bring the burden of my grief
　　Hither to Thee;
And feel, O Jesus, Son of man,
　　Thy sympathy. — Mother Loyola.

Act of Contrition, Hope, Confidence

O Jesus, loving Spouse of my soul, the longed-for moment draws near; the happy moment, in which I, Thy unworthy creature, shall receive the most holy sacrament of Thy body and blood, as the most effectual remedy for all my miseries. For the love of Thee I grieve most bitterly for every one of my sins

and for all my negligences, whereby I have offended
Thy tender goodness, and defiled my soul, which Thou
didst ransom with Thine own most precious blood.
How shall I presume to receive Thee into a heart all
surrounded with briers and thorns of earthly attachments, reeking with unwholesome vapors of worldliness
and vain desires! But, my merciful Jesus, though I am
sick of soul, I remember the words which fell from
Thine own gracious lips — that they who are whole
need not the physician, but they who are sick — and
this gives me confidence. Surely, my Lord, if any one
has cause to trust Thee it is I! Others may have their
innocence or their virtues to fall back upon, but I have
Thy mercy, Thy *great mercy*, only. I have made myself
undeserving of it, but when hast Thou ever treated me
as I deserved? Where should I be now if justice and
not mercy had had its way? Good Jesus, Who didst
invite the blind and the lame, the poor and the needy,
to Thy supper, behold, as one of them, yea, even as the
poorest and most wretched of them all, I will draw
near to the most sacred feast of Thy body and blood,
the banquet of the angels, not in presumption, but with
a contrite and humble heart, with lowly confidence,
with hope in Thy goodness and mercy, with love in
return for all Thy love, with fervent desire to please
Thee, to live henceforth according to Thy Spirit, and
in the imitation of the virtues of Thy sacred Heart
that I may praise and glorify Thee eternally.

Act of Humility

HE COMES to Me Who is the Judge of the living
and the dead. Before Him the pillars of heaven
tremble, and the pure angels veil their faces with their

wings. Whither shall I flee from His face? Two places are safe for me — the depths of my misery and the Heart of my Judge. In them will I hide myself.

O my God, I detest all the sins of my whole life because they displease Thee, and especially I am sorry for those which I have committed against this sacrament, by my irreverence and the little profit I have drawn from so many communions, by my negligence in guarding my senses, particularly my tongue, which has been so often consecrated by Thy divine presence.

My Lord and my God, what confusion I feel at beholding myself so unworthy to approach Thy holy table. Suffer me, dear Jesus, to seek the remedy for my evils in the wound of Thy sacred Heart. Let Thy sacred Heart be to me as the burning coal which purified the lips of Isaias; place it, all inflamed with charity, I beseech Thee, dear Lord, on my heart, my tongue, my senses, and all the powers of my soul, so that it may burn and annihilate all that is displeasing to Thee.

Jesus, Jesus, be to me Jesus, and save me. Remember Thou hast said, "*The Son of man is come to seek and to save that which was lost*" (*Luke* xix. 10). *They that are in health need not a physician, but they that are sick. I am not come to call the just, but sinners* (*Matt.* ix. 13). Dear Lord, I am sick, I am sinful, as Thou knowest; come to me and say, *I am thy salvation* (*Ps.* xxxiv. 3).

Grant me, O Lord, the grace of beginning a new, a fervent life, and deign to give me in this holy sacrament the pledge of eternal life promised to those who receive Thee worthily. Amen.

Act of Love and Desire

O H, THAT I could love Thee, Jesus, as if I had knelt at Thy feet and felt the touch of Thy hand on my brow, and heard Thy gentle voice that uttered absolutions and gave encouragement to the sick and the unfortunate. Oh, that I could love Thee, as the poor of Galilee loved Thee, as Mary Magdalen loved Thee, as St. Peter and St. John, the beloved disciple, loved Thee, as she, who knew Thee best — Thy blessed Mother — loved Thee, and, most of all, O Lord, as Thou hast loved me.

Let me at least love Thee with all my heart and soul and mind and strength. And let my love be worthy of the name — showing itself by confidence, by generosity, by sacrifice — acknowledging cheerfully that all Thy dispensations are best for me — counting no cost when I work for Thee — giving up gladly what is dear to me when Thou dost ask it, when it will help to serve Thee better and to further the interests of Thy sacred Heart.

Dispose of me, O Lord, as Thou pleasest; for from henceforth I am entirely Thine. I offer Thee all that I am and all that I have. I shall labor and suffer for Thy glory, for the salvation of others, and for my own sanctification.

Come, my Jesus, crucified for love of me. Come, dear Jesus, in the sacrament of Thy love, and be Thou all mine, as I desire to be all Thine.

O blessed Virgin, my tender Mother, who didst obtain from thy divine Son a wonderful miracle at the wedding-feast at Cana, behold my misery and the need I have of thy assistance; obtain for me of Jesus a prodigy of His almighty power, that my coldness and tepidity may be changed into ardent charity.

Veni, Domine Jesu!

O Jesus, hidden God, I cry to Thee;
O Jesus, hidden Light, I turn to Thee;
O Jesus, hidden Love, I run to Thee;
With all the strength I have I worship Thee;
With all the love I have I cling to Thee;
With all my soul I long to be with Thee,
And fear no more to fail, or fall from Thee.

O Jesus, deathless Love, Who seekest me,
Thou Who didst die for longing love of me,
Thou King, in all Thy beauty, come to me,
White-robed, blood-sprinkled, Jesus, come to me,
And go no more, dear Lord, away from me.

O sweetest Jesus, bring me home to Thee;
Free me, O dearest God, from all but Thee,
And all the chains that keep me back from Thee;
Call me, O thrilling Love, I follow Thee;
Thou art my All, and I love nought but Thee.

O hidden Love, Who now art loving me;
O wounded Love, Who once wast dead for me;
O patient Love, Who weariest not of me —
O bear with me till I am lost in Thee;
O bear with me till I am found in Thee.

            — Fr. Rawes.

"DOMINE, *non sum dignus!*" "Lord, I am not worthy, that Thou shouldst enter under my roof." Blessed be the Lamb of God, that comes to me, a sinner! Lord, have mercy on me! O God of purity and majesty, how canst Thou vouchsafe to lower Thyself to me, so unworthy of Thy presence.

But Thou dost invite me to this sacred Banquet. I come with confidence, trusting in Thy goodness and mercy. Say but the word, and my soul shall be healed. Come to me, Jesus, and remain with me forever. I humbly adore Thee, with my whole heart I love Thee.

Method of Thanksgiving after Communion

Look upon Our Lord as a treasure you carry away and have all to yourself. God is looking upon this treasure in your heart, wondering what you will do with it, to whom you will give it. This treasure is the One Whom He loves — His only Son! You are no longer a poor, miserable beggar, you are now rich and can offer a gift infinite in value. For what will you offer it? Know what you are about, and do not spend the time in a fruitless manner for want of a method. Realize Who is within you — and as soon as your devotion flags use a book, if only for two minutes, until you collect your thoughts again.

Adoration. — Jesus is in your soul, seated as a king on His throne, expecting your homage. Prostrate at His feet, tell Him again that He is your Lord, your God, and your all . . . that you wish to belong entirely to Him . . . to obey Him in all and live only for His glory. "O Godhead, hid devoutly, I adore Thee."

Thanksgiving and Reparation. — What return can you make for this infinite gift? You are so poor. . . . Offer at least your love . . . your gratitude.

"Praised, loved, and adored forever be Jesus, in the most blessed Sacrament of the Altar." Beg Mary and the angels to supply for your inability by their ardor.

Petition. — Jesus wishes to give you everything . . . and He can. . . . Ask earnestly, with immense confidence, for all necessary graces for yourself, for your dear ones, for the Church, sinners, the souls in purgatory.

Offering (or oblation). — Jesus has just given you all, . . . Himself, the source of all graces. . . . Will *you* keep anything back? . . . He has a right to all that you are and all that you possess. . . . Offer then all to Him, that He may govern it according to His good pleasure. "Take, O Lord, and receive all that I am and have." — (Prayer: *"Suscipe"* of St. Ignatius.)

Resolutions. — Renew, with strong determination, your promises and good resolutions to lead a more perfect life, to overcome your predominant passion, to become like to your divine Master, by the exercise of His virtues, to be more charitable and more faithful in the discharge of your duties.

You carry God away with you. Let every one see it by your modesty, your recollection, your devotedness, your spiritual progress, your charity, your kindness.

"In all places and times I will never depart
From the Heart of my God and the God of my heart."

☩ Sacrum Convivium

O SACRUM Convivium, in quo Christus sumitur; recolitur memoria passionis ejus; mens impletur gratia, et futuræ gloriæ nobis pignus datur.

O SACRED Banquet, wherein Christ is received; the memory of His passion is renewed, the mind is filled with grace, and the pledge of future glory is given unto us.

ACTS AND PRAYERS AFTER HOLY COMMUNION

Faith, Adoration, Reparation, Praise, and Thanksgiving

MY JESUS my Lord, my God, and my All! Jesus, my Life, my Love, Thou art really mine! Thou art truly within me, Thou art all mine! With the angels and saints I adore Thee. In union with the blessed Virgin Mary, in her transports of joyful praise and thanksgiving, when the Angel Gabriel announced to her the mystery of Thy incarnation, and when later she received Thee in the Most Holy Sacrament at the hands of St. John, Thy beloved disciple, I adore Thee with the liveliest faith, the most profound respect, the deepest gratitude, the most ardent devotion. "My soul doth magnify the Lord and my spirit hath rejoiced in God my Saviour, for He hath regarded the humility of His handmaid" (*Luke* i. 46, 47, 48). With Mary Magdalen I fall at Thy feet and cry with her faith and love and devotedness! *Rabboni! Master!* Master of my heart! Master of all I am and have!

> O hidden God, devoutly unto Thee,
>   Bends my adoring knee;
> With lowly semblances from sight concealed,
>   To faith alone revealed.

O MY God, my supreme Good, my divine Friend and Benefactor in this wonderful sacrament, I praise Thee, I thank Thee, and in reparation for all my ingratitude and infidelities of the past, I consecrate to Thee my heart with all its affections, my soul with all its powers, my body with all its senses; I offer to Thee all my prayers, works, and sufferings, in union with Thy sacred Heart, for all the intentions for which Thou dost plead on our altars in the holy sacrifice of the Mass; I am determined to honor and glorify Thee more than ever in the Holy Eucharist; I offer to Thee, with a contrite and humble heart, Thy own bitter passion, the sorrows of Thy blessed Mother, and the merits of all the saints.

By the fervor of my love, by my devotedness to Thy interests, by my fidelity to all my duties, and by cultivating and exercising the virtues of Thy sacred Heart, in particular, meekness, humility, charity, and zeal for the salvation of souls, I wish to show my gratitude to Thee for all the benefits I have received from Thy real presence on our altars and to make amends to Thee for the injuries inflicted on Thy sacred Heart in the sacrament of Thy love. To Thee be adoration, praise, and thanksgiving from all creatures forevermore.

> "That He Who lay on Mary's knee,
> Who stilled the waves of Galilee,
> Was the dear Guest at Bethany,
> And bled and died on Calvary,
> That He in truth abides with me
> I hold with faith's sure certainty.
> O God, O hidden Deity,
> Profoundly I here worship Thee,
> Rabboni! Master!
>
> "O God, most wonderful in all Thy ways,
> Most in this mystery of love, upraise
> My heart to Thee in canticles of praise,
> Rabboni! Master!
>
> "And since my hungry soul this day is fed
> With 'meat indeed,' with Thee the living Bread,
> Give me to live by Thee as Thou hast said,
> Rabboni! Master!"
> — MOTHER LOYOLA.

O my soul, bless the Lord! (*Ps.* ciii. 2.)
Blessed be Jesus Christ, true God and true Man.
Blessed be the Name of Jesus.
Blessed be His most sacred Heart.
Blessed be Jesus Christ in the most holy Sacrament of the Altar.

O Sacrament most holy, O Sacrament divine,
All praise and all thanksgiving be every moment Thine

Praise the Lord, O my soul; in my life I will praise the Lord, I will sing to my God as long as I shall be (*Ps.* cxlv. 1).

Praise ye Him, all His angels: praise ye Him all His hosts (*Ps.* cxlviii. 2).

Bless the Lord, O my soul, and let all that is within me bless His holy name. Bless the Lord, O my soul, and never forget all He hath done for thee (*Ps.* cii. 1, 2).

What shall I render to the Lord, for all that He hath rendered to me. . . . I will pay my vows to the Lord in the courts of the house of the Lord, in the midst of thee, O Jerusalem! (*Ps.* cxv. 12, 14).

Bless the Lord, all ye His angels, you that are mighty in strength (*Ps.* cii. 20).

Give glory to the Lord, for He is good: for His mercy endureth forever. . . . For He hath satisfied the empty soul, and hath filled the hungry soul with good things (*Ps.* cvi. 1, 9).

Blessed be the Lord forevermore (*Ps.* lxxxviii. 53). He is my hope and my salvation.

Act of Love

IN THY excess of love, O divine Lord! Thou hast given Thyself to me. Tell me, O Jesus! what Thou desirest of me. Is there any sacrifice Thy love demands of me? Speak, Lord! for Thy child, Thy servant, listeneth, and, with Thy gracious assistance, will accomplish Thy divine pleasure. I love Thee, O my God! I love Thee, and love Thee alone. I love all Thy creatures for Thee and in Thee; and, with St. Paul, I will labor to become all to all, in order to gain all to Thee, O sweetest Jesus, O most amiable, most loving Lord Jesus.

O sweetest Heart of Jesus! I implore
That I may ever love Thee more and more!

Indulgence 300 days, each time. — Pius IX, Nov. 26, 1876.

Thanksgiving of St. Thomas Aquinas

From the Roman Missal

I GIVE Thee thanks, eternal Father, for having, out of Thy pure mercy, without any deserts of mine, been pleased to feed my soul with the body and blood of Thy only Son, Our Lord Jesus Christ. I beseech Thee that this holy communion may not be to my condemnation, but prove an effectual remission of all my sins. May it strengthen my faith; encourage me in all that is good; deliver me from my vicious customs; remove all concupiscence; perfect me in charity, patience, humility, and obedience, and in all other virtues. May it secure me against all the snares of my enemies, both visible and invisible; perfectly moderate all my inclinations, closely unite me to Thee, the true and only good, and happily settle me in unchangeable bliss. I now make it my hearty request, that Thou wilt one day admit me, though an unworthy sinner, to be a guest at Thy divine Banquet where Thou, with Thy Son and the Holy Ghost, art the true light, complete satiety, everlasting joy, supreme pleasure, and perfect happiness. Through the same Jesus Christ our Lord. Amen.

O THOU Memorial of Our Lord's own dying!
O Bread that living art and vivifying!
Make ever Thou my soul on Thee to live;
Ever a taste of heavenly sweetness give.

O loving Pelican! O Jesus, Lord!
Unclean I am, but cleanse me in Thy blood;
Of which a single drop, for sinners spilt,
Is ransom for a world's entire guilt.

Jesus! Whom for the present veiled I see,
What I so thirst for, oh, vouchsafe to me,
That I may see Thy countenance unfolding,
And may be blest Thy glory in beholding.
—St. Thomas, *Adoro Te Devote*

Peace with Jesus

MY LOVING Saviour! ah, what depth of love
Hath made Thee leave Thy heavenly throne above
And come to visit me, to be my food,
To make my sinful body Thy abode;
To shield me from the world, to make me pure,
To give me strength, with patience to endure.
Ah, let me with a burning soul draw near,
And fondly, with St. John, without a fear,
Lean my poor head upon Thy loving breast,
And in Thy sacred arms serenely rest.
Depart, each earthly care, each worldly smile;
Leave me alone with Jesus for a while.

Sweet Jesus! by this sacrament of love
All gross affections from my heart remove;
Let but Thy loving kindness linger there,
Preserved by grace and perfected by prayer;
And let me to my neighbor strive to be
As mild and gentle as Thou art with me.
Take Thou the guidance of my whole career,
That to displease Thee be my only fear;
Give me that peace the world can never give,
And in Thy loving presence let me live.
Ah! show me always, Lord, Thy holy will
And to each troubled thought say, "*Peace, be still.*"
— R. Trainer.

To Jesus in the Holy Eucharist

Indulgenced Prayer

DEAR Jesus, in the Sacrament of the Altar, be forever thanked and praised. Love, worthy of all celestial and terrestrial love! Who, out of infinite love for me, ungrateful sinner, didst assume our human nature, didst shed Thy most precious blood in the cruel scourging, and didst expire on a shameful cross for our eternal welfare! Now, illumined with lively faith, with the outpouring of my whole soul and the fervor of my heart, I humbly beseech Thee, through the infinite merits of Thy painful sufferings, give me strength and courage to destroy every evil passion which sways my heart, to bless Thee in my greatest afflictions, to glorify Thee by the exact fulfilment of all my duties, supremely to hate all sin, and thus to become a saint.

Indulgence of 100 days, once a day. — Pius IX, Jan. 1, 1866.

OBLATION

Prayer of St. Ignatius Loyola

Indulgenced

SUSCIPE, Domine, universam meam libertatem. Accipe memoriam, intellectum atque voluntatem omnem. Quidquid habeo vel possideo, mini largitus es; id tibi totum restituo ac tuæ prorsus voluntati trado gubernandum. Amorem tui

TAKE, O Lord, and receive all my liberty, my memory, my understanding and my whole will. Thou hast given me all that I am and all that I possess; I surrender it all to Thee that Thou mayest dispose of it according to Thy will. Give me only

solum cum gratia tua mi-
hi dones et dives sum satis,
nec aliud quidquam ultra
posco.

Thy love and Thy grace;
with these I will be rich
enough, and will have no
more to desire.

His Holiness, Pope Leo XIII, by a rescript of the Sacred
Congregation of Indulgences, May 26, 1883, granted to
all the faithful who, with at least contrite heart and devotion, shall recite the above prayer, an *indulgence of
three hundred days*, once a day.

Anima Christi

ANIMA Christi, sancti-
fica me.
Corpus Christi, salva me.
Sanguis   Christi,   inebria
me.
Aqua lateris Christi, lava
me.
Passio Christi, conforta me.
O bone Jesu, exaudi me.
Intra tua vulnera absconde
me.
Ne permittas me separari
a te.
Ab hoste maligno defende
me.
In hora mortis meæ voca
me,
Et jube me venire ad te,
Ut cum sanctis tuis laudem
te
In sæcula sæculorum.
Amen.

SOUL of Christ, sanc-
tify me.
Body of Christ, save me.
Blood of Christ, inebriate
me.
Water from the side of
Christ, wash me.
Passion of Christ, strength-
en me.
O good Jesus, hear me.
Within Thy wounds hide
me.
Permit me not to be sepa-
rated from Thee.
From the malignant enemy
defend me.
In the hour of my death call
me,
And bid me come to Thee,
That, with Thy saints, I
may praise Thee
Forever and ever. Amen.

Indulgence of 300 days, every time. — Pius IX, Jan. 9,
1854.

Petitions and Offerings after Holy Communion

SINCE Thou hast been pleased, most loving Jesus, to come and dwell within my heart, I expect many favors of Thee; for how canst Thou refuse to give me Thy gifts, since Thou hast given me Thyself? No, this is not possible, my dearest Lord, and therefore I am quite confident of obtaining all from Thy goodness. I confess, O Lord, that I deserve nothing; but the more undeserving I am, the more is Thy goodness glorified in bestowing Thy grace upon me. I ask, then, O most loving Redeemer, a full pardon and remission of the guilt of all my sins, which I once more detest and abominate with all my heart; and for the remission of the temporal punishment which is due for them, I desire to gain all the indulgences I can, and beseech Thee to give me the grace to accomplish this purpose.

By Thy most precious blood, by Thy body, soul, and divinity, which I have this morning received, I beg of Thee with all humility to cleanse my heart from all defilement. Create, O my Jesus, a clean heart within me, and grant me a new spirit truly just and upright. Fill my heart with all the gifts of Thy holy Spirit, and adorn it with every virtue, especially with humility, patience, meekness, and mortification. Detach my heart from all created things, fashion it after Thine own most sacred Heart, and unite it forever to Thyself in the bonds of perfect charity. Give me a heart conformable in all things to Thy holy will, that it may seek only what is pleasing to Thee and have no other desire than Thy holy love. No matter what may happen to me, with Thy love and Thy grace, I shall be perfectly happy. Give me strength and courage to resist

bravely all temptations until death; I purpose to
banish them at once, and promise to avoid every
occasion of sin. But, my Lord, Thou knowest that of
myself I can do nothing, and therefore I implore
Thee to help me and to strengthen me by Thy blood.

I beseech Thee to engrave upon my heart so lively
a remembrance of Thy passion and death, and the bitter sorrows of my Mother Mary, that they may
be my continual meditation; so that henceforth
and to my last breath I may dwell on Calvary at the
foot of Thy cross, in company with our dear Lady of
Sorrows.

I beseech Thee, too, my dearest Lord, most earnestly,
to give me the grace to free myself once for all from my
predominant passion, and the sin into which I most often
fall. (*Here mention the particular passion, or sin, or
fault.*) I ask, moreover, for those temporal graces Thou
knowest to be most expedient for me, for Thy greater glory
and the salvation of my soul. I trust that Thou in
Thy infinite goodness and wisdom wilt give me what
Thou knowest to be best for me. To all these
graces add that highest and most precious gift, the
crown and perfection of all Thy other gifts, the grace
of final perseverance. Bless me that I may live a
holy life, die a happy death and glorify Thee eternally
in heaven.

[You may here add any particular petitions for yourself
and for your neighbor. Do not forget to pray for the
Church, the Sovereign Pontiff, and all superiors, both
ecclesiastical and secular. Recommend to our dear
Lord the regular and secular clergy, as also the members
of all Religious Orders, and pray Him to give them the
true spirit of their holy vocation. Pray for your relatives,
friends, and benefactors, for the afflicted, the sick, and

those in their agony. Pray for the poor holy souls in purgatory. Recommend all poor sinners, and pray for their conversion and salvation. Pray for heretics and infidels, beseeching God to enlighten them and to lead them to the true faith.]

I SHOULD, indeed, be ungrateful, O my Jesus, if after Thou hast given me Thyself in this holy communion, I were to delay an instant in giving myself entirely to Thee. I offer Thee, most loving Lord, my soul, together with my liberty. I offer Thee my understanding, that, sanctified by Thee, it may be occupied earnestly in the consideration of Thy blessed passion and death, and Thy divine attributes. I give Thee my memory, that I may ever have in remembrance the infinite mercies Thou hast shown me. I give Thee my will, that by Thy holy love I may be entirely conformed to Thy divine will, desiring nothing but what Thou willest, and rejecting everything that is displeasing to Thee. I give Thee my whole self, to be sanctified by Thee in soul and body. O my Jesus, detach my heart from creatures, unite it perfectly to Thine own, and, hiding it within the loving wound of Thy side, imprint deeply in it the memory of Thy bitter passion and the sorrows of Thy most holy Mother; so that, by frequent meditation on these mysteries, I may be filled with sorrow for my past sins, and for the time to come faithfully correspond to Thine infinite love.

Blessed and praised every moment be the Most Holy and Most Divine Sacrament!

"O sweetest Heart of Jesus, I implore that I may ever love Thee more and more."

Indulgence of 300 days, each time. — Pius IX, Nov. 26, 1876.

Sweet heart of Mary, be my salvation!

Indulgence of 300 days, each time. — Pius IX, Sept. 30, 1852.

O Mary, who didst come into this world free from stain! obtain of God for me that I may leave it without sin.

Indulgence of 100 days, once a day. — Pius IX, March 27, 1863.

Virgin Mother of God, Mary, pray to Jesus for me.

Indulgence of 50 days, once a day. — Leo XIII, March 29, 1894.

Holy Virgin Mary, immaculate Mother of God and our Mother, speak thou for us to the Heart of Jesus, Who is thy Son, and our Brother.

Indulgence of 100 days, once a day. — Leo XIII, Dec. 20, 1890.

Jesus, Mary, and Joseph, I give you my heart and my soul.

Jesus, Mary, and Joseph, assist me in my last agony. Jesus, Mary, and Joseph, may I breathe out my soul in peace with you!

Indulgence of 300 days, each time, for all three. — Pius VII, Aug. 26, 1814.

JESUS, gentle Saviour,
God of might and power,
Thou Thyself art dwelling
In me at this hour.

Multiply Thy graces,
Chiefly love and fear,
And, dear Lord, the chiefest,
Grace to persevere.

When my heart Thou leavest,
Lord, worthless though it be,
Give it to Thy Mother
To be kept for Thee.

Prayer to the Blessed Virgin

O MARY, you desire so much to see Jesus loved; if you love me, this is the favor which I ask of you, to obtain for me a great personal love of Jesus Christ. You obtain from your Son whatever you please; pray then for me that I may never lose the grace of God and that I may increase in holiness and perfection from day to day. By that grief which you suffered on Calvary, when you beheld Jesus expire on the cross, obtain for me a happy death, that by loving Jesus, and you, my Mother, on earth I may receive the reward of loving and blessing you eternally in heaven.

Petitions of St. Augustine

O LORD Jesus, let me know myself, let me know Thee,
And desire nothing else but Thee.
Let me hate myself and love Thee,
And do all things for the sake of Thee.
Let me humble myself, and exalt Thee,
And think of nothing else but Thee.
Let me die to myself, and live in Thee,
And take whatever happens as coming from Thee.
Let me forsake myself and walk after Thee,
And ever desire to follow Thee.
Let me flee from myself, and turn to Thee,
That so I may merit to be defended by Thee.
Let me fear for myself, let me fear Thee,

And be amongst those who are chosen by Thee.
Let me distrust myself, and trust in Thee,
And ever obey for the love of Thee.
Let me cleave to nothing but only to Thee,
And ever be poor for the sake of Thee.
Look upon me, that I may love Thee;
Call me, that I may see Thee
And forever possess Thee. Amen.

Indulgence of 50 days, once a day. — Leo XIII, Sept. 25, 1883.

Prayer to Jesus Crucified

EN EGO, O bone et dulcissime Jesu, ante conspectum tuum genibus me provolvo ac maximo animi ardore te oro atque obtestor ut meum in cor vividos fidei, spei, et charitatis sensus, atque veram peccatorum meorum pœnitentiam, eaque emendandi firmissimam voluntatem velis imprimere: dum magno animi affectu et dolore tua quinque vulnera mecum ipse considero, ac mente contemplor, illud præ oculis habens quod jam in ore ponebat tuo David propheta de te, O bone Jesu: "Foderunt manus meas et pedes meos; dinumeraverunt omnia ossa mea."

LOOK down upon me, good and gentle Jesus, while before Thy face I humbly kneel, and with burning soul pray and beseech Thee to fix deep in my heart lively sentiments of faith, hope, and charity, true contrition for my sins, and a firm purpose of amendment; while I contemplate with great love and tender pity Thy five wounds, pondering over them within me, and calling to mind what the prophet David put in Thy mouth concerning Thee, O, good Jesus: "They have pierced my hands and my feet; they have numbered all my bones" (*Ps.* xxi. 17, 18).

His Holiness, Pope Pius IX, by a decree of the Sacred Congregation of Indulgences, July 31, 1858, following the decrees already issued by his predecessors, confirmed anew the *plenary indulgence* granted by Clement VIII and Benedict XIV, and confirmed by Pius VII and Leo XII, to those who shall say this prayer. He declared, moreover, that those who wish to gain this plenary indulgence, must say this prayer with devotion before an image or picture of our crucified Redeemer; and, being truly penitent, after confession and communion, spend some time in prayer for the intention of the Pope.

Reflections after Communion

1. CALL to mind frequently during the day that you have received Jesus in the Blessed Sacrament and say to yourself: "*This morning Jesus Christ, the Son of God, condescended to come and dwell within me, and gave Himself to me.*" By doing this, you will derive greater fruit from your communion; you will gain more patience under difficulties, and be more careful in keeping the grace of God in your soul; you will more easily acquire true and real devotion; you will set a good example to others, and have a continual inducement to lead a good Christian life. Make Father Russell's thought and prayer your own:

"DURING all the hours that follow of this day, my thoughts, my words, and my deeds must be the thoughts and words and deeds that are fitting one on whom so many graces are showered hour by hour, the latest being this sacramental communion. And so from day to day, from communion to communion, may I sanctify my soul and serve Thee, my almighty and all-merciful God, my Creator, my Redeemer, my Judge — from day to day, and from communion to communion, on to the last communion which I hope to receive as my

Viaticum. May that Viaticum 'conduct my soul, pure from sin, safe to the feet of my Jesus, Who has just now come to me as my Saviour, but then must be my Judge. O Jesus, my Saviour, be to me indeed a Saviour then and now and forever."

2. Retire frequently into your heart, in order to renew an act of adoration of Jesus, or of thanksgiving for the loving visit He made you in the morning, and rekindle the fire of divine charity by some holy aspiration. We would not so quickly lose the fervor of devotion and the love of God, if we took greater pains about this; and Jesus Christ would not have to lament the coldness of men toward Him, if they only thought oftener of His benefits and His love, especially in the Most Holy Sacrament, and thanked Him becomingly.

3. Frequently renew the offering of your heart to our dear Lord. By giving Himself to you, He desires to gain you to His love; He earnestly asks you to give Him your heart in exchange for the infinite gift He has bestowed upon you. Will you be so ungrateful as to deny Him your heart, and to give it to the world and the devil on the very day on which He has come to take possession of it? Ah! no; this must not be; you have consecrated your heart to Jesus in your communion; you must ratify and confirm this offering; and if the world, with its enticements, vanities, and false pleasures, wishes to enter into your heart, say that you have given it forever to Jesus. If the devil with his suggestions, and the flesh with its temptations, assail your heart, answer generously and courageously that you have given it to Jesus, to be His and His alone and forever. Oh, if all Christians were but to do this after their communion, they would preserve the grace of God, and not relapse into sin.

4. Remember that your tongue has received Jesus, that it has touched His sacred body when you went to communion. Only recall this thought to mind when you feel tempted to speak impatiently, or so as to offend or injure

your neighbor; and surely it will keep you from offending Jesus with that tongue which has been sanctified by the touch of His sacred flesh.

5. In connection with your visits to the Blessed Sacrament, make a *spiritual communion*, renewing in the most lively manner your desire to receive our dear Lord into your heart. Remember, for love of us Jesus remains night and day in the tabernacle, ardently desiring to communicate Himself to our souls, and bestow His graces upon us. Ah! what monstrous forgetfulness and ingratitude, if, when we can easily visit Him, we neglect to go to Him during the day, to pay our homage and adoration to Him in return for all His love.

N.B. — To these devotions after communion may be added (or in place of them may be substituted), according to one's time and pleasure, other acts and prayers in honor of the Blessed Sacrament, the passion of Our Lord, or the Sacred Heart of Jesus.

Extract from the Decree on Daily Communion

Given at Rome the 20th day of December, 1905

1. FREQUENT and daily communion as a thing most earnestly desired by Christ our Lord and by the Catholic Church should be open to all the faithful, of whatever rank and condition of life; so that no one who is in the state of grace, and who approaches the Holy Table with a right and devout intention, can lawfully be hindered therefrom.

2. A right intention consists in this: That he who approaches the Holy Table should do so, not out of routine, or vainglory, or human respect, but for the purpose of pleasing God, or being more closely united with Him by charity, and of seeking this divine remedy for his weaknesses and defects.

3. Although it is more expedient that those who communicate frequently or daily should be free from venial sins, especially from such as are fully deliberate, and from any affection thereto; nevertheless it is sufficient that they be free from mortal sin, with the purpose of never sinning mortally in future; and, if they have this sincere purpose, it is impossible but that daily communicants should gradually emancipate themselves from even venial sins, and from all affection thereto.

4. But whereas the sacraments of the New Law, though they take effect *ex opere operato*, nevertheless produce a greater effect in proportion as the dispositions of the recipient are better; therefore, care is to be taken that holy communion be preceded by serious preparation, and followed by a suitable thanksgiving according to each one's strength, circumstances, and duties.

5. That the practice of frequent and daily communion may be carried out with greater prudence and more abundant merit, the confessor's advice should be asked. Confessors, however, are to be careful not to dissuade any one from frequent and daily communion, provided that he is in a state of grace and approaches with a right intention.

6. But since it is plain that, by the frequent or daily reception of the Holy Eucharist, union with Christ is fostered, the spiritual life more abundantly sustained, the soul more richly endowed with virtues, and an even surer pledge of everlasting happiness bestowed on the recipient, therefore parish priests, confessors, and preachers — in accordance with the approved teaching of the Roman Catechism (Part ii. cap. 4, n. 60) — are frequently and with great zeal, to exhort the faithful to this devout and salutary practice.

Our Lord Himself more than once, and in no ambiguous terms, pointed out the necessity of eating His flesh and drinking His blood, especially in these words: "This is the bread that cometh down from heaven; not as your fathers did eat manna and are dead: he that eateth this bread shall live forever " (*John* vii. 59).   **Now from this** comparison of the food of angels with bread and with the manna, it was easily to be understood by His disciples that, as the body is daily nourished with bread, and as the Hebrews were daily nourished with manna in the desert, so the Christian soul might daily partake of this heavenly Bread and be refreshed thereby. Moreover, whereas, in the Lord's Prayer, we are bidden to ask for "our daily bread," the holy Fathers of the Church all but unanimously teach that by these words must be understood not so much that material bread which is the support of the body, as the eucharistic Bread which ought to be our daily food.

Moreover, the desire of Jesus Christ and of the Church that all the faithful should daily approach the sacred Banquet is directed chiefly to this end, that the faithful, being united to God by means of the sacrament, may thence derive strength to resist their sensual passions, to cleanse themselves from the stains of daily faults, and to avoid these graver sins to which human frailty is liable; so that its primary purpose is not that the honor and reverence due to Our Lord may be safeguarded, or that the sacrament may serve as a reward of virtue bestowed on the recipients (St. Augustine, Serm. 57 in Matt., de Orat. Dom. n. 7).   Hence the holy Council of Trent calls the Eucharist "the antidote whereby we are delivered from daily faults and preserved from deadly sins " (Sess. xiii. c. 11).

Prayer for the Propagation of the Pious Custom of Daily Communion

O SWEET Jesus, Who didst come into the world to give to all souls the life of Thy grace, and Who, to preserve and nourish in them this life, hast wished to be their daily food and the daily remedy of their daily weakness, we humbly supplicate Thee, by Thy

Heart so inflamed with love for us, to shed upon all souls Thy divine Spirit, that they who, unhappily, are in mortal sin may be converted to Thee and recover the life of grace that they have lost, and that they who, by Thy help, already live this divine life, may devoutly approach Thy Holy Table every day that they can; so that by means of daily communion, receiving daily the antidote of their daily venial sins, and feeding daily the life of Thy grace in their soul, and thus purifying themselves always more and more, they may, at last, arrive at the possession of the life of beatitude with Thee! Amen.

Indulgence of 300 days, every day. — Pius X.

Third Exercise

Before Holy Communion

Prayer for Help

MY GOD, help me to make a good communion. To Thy glory and for the good of my soul I wish to receive the Most Holy Sacrament. Mary, my Mother, pray to Jesus for me. My good angel guardian, lead me to the altar of God. My patron saints, pray for me that I may receive the Lord with a heart that is pleasing to Him and with great profit to my soul.

Act of Faith and Adoration

MY LORD Jesus Christ, I believe that Thou art truly present in the Blessed Sacrament. I believe that in holy communion I shall receive Thy sacred body and Thy precious blood. My faith in Thy real presence in the Holy Eucharist is firmly founded on Thy word, O eternal Truth. My Saviour and my God, with the angels who surround Thy altar-throne, I bow down in humble adoration before Thy Majesty.

Act of Hope

O JESUS! relying on Thy promises, goodness, and power, I hope to obtain from Thee the graces necessary for the sanctification and salvation of my soul.

Act of Love and Desire

JESUS, my God, Thou art infinitely good and perfect. I love Thee above all things and with my whole heart. I desire to receive Thee in holy communion that I may love Thee more and serve Thee better. Come to me and strengthen me, so that I may never be separated from Thee on earth and that I may live with Thee eternally in heaven.

Act of Contrition

MY GOD, I detest all the sins of my life. I am truly sorry that I have sinned, because Thou art infinitely good and sin displeases Thee. Have mercy on me and pardon my offenses. I am resolved to avoid the occasions of sin and never again to offend Thee.

Act of Humility and Confidence

JESUS, my Lord, I confess that I am a sinner. But in Thy goodness Thou dost invite me to approach Thy Holy Table and to partake of Thy heavenly Banquet. Trusting in Thy mercy I come to Thee with confidence, albeit with it a contrite and humble heart. Lord, I am not worthy that Thou shouldst enter under my roof; but say only the word, and my soul shall be healed. Come to me, Jesus, come to me, and keep me in Thy love and Thy grace forevermore.

Prayer

SEE where Thy boundless love has reached, my loving Jesus! Thou, of Thy flesh and precious blood, hast made ready for me a banquet whereby to give me all Thyself. Who drove Thee to this excess of love for me? Thy Heart, Thy loving Heart. O adorable Heart of Jesus, burning furnace of divine love! within Thy sacred wound take Thou my soul; so that, in that school of charity, I may learn to love Him Who has given me such wondrous proofs of His great love. Amen.

Indulgence of 100 days, once a day. — Pius VII, Feb. 9, 1818.

JESUS, hidden God, I cry to Thee;
O Jesus, hidden Light, I turn to Thee;
O Jesus, hidden Love, I run to Thee;
With all the strength I have I worship Thee;
With all the love I have I cling to Thee;
With all my soul I long to be with Thee,
And fear no more to fail, or fall from Thee.
O Jesus, deathless Love, Who seekest me,
Thou Who didst die for longing love of me,
Thou King, in all Thy beauty, come to me,
White-robed, blood-sprinkled, Jesus, come to me,
And go no more, dear Lord, away from me.

IN RECEIVING HOLY COMMUNION

(1) In going to the altar rail, and returning to your place, keep your *hands* joined, your *eyes* cast down, and your *thoughts* on Jesus Christ.

(2) At the altar rail, take the communion cloth and spread it before you, under your chin.

(3) Hold your head straight up, keep your eyes closed, your mouth well open, and your tongue out, resting on the lower lip. Then, with great reverence, receive the sacred Host, saying in your heart, with all the faith of St. Thomas — "*My Lord and my God!*"

AFTER HOLY COMMUNION
Prayer of Adoration and Praise

"BLESS the Lord, O my soul! and let all that is within me bless His holy name."

"Bless the Lord, O my soul! and never forget all that He hath done for thee."

"Now your King is here, Whom you have chosen and desired" (1 *Kings* xii).

"I will extol Thee, O God, my King" (*Ps.* cxliv).

Thou alone art my King and my God, "the King of kings, and Lord of lords" (1 *Tim.* vi), "my King Who is in His sanctuary" (*Ps.* lxvii).

"Sing praises to our God, sing praises to our King" (*Ps.* xlvi).

"For this is God, our God unto eternity, and forever and ever; He shall rule forevermore" (*Ps.* xlvii).

"O bless our God and make the voice of His praise to be heard" (*Ps.* lxv).

"I will cry to God, the most High, to God Who hath done good to me" (*Ps.* lvi).

"Bless the Lord, all ye servants of the Lord, who stand in the house of the Lord, in the courts of the house of our God" (*Ps.* cxxxiii).

"Oh, magnify the Lord with me, and let us extol His name together" (*Ps.* xxxiii).

"Blessed be the Lord, for He hath shown His wonderful mercy to me" (*Ps.* xxx).

"My soul doth magnify the Lord, and my spirit hath rejoiced in God my Saviour" (*Luke* i).

"Give glory to the Lord for He is good. for His mercy endureth forever" (*Ps.* cvi).

"For He is our peace" (*Eph.* ii), "making peace through the blood of His cross" (*Col.* i).

Blessed be God.

Blessed be His holy name.

Blessed be Jesus Christ, true God and true man.

Blessed be Jesus in the most holy Sacrament of the Altar.

"Thanks be to God for His unspeakable gift" (2 *Cor.* ix).

"My God and my Saviour!" (*Ps.* lxi).

"Say to my soul: I am thy salvation" (*Ps.* xxxiv).

"This day is salvation come to this house" (*Luke* xix).

"Behold, God is my Saviour: I will deal confidently" (*Is.* xii).

"The Lord is my rock, and my strength, and my Saviour" (*2 Kings* xxii).

"He loved me and delivered Himself for me" (*Gal.* ii).

"It is good for me to adhere to my God, to put my hope in the Lord God. I will hear what the Lord God will speak in me."

Here pause a while, and commune with your God, your Lord and Redeemer. Tell Him how grateful you are for this holy communion and for all His graces and blessings. Tell Him again how sorry you are on account of your sins; how much you love Him now, and what you intend to do to prove your love. You want to imitate the virtues of the Sacred Heart of Jesus; resolve to become more like to Jesus. Offer Him your heart and ask Him to make it like to His own most sacred Heart. Resolve to struggle valiantly against your predominant passion, and your evil inclinations. Be generous in your sacrifices for the love of God, and He will be generous in His rewards — generous in accordance with His infinite goodness and power.

If you love God, you will keep His commandments. That is the visible proof of charity. Love can not rest .in words — it must go out into action. If you love God, you will do something for Him. Love is ingenious at finding ways in which to show itself. It manifests itself in acts of praise, in acts of self-denial, in acts of kindness to God's other creatures. Love without works is dead.

Approach Our Lord with confidence and ask Him for whatever temporal and spiritual favor you desire, but above all things pray for the gift of final perseverance. The love and the grace of God are the most precious gifts. "Seek ye first the kingdom of God and all these things shall be added unto you" (*Luke* xii. 31). In your sufferings and in your prayers resolve to say with Christ in the Garden: "Not my will but Thine be done." Saints and spiritual writers agree that in Holy Mass and after communion our prayers are most acceptable and most likely to be granted.

Act of Faith

O JESUS, my God and my Saviour, Thy word is Truth. I firmly believe that this is Thy sacred body and blood which I have just received, and that Thou art now really and truly present within me. I can only prostrate myself before Thee, and cry out from the depths of my heart, "Thou art my Lord, my God, and my All!"

Act of Hope and Confidence

MY SOUL, confide in Jesus. He can do thee every good. He is God and He loves thee. In the Blessed Eucharist He is sweet and mild and generous. Urged by love, He comes to manifest His love to thee. Yes, my dear Jesus, Thou art my hope and my salvation. Sacred Heart of Jesus, I place my trust in Thee. I trust, O Lord, that Thou wilt enkindle in my heart the flame of Thy pure love, and a real desire to please Thee; so that, from this day forward, I may never will anything but what Thou willest.

Act of Humility

O JESUS, my God! Thou art infinite in all perfections; and I am but dust, and unto dust shall I return. Depart from me, O Lord, for I am a sinful man. Yet, O my sweet Jesus, if Thou leavest me, to whom shall I go? What will become of me? Rather will I say, "Stay with me, Lord; abide always within my heart; and may my heart make every sacrifice for Thee."

Act of Love

O JESUS, my God, infinite Love, Source, and Fount of all that is true, of all that is good, of all that is beautiful, how can I help loving Thee, both because of Thine own infinite goodness and because of Thy goodness and kindness to me! My Jesus! I love Thee with my whole heart. Oh! may I love Thee daily more and more! Amen.

Act of Thanksgiving

MY GOOD Jesus, I thank Thee with all my heart for giving me Thyself, the Source of all graces, in holy communion. I thank Thee for all the blessings that I have received from Thee, especially through the Holy Eucharist, in which Thou art ever present to console us and to help us in our needs.

In thanksgiving for all Thy favors, I offer Thee all that I am and have. Dispose of me according to Thy pleasure. May Thy will be done in me and through me now and forever.

Jesus, receive my poor offering.

What can I give Thee?

I give myself to Thee, that I may always serve Thee.

I give Thee my *body*, that it may be chaste and pure.

I give Thee my *soul*, that it may be free from sin.

I give Thee my *heart*, that it may always love Thee.

I give Thee every breath that I shall breathe, and

especially my last; I give Thee *myself* in life and in death, that I may be Thine forever and glorify Thee eternally.

Remember the words of Jesus: "Ask and you shall receive," and *pray for yourself*.

O JESUS, wash away my sins with Thy precious blood.

O Jesus, the struggle against temptation is not yet finished. My Jesus, when temptation comes near me, make me strong against it. In the moment of temptation may I always say, "Jesus, mercy!" "Mary, help of Christians, help me."

O Jesus, may I lead a good life; may I die a happy death. May I receive Thee in Holy Viaticum before I die. May I say when I am dying, "Jesus, Mary and Joseph, I give you my heart and my soul."

Listen now for a moment to Jesus; perhaps He has something to say to you. There may be some promise you have made and broken, which He wishes you to make again and keep.

Answer Jesus in your heart, and tell Him all your troubles. Then, *pray for others*.

O JESUS, have mercy on Thy holy Church. Bless our Holy Father, and grant what he asks of Thee.

O Jesus, have pity on all *sinners, heretics*, and *infidels*. Save them by Thy most precious blood.

O Jesus, bless my father, my mother, my brothers, and sisters; my relatives, friends, and benefactors; and all for whom I have promised to pray; bless them as Thy kind Heart knows how to bless them.

O Jesus, have pity on the *poor souls suffering in purgatory*, and give them eternal rest.

Act of Petition

O JESUS, merciful Saviour, relying on Thy infinite goodness, I hope to obtain through this holy communion all the graces of which I stand in need for my greater sanctification and eternal salvation. Begging Thy pardon for all the transgressions of my past life, I first of all beseech Thee to give me the grace that I may never again fall into any mortal sin. I would rather be dead than live a moment without Thy grace and Thy love. But Thou, O Lord, knowest how weak I am and how prone to evil. Do Thou strengthen me by Thy grace that I may be faithful in doing Thy will. Thou canst heal all the evils of my soul since Thou art its true Physician, Who givest me Thy body and blood in this Blessed Sacrament as a sovereign medicine for all my infirmities. Dispel the darkness of ignorance from my understanding by Thy heavenly light; banish the corruption and malice of my will by the fire of Thy divine love; subdue in me all evil passions and help me especially to overcome my predominant fault; stand by me in all temptations of the devil, the world, and the flesh, that I may not fall into their snares. Increase my faith, and grant that in my daily life I may be guided by Thy example and the maxims of Thy holy Gospel. Teach me to be poor in spirit; to place no value upon the world's transitory pleasures and honors; to be meek and humble of heart and in patience to possess my soul; to love Thee more and more and to walk always in Thy presence; to be kind and generous to my neighbor; to strive earnestly to advance every day in holiness and perfection. May Thy holy will be accomplished in me. Grant me, above all, the grace of final perseverance, that I may become a saint.

O Mary, immaculate Mother of God! All ye angels and saints of heaven! unite your prayers with mine as you stand before the throne of divine grace, and, above all, pray that I may be united with you in loving, praising, and enjoying God for all eternity.

Say the prayer before a crucifix, *Look down upon me, good and gentle Jesus* (p. 417), to obtain a plenary indulgence.

Sweet Heart of Jesus, be my love!

Indulgence of 300 days, once a day. — Leo XIII, May 21, 1892.

Sweet Heart of Mary, be my salvation!

Indulgence of 300 days, each time. — Pius IX, Sept. 30. 1852.

Holy Archangel Michael, defend us in battle, that we may not perish in the tremendous judgment.

Indulgence of 100 days, once a day. — Leo XIII, Aug. 19, 1893.

St. Joseph, model and patron of those who love the Sacred Heart of Jesus, pray for us.

Indulgence of 100 days, once a day. — Leo XIII Dec. 19, 1891.

St. Joseph, reputed father of Our Lord Jesus Christ and true spouse of Mary, ever Virgin, pray for us.

Indulgence of 300 days, once a day. — Leo XIII, May 15, 1891.

> Help us, Joseph, in our earthly strife,
> E'er to lead a pure and blameless life.

Indulgence of 300 days, once a day. — Leo XIII, March 18, 1882.

Benediction of the Blessed Sacrament

Prayers at Benediction

I

O JESUS, Who art about to give Thy benediction to me, and to all who are here present, I humbly beseech Thee that it may impart to each and all of us the special graces we need. Yet more than this I ask. Let Thy blessing go forth far and wide. Let it be felt in the souls of the afflicted who can not come here to receive it at Thy feet. Let the weak and tempted feel its power wherever they may be. Let poor sinners feel its influence, arousing them to come to Thee. Grant to me, O Lord, and to all here present, a strong, personal love of Thee, a lively horror of sin, a higher esteem of grace, great zeal for Thy honor and glory, for the interest of Thy sacred Heart, for our own sanctification and for the salvation of souls. Amen.

II

O DIVINE Redeemer, Who in Thy infinite goodness hast been pleased to leave us Thy precious body and blood in the Blessed Eucharist, we adore Thee with the most profound respect, and return Thee our most humble thanks for all the favors Thou hast bestowed upon us, especially for the institution

434

of this most holy sacrament. As Thou art the source of every blessing, we entreat Thee to pour down Thy benediction this day upon us and our relations, and upon all those for whom we offer our prayers. And that nothing may interrupt the course of Thy blessing, take from our hearts whatever is displeasing to Thee. Pardon our sins, O my God, which, for the love of Thee, we sincerely detest; purify our hearts, sanctify our souls, and bestow a blessing on us like that which Thou didst grant to Thy disciples at Thy ascension into heaven; grant us a blessing that may change us, consecrate us, unite us perfectly to Thee, fill us with Thy spirit, and be to us in this life a foretaste of those blessings which Thou hast prepared for. Thy elect in Thy heavenly kingdom. Amen.

✠ Salutaris Hostia

O SALUTARIS
    Hostia,
  Quæ cœli pandis
    ostium.
Bella premunt
   hostilia;
  Da robur fer
    auxilium.

Uni trinoque
    Domino,
  Sit sempiterna
   gloria:
Qui vitam sine
   termino,
  Nobis donet in
    patria. Amen.

O SAVING Victim, open-
    ing wide
The gate of heav'n to man
   below!
Our foes press on from every
   side;
Thine aid supply, Thy
   strength bestow.

To Thy great name be end-
   less praise,
Immortal Godhead, One
   in Three;
Oh, grant us endless length
   of days,
In our true native land with
   Thee. Amen.

Tantum Ergo Sacramentum

TANTUM ergo sacra-
   mentum,
   Veneremur cernui;
Et antiquum docu-
   mentum
   Novo cedat ritui;
Præstet fides supple-
   mentum
   Sensuum defectui.

DOWN in adoration fall-
   ing,
Lo! the sacred Host we hail!
Lo! o'er ancient forms de-
   parting,
Newer rites of grace prevail;
Faith for all defects supply-
   ing,
Where the feeble senses fail.

Genitori, Genito-
   que,
   Laus et jubilatio;
Salus, honor, virtus quo-
   que
   Sit et benedictio:
Procedenti ab utroque
   Compar sit laudatio.
           Amen.

To the everlasting Father,
And the Son Who reigns on
   high,
With the Holy Ghost pro-
   ceeding
Forth from each eternally,
Be salvation, honor, blessing,
Might, and endless majesty.
           Amen.

V. Panem de cœlo præ-
stitisti eis.
R. Omne delectamentum
in se habentem.

V. Thou hast given them
bread from heaven.
R. Replenished with all
sweetness and delight.

Prayer

DEUS, qui nobis, sub
   sacramento mirabili,
passionis tuæ memoriam
reliquisti, tribue quæ-
sumus, ita nos corporis et
sanguinis tui sacra mys-
teria venerari, ut re-

O GOD, Who hast left
   us in this wonderful
sacrament a perpetual me-
morial of Thy passion; grant
us the grace, we beseech
Thee, so to venerate the
sacred mysteries of Thy

demptionis tui fructum in nobis jugiter sentiamus. Qui vivis et regnas in sæcula sæculorum. *R.* Amen.

body and blood that we may ever feel within us the fruit of Thy Redemption. Who livest and reignest world without end. *R.* Amen.

AT THE BLESSING

O SACRAMENT most holy! O Sacrament divine! All praise and all thanksgiving be every moment Thine.

May Thy blessing come down upon me, O Lord! ✠ in the name of the Father, and of the Son, and of the Holy Ghost. Amen.

An Act of Reparation for Profane Language

BLESSED be God.
Blessed be His holy name.
Blessed be Jesus Christ, true God and true man.
Blessed be the name of Jesus.
Blessed be His most sacred Heart.
Blessed be Jesus in the most holy Sacrament of the Altar.
Blessed be the great Mother of God, Mary most holy.
Blessed be her holy and immaculate conception.
Blessed be the name of Mary, virgin and mother
Blessed be St. Joseph, her most chaste spouse.
Blessed be God in His angels and in His saints.

Indulgence of two years for every public recital after Mass or Benediction.—Leo XIII, Feb. 2, 1897.

Te Deum Laudamus

TE Deum laudamus: Te Dominum confitemur.

Te æternum Patrem, omnis terra veneratur.

Tibi omnes angeli : tibi cœli et universæ potestates:

Tibi cherubim et seraphim incessabili voce proçlamant:

Sanctus, sanctus, sanctus, Dominus Deus Sabaoth.

Pleni sunt cœli et terra majestatis gloriæ tuæ.

Te gloriosus apostolorum chorus:

Te prophetarum laudabilis numerus:

Te martyrum candidatus laudat cxercitus.

Te per orbem terrarum sancta confitetur Ecclesia.

Patrem immensæ majestatis;

Venerandum tuum verum et unicum Filium;

Sanctum quoque Paraclitum Spiritum.

Tu Rex gloriæ, Christe.

Tu Patris sempiternus es Filius.

Tu ad liberandum suscepturus hominem,

WE praise Thee, O God; we acknowledge Thee to be our Lord.

All the earth worships Thee, the Father everlasting.

To Thee all the angels cry aloud; the heavens, and all the heavenly powers,

To Thee the cherubim and seraphim continually do cry:

Holy, holy, holy, Lord God of Sabaoth.

Heaven and earth are full of the majesty of Thy glory.

The glorious choir of the apostles praises Thee.

The admirable company of the prophets praises Thee.

The noble army of the martyrs praises Thee.

The holy Church throughout the world acknowledges Thee.

The Father of infinite majesty;

Thy adorable, true, and only Son;

Also, the Holy Ghost, the Comforter.

Thou, O Christ, art the King of glory.

Thou art the everlasting Son of the Father.

When Thou didst take upon Thee to deliver man,

non horruisti Virginis uterum.

Thou didst not disdain the Virgin's womb.

Tu devicto mortis aculeo, aperuisti credentibus regna cœlorum.

Having overcome the sting of death, Thou didst open the kingdom of heaven to all believers.

Tu ad dexteram Dei sedes in gloria Patris.

Thou sittest at the right hand of God, in the glory of the Father.

Judex crederis esse venturus.

We believe that Thou shalt come to be our Judge.

Te ergo quæsumus, tuis famulis subveni, quos pretioso sanguine redemisti.

We therefore pray Thee to help Thy servants, whom Thou hast redeemed with Thy precious blood.

Æterna fac cum sanctis tuis in gloria numerari.

Make them to be numbered with Thy saints in glory everlasting.

Salvum fac populum tuum, Domine, et benedic hæreditati tuæ.

Save Thy people, O Lord, and bless Thy inheritance.

Et rege eos, et extolle illos usque in æternum.

Govern them, and raise them up forever.

Per singulos dies benedicimus Te.

Every day we bless Thee.

Et laudamus nomen tuum in sæculum, et in sæculum sæculi.

And we praise Thy name forever; yea, forever and ever.

Dignare, Domine, die isto, sine peccato nos custodire.

Vouchsafe, O Lord, this day, to keep us from sin.

Miserere nostri, Domine, miserere nostri.

Have mercy on us, O Lord, have mercy on us.

Fiat misericordia tua, Domine, super nos: quemadmodum speravimus in Te.

Let Thy mercy, O Lord, be upon us, as we have hoped in Thee.

In Te, Domine, speravi; non confundar in æternum.

In Thee, O Lord, I have hoped; let me never be confounded.

On occasions of solemn thanksgiving the following prayers are added:

V. **B**ENEDICTUS es, Domine, Deus Patrum nostrorum.

R. Et laudabilis, et gloriosus in sæcula.

V. Benedicamus Patrem et Filium, cum Sancto Spiritu.

R. Laudemus et superexaltemus eum in sæcula.

V. Benedictus es, Domine Deus, in firmamento cœli.

R. Et laudabilis, et gloriosus, ·et superexaltatus in sæcula.

V. Benedic, anima mea, Dominum.

R. Et noli oblivisci omnes retributiones ejus.

V. Domine, exaudi orationem meam.

R. Et clamor meus ad te veniat.

V. Dominus vobiscum.

R. Et cum spiritu tuo.

V. **B**LESSED art Thou, O Lord, the God of our fathers.

R. And worthy to be praised, and glorified forever.

V. Let us bless the Father and the Son, with the Holy Ghost.

R. Let us praise and magnify Him forever.

V. Blessed art Thou, O Lord, in the firmament of heaven.

R. And worthy to be praised, glorified, and exalted forever.

V. Bless the Lord, O my soul.

R. And forget not all His benefits.

V. O Lord, hear my prayer.

R. And let my cry come unto Thee.

V. The Lord be with you.

R. And with thy spirit.

Oremus

DEUS, cujus misericordiæ non est numerus, et bonitatis infinitus est thesaurus: piissimæ majestati tuæ pro col-

Let us pray

O GOD, Whose mercies are without number, and the treasure of Whose goodness is infinite; we render thanks to Thy most

latis donis gratias agimus, tuam semper clementiam exorantes; ut qui petentibus postulata concedis, eosdem non deserens, ad præmia futura disponas.

gracious Majesty for the gifts Thou hast bestowed upon us, evermore beseeching Thy clemency; that as Thou grantest the petitions of those who ask Thee, Thou wilt never forsake them, but wilt prepare them for the rewards to come.

DEUS, qui corda fidelium Sancti Spiritus illustratione docuisti: da nobis in eodem Spiritu recta sapere, et de ejus semper consolatione gaudere.

O GOD, Who hast taught the hearts of the faithful by the light of the Holy Spirit: grant us, by the same Spirit, to relish what is right, and evermore to rejoice in His consolation.

DEUS, qui neminem in Te sperantem nimium affligi permittis, sed pium precibus præstas auditum; pro postulationibus nostris, votisque susceptis gratias agimus, Te piissime deprecantes, ut a cunctis semper muniamur adversis. Per Christum Dominum nostrum.

O GOD, Who sufferest none that hope in Thee to be afflicted overmuch, but dost listen graciously to their prayers; we render Thee thanks because Thou hast received our supplications and vows; and we most humbly beseech Thee that we may evermore be protected from all adversities. Through Christ our Lord.

R. Amen.

R. Amen.

The Stations of the Cross

PREPARATORY PRAYER

MOST merciful Jesus! With a contrite heart and penitent spirit I purpose now to perform this devotion in honor of Thy bitter passion and death. I adore Thee most humbly as my Lord and my God. I thank Thee most heartily, my divine Saviour, for the infinite love wherewith Thou didst make the painful journey to Calvary for me, a wretched sinner, and didst die upon the cross for my salvation. I am truly sorry for all my sins, because by them I have offended Thee, Who art infinitely good. I detest them and I am resolved to amend my life. Grant that I may gain all the indulgences which are attached to this devotion, and since Thou hast promised to draw all things to Thyself, draw my heart and my love to Thee, that I may live and die in union with Thee. Amen.

First Station

Jesus is Condemned to Death

V. We adore Thee, O Christ, and praise Thee:
R. Because by Thy holy cross Thou hast redeemed the world!

MEDITATION

JESUS, most innocent and perfectly sinless, was condemned to death, and, moreover, to the most ignominious death of the cross. To remain a friend

442

of Cæsar, Pilate delivered Him into the hands of His enemies. A fearful crime — to condemn Innocence to death, and to offend God in order not to displease men!

Prayer

O INNOCENT Jesus! Having sinned, I am guilty of eternal death, but Thou willingly dost accept the unjust sentence of death, that I might live. For whom, then, shall I henceforth live, if not for Thee, my Lord? Should I desire to please men, I could not be Thy servant. Let me, therefore, rather displease men and all the world than not please Thee, O Jesus.

Our Father, etc.; Hail Mary, etc.

V. Lord Jesus, crucified:
R. Have mercy on us!

Second Station

Jesus Carries His Cross

V. We adore Thee, O Christ, and praise Thee:
R. Because by Thy holy cross Thou hast redeemed the world!

MEDITATION

WHEN our divine Saviour beheld the cross, He stretched out His bleeding arms toward it with eager desire, lovingly embraced it, tenderly kissed it, and, placing it on His bruised shoulders, joyfully carried it, although He was worn and weary unto death.

Prayer

O MY Jesus! I can not be Thy friend and follower if I refuse to carry the cross. O dearly beloved cross! I embrace thee, I kiss thee, I joyfully accept thee from the hands of my God. Far be it from me to glory in anything, save in the cross of my Redeemer. By it the world shall be crucified to me·and I to the world, that I may be Thine, O Jesus, forever.

Our Father, etc.; Hail Mary, etc.

V. Lord Jesus, crucified:
R. Have mercy on us!

Third Station

Jesus Falls the First Time

V. We adore Thee, O Christ, and praise Thee:
R. Because by Thy holy cross Thou hast redeemed the world!

MEDITATION

O UR dear Saviour carrying the cross was so weakened by its heavy weight as to fall exhausted to the ground. Our sins and misdeeds were the heavy burden which oppressed Him; the cross was to Him light and sweet, but our sins were galling and insupportable.

Prayer

O MY Jesus! Thou didst bear my burden and the heavy weight of my sins. Should I, then, not bear in union with Thee my easy burden of suffering, and accept the sweet yoke of Thy commandments? Thy yoke is sweet and Thy burden is light: I therefore willingly accept it. I will take up my cross and follow Thee.

Our Father, etc.; Hail Mary, etc.

V. Lord Jesus, crucified:

R. Have mercy on us!

Fourth Station

Jesus Meets His Afflicted Mother

V. We adore Thee, O Christ, and praise Thee:

R. Because by Thy holy cross Thou hast redeemed the world!

MEDITATION

How painful and sad it must have been for Mary, the sorrowful Mother, to behold her beloved Son laden with the burden of the cross. What unspeakable pangs her most tender heart experienced! How earnestly did she desire to die in place of Jesus, or at least with Him! Implore this sorrowful Mother to assist you graciously in the hour of your death.

Prayer

O Jesus! O Mary! I am the cause of the great and manifold pains which pierce your loving hearts. O that my heart also would experience at least some of your sufferings! Mother of sorrows! pray for me that I may be truly sorry for my sins, bear my sufferings patiently in union with Thee, and merit to enjoy thy assistance in the hour of my death.

Our Father, etc.; Hail Mary, etc.
V. Lord Jesus, crucified:
R. Have mercy on us!

Fifth Station

Simon of Cyrene Helps Jesus to Carry the Cross

V. We adore Thee, O Christ, and praise Thee:
R. Because by Thy holy cross Thou hast redeemed the world!

MEDITATION

SIMON of Cyrene was compelled to assist Jesus in carrying His cross, and Jesus accepted his assistance. How willingly would He also permit you to carry the cross. He calls, but you hear Him not; He invites you, but you decline His invitation. What a reproach it is to bear the cross reluctantly!

Prayer

O JESUS! Whosoever does not take up his cross and follow Thee is not worthy of Thee. Behold, I will accompany Thee on the way of the cross; I will carry my cross cheerfully; I will walk in Thy bloodstained footsteps, and follow Thee, that I may be with Thee in life eternal.
Our Father, etc.; Hail Mary, etc.
V. Lord Jesus, crucified:
R. Have mercy on us!

Sixth Station

Veronica Wipes the Face of Jesus

V. We adore Thee, O Christ, and praise Thee:
R. Because by Thy holy cross Thou hast redeemed the world!

MEDITATION

VERONICA, impelled by devotion and compassion, wipes the disfigured face of Jesus with her veil. And Jesus imprints on it His holy countenance: a great recompense for so small a service. What return do you make to your Saviour for His great and manifold benefits?

Prayer

MOST merciful Jesus! What return shall I make for all the benefits Thou hast bestowed upon me? Behold I consecrate myself entirely to Thy service. I offer and consecrate to Thee my heart: imprint on it Thy sacred image, never again to be effaced by sin.

Our Father, etc.; Hail Mary, etc.
V. Lord Jesus, crucified:
R. Have mercy on us!

Seventh Station

Jesus Falls the Second Time

V. We adore Thee, O Christ, and praise Thee:
R. Because by Thy holy cross Thou hast redeemed the world!

MEDITATION

THE suffering Jesus, under the weight of His cross, again falls to the ground; but the cruel executioners do not permit Him to rest a moment. Pushing and striking Him, they urge Him onward. It is the frequent repetition of our sins which oppresses Jesus. Knowing and realizing this, how can I continue to sin?

Prayer

O JESUS, Son of David! Have mercy on me! Extend to me Thy gracious hand and support me, that I may never fall again into my old sins. From this very moment I will earnestly strive to reform my life and to avoid every sin. Help of the weak, strengthen me by Thy grace, without which I can do nothing, that I may carry out faithfully my good resolution.

Our Father, etc.; Hail Mary, etc.

V. Lord Jesus, crucified:

R. Have mercy on us!

Eighth Station

The Daughters of Jerusalem Weep over Jesus

V. We adore Thee, O Christ, and praise Thee:

R. Because by Thy holy cross Thou hast redeemed the world!

MEDITATION

THESE devoted women, moved by compassion, weep over the suffering Saviour. But He turns to them, saying: *"Weep not for Me Who am innocent, but weep for yourselves and for your children."* Weep *thou* also; for there is nothing more pleasing to Our Lord, and nothing more profitable for *thyself*, than tears that are shed in contrition for sin.

Prayer

O JESUS! Who will give to my eyes a fountain of tears, that day and night I may weep for my sins. I beseech Thee, through Thy bitter tears, to move my heart to compassion and repentance, so that I may weep all my days over Thy sufferings and still more over their cause, my sins.

Our Father, etc.; Hail Mary, etc.

V. Lord Jesus, crucified:

R. Have mercy on us!

Ninth Station

Jesus Falls the Third Time

V. We adore Thee, O Christ, and praise Thee:

R. Because by Thy holy cross Thou hast redeemed the world!

MEDITATION

JESUS, arriving exhausted at the foot of Calvary, falls the third time to the ground. His love for us, however, remains strong and fervent.

What a fearfully oppressive burden our sins must be to cause Jesus to fall so often! Had He, however, not taken them upon Himself, they would have plunged us into the abyss of hell.

Prayer

OST merciful Jesus! I return Thee infinite thanks for not permitting me to continue in sin and to fall, as I have so often deserved, into the depths of hell.   Enkindle in me an earnest desire of amendment; let me never again relapse, but vouchsafe me the grace to persevere in penance to the end of my life.

Our Father, etc.; Hail Mary, etc.
V. Lord Jesus, crucified:
R. Have mercy on us!

Tenth Station

Jesus is Stripped of His Garments

V. We adore Thee, O Christ, and praise Thee:
R. Because by Thy holy cross Thou hast redeemed the world!

MEDITATION

HEN Our Saviour had arrived on Calvary, He was cruelly despoiled of His garments.   How painful must this have been, because they adhered to His wounded and torn body and with them parts of His bloody skin were removed!   All the wounds of Jesus are renewed.   Jesus is despoiled of His garments that He might die possessed of nothing; how happy shall I also die after casting off my evil self with all its sinful inclinations!

Prayer

ELP me, Jesus! to conquer myself and to be renewed according to Thy will and desire.   I will not count the cost but will struggle bravely to cast off my evil propensities; despoiled of things temporal, of my own will, I desire to die, that I may live to Thee forevermore.

Our Father, etc.; Hail Mary, etc.

V. Lord Jesus, crucified:

R. Have mercy on us!

Eleventh Station

Jesus is Nailed to the Cross

V. We adore Thee, O Christ, and praise Thee:

R. Because by Thy holy cross Thou hast redeemed the world!

MEDITATION

JESUS, after He had been stripped of His garments, was violently thrown upon the cross, to which His hands and His feet were nailed most cruelly. In this excruciating pain He remained silent, and perfectly resigned to the will of His heavenly Father. He suffered patiently, because He suffered for me. How do I act in sufferings and in trouble? How fretful and impatient, how full of complaints I am!

Prayer

O JESUS, meek and gentle Lamb of God! I renounce forever my impatience. Crucify, O Lord! my flesh and its concupiscences. Punish me, afflict me in this life, as Thou willest, only spare me in eternity. I commit my destiny to Thee, resigning myself to Thy holy will: Not my will but Thine be done!

Our Father, etc.; Hail Mary, etc.
V. Lord Jesus, crucified:
R. Have mercy on us!

Twelfth Station

Jesus Dies on the Cross

V. We adore Thee, O Christ, and praise Thee:
R. Because by Thy holy cross Thou hast redeemed
the world!

MEDITATION

BEHOLD Jesus crucified! Behold His wounds, received for love of you! His whole appearance
betokens love! His head is bent to kiss you, His
arms are extended to embrace you, His Heart is open
to receive you. O superabundance of love! Jesus,
the Son of God, dies upon the cross, that man may
live and be delivered from everlasting death.

Prayer

O MOST amiable Jesus! If I can not sacrifice my
life for love of Thee, I will at least endeavor to
die to the world. How must I regard the world and
its vanities, when I behold Thee hanging on the
cross, covered with wounds? O Jesus! receive me
into Thy wounded Heart: I belong entirely to Thee;
for Thee alone do I desire to live and to die.
Our Father, etc.; Hail Mary, etc.
V. Lord Jesus, crucified:
R. Have mercy on us!

Thirteenth Station

Jesus is Taken Down from the Cross

V. We adore Thee, O Christ, and praise Thee:
R. Because by Thy holy cross Thou hast redeemed the world!

MEDITATION

JESUS did not descend from the cross, but remained on it until He died. And when taken down from it, He, in death as in life, rested on the bosom of His blessed Mother. Persevere in your resolutions of reform and do not part from the cross: he who persevereth to the end shall be saved. Consider, moreover, how pure the heart should be that receives the body and blood of Christ in the adorable Sacrament of the Altar.

Prayer

O LORD, Jesus! Thy lifeless body, mangled and lacerated, found a worthy resting-place on the bosom of Thy virgin Mother. Have I not often compelled Thee to dwell in my heart, despite its unworthiness to receive Thee? Create in me a new heart, that I may worthily receive Thy most sacred body in holy communion, and that Thou mayest remain in me and I in Thee, for all eternity.

Our Father, etc.; Hail Mary, etc.
V. Lord Jesus, crucified:
R. Have mercy on us!

Fourteenth Station

Jesus is Laid in the Sepulcher

V. We adore Thee, O Christ, and praise Thee:
R. Because by Thy holy cross Thou hast redeemed the world!

MEDITATION

THE body of Jesus is interred in a stranger's sepulcher. He Who in this world had not whereupon to rest His head would not even have a grave of His own, because He was not of this world. You who are so attached to the world, henceforth despise it, that you may not perish with it.

Prayer

O JESUS! Thou hast set me apart from the world: what, then, shall I seek therein? Thou hast created me for heaven; what, then, have I to do with the world? Depart from me, deceitful world, with thy vanities! Henceforth I will follow the way of the cross traced out for me by my Redeemer, and journey onward to my heavenly home, my eternal dwelling place.

Our Father, etc.; Hail Mary, etc.
V. Lord Jesus, crucified:
R. Have mercy on us!

CONCLUSION

ALMIGHTY and eternal God! merciful Father! Who hast given to the human race Thy beloved Son as an example of humility, obedience, and patience, to precede us on the Way of the Cross and on the Way of Life, graciously grant that we, inflamed by His infinite

love, may take upon us the sweet yoke of His Gospel
and the mortification of the cross, following Him as
His true disciples, so that we may one day gloriously
rise with Him and joyfully hear the final sentence:
"*Come ye blessed of My Father, possess you the kingdom prepared for you from the foundation of the world*"
(*Matt.* xxv. 34).

Stabat Mater

STABAT Mater dolo-
   rosa,
  Juxta crucem lacry-
    mosa,
    Dum pendebat Filius.

AT the cross her sta-
   tion keeping,
Stood the mournful Mother
    weeping,
Close to Jesus to the last.

Cujus animam gemen-
   tem,
  Contristatam et dolen-
    tem,
    Pertransivit glad-
    ius.

Through her heart, His
   sorrow sharing,
All His bitter anguish
    bearing,
Now at length the sword
    had passed.

O quam tristis et
   afflicta
  Fuit illa bene-
    dicta
    Mater Unigeniti!

Oh, how sad and sore dis-
   tressed
Was that Mother highly
    blessed
Of the sole-begotten One!

Quæ mœrebat, et dole-
   bat,
  Pia Mater dum vide-
    bat
    Nati pœnas inclyti.

Christ above in torment
   hangs,
She beneath beholds the
    pangs
Of her dying, glorious Son.

Quis est homo qui non fleret
  Matrem Christi si videret
    In tanto supplicio ?
	Is there one who would not weep
	  Whelmed in miseries so deep
	    Christ's dear Mother to behold?

Quis non posset contristari,
  Christi Matrem contemplari
    Dolentem cum Filio?
	Can the human heart refrain
	  From partaking in her pain,
	    In that Mother's pain untold?

Pro peccatis suæ gentis,
  Vidit Jesum in tormentis,
    Et flagellis subditum,
	Bruised, derided, cursed, defiled,
	  She beheld her tender Child,
	    All with bloody scourges rent,

Vidit suum dulcem natum Moriendo, desolatum, Dum emisit spiritum.	For the sins of His own nation Saw Him hang in desolation Till His spirit forth He sent.

Eia mater, fons amoris,
  Me sentire vim doloris
    Fac, ut tecum lugeam.
	O thou Mother! fount of love,
	  Touch my spirit from above.
	  Make my heart with thine accord:

Fac, ut ardeat cor
 meum
  In amando Christum
  Deum,
   Ut sibi complaceam.

Make me feel as thou hast
 felt:
Make my soul to glow and
 melt
With the love of Christ,
 my Lord.

Sancta Mater istud
 agas,
  Crucifixi fige pla-
  gas
   Cordi meo valide.

Holy Mother! pierce me
 through.
In my heart each wound
 renew
Of my Saviour crucified.

Tui nati vulne-
 rati,
  Tam dignati pro me
  pati,
   Pœnas mecum di-
   vide.

Let me share with thee His
 pain,
Who for all our sins was
 slain,
Who for me in torments
 died.

Fac me tecum pie
 flere,
  Crucifixo condo-
  lere,
   Donec ego vixero.

Let me mingle tears with
 thee,
Mourning Him Who
 mourned for me,
All the days that I may live.

Juxta crucem tecum
 stare,
  Et me tibi soci-
  are,
   In planctu desidero.

By the cross with thee to
 stay,
There with thee to weep
 and pray,
Is all I ask of thee to give.

Virgo virginum præclara,
 Mihi jam non sis amara,
  Fac me tecum plan-
 gere.

Virgin of all virgins best!
 Listen to my fond request:
  Let me share thy grief
 divine;

Fac, ut portem Christi
  mortem,
 Passionis fac consortem,
  Et plagas recolere.

Let me, to my latest
  breath,
 In my body bear the death
 Of that dying Son of thine.

Fac me plagis vulne-
  rari,
 Fac me cruce ineb-
 riari,
  Et cruore Filii.

Wounded with His every
  wound,
 Steep my soul till it hath
  swooned
 In His very blood away;

Flammis ne urar succen-
 sus
 Per te, Virgo, sim defen-
 sus
  In die judicii.

Bè to me, O Virgin,
  nigh,
 Lest in flames I burn and
  die,
 In His awful judgment day.

Christe, cum sit hinc
  exire,
 Da per Matrem me
 venire
  Ad palmam victoriæ.

Christ, when Thou shalt
  call me hence,
 Be Thy Mother my de-
 fence,
 Be Thy cross my victory;

Quando corpus morietur,
 Fac ut animæ don-
 etur
  Paradisi gloria.
    Amen.

While my body here decays,
 May my soul Thy good-
 ness praise,
 Safe in paradise with Thee.
    Amen.

V. Ora pro nobis, Virgo dolorosissima.

R. Ut digni efficiamur promissionibus Christi.

V. Pray for us, Virgin most sorrowful.

R. That we may be made worthy of the promises of Christ.

Oremus

INTERVENIAT pro nobis, quæsumus, Domine Jesu Christe, nunc et in hora mortis nostræ, apud tuam clementiam, beata Virgo Maria Mater tua, cujus sacratissimam animam in hora tuæ passionis doloris gladius pertransivit. Per te, Jesu Christe, salvator mundi, qui cum Patre et Spiritu Sancto vivis et regnas, per omnia sæcula sæculorum.

Amen.

Let us pray

GRANT, we beseech Thee, O Lord Jesus Christ, that the most blessed Virgin Mary, Thy Mother, through whose most holy soul, in the hour of Thine own passion, the sword of sorrow passed, may intercede for us before the throne of Thy mercy, now and at the hour of our death, through Thee, Jesus Christ, Saviour of the world, Who livest and reignest, with the Father and the Holy Ghost, now and forever. Amen.

Litanies

Litany of the Most Holy Name of Jesus

LORD, have mercy on us.
Christ, have mercy on us.
Lord, have mercy on us.
Jesus, hear us.
Jesus, graciously hear us.
God, the Father of heaven,[1]
God, the Son, Redeemer of the world,
God, the Holy Ghost,
Holy Trinity, one God,
Jesus, Son of the living God,
Jesus, splendor of the Father,
Jesus, brightness of eternal light,
Jesus, king of glory,
Jesus, the sun of justice,
Jesus, son of the Virgin Mary,
Jesus, amiable,
Jesus, admirable,
Jesus, the powerful God,
Jesus, father of the world to come,
Jesus, angel of great counsel,
Jesus, most powerful,
Jesus, most patient,
Jesus, most obedient,
Jesus, meek and humble of heart,
Jesus, lover of chastity,
Jesus, lover of us,

[1] Have mercy on us.

Jesus, God of peace,[1]
Jesus, author of life,
Jesus, model of all virtues,
Jesus, zealous for souls,
Jesus, our God,
Jesus, our refuge,
Jesus, father of the poor,
Jesus, treasure of the faithful,
Jesus, good shepherd,
Jesus, true light,
Jesus, eternal wisdom,
Jesus, infinite goodness,
Jesus, our way and our life,
Jesus, joy of angels,
Jesus, king of patriarchs,
Jesus, master of apostles,
Jesus, teacher of the evangelists,
Jesus, strength of martyrs,
Jesus, light of confessors,
Jesus, purity of virgins,
Jesus, crown of all saints,
Be merciful, Spare us, O Jesus.
Be merciful, Graciously hear us, O Jesus.
From all evil,[2]
From all sin,
From Thy wrath,
From the snares of the devil,
From the spirit of fornication,
From eternal death,
From a neglect of Thy inspirations,
By the mystery of Thy holy Incarnation,
By Thy nativity,
By Thy infancy,

---

[1] Have mercy on us.   [2] Deliver us, O Jesus.

By Thy most divine life,[1]
By Thy labors,
By Thy agony and passion,
By Thy cross and dereliction,
By Thy languors,
By Thy death and burial,
By Thy resurrection,
By Thy ascension,
By the most holy institution of Thy Eucharist,
By Thy joys,
By Thy glory,
Lamb of God, Who takest away the sins of the world,
    Spare us, O Jesus!
Lamb of God, Who takest away the sins of the world,
    Hear us, O Jesus!
Lamb of God, Who takest away the sins of the world,
    Have mercy on us, O Jesus!
Jesus, hear us.
Jesus, graciously hear us.

Let us pray

O LORD Jesus Christ, Who hast said, "Ask and you shall receive, seek and you shall find, knock and it shall be opened unto you!" mercifully attend to our supplications, and grant us the gift of Thy divine charity, that we may ever love Thee with our whole heart, and never desist from Thy praise.

Give us, O Lord, a perpetual fear and love of Thy holy name; for Thou never ceasest to govern those

---

[1] Deliver us, O Jesus.

whom Thou instructest in the solidity of Thy love.
Who livest and reignest one God, world without end.
Amen.

[1] Indulgence of 300 days, once a day. — Leo XIII, Jan. 16, 1886.

Litany of the
Sacred Heart of Jesus

LORD, have mercy on us.
   Christ, have mercy on us.
Lord, have mercy on us.
Christ, hear us.
Christ, graciously hear us.
God, the Father of heaven,[1]
God, the Son, Redeemer of the world,
God, the Holy Ghost,
Holy Trinity, one God,
Heart of Jesus, Son of the Eternal Father,
Heart of Jesus, formed by the Holy Ghost in the womb
   of the Virgin Mother,
Heart of Jesus, substantially united to the Word of God,
Heart of Jesus, of infinite majesty,
Heart of Jesus, sacred temple of God.
Heart of Jesus, tabernacle of the Most High,
Heart of Jesus, house of God and gate of heaven,
Heart of Jesus, burning furnace of charity,
Heart of Jesus, abode of justice and love,
Heart of Jesus, full of goodness and love,
Heart of Jesus, abyss of all virtues,
Heart of Jesus, most worthy of all praise,
Heart of Jesus, king and center of all hearts,

[1] Have mercy on us.

Heart of Jesus, in Whom are all the treasures of wisdom
   and knowledge,[1]
Heart of Jesus, in Whom dwells the fulness of divinity,
Heart of Jesus, in Whom the Father was well pleased,
Heart of Jesus, of Whose fulness we have all received,
Heart of Jesus, desire of the everlasting hills,
Heart of Jesus, patient and most merciful,
Heart of Jesus, enriching all who invoke Thee,
Heart of Jesus, fountain of life and holiness,
Heart of Jesus, propitiation for our sins,
Heart of Jesus, loaded down with opprobrium,
Heart of Jesus, bruised for our offences,
Heart of Jesus, obedient unto death,
Heart of Jesus, pierced with a lance,
Heart of Jesus, source of all consolation,
Heart of Jesus, our life and resurrection,
Heart of Jesus, our peace and reconciliation,
Heart of Jesus, victim for sin,
Heart of Jesus, salvation of those who trust in Thee,
Heart of Jesus, hope of those who die in Thee,
Heart of Jesus, delight of all the saints,
Lamb of God, Who takest away the sins of the world,
   Spare us, O Lord.
Lamb of God, Who takest away the sins of the world,
   Graciously hear us, O Lord.
Lamb of God, Who takest away the sins of the world,
   Have mercy on us.
   V. Jesus, meek and humble of heart,
   R. Make our hearts like unto Thine.

Let us pray

O ALMIGHTY and eternal God, look upon the heart
   of Thy dearly beloved Son, and upon the praise

---

[1] Have mercy on us.

and satisfaction He offers Thee in the name of sinners and for those who seek Thy mercy, be Thou appeased and grant us pardon in the name of the same Jesus Christ, Thy Son, Who liveth and reigneth with Thee in the unity of the Holy Ghost, world without end.   Amen.

Indulgence of 300 days, once a day. — Leo XIII, April 2, 1899.

Litany of the Blessed Virgin

LORD, have mercy on us.
Christ, have mercy on us.
Lord, have mercy on us.
Christ, hear us.
Christ, graciously hear us.
God, the Father of heaven, Have mercy on us.
God, the Son, Redeemer of the world, Have mercy on us.
God, the Holy Ghost, Have mercy on us.
Holy Trinity, one God, Have mercy on us.
Holy Mary,[1]
Holy Mother of God,
Holy Virgin of virgins,
Mother of Christ,
Mother of divine grace,
Mother most pure,
Mother most chaste,
Mother inviolate,
Mother undefiled,
Mother most amiable,
Mother most admirable,
Mother of good counsel,
Mother of our Creator,

[1] Pray for us.

Mother of our Saviour,[1]
Virgin most prudent,
Virgin most venerable,
Virgin most renowned,
Virgin most powerful,
Virgin most merciful,
Virgin most faithful,
Mirror of justice,
Seat of wisdom,
Cause of our joy,
Spiritual vessel,
Vessel of honor,
Singular vessel of devotion,
Mystical rose,
Tower of David,
Tower of ivory,
House of gold,
Ark of the covenant,
Gate of heaven,
Morning star,
Health of the sick,
Refuge of sinners,
Comforter of the afflicted,
Help of Christians,
Queen of angels,
Queen of patriarchs,
Queen of prophets,
Queen of apostles,
Queen of martyrs,
Queen of confessors,
Queen of virgins,
Queen of all saints,
Queen conceived without original sin,
Queen of the most holy Rosary,

[1] Pray for us.

Queen of peace,[1]

Lamb of God, Who takest away the sins of the world,
  Spare us, O Lord!

Lamb of God, Who takest away the sins of the world,
  Graciously hear us, O Lord!

Lamb of God, Who takest away the sins of the world,
  Have mercy on us!

V. Pray for us, O holy Mother of God, '

R. That we may be made worthy of the promises of Christ.

Indulgence of 300 days, every time; plenary indulgence on usual conditions. — Pius VII, Sept. 30, 1817.

Let us pray

POUR forth, we beseech Thee, O Lord, Thy grace into our hearts; that we, to whom the incarnation of Christ Thy Son was made known by the message of an angel, may, by His passion and cross, be brought to the glory of His resurrection; through the same Christ our Lord. Amen.

May the divine assistance remain always with us.

May the souls of the faithful departed, through the mercy of God, rest in peace. Amen.

We fly to thy patronage, O holy Mother of God, despise not our petitions in our necessities; but deliver us from all dangers, O ever glorious and blessed Virgin. Amen.

Prayer to St. Joseph

O BLESSED Joseph, father and guide of Jesus Christ in His childhood and youth, who didst lead Him safely in His flight through the desert and in all the ways of His earthly pilgrimage, be also my companion and

---

[1] P ay f·r us.

guide in this pilgrimage of life, and never permit me to turn aside from the way of God's commandments; be my refuge in adversity, my support in temptation, my solace in affliction, until at length I arrive at the land of the living, where with thee, and Mary, thy most holy spouse, and all the saints, I may rejoice forever in Jesus, my Lord.   Amen.

Litany of the Saints

LORD, have mercy on us.
Christ, have mercy on us.
Lord, have mercy on us.
Christ, hear us.
Christ, graciously hear us.
God, the Father of heaven, Have mercy on us.
God the Son, Redeemer of the world, Have mercy on us.
God the Holy Ghost, Have mercy on us.
Holy Trinity, one God, Have mercy on us.
Holy Mary,[1]
Holy Mother of God,
Holy Virgin of virgins
St. Michael,
St. Gabriel,
St. Raphael,
All ye holy angels and archangels,
All ye holy orders of blessed spirits,
St. John Baptist,
St. Joseph,
All ye holy patriarchs and prophets,
St. Peter,

[1] Pray for us.

St. Paul,[1]
St. Andrew,
St. James,
St. John,
St. Thomas,
St. James,
St. Philip,
St. Bartholomew,
St. Matthew,
St. Simon,
St. Thaddeus,
St. Matthias,
St. Barnabas,
St. Luke,
St. Mark,
All ye holy apostles and evangelists,
All ye holy disciples of Our Lord,
All ye holy innocents,
St. Stephen,
St. Lawrence,
St. Vincent,
SS. Fabian and Sebastian,
SS. John and Paul,
SS. Cosmas and Damian,
SS. Gervase and Protase,
All ye holy martyrs,
St. Sylvester,
St. Gregory,
St. Ambrose,
St. Augustine,
St. Jerome,
St. Martin,
St. Nicholas,

[1] Pray for us.

All ye holy bishops and confessors,[1]
All ye holy doctors,
St. Anthony,
St. Benedict,
St. Bernard,
St. Dominic,
St. Francis,
All ye holy priests and levites,
All ye holy monks and hermits,
St. Mary Magdalen,
St. Agatha,
St. Lucy,
St. Agnes,
St. Cecilia,
St. Catharine,
St. Anastasia,
All ye holy virgins and widows,
All ye men and women, saints of God, Make inter-
cession for us.
Be merciful, Spare us, O Lord!
Be merciful, Graciously hear us, O Lord!
From all evil,[2]
From all sin,
From Thy wrath,
From a sudden and unprovided death,
From the deceits of the devil,
From anger, hatred, and all ill will,
From the spirit of fornication,
From lightning and tempest,
From the scourge of earthquake,
From pestilence, famine, and war,
From everlasting death,
Through the mystery of Thy holy incarnation,

[1] Pray for us.   [2] O Lord, deliver us.

Through Thy coming,[1]
Through Thy nativity,
Through Thy baptism and holy fasting,
Through Thy cross and passion,
Through Thy death and burial,
Through Thy holy resurrection,
Through Thy admirable ascension,
Through the coming of the Holy Ghost, the Paraclete,
In the day of judgment, We sinners beseech Thee, hear us.
That Thou wouldst spare us,[2]
That Thou wouldst pardon us,
That Thou wouldst vouchsafe to bring us to true penance,
That Thou wouldst vouchsafe to govern and preserve Thy holy Church,
That thou wouldst vouchsafe to preserve our Apostolic Prelate and all ecclesiastical Orders in holy religion,
That Thou wouldst vouchsafe to humble the enemies of Thy holy Church,
That Thou wouldst vouchsafe to give peace and true concord to Christian kings and princes,
That Thou wouldst vouchsafe to grant peace and unity to all Christian people,
That Thou wouldst vouchsafe to bring back to the unity of the Church all those who have strayed away, and lead to the light of the Gospel all unbelievers,
That Thou wouldst vouchsafe to confirm and preserve us in Thy holy service,
That Thou wouldst lift up our minds to heavenly desires,
That Thou wouldst render eternal good things to all our benefactors,

[1] O Lord, deliver us.   [2] We beseech Thee, hear us.

That Thou wouldst deliver our souls and those of
   our brethren, kinsfolk, and benefactors from eter-
   nal damnation,[1]
That Thou wouldst vouchsafe to give and preserve
   the fruits of the earth,
That Thou wouldst vouchsafe to give eternal rest to
   all the faithful departed,
That Thou wouldst vouchsafe graciously to hear us,
Son of God,
Lamb of God, Who takest away the sins of the
   world, Spare us, O Lord!
Lamb of God, etc., Hear us, O Lord!
Lamb of God, etc., Have mercy upon us, O Lord!
Christ, hear us; Christ, graciously hear us.
Lord, have mercy upon us.
Christ, have mercy upon us.
Lord, have mercy upon us.
   Our Father, etc.   (*In secret.*)
   V. And lead us not into temptation.
   R. But deliver us from evil.   *Amen.*

Psalm lxix

INCLINE unto my aid, O God.   O Lord, make haste to
   help me.
   Let them be confounded and ashamed that seek my soul.
   Let them be turned backward and blush for shame that
desire evils to me.
   Let them be presently turned away blushing for shame
that say to me, 'Tis well, 'tis well.
   Let all that seek Thee rejoice and be glad in Thee;
and let such as love Thy salvation say always, The Lord
be magnified.
   But I am needy and poor: O God, help me.
   Thou art my helper and my deliverer: O Lord, make
no delay.

[1] We beseech Thee, hear us.

Glory be to the Father, etc.

V. Save Thy servants.

R. Trusting in Thee, O my God.

V. Be unto us, O Lord, a tower of strength.

R. From the face of the enemy.

V. Let not the enemy prevail against us.

R. Nor the son of iniquity have power to hurt us.

V. O Lord, deal not with us according to our sins

R. Neither reward us according to our iniquities.

V. Let us pray for our chief bishop N.

R. The Lord preserve him, and give him life, and make him blessed upon earth, and deliver him not to the will of his enemies.

V. Let us pray for our benefactors.

R. Vouchsafe, O Lord, for Thy name's sake, to reward with eternal life all those who have done us good.

V. Let us pray for the faithful departed.

R. Eternal rest give to them, O Lord, and let perpetual light shine upon them.

V. May they rest in peace.

R. Amen.

V. For our absent brethren.

R. O my God, save Thy servants trusting in Thee.

V. Send them help, O Lord, from Thy holy place.

R. And from Sion protect them.

V. O Lord hear my prayer.

R. And let my cry come unto Thee.

Let us pray

O GOD, Whose property it is always to have mercy and to spare, receive our petitions, that we, and all Thy servants who are bound by the chain of sin, may, by the compassion of Thy goodness, mercifully be absolved.

Hear, we beseech Thee, O Lord, the prayer of Thy suppliants, and pardon the sins of those who confess to Thee, that, of Thy bounty, Thou mayest grant us pardon and peace.

Out of Thy clemency, O Lord, show Thy unspeakable mercy to us, that so Thou mayest both acquit us of our sins and deliver us from the punishment we deserve for them.

O God, Who by sin art offended and by penance pacified, mercifully regard the prayers of Thy people, who make supplication to Thee, and turn away the scourges of Thy anger, which we deserve for our sins.

O almighty and eternal God, have mercy on Thy servant N., our chief bishop, and direct him, according to Thy clemency, in the way of everlasting salvation, that, by Thy grace, he may desire the things that are agreeable to Thy will, and perform them with all his strength.

O God, from Whom are all holy desires, righteous counsels, and just works, give to Thy servants that peace which the world can not give; that, our hearts being disposed to keep Thy commandments, and the fear of enemies taken away, the times, by Thy protection, may be peaceable.

Inflame, O Lord, our reins and hearts with the fire of Thy holy Spirit; to the end that we may serve Thee with a chaste body, and please Thee with a clean heart.

O God, the Creator and Redeemer of all the faithful, give to the souls of Thy servants departed the remission of all their sins, that by pious supplications they may obtain the pardon they have always desired.

Direct, we beseech Thee, O Lord, our actions by Thy holy inspirations, and carry them on by Thy gracious assistance; that every prayer and work of ours may always begin from Thee, and by Thee be happily ended.

O almighty and eternal God, Who hast dominion over the living and the dead, and art merciful to all of whom Thou foreknowest that they will be Thine by faith and good works: we humbly beseech Thee that they for whom we have purposed to offer our prayers, whether this present world still detains them in the flesh or the next world hath already received them divested of their bodies, may, by the clemency of Thine own goodness and the intercession of Thy saints, obtain pardon and full remission of all their sins. Through Our Lord Jesus Christ, Who liveth and reigneth with Thee in the unity of the Holy Ghost, one God, world without end.

R. Amen.

V. O Lord, hear my prayer.

R. And let my cry come unto Thee.

V. May the almighty and merciful Lord graciously hear us.

R. Amen.

V. May the souls of the faithful departed through the mercy of God rest in peace.

R. Amen.

Litany of the Blessed Sacrament[1]

LORD, have mercy on us.

Christ, have mercy on us.

Lord, have mercy on us.

Christ, hear us.

Christ, graciously hear us.

God the Father of heaven,[2]

God the Son, Redeemer of the world,

God the Holy Ghost,

Holy Trinity, one God,

Living Bread, that camest down from heaven,

Hidden God and Saviour,

Wheat of the elect,

Wine of which virgins are the fruit,

Bread of fatness and royal dainties,

Perpetual sacrifice,

Clean oblation,

Lamb without spot,

Most pure feast,

Food of angels,

Hidden manna,

[1] For private devotion.   [2] Have mercy on us.

Memorial of the wonders of God,[1]
Super-substantial bread,
Word made flesh, dwelling in us,
Sacred Host,
Chalice of benediction,
Mystery of faith,
Most high and adorable sacrament,
Most holy of all sacrifices,
True propitiation for the living and the dead,
Heavenly antidote against the poison of sin,
Most wonderful of all miracles,
Most holy commemoration of the passion of Christ,
Gift transcending all fulness,
Special memorial of divine love,
Affluence of divine bounty,
Most august and holy mystery,
Medicine of immortality,
Tremendous and life-giving sacrament,
Bread made flesh by the omnipotence of the Word,
Unbloody sacrifice,
Our feast at once and our fellow-guest,
Sweetest banquet, at which angels minister,
Sacrament of piety,
Bond of charity,
Priest and victim,
Spiritual sweetness tasted in its proper source,
Refreshment of holy souls,
Viaticum of such as die in the Lord,
Pledge of future glory,
Be merciful, Spare us, O Lord,
Be merciful, Graciously hear us, O Lord,
From an unworthy reception of Thy body and blood,[2]
From the lust of the flesh,

---

[1] Have mercy on us.   [2] O Lord, deliver us.

From the lust of the eyes,[1]
From the pride of life,
From every occasion of sin,
Through the desire wherewith Thou didst long to eat
  this passover with Thy disciples,
Through that profound humility wherewith Thou didst
  wash their feet,
Through that ardent charity whereby Thou didst in-
  stitute this divine sacrament,
Through Thy precious blood, which Thou hast left us
  on our altars,
Through the five wounds of this Thy most holy body,
  which Thou didst receive for us,
We sinners beseech Thee, hear us,
That Thou wouldst vouchsafe to preserve and increase
  our faith, reverence, and devotion toward this admirable sacrament,[2]
That Thou wouldst vouchsafe to conduct us, through a
  true confession of our sins, to a frequent reception of
  the Holy Eucharist,
That Thou wouldst vouchsafe to deliver us from all
  heresy, perfidy, and blindness of heart,
That Thou wouldst vouchsafe to impart to us the pre-
  cious and heavenly fruits of this most holy sacrament,
That at the hour of death Thou wouldst strengthen and
  defend us by this heavenly viaticum,
Son of God,
Lamb of God, Who takest away the sins of the world,
  Spare us, O Lord.
Lamb of God, Who takest away the sins of the world,
  Graciously hear us, O Lord.
Lamb of God, Who takest away the sins of the world,
  Have mercy on us.

[1] O Lord, deliver us.   [2] We beseech Thee, hear us.

Christ, hear us. Christ, graciously hear us.

V. Thou didst give them bread from heaven. **Alleluia.**

R. Containing in itself all sweetness. **Alleluia.**

Let us pray

O God, Who in this wonderful sacrament has left us a memorial of Thy passion, grant us the grace, we beseech Thee, so to venerate the sacred mysteries of Thy body and blood, that we may ever continue to feel within ourselves the blessed fruit of Thy redemption. Who livest and reignest God forever and ever. Amen.

Litany of the Passion [1]

LORD, have mercy on us.

Christ, have mercy on us.

Lord, have mercy on us.

Christ, hear us. Christ, graciously hear us.

God, the Father of heaven,[2]

God, the Son, Redeemer of the world,

God, the Holy Ghost,

Holy Trinity, one God,

Jesus, the Eternal Wisdom,

Jesus, sold for thirty pieces of silver,

Jesus, prostrate on the ground in prayer,

Jesus, strengthened by an angel,

Jesus, in Thine agony bathed in a bloody sweat,

Jesus, betrayed by Judas with a kiss,

Jesus, bound by the soldiers,

Jesus, forsaken by Thy disciples,

[1] For private devotion.   [2] Have mercy on us.

Jesus, brought before Annas and Caiphas,[1]
Jesus, struck in the face by a servant,
Jesus, accused by false witnesses,
Jesus, declared guilty of death,
Jesus, spat upon,
Jesus, blindfolded,
Jesus, smitten on the cheek,
Jesus, thrice denied by Peter,
Jesus, delivered up to Pilate,
Jesus, despised and mocked by Herod,
Jesus, clothed in a white garment,
Jesus, rejected for Barabbas,
Jesus, torn with scourges,
Jesus, bruised for our sins,
Jesus, esteemed a leper,
Jesus, covered with a purple robe,
Jesus, crowned with thorns,
Jesus, struck with a reed upon the head,
Jesus, demanded for crucifixion by the Jews,
Jesus, condemned to an ignominious death,
Jesus, given up to the will of Thine enemies,
Jesus, loaded with the heavy weight of the cross,
Jesus, led like a sheep to the slaughter,
Jesus, stripped of Thy garments,
Jesus, fastened with nails to the cross,
Jesus, reviled by the malefactors,
Jesus, promising paradise to the penitent thief,
Jesus, commending St. John to Thy Mother as her son,
Jesus, declaring Thyself forsaken by Thy Father,
Jesus, in Thy thirst given gall and vinegar to drink,
Jesus, testifying that all things written concerning Thee were accomplished,

---

[1] Have mercy on us.

Jesus, commending Thy spirit into the hands of Thy
Father,[1]
Jesus, obedient even to the death of the cross,
Jesus, pierced with a lance,
Jesus, made a propitiation for us,
Jesus, taken down from the cross,
Jesus, laid in the sepulcher,
Jesus, rising gloriously from the dead,
Jesus, ascending into heaven,
Jesus, our advocate with the Father,
Jesus, sending down on Thy disciples the Holy Ghost,
the Paraclete,
Jesus, exalting Thy Mother above the choirs of
angels,
Jesus, Who shalt come to judge the living and the
dead,
Be merciful, Spare us, O Lord.
Be merciful, Graciously hear us, O Lord.
From all evil,[2]
From all sin,
From anger, hatred, and every evil will,
From war, famine, and pestilence,
From all dangers of mind and body,
From everlasting death,
Through Thy most pure conception,
Through Thy miraculous nativity,
Through Thy humble circumcision,
Through Thy baptism and holy fasting,
Through Thy labors and watchings,
Through Thy cruel scourging and crowning,
Through Thy thirst, and tears, and nakedness,
Through Thy precious death and cross,
Through Thy glorious resurrection and ascension,

[1] Have mercy on us.   [2] Lord Jesus, deliver us.

Through Thy sending forth the Holy Ghost, the Paraclete,[1]

In the day of judgment,

We sinners beseech Thee, hear us

That Thou wouldst spare us,[2]

That Thou wouldst pardon us,

That Thou wouldst vouchsafe to bring us to true penance,

That Thou wouldst vouchsafe mercifully to pour into
our hearts the grace of the Holy Spirit,

That Thou wouldst vouchsafe to defend and propagate
Thy holy Church,

That Thou wouldst vouchsafe to preserve and increase
all societies assembled in Thy holy name,

That Thou wouldst vouchsafe to bestow upon us true
peace,

That Thou wouldst vouchsafe to give us perseverance in
grace and in Thy holy service,

That Thou wouldst vouchsafe to deliver us from unclean
thoughts, the temptations of the devil, and everlasting
damnation,

That Thou wouldst vouchsafe to unite us to the com·
pany of Thy saints,

That Thou wouldst vouchsafe graciously to hear us,

Lamb of God, Who takest away the sins of the world,
Spare us, O Lord.

Lamb of God, Who takest away the sins of the world,
Graciously hear us, O Lord.

Lamb of God, Who takest away the sins of the world,
Have mercy on us, O Lord.

Christ, hear us; Christ, graciously hear us.

V. We adore Thee, O Christ, and praise Thee:

R. Because by Thy holy cross Thou hast redeemed
the world.

[1] Lord Jesus, deliver us.   [2] We beseech Thee, hear us.

Let us pray

ALMIGHTY and eternal God, Who hast appointed Thine only-begotten Son the Saviour of the world, and hast willed to be appeased with His blood, grant that we may so venerate this price of our salvation, and by its might be so defended upon earth from the evils of this present life, that in heaven we may rejoice in its everlasting fruit. Who liveth and reigneth with Thee in the unity of the Holy Ghost, world without end. Amen.

General Devotions

The Holy Trinity: One God

THE SIGN OF THE CROSS

Make the Sign of the Cross, ✠ Saying:

IN THE name of the Father, and of the Son, and of the Holy Ghost. Amen.

This sacred sign may be regarded as a compendium of all the mysteries of our Faith, as a homage rendered to the three Persons of the adorable Trinity, as an act of gratitude for all that the Godhead — the Father, the Son, and the Holy Spirit — has condescended to do in favor of man.

Indulgence of 100 days. — Pius IX, March 23, 1876.

PRAYERS TO THE MOST HOLY TRINITY TO BE SAID AT THE END AND AT THE BEGINNING OF THE YEAR

Pope Pius IX, by a brief, Dec. 5, 1876, granted to all the faithful, who, with at least contrite heart, during the last half hour of the year and the first half hour of the following year, shall pray to the Most Holy Trinity in thanksgiving for benefits received ; beseeching the same Holy Trinity for peace among Christian nations, for concord among Christian princes, for the conversion of sinners, and for the triumph of holy Mother Church and its visible head, the Roman Pontiff, an indulgence of seven years.

The Canticle of the Seraphim
or
The Angelic Trisagion

HOLY, holy, holy, Lord God of hosts! the earth is full of Thy glory. Glory be to the Father, glory be to the Son, glory be to the Holy Ghost.

Indulgence of 100 days, once a day; three times every Sunday and during the octave of the festival of the Most Holy Trinity. — Clement XIV, June 6, 1769.

Prayer for Sunday to the Blessed Trinity

O BLESSED Trinity, Father, Son, and Holy Ghost, the source and fountain of all good, I most firmly believe in You, I most humbly adore You, and thank You with a grateful heart for all the blessings and benefits I have received from Your infinite goodness. I most fervently consecrate and offer to You an unreserved sacrifice of my whole being. O my God, Who hast a right to every day, hour, and moment of my existence, accept the thoughts, words, and actions of this day, which I offer Thee in testimony of my sincere desire to satisfy my obligation of keeping it holy and as the first-fruits of the week; mercifully assist me to spend it in such a manner as may draw down Thy blessing. Increase in my soul the heavenly virtues of faith, hope, and charity which I received at Baptism, and teach me to make faith the rule of my conduct, that thereby it may avail me to life everlasting. Eternal Father, take possession of my memory; efface from it all images of vanity, and engrave therein the recollection of Thy adorable presence. Eternal Son, enlighten my understanding, and conduct me in the path of salvation by the light of faith. Holy Spirit, sanctify my will by the most ardent love; render it submissive under the contradictions of this life, and never permit that by attachment to my own ideas or judgment, I should forfeit the blessings of peace offered to men of good-will and obedient minds. Holy, adorable, undivided Trinity, by Whose power, mercy, and providence I was created, redeemed, regenerated, and preserved to this moment, receive the oblation of my whole being, and take me out of the world rather than permit me to efface Your sacred image in my soul by mortal sin. I adore You, O Holy Trinity, I worship You, I most humbly give You thanks for having revealed to man this glorious, this incomprehensible mystery, and for granting to those who persevere until death in the faithful profession of it, the reward of beholding and enjoying in heaven what we now believe and adore upon earth, one God in three Persons, the Father, the Son, and the Holy Ghost. Amen.

Aspiration

GLORY be to the Father, and to the Son, and to the Holy Ghost; as it was in the beginning, is now, and ever shall be, world without end. Amen.

The Holy Ghost

Hymn

Veni Creator Spiritus,
Mentes tuorum visita,
Imple superna gratia
Quæ tu creasti pectora.

Qui diceris Paraclitus,
Altissimi donum Dei,
Fons vivus, ignis, charitas,
Et spiritalis unctio.

Tu septiformis munere,
Digitus paternæ dexteræ,
Tu rite promissum Patris,
Sermone ditans guttura.

Accende lumen sensibus,

Come, Holy Ghost, Creator, come,
From Thy bright, heavenly throne;
Come, take possession of our souls,
And make them all Thine own.

Thou Who art called the Paraclete,
Best gift of God above;
The living spring, the living fire,
Sweet unction and true love.

Thou Who art sevenfold in Thy grace,
Finger of God's right hand;
His promise, teaching little ones
To speak and understand.

Oh! guide our minds with Thy blest light,

Infunde amorem cordibus,
Infirma nostri corporis
Virtute firmans perpeti.

Hostem repellas longius,
Pacemque dones protinus:
Ductore sic Te prævio,
Vitemus omne noxium.

Per Te sciamus da Patrem
Noscamus atque Filium,
Teque utriusque Spiritum
Credamus omni tempore.

Deo Patri sit gloria,
Et Filio, qui a mortuis
Surrexit, ac Paraclito,
In sæculorum sæcula.
Amen.

With love our hearts inflame;
And with Thy strength which ne'er decays,
Confirm our mortal frame.

Far from us drive our hellish foe, ,
True peace unto us bring;
And through all perils lead us safe
Beneath Thy sacred wing.

Through Thee may we the Father know,
Through Thee, th' eternal Son,
And Thee, the Spirit of them both, —
Thrice-blessed Three in one.

All glory to the Father be,
And to His risen Son,
The like to Thee, great Paraclete.
While endless ages run.
Amen.

Sequence

VENI Sancte Spiritus,
Et emitte cœlitus
Lucis tuæ radium.

HOLY Spirit! Lord of light!
From Thy clear celestial height,
Thy pure, beaming radiance give:

Veni pater pauper-	Come, Thou Father of the
um,	poor!
Veni dator mune-	Come, with treasures
rum,	which endure!
Veni lumen cor-	Come, Thou light of all
dium.	that live!

Consolator optime, Thou, of all consolers best,
Dulcis hospes animæ, Visiting the troubled breast,
Dulce refrige- Dost refreshing peace be-
rium. stow:

In labore re- Thou in toil art comfort
quies, sweet;
In æstu tempe- Pleasant coolness in the
ries, heat;
In fletu solatium. Solace in the midst of woe

O lux beatis- Light immortal! light di
sima, vine!
Reple cordis in- Visit Thou these hearts of
tima Thine,
Tuorum fidelium. And our inmost being fill.

Sine tuo no- If Thou take Thy grace
mine away,
Nihil est in ho- Nothing pure in man will
mine, stay;
Nihil est innoxium. All his good is turn'd to ill.

Lava quod est sor- Heal our wounds — our
didum, strength renew;
Riga quod est ari- On our dryness pour Thy
dum, dew;
Sana quod est sau- Wash the stains of guilt
cium. away:

Flecte quod est rigidum,	Bend the stubborn heart and will;
Fove quod est frigidum,	Melt the frozen, warm the chill;
Rege quod est devium.	Guide the steps that go astray.
Da tuis fidelibus	Thou, on those who evermore
In Te confitentibus	Thee confess and Thee adore,
Sacrum septenarium.	In Thy sevenfold gifts descend.
Da virtutis meritum,	Give them comfort when they die;
Da salutis exitum,	Give them life with Thee on high;
Da perenne gaudium. Amen.	Give them joys which never end. Amen.

Indulgence of 100 days, each time for reciting either the hymn or the sequence. — Pius VI, May 26, 1796.

Versicle, Response, and Prayer to the Holy Ghost

V. Emitte Spiritum tuum et creabuntur.

R. Et renovabis faciem terræ.

V. Send forth Thy Spirit, and they shall be created.

R. And Thou shalt renew the face of the earth.

Oremus

Deus, qui corda fidelium Sancti Spiritus illustratione docuisti, da nobis

Let us pray

O God, Who hast taught the hearts of the faithful by the light of the Holy

in eodem Spiritu recta sapere, et de ejus semper consolatione gaudere. Per Christum Dominum nostrum. Amen.	Spirit; grant that, by the gift of the same Spirit, we may be always truly wise, and ever rejoice in His consolation. Through Christ our Lord. Amen.

THE PRACTICE OF THE SEVEN GLORIA PATRIS IN HONOR OF THE HOLY SPIRIT, ACCORDING TO THE INTENTIONS OF THE SOVEREIGN PONTIFF

Indulgence of 7 days. — Pius IX, March 12, 1857.

INDULGENCES FOR NOVENA TO THE HOLY GHOST

Pope Leo XIII, May 9, 1897, decreed that a novena to the Holy Ghost should be made every year in preparation for the feast of Pentecost, and granted an indulgence of seven years and seven quarantines for each day of the novena; and plenary indulgence any one day of the novena on the usual conditions. The same indulgences may be gained any day of the week between Pentecost and Trinity Sunday.

Novena to the Holy Ghost in Preparation for the Feast of Pentecost

(*Commencing on Ascension Day*)

THE novena of the Holy Spirit is the chief of all the novenas, because it was the first that was ever celebrated, and that by the holy apostles and the most holy Mary in the supper room, being distinguished by so many remarkable wonders and gifts; principally by the gift of the same Holy Spirit, a gift merited for us by the passion of Jesus Christ Himself. Jesus Himself made this known to us when He said to His disciples that if He did not die He could not send us the Holy Ghost: " If I go not, the Paraclete will not come to you; but if I go, I will send

Him to you" (*John* xvi. 7). We know well by faith that the Holy Ghost is the love that the Father and the Eternal Word bear one to the other; and therefore the gift of love which the Lord infuses into our souls, and which is the greatest of all gifts, is particularly attributed to the Holy Ghost. As St. Paul says, "The charity of God is poured forth in our hearts by the Holy Ghost, Who is given to us" (*Rom.* v. 5). In this novena, therefore, we must consider, above all, the great value of divine love, in order that we may desire to obtain it, and endeavor, by devout exercises, and especially by prayer, to be made partakers of it, since God has promised it to him who asks for it with humility: "Your Father from heaven will give the good Spirit to them that ask Him" (*Luke* xi. 13).[1]

Prayer to the Holy Spirit for the Church

O HOLY Spirit, Creator, propitiously help the Catholic Church, and by Thy supernal power strengthen and confirm it against the assaults of the enemy; by Thy charity and grace renew the spirit of Thy servants whom Thou hast anointed, that in Thee they may glorify the Father and His only-begotten Son, Jesus Christ our Lord. Amen.

Indulgence of 300 days, once a day. — Leo XIII, Aug. 26, 1889.

Short Indulgenced Prayer to the Holy Ghost

HOLY Spirit, Spirit of truth, come into our hearts; give to all peoples the brightness of Thy light, that they may be well-pleasing to Thee in unity of faith.

Indulgence of 100 days, once a day. — Leo XIII, July 31, 1897.

[1] During this novena no particular form of prayer is of obligation. Any prayer to the Holy Ghost will suffice.

Prayer for the Feast of Pentecost

O HOLY Spirit, O my God, I adore Thee, and acknowledge, here in Thy divine presence, that I am nothing and can do nothing without Thee. Come, great Paraclete, Thou father of the poor, Thou comforter the best, fulfil the promise of our blessed Saviour, Who would not leave us orphans, and come into the mind and the heart of Thy poor, unworthy creature, as Thou didst descend on the sacred day of Pentecost on the holy Mother of Jesus and on His first disciples. Grant that I may participate in those gifts which Thou didst communicate to them so wonderfully, and with so much mercy and generosity. Take from my heart whatever is not pleasing to Thee, and make of it a worthy dwelling-place for Thyself. Illumine my mind, that I may see and understand the things that are for my eternal good. Inflame my heart with pure love of Thee, that it may be cleansed from the dross of all inordinate attachments, and that my whole life may be hidden with Jesus in God. Strengthen my will, that it may be made conformable to Thy divine will, and be guided by Thy holy inspirations. Aid me by Thy grace to practise the divine lessons of humility, poverty, obedience, and contempt of the world, which Jesus taught us in His mortal life.

Oh, rend the heavens, and come down, consoling Spirit! that inspired and encouraged by Thee, I may faithfully comply with the duties of my state, carry my daily cross most patiently, and endeavor to accomplish the divine will with the utmost perfection. Spirit of love! Spirit of purity! Spirit of peace! Sanctify my soul more and more, and give me that heavenly peace which the world can not give. Bless our Holy

Father the Pope, bless the Church, bless our bishops, our priests, all Religious Orders, and all the faithful, that they may be filled with the spirit of Christ, and labor earnestly for the spread of His kingdom.

O Holy Spirit, Thou Giver of every good and perfect gift, grant me, I beseech Thee, the intentions of this novena. May Thy will be done in me and through me. Mayest Thou be praised and glorified forevermore! Amen.

Offering to the Holy Ghost

ON my knees, before the multitude of heavenly witnesses, I offer myself, soul and body, to Thee, Eternal Spirit of God! I adore Thee, great God, and acknowledge Thy dominion over me.

Thou art the light and the strength of my soul. In Thee I live and move and have my being. I desire never to grieve Thee by unfaithfulness to grace, and I pray with all my heart to be kept from the smallest sin against Thee. Make me faithful in every thought, and grant that I may always listen to Thy voice, watch for Thy light, and follow Thy gracious inspirations. I cling to Thee, and give myself to Thee, and ask Thee, by Thy compassion, to watch over me in my weakness. Holding the pierced feet of Jesus, and looking at His five wounds, trusting in His precious blood, and adoring His sacred Heart, lacerated for love of me, I implore Thee, Holy Spirit, Helper of my infirmity, so to keep me in Thy grace that I may never sin against Thee with the sin which Thou canst not forgive. Give me grace, O Holy Ghost, Spirit of the Father and the Son, to say to Thee, always and everywhere, "Speak, Lord, for Thy servant heareth."

Our Divine Lord

Act of Adoration, Thanksgiving, Reparation, and Supplication

IN MY moments before the tabernacle, I will try to obey the pious counsels contained in the Latin distich :

"Crede, dole, spera, grates age, dilige, adora,
Vulnera pande animæ, donaque sancta pete."

BELIEVING all that Thou, my God, hast in any way revealed to us — grieving for all my sins, offenses, and negligences — hoping in Thee, O Lord, Who wilt never let me be confounded — thanking Thee for this supreme gift, and for all the gifts of Thy goodness — loving Thee, above all in this sacrament of Thy love — adoring Thee in this deepest mystery of Thy condescension: I lay before Thee all the wounds and wants of my poor soul, and ask for all that I need and desire. But I need only Thyself, O Lord; I desire none but Thee — Thy grace, and the grace to use well Thy graces, the possession of Thee by grace in this life, and the possession of Thee forever in the eternal kingdom of Thy glory. Thus, day by day, especially during my moments before the tabernacle, I will

" Believe, and grieve, and hope; thank, love, adore,
Show my soul's wounds, and holy gifts implore."

494

There is no aspect of God's love for us which ought to affect our hearts more tenderly than the mere fact of His wishing to be loved by us; and there is no manifestation of that tenderness of the Sacred Heart more touching than the yearning to be remembered, expressed at many times and in many ways, but especially in the eucharistic *Do this in commemoration of Me,* which becomes at the altar even more simple and affecting, *In Mei memoriam facietis* — "In memory of Me." When such infinite and utterly incomprehensible love as this has Omnipotence for the instrument of its behests, how can any poor little creature of God — whose sole dignity is that he has a heart to love Him — how can he presume for one moment to discuss the limits of the possibilities of the divine condescension? — FR. RUSSELL, S.J.

𝔄 𝔓rayer for a 𝔙isit to t𝔥e 𝔅lesse𝔡 𝔖acrament

(*Including all the Acts Recommended*)

MY Lord and my God, I firmly *believe* that Thou art really present in the sacred Host. I *adore* Thee beneath the sacramental veil which Thou hast mercifully chosen in order to approach us. Permit me, O dearest Jesus, to render Thee my *homage* together with the angels who surround Thy altar-throne. I believe that Thou dwellest on our altars not only to receive our humble adoration, but also to be the food of our souls, our sacrifice to the infinite majesty of the heavenly Father, our light in darkness, our counsel in doubt, our consolation in affliction, our strength in temptation, our friend in every need, our teacher in the school of perfection, our model in the way of sanctity.

I am a poor sinner, but I *hope* in that boundless mercy which detains Thee a prisoner of love in the tabernacle. I come to Thee with a *contrite* heart, and I beg Thy pardon and mercy. Thou art truly called the "Lover of souls," for Thou hast sacrificed Thy life for our salvation; Thou hast said: "My delights are to be with the children of men"; and Thy death-bed gift to us was the Holy Eucharist. I behold the tabernacle surmounted by a cross, and this reminds me, dear Lord and Saviour, that the Blessed Sacrament is a memorial of Thy passion and death. I *love* that infinite goodness which induced Thee to institute this holy sacrament of the altar, the grandest memorial of all Thy works, wherein Thou dost communicate Thyself so wonderfully to Thy creatures. I *thank* Thee for this sublime proof of Thy love, and ardently wish that I could worthily acknowledge all the blessings that I have ever received from this fountain of grace and mercy. I sincerely *regret* that this precious pledge of Thy love is received by so many Christians with coldness and indifference. I wish to make amends for my own ingratitude, and heartfelt *atonement* for all those sinful acts of my life, by which I have wounded Thy sacred Heart. I offer Thee my profound *adoration*, my *sorrow*, and my *love*, to appease and to rejoice, as much as I can, Thy sacred Heart, in this sacrament of love and to make reparation for all the acts of irreverence and profanation, which have been committed against Thee. I love Thee with my whole soul; I acknowledge Thee as my only Master; I offer Thee all that I have, and all that I am. Jesus! I give Thee my heart with all its affections; I give Thee my soul with all its powers; I give Thee my body with all its senses. Jesus! I consecrate myself entirely to Thee; I wish to live and labor and suffer and die for the love of Thee. I abandon myself to Thee. Give me but Thy *love* and Thy *grace;* I will ask for nothing more. Thy kingdom come, Thy will be done! I desire to adore and love Thee now, not only to supply the defect of those Catholics who do not adore and love Thee, but also for the conversion of heretics, schismatics, atheists, blasphemers, Jews, and idolaters. O silent dweller in the tabernacle, Thou art, indeed, a hidden God! here Thou art still the victim of the cross! As I gaze upon the sacred Host, I recall that pathetic word of Thine, O Lord, at the Last Supper: "Do this in commemoration of Me" — "Remember Me!" Yes, the Blessed Sacrament is a memorial of the "*Man of sorrows,*" a memorial of the greatest pain a creature on earth ever endured, a memorial of the most tender, most constant, most unselfish, and most heroic love the world shall ever know — the last sweet gift of a heart that fears to be forgotten. Oh, yes! Lord, I shall remember Thee. How could I forget Thy love, dearest Jesus! Mayest Thou be known, adored, and loved by all, and may thanks and praise forevermore be given to Thee in the most holy and most adorable sacrament. Amen.

Prayer of St. Alphonsus Liguori for a Visit to the Blessed Sacrament

LORD Jesus Christ, Who, through the love which Thou bearest to men, dost remain with them day and night in this sacrament, full of mercy and of love, expecting, inviting, and receiving all who come to visit Thee, I believe that Thou art present in the Sacrament of the Altar. From the abyss of my nothingness I adore Thee, and I thank Thee for all the favors which

Thou hast bestowed upon me, particularly for having given me Thyself in this sacrament, for having given me for my advocate Thy most holy Mother, Mary, and for having called me to visit Thee in this church.

I this day salute Thy most loving Heart, and I wish to salute it for three ends: first, in thanksgiving for this great gift; secondly, in compensation for all the injuries Thou hast received from Thy enemies in this sacrament; thirdly, I wish by this visit, to adore Thee in all places in which Thou art least honored and most abandoned in the holy sacrament. My Jesus, I love Thee with my whole heart. I am sorry for having hitherto offended Thine infinite goodness. I purpose, with the assistance of Thy grace, never more to offend Thee; and, at this moment, miserable as I am, I consecrate my whole being to Thee. I give Thee my entire will, all my affections and desires, and all that I have. From this day forward, do what Thou wilt with me, and with whatever belongs to me. I ask and desire only Thy holy love, the gift of final perseverance, and the perfect accomplishment of Thy will. I recommend to Thee the souls in purgatory, particularly those who were most devoted to the Blessed Sacrament and to most holy Mary; and I also recommend to Thee all poor sinners. Finally, my dear Saviour, I unite all my affections with the affections of Thy most loving Heart; and, thus united, I offer them to Thy eternal Father, and I entreat Him, in Thy name, and for Thy sake, to accept them.

Indulgence of 300 days when said before the Blessed Sacrament. Plenary indulgence on usual conditions. — Pius IX, Sept. 7, 1854.

𝔓ious 𝔈jaculations

ᴹAY the Heart of Jesus in the Most Blessed Sacrament be praised, adored, and loved with grateful affection, at every moment, in all the tabernacles of the world, even to the end of time. Amen.

Indulgence of 100 days. — Pius IX, Feb. 29, 1868.

O SACRAMENT most holy! O Sacrament divine! All praise and all thanksgiving be every moment Thine!

Indulgence of 100 days.

Heart of Jesus burning with love for us, inflame our hearts with love of Thee.

Indulgence of 100 days, once a day. — Leo XIII, June 16, 1893.

ACTS IN THE PRESENCE OF THE BLESSED SACRAMENT

At the Hour of Adoration and also at Holy Communion

𝔄ct of 𝔉aith

O JESUS! my Lord, my God, and my all! I believe that Thou art in Thy living manhood as truly present here in the Blessed Sacrament as when Thou didst walk amidst men, and converse with them. Relying on Thy word, which *shall not pass away*, I believe that Thou art here, *ever living to make intercession* for us. Here is Thy sacred body, which hung upon the cross; here is Thy soul, which was *sorrowful unto death* and agonized in the Garden of Olives on account of my sins; here are those sacred wounds made by the nails and spear; here are those eyes which looked with pity and love on the penitent Peter, now gazing into my heart, now raised to plead for me with the heavenly Father; here are those ears, which heard the cruel cry of the Jews, "Crucify Him," which listened so compassionately to all the ills of men, and which now are listening to me.

Lord, I believe that here on the altar Thy wounded Heart is beating for love of me, and I recall Thy blessed words: "My Heart is so consumed with love for men, that it can no longer restrain the flames of its charity." Sweet words of Thine, O blessed Saviour! I believe that they are true, and true as regards myself. — FR. RAMIÈRE, S.J.

An Act of Hope and Confidence in God

MY GOD, I believe most firmly that Thou watchest over all who hope in Thee, and that we can want for nothing when we rely upon Thee in all things; therefore I am resolved for the future to have no anxieties, and to cast all my cares upon Thee. *"In peace in the self-same I will sleep and I will rest; for Thou, O Lord, singularly hast settled me in hope."*

Men may deprive me of worldly goods and of honors; sickness may take from me my strength and the means of serving Thee; I may even lose Thy grace by sin; but my trust shall never leave me. I will preserve it to the last moment of my life, and the powers of hell shall seek in vain to wrest it from me. *"In peace in the self-same I will sleep and I will rest."*

Let others seek happiness in their wealth, in their talents: let them trust to the purity of their lives, the severity of their mortifications, to the number of their good works, the fervor of their prayers; as for me, O my God, in my very confidence lies all my hope. *"For Thou, O Lord, singularly hast settled me in hope."* This confidence can never be vain. *"No one has hoped in the Lord and has been confounded."*

I am assured, therefore, of my eternal happiness, for I firmly hope for it, and all my hope is in Thee. *"In Thee, O Lord, have I hoped; let me never be confounded."*

I know, alas! I know but too well that I am frail and changeable; I know the power of temptation against the strongest virtue. I have seen stars fall from heaven, and pillars of the firmament totter; but these things alarm me not. While I hope in Thee I am sheltered from all misfortune, and I am sure that my trust shall endure, for I rely upon Thee to sustain this unfailing hope.

Finally, I know that my confidence can not exceed Thy bounty, and that I shall never receive less than I have hoped for from Thee. Therefore I hope that Thou wilt sustain me against my evil inclinations; that Thou wilt protect me against the most furious assaults of the evil one, and that Thou wilt cause my weakness to triumph over my most powerful enemies. I hope that Thou wilt never cease to love me, and that I shall love Thee unceasingly. *"In Thee, O Lord, have I hoped; let me never be confounded."* — REV. CLAUDE DE LA COLOMBIÈRE, S.J.

Act of Charity
According to Saint Margaret Mary

O GOOD and merciful Saviour, it is the desire of my heart to return Thee love for love. My greatest sorrow is that Thou art not loved by men, and, in particular, that my own heart is so cold, so selfish, so ungrateful. Deeply sensible of my own weakness and poverty, I trust that Thy own grace will enable me to offer Thee an act of pure love. And I wish to offer Thee this act of love in reparation for the coldness and neglect that are shown to Thee by Thy creatures in the sacrament of Thy love. O Jesus, my sovereign Good, I love Thee, not for the sake of the reward which Thou hast promised to those who love Thee, but purely for Thyself. I love Thee above all things that can be loved, above all pleasures, and in fine above myself and all that is not Thee, protesting in the presence of heaven and earth, that I will live and die purely and simply in Thy holy love, and that if to love Thee thus I must be persecuted, tormented, and put to death, I am perfectly satisfied, and I will ever say with St. Paul: Nothing shall separate me from the love of Christ. O Jesus, supreme Master of all hearts, I love Thee, I adore Thee, I praise Thee, I thank Thee, because I am now all Thine own. Rule over me, and transform my soul into the likeness of Thyself, so that it may bless and glorify Thee forever in the abode of the saints.

Indulgenced Acts of Adoration and Thanksgiving

ADORAMUS Te, Christe, et benedicimus Tibi.

Quia per sanctam crucem Tuam redemisti mundum.

WE ADORE Thee, Christ, and we bless Thee.

Because by Thy holy cross Thou hast redeemed the world.

I ADORE Thee, eternal Father, and I give Thee thanks for the infinite love with which Thou didst deign to send Thy only-begotten Son to redeem me, and to become the food of my soul. I offer Thee all the acts of adoration and thanksgiving that are offered to Thee by the angels and saints in heaven, and by the just on earth. I praise, love, and thank Thee with all the praise, love, and thanksgiving that are offered to Thee by Thine own Son in the Blessed Sacrament; and I beg Thee to grant that He may be known, loved, honored, praised, and worthily received by all, in this most divine sacrament.

Our Father, Hail Mary, Glory be to the Father.

I adore Thee, eternal Son, and I thank Thee for the infinite love which caused Thee to become man for me, to be born in a stable, to live in poverty, to suffer hunger, thirst, heat, cold, fatigue, hardships, contempt, persecutions, the scourging, the crowning with thorns, and a cruel death upon the hard wood of the cross. I thank Thee, with the Church militant and triumphant, for the infinite love with which Thou didst institute the most blessed sacrament to be the food of my soul.

I adore Thee in all the consecrated hosts throughout the whole world, and I return thanks for those who know Thee not, and who do not thank Thee. Would that I were able to give my life to make Thee known, loved, and honored by all, in this sacrament of love, and to prevent the irreverences and sacrileges that are committed against Thee! I love Thee, divine Jesus, and I desire to receive Thee with all the purity, love, and affection of Thy blessed Mother, and with the love and affection of Thy own most pure Heart. Grant, O most amiable Spouse of my soul! in coming to me in this most holy sacrament, that I may receive all the graces and blessings which Thou dost come to bestow on us, and let me rather die than receive Thee unworthily.

Our Father, Hail Mary, Glory be to the Father.

I adore Thee, eternal Holy Ghost, and I give Thee thanks for the infinite love with which Thou didst work the ineffable mystery of the Incarnation, and for the infinite love with which Thou didst form the sacred body of Our Lord Jesus Christ out of the most pure blood of the blessed virgin Mary, become in this sacrament the food of my soul. I beg Thee to enlighten my mind, and to purify my heart and the hearts of all men, that all may know the benefit of Thy love, and receive worthily this most blessed sacrament.

Our Father, Hail Mary, Glory be to the Father.

Tantum Ergo

TANTUM ergo Sacramentum
 Veneremur cernui:
Et antiquum documentum
 Novo cedat ritui:
Præstet fides supplementum
 Sensuum defectui.

Genitori, Genitoque
 Laus et jubilatio:
Salus, honor, virtus quoque,
 Sit et benedictio:
Procedenti ab utroque
 Compar sit laudatio.

V. Panem de cœlo præstitisti eis.

DOWN in adoration falling.
Lo! the sacred Host we hail.
Lo! o'er ancient forms departing,
Newer rites of grace prevail;
Faith for all defect supplying
Where the feeble senses fail.

To the everlasting Father,
And the Son Who reigns on high,
With the Holy Ghost proceeding
Forth from each eternally,
Be salvation, honor, blessing,
Might and endless majesty!

V. Thou gavest them bread from heaven.

℟. Omne delectamentum in se habentem.

℟. And therein was sweetness of every kind.

Oremus

Let us pray

DEUS, qui nobis, sub sacramento mirabili passionis tuæ memoriam reliquisti: tribue, quæsumus, ita nos corporis et sanguinis tui sacra mysteria venerari, ut redemptionis tuæ fructum in nobis jugiter sentiamus. Qui vivis et regnas, in unitate Spiritus Sancti Deus, etc.

GOD, Who, beneath this marvelous sacrament, hast left us a memorial of Thy passion: grant us the grace, we beseech Thee, so to venerate the sacred mysteries of Thy body and blood, that we may ever feel within us the fruit of Thy redemption, Who livest and reignest, etc.

Plenary indulgence on usual conditions to all who, after confession and communion, on the first Thursday of the month, shall visit with devotion the Blessed Sacrament; seven years and seven quarantines, on all the other Thursdays of the year; one hundred days on any other day of the year, to those who say them with a contrite heart before the Blessed Sacrament. — Pius VI, Oct. 17, 1796.

An Act of Reparation in Honor of the Blessed Sacrament

MOST adorable Saviour, in Thy wondrous love for us Thou dost remain in the blessed Sacrament of the Altar, in order to be the perpetual sacrifice of the New Law, the propitiatory Victim for our sins, the life-giving Manna of our souls, our powerful Mediator, our good Master, our best and kindest Friend.

But, alas! with what ingratitude on our part has Thine infinite goodness been repaid. Prostrate before Thy veiled majesty, at the foot of the altar, where Thou art as truly and really present as in heaven, we come to make reparation and offer atonement for all the injuries and for all the ingratitude inflicted on Thee in the sacrament of Thy love.

O divine Jesus, O meek and humble Jesus, accept our feeble efforts to compassionate Thy suffering Heart, and to make a fitting reparation to Thy outraged majesty for all blasphemies, profanations, and sacrileges ever committed; for our own want of devotion and reverence in Thy sacred presence, for our poor preparations and thanksgivings at holy communion, and for the little fruit we have drawn from holy communion through our own fault.

Pardon, O Lord, pardon, we beseech Thee, these and all our offenses against Thee. We are truly sorry for having sinned, because Thou art infinitely good and sin displeases Thee. Thou wilt not despise a contrite and humble heart. We offer Thee our poor hearts filled with sentiments of sincere repentance and deep affection. We offer Thee, in atonement, Thy own bitter sufferings, the sorrows of Thy blessed Mother, and the merits of all the saints. By the fervor of our love we desire to make amends to Thee for the injuries inflicted on Thee by ourselves, by infidels, heretics, and all negligent Christians. Yes, Jesus, we love Thee now above all things, and we are resolved to please Thee by doing Thy will and by faithfully discharging the obligations of our state of life. Thy kingdom come; Thy will be done on earth as it is in heaven!

How happy should we be, O Jesus, could we but make reparation to Thy glory, by our respect, by our zeal, aye, even by the shedding of our blood. At least, most adorable Saviour, grant us the grace to love Thee in the most holy Sacrament of the Altar, with the most tender, the most generous, the most perfect, the most constant love.

O Sacrament most holy, O Sacrament divine,
All praise and all thanksgiving be every moment Thine!

Virgin most holy, by thy holy and immaculate heart, make us enter into the adorable Heart of thy divine Son, Jesus Christ.

O sweet St. Joseph! obtain for us the gift of prayer and of perpetual union with Jesus and Mary.   Amen.

Morning Prayer to the Blessed Sacrament

O SWEETEST Jesus, Thou hast been waiting patiently all through the night, watching for the moment which should find me once more at Thy blessed feet. And now, dearest Jesus, I have come with my heart full of thanks to Thee for having spared me during the night past, and for having given me another day to labor for Thy greater honor and glory, and the salvation of my soul.   I offer myself entirely to Thee.   Deign to make my heart like Thine, meek and humble; let me resemble 'Thee in charity and kindness to all; make me resigned to Thy holy will, and grant that I may be worthy of that reward which Thou hast promised to those who love Thee faithfully here upon earth.   Amen.

Evening Prayer to the Blessed Sacrament

O DIVINE Jesus, alone to-night in so many tabernacles, without a visitor or a worshiper, I offer Thee my lowly heart.   May every beating be a prayer of love to Thee.   In Thy love Thou art ever watching under the sacramental veils.   Thou never sleepest, and Thou art never weary of Thy vigil for sinners.

O loving Jesus, O lonely Jesus, may my heart be a lamp, the light of which shall burn and beam for Thee alone in time and in eternity.

May Thy will be done in me. Keep me in Thy love; grant me the grace of perseverance.

Lord, into thy hands I commend my spirit. Jesus, my God and my All!

A SIMPLE INDULGENCED VISIT TO THE BLESSED SACRAMENT

His Holiness, Pope Pius IX, granted an Indulgence of 300 days, each time, to all the faithful who shall visit the Most Blessed Sacrament, and recite the Our Father, the Hail Mary, and the Glory be to the Father, each five times, and another Our Father, Hail Mary, and Glory be to the Father, for the intention of the Pope.

Petition for the Holy Souls in Purgatory

O MY God, I recommend to Thy clemency the holy souls in purgatory, and especially those to whom I am most indebted by the bond of charity or of justice; and chiefly I implore Thee in behalf of those who, during their life, have been most devout to the Blessed Sacrament; as also those who have most loved the Blessed Virgin. For this I offer Thee, my good Jesus, Thy wounds, Thy agony, Thy death, and all the merits of Thy most bitter passion. I know that it is Thy pleasure I should pray for these holy souls, who are so worthy of Thy love. Hear, then, dear Lord, and grant this my prayer in their behalf, which I present to Thee in the words of Thy holy Church: *"Requiem æternam dona eis, Domine, et lux perpetua luceat eis."* — "Eternal rest give unto them, O Lord, and let perpetual light shine upon them."

Spiritual Communion

By St. Alphonsus Liguori

1. "MY JESUS, I believe that Thou art truly present in the most blessed sacrament. I love Thee above all things and I desire to possess Thee within my soul. Since I am unable now to receive Thee sacramentally, come at least spiritually into my heart. I embrace Thee as being already there, and unite myself wholly to Thee ; never, never permit me to be separated from Thee."

2. St. Teresa was wont to say to her spiritual daughters: "As often as you hear Holy Mass, although you be unable to communicate sacramentally, you can make a spiritual communion, which is of great value." The Council of Trent requires for a spiritual communion an *ardent desire, lively faith*, and *fervent charity*. How often shall we communicate spiritually? As often as God inspires the holy desire, at any time, but especially at *Mass*, at *Benediction*, and at *Visits*. No particular form is required. With a contrite and loving heart, we may simply say: "Come, dearest Jesus, come into my heart; come and satiate my longing; come and sanctify my soul; come, my sweetest Jesus, come."

3. We read in the lives of some of the saints how Our Lord, to satisfy their burning desire to receive the Holy Eucharist, communicated Himself to them in miraculous ways, as by going from the priest's hand to St. Catharine of Sienna, and to blessed Imelda, or piercing through the breast of St. Juliana Falconieri, or as by the hands of angels or of His blessed Mother to St. Bonaventure and St. Stanislaus. In various ways and by signal miracles, Jesus has manifested His approbation of *spiritual communion*.

Another Prayer for Spiritual Communion

JESUS, my Saviour and my God! I am not worthy to appear before Thee, for I am a poor sinner; yet I approach Thee with confidence, for Thou hast said, "Come to Me, all you that labor and are heavy-laden, and I will refresh you." Thou wilt not despise a contrite and humble heart. I am truly sorry for my sins, because by them I have offended Thee, Who art infinitely good. Whatever may have been my foolish transgressions in the past, I love Thee now above all things, and with all my heart. I desire, good Jesus, to receive Thee in holy communion, and since I can not now receive Thee in the Blessed Sacrament, I beseech Thee to come to me spiritually and to refresh my soul with Thy sweetness.

Come, my Lord, my God, and my All! Come to me, and let me never again be separated from Thee by sin. Teach me Thy blessed ways; help me with Thy grace to imitate Thy example; to practise meekness, humility, charity, and all the virtues of Thy sacred Heart. My divine Master, my one desire is to do Thy will and to love Thee more and more; help me that I may be faithful to the end in Thy service. Bless me in life and in death, that I may praise Thee forever in heaven. Amen.

O JESUS, sweetest Love, come Thou to me;
   Come down in all Thy beauty unto me;
Thou Who didst die for longing love of me;
And never, never more depart from me.
Free me, O beauteous God, from all but Thee;
Sever the chain that holds me back from Thee;
Call me, O tender Love, I cry to Thee;
Thou art my all! O bind me close to Thee.

O suffering Love, Who hast so loved me;
O patient Love, Who weariest not of me;
Alone, O Love! Thou weariest not of me!
Ah! weary not till I am lost in Thee;
Nay, weary not till I am found in Thee.

Say the *Anima Christi*, "Soul of Christ," etc.

Petitions

O JESUS, I thank Thee for all the graces I have received through Thy real presence in the tabernacle; grant me an ardent love for the sacrament of Thy love; grant that my visits to Thee in the Blessed Eucharist may sanctify me, make me resemble Thee, and render me more pleasing to Thee.

Dispose me better for the worthy and fruitful reception of holy communion and increase in me the desire of honoring Thee and of causing others to love and honor Thee more in the Blessed Sacrament.

I recommend to Thee the wants of my soul, those of my family, of my friends and benefactors, and of all who have asked me to pray for them. Preserve us from all deliberate sins, forgive us those that we have committed, and fill us with the penitential spirit. Send Thine aid to the Holy Church, the Sovereign Pontiff, the bishops, priests, Religious, and all the faithful. Direct the labors of apostolic missionaries. Convert infidels, heretics, and sinners, and lead them to sincere repentance. O my Jesus, grant me the inestimable gift of final perseverance. Let me attain to that degree of virtue which is requisite for obtaining the degree of glory to which Thou hast destined me. Preserve me from sudden and unforeseen death, and let me be fortified in my departure for eternity by the grace of

Extreme Unction and the Holy Viaticum. Save me through the mercy of Thy divine Heart, grant me the grace at the hour of my death to love Thee with a disinterested love like that with which Thou didst love me in Thy last hour on the cross. Amen.

Prayer to the Eucharistic Jesus

Indulgenced

DEAR Jesus, in the Sacrament of the Altar, be forever thanked and praised. Love, worthy of all celestial and terrestrial love! Who, out of infinite love for me, ungrateful sinner, didst assume our human nature, didst shed Thy most precious blood in the cruel scourging, and didst expire on a shameful cross for our eternal welfare! Now, illumined with lively faith, with the outpouring of my whole soul and the fervor of my heart, I humbly beseech Thee, through the infinite merits of Thy painful sufferings, give me strength and courage to destroy every evil passion which sways my heart, to bless Thee in my greatest afflictions, to glorify Thee by the exact fulfilment of all my duties, supremely to hate all sin, and thus to become a saint.

His Holiness, Pope Pius IX, by an autograph rescript, Jan. 1, 1866, granted an indulgence of one hundred days, once a day, to all the faithful who, with at least contrite heart and devotion, shall say this prayer.

Indulgenced Devotions to the Blessed Sacrament

The archbishop of Port-au-Prince in Haiti entreats the Holy Father, in order to move the faithful more and more to show their faith and reverence toward the

Blessed Sacrament, that he would grant the following indulgences, applicable to the holy souls in purgatory:

1. For reciting in any language the invocation, " Jesus, my God, I adore Thee here present in the sacrament of Thy love," whilst devoutly genuflecting before the Blessed Sacrament enclosed in the tabernacle, one hundred days indulgence each time.

2. For reciting the same invocation whilst adoring with a double genuflection the Blessed Sacrament solemnly exposed, three hundred days each time.

3. For making an exterior act of reverence in passing by a church or oratory where the Blessed Sacrament is kept, one hundred days each time.

The Holy Father granted these indulgences as asked (S. Cong. Indul., July 3, 1908).

(These indulgences will encourage the slow and reverent genuflection before the Blessed Sacrament, and the pious custom so common amongst Irish Catholics of always raising the hat or slightly bowing in passing before a church door.

Indulgenced Chaplet of the Sacred Heart of Jesus

Consisting of Acts of Thanksgiving, Contrition, Love, and Supplication

V. Incline unto mine aid, O God!
R. O Lord, make haste to help me!

1. MOST loving Jesus! my heart leaps for joy while contemplating Thy loving Sacred Heart, all tenderness and sweetness for sinful man; and, with trust unbounded, it never doubts Thy ready welcome. Ah me! my sins! how many and how great! With Peter and Magdalen, in tears, I bewail

and abhor them, because they are an offense to Thee, my sovereign good. Grant me, O grant me pardon for them all! O may I die, I beseech Thee, by Thy loving Heart, may I die rather than offend Thee, and may I live only to correspond to Thy love.

Say the Our Father once, the Glory be to the Father five times; and then:

> O sweetest Heart of Jesus! I implore
> That I may ever love thee more and more.

2. My Jesus! I bless Thy most humble Heart; and I give thanks to Thee, Who, in making it my model, not only dost urge me with much pressing to imitate it, but, at the cost of so many humiliations, dost Thyself stoop to point me out the path and smooth for me the way to follow Thee. Foolish and ungrateful that I am, how have I wandered far away from Thee! Mercy, my Jesus, mercy! Away, hateful pride and love of worldly honor! With lowly heart I wish to follow Thee, my Jesus, through humiliations and the cross, and thus to gain peace and salvation. Only be Thou at hand to strengthen me, and I will ever bless Thy sacred Heart.

Our Father once, Glory be to the Father five times.

O sweetest Heart of Jesus, etc.

3. My Jesus! I marvel at Thy most patient Heart, and I thank Thee for all those wondrous examples of unwearied patience which Thou didst leave me to guide me on my way. It grieves me that I have still to reproach myself with my extravagant delicacy, shrinking from the slightest pain. Oh, pour, then, into my heart, dear Jesus, eager and enduring love of suffering and of the cross, of mortification and of

penance, that, following Thee to Calvary, I may with Thee attain to the joys of paradise!

Our Father once, Glory be to the Father five times.

O sweetest Heart of Jesus, etc.

4. Dear Jesus! at the sight of Thy most gentle Heart, I shudder to see how unlike mine is to Thine, since at a shadow, at a look, at a word of opposition, I fret and grieve. Oh, then, pardon my excesses, and give me grace that, in every contradiction, I may follow the example of Thy unchangeable meekness, and so enjoy an everlasting holy peace.

Our Father once, Glory be to the Father five times.

O sweetest Heart of Jesus, etc.

5. Sing praise to Jesus for His most generous Heart, the conqueror of death and hell; yet never wilt thou reach its due with all thy praise. More than ever am I confounded, looking upon my coward heart, which, through human respect, dreads even a passing word. Courage, my soul! it shall be so with thee no more. My Jesus, I pray Thee for such strength that, fighting and conquering on earth, I may one day rejoice triumphantly with Thee in heaven.

Our Father once, Glory be to the Father five times.

O sweetest Heart of Jesus, etc.

Let us turn to Mary, consecrating ourselves to her more and more, and, trusting in her maternal heart, let us say to her:

By the precious gifts of thy sweetest heart, obtain for me, great Mother of my God and my Mother Mary, a true and lasting devotion to the Sacred Heart of Jesus, thy well-beloved Son, that, united in every thought and affection with that Heart, I may fulfil all the duties of my state of life with ready heart, serving my Jesus ever more, but especially on this day.

Offering to the Sacred Heart of Jesus

MY LOVING Jesus! I [N.N.] give Thee my heart, and I consecrate myself wholly to Thee, out of the grateful love I bear Thee, and as a reparation for all my unfaithfulness, and with Thy aid I purpose never to sin again.

V. Cor Jesu flagrans amore nostri,

R. Inflamma cor nostrum amore tui.

V. Heart of Jesus, burning with love of us,

R. Inflame our hearts with love of Thee.

Oremus

ILLO nos igne, quæsumus, Domine, Spiritus Sanctus inflammet, quem Dominus noster Jesus Christus e penetralibus cordis sui misit in terram et voluit vehementer accendi. Qui tecum vivit et regnat in unitate ejusdem Spiritus Sancti Deus per omnia sæcula sæculorum.
Amen.

Let us pray

LORD, we beseech Thee, let Thy Holy Spirit kindle in our hearts that fire of charity which Our Lord Jesus Christ, Thy Son, sent forth from His inmost Heart upon this earth, and willed that it should burn with vehemence. Who liveth and reigneth with Thee, in the unity of the same Holy Spirit, God, forever and ever.
Amen.

Indulgence of 300 days, every time, and plenary indulgence once a month on usual conditions. — Pius VII, March 20, 1815.

An Act of Reparation to the Sacred Heart of Jesus

(For the First Friday of the Month)

ADORABLE Heart of Jesus, glowing with love for us and inflamed with zeal for our salvation: O Heart! ever sensible of our misery and the wretchedness to which our sins have reduced us, infinitely rich in mercy to heal the wounds of our souls, behold us humbly prostrate before Thee to express the sorrow that fills our hearts for the coldness and indifference with which we have so long requited the numberless benefits that Thou hast conferred upon us. With a deep sense of the outrages that have been heaped upon Thee by our sins and the sins of others, we come to make a solemn reparation of honor to thy most sacred majesty. It was our sins that overwhelmed Thy Heart with bitterness; it was the weight of our iniquities that pressed down Thy face to the earth in the Garden of Olives, and caused Thee to expire in anguish and agony on the cross. But now, repenting and sorrowful, we cast ourselves at Thy feet, and implore forgiveness. Adorable Heart of Jesus, source of true contrition and ever merciful to the penitent sinner, impart to our hearts the spirit of penance, and give to our eyes a fountain of tears, that we may sincerely bewail our sins now and for the rest of our days. Oh, would that we could blot them out, even with our blood! Pardon them, O Lord, in Thy mercy, and pardon and convert to Thee all that have committed irreverences and sacrileges against Thee in the sacrament of Thy love, and thus give another proof that Thy mercy is above all Thy works. Divine Jesus, with Thee there are mercy and plentiful redemption: deliver us from our sins, accept the sincere desire we now entertain, and our holy resolution, relying on the assistance of Thy grace, henceforth to be faithful to Thee. And in order to repair the sins of ingratitude by which we have grieved Thy most tender and loving Heart, we are resolved in the future ever to love and honor Thee in the most adorable Sacrament of the Altar, where Thou art ever present to hear and grant our petitions, and to be the food and life of our souls. Be Thou, O compassionate Jesus! our Mediator with Thy heavenly Father, Whom we have so grievously offended, strengthen our weakness, confirm these our resolutions of amendment, and as Thy sacred Heart is our refuge and our hope when we have sinned, so may it be the strength and support of our repentance, that nothing in life or death may ever again separate us from Thee. Amen.

An Act of Consecration and Reparation to the Most Sacred Heart of Jesus

MOST sacred Heart of Jesus! I adore Thee; I offer to Thee all that I am and all that I possess; I consecrate to Thee my soul with its faculties, my body with all its senses, my heart with all its affections, desiring in all things to honor, love, and glorify Thee; in thanksgiving for the numberless benefits that I have received from Thee, especially in the Holy Eucharist; in atonement for my own sins as well as in reparation for all the offenses that are committed against Thee in the sacrament of Thy love, and, finally, in humble supplication, that I may henceforth be faithful to Thee, that I may please Thee in thought, word, and deed, that I may suffer in patience and in perfect resignation to Thy holy will, that I may become like to Thee in meekness and humility, that I may persevere in

Thy love and Thy grace to the end of my life, and that I may praise Thee and bless Thee with the saints and angels in eternity.

We beseech Thee, also, O good Jesus, by Thy sacred Heart, overflowing with sweetness and mercy, to bless our Holy Father, the Pope, and our Holy Mother, the Church; to take under Thy special protection this congregation, our homes, our country, our rulers, our legislators, our bishops, our priests, and all Religious Orders. We recommend to Thee all our concerns, our friends, relatives, benefactors, and all those who have asked us to pray for them; those who are sick and those who are dying, and all who are under any affliction. Cast an eye of compassion on obstinate sinners and heretics and unbelievers.

Give eternal rest to the faithful departed.

Bless in particular the apostolic labors of those who are engaged in giving missions and retreats, in propagating the Faith in heathen lands, in spreading Thy kingdom on earth, and in fostering devotion to Thy most sacred Heart and to the most holy Sacrament of the Altar. Amen.

Form of Consecration

Issued with the Encyclical Letter of His Holiness, Leo XIII, dated May 25, 1899, on the consecration of mankind to the Sacred Heart of Jesus.

MOST sweet Jesus, Redeemer of the human race, look down upon us, humbly prostrate before Thy altar. We are Thine and Thine we wish to be; but to be more surely united with Thee, behold each one of us freely consecrates himself to-day to Thy most sacred Heart. Many, indeed, have never known Thee; many, too, despising Thy precepts, have rejected Thee. **Have mercy** on them all, most merciful Jesus, and **draw** them to Thy sacred Heart. Be Thou King, O Lord, **not** only of the faithful who have never forsaken Thee, but also of the prodigal children who have abandoned Thee; grant that they may quickly return to their Father's house, lest they die of wretchedness and hunger. Be Thou King of those who are deceived by erroneous opinions, or whom discord keeps aloof, and call them back to the harbor of truth and unity of faith, so that soon there may be but one flock and one shepherd. Be Thou King also of all those who sit in the ancient superstition of the Gentiles, and refuse not Thou to deliver them out of darkness into the light and kingdom of God. Grant, O Lord, to Thy Church, assurance of freedom and immunity from harm; give peace and order to all nations, and make the earth resound from pole to pole with one cry: Praise to the divine Heart that wrought our salvation; to it be glory and honor forever. Amen.

An Act of Consecration to the Sacred Heart of Jesus for Promoters

O JESUS, Saviour of mankind, Thou hast mercifully revealed to us the wonderful riches of Thy Heart; in thanksgiving for Thy benefits, especially for the institution of the Holy Eucharist — in reparation for the offenses against the Blessed Sacrament — in union with Thy mediation in heaven for us poor sinners, I consecrate myself entirely to Thee, for the glory of God and the salvation of souls. I promise to aid in spreading the worship and in promoting the interests of Thy sacred Heart.

. I choose, moreover, the Blessed Virgin Mary for my queen, my advocate, and my mother, and I am resolved to imitate her virtues, in particular her love for sinners, and to foster and promote devotion to her immaculate conception. I beseech Thee humbly to accept this promise. Thou hast inspired me to make it; grant me the grace to fulfil it. Amen.

Sweet Heart of Jesus, be my love!
Sweet heart of Mary, be my salvation!

Rosary of the Sacred Heart

THERE are various forms of the "Beads of the Sacred Heart," composed of different sets of indulgenced prayers. There is no need, however, for special beads. By repeating certain indulgenced ejaculations, according to one's choice, with the ordinary string of beads, a perfect treasury of indulgences is obtained. As a private form of devotion, it can be adapted to one's inclination.

Some printed forms of the Sacred Heart Beads are misleading, because they do not discriminate carefully enough between ejaculations that have an indulgence attached for *each* recitation, and such as have an indulgence that can be gained but *once a day*.

ON THE CROSS

SOUL of Christ, sanctify me! Body of Christ, save me! Blood of Christ, inebriate me! Water from the side of Christ, wash me! Passion of Christ, strengthen me! O good Jesus, hear me; within Thy wounds, hide me; permit me not to be separated from

Thee; from the malignant enemy, defend me; in the hour of death call me and bid me come to Thee, that with Thy saints, I may praise Thee, forever and ever. Amen.

Indulgence of 300 days, each time. Pius IX, Jan. 9, 1854.

Or say the following:

Eternal Father! I offer Thee the precious blood of Jesus in satisfaction for my sins, and for the wants of holy Church.

Indulgence of 100 days, each time. — Pius VII, Sept. 22, 1817.

ON THE LARGE BEADS AFTER EACH DECADE

O sweetest Heart of Jesus, I implore that I may ever love Thee more and more.

Indulgence of 300 days, each time; plenary indulgence, once a month, on the usual conditions. — Pius IX, Nov. 26, 1876.

OR

Jesus, meek and humble of heart, make my heart like unto Thine.

Indulgence of 300 days, every time.—Pius X, Sept. 15, 1905.

OR

Heart of Jesus, inflamed with love of us, inflame our hearts with love of Thee.

Indulgence of 100 days, once a day. — Leo XIII, June 16, 1893.

ON THE SMALL BEADS

Sweet Heart of Jesus, be my love.

Indulgence of 300 days, once a day. — Leo XIII, May 21, 1892.

Sweet heart of Mary, be my salvation.

The latter invocation to the heart of Mary has attached to it for each recitation 300 days' indulgence. — Pius IX, Sept. 30, 1852.

AT THE CONCLUSION

Jesus, Mary, and Joseph, I give you my heart and my soul. Jesus, Mary, and Joseph, assist me in my last agony. Jesus, Mary, and Joseph, may I breathe forth my soul in peace with you.

Indulgence of 300 days, each time that all three invocations are recited; 100 days, when only one is recited. — Pius VII, April 28, 1807.

Or any of the following prayers:

May the Heart of Jesus in the Most Blessed Sacrament be praised, adored, and loved with grateful affection, at every moment, in all the tabernacles of the world. even to the end of time. Amen.

Indulgence of 100 days, once a day, — Pius IX, Feb. 29, 1868.

Blessed be the holy and immaculate conception of the most blessed Virgin Mary, Mother of God.

Indulgence of 300 days, each time. — Leo XIII, Sept. 10, 1878.

O Mary, who didst come into this world free from stain, obtain of God for me that I may leave it without sin.

Indulgence of 100 days, once a day. — Pius IX, March 27, 1863.

St. Joseph, model and patron of those who love the Sacred Heart of Jesus, pray for us.

Indulgence of 100 days, once a day. — Leo XIII, Dec. 19, 1891.

An Act of Consecration to the Most Sacred Heart of Jesus

O THEE, most sacred Heart of Jesus, I devote my life. To Thee I consecrate all my thoughts, words, actions, and sufferings. My whole being shall be employed henceforth in loving, serving, and glorifying Thee. Be Thou, most blessed and adorable Heart, the sole object of my love, the protector of my life, the pledge of my salvation, and my secure refuge at the hour of my death. Be Thou my advocate at the throne of Divine Justice, and screen me from the wrath which my sins deserve.

I trust entirely in Thy mercy. I place all my confidence in Thee. Destroy in me all that is displeasing to Thee. Jesus, meek and humble of heart, make my heart like unto Thine. Imprint Thyself like a seal upon my heart in order that I may never be separated from Thee. May I be a victim forever consecrated to Thy glory — ever burning with the flames of Thy pure love in time and for eternity. This is my whole desire — to live in Thee. This shall be my happiness, to live and die as Thy devoted servant.

Sweet Heart of Jesus, I implore that I may love Thee more and more. Amen.

V. Heart of Jesus, burning with love for us.

R. Inflame our hearts with love of Thee.

Let us pray

Lord, we beseech Thee, let Thy Holy Spirit kindle in our hearts that fire of charity which Our Lord Jesus Christ, Thy Son, sent forth from His inmost heart upon this earth, and willed that it should burn with vehemence. Who liveth and reigneth with Thee, in the unity of the same Holy Spirit, God, for ever and ever. Amen.

Prayer in Honor of the Passion of Our Saviour

O GOD, Who for the world's redemption wast pleased to be born, circumcised, rejected by the Jews, betrayed by the kiss of the traitor Judas, bound with chains, led like an innocent lamb to sacrifice, and shamefully presented before Annas, Caiphas, Pilate, and Herod, accused by false witnesses, beaten with whips, buffeted, insulted, spit upon, crowned with thorns, smitten with a reed, blindfolded, stripped of Thy garments, fastened with nails to the cross, and lifted up on high, reputed among thieves, and made to drink gall and vinegar, and wounded by a lance; oh, by these most sacred sufferings, which, unworthy as I am, I thus commemorate, and by Thy holy cross and death, deliver me, Lord, from the pains of hell, and deign to lead me where Thou didst lead the penitent thief, who was crucified by Thy side; Thou Who, with the Father and the Holy Ghost, livest and reignest, world without end. Amen.

Our Father, Hail Mary, Glory be to the Father, etc., five times.

The Sovereign Pontiff, Pius VII, by a decree of the Sacred Congregation of Indulgences, Aug. 25, 1820, granted to all the faithful who, with at least contrite heart and devotion, shall say this prayer, and the *Our Father*, the *Hail Mary* and the *Glory be to the Father*, each five times, an *indulgence of three hundred days,* once a day, also a *plenary indulgence*, on any one of the last three days of the month, to all those who having said these prayers every day for a month and being truly penitent after confession and communion, shall pray devoutly for some time for the intention of His Holiness.

EJACULATION

Adoramus Te, sanctissime Domine Jesu Christe, benedicimus Tibi; quia per sanctam crucem Tuam redemisti mundum.

We adore Thee, O most blessed Lord, Jesus Christ, we bless Thee; because by Thy holy cross Thou hast redeemed the world.

His Holiness, Pope Leo XIII, by a rescript of the Sacred Congregation of Indulgences, March 4, 1882, granted to all the faithful who, with at least contrite heart and devotion, shall recite this ejaculation, an *indulgence of one hundred days*, once a day.

Seven Offerings of the Precious Blood of Jesus Christ

1. ETERNAL Father! I offer Thee the merit of the precious blood of Jesus, Thy well-beloved Son, my Saviour and my God, for my dear Mother, the holy Church, that she may enlarge her borders and be magnified among all the nations of the earth; for the safety and well-being of her visible head,

the sovereign Roman Pontiff; for the cardinals, bishops, and pastors of souls, and for all the ministers of Thy sanctuary.

Then say the " Glory be to the Father," and the ejaculation, " Blessing and thanksgiving be to Jesus, Who with His blood hath saved us ! "

II. Eternal Father! I offer Thee the merit of the precious blood of Jesus, Thy well-beloved Son, my Saviour and my God, for peace and union among all Catholic kings and princes, for the humiliation of the enemies of our holy Faith, and for the welfare of all Christian people.

" Glory be to the Father," and, " Blessing and thanksgiving," etc.

III. Eternal Father! I offer Thee the merit of the precious blood of Jesus, Thy well-beloved Son, my Saviour and my God, for the repentance of unbelievers, for the uprooting of heresy, and for the conversion of sinners.

" Glory be to the Father," and, " Blessing and thanksgiving," etc.

IV. Eternal Father! I offer Thee the merit of the precious blood of Jesus, Thy well-beloved Son, my Saviour and my God, for all my kindred, friends, and enemies; for the poor, the sick, and wretched, and for all for whom Thou, my God, knowest that I ought to pray, or wouldst have me pray.

" Glory be to the Father," and, " Blessing and thanksgiving," etc.

V. Eternal Father! I offer Thee the merit of the precious blood of Jesus, Thy well-beloved Son, my Saviour and my God, for all who, this day, are passing to the other life; that Thou wouldst save them from the pains of hell, and admit them quickly to the possession of Thy glory.

"Glory be to the Father," and, "Blessing and thanksgiving," etc.

VI. Eternal Father! I offer Thee the merit of the precious blood of Jesus, Thy well-beloved Son, my Saviour and my God, for all those who love this great treasure, for those who join with me in adoring it and honoring it, and who strive to spread devotion to it.

"Glory be to the Father," and, "Blessing and thanksgiving," etc.

VII. Eternal Father! I offer Thee the merit of the precious blood of Jesus, Thy well-beloved Son, my Saviour and my God, for all my wants, spiritual and temporal, in aid of the holy souls in purgatory, and chiefly for those who most loved this precious blood, the price of our redemption, and who were most devout to the sorrows and pains of most holy Mary, our dear Mother.

"Glory be to the Father," and, "Blessing and thanksgiving," etc.

Glory be to the blood of Jesus, now and forever, and throughout all ages. Amen.

Indulgence of 300 days, each time.—Pius VII, Sept. 22, 1817. Plenary indulgence once a month, under usual conditions.

EJACULATION

Eternal Father! I offer Thee the precious blood of Jesus in satisfaction for my sins, and for the wants of the holy Church.

Indulgence of 100 days, each time.—Pius VII, Sept. 22. 1817.

Prayer, "O Most Compassionate Jesus"

O MOST compassionate Jesus! Thou alone art our salvation, our life, and our resurrection. We implore Thee, therefore, do not forsake us in our needs and afflictions, but, by the agony of Thy most sacred Heart, and by the sorrows of Thy immaculate Mother, succor Thy servants whom Thou hast redeemed by Thy most precious blood.

Indulgence of 100 days, once a day. — Pius IX, Oct. 6, 1870.

EJACULATION

Jesu, Deus meus, super omnia amo Te.

Jesus, my God, I love Thee above all things.

His Holiness, Pope Pius IX, by an autograph rescript, May 7, 1854, granted to all the faithful, every time that, with at least contrite heart and devotion, they shall say this ejaculation, or induce others to say it, an *indulgence of fifty days*.

Prayer, "Divine Jesus"

D IVINE Jesus, incarnate Son of God, Who for our salvation didst vouchsafe to be born in a stable, to pass Thy life in poverty, trials, and misery, and to die amid the sufferings of the cross, I entreat Thee, say to Thy divine Father at the hour of my death: *Father, forgive him;* say to Thy beloved Mother: *Behold thy son;* say to my soul: *This day thou shalt be with Me in paradise.* My God, my God, forsake me not in that hour. *I thirst;* yes, my God, my soul thirsts after Thee, Who art the fountain of living waters. My life passes like a shadow; yet a little while, and all will be consummated. Wherefore, O my adorable Saviour! from this moment, for all eternity, *into Thy hands I commend my spirit.* Lord Jesus, receive my soul. Amen.

His Holiness, Pope Pius IX, by a decree of the Sacred Congregation of Indulgences, June 10, 1856, confirmed an *indulgence of three hundred days,* to be gained by all the faithful every time that they shall say this prayer with contrite heart and devotion.

Prayer for Greater Love of Jesus

O MY Jesus, Thou knowest well that I love Thee; but I do not love Thee enough; O grant that I may love Thee more. O love that burnest ever and never failest, my God, Thou Who art charity itself, enkindle in my heart that divine fire which consumes the saints and transforms them into Thee. Amen.

His Holiness, Leo XIII, by a rescript of the Sacred Congregation of Indulgences, Feb. 6, 1893, granted to the faithful who recite the above prayer an *indulgence of fifty days,* twice a day.

Prayer

GRANT us, Lord Jesus, always to follow the example of Thy holy family, that at the hour of our death Thy glorious Virgin Mother with blessed Joseph may come to meet us, and so we may deserve to be received by Thee into Thy everlasting dwelling-place.

His Holiness, Leo XIII, by a rescript of the Sacred Congregation of Indulgences, March 25, 1897, granted to the faithful who shall recite the above prayer an *indulgence of two hundred days,* once a day.

Novena in Honor of the Holy Name of Jesus

O MERCIFUL Jesus, Who didst in Thy early infancy commence Thy office of Saviour by shedding Thy precious blood, and assuming for us that name which is above all names; we thank Thee for such early proofs of Thy infinite love. We venerate Thy sacred name, in union with the profound respect of the angel who first announced it to the earth, and unite our affections to the sentiments of tender devotion which the adorable name of Jesus has in all ages enkindled in the hearts of Thy saints. Animated with a firm faith in Thy unerring word, and penetrated with confidence in Thy mercy, we now most humbly remind Thee of the promise Thou hast made, that where two or three should assemble in Thy name, Thou Thyself wouldst be in the midst of them. Come, then, into the midst of us, most amiable Jesus, for it is in Thy sacred name we are here assembled; come into our hearts, that we may be governed by Thy holy spirit; mercifully grant us, through that adorable name, which is the joy of heaven, the terror of hell, the consolation of the afflicted, and the solid ground of our unlimited confidence, all the petitions we make in this novena.

Oh! blessed Mother of our Redeemer! who didst participate so sensibly in the sufferings of thy dear Son when He shed His sacred blood and assumed for us the name of Jesus, obtain for us, through that adorable name, the favors we petition in this novena. Beg also, that the most ardent love may imprint on our hearts that sacred name, that it may be always in our minds and frequently on our lips; that it may be our defense and our refuge in the temptations and trials of life, and our consolation and support in the hour of death. Amen.

INDULGENCED INVOCATIONS

My Jesus, mercy!

Indulgence of 100 days, for each recital. — Pius IX, Sept. 24, 1846.

My sweetest Jesus, be not my judge, but my Saviour.

Indulgence of 50 days, for each recital. — Pius IX, Aug. 11, 1851.

Jesus, my God, I love Thee above all things.

Indulgence of 50 days, each time. — Pius IX, May 7, 1854.

Jesus, Son of David, have mercy on me! (*Luke* xviii. 38.)

Indulgence of 100 days, once a day. — Leo XIII, Feb. 27, 1886.

Prayer to the Infant Jesus
Before an Image of
St. Anthony of Padua

O JESUS, my Saviour! Who didst vouchsafe to appear to St. Anthony in the form of an infant, I implore Thee, through the love Thou didst bear to this saint when he dwelt on earth, and which Thou now bearest to him in heaven, graciously hear my prayer, and assist me in my necessities. Who livest and reignest, world without end. Amen.

Our Father; Hail Mary; Glory, etc. St. Anthony, pray for us.

Thirty-three Petitions in Honor of the Sacred Humanity of Our Lord Jesus Christ

O GOOD Jesus! Word of the Eternal Father, convert me!

O good Jesus! Son of Mary, make me her child!

O good Jesus! my Master, teach me!

O good Jesus! Prince of peace, give me peace!

O good Jesus! my Refuge, receive me!

O good Jesus! my Pastor, feed my soul!

O good Jesus! Model of patience, comfort me!

O good Jesus! meek and humble of Heart, help me to become like to Thee!

O good Jesus! my Redeemer, save me!

O good Jesus! my God and my All, possess me!

O good Jesus! the true Way, direct me!

O good Jesus! eternal Truth, instruct me!

O good Jesus! Life of the blessed, make me live in Thee!

O good Jesus! my Support, strengthen me!

O good Jesus! my Justice, justify me!

O good Jesus! my Mediator, reconcile me to Thy Father!

O good Jesus! Physician of my soul, heal me!

O good Jesus! my Judge, absolve me!

O good Jesus! my King, govern me!

O good Jesus! my Sanctification, sanctify me!

O good Jesus! Abyss of goodness, pardon me!

O good Jesus! living Bread from heaven, satiate me!

O good Jesus! the Father of the prodigal, receive me!

O good Jesus! Joy of my soul, refresh me!

O good Jesus! my Helper, assist me!

O good Jesus! Magnet of love, attract me!

O good Jesus! my Protector, defend me!

O good Jesus! my Hope, sustain me!

O good Jesus! Object of my love, make me love Thee!

O good Jesus! Fountain of life, cleanse me!

O good Jesus! my Propitiation, purify me!

O good Jesus, my last End, let me obtain Thee!

O good Jesus! my Glory, glorify me. Amen.

Jesus, hear my prayer!

Jesus, graciously hear me.

Let us pray

` O Lord Jesus Christ, Who hast said, *Ask and you shall receive, seek and you shall find, knock and it shall be opened unto you!* mercifully attend to our supplication, and grant us the gift of Thy divine charity, that we may ever love Thee with our whole heart, and never desist from Thy praise: who livest and reignest one God, world without end. Amen.

O God, Who didst appoint Thine only begotten Son savior of mankind, and didst command that He should be called Jesus; mercifully grant that we may enjoy the vision of Him in heaven, Whose holy name we venerate on earth. Through the same Christ our Lord. Amen.

Prayer in Honor of the Most Holy and Adorable Name of Jesus

JESUS! O name of Jesus! sweet name! delightful name! consoling name! for what else is Jesus than Saviour! Therefore, O Jesus, for Thy sweet name's sake, be to me a Jesus, and save me. Suffer me not to be eternally lost. O good Jesus! let not my iniquities destroy me, whom Thy bounty made. O sweet Jesus! recognize in me what is Thine, and efface all that is not Thine. O sweet Jesus! show mercy now in the time of mercy, and condemn me not in the day of justice. What profit to Thy precious blood, or what honor will my destruction give Thy holy name, O Jesus! "The dead shall not praise Thee, O Lord Jesus! nor all they that go down to hell." Most amiable Jesus! most meek, most loving Jesus! O Jesus, Jesus, Jesus! admit me to the number of Thy elect.

O Jesus, salvation of those who believe in Thee! comfort of those who fly to Thee! O Jesus, Son of the virgin Mary! give me grace, wisdom, charity, purity, and humility, that I may love Thee perfectly, praise Thee, enjoy Thee, serve Thee, and be glorified in Thee, with all those who call upon Thy name, Thy holy name, Thy sweet name — Jesus. Amen.

HYMNS IN HONOR OF THE MOST HOLY NAME OF JESUS

Jesu Dulcis Memoria

JESU dulcis memoria, Dans vera cordi gaudia; Sed super mel et omnia, Ejus dulcis praesentia.	JESUS! the very thought of Thee With sweetness fills my breast; But sweeter far Thy face to see, And in Thy presence rest.

Nil canitur sua-
vius,
  Nil auditur jucun-
  dius,
Nil cogitatur dul-
cius,
  Quam Jesu Dei Fi-
  lius!

Nor voice can sing, nor
heart can frame,
  Nor can the memory
  find,
A sweeter sound than Thy
blest name,
  O Saviour of man-
  kind!

Jesu spes pœniten-
tibus,
  Quam pius es peten-
  tibus!
Quam bonus Te quæ-
rentibus!
  Sed quid invenien-
  tibus! .

O hope of every contrite
heart!
  O joy of all the
  meek!
To those who fall, how kind
Thou art!
  How good to those who
  seek!

Nec lingua valet dic-
ere
  Nec littera expri-
  mere;
Expertus potest cre-
dere,
  Quid sit Jesum dili-
  gere.

But what to those who find?
Ah! this
  Nor tongue nor pen can
  show:
The love of Jesus — what
it is,
  None but His loved ones
  know.

Sis, Jesu, nostrum gau-
dium,
  Qui es futurum præ-
  mium;
Sit nostra in Te glo-
ria,
  Per cuncta semper
  sæcula. Amen.

Jesus! our only joy be
Thou,
  As Thou our prize wilt
  be;
Jesus! be Thou our glory
now
  And through eternity.
            Amen.

Jesu Rex Admirabilis

Jesu! Rex admira-
  bilis!
Et triumphator nobilis,
Dulcedo   ineffa-
  bilis
Totus   desidera-
  bilis.

O Jesus! King most
  wonderful!
Thou conqueror renowned!
Thou sweetness most in-
  effable!
In whom all joys are
  found!

Quando cor nostrum
  visitas,
Tunc lucet ei veri-
  tas;
Mundi vilescit vani-
  tas,
Et intus fervet chari-
  tas.

When once Thou visitest
  the heart,
Then truth begins to
  shine:
Then earthly vanities de-
  part,
Then kindles love di-
  vine.

Jesu dulcedo cor-
  dium,
Fons vivus, lumen
  mentium,
Excedens omne gaud-
  ium,
Et omne deside-
  rium.

O Jesus! light of all be-
  low!
Thou fount of life and
  fire!
Surpassing all the joys we
  know,
All that we can de-
  sire.

Jesum omnes agnos-
  cite,
Amorem ejus poscite;
Jesum ardenter quæ-
  rite,
Quærendo inardes-
  cite.

May every heart confess Thy
  name,
And ever Thee adore;
And seeking Thee, itself inflame,
To seek Thee more and
  more.

Te nostra, Jesu, vox so-
net;
Nostri te mores expri-
mant;
Te corda nostra dili-
gant
Et nunc, et in perpe-
tuum. Amen.

Thee may our tongues for-
ever bless;
Thee may we love
alone;
And ever in our lives ex-
press
The image of Thine own.
Amen.

V. Sit nomen Domini
benedictum.
R. Ex hoc nunc, et usque
in sæculum.

V. Blessed be the name
of the Lord.
R. From henceforth and
forevermore.

Oremus

DEUS, Qui unigenitum
Filium tuum constitu-
isti humani generis salvatorem, et Jesum vocari
jussisti: concede propi-
tius; ut cujus sanctum
nomen veneramur in terris,
ejus quoque aspectu per-
fruamur in cœlis. Per eumdem Christum Dominum
nostrum. Amen.

GOD, Who didst appoint
Thine only begotten
Son Saviour of mankind, and
didst command that He
should be called Jesus;
mercifully grant that we
may enjoy the vision of
Him in heaven, Whose holy
name we venerate on earth.
Through the same Christ
our Lord. Amen.

Devotions in honor of the Blessed Virgin Mary

Dedication to Mary

My Queen! my Mother! I give myself entirely to thee; and to show my devotion to thee, I consecrate to thee this day my eyes, my ears, my mouth, my heart, my whole being, without reserve. Wherefore, good Mother, as I am thine own, keep me, guard me, as thy property and possession.

His Holiness, Pope Pius IX, by a decree of the Sacred Congregation of Indulgences, Aug. 5, 1851, granted to all the faithful who, with fervor and at least contrite heart, shall say, morning and evening, one *Hail Mary*, together with this prayer, to implore of the Blessed Virgin victory over temptations, especially over those against chastity, an *indulgence of one hundred days*, once a day.

Prayer to the Blessed Virgin

O Mary, you desire above all things to see Jesus loved; if you love me, this is the favor which I ask of you, to obtain for me a great love of Jesus Christ. You obtain from your Son whatever you please; pray then for me, that I may forever remain in His love and in His grace, and that by imitating you I may practise every virtue that is pleasing to His sacred Heart. Obtain for me a great love toward you, who, of all creatures, are the most pure and most beloved of God. And through that grief which you suffered on Calvary, when you beheld Jesus expire on the cross, obtain for me a happy death, that by loving Jesus, and you, my Mother, all through life, I may come to love you and bless you forever in heaven:

Three Offerings in Honor of the Blessed Virgin Mary

I. Holiest Virgin, with all my heart I worship thee above all the angels and saints in paradise as the daughter of the eternal Father, and to thee I consecrate my soul and all its powers. Hail Mary, etc.

II. Holiest Virgin, with all my heart I worship thee above all the angels and saints in paradise as the Mother of the only-begotten Son, and to thee I consecrate my body with all its senses. Hail Mary, etc.

III. Holiest Virgin, with all my heart I worship thee above all the angels and saints in paradise as the spouse of the Holy Ghost, and to thee I consecrate my heart and all its affections, praying thee to obtain for me from the ever blessed Trinity all the graces which I need for my salvation. Hail Mary, etc.

Indulgence of 300 days, each time. — Leo XII, Oct. 21, 1823.

Memorare of Our Lady of the Sacred Heart

Remember, O our Lady of the Sacred Heart! the unlimited power that thou possessest over the Heart of thy adorable Son. Full of confidence in thy merits, I come to implore thy protection. O sovereign Mistress of the Heart of Jesus! of that Heart which is the inexhaustible source of all graces, and which thou canst open at thy pleasure, and cause all the treasures of love and mercy, of light and salvation, that this Heart incloses, to descend upon man, grant me, I conjure thee, the favor I solicit. No, I can not bear a refusal, and because thou art my Mother, O our Lady of the Sacred Heart! favorably receive my prayer, and vouchsafe to grant my petition. Amen.

An Act of Consecration to the Most Holy Heart of Mary

O HEART of Mary, ever Virgin! O heart the holiest, the purest, the most perfect, that the Almighty hath formed in any creature; O heart, full of all grace and sweetness, throne of love and mercy, image of the adorable Heart of Jesus, heart that didst love God more than all the seraphim, that didst procure more glory to the most holy Trinity than all the saints together, that didst endure for love of us the bitter dolors at the foot of the cross, and dost so justly merit the reverence, love, and gratitude of all mankind, I give thee thanks for all the benefits which thou hast obtained for me from the divine Mercy; I unite myself to all the souls that find their joy and consolation in loving and honoring thee. O heart most amiable, the delight and admiration of the angels and the saints, henceforth thou shalt be to me, next to the Heart of Jesus, the object of my tenderest devotion, my refuge in affliction, my consolation in sorrow, my place of retreat from the enemies of my salvation, and, at the hour of my death, the surest anchor of my hope. Amen.

O HOLY Mother of God, glorious Queen of heaven and earth! I choose thee this day for my Mother, and my advocate at the throne of thy divine Son. Accept the offering I here make of my heart. May it be irrevocable. It never can be out of danger whilst at my disposal; never secure but in thy hands. Obtain for me at present the gift of true repentance, and such graces as I may afterward stand in need of, for the gaining of life everlasting. Amen.

This and the following prayer are from the " Visitation Manual."

Prayer in Honor of Our Sorrowful Mother

O LORD, in Whose passion, according to the prophecy of Simeon, a sword of sorrow pierced the most sweet soul of Mary, mother and virgin, grant, in Thy mercy, that we may call to mind with veneration her transfixion and sufferings; and that by the glorious merits and prayers of all the saints who stood faithfully by the cross, we may experience the happy effects of Thy passion. Who livest and reignest forever and ever. Amen.

Prayer of St. Alphonsus de Liguori

To the Blessed Virgin Mary

MOST holy and immaculate Virgin! O my Mother! thou who art the Mother of my Lord, the Queen of the world, the advocate, hope, and refuge of sinners! I, the most wretched among them, now come to thee. I worship thee, great Queen, and give thee thanks for the many favors thou hast bestowed on me in the past; most of all do I thank thee for having saved me from hell, which I had so often deserved. I love thee, Lady most worthy of all love, and, by the love which I bear thee, I promise ever in the future to serve thee, and to do what in me lies to win others to thy love. In thee I put all my trust, all my hope of salvation. Receive me as thy servant, and cover me with the mantle of thy protection, thou who art the Mother of mercy! And since thou hast so much power with God, deliver me from all temptations, or at least obtain for me the grace ever to overcome them. From thee I ask a true love of Jesus Christ and the grace of a happy death. O my Mother! by thy love for God I beseech thee to be at all times my helper, but above all at the last moment of my life. Leave me not until thou seest me safe in heaven, there for endless ages to bless thee and sing thy praises. Amen.

Indulgence of 300 days, each time, if said before a representation of Our Lady; plenary indulgence once a month, on the usual conditions.—Pius IX, Sept. 7, 1854.

Prayer of St. Aloysius Gonzaga to the Blessed Virgin

OST holy Mary, my Lady, to thy faithful care and special keeping and to the bosom of thy mercy, to-day and every day, and particularly at the hour of my death, I commend my soul and my body. All my hope and consolation, all my trials and miseries, my life and the end of my life I commit to thee, that through thy most holy intercession and by thy merits all my actions may be directed and ordered according to thy will and that of thy divine Son. Amen.

His Holiness, Leo XIII, by a rescript of the Sacred Congregation of Indulgences, March 15, 1890, granted to the faithful who recite the above prayer, an *indulgence of two hundred days,* once a day.

Prayer and Consecration to Our Lady of Perpetual Help

OST holy Virgin Mary, Mother of God, whom I love to honor under the lovely title of Mother of Perpetual Help, I, N., although most unworthy to be thy servant, yet moved by thy wonderful compassion, and by my desire to serve thee, now choose thee, in presence of my guardian angel and of the whole celestial court, for my queen, advocate, and mother: and I firmly purpose always to love and serve thee for the future, and to do whatever I can to induce others to love and serve thee also. I beseech thee, O Mother of God, and my most compassionate and loving Mother, by the blood which thy Son shed for me, to receive me into the number of thy servants, to be thy child and servant forever. Assist me in my thoughts, words, and actions every moment of my life, so that all may be directed to the greater glory of my God; and through thy most powerful intercession, may I never more offend my beloved Jesus, but may I glorify Him, and love Him in this life, and love thee also, my most tender and dear Mother, so that I may love thee and enjoy thee in heaven and bless God for all eternity. Amen.

Chaplet in Honor of the Immaculate Heart of Mary, Our Lady of Sorrows

Suitable for a Novena

V. DEUS in adjutorium meum intende.
R. Domine ad adjuvandum me festina.
V. Gloria Patri, et Filio, etc.
R. Sicut erat, etc.

V. INCLINE unto my aid, O God!
R. O Lord! make haste to help me.
V. Glory be to the Father, etc.
R. As it was, etc.

I. IMMACULATE Virgin, who, conceived without sin, didst direct every movement of thy most pure heart to that God Who was ever the object of thy love, and who wast ever most submissive to His will; obtain for me the grace to hate sin with my whole heart, and to learn of thee to live in perfect resignation to the will of God.

Our Father, once, Hail Mary, seven times.

> Heart transpierced with pain and woe!
> Set my heart with love aglow.

II. **I** MARVEL, Mary, at thy deep humility, through which thy blessed heart was troubled at the gracious message brought thee by Gabriel, the archangel, that thou wast chosen Mother of the Son of the Most High, and through which thou didst proclaim thyself His humble handmaid; wherefore, in great confusion at the sight of my pride, I ask thee for the grace of a contrite and humble heart, that, knowing my own misery, I may obtain that crown of glory promised to the truly humble of heart.

Our Father, etc., Heart, etc.

III. **B**LESSED Virgin, who, in thy sweetest heart, didst keep as a precious treasure the words of Jesus, thy Son, and, pondering on the lofty mysteries they contained, didst learn to live for God alone; how doth my cold heart confound me! O dearest Mother! get me grace so to meditate within my heart upon God's holy law that I may strive to follow thee in the fervent practice of every Christian virtue.

Our Father, etc., Heart, etc.

IV. **G**LORIOUS Queen of martyrs, whose sacred heart was pierced in thy Son's bitter passion by the sword whereof the holy old man Simeon had prophesied; gain for my heart true courage and a holy patience to bear the troubles and misfortunes of this miserable life, so that, by crucifying my flesh with its desires, while following the mortification of the cross, I may, indeed, show myself to be a true son of thine.

Our Father, etc., Heart, etc.

V. O MARY, mystical rose, with loving heart, burning with the living fire of charity, Thou didst accept us for thy children at the foot of the cross, becoming thus our tender Mother! make me feel the sweetness of thy maternal heart and thy power with Jesus, that, when menaced by the perils of this mortal life, and most of all in the dread hour of death, my heart, united with thine, may love my Jesus then and through all ages. Amen.

Our Father, etc., Heart, etc.

LET us now turn to the most sacred Heart of Jesus, that He may inflame us with His holy love.

O divine Heart of Jesus! to Thee I consecrate myself, full of deep gratitude for the many blessings I have received and daily do receive from Thy boundless charity. With my whole heart I thank Thee for having, in addition to them all, vouchsafed to give me Thy own most holy Mother, giving me to her as a son, in the person of the beloved disciple. Let my heart ever burn with love for Thee, finding in Thy sweetest Heart its peace, its refuge, and its happiness.

Indulgence of 300 days, once a day. — Pius IX, Dec. 11, 1854.

Novena to Our Lady of Perpetual Help

To Obtain some Spiritual or Temporal Favor

Recite each day nine Hail Marys, and then say the following prayer:

OUR Lady of Perpetual Help, show that thou art indeed our Mother, and obtain for me the favor I desire (*here specify the desired favor*) and the grace to use it for the glory of God and the salvation of my soul.

Glorious St. Alphonsus, who by thy confidence in the Blessed Virgin didst obtain from her so many favors, and who, by thy writings, hast shown us what graces God bestows on us by the hands of Mary! Obtain for me the greatest confidence in our good Mother of Perpetual Help, and beg of her to grant me the favor I am asking of her power and maternal goodness.

Eternal Father, in the name of Jesus, and by the intercession of our Mother of Perpetual Help, and of St. Alphonsus, I pray Thee to hear me and to grant my request, if it be to Thy greater glory and the good of my soul. Amen.

Prayer to Our Lady of Good Counsel

MOST glorious Virgin, chosen by the eternal Counsel to be the Mother of the eternal Word made flesh, treasure of divine grace, and advocate of sinners, we, the most unworthy of thy servants, supplicate thee to be our guide and counselor in this valley of tears. Obtain for us, by the most precious blood of thy Son, pardon for our sins, and the salvation of our souls. Grant that the holy Catholic Church may triumph

over her enemies and that the kingdom of Christ may
be propagated on earth.   Amen.

Oh! most loving and tender Mother, it is sufficient
for me to tell thee my need and difficulty, for thy loving
heart always longs to help thy children.   Remember the
Holy Ghost has made Thee the Mother of good counsel
in order that we might find in thee a guardian and a
guide.   Turn to me, then, I beseech thee, and listen
to my prayer.   Show me how to act in this matter, for
the glory of God and the good of my soul.   Amen.

Indulgenced Novenas in Honor of the Blessed Virgin Mary

ELEVEN NOVENAS TO THE BLESSED VIRGIN

THE Sovereign Pontiff, Pius IX, granted to all the
faithful who devoutly and with contrite heart
shall make at any time during the year any of the following
novenas in honor of the Blessed Virgin Mary, with any
formula of prayer, provided it be approved by competent
ecclesiastical authority, an *indulgence of three hundred days*,
each day; a *plenary indulgence*, either during the course of
each novena, or upon one of the eight days immediately
following, on the usual conditions.

LIST OF THESE NOVENAS

1. In honor of the Immaculate Conception of the
Blessed Virgin Mary.
2. In honor of the Birth of Mary most holy.
3. In honor of the Presentation of Mary in the Temple.
4. In honor of the Annunciation.
5. In honor of the Visitation.
6. In honor of Mary's holy Delivery and of the Birth
of the Child Jesus.

7. In honor of the Purification of the Blessed Virgin Mary.

8. In honor of the Dolors of Mary.

9. In honor of the Assumption of Mary.

10. In honor of the Sacred Heart of Mary and of her Patronage.

11. In honor of the Feast of the Most Holy Rosary of the Blessed Virgin.

N. B. — The prayers in this book are all approved by ecclesiastical authority, and hence may be used at pleasure in making the above-mentioned novenas.

A very simple and satisfactory method of making a novena in honor of the Blessed Virgin Mary consists in reciting the following prayers:

1. The Litany of Loreto.

2. The Memorare, and an act of consecration.

3. Three Our Fathers, Hail Marys, and Glorys in thanksgiving to the Blessed Trinity for the prerogatives and graces bestowed upon the Blessed Virgin Mary. Conclude with an ejaculation appropriate to the season or to the festival commemorated. The following will suffice for all seasons.

EJACULATION

O DOMINA mea! O Mater mea! memento me esse tuum.

Serva me, defende me, ut rem et possessionem tuam.

O Y Queen! my Mother! remember I am thine own.

Keep me, guard me, as thy property and possession.

Indulgence of 40 days, each time. — Pius IX, Aug. 5, 1851.

OTHER EJACULATIONS

Sweet heart of Mary, be my salvation!

Indulgence of 300 days, each time. — Pius IX, Sept. 30, 1852.

O Mary, conceived without sin, pray for us who have recourse to thee!

Indulgence of 100 days, once a day. — Leo XIII, March 15, 1884.

Mary, Mother of God, and Mother of mercy, pray for me and for the departed.

Indulgence of 100 days, once a day. — Leo XIII, Dec. 15, 1883.

Novena in Honor of the Blessed Virgin Mary for any Festival and for any Special Occasion

In connection with the *Litany of Loreto* and the *Memorare*, the following prayer may be said occasionally.

O MARY, ever blessed Virgin, Mother of God, Queen of the angels and of the saints, I salute thee with the most profound veneration and filial devotion. I renew the consecration of myself and all I have to thee. I thank thee for thy maternal protection and for the many blessings that I have received through thy wondrous mercy and most powerful intercession. In all my necessities I have recourse to thee with unbounded confidence. O Help of Christians, O Mother of mercy, I beseech thee now to hear my prayer, and to obtain for me of thy divine Son the favor that I request in this novena.

Obtain for me, also, dearest Mother, the grace that I may imitate thee and become more like to thee in the practice of the virtues of humility, obedience, purity, poverty, submission to the will of God, and charity. Be my protectress in life, guard and guide me in dangers, direct me in perplexities, lead me in the way of perfection, and assist me in the hour of my death, that I may come to Jesus, and with thee enjoy Him, bless Him, and love Him eternally in heaven. Amen.

MEMORARE, O piissima Virgo Maria, non esse auditum a sæculo quemquam ad tua currentem præsidia, tua implorantem auxilia, tua petentem suffragia, esse derelictum. Ego tali animatus confidentia, ad te, Virgo virginum, Mater, curro, ad te venio, coram te gemens peccator assisto; noli, Mater Verbi, verba mea despicere, sed audi propitia et exaudi. Amen.

REMEMBER, O most gracious Virgin Mary! that never was it known that any one who fled to thy protection, implored thy help, and sought thy intercession, was left unaided. Inspired with this confidence, I fly unto thee, O Virgin of virgins, my Mother! To thee I come; before thee I stand, sinful and sorrowful. O Mother of the Word incarnate! despise not my petitions, but, in thy mercy, hear and answer me. Amen.

His Holiness, Pope Pius IX, by a rescript of the Sacred Congregation of Indulgences, Dec. 11, 1846, granted to all the faithful every time that, with at least contrite heart and devotion, they shall say this prayer, an *indulgence of three hundred days;* also a *plenary indulgence,* once a month, to all those who, having said it at least once a day for a month, on any day, being truly penitent, after confession and communion, shall visit a church or public oratory, and pray there, for some time, for the intention of His Holiness.

A Visit to Our Lady of Sorrows

To be Made Before her Altar or Image, immediately after Performing the Stations, or at any Other Time

O MOST holy Mother, Queen of sorrows, who didst follow thy beloved Son through all the way of the cross, and whose heart was pierced with a fresh sword of grief at all the stations of that most sorrowful journey; obtain for us, we beseech thee, O most loving Mother, a perpetual remembrance of our blessed Saviour's cross and death, and a true and tender devotion to all the mysteries of His most holy passion; obtain for us the grace to hate sin, even as He hated it in the agony in the garden; to endure wrong and insult with all patience, as He endured them in the judgment hall; to be meek and humble in all our trials, as He was before His judges; to love our enemies even as He loved His murderers, and prayed for them upon the cross; and to glorify God and do good to our neighbors, even as He did in every mystery of His sufferings. O Queen of martyrs, who, by the dolors of thy immaculate heart on Calvary, didst merit to share the passion of our blessed Redeemer, obtain for us some portion of thy compassion, that for the love of Jesus crucified we may be crucified to the world in this life; and in the life to come, may, by His infinite merits and thy powerful intercession, reign with Him in glory everlasting. Amen.

Pious Exercise in Honor of Our Lady of Dolors

SANCTA mater istud agas,
 Crucifixi fige plagas
  Cordi meo valide.

BID me bear, O Mother blessed!
 On my heart the wounds impressed,
  Suffered by the Crucified.

An indulgence of 300 days, once a day, to those who, with contrite heart, shall say the Hail Mary seven times. and, after each Hail Mary, the stanza. as above. — Pius VII, Dec. 1, 1815.

Prayer to Our Lady of Sorrows

O MARY! I beseech thee by the sorrows thou didst experience in beholding thy divine Son dying on the cross, procure for me a good death; obtain for me that, having loved Jesus and thee, my most tender Mother, here on earth, I may love you both and bless you eternally in heaven. Amen.

Novena in Honor of the Dolors of the Blessed Virgin

O MOST holy and afflicted Virgin! Queen of martyrs! thou who didst stand beneath the cross, witnessing the agony of thy divine Son — through the unceasing sufferings of thy life of sorrow, and the bliss which now more than amply repays thee for thy past trials, look down with a mother's tenderness and pity on me, who kneel before thee to venerate thy dolors, and place my requests, with filial confidence, in the sanctuary of thy wounded heart; present them, I beseech thee on my behalf, to Jesus Christ. Through the merits of His most sacred death and passion, and through thy sufferings at the foot of the cross, I hope to obtain the grant of my present petition. To whom shall I recur in my wants and miseries if not to thee, O Mother of mercy, who, having so deeply drunk of the chalice of thy Son, canst compassionate the woes of those who still sigh in the land of exile? *Sancta Maria, Mater Dolorosa, ora pro me!*

Novena in Honor of the Immaculate Conception

O IMMACULATE Virgin! Mary, conceived without sin! Remember, thou wert miraculously preserved from even the shadow of sin, because thou wert destined to become not only the Mother of God, but also the mother, the refuge, and the advocate of man; penetrated therefore, with the most lively confidence in thy never-failing intercession, we most humbly implore thee to look with favor upon the intentions of this novena, and to obtain for us the graces and the favors we request. Thou knowest, O Mary, how often our hearts are the sanctuaries of God, Who abhors iniquity. Obtain for us, then, that angelic purity which was thy favorite virtue, that purity of heart which will attach us to God alone, and that purity of intention which will consecrate every thought, word, and action to His greater glory. Obtain also for us a constant spirit of prayer and self-denial, that we may recover by penance that innocence which we have lost by sin, and at length attain safely to that blessed abode of the saints, where nothing defiled can enter.

O Mary, conceived without sin, pray for us who have recourse to thee.

Recite the "Litany of the Blessed Virgin," or the following Hymn.

Hymn

V. Tota pulchra es, Maria.

R. Tota pulchra es, Maria.

V. Et macula originalis non est in te.

R. Et macula originalis non est in te.

V. Tu gloria Jerusalem.

V. Thou art all fair, O Mary.

R. Thou art all fair, O Mary.

V. And the original stain is not in thee.

R. And the original stain is not in thee.

V. Thou art the glory of Jerusalem.

R. Tu lætitia Is-
rael.

V. Tu honorificentia po-
puli nostri.

R. Tu advocata peccato-
rum.

V. O Maria.

R. O Maria.

V. Virgo prudentissima.

R. Mater clementissima.

V. Ora pro nobis.

R. Intercede pro nobis ad
Dominum Jesum Christum.

V. In conceptione tua,
Virgo Immaculata
fuisti.

R. Ora pro nobis Pa-
trem cujus Filium pepe-
risti.

V. Domina, protege ora-
tionem meam.

R. Et clamor meus ad te
veniat.

R. Thou art the joy of
Israel.

V. Thou art the honor of
our people.

R. Thou art the advocate
of sinners.

V. O Mary.

R. O Mary.

V. Virgin, most prudent.

R. Mother, most tender.

V. Pray for us.

R. Intercede for us with
Jesus Christ our Lord.

V. In thy conception,
Holy Virgin, thou wast
immaculate.

R. Pray for us to the
Father, Whose Son thou
didst bring forth.

V. O Lady! aid my
prayer.

R. And let my cry come
unto thee.

Oremus

SANCTA Maria, regina
cœlorum, mater Do-
mini nostri Jesu Christi, et
mundi domina, quæ nul-
lum derelinquis, et nullum
despicis: respice me, do-
mina, clementer oculo pietatis, et impetra mihi apud
tuum dilectum Filium cunctorum veniam peccatorum:
ut qui nunc tuam sanctam et
immaculatam conceptionem

Let us pray

HOLY Mary, Queen of
heaven, Mother of our
Lord Jesus Christ, and mistress of the world, who
forsakest no one, and de-
spisest no one, look upon
me, O Lady! with an eye
of pity, and entreat for
me of thy beloved Son
the forgiveness of all my
sins; that, as I now celebrate, with devout affec-

devoto affectu recolo, æternæ in futurum beatitudinis, bravium capiam, ipso, quem / virgo peperisti, donante Domino nostro Jesu Christo: qui cum Patre et Sancto Spiritu vivit et regnat, in Trinitate perfecta, Deus, in sæcula sæculorum. Amen.

tion, thy holy and immacu late conception, so, hereafter, I may receive the prize of eternal blessedness, by the grace of Him whom thou, in virginity, didst bring forth, Jesus Christ our Lord: Who, with the Father and the Holy Ghost, liveth and reigneth, in perfect Trinity, God, world without end. Amen.

Then Add the Following Prayer:

O GOD, the Shepherd and Ruler of all the faithful, look mercifully down on Thy servant, our Holy Father, Pope N., whom Thou hast chosen to be the shepherd of Thy Church.

Grant, we beseech Thee, that he may both by word and example benefit those over whom he governs, that, together with the flock entrusted to his care, he may come to life everlasting.

O God, our refuge and our strength, listen to the prayers of Thy servants, and grant that we may obtain what we ask for with faith and confidence, through Christ our Lord. Amen.

Anthem, Versicle, and Prayer in Honor of the Immaculate Mary

Ant. HÆC est virga in qua nec nodus originalis, nec cortex actualis culpæ fuit.

Ant. THIS is the rod in which was neither knot of original sin, nor rind of actual guilt.

V. In conceptione tua virgo immaculata fuisti.

R. Ora pro nobis Patrem, cujus Filium peperisti.

V. In thy conception, O Virgin! thou wast immaculate.

R. Pray for us to the Father, whose Son thou didst bring forth.

Oremus

DEUS qui per immaculatam Virginis conceptionem dignum Filio tuo habitaculum p r æ p a r a s t i: quæsumus, ut qui ex morte ejusdem Filii tui prævisa eam ab omni labe præservasti, nos quoque mundos ejus intercessione ad te pervenire concedas. Per eumdem Christum Dominum nostrum. Amen.

Let us pray

O GOD, Who, by the immaculate conception of the Virgin, didst prepare a worthy habitation for Thy Son; we beseech Thee that, as in view of the death of that Son, Thou didst preserve her from all stain of sin, so thou wouldst enable us, being made pure by her intercession, to come unto Thee. Through the same Christ our Lord. Amen.

His Holiness, Pope Pius IX, by a brief, March 31, 1876, granted to all the faithful, as often as they shall say, with at least contrite heart and devotion, this anthem, versicle, and prayer, an *indulgence of one hundred days.*

The October Rosary

His Holiness, Leo XIII, by his encyclical *Supremi Apostolatus*, Sept. 1, 1883, and by a decree of the Sacred Congregation of Rites, Aug. 20, 1885, had granted and confirmed some indulgences for the saying of the Rosary during the month of October; then, by a rescript of the Sacred Congregation of Indulgences, July 23, 1898, he made them perpetual and modified them, granting to the faithful who, during the said month, publicly in church or privately anywhere, recite at least a third part of the Rosary, an *indulgence of seven years and as many quarantines* on each day of that month; also a *plenary indulgence* on the feast of Our Lady of the Rosary, or on any one day of its octave, to those who, both on the feast itself and on every day of its octave, shall have recited at least a third part of the Rosary on the usual conditions, confession, communion, and a visit to some church or public oratory, and there pray according to the intention of the Pope; also a *plenary indulgence,* on any one day, to those who, after the said octave, shall have recited at least the third part of the Rosary for ten days during the same month, on the same conditions.

Pious Recommendation to the Blessed Virgin Mary

M OST holy Virgin, mother of the incarnate Word, treasure-house of grace, and refuge of us wretched sinners, with lively faith we have recourse to thy motherly love, and ask of thee the grace of ever doing God's will and thine. In thy most holy hands we place our hearts, and of thee we ask health of body and soul; and, as we have the sure hope that thou, our most loving mother, wilt hear us, we say to thee with lively faith, Hail Mary, etc. (*Three times.*)

Oremus	*Let us pray*
D EFENDE, quæsumus Domine, ab omni infirmitate, beata Maria semper Virgine intercedente, famulos tuos; et toto corde tibi prostratos ab hostium propitius	D EFEND, we beseech Thee, O Lord! by the intercession of the blessed Mary, ever virgin, Thy servants from all infirmity; and mercifully deign to guard them, prostrate in the sin-

tuere clementer insidiis.
Per Christum Dominum
nostrum. Amen.

cerity of their hearts before
Thee, against the snares of
the enemy. Through Christ
our Lord. Amen.

The Sovereign Pontiff, Leo XII, by a decree of the Sacred
Congregation of Indulgences, Aug. 11, 1824, confirmed
forever an *indulgence of one hundred days*, once a day, to
all those who, with at least contrite heart and devotion,
shall say these prayers.

Indulgences for the Month of May

The Sovereign Pontiff, Pius VII, by a rescript from the
Office of the Secretary of Memorials, March 21, 1815,
granted to all the faithful who, either in public or in private,
shall honor the Blessed Virgin with some special homage
and devout prayers, or the practice of other virtuous acts,
an indulgence of three hundred days, every day; a plenary
indulgence, once in this month, or according to the rule
already established on one of the first eight days of June,
on the day when, being truly penitent, after confession and
communion, they shall pray for the intention of His Holiness.
By a rescript of the Sacred Congregation of Indulgences,
June 18, 1822, the same Sovereign Pontiff confirmed forever these indulgences.

Recite the *Litany of Loreto*, the *Memorare*, or any of the
prayers in honor of the Blessed Virgin Mary contained in
this book.

St. Aloysius' Act of Consecration

MOST holy Mary, my Lady, to thy faithful care and
particular protection and to the bosom of thy
mercy, to-day and every day, and particularly at the
hour of my death, I commend my soul and my body.
All my hope and consolation, all my trials and miseries,

my life and the end of my life, I commit to thee, that through thy most holy intercession and by thy merits all my actions may be directed and ordered according to thy will and that of thy divine Son. Amen.

Indulgence of 200 days, once a day. — Leo XIII, March 15, 1890.

Prayer for the Month of May

O MOST august and blessed Virgin Mary! holy Mother of God! glorious Queen of heaven and earth! powerful protectress of those who love thee, and unfailing advocate of all who invoke thee! look down, we beseech thee, from thy throne of glory on thy devoted children; accept the solemn offering we present thee of this month, especially dedicated to thee, and receive our ardent, humble desire, that by our love and fervor we may worthily honor thee, who, next to God, art deserving of all honor. Receive us, O Mother of mercy, among thy best beloved children; extend to us thy maternal tenderness and solicitude; obtain for us a place in the Heart of Jesus and a special share in the gifts of His grace. Oh, deign, we beseech thee, to recognize our claims on thy protection, to watch over our spiritual and temporal interests, as well as those of all who are dear to us; to infuse into our souls the spirit of Christ and to teach us thyself to become meek, humble, charitable, patient, and submissive to the will of God.

May our hearts burn with the love of thy divine Son, and of thee, His blessed Mother, not for a month alone, but for time and eternity; may we thirst and labor for the promotion of His glory and for thy greater veneration. Receive us, O Mary, the refuge of sinners;

grant us a mother's blessing and a mother's care now and at the hour of our death. Amen.

Prayer to Our Lady of Lourdes

O EVER immaculate Virgin,, Mother of mercy, health of the sick, refuge of sinners, comfort of the afflicted, you know my wants, my troubles, my sufferings; deign to cast upon me a look of mercy. By appearing in the Grotto of Lourdes, you were pleased to make it a privileged sanctuary, whence you dispense your favors, and already many sufferers have obtained the cure of their infirmities, both spiritual and corporal. I come, therefore, with unbounded confidence, to implore your maternal intercession. Obtain, O loving Mother, the grant of my requests. I will endeavor to imitate your virtues, that I may one day share your glory, and bless you in eternity. Amen.

INVOCATION

O MARY! conceived without sin, pray for us who have recourse to thee.

His Holiness, Pope Leo XIII, by a rescript of the Sacred Congregation of Indulgences, March 15, 1884, granted to all the faithful who, with contrite hearts, devoutly recite this invocation, an *indulgence of one hundred days*, once a day.

EJACULATION

BLESSED be the holy and immaculate conception of the most blessed Virgin Mary, Mother of God.

His Holiness, Pope Leo XIII, revoking the concession made Nov. 21, 1793, by the Sovereign Pontiff, Pius VI, granted by brief, Sept. 10, 1878, to all the faithful each time that, devoutly and with contrite hearts, they recite this ejaculation, an *indulgence of three hundred days*.

INVOCATION

SANCTA Virgo Maria immaculata, Mater Dei, Mater nostra, Tu pro nobis loquere ad Cor Jesu, qui tuus Filius est et Frater noster.

HOLY Virgin Mary immaculate, Mother of God and our Mother, speak thou for us to the Heart of Jesus, Who is thy Son and our Brother.

His Holiness, Leo XIII, by a rescript of the Sacred Congregation of Indulgences, Dec. 20, 1890, granted to the faithful who shall recite the above invocation an *indulgence of one hundred days*, once a day.

Indulgenced Acts of Consecration to the Blessed Virgin Mary

FOR THE MEMBERS OF THE BLESSED VIRGIN MARY SODALITY

I

ACT OF CONSECRATION

By St. John Berchmans

HOLY Mary, Mother of God and Virgin, I choose thee this day for my queen, patron, and advocate, and firmly resolve and purpose never to abandon thee, never to say or do anything against thee, nor to permit that aught be done by others to dishonor thee. Receive me, then, I conjure thee, as thy perpetual servant; assist me in all my actions, and do not abandon me at the hour of my death. Amen.

Indulgence of 300 days, for each recitation. — Pius X, Nov. 17, 1906.

II

ACT OF CONSECRATION

By St. Fráncis de Sales

MOST Holy Mary, virgin Mother of God, I (*full name*), most unworthy though I am to be thy servant, yet touched by thy motherly care for me and longing to serve thee, do, in the presence of my guardian angel and all the court of heaven, choose thee this day to be my queen, my advocate, and my mother, and I firmly purpose to serve thee evermore myself and to do what I can that all may render faithful service to thee.

Therefore, most devoted Mother, through the precious blood thy Son poured out for me, I beg thee and beseech thee, deign to take me among thy clients and receive me as thy servant forever.

Aid me in my every action, and beg for me the grace never, by word or deed or thought, to be displeasing in thy sight and that of thy most holy Son.

Think of me, my dearest Mother, and desert me not at the hour of death.   Amen.

Indulgence of 300 days, for each recitation. — Pius X, Nov. 17, 1906.

N. B.   By request of the Rev. Fr. Elder Mullan, S.J., an indulgence of 300 days, applicable to the souls in purgatory, has been attached to the devout recitation, every time, of each of the acts of consecration, by members regularly enrolled in the Sodality of the Blessed Virgin. The first of the two forms was used by St. John Berchmans, the other by St. Francis de Sales.   The Sacred Congregation authenticates the concession of the indulgence under date of Nov. 17, 1906.   Signed by Cardinal Tripepi, Prefect, and by Archbishop Panici, Secretary. — *American Ecclesiastical Review.*   May, 1907, p. 555.

The Canticle of the Blessed Virgin Mary

MAGNIFICAT anima mea Dominum.

Et exultavit Spiritus meus in Deo salutari meo.

Quia respexit humilitatem ancillæ suæ; ecce enim ex hoc beatam me dicent omnes generationes.

Quia fecit mihi magna Qui potens est; et sanctum nomen Ejus.

Et misericordia Ejus a progenie in progenies, timentibus eum.

Fecit potentiam in brachio suo; dispersit superbos mente cordis sui.

Deposuit potentes de sede, et exaltavit humiles.

Esurientes implevit bonis: et divites dimisit inanes.

Suscepit Israel puerum Suum; recordatus misericordiæ Suæ.

Sicut locutus est ad patres nostros, Abraham, et semini ejus in sæcula.

MY SOUL doth magnify the Lord;

And my spirit hath rejoiced in God my Saviour.

Because He hath regarded the humility of His handmaid, for behold from henceforth all generations shall call me blessed.

For He that is mighty hath done great things to me; and holy is His name.

And His mercy is from generation to generation, to them that fear Him.

He hath shown might in His arm; He hath scattered the proud in the conceit of their heart.

He hath put down the mighty from their seat, and hath exalted the humble.

He hath filled the hungry with good things; and the rich He hath sent away empty.

He hath received Israel His servant; being mindful of His mercy.

As He spoke to our fathers, to Abraham, and to his seed forever.

Indulgence of 100 days, once a day. — Leo XIII, Feb. 22, 1888.

The Hymn Ave Maris Stella

Ave, maris stella,
 Dei Mater alma,
Atque semper Virgo,
Felix cœli porta.

Hail, thou star of ocean!
 Portal of the sky!
Ever virgin Mother
 Of the Lord most high.

Sumens illud ave
Gabrielis ore,
Funda nos in pace,
Mutans Hevæ nomen.

Oh! by Gabriel's Ave,
 Uttered long ago,
Eva's name reversing,
 Establish peace below.

Solve vincla reis,
Profer lumen cæcis,
Mala nostra pelle,
Bona cuncta posce.

Break the captives' fetters,
 Light on blindness pour;
All our ills expelling,
 Every bliss implore.

Monstra te esse Matrem,
Sumat per te preces,
Qui pro nobis natus,
Tulit esse tuus.

Show thyself a Mother;
 Offer Him our sighs,
Who for us incarnate
 Did not thee despise.

Virgo singularis,
Inter omnes mitis,
Nos culpis solutos,
Mites fac et castos.

Virgin of all virgins!
 To thy shelter take us;
Gentlest of the gentle!
 Chaste and gentle make us,

Vitam præsta puram,
Iter para tutum,
Ut videntes Jesum
Semper collætemur.

Still, as on we journey,
 Help our weak endeavor,
Till with thee and Jesus
 We rejoice forever.

Sit laus Deo Patri,
Summo Christo decus,
Spiritui sancto,
Tribus honor unus.
                Amen.

Through the highest heaven,
 To the almighty Three,
Father, Son, and Spirit,
 One same glory be.
                Amen.

His Holiness Leo XIII, by a rescript of the Sacred Congregation of Indulgences, Jan. 27, 1888, granted to the faithful who shall recite the above hymn, an *indulgence of three hundred days*, once a day.

The Four Great Anthems of the Blessed Virgin Mary

Alma Redemptoris
Ave Regina Cœlorum
Regina Cœli

and

Salve Regina

They are to be recited in the following order, in the course of the year.

A Sabbato ante I Dom. Adventus usque ad Purificationem inclusive.

From the Saturday before the first Sunday of Advent to Candlemas inclusive.

ALMA Redemptoris Mater, quæ pervia cœli
Porta manes, et stella maris, succurre cadenti
Surgere qui curat, populo: tu quæ genuisti,
Natura mirante, tuum sanctum Genitorem,
Virgo prius ac posterius, Gabrielis ab ore,
Sumens illud Ave, peccatorum miserere.

MOTHER of Christ! hear thou thy people's cry,
Star of the deep, and portal of the sky,
Mother of Him Who thee from nothing made,
Sinking we strive and call to thee for aid.
Oh, by that joy which Gabriel brought to thee,
Pure Virgin, first and last, look on our misery.

In Adventu

V. Angelus Domini nuntiavit Mariæ.

R. Et concepit de Spiritu sancto.

In Advent

V. The angel of the Lord declared unto Mary.

R. And she conceived of the Holy Ghost.

Oremus

GRATIAM Tuam, quæsumus Domine, mentibus nostris infunde:

Let us pray

POUR forth, we beseech Thee, O Lord, Thy grace into our hearts,

ut Qui, angelo nuntiante, Christi Filii Tui incarnationem 'cognovimus, per passionem ejus et crucem, ad resurrectionis gloriam perducamur. Per eumdem Christum Dominum nostrum.

R. Amen.

V. Divinum auxilium maneat semper nobiscum.

R. Amen.

A Vigilia Nativitatis usque ad totam diem Purificationis.

V. Post partum Virgo Inviolata permansisti.

R. Dei Genitrix, intercede pro nobis.

Oremus

DEUS, Qui salutis æternæ, beatæ Mariæ Virginitate fœcunda, humano generi præmia præstitisti: tribue, quæsumus; ut ipsam pro nobis intercedere sentiamus, per quam meruimus auctorem vitæ suscipere, Dominum nostrum Jesum Christum Filium tuum: qui tecum vivit et regnat in unitate Spiritus Sancti Deus, per omnia sæcula sæculorum.

that we, to whom the incarnation of Christ, Thy Son, was made known by the message of an angel, may by His passion and cross be brought to the glory of His resurrection. Through the same Christ our Lord.

R. Amen.

V. May the divine assistance remain always with us.

R. Amen.

From the First Vespers of Christmas to Candlemas.

V. After childbirth, O Virgin, thou didst remain inviolate.

R. O Mother of God, plead for us.

Let us pray

O GOD, Who by the fruitful virginity of blessed Mary hast given to mankind the rewards of eternal salvation: grant, we beseech Thee, that we may experience her intercession for us, by Whom we deserved to receive the Author of life, Our Lord Jesus Christ, Thy Son, Who liveth and reigneth with Thee in the unity of the Holy Ghost, God, world without end.

R. Amen.
V. Divinum auxilium maneat semper nobiscum.
R. Amen.

R. Amen.
V. May the divine assistance remain always with us.
R. Amen.

A Purificatione usque at Completorium Sabbati Sancti exclusive.

From Candlemas until Compline on Holy Saturday exclusively.

ANTIPHONA

AVE Regina coelorum,
Ave Domina Angelorum:
Salve radix, salve porta,
Ex qua mundo lux est orta.
Gaude Virgo gloriosa,
Super omnes speciosa:
Vale, O valde decora,
Et pro nobis Christum exora.

V. Dignare me laudare te, Virgo sacrata.
R. Da mihi virtutem contra hostes tuos.

ANTHEM

HAIL, O Queen of heav'n enthroned!
Hail, by angels Mistress owned!
Root of Jesse! Gate of morn,
Whence the world's true Light was born:
Glorious Virgin, joy to thee,
Beautiful surpassingly!
Fairest thou where all are fair!
Plead for us a pitying prayer.

V. Grant that I may praise thee, O blessed Virgin.
R. Give me strength against thine enemies.

Oremus

CONCEDE, misericors Deus, fragilitati nostræ præsidium: ut qui sanctæ Dei Genitricis memoriam agimus, intercessionis ejus auxi-

Let us pray

O MOST merciful God, grant succor unto our frailty; that as we celebrate the memory of the holy Mother of God, so by

lio a nostris iniquitatibus resurgamus. Per eumdem Christum Dominum nostrum.

R. Amen.

V. Divinum auxilium maneat semper nobiscum.

R. Amen.

A Completorio Sabbati Sancti usque ad Nonam Sabbati post Pentecosten inclusive.

ANTIPHONA

R EGINA cœli, lætare, Alleluia,

Quia quem meruisti portare, Alleluia,

Resurrexit sicut dixit, Alleluia.

Ora pro nobis Deum, Alleluia.

V. Gaude et lætare, Virgo Maria, Alleluia.

R. Quia surrexit Dominus vere, Alleluia.

Oremus

D EUS, Qui per resurrectionem Filii Tui Domini nostri Jesu Christi mundum lætificare dignatus es; præsta quæsumus; ut per ejus Genitricem Virginem Mariam

the help of her intercession we may rise again from our sins. Through the same Christ our Lord.

R. Amen.

V. May the divine assistance remain always with us.

R. Amen.

From Compline of Holy Saturday until None on the Saturday after Pentecost inclusively.

ANTHEM

O QUEEN of heaven, rejoice, Alleluia,

For He Whom thou wast meet to bear, Alleluia,

Hath risen, as He said, Alleluia.

Pray for us to God, Alleluia.

V. Rejoice and be glad, O Virgin Mary, Alleluia.

R. For the Lord hath risen indeed, Alleluia.

Let us pray

O GOD, Who didst vouchsafe to give joy to the world through the Resurrection of Thy Son, Our Lord Jesus Christ; grant, we beseech Thee, that, through His Mother, the

perpetuæ capiamus gaudia vitæ. Per eumdem Christum Dominum nostrum.

R. Amen.

V. Divinum auxilium maneat semper nobiscum.

R. Amen.

A Completorio Sabbati post Pentecosten usque ad Adventum.

ANTIPHONA

SALVE Regina, Mater misericordiæ, vita, dulcedo, et spes nostra salve.

Ad te clamamus, exsules filii Hevæ;

Ad te suspiramus, gementes et flentes in hac lacrimarum valle.

Eia ergo, advocata nostra illos tuos misericordes oculos ad nos converte.

Et Jesum, benedictum fructum ventris tui, nobis post hoc exilium ostende.

O clemens, O pia, O dulcis Virgo Maria.

V. Ora pro nobis, sancta Dei Genitrix.

R. Ut digni efficiamur promissionibus Christi.

Virgin Mary, we may obtain the joys of everlasting life. Through the same Christ our Lord.

R. Amen.

V. May the divine assistance remain always with us.

R. Amen.

From Compline of the Saturday after Pentecost until Advent.

ANTHEM

HAIL, holy Queen, Mother of mercy. Hail, our life, our sweetness, and our hope!

To thee do we cry, poor banished children of Eve;

To thee do we send up our sighs, mourning and weeping in this vale of tears.

Turn then, most gracious advocate, thine eyes of mercy toward us.

And after this our exile show unto us the blessed fruit of thy womb, Jesus.

O clement, O loving, O sweet Virgin Mary.

V. Pray for us, O holy Mother of God.

R. That we may be made worthy of the promises of Christ.

Oremus	*Let us pray*
OMNIPOTENS sempiterne Deus, qui gloriosæ Virginis Matris Mariæ corpus et animam ut dignum Filii tui habitaculum effici mereretur, Spiritu sancto cooperante præparasti: da, ut cujus commemoratione lætamur, ejus pia intercessione ab instantibus malis, et a morte perpetua liberemur. Per eumdem Christum Dominum nostrum.	ALMIGHTY, everlasting God, Who, by the co-operation of the Holy Ghost, didst so make ready the body and soul of the glorious virgin Mother Mary that she deserved to become a meet dwelling for Thy Son: grant that we, who rejoice in her memory, may by her loving intercession be delivered from the evils that hang over us, and from everlasting death. Through the same Christ our Lord.
R. Amen.	R. Amen.
V. Divinum auxilium maneat semper nobiscum.	V. May the divine assistance remain always with us.
R. Amen.	R. Amen.

Indulgenced Ejaculations in Honor of Our Lady

Mary!

Indulgence of 25 days, each time. — Clement XIII, Sept. 5, 1758.

In thy conception, O Virgin Mary, thou wast immaculate! Pray for us to the Father, Whose Son, Jesus, conceived in thy womb by the Holy Ghost, thou didst bring forth.

Indulgence of 100 days, each time. — Pius VI, Nov. 21, 1793.

My Queen! my Mother! Remember I am thine own;
Keep me, guard me, as thy property and possession.

Indulgence of 40 days, each time, when tempted. — Pius IX, Aug. 5, 1851.

Sweet heart of Mary, be my salvation!

Indulgence of 300 days, each time. — Pius IX, Sept. 30, 1852.

O Mary, who didst come into this world free from stain! obtain of God for me that I may leave it without sin.

Indulgence of 100 days, once a day. — Pius IX, March 27, 1863.

Virgin Mother of God, Mary, pray to Jesus for me.

Indulgence of 50 days, once a day. — Leo XIII, March 29, 1894.

Holy Virgin, Mary immaculate, Mother of God and our Mother, speak thou for us to the Heart of Jesus, Who is thy Son, and our Brother.

Indulgence of 100 days, once a day. — Leo XIII, Dec. 20, 1890.

Jesus, Mary, and Joseph, I give you my heart and my soul.

Jesus, Mary, and Joseph, assist me in my last agony.

Jesus, Mary, and Joseph, may I breathe out my soul in peace with you!

Indulgence of 300 days, each time, for all three. — Pius VII, Aug. 26, 1814.

O Mary, conceived without sin, pray for us who have recourse to thee.

Indulgence of 100 days, once a day. — Leo XIII, March 15 1884.

Our Lady of Lourdes, pray for us!

Indulgence of 100 days, once a day. — Leo XIII, June 25, 1902.

Mary, most sorrowful Mother of all Christians, pray for us.

Indulgence of 300 days. — Pius X, June 27, 1906.

Our Lady of Good Studies, pray for us.

Indulgence of 300 days. — Pius X, May 22, 1906.

Mary, our hope, have pity on us!

Indulgence of 300 days. — Pius X, Jan. 8, 1906.

Devotions to the Angels

And in Particular to the Angel Guardian

Prayer to the Angel Guardian

NGELE Dei, qui custos es mei,
Me tibi commissum pie-
tate superna
Illumina, custodi, rege, et
guberna.
Amen.

NGEL of God, m.
guardian dear,
To whom His love com-
mits me here,
Ever this day be at my side,
To light and guard, to rule
and guide. Amen.

Indulgence of 100 days; plenary indulgence on the feast of the holy guardian angels (Oct. 2), to those who shall have said this prayer, morning and evening, throughout the year, on usual conditions; plenary indulgence at the hour of death. — Pius VI, Oct. 2, 1795; June 11, 1796.

Pius VII, on May 15, 1821, granted a plenary indulgence, once a month, to all the faithful who shall have said it every day for a month, as above directed.

Little Office of the Holy Angels

At Matins

Ant. OD hath given His angels charge of thee, that they keep thee in all thy ways. Amen.

O Lord, open Thou my lips,
And my tongue shall declare Thy praise.
O God, incline unto my aid.
O Lord, make haste to help me.
Glory be to the Father, etc. Alleluia.

HYMN

O LORD, permit us here to raise our voice;
  And waft before Thy throne our feeble praise,
And thank Thee for those angels whom Thy choice
  Hath lent our weakness to direct its ways,
And free us from the envious foes that lurk
To spoil the beauty of Thy cherished work.

Ant. O holy angels, our guardians, defend us in the combat, that we perish not in the dreadful judgment.

V. In sight of Thy angels I will sing to Thee, my God.

R. I will adore at Thy holy temple, and confess to Thy name.

PRAYER

O GOD, Who, with unspeakable providence, hast vouchsafed to appoint Thy holy angels to be our guardians grant to Thy humble suppliants to be always defended by their protection, and to enjoy their everlasting society through Jesus Christ, Thy Son, Our Lord, Who liveth and reigneth, etc.   Amen.

At Prime

Ant. GOD hath given His angels charge of thee, that they keep thee in all thy ways.   Amen.
O God, incline unto, etc.
O Lord, make haste, etc.
Glory be to the Father, etc.   Alleluia.

HYMN

FOR Satan, driven from the happy land
  Where once he shone in splendor, ill can brook
The kindly justice of the Almighty hand,
  That gives to man the throne that he forsook;
And seeks to drag into his own disgrace
Poor mortals thus designed to fill his place.

Ant. O holy angels, our guardians, etc.

V. In sight of Thy angels I will sing unto Thee, my God.

R. I will adore at Thy holy temple, and confess to Thy name.

PRAYER

O God, Who with unspeakable providence, etc.

At Tierce

Ant. GOD hath given His angels, etc.
O God, incline unto my aid.
O Lord, make haste to help me.
Glory be to the Father, etc. Alleluia.

HYMN

BRIGHT Spirit! whom a God supremely wise
Hath given to be the guardian of this land,
Come, arm'd with all thy power from the skies,
And bear its children harmless in thy hand —
Safe from all evil that defiles the soul,
Safe from disunion's withering control.
Ant. O holy angels, etc.
V. In the sight of Thy angels, etc.
R. I will adore at Thy holy temple, etc.

PRAYER

O God, Who with unspeakable providence, etc

At Sext

Ant. GOD hath given His angels, etc
O God, incline unto my aid.
O Lord, make haste to help me.
Glory be to the Father, etc. Alleluia.

HYMN

O JESUS! glory of the angelic choirs,
Light of their brightness, sweetness of their bliss;
Thou Who didst leave a world where nothing tires,
To taste the pains and miseries of this;

Be these same pains, endured to set us free,
The germ of endless happiness with Thee.
    Ant. O holy angels, our guardians, etc.
    V. In the sight of Thy angels, etc.
    R. I will adore at Thy holy temple, etc.

PRAYER

O God, Who with unspeakable providence, etc.

At None

Ant. GOD hath given His angels charge over, etc.
        R. Amen.
    V. O God, incline unto my aid.
    R. O Lord, make haste to help me.
Glory be to the Father, etc. Alleluia.

HYMN

ANGEL of peace! come, Michael, to our aid,
    Thou who didst once chase discord from the sky:
Come, calm those boisterous passions that have made
  Such havoc here as they have made on high;
Drive strife and rancor to their kindred gloom,
To hell, their fitting, their eternal tomb.
    Ant. Holy angels, our guardians, defend, etc.
    V In the sight of Thy angels I will sing to, etc.
    R. I will adore at Thy holy temple, etc.

PRAYER

O God, Who with unspeakable providence, etc.

At Vespers

Ant. GOD hath given His angels charge over, etc.
        V. O God, incline unto my aid.
    R. O Lord, make haste to help me.
Glory be to the Father, etc. Alleluia.

HYMN

SPIRIT of might ! O Gabriel, display
    Thy matchless power against our ancient foes;
Visit those sacred temples where we pray —
    'Twas at thy potent word those temples rose;
Whose worship raised these shrines throughout the earth;
Thou wert the herald of His future birth.
    Ant. O holy angels, our guardians, etc.
    V. In the sight of Thy angels, etc.

PRAYER

O God, Who with unspeakable providence, etc.

At Compline

Ant. **G**OD hath given His angels, etc.
        V. Convert us, O God, our Saviour.
  R. And avert Thy anger from us.
O God, incline unto my aid.
Glory be to the Father, etc. Alleluia.

HYMN

AND Raphael ! of the glorious seven who stand
    Before the throne of Him Who lives and reigns;
Angel of health ! the Lord hath filled thy hand
    With balm from heaven to soothe or cure our pains,
Heal or console the victim of disease,
And guide our steps when doubtful of our ways.
    Ant. O holy angels, etc.
    V. In the sight of Thy angels, etc.
    R. I will adore at Thy holy temple, etc.

PRAYER

O God, Who with unspeakable providence, etc.

COMMENDATION

O HOLY guardian! at thy feet
  This wreath of humble flowers I lay;
O that their odor were as sweet
  As he desires, who sings the lay,
Protect me at death's awful hour,
  Receive my soul to thy embrace,
Rich with the wonders of thy power,
  To thank, to praise thee, face to face.
                                Amen.

Antiphon to the Archangel Michael

SANCTE Michael arch-angele, defende nos in prælio, ut non pereamus in tremendo judicio.

HOLY archangel Michael, defend us in battle, that we may not perish in the tremendous judgment.

Indulgence of 100 days. — Leo XIII, Aug. 19, 1893.

Prayer to St. Raphael, Archangel

GLORIOUS archangel, St. Raphael, great prince of the heavenly court, illustrious by thy gifts of wisdom and grace, guide of travelers by land and sea, consoler of the unfortunate and refuge of sinners, I entreat thee to help me in all my needs and in all the trials of this life, as thou didst once assist the young Tobias in his journeying. And since thou art the "physician of God," I humbly pray thee to heal my soul of its many infirmities and my body of the ills that afflict it, if this favor is for my greater good. I ask, especially, for angelic purity, that I may be made fit to be the living temple of the Holy Ghost. Amen.

Indulgence of 100 days. — Leo XIII, June 21, 1890.

Prayer to the Archangel Gabriel

O BLESSED archangel Gabriel, we beseech thee, do thou intercede for us at the throne of divine mercy in our present necessities that, as thou didst announce to Mary the mystery of the incarnation, so through thy prayers and patronage in heaven we may obtain the benefits of the same, and sing the praise of God forever in the land of the living. Amen.

Devotions in honor of St. Joseph

Devotion of the Seven Sundays in Honor of St. Joseph

THE Sovereign Pontiffs who have so gloriously occupied the chair of St. Peter in later days have enriched with great indulgences this tender devotion, in order to stimulate the faithful to its practice.

In virtue of a concession of Pope Gregory XVI we may gain an indulgence of 300 days on each of the first six Sundays, and a plenary indulgence on the seventh Sunday, for saying the prayers of the Seven Sorrows and Joys of St. Joseph on any seven consecutive Sundays of the year.

On February 1, 1847, Pope Pius IX, of holy memory, wishing to extend this devotion, added to the indulgences already granted a plenary indulgence on each Sunday, applicable to the souls in purgatory.

On March 22 of the same year his Holiness extended this indulgence to those who, owing to some good cause, being unable to recite the prayers of the Seven Sorrows and Joys of St. Joseph, say seven Our Fathers, seven Hail Marys, and seven Glorias, fulfilling the usual conditions for gaining a plenary indulgence; namely, confession, communion, and prayers for our holy mother the Church.

The Sovereign Pontiff, Pius VII, Dec. 9, 1819, granted an indulgence of 100 days, once a day; an indulgence of 300 days, every Wednesday in the year, and on every day of the two novenas preceding the feasts of St. Joseph, viz., the principal feast, March 19, and the feast of the patronage, the third Sunday after Easter. A plenary indulgence, on these two feasts, to all those who, moreover, being truly penitent, shall have gone to confession and communion. A plenary indulgence, once a month, to all those who shall have said them every day for a month, on the day when, being truly penitent, they shall go to confession and communion.

Devout Exercise in Honor of the Seven Sorrows and Seven Joys of St. Joseph

1. PURE husband of most holy Mary, glorious St. Joseph, great was the travail and anguish of thy heart when, in sore perplexity, thou didst feel inclined to put away thy stainless spouse; but unspeakable was thy joy when the angel revealed to thee the high mystery of the Incarnation.

By this thy sorrow and thy joy, we pray thee, comfort our souls now and in their dying agony with the sweet consolation of a well-spent life, and a death like unto thine own, in the embrace of Jesus and of Mary.

Our Father, Hail Mary, Glory be to the Father.

2. Thrice happy patriarch, glorious St. Joseph, chosen to be the foster-father of the Word made man, keen was the pain thou didst feel when thou didst see the infant Jesus born in abject poverty; but thy pain was suddenly changed into heavenly joy when upon thee burst the harmony of the angel choirs, and thou didst behold the glory of that refulgent night.

By this thy sorrow and thy joy, we pray thee, obtain for us that, when the journey of our life is over, we too may pass to that blessed land where we shall hear the angel-chants, and enjoy the brightness of celestial glory.

Our Father, Hail Mary, Glory be to the Father.

3. O thou who wast ever most obedient in fulfilling the law of God, glorious St. Joseph! when, at His circumcision, the infant Saviour's precious blood was shed, thy heart was pierced through and through; but

with the name of Jesus came again to thee new life and heavenly joy.

By this thy sorrow and thy joy, obtain for us that, freed in life from the vile yoke of sin, we too may die with joy, with the sweet name of Jesus in our hearts and on our lips.

Our Father, Hail Mary, Glory be to the Father.

4. Faithful saint, who wast admitted to take part in man's redemption, glorious St. Joseph, Simeon's prophecy of the coming woes of Jesus and of Mary filled thy soul with agony like death but thy soul was filled with blessedness when he foretold salvation and glorious resurrection to innumerable souls.

By this thy sorrow and thy joy, help us with thy prayers to be of those who, by the merits of Jesus and His virgin Mother, shall be partakers of the glorious resurrection.

Our Father, Hail Mary, Glory be to the Father.

5. Watchful guardian, bosom friend of the incarnate Son of God, glorious St. Joseph, how didst thou toil to nurture and to serve the Son of the Most High, especially in the flight into Egypt; but far greater was thy joy in having with thee God Himself, and in seeing Egypt's idols fall to the earth!

By this thy sorrow and thy joy, obtain for us to keep aloof from the infernal tyrant, quitting all dangerous occasions, that all earthly idols may be cast out from our hearts, and that, employed in the service of Jesus and Mary, we may ever live for them alone, and with them calmly die.

Our Father, Hail Mary, Glory be to the Father.

6. Angel on earth, glorious St. Joseph, while thou didst marvel at seeing the King of heaven obedient to thy bidding, fear of the tyrant mingled with thy joy when

thou didst bring him back from Egypt; but, reassured by the angel, thou didst dwell at Nazareth with glad heart, in the sweet company of Jesus and Mary.

By this thy sorrow and thy joy, obtain for us that, with hearts set free from every hurtful fear, we too may taste the quiet of a tranquil conscience, safely dwelling with Jesus and with Mary, and one day die within their loving arms.

Our Father, Hail Mary, Glory be to the Father.

7. Pattern of all holiness, glorious St. Joseph, without fault of thine, thou didst lose the holy child Jesus, and for three days, to thy great sorrow, didst seek for Him, until, with joy unspeakable, thou didst find thy Life amid the Doctors in the Temple.

By this thy sorrow and thy joy, we pray thee with all our heart, stand between us and danger, that we may never lose Jesus by mortal sin; but if, to our shame and disgrace, we lose Him, may we seek Him with such ceaseless grief that we may find Him propitious to us, especially at the hour of our death, and thus go to enjoy Him in heaven, and there with thee sing His divine mercy forever!

Our Father, Hail Mary, Glory be to the Father.

Ant. Jesus was about thirty years old, being, as was supposed, the son of Joseph.

V. Pray for us, blessed Joseph,

R. That we may be made worthy of the promises of Christ.

Let us pray

GOD, Who in Thine ineffable providence didst vouchsafe to choose blessed Joseph to be the husband of Thy most holy Mother: grant, we beseech Thee, that we may be made worthy to receive him for our intercessor in heaven, whom on earth we venerate as our holy protector. Who livest and reignest world without end. Amen.

Prayer to St. Joseph for the October Devotions
Ordered by Pope Leo XIII to be said as Part of the Devotions for the Month of October

To THEE, O blessed Joseph, do we fly in our tribulation, and *having implored the help of thy most holy spouse, we* confidently crave thy patronage *also.* Through that charity which bound thee to the immaculate, virgin Mother of God, and through the paternal love with which thou didst embrace the Child Jesus, we humbly beseech thee graciously to regard the inheritance which Jesus Christ hath purchased by His blood, and with thy power and strength to aid us in our necessities.

O most watchful Guardian of the Divine Family, defend the chosen children of Jesus Christ; O most loving Father, ward off from us every contagion of error and corrupting influence; O our most mighty Protector, be propitious to us and from heaven assist us in this our struggle with the power of darkness: and, as once thou didst rescue the Child Jesus from deadly peril, so now protect God's holy Church from the snares of the enemy and from all adversity: shield, too, each one of us by thy constant protection, so that, supported by thine example and thine aid, we may be able to live piously, to die holily, and to obtain eternal happiness in heaven. Amen.

Indulgences: I. Seven years and seven quarantines, if said after the Rosary in October. II. 300 days, once a day, at other times (and in this case the words in italics are omitted).—Leo XIII, Enc., Aug. 15, 1889; Indul., Sept. 21, 1889.

Another Approved Version of This Favorite Prayer to St. Joseph, as Recited in Some Parts of the United States

WE COME to thee, O blessed Joseph, in our sore distress and having sought the help of thy most blessed spouse, we now confidently implore thy assistance also. We humbly beg that, mindful of the dutiful affection which bound thee to the immaculate, virgin Mother of God and of the fatherly love wherewith thou didst cherish the Child Jesus, thou wilt lovingly watch over the heritage which Jesus Christ purchased with His blood, and of thy strength and power help us in our urgent need.

O most provident Guardian of the Divine Family, protect the chosen race of Jesus Christ; drive far from us, most loving Father, every pest of error and corrupting sin; from thy place in heaven, most powerful Deliverer, graciously come to our aid in this conflict with the powers of darkness; and as of old thou didst deliver the Child Jesus from supreme peril of life, so now defend the holy Church of God from the snares of her enemies and from all adversity; have each of us always in thy keeping that following thine example, and borne up by thy strength we may be able to live holily, die happily, and so enter into the everlasting bliss of heaven. Amen.

Novena to St. Joseph, Spouse of Mary Most Holy

PIUS IX, Nov. 28, 1876, granted to all the faithful who, with contrite heart, devoutly make at any time during the year the novena to St. Joseph, spouse of Mary most holy, with any formula of prayer, if it be approved by ecclesiastical authority, an indulgence of 300 days, once a day; plenary indulgence on usual conditions.

EJACULATION

St. Joseph, model and patron of those who love the Sacred Heart of Jesus, pray for us.

Indulgence of 100 days, once a day. — Leo XIII, Dec. 19, 1891.

Prayer

REMEMBER, O most pure spouse of the Blessed Virgin Mary, my sweet protector St. Joseph! that no one ever had recourse to thy protection or implored thy aid without obtaining relief. Confiding therefore in thy goodness, I come before thee, and humbly supplicate thee. Oh, despise not my petitions, foster-father of the Redeemer, but graciously receive them. Amen.

Indulgence of 300 days, once a day. — Pius IX, June 26, 1863.

Prayers in Honor of St. Joseph for the Agonizing

ETERNAL Father, by Thy love for St. Joseph, whom Thou didst select from among all men to represent Thee upon earth, have mercy on us and on the dying.

Our Father, Hail Mary, Glory be to the Father.

Eternal divine Son, by Thy love for St. Joseph, who was Thy faithful guardian upon earth, have mercy upon us and upon the dying.

Our Father, Hail Mary, Glory be to the Father.

Eternal divine Spirit, by Thy love for St. Joseph, Who so carefully watched over Mary, Thy beloved spouse, have mercy on us and on the dying.

Our Father, Hail Mary, Glory be to the Father.

Indulgence of 300 days, once a day. — Leo XIII, May 17, 1884.

Act of Consecration to St. Joseph

O BLESSED St. Joseph! I consecrate myself to thy honor, and give myself to thee, that thou mayest always be my father, my protector, and my guide in the way of salvation. Obtain for me a great purity of heart and a fervent love of the interior life. After thy example may I do all my actions for the greater glory of God, in union with the divine Heart of Jesus and the immaculate heart of Mary! And do thou, O blessed Joseph, pray for me, that I may experience the peace and joy of thy holy death. Amen.

INVOCATION TO ST. JOSEPH

Help us, Joseph, in our earthly strife;
Ever to lead a pure and blameless life.

Indulgence of 300 days. — Leo XIII, March 18, 1882.

Jesus, Mary, and Joseph, I give you my heart and my soul; Jesus, Mary, and Joseph, assist me in my last agony; Jesus, Mary, and Joseph, may I breathe forth my soul in peace with you.

Indulgence of 300 days, each time. — Pius VII, Aug. 26, 1814.

Prayer to St. Joseph in any Great Necessity

O MOST faithful guardian of Jesus and spouse of Mary, thou seest the anguish of my heart. I am disturbed and perplexed. Obtain for me the light of the Holy Ghost and all the helps I need to enable me at all times and in all things to fulfil the adorable will of God. I choose thee this day, in the presence of Jesus and Mary, as my angel of good counsel, to direct me in all my necessities. Guide me, I entreat thee, by the many bitter dolors which rent thy tender heart during the course of thy mortal pilgrimage. Amen.

Every good Catholic should foster devotion to the good St. Joseph, and now more than ever, since he has been declared the patron and protector of the whole Church. No mortal man had ever such honor conferred upon him as that which was conferred on St. Joseph. This great saint, who took such care of the infant Jesus and of His blessed Mother Mary, will take most especial care of us, in all our necessities, temporal and spiritual, if we only ask him. Fathers of families, and those who have charge of others, should pray in a particular manner to St. Joseph.

Prayer for a Novena to St. Joseph

(Feast March 19)

Illustrious Saint! inheritor of the virtues of all the patriarchs! Good and faithful guardian of the Holy Family! Thou art my glorious protector, and shalt ever be, after Jesus and Mary, the object of my most profound veneration and tender confidence. Thou art the most hidden saint and particularly the patron of those who serve God with the greatest purity of intention and fervor of devotion. O thou model and guardian of pure souls, who hast given us so illustrious an example of purity, unselfish devotedness to duty, fidelity, humility, patience, obedience, and trust in divine Providence, be moved with the confidence I place in thy intercession, and obtain for me the grace to practise every virtue which will make me pleasing to God.

I thank God for the signal favors He has bestowed upon thee, and I beg through thy intercession grace to imitate thy virtues. In union with all those who have ever been most devoted to thee, I now dedicate myself to thy service, beseeching thee, for the sake of Jesus Christ, Who vouchsafed to love and obey thee as a son, to become a father to me, and to obtain for me the filial respect, confidence, and love of a child toward thee. O powerful advocate of all Christians! whose intercession, as St. Teresa assures us, has never been found to fail, deign to intercede for me now, and to obtain for me the particular object of this novena. [Specify it.] Present me, O great saint, to the adorable Trinity, with Whom thou hadst so glorious and so intimate a correspondence. Obtain that I may never efface by sin the sacred image according to the likeness of which I was created. Beg for me that my divine Redeemer may enkindle in my heart, and in all hearts, the fire of His love, and infuse therein the virtues of His adorable infancy, His purity, simplicity, obedience, and humility. Obtain for me likewise a lively devotion to thy virgin spouse, and protect me so powerfully in life and death that I may have the happiness of dying as thou didst, in the friendship of my Creator, and under the immediate protection of the Mother of God.

Pius IX, by a rescript of the S. C. of Indulgences, Nov. 28, 1876, granted to all the faithful who, with contrite heart, devoutly make at any time during the year a *novena in honor of St. Joseph, spouse of Mary most holy*, with any formula of prayer, provided it be approved by competent ecclesiastical authority, *an indulgence of three hundred days*, once a day; *a plenary indulgence*, during the course of the novena, if, being truly penitent, having confessed and communicated, they pray for the intention of the Sovereign Pontiff.

Devotions for the Faithful Departed

Reflections

A TRULY pious soul will not fail to offer the holy sacrifice of the Mass and holy communion very frequently for the faithful departed. The Way of the Cross, the Rosary, novenas, and litanies are good devotions for the same purpose. The *De Profundis*, besides other indulgenced prayers and ejaculations, should be made use of daily for the relief of the poor holy souls in purgatory.

Nourish the most tender compassion for those who are now absolutely incapable of assisting themselves, and who must remain separated from God until the last farthing is paid, either by their own sufferings, or by the interposition of the faithful. Many powerful motives should induce you to be most fervent in assisting them. By this spiritual work of mercy you prove your love for God, you benefit your neighbor, and acquire great merit for yourself. You prove your love for God by interceding for those holy souls who are so dear to His divine Majesty, and whom He so ardently longs to glorify forever. You perform an act of the greatest charity toward these suffering, holy souls, by endeavoring to shorten their banishment where they are tortured by a fire far more terrible than any earthly fire, and deprived of the sight of God, a torment more excruciating than all other pains; and you essentially serve your own soul by providing for yourself powerful advocates who will not forget you when they stand before God.

Let these considerations animate you to do all you can for the souls in purgatory. Devote fervently many prayers, good works, and various actions and mortifications to their relief, and endeavor to gain many indulgences for their benefit.

591

Short Indulgenced Prayer for the Souls in Purgatory

V. Requiem æter-
nam dona eis,
Domine;

R. Et lux perpetua luceat
eis.

V. Eternal rest
give to them,
O Lord;

R. And let perpetual light
shine upon them.

Indulgence applicable to the poor souls alone, 50 days each time. — Leo XIII, March 22, 1902.

The Month of November

His Holiness, Leo XIII, Jan. 17, 1888, granted to the faithful who shall perform some pious practice for the relief of the souls in purgatory, every day during the whole month of November, whether in public or in private, an indulgence of seven years and as many quarantines on each day of the month; a plenary indulgence, once during the same month, on any day of the month, on the usual conditions: confession and communion, and a visit to a church or public oratory, and there praying for the intention of the Sovereign Pontiff.

PRAYERS FOR EVERY DAY IN THE WEEK IN AID OF THE SOULS IN PURGATORY

For Sunday

Lord God almighty, I beseech Thee, by the precious blood which Thy divine Son Jesus shed in the garden, deliver the souls in purgatory, and amongst them all especially that soul which is most destitute of aid; and bring it to Thy glory, there to praise and bless Thee forever. Amen.
Our Father, Hail Mary, and the *De Profundis*.

For Monday

LORD God almighty, I beseech Thee, by the precious blood which Thy divine Son Jesus shed in His cruel scourging, deliver the souls in purgatory, and amongst them all, especially that soul which is nearest to its entrance into Thy glory; that so it may soon begin to praise and bless Thee forever. Amen.

Our Father, Hail Mary, and the *De Profundis.*

For Tuesday

LORD God almighty, I beseech Thee, by the precious blood which Thy divine Son Jesus shed in His bitter crowning with thorns, deliver the souls in purgatory, and in particular, amongst them all, deliver that one which would be the last to issue from those pains, that it tarry not so long a time before it comes to praise Thee in Thy glory and bless Thee forever. Amen.

Our Father, Hail Mary, and the *De Profundis.*

For Wednesday

LORD God almighty, I beseech Thee, by the precious blood which Thy divine Son Jesus shed through the streets of Jerusalem when He carried the cross upon His sacred shoulders, deliver the souls in purgatory, and especially that soul which is richest in merits before Thee; that so, on that throne of glory which awaits it, it may magnify Thee and bless Thee forever. Amen.

Our Father, Hail Mary, and the *De Profundis.*

For Thursday

LORD God almighty, I beseech Thee, by the precious body and blood of Thy divine Son Jesus, which He gave with His own hand upon the eve of His passion to His beloved apostles to be their meat and drink, and which He left to His whole Church to be a perpetual sacrifice and life-giving food of His own faithful people, deliver the souls in purgatory, and especially that one which was most devoted to this mystery of infinite love; that, with Thy divine Son, and with Thy Holy Spirit, it may ever praise Thee for this Thy wondrous love in Thy eternal glory. Amen.

Our Father, Hail Mary, and the *De Profundis*.

For Friday

LORD God almighty, I beseech Thee, by the precious blood which Thy divine Son shed on this day, upon the wood of the cross, from His most sacred hands and feet, deliver the souls in purgatory, and especially that soul for which I am most bound to pray; that the blame rest not with me that Thou bringest it not forthwith to praise Thee in Thy glory and to bless Thee forever. Amen.

Our Father, Hail Mary, and the *De Profundis*.

For Saturday

LORD God almighty, I beseech Thee, by the precious blood which gushed forth from the side of Thy divine Son Jesus, in the sight and to the extreme pain of His most holy Mother, deliver the souls in purgatory, and especially that one amongst them all which was ever the most devout to this great Lady; that it may soon attain unto Thy glory, there to praise Thee in her, and her in Thee, world without end. Amen.

Our Father, Hail Mary, and the *De Profundis*.

Indulgence of 100 days, once a day. — Leo XII, Nov. 18, 1826.

Miscellaneous Prayers

Prayer to Saint Anne

MOST august St. Anne! Heaven admires you, earth blesses you; God the Father loves you as the mother of His cherished daughter; the incarnate Word loves you as the parent of His well-beloved Mother; the Holy Spirit loves you as the mother of His perfect Spouse. The angels and the elect honor you as the tree producing a flower, the celestial perfume and beauty of which charms them, and whose divine fruit is their life and their joy. Repentant sinners look on you as their powerful advocate with God, the just through your intercession hope for an increase of grace, and penitents the expiation of their faults. Be propitious to us, O most merciful mother; unite with Mary, your dear and admirable Child, and by her intercession and yours, we shall confidently expect mercy from Jesus, to Whom you were so intimately allied; also the intentions of this devotion, every grace during life, and, above all, the grace of a happy death. Amen. — *A Gleaner's Sheaf.*

Prayer to any Virgin-Saint

O WORTHY spouse of that Lamb of God which feeds among the lilies, St. ——, you preserved intact the flower of your purity, edifying all by the constant practice of this lovely virtue; obtain for me, I pray, the grace to follow your example, that, overcoming all inordinate earthly affections and living according to the spirit of Jesus Christ, I may abound in charity and all good works. Make me to be enamored of the angelical virtue of purity, that by word and deed I may inspire others with a love of it, and may become worthy to join the happy choir of your companions, who, together with you, enjoy the Beatific Vision, and follow the Lamb "whithersoever He goeth."

To Any Other Saint

O GLORIOUS St. ——, who, burning with the desire of increasing the glory of God and of His Spouse the Church, invariably attended to the sanctification of your own soul and the edification of others, by the constant practice of prayer and charity, penance, and all Christian virtues; so that, becoming in the Church a model of holiness, you are now in heaven the protector of all those who have recourse to you in faith: cast a benign eye upon us who invoke your powerful patronage. Increase in us that true piety which forms the characteristic of the sons of God. Cause us, in imitation of you, to have, like faithful servants, our loins girt, and our lamps burning in our hands, and to live in edifying penitence; that when the eternal Master comes we may be found ready to depart from this exile, and merit to be admitted to those eternal tabernacles, where we shall see what we now believe, and obtain what now we hope for, the enjoyment of the immortal King of ages, to Whom be honor, glory, and benediction given, forever and ever.

Prayer for Youth to beg the Divine Direction in the Choice of a State of Life

O ALMIGHTY God! Whose wise and amiable providence watches over every human event, deign to be my light and my counsel in all my undertakings, particularly in the choice of a state of life. I know that on this important step my sanctification and salvation may in a great measure depend. I know that I am incapable of discerning what may be best for me; therefore I cast myself into Thy arms, beseeching Thee, my God, Who hast sent me into this world only to love and serve Thee, to direct by Thy grace every moment and action of my life to the glorious end of my creation. I renounce most sincerely every other wish, than to fulfil Thy designs on my soul, whatever they may be; and I beseech Thee to give me the grace, by imbibing the true spirit of a Christian, to qualify myself for any state of life to which Thy adorable providence may call me. O my God! whenever it may become my duty to make a choice, do Thou be my light and my counsel, and mercifully deign to *make the way known to me wherein I should walk, for I have lifted up my soul to Thee.* Preserve me from listening to the suggestions of my own self-love, or worldly prudence, in prejudice to Thy holy inspirations. Let *Thy good Spirit lead me into the right way*, and let Thy adorable providence place me, not where I may naturally feel inclined to go, but where all things may be most conducive to Thy glory and to the good of my soul. Mary, Mother of Good Counsel, Seat of Wisdom, Help of Christians, pray for me.

Lead, Kindly Light

LEAD, kindly Light, amid the encircling gloom
    Lead Thou me on!
The night is dark, and I am far from home.
    Lead Thou me on!
Keep Thou my feet; I do not ask to see
The distant scene, — one step enough for me.

I was not ever thus, nor pray'd that Thou
    Shouldst lead me on.
I loved to choose and see my path, but now
    Lead Thou me on!
I loved the garish day, and, spite of fears,
Pride ruled my will: remember not past years.

So long Thy power hath blest me, sure it still
    Will lead me on.
O'er moor and fen, o'er crag and torrent, till
    The night is gone;
And with the morn those angel faces smile
Which I have loved long since, and lost awhile.
                — CARDINAL NEWMAN

To-Day

LORD, for to-morrow and its needs
      I do not pray;
Keep me, my God, from stain of sin
      Just for to-day.
Let me both diligently work
      And duly pray;
Let me be kind in word and deed
      Just for to-day.
Let me be slow to do my will,
      Prompt to obey;
Help me to mortify my flesh,
      Just for to-day.
Let me no wrong or idle word,
      Unthinking, say;
Set Thou a seal upon my lips,
      Just for to-day.

Let me in season, Lord, be grave,
      In season, gay;
Let me be faithful to Thy grace
      Just for to-day.
And if to-day my tide of life
      Should ebb away,
Give me Thy sacraments divine,
      Sweet Lord, to-day.
In purgatory's cleansing fires
      Brief be my stay;
O bid me, if to-day I die,
      Go home to-day.

So, for to-morrow and its needs,
      I do not pray;
But keep me, guide me, love me, Lord,
      Just for to-day.

Prayers for the Church and for the Civil Authorities

(Composed by Archbishop Carroll)

WE pray Thee, O almighty and eternal God! Who through Jesus Christ hast revealed Thy glory to all nations, to preserve the works of Thy mercy, that Thy Church, being spread through the whole world, may continue with unchanging faith in the confession of Thy name.

We pray Thee, Who alone art good and holy, to endow with heavenly knowledge, sincere zeal, and sanctity of life, our chief bishop, N.N., the vicar of Our Lord Jesus Christ, in the government of His Church; our own bishop, N.N. (or archbishop); all other bishops, prelates, and pastors of the Church; and especially those who are appointed to exercise amongst us the functions of the holy ministry, and conduct Thy people into the ways of salvation.

We pray Thee, O God of might, wisdom, and justice! through Whom authority is rightly administered, laws are enacted, and judgment decreed, assist with Thy holy spirit of counsel and fortitude the President of the United States, that his administration may be conducted in righteousness, and be eminently useful to Thy people over whom he presides; by encouraging due respect for virtue and religion; by a faithful execution of the laws in justice and mercy; and by restraining vice and immorality. Let the light of Thy divine wisdom direct the deliberations of Congress, and shine forth in all the proceedings and laws framed for our rule and government, so that they may tend to the preservation of peace, the promotion of national happiness, the increase of industry, sobriety, and useful knowledge; and may perpetuate to us the blessing of equal liberty.

We pray for his excellency, the Governor of this State, for the members of the Assembly, for all judges, magistrates, and other officers who are appointed to guard our political welfare, that they may be enabled, by Thy powerful protection, to discharge the duties of their respective stations with honesty and ability.

We recommend likewise, to Thy unbounded mercy, all our brethren and fellow-citizens throughout the United States, that they may be blessed in the knowledge and sanctified in the observance of Thy most holy law; that they may be preserved in union, and in that peace which the world can not give; and after enjoying the blessings of this life, be admitted to those which are eternal.

Finally, we pray to Thee, O Lord of mercy, to remember the souls of Thy servants departed who are gone before us with the sign of faith, and repose in the sleep of peace; the souls of our parents, relatives, and friends; of those who, when living, were members of this congregation, and particularly of such as are lately deceased; of all benefactors who, by their donations or legacies to this church, witnessed their zeal for the decency of divine worship and proved their claim to our grateful and charitable remembrance. To these, O Lord, and to all that rest in Christ, grant, we beseech Thee, a place of refreshment, light, and everlasting peace, through the same Jesus Christ, our Lord and Saviour. Amen.

A Universal Prayer

For All Things Necessary to Salvation

(Composed by Pope Clement XI, A.D. 1721)

O MY God, I believe in Thee; do Thou strengthen my faith. All my hopes are in Thee; do Thou secure them. I love Thee; teach me to love Thee daily more and more. I am sorry that I have offended Thee; do Thou increase my sorrow.

I adore Thee as my first beginning; I aspire after Thee as my last end. I give Thee thanks as my constant benefactor; I call upon Thee as my sovereign protector.

Vouchsafe, O my God! to conduct me by Thy wisdom, to restrain me by Thy justice, to comfort me by Thy mercy, to defend me by Thy power.

To Thee I desire to consecrate all my thoughts, words, actions, and sufferings; that henceforward I may think of Thee, speak of Thee, refer all my actions to Thy greater glory, and suffer willingly whatever Thou shalt appoint.

Lord, I desire that in all things Thy will may be done because it is Thy will, and in the manner that Thou willest.

I beg of Thee to enlighten my understanding, to inflame my will, to purify my body, and to sanctify my soul.

Give me strength, O my God! to expiate my offenses, to overcome my temptations, to subdue my passions, and to acquire the virtues proper for my state of life.

Fill my heart with tender affection for Thy goodness,

hatred of my faults, love of my neighbor, and contempt of the world.

May Thy grace help me to be submissive to my superiors, condescending to my inferiors, faithful to my friends, and charitable to my enemies.

Assist me to overcome sensuality by mortification, avarice by alms-deeds, anger by meekness, and tepidity by devotion.

O my God! make me prudent in my undertakings, courageous in dangers, patient in affliction, and humble in prosperity.

Grant that I may be ever attentive at my prayers, temperate at my meals, diligent in my employments, and constant in my resolutions.

Let my conscience be ever upright and pure, my exterior modest, my conversation edifying, and my comportment regular.

Assist me, that I may continually labor to overcome nature, to correspond with Thy grace, to keep Thy commandments, and to work out my salvation.

Make me realize, O my God! the nothingness of this world, the greatness of heaven, the shortness of time, and the length of eternity.

Grant that I may prepare for death; that I may fear Thy judgments, and in the end obtain heaven; through Jesus Christ our Lord. Amen.

Aspirations to St. Anthony of Padua

ST. ANTHONY, we beseech thee, obtain for us the grace that we desire.

St. Anthony, great wonder-worker, intercede for us that God may grant us our request, if it be for the good of our soul.

St. Anthony, be our patron, our protector, and our advocate in life and in death.

St. Anthony, attentive to those who invoke thee, grant us the aid of thy powerful intercession for the grace of holy purity, meekness, humility, obedience, the spirit of poverty, and perfect abandonment to the will of God.

St. Anthony, glory of the church and hammer of heretics, pray for our Holy Father, our bishops, our priests, our Religious Orders, that, through their pious zeal and apostolic labors, infidels, heretics, and all those outside the true Church of Christ may be converted and, united in faith, give greater glory to God.

St. Anthony, servant of Mary, obtain for us greater devotion to the blessed Mother of God.

St. Anthony, obtain for us the grace of perseverance, the grace of a happy death.

Indulgenced Responsory in Honor of St. Anthony

SI QUÆRIS miracula,
Mors, error, calamitas,
Dæmon, lepra fugiunt,
Ægri surgunt sani.

Cedunt mare, vincula;
Membra resque perditas
Petunt et accipiunt

IF, THEN, you ask for miracles,
Death, error, all calamities,
The leprosy, and demons fly,
And health succeeds infirmities.

The sea obeys, and fetters break;
And lifeless limbs thou dost restore;
Whilst treasures lost are found again,

Juvenes et
cani.

When young or old thine
aid implore.

Pereunt peri-
cula,
Cessat et necessi-
tas;
Narrent hi, qui sen-
tiunt,
Dicant Padua-
ni.

All dangers vanish at thy
prayer,
And direst need doth quickly
flee;
Let those who know, thy
power proclaim,
Let Paduans say: These
are of thee.

Cedunt mare, vinc-
ula;
Membra resque per-
ditas
Petunt et accipi-
unt
Juvenes et
cani.

The sea obeys, and fetters
break;
And lifeless limbs thou dost
restore;
Whilst treasures lost are
found again,
When young or old thine
aid implore.

Gloria Patri et Fi-
lio,
Et Spiritui Sancto.
Cedunt mare, vincula, etc.

To Father, Son, may glory
be,
And Holy Ghost, eternally.
The sea obeys, etc.

V. Ora pro nobis, B.
Antoni.
R. Ut digni efficiamur
promissionibus Chri-
sti.

V. Pray for us, blessed
Anthony.
R. That we may be
made worthy of the prom-
ises of Christ.

Oremus

Let us pray

Ecclesiam Tuam, Deus,
beati Antonii confes-
soris Tui commemoratio vo-
tiva lætificet, ut spiritualibus
semper muniatur auxiliis

O God! may the votive
commemoration of
blessed Anthony, Thy con-
fessor, be a source of joy
to Thy Church, that she

et gaudiis perfrui mereatur æternis. Per Christum Dominum nostrum. Amen.	may always be fortified with spiritual assistance, and deserve to enjoy eternal rewards. Through Christ our Lord. Amen.

His Holiness, Pope Pius IX, by a decree of the Sacred Congregation of Indulgences, Jan. 25, 1866, granted to all the faithful, as often as they shall, with at least contrite heart and devotion, say this responsory, with the versicle and prayer annexed, an *indulgence of one hundred days;* also a *plenary indulgence,* once a month, on any day, to all those who have said it for a month, provided that, being truly penitent, after confession and communion, they shall visit a church or public oratory, and there pray, for some time, for the intention of His Holiness.

The Novena of Grace

ORIGIN OF THE NOVENA

The Novena of Grace, which begins on March 4th and ends on the 12th, the day of the canonization of St. Francis Xavier, owes its origin to the saint himself. At Naples, in December, 1633, Father Marcello Mastrilli, S.J., was at the point of death. The saint appeared to him, and bidding him renew a vow he had made to labor in Japan, said: "All those who implore my help daily for nine consecutive days, from the 4th to the 12th of March included, and worthily receive the sacraments of Penance and the Holy Eucharist on one of the nine days, will experience my protection and may hope with entire assurance to obtain from God *any grace* they ask for the good of their souls and the glory of God." The Father arose, instantly cured. So well has the saint kept this promise, that this devotion in his honor became universally known as the Novena of Grace. Its efficacy is not restricted to the dates mentioned. It may be made very appropriately in preparation for the feast of St. Francis Xavier, *viz.*, the 3d of December. Though any prayers may be said in honor of the saint, the following are generally recommended.

PRAYERS FOR THE NOVENA

Prayer to St. Francis Xavier

Used for the novena from the beginning and attributed to Father Mastrilli, S.J.

MOST amiable and most loving Saint Francis Xavier, in union with thee I reverently adore the divine Majesty. I rejoice exceedingly on account of the marvelous gifts which God bestowed upon thee. I thank God for the special graces He gave thee during thy life on earth and for the great glory that came to thee after thy death. I implore thee to obtain for me, through thy powerful intercession, the greatest of all blessings — that of living and dying in the state of grace. I also beg of thee to secure for me the special favor I ask in this novena.

Here you may mention the grace, spiritual or temporal, you wish to obtain.

In asking this favor I am fully resigned to the divine will. I pray and desire only to obtain that which is most conducive to the greater glory of God and the greater good of my soul.

V. Pray for us, St. Francis Xavier.

R. That we may be made worthy of the promises of Christ.

Let us pray

O God, Who didst vouchsafe, by the preaching and miracles of St. Francis Xavier, to join unto Thy Church the nations of the Indies; grant, we beseech Thee, that we who reverence his glorious merits, may also imitate his example, through Jesus Christ, our Lord. Amen.

Then add an *Our Father* and *Hail Mary*, three times, in memory of St. Francis Xavier's devotion to the most holy Trinity, and *Glory be to the Father*, ten times, in thanksgiving for the graces received during his ten years of apostleship.

Prayer of St. Francis Xavier for the Conversion of the Infidels

ETERNAL God, Creator of all things, remember that Thou alone didst create the souls of infidels, framing them to Thy own image and likeness; behold, O Lord! how, to Thy dishonor, hell is daily replenished with them. Remember, O Lord! Thy only Son, Jesus Christ, Who suffered for them, most bountifully shedding His precious blood: suffer not, O Lord! Thy Son and our Lord to be any longer despised by infidels; but rather, being appeased by the entreaties and prayers of the elect, the saints, and of the Church, the most blessed spouse of Thy Son, vouchsafe to be mindful of Thy mercy, and forgetting their idolatry and infidelity, cause them also to know Him Whom Thou didst send, Jesus Christ Thy Son, our Lord, Who is our health, life, and resurrection, through Whom we are freed and saved, to Whom be all glory forever.

An *indulgence of three hundred days*, once a day, to all the faithful who, with at least contrite heart and devotion, shall say this prayer.—Pius IX, May 24, 1847.

St. Francis Xavier's Hymn of Love

O God, I love Thee for Thou,
Thyself
And not that I may heaven
gain,
Nor because those who love
Thee not,
Must suffer hell's eternal
pain.

O my Jesus! Thou
didst me
Upon the cross embrace;
For me didst bear the nails
and spear
And manifold disgrace;

And griefs and torments
   numberless,
And sweat of agony;
E'en death itself—and all
   for one
Who was Thine enemy.

Then why, O blessed Jesus
   Christ,
Should I not love Thee well:
Not for the sake of winning
   heaven,

Or of escaping hell;
Not with the hope of gaining
   aught, not seeking a
   reward;
But, as Thyself hast loved
   me, O ever-loving Lord?

E'en so I love Thee, and will
   love, and in Thy praise
   will sing;
Solely because Thou art my
   God
And my eternal King.

Prayer to the Holy Family

O MOST loving Jesus, Who by Thy sublime and beautiful virtues of humility, obedience, poverty, modesty, charity, patience, and gentleness, and by the example of Thy domestic life, didst bless with peace and happiness the family which Thou didst choose on earth; in Thy clemency look down upon this household, humbly prostrate before Thee and imploring Thy mercy. Remember that this family belongs to Thee; for to Thee we have in a special way dedicated and devoted ourselves. Look upon us in Thy loving-kindness, preserve us from danger, give us help in time of need, and grant us the grace to persevere to the end in the imitation of Thy Holy Family; that having revered Thee and loved Thee faithfully on earth, we may bless and praise Thee eternally in heaven. O Mary, most sweet Mother, to thy intercession we have recourse, knowing that thy divine Son will hear thy prayers. And do thou, O glorious Patriarch, St. Joseph, assist us by thy powerful mediation and offer, by the hands of Mary, our prayers to Jesus. Amen.

Indulgenced Prayer for a Christian Family

•

GOD of goodness and mercy, we commend to Thy all-powerful protection our home, our family, and all that we possess. Bless us all as Thou didst bless the holy family of Nazareth.

O Jesus, our most holy Redeemer, by the love with which Thou didst become man in order to save us, by the mercy through which Thou didst die for us upon the cross, we entreat Thee to bless our home, our family, our household. Preserve us from all evil and from the snares of men; preserve us from lightning and hail and fire, from flood and from the rage of the elements; preserve us from Thy wrath, from all hatred and from the evil intentions of our enemies, from plague, famine, and war. Let not one of us die without the holy sacraments. Bless us, that we may always openly confess our faith, which is to sanctify us, that we may never falter in our hope, even amid pain and affliction, and that we may ever grow in love for Thee and in charity toward our neighbor.

O Jesus, bless us, protect us.

O Mary, Mother of grace and mercy, bless us, protect us against the evil spirit; lead us by the hand through this vale of tears; reconcile us with thy divine Son; commend us to Him, that we may be made worthy of His promises.

St. Joseph, reputed father of Our Saviour, guardian of His most holy Mother, head of the holy family, intercede for us, bless and protect our home always.

St. Michael, defend us against all the wicked wiles of hell.

St. Gabriel, obtain for us that we may understand the holy will of God.

St. Raphael, preserve us from ill health and all danger to life.

Holy guardian angels, keep us day and night in the way to salvation.

Holy patrons, pray for us before the throne of God.

Bless this house, Thou, God our Father, Who didst create us; Thou, divine Son, Who didst suffer for us on the cross; Thou, Holy Spirit, Who didst sanctify us in Baptism. May God, in His three divine Persons, preserve our body, purify our soul, direct our heart, and lead us to life everlasting.

Glory be to the Father, glory be to the Son, glory be to the Holy Ghost. Amen.

His Holiness, Leo XIII, by a rescript of the Sacred Congregation of Indulgences, Jan. 19, 1889, granted to the faithful who recite the above prayer, an *indulgence of two hundred days*, once a day.

prayer for travelers

The breviary contains prayers for travelers that have received the consecration of the Church and of centuries — the "Itinerary," which priests seldom fail to recite for themselves and their companions as often as they begin a journey. As it may seem rather long for general use, we give an abridgment for the use of those who may wish to know and learn it.

MAY the almighty and merciful Lord direct us on our journey; may He make it prosper and maintain us in peace.

May the Archangel Raphael accompany us along the way, and may we return to our homes in peace, joy, and health.

Lord, have mercy on us! Jesus Christ, have mercy on us! Lord, have mercy on us!

Prayer

O GOD, Who didst cause the children of Israel to traverse the Red Sea dryshod; Thou Who didst point out by a star to the Magi the road that led them to Thee; grant us, we beseech Thee, a prosperous journey and propitious weather; so that, under the guidance of Thy holy angels, we may safely reach that journey's end, and later the haven of eternal salvation.

Hear, O Lord, the prayers of Thy servants. Bless their journeyings. Thou Who art everywhere present, shower everywhere upon them the effects of Thy mercy; so that, insured by Thy protection against all dangers, they may return to offer Thee their thanksgiving. Through Jesus Christ our Lord. Amen.

(Those who have a special confidence in St. Joseph may make use of the following prayer which solicits also supernatural graces, and especially that of traveling always in the way of the commandments, so as ultimately to reach the celestial terminus.)

O BLESSED St. Joseph, who didst accompany Jesus and Mary in all their journeys, and who hast therefore merited to be called the patron of all travelers, accompany us in this journey that we are about to undertake. Be our guide and our protector; watch over us; preserve us from all accidents and dangers to soul and body; support us in our fatigue, and aid us to sanctify it by offering it to God. Make us ever mindful that we are strangers, sojourners here below; that heaven is our true home; and help us to persevere on the straight road that leads thereunto. We beseech thee especially to protect and aid us in the last great voyage from time to eternity, so that, under thy guidance, we may reach the realm of happiness and glory, there to repose eternally with thee in the company of Jesus and Mary. Amen.

Still another prayer for travelers, asking in a special manner for the protection of the guardian angels, was composed by the saintly Msgr. Dupanloup.   It reads:

O ALMIGHTY and merciful God, Who hast commissioned Thy angels to guide and protect us, command them to be our assiduous companions from our setting out until our return; to clothe us with their invisible protection; to keep from us all danger of collision, of fire, of explosion, of falls and bruises; and finally, having preserved us from all evil, and especially from sin, to guide us to our heavenly home.   Through Jesus Christ our Lord.   Amen.

Another not less beautiful prayer runs thus:

M Y HOLY angel guardian, ask the Lord to bless the journey which I undertake, that it may profit the health of my soul and body; that I may reach its end; and that, returning safe and sound, I may find all at home in good health.   Do thou guard, guide, and preserve us.   Amen.

The following couplet was a favorite ejaculation of Columbus:

Jesus cum Maria	Jesus and Mary, we pray,
Sit nobis in via.	Be with us ever on our way.

One should not fail at least to make the sign of the cross on beginning a journey.   The neglect or performance of such acts of piety may make all the difference between having our names figure on the list of "killed and wounded" in some railway catastrophe, and having them appear as those of passengers "saved by a miracle." — *Ave Maria Press.*

The Little Flower

Prayers in Honor of St. Teresa of the Infant Jesus

St. Teresa of the Infant Jesus, who didst show so much love for thy Divine Spouse, and didst ever hold "that deeds, even the most brilliant, without love count as nothing—that true love is nourished by sacrifice"; obtain for me, I beseech thee, from the Lord Jesus, a faith strong enough to raise me above all earthly things, a love without bound or limit, grace to do His holy will, so that no trial or suffering shall ever be able to separate me from Jesus and His blessed Mother. I likewise entreat thee, St. Teresa, to obtain for me the particular favor I ask in this Novena, if it be for the honor and glory of God, the salvation of my own soul, and the welfare of those for whom I pray.

Prayer

(*From the Mass of her feast*)

O Lord, Who hast said: Unless ye become as little children, ye shall not enter into the kingdom of heaven, grant unto us, we beseech Thee, so to follow the footsteps of blessed Teresa, virgin, in lowliness and simplicity of heart that we may gain everlasting rewards. Who livest and reignest, with God the Father, in the unity of the Holy Ghost, world without end. Amen.

St. Teresa of the Infant Jesus, pray for us.

Petitions of St. Augustine

O LORD Jesus, let me know myself, let me know
        Thee
And desire nothing else but only Thee.
Let me hate myself and love Thee;
And do all things for the sake of Thee.
Let me humble myself, and exalt Thee,
And think of nothing but only of Thee.
Let me die to myself, and live in Thee,
And take whatever happens as coming from Thee.
Let me forsake myself and walk after Thee;
And ever desire to follow Thee.
Let me flee from myself, and turn to Thee;
That so I may merit to be defended by Thee.
Let me fear for myself, let me fear Thee;
And be amongst those who are chosen by Thee.
Let me distrust myself, and trust in Thee,
And ever obey for the love of Thee.
Let me cleave to nothing but only to Thee,
And ever be poor for the sake of Thee.
Look upon me, that I may love Thee;
Call me, that I may see Thee,
And forever possess Thee.   Amen.

His Holiness, Pope Leo XIII, by a brief, Sept. 25, 1883, granted to all the faithful who, with at least contrite heart and devotion, shall recite this petition, an *indulgence of fifty days*, once a day.

Indulgenced Prayer to St. Joachim

SAINT Joachim, spouse of Anne, father of the be- nign Virgin, aid thy clients here on the way to sal- vation.

Indulgence of 300 days. — Pius X, June 16, 1906.

A Most Commendable Indulgenced Prayer to the Sacred Heart of Jesus

MOST sacred Heart of Jesus, shower copiously Thy blessings on Thy holy Church, on the Supreme Pontiff, and on all the clergy; grant perseverance to the just, convert sinners, enlighten infidels, bless our parents, friends, and benefactors, assist the dying, liberate the souls of purgatory, and extend over all hearts the sweet empire of Thy love.

Indulgence of 300 days. — Pius X, June 16, 1906.

EJACULATION

JESUS, Mary, and good Joseph, bless us, now and in the agony of death.

Indulgence of 50 days. — Pius X, June 9, 1906.

Prayer for a Happy Death

By Cardinal Newman

O MY Lord and Saviour, support me in my last hour by the strong arms of Thy sacraments, and the fragrance of Thy consolations. Let Thy absolving words be said over me, and the holy oil sign and seal me; and let Thine own body be my food, and Thy blood my sprinkling; and let Thy Mother Mary come to me, and my angel whisper peace to me, and Thy glorious saints and my own dear patrons smile on me, that in and through them all I may die as I desire to live, in Thy Church, in Thy faith, and in Thy love. Amen.

My Jesus, mercy.

Indulgence of 100 days, each time. — Pius IX, Sept. 24, 1846.

Prayer for a Sick Person

OST merciful Jesus, Who art the consolation and salvation of all who put their trust in Thee, we humbly beseech Thee, by Thy most bitter passion, grant the recovery of his health to Thy servant N.N., provided this be for his soul's welfare, that with us he may praise and magnify Thy holy name. But if it be Thy holy will to call him out of this world, strengthen him in his last hour, grant him a peaceful death and life everlasting. Amen.
Our Father. Hail Mary. Glory.

Prayer for a Deceased Person

O GOD, Whose property it is ever to have mercy and to spare, we beseech Thee on behalf of the soul of Thy servant whom Thou hast called out of this world; look upon him with pity and let him be conducted by the holy angels to paradise, his true country. Grant that he who believed in Thee and hoped in Thee may not be left to suffer the pains of the purgatorial fire, but may be admitted to eternal joys. Through Jesus Christ, Thy Son, our Lord, Who with Thee and the Holy Ghost liveth and reigneth world without end. Amen.
Our Father. Hail Mary.
V. Eternal rest give unto him, O Lord;
R. And let perpetual light shine upon him.

Litany, and Other Prayers for a happy Death

ORD, have mercy on us.
Christ, have mercy on us
Lord, have mercy on us.
Christ, hear us.
Christ, graciously hear us.
God, the Father of heaven. **Have mercy on us.**

God, the Son, Redeemer of the world. Have mercy on us.
God, the Holy Ghost. Have mercy on us.
Holy Trinity, one God. Have mercy on us.
Holy Mary,[1]
All ye holy angels and archangels,
Holy Abraham,
St. John the Baptist,
St. Joseph,
All ye holy patriarchs and prophets,
St. Peter,
St. Paul,
St. Andrew,
St. John,
St. Jude,
All ye holy apostles and evangelists,
All ye holy disciples of Our Lord,
All ye holy innocents,
St. Stephen,
St. Lawrence,
All ye holy martyrs,
St. Sylvester,
St. Gregory,
St. Augustine,
St. Basil,
St. Ambrose,
St. Francis de Sales,
St. Vincent de Paul,
St. Aloysius,
St. Stanislaus,
All ye holy bishops and confessors,
St. Benedict,
St. Dominic,
St. Francis of Assisi,
St. Ignatius,
St. Philip Neri,
St. Camillus de Lellis,
St. John of God,

[1] Pray for us.

All ye holy monks, hermits, and founders of Religious
    Orders,[1]
St. Mary Magdalene,
St. Lucy,
St. Scholastica,
St. Teresa,
St. Catharine,
St. Clara,
St. Ursula,
St. Angela Merici,
St. Jane Frances de Chantal,
St. Barbara,
All ye holy virgins and widows,
All ye saints of God, intercede for us.
Be merciful unto us.   Spare us, O Lord.
Be merciful unto us.   Hear us, O Lord.
From Thine anger,[2]
From the peril of death,
From an evil death,
From the pains of hell,
From all evil,
From the power of the devil,
By Thy nativity,
By Thy cross and passion,
By Thy death and burial,
By Thy glorious resurrection,
By the grace of the Holy Ghost the Comforter,
In the day of judgment,
We sinners, beseech Thee, hear us.
That Thou wouldst spare us,[3]
That Thou wouldst vouchsafe to bring us unto true re-
    pentance,
That Thou wouldst vouchsafe to grant eternal rest to all
    the faithful departed,
Lamb of God, Who takest away the sins of the world.
    Have mercy on us!

[1] Pray for us.   [2] O Lord, deliver us.
[3] We beseech Thee, hear us.

Lamb of God, forgive us our sins. Grant that we may die in Thy love and Thy grace!

Lamb of God, by Thy precious blood. We beseech Thee to hear us and to lead us to life everlasting.

Lord, have mercy on us. Christ, have mercy on us. Lord, have mercy on us.

Let us pray

WE beseech Thy clemency, O Lord, that Thou wouldst vouchsafe so to strengthen Thy servants in Thy grace, that, at the hour of death, the enemy may not prevail over us, and that we may deserve to pass with Thy angels into everlasting life.

Almighty and most merciful God, Who, for Thy thirsting people, didst bring forth from the rock a stream of living water, draw forth from the hardness of our hearts tears of compunction, that we may bewail our sins, and receive forgiveness of them from Thy mercy.

O Lord Jesus Christ, Redeemer of the world, behold us prostrate at Thy feet. With our whole heart we detest our sins of thought, word, and deed, and because we love Thee above all created things we steadfastly purpose, by the help of Thy grace, never more to offend Thee, and rather to die than to commit one mortal sin. Amen.

O Jesus, Who, during Thy prayer to the Father in the garden, wast so filled with sorrow and anguish that there came forth from Thee a bloody sweat; have mercy on us.

Have mercy on us, O Lord; have mercy on us.

O Jesus, Who wast betrayed by the kiss of a traitor into the hands of the wicked, seized and bound like a thief, and forsaken by Thy disciples; have mercy on us.

Have mercy on us, O Lord; have mercy on us.

O Jesus, Who, by the unjust council of the Jews, was sentenced to death, led like a malefactor before Pilate, scorned and derided by impious Herod; have mercy on us.

Have mercy on us, O Lord; have mercy on us.

O Jesus, Who wast stripped of Thy garments, and most cruelly scourged at the pillar; have mercy on us.

Have mercy on us, O Lord; have mercy on us.

O Jesus, Who wast crowned with thorns, buffeted, struck with a reed, blindfolded, clothed with a purple garment, in many ways derided, and overwhelmed with reproaches; have mercy on us.

Have mercy on us, O Lord; have mercy on us.

O Jesus, Who wast less esteemed than the murderer Barabbas, rejected by the Jews, and unjustly condemned to the death of the cross; have mercy on us.

Have mercy on us, O Lord; have mercy on us.

O Jesus, Who wast loaded with a cross, and led to the place of execution as a lamb to the slaughter; have mercy on us.

Have mercy on us, O Lord; have mercy on us.

O Jesus, Who wast numbered among thieves, blasphemed, and derided, made to drink of gall and vinegar, and crucified in dreadful torment from the sixth to the ninth hour; have mercy on us.

Have mercy on us, O Lord; have mercy on us.

O Jesus, Who didst expire on the cross, Who wast pierced with a lance in presence of Thy holy Mother, and from Whose side poured forth blood and water; have mercy on us.

Have mercy on us, O Lord; have mercy on us.

O Jesus, Who wast taken down from the cross, and bathed in the tears of Thy most sorrowing Virgin Mother; have mercy on us.

Have mercy on us, O Lord; have mercy on us.

O Jesus, Who wast covered with bruises, marked with the five wounds, embalmed with spices, and laid in the sepulcher; have mercy on us.

Have mercy on us, O Lord; have mercy on us.

V. He hath truly borne our sorrows.

R. And He hath carried our griefs.

Let us pray

O GOD, Who, for the redemption of the world, didst deign to be born, to be circumcised, to be rejected by the Jews, and betrayed by Judas with a kiss; to be bound with fetters, and led like an innocent lamb to the slaughter; to be ignominiously brought before Annas, Caiphas, Pilate, and Herod; to be accused by false witnesses, to be scourged, buffeted, and reviled; to be spit upon, to be crowned with thorns, and struck with a reed; to be blindfolded, to be stripped of Thy garments, to be nailed to a cross and raised thereon, to be numbered among thieves, to be made to drink of gall and vinegar, and to be pierced with a lance: do Thou, O Lord, by these Thy most holy sufferings, which we Thy servants, commemorate, and by Thy most holy cross and death, deliver us from the pains of hell, and conduct us, as Thou didst conduct the penitent thief, into Thy paradise. Who liveth and reigneth, world without end. Amen.

Prayer for the Faithful in their Agony

O MOST merciful Jesus, Lover of souls! I pray Thee, by the agony of Thy most sacred Heart, and by the sorrows of Thy immaculate Mother, cleanse in Thine own blood the sinners of the whole world who are now in their agony and to die this day. Amen.

Heart of Jesus, once in agony, pity the dying.

Act of Resignation and Prayer for a Happy Death

LORD Jesus, incarnate Son of God, Who for our salvation didst will to be born in a stable, to endure poverty, suffering, and sorrow throughout Thy life, and finally to die the bitter death of the cross, I implore Thee, in the hour of my death, to say to Thy divine Father: O Father, forgive him (her)! Say to Thy beloved Mother: Behold thy son --

thy child! Say to my soul: This day shalt thou be with **Me**
in paradise! O my God, my God! forsake me not at that
moment! I thirst! O my God! Truly my soul is athirst
for Thee, the fountain of living water. My life has passed
away like unto smoke; yet a little while and all is consummated. O adorable Saviour, into Thy hands I commend my spirit for all eternity. Lord Jesus, receive my
soul. Amen.

To Mary

O DEAREST Lady, sweet Mother mine, watch the hour
when my departing soul shall lose its hold on all
earthly things, and stand unveiled in the presence of its
Creator. Show thyself my tender Mother then, and offer
to the Eternal Father the precious blood of thy Son Jesus
for my poor soul, that it may, thus purified, be pleasing in
His sight. Plead for thy poor child at the moment of his
(or her) departure from this world, and say to the heavenly
Father: Receive him (her) this day into Thy kingdom!
Amen.

Jesus, Mary, and Joseph, I give you my heart and my
soul.

Jesus, Mary, and Joseph, assist me in my last agony.

Jesus, Mary, and Joseph, may I breathe forth my soul
in peace with you.

Ejaculations to be used in Prepara- tion for a Good Death

T HOSE who wish to make sure of dying well should frequently pray for the grace of perseverance and make
use of indulgenced invocations, many of which are contained in this book, and also of such pious ejaculations as the
following by St. Alphonsus, especially in time of sickness.

As for those persons who are in attendance on the sick,
their duty is from time to time to suggest or recite the

Christian Acts, short prayers, etc., but always with great sweetness and discretion.

Confidence in God

H E who has placed his confidence in God is never abandoned by Him.

Jesus Christ died to obtain for us the pardon of our sins.

God gave us His only Son to die for us; therefore how can He refuse to pardon us?

The Lord is my light and my salvation; of whom, then, shall I be afraid?

Into Thy hands I commend my spirit; Thou didst redeem me, Lord, Thou God of truth.

We pray thee, therefore, help Thy servants whom Thou hast redeemed with Thy precious blood.

In Thee, O Lord, have I trusted; let me never be confounded. Good Jesus, hide me in Thy sacred wounds.

Thy wounds will plead for me.

My Jesus, Thou wilt not refuse me the pardon of my sins, since Thou hast not refused me Thy blood and Thy life.

Passion of Jesus, thou art my hope.

Blood of Jesus, thou art my hope.

Death of Jesus, thou art my hope.

Eternally will I sing the Lord's mercy.

O Mary, my Mother, thou canst save me; thou must save me; have pity on me. Hail! our Queen! Hail! our hope!

Holy Mary, pray for me.

My God, I regret that I have sinned because sin displeases Thee, O infinite Good! My God, I love Thee with my whole heart and above all things. Oh, grant that I may love Thee more and more.

My God, would that I could love Thee as Thou dost deserve to be loved.

O Mary, my Mother, I love Thee with all the ardor of my soul, and I desire to love Thee eternally in paradise.

Conformity to God's Will

BEHOLD me, Lord; do with me what Thou wilt. May Thy will be ever done; I only desire what Thou wilt. I desire to suffer what Thou willest; I desire to die when Thou willest.

Into Thy hands I commend my body, my soul, my life, and my death. I love Thee, O my God, whether it pleaseth Thee to send me consolations or afflictions, and I desire to love Thee always.

Eternal Father, I unite my death to that of Jesus Christ, and I offer it to Thee in order to please Thee.

Will of my God, Thou art my love.

Good pleasure of my God, I devote myself entirely to Thee.

Desire of Paradise

O MY God, when shall I behold Thine infinite beauty; when shall I behold Thee face to face?

In paradise I shall love Thee, and Thou wilt love me to all eternity, my God and my All!

My Jesus, when shall I behold Thee and kiss those wounds which were inflicted on Thee for my sake?

O Mary, when shall I find myself at the feet of the Mother who has loved and aided me so tenderly?

My sweet Protectress, turn thou on me thine eyes of mercy. Take me from this land of exile, and show me the blessed fruit of thy womb, Jesus.

On Kissing the Crucifix

MY JESUS, look not on my sins, but look on what Thou didst suffer for me.

Remember, I am a sheep of that flock for which Thou didst lay down Thy life.

I consent to being consumed for Thee, my Jesus, Who didst consume Thyself entirely for me.

Thou didst give thyself entirely to me; I now give myself entirely to Thee.

My innocent Lord, Thou didst suffer for me far more than I, a sinner, am now suffering.

My beloved Redeemer, like Magdalen I kiss Thy sacred feet; vouchsafe me a pardoning word.

My God, for the love of Jesus Christ, pardon me, and grant me a good death.

My Jesus, I have repaid Thee with ingratitude; have pity on me; I pray Thee to punish me in this life rather than in the next.

Thou didst not abandon me when I strayed away from Thee; abandon me not, I pray Thee, now that I would seek Thee.

Sweet Jesus, let me not be separated from Thee. Who can separate me from the love of Jesus?

Lord Jesus Christ, by Thy sufferings when Thy pure and innocent soul left Thy most holy body, have pity on my poor soul when it shall leave my body. Amen.

My Jesus, Thou didst die for love of me; I would die for love of Thee.

Prayer

I THROW myself on Thy mercy, hoping through Thy precious blood to die in Thy friendship, and to receive Thy blessing when I shall see Thee first as my judge. Into Thy hands, wounded for love of me, I commend my soul. I hope in Thee, that Thou wilt not then condemn me to hell. *In te, Domine, speravi, non confundar in æternum.* Ah, help me always, but especially at my death; grant me to die loving Thee, so that the last sigh of life may be an act of love, which shall transport me from this earth to love Thee forever in paradise.

EJACULATIONS

Eternal Father! I offer Thee the precious blood of Jesus in satisfaction for my sins and for the wants of holy Church.

Indulgence of 100 days, every time. — Pius VII, Sept. 22, 1817.

My sweetest Jesus, be not my Judge, but my Saviour.

Indulgence of 50 days, every time. — Pius IX, Aug. 11, 1851.

My Queen, my Mother, remember I am thine own. Keep me, guard me, as thy property and possession.

Indulgence of 40 days, every time. — Pius IX, Aug. 5, 1851.

O Mary, who didst come into this world free from stain, obtain of God for me that I may leave it without sin.

Indulgence of 100 days, once a day. — Pius IX, March 27, 1863.

My Jesus, mercy!

Indulgence of 100 days, every time. — Pius IX, Sept. 24, 1846.

May the most just, most high, and most amiable will of God be done in all things — praised and magnified forever.

Indulgence of 100 days, once a day. — Pius VII, May 19, 1818.

Jesus, Son of David, have mercy on me!

Indulgence of 100 days, once a day. — Leo XIII, Feb. 27, 1886.

O sweetest Heart of Jesus! I implore
That I may ever love Thee more and more.

Indulgence of 300 days, every time. — Pius IX, Nov. 26, 1876.

Jesus, my God, I love Thee above all things!

Indulgence of 50 days, every time. — Pius IX, May 7, 1854.

Sweet heart of Mary, be my salvation.

Indulgence of 300 days, every time; plenary indulgence once a month. — Pius IX, Sept. 30, 1852.

The Seven Penitential Psalms

Ant. Ne reminiscaris, delicta nostra, Domine, vel parentum nostrorum, neque vindictam sumas de peccatis nostris.

Ant. Remember not, O Lord, our offenses, nor those of our parents; and take not revenge of our sins.

1. Psalm VI. Domine, ne in furore

Verse 1. David, in deep affliction, prays for a mitigation of the divine anger. 4. In consideration of God's mercy. 5. His glory. 6. His own repentance. 8. By faith he triumphs over his enemies.

1. DOMINE, ne in furore Tuo arguas me, neque in ira Tua corripias me.

2. Miserere mei, Domine, quoniam infirmus sum: sana me, Domine, quoniam conturbata sunt ossa mea.

3. Et anima mea turbata est valde; sed Tu, Domine, usquequo?

4. Convertere, Domine, et eripe animam meam; salvum me fac propter misericordiam tuam.

1. O LORD, rebuke me not in Thine indignation: nor chastise me in Thy wrath.

2. Have mercy upon me, O Lord, for I am weak: heal me, O Lord, for my bones are troubled.

3. My soul also is troubled exceedingly: but Thou, O Lord, how long?

4. Turn Thee, O Lord, and deliver my soul: O save me for Thy mercy's sake.

5. Quoniam non est in morte qui memor sit Tui; in inferno autem quis confitebitur Tibi?

6. Laboravi in gemitu meo; lavabo per singulas noctes lectum meum: lacrymis meis stratum meum rigabo.

7. Turbatus est a furore meus; inveteravi inter omnes inimicos meos.

8. Discedite a me omnes qui operamini iniquitatem, quoniam exaudivit Dominus vocem fletus mei.

9. Exaudivit Dominus deprecationem meam; Dominus orationem meam suscepit.

10. Erubescant, et conturbentur vehementer omnes inimici mei; convertantur, et erubescant valde velociter.

Gloria, etc.

5. For in death there is no one that remembereth Thee: and who shall give Thee thanks in hell?

6. I have labored in my groanings: every night will I wash my bed, and water my couch with my tears.

7. Mine eye is troubled through indignation: I have grown old among all mine enemies.

8. Depart from me, all ye that work iniquity: for the Lord hath heard the voice of my weeping.

9. The Lord hath heard my supplication: the Lord hath received my prayer.

10. Let all mine enemies be ashamed and sore vexed: let them be turned back, and be ashamed very speedily.

Glory, etc.

2. Psalm XXXI. Beati Quorum

1. The blessedness of those whose sins are forgiven. 3. The misery of impenitence. 6. Confession of sin brings ease; 8. safety; 14. joy.

1. **B**EATI quorum remissæ sunt iniquitates, et quorum tecta sunt peccata.

2. Beatus vir cui non imputavit Dominus peccatum, nec est in spiritu ejus dolus.

3. Quoniam tacui, inveteraverunt ossa mea, dum clamarem tota die.

4. Quoniam die ac nocte gravata est super me manus Tua, conversus sum in ærumna mea, dum configitur spina.

5. Delictum meum cognitum Tibi feci, et injustitiam meam non abscondi.

6. Dixi: Confitebor adversum me injustitiam meam Domino et Tu remisisti impietatem peccati mei.

7. Pro hac orabit ad Te omnis sanctus in tempore opportuno.

8. Verumtamen in diluvio aquarum multarum, ad eum non approximabunt.

9. Tu es refugium meum a tribulatione quæ circum-

1. **B**LESSED are they whose iniquities are forgiven: and whose sins are covered.

2. Blessed is the man to whom the Lord hath not imputed sin: and in whose spirit there is no guile.

3. Because I was silent, my bones grew old: while I cried aloud all the day long.

4. For day and night Thy hand was heavy upon me: I turned in my anguish, while the thorn was fastened in me.

5. I acknowledged my sin unto Thee: and my injustice have I not concealed.

6. I said I will confess against myself my injustice to the Lord: and Thou forgavest the wickedness of my sin.

7. For this shall every one that is holy pray unto Thee: in seasonable time.

8. But in the flood of many waters: they shall not come nigh unto him.

9. Thou art my refuge from the trouble which

dedit me exultatio mea, erue me a circumdantibus me.

10. Intellectum tibi dabo, et instruam te in via hac qua gradieris firmabo super te oculos meos.

11. Nolite fieri sicut equus et mulus, quibus non est intellectus.

12. In camo et freno maxillas eorum constringe, qui non approximant ad te.

13. Multa flagella peccatoris; sperantem autem in Domino misericordia circumdabit.

14. Lætamini in Domino, et exultate, justi; et gloriamini, omnes recti corde.

Gloria, etc.

hath surrounded me: my joy, deliver me from them that compass me about.

10. I will give thee understanding, and will instruct thee in the way wherein thou shalt go: I will fix Mine eyes upon thee.

11. Be ye not like unto horse and mule, which have no understanding.

12. With bit and bridle bind fast the jaws of those who come not nigh unto thee.

13. Many are the scourges of the sinner: but mercy shall compass him about that hopeth in the Lord.

14. Be glad, O ye just, and rejoice in the Lord; and glory all ye that are right of heart.

Glory, etc.

3. Psalm XXXVII. Domine, ne in furore

1. David's extreme anguish. His resignation and grief. 15. He hopes in God. 18. 22. Prayer.

1. DOMINE, ne in furore Tua arguas me, neque in ira Tua corripias me.

1. O LORD, rebuke me not in Thine indignation: nor chastise me in Thy wrath.

2. Quoniam sagittæ Tuæ infixæ sunt mihi, et confirmasti super me manum Tuam.

3. Non est sanitas in carne mea, a facie iræ Tuæ; non est pax ossibus meis, a facie peccatorum meorum.

4. Quoniam iniquitates meæ supergressæ sunt caput meum, et sicut onus grave gravatæ sunt super me.

5. Putruerunt et coruptæ sunt cicatrices meæ, a facie insipientiæ meæ.

6. Miser factus sum et curvatus sum usque in finem; tota die contristatus ingrediebar.

7. Quoniam lumbi mei impleti sunt illusionibus; et non est sanitas in carne mea.

8. Afflictus sum, et humiliatus sum nimis; ruiebam a gemitu cordis mei.

9. Domine, ante Te omne desiderium meum, et gemitus meus a Te non est absconditus.

10. Cor meum conturbatum est, dereliquit

2. For Thine arrows stick fast in me: and Thou hast laid Thy hand heavily upon me.

3. There is no health in my flesh because of Thy wrath: there is no rest in my bones because of my sins.

4. For my iniquities are gone over my head: and, like a heavy burden, press sorely upon me.

5. My wounds have putrefied and are corrupt: because of my foolishness.

6. I am become miserable and am bowed down even to the end: I go sorrowfully all the day long.

7. For my loins are filled with illusions: and there is no soundness in my flesh.

8. I am afflicted and humbled exceedingly: I have roared for the groaning of my heart.

9. Lord, all my desire is before Thee: and my groaning is not hidden from Thee.

10. My heart is troubled, my strength hath failed

me virtus mea, et lumen oculorum /meorum, et ipsum non est mecum.

11. Amici mei et proximi mei adversum me appropinquaverunt, et steterunt.

12. Et qui juxta me erant, de longe steterunt, et vim faciebant qui quærebant animam meam.

13. Et qui inquirebant mala mihi, locuti sunt vanitates, et dolos tota die meditabantur.

14. Ego autem, tanquam surdus, non audiebam; et sicut mutus non aperiens os suum.

15. Et factus sum sicut homo non audiens, et non habens in ore suo redargutiones.

16. Quoniam in Te, Domine, speravi; Tu exaudies me, Domine Deus meus.

17. Quia dixi: Nequando supergaudeant mihi inimici mei; et dum commoventur pedes mei, super me magna locuti sunt.

18. Quoniam ego in flagella paratus sum, et

me: the very light of mine eyes is gone from me.

11. My friends and my neighbors drew near, and stood up against me.

12. They that were once nigh me stood afar off: and they that sought after my soul did violence against me.

13. And they that sought to do me evil talked vanities: and imagined deceits all the day long.

14. But I, as a deaf man, heard not: and as one that is dumb, who openeth not his mouth.

15. I became as a man that heareth not: and that hath no reproofs in his mouth.

16. For in Thee, O Lord, have I hoped: Thou wilt hear me, O Lord my God.

17. For I said, Let not mine enemies at any time triumph over me: and when my feet slip, they have spoken great things against me.

18. For I am prepared for scourges; and my

dolor meus in conspectu meo semper.

sorrow is always before me.

19. Quoniam iniquitatem meam annuntiabo, et cogitabo pro peccato meo.

19. For I will confess mine iniquity: and will think upon my sin.

20. Inimici autem mei vivunt, et confirmati sunt super me: et multiplicati sunt qui oderunt me inique.

20. But mine enemies live, and are strengthened against me: and they that hate me wrongfully are multiplied.

21. Qui retribuunt mala pro bonis, detrahebant mihi, quoniam sequebar bonitatem.

21. They that render evil for good spake against me, because I followed goodness.

22. Ne derelinquas me, Domine Deus meus; ne discesseris a me.

22. Forsake me not, O Lord my God: go not Thou far from me.

23. Intende in adjutorium meum, Domine, Deus salutis meæ.

23. Haste Thee to my help, O Lord God of my salvation.

Gloria, etc.

Glory, etc.

4. Psalm L. Miserere

1. David prays for remission of his sins; 8. for perfect sanctity. 17. Sacrifice without contrition will not pardon sin. 19. David prays for the exaltation of the Church.

1. MISERERE mei Deus: secundum magnam misericordiam Tuam.

1. HAVE mercy upon me, O God; according to Thy great mercy.

2. Et secundum multitudinem miserationum Tuarum: dele iniquitatem meam.

2. And according to the multitude of Thy tender mercies: blot out my iniquity.

3. Amplius lava me ab iniquitate mea: et a peccato meo munda me.

4. Quoniam, iniquitatem meam ego cognosco: et peccatum meum contra me est semper.

5. Tibi soli peccavi, et malum coram Te feci: ut justificeris in sermonibus Tuis, et vincas cum judicaris.

6. Ecce enim in iniquitatibus conceptus sum: et in peccatis concepit me mater mea.

7. Ecce enim veritatem dilexisti: incerta et occulta sapientiæ Tuæ manifestasti mihi.

8. Asperges me hyssopo, et mundabor: lavabis me, et super nivem dealbabor.

9. Auditui meo dabis gaudium et lætitiam: et exultabunt ossa humiliata.

10. Averte faciam Tuam a peccatis meis: et omnes iniquitates meas dele.

3. Wash me more yet from my iniquity: and cleanse me from my sin.

4. For I acknowledge my iniquity: and my sin is always before me.

5. Against Thee only have I sinned, and done evil in Thy sight: that Thou mayest be justified in Thy words, and mayest overcome when Thou art judged.

6. For behold, I was conceived in iniquities: and in sins did my mother conceive me.

7. For behold, Thou hast loved truth: the uncertain and hidden things of Thy wisdom Thou hast made manifest unto me.

8. Thou shalt sprinkle me with hyssop, and I shall be cleansed: Thou shalt wash me, and I shall be made whiter than snow.

9. Thou shalt make me hear of joy and gladness: and the bones that were humbled shall rejoice.

10. Turn away Thy face from my sins and blot out all my iniquities.

11. Cor mundum crea in me, Deus: et spiritum rectum innova in visceribus meis.

12. Ne projicias me a facie Tua: et Spiritum sanctum Tuum ne auferas a me.

13. Redde mihi lætitiam salutaris Tui: et spiritu principali confirma me.

14. Docebo iniquos vias Tuas; et impii ad Te convertentur.

15. Libera me de sanguinibus, Deus, Deus salutis meæ: et exultabit lingua mea justitiam Tuam.

16. Domine, labia mea aperies: et os meum annuntiabit laudem Tuam.

17. Quoniam si voluisses sacrificium, dedissem utique: holocaustis non delectaberis.

18. Sacrificium Deo spiritus contribulatus: cor contritum et humiliatum, Deus non despicies.

11. Create in me a clean heart, O God: and renew a right spirit within my bosom.

12. Cast me not away from Thy presence: and take not Thy holy Spirit from me.

13. Restore unto me the joy of Thy salvation: and strengthen me with a perfect spirit.

14. I will teach the unjust Thy ways: and the wicked shall be converted unto Thee.

15. Deliver me from blood-guiltiness, O God, Thou God of my salvation: and my tongue shall extol Thy justice.

16. Thou shalt open my lips, O Lord: and my mouth shall declare Thy praise.

17. For if Thou hadst desired sacrifice, I would surely have given it: with burnt offerings Thou wilt not be delighted.

18. The sacrifice of God is an afflicted spirit: a contrite and humble heart, O God, Thou wilt not despise.

19. Benigne fac, Domine, in bona voluntate Tua Sion: ut ædificentur muri Jerusalem.

20. Tunc acceptabis sacrificium justitiæ, oblationes, et holocausta: tunc imponent super altare Tuum vitulos.

Gloria, etc.

19. Deal favorably, O Lord, in Thy good-will with Sion: that the walls of Jerusalem may be built up.

20. Then shalt Thou accept the sacrifice of justice, oblations, and whole burnt offerings: then shall they lay calves upon Thine altars.

Glory, etc.

5. Psalm CI. Domine Exaudi

1. The extreme affliction of the Psalmist. 12. The eternity and the mercy of God. 19. To be recorded and praised by future generations. 26. The unchangeableness of God.

1. DOMINE, exaudi orationem meam, et clamor meus ad Te veniat.

2. Non avertas faciem Tuam a me; in quacumque die tribulor, inclina ad me aurem tuam.

3. In quacumque die invocavero Te, velociter exaudi me.

4. Quia defecerunt sicut fumus dies mei, et ossa mea sicut cremium aruerunt.

5. Percussus sum ut fœnum, et aruit cor meum,

1. O LORD, hear my prayer: and let my cry come unto Thee.

2. Turn not away Thy face from me: in the day when I am in trouble, incline Thine ear unto me.

3. In what day soever I shall call upon Thee: oh, hearken unto me speedily.

4. For my days are vanished like smoke: and my bones are dried up like fuel for the fire.

5. I am smitten as grass, and my heart is withered:

quia oblitus sum comedere panem meum.

6. A voce gemitus mei adhæsit os meum carni meæ.

7. Similis factus sum pellicano solitudinis; factus sum nycticorax in domicilio.

8. Vigilavi, et factus sum sicut passer solitarius in tecto.

9. Tota die exprobrabant mihi inimici mei, et qui laudabant me adversum me jurabant:

10. Quia cinerem tamquam panem manducabam, et potum meum cum fletu miscebam.

11. A facie iræ et indignationis Tuæ, quia elevans allisisti me.

12. Dies mei sicut umbra declinaverunt, et· ego sicut fœnum arui.

13. Tu autem, Domine, in æternum permanes, et memoriale Tuum in generationem et generationem.

14. Tu exurgens mis-

for I have forgotten to eat my bread.

6. Through the voice of my groaning: my bones have cleaved to my flesh.

7. I am become like a pelican in the wilderness: and like a night-raven in the house.

8. I have watched: and am become like a sparrow that sitteth alone on the housetop.

9. Mine enemies reviled me all the day long: and they that praised me have sworn together against me.

10. For I have eaten ashes as it were bread; and mingled my drink with weeping.

11. Because of Thine indignation and wrath: for Thou hast lifted me up and cast me down. .

12. My days are gone down like a shadow: and I am withered like grass.

13. But Thou, O Lord, endurest forever: and Thy memorial to all generations.

14. Thou shalt arise and

creberis Sion, quia tempus miserendi ejus, quia venit tempus.

15. Quoniam placuerunt servis Tuis lapides ejus, et terræ ejus miserebuntur.

16. Et timebunt gentes nomen Tuum, Domine, et omnes reges terræ gloriam Tuam.

17. Quia ædificavit Dominus Sion, et videbitur in gloria Sua.

18. Respexit in orationem humilium, et non sprevit precem eorum.

19. Scribantur hæc in generatione altera, et populus qui creabitur laudabit Dominum.

20. Quia prospexit de excelso sancto Suo, Dominus de cælo in terram aspexit.

21. Ut audiret gemitus compeditorum, ut solveret filios interemptorum.

22. Ut annuntient in Sion nomen Domini, et

have mercy upon Sion: for it is time that Thou have mercy upon her, yea, the time is come.

15. For Thy servants delighted in her stones: and they shall have compassion on the earth thereof.

16. The Gentiles shall fear Thy name, O Lord. and all the kings of the earth Thy glory.

17. For the Lord hath built up Sion: and He shall be seen in His glory.

18. He hath had regard unto the prayer of the lowly: and hath not despised their petition.

19. Let these things be written for another generation: and the people that shall be created shall praise the Lord.

20. For He hath looked down from His high, holy place, from heaven hath the Lord looked upon the earth.

21. That He might hear the groaning of them that are in fetters: that He might deliver the children of the slain.

22. That they may declare the name of the Lord

laudem ejus in Jerusalem.

23. In conveniendo populos in unum, et reges ut serviant Domino.

24. Respondit ei in via virtutis suæ: Paucitatem dierum meorum nuntia mihi.

25. Ne revoces me in dimidio dierum eorum; in generationem et generationem anni Tui.

26. Initio Tu, Domine, terram fundasti; et opera manuum Tuarum sunt cœli.

27. Ipsi peribunt, Tu autem permanes; et omnes sicut vestimentum veterascent.

28. Et sicut opertorium mutabis eos, et mutabuntur; Tu autem idem ipse es, et anni Tui non deficient.

29. Filii servorum tuorum habitabunt; et semen eorum in sæculum dirigetur.

Gloria, etc.

---

in Sion: and His praise in Jerusalem.

23. When the people assemble together: and kings to serve the Lord.

24. He answered him in the way of his strength: Declare unto me the fewness of my days.

25. Call me not away in the midst of my days: Thy years are unto generation and generation.

26. In the beginning, O Lord, Thou foundedst the earth: and the heavens are the work of Thy hands.

27. They shall perish but Thou endurest: and they all shall grow old as a garment.

28. And as a vesture shalt Thou change them, and they shall be changed; but Thou art the same, and Thy years shall not fail.

29. The children of Thy servants shall continue; and their seed be directed forever.

Glory, etc.

6. Psalm CXXX. De Profundis

The just, afflicted by his sins, implores the divine mercy.

1. DE PROFUNDIS clamavi ad Te, Domine: Domine, exaudi vocem meam.

2. Fiant aures Tuæ intendentes in vocem deprecationis meæ.

3. Si iniquitates observaveris, Domine: Domine, quis sustinebit?

4. Quia apud Te propitiatio est: et propter legem Tuam sustinui Te, Domine.

5. Sustinuit anima mea in verbo ejus: speravit anima mea in Domino.

6. A custodia matutina usque ad noctem: speret Israel in Domino.

7. Quia apud Dominum misericordia: et copiosa apud eum redemptio.

8. Et ipse redimet Israel, ex omnibus iniquitatibus ejus.

Gloria, etc.

1. OUT of the depths have I cried unto Thee, O Lord: Lord, hear my voice.

2. Let Thine ears be attentive to the voice of my supplication.

3. If Thou, O Lord, wilt mark iniquities: Lord, who shall abide it?

4. For with Thee there is merciful forgiveness: and because of Thy law I have waited for Thee, O Lord.

5. My soul hath waited on His word: my soul hath hoped in the Lord.

6. From the morning watch even until night let Israel hope in the Lord.

7. For with the Lord there is mercy; and with Him is plenteous redemption.

8. And He shall redeem Israel from all his iniquities.

Glory, etc.

When said for the departed:

Requiem, etc.

Eternal rest give, etc.

7. Psalm CXLII. Domine Exaudi

1. **David** prays for favor in judgment. *3.* He represents his distress. He prays for grace; *9.* for deliverance; *10.* for sanctification; *12.* for victory over his enemies.

1. **D**OMINE, exaudi orationem meam; auribus percipe obsecrationem meam in veritate Tua; exaudi me in Tua justitia.

2. Et non intres in judicium cum servo Tuo, quia non justificabitur in conspectu tuo omnis vivens.

3. Quia persecutus est inimicus animam meam, humiliavit in terra vitam meam: collocavit me in obscuris, sicut mortuos sæculi.

4. Et anxiatus est super me spiritus meus; in me turbatum est cor meum.

5. Memor fui dierum antiquorum; meditatus sum in omnibus operibus Tuis, in factis manuum Tuarum meditabar.

6. Expandi manus meas ad Te; anima mea sicut terra sine aqua Tibi.

1. **H**EAR my prayer, O Lord; give ear to my supplication in Thy truth; hearken unto me for Thy justice' sake.

2. And enter not into judgment with Thy servant: for in Thy sight shall no man living be justified.

3. For the enemy hath persecuted my soul: he hath brought my life down unto the ground. He hath made me to dwell in darkness, as those that have been long dead.

4. And my spirit is vexed within me, my heart within me is troubled.

5. I remembered the days of old, I meditated all Thy works: I have mused upon the works of Thy hands.

6. I have stretched forth my hands unto Thee; my soul gaspeth unto Thee, as a land where no water is.

7. Velociter exaudi me, Domine; defecit spiritus meus.

8. Non avertas faciem Tuam a me, et similis ero descendentibus in lacum.

9. Auditam fac mihi mane misericordiam Tuam, quia in Te speravi.

10. Notam fac mihi viam in qua ambulem, quia ad Te levavi animam meam.

11. Eripe me de inimicis meis, Domine, ad Te confugi.

12. Doce me facere voluntatem tuam, quia Deus meus es Tu. Spiritus Tuus bonus deducet me in terram rectam.

13. Propter nomen Tuum, Domine, vivificabis me; in æquitate Tua, educes de tribulatione animam meam.

14. Et in misericordia Tua disperdes inimicos meos, et perdes omnes qui tribulant animam meam, quoniam ego servus Tuus sum.

Gloria, etc.

7. Hear me speedily, O Lord; my spirit hath fainted away.

8. Turn not away Thy face from me: lest I be like unto them that go down into the pit.

9. Make me to hear Thy mercy in the morning: for in Thee have I hoped.

10. Make me to know the way wherein I should walk: for to Thee have I lifted up my soul.

11. Deliver me from mine enemies, O Lord, unto Thee have I fled.

12. Teach me to do Thy will, for Thou art my God. Thy good spirit shall lead me into the right land.

13. For Thy name's sake, O Lord, Thou shalt quicken me in Thy justice. Thou shalt bring my soul out of trouble.

14. And in Thy mercy Thou shalt destroy mine enemies. Thou shalt destroy all them that afflict my soul: for I am Thy servant.

Glory, etc.

Ant. Ne reminiscaris Domine, delicta nostra vel parentum nostrorum, neque vindictam sumas de peccatis nostris.	*Ant.* Remember not, O Lord, our offenses, nor those of our parents; and take not revenge of our sins.

Indulgence of 50 days. — St. Pius V, April 5, 1571.

The Psalms

Excellent Spiritual Reading

DURING many weeks of extreme languor the Psalms have never been out of my hands. I was never wearied of reading over and over those sublime lamentations, those flights of hope, those supplications full of love, which answer to all the wants and all the miseries of human nature. It is nearly three thousand years since a king composed those songs in his days of repentance and desolation; and we still find in them the expression of our deepest anguish, and the consolation of our sorrows. The priest recites them daily; thousands of monasteries have been founded in order that these psalms might be chanted at every hour, and that this voice of supplication might never be silent. The Gospel alone is superior to the hymns of David, and this only because it is their fulfilment, because all the yearnings, all the ardors, all the holy impatience of the prophet find their accomplishment in the Redeemer issued of his race. — OZANAM.

An excellent *daily* spiritual reading would be a combination of extracts from Holy Scripture, "The Imitation of Christ" by Thomas á Kempis, and "The Lives of the Saints" (or St. Francis de Sales' "Devout Life"). A very serviceable book for this purpose is Le Masson's "Spiritual Reading for Every Day," edited by Kenelm Digby Best of the Oratory of Saint Philip Neri.

Books That Have Had the Most Powerful and Lasting Influence on Our Life

IF WE were asked to name the books that influenced us most in the whole course of our life, and if in our reply to this question we were permitted to name only *four* books, we would mention the following:

1. The Holy Bible, and especially the New Testament and the Psalms.

2. Butler's "Lives of the Saints." We have special pleasure, however, in recommending to the pious reader Bowden's "Miniature Lives of the Saints."

3. "The Imitation of Christ" (or "The Following of Christ") by Thomas á Kempis.

4. St. Ignatius Loyola's "Book of the Spiritual Exercises."

We would add to these, if we were permitted to name just one more book, St. Francis de Sales' "Devout Life."

We owe a vast debt of gratitude also to St. Alphonsus de Liguori, especially for his "Devout Reflections on Various Spiritual Subjects," on "The Passion of Our Lord," on "The Love of Our Lord Jesus Christ," on "The Holy Eucharist," and on "The Blessed Virgin Mary."

Concerning the two first-mentioned works of St. Alphonsus, we read in the preface to "Devout Reflections on Various Spiritual Subjects," newly translated from the Italian by Father Edmund Vaughan, C.SS.R.:

"The 'Devout Reflections on Spiritual Subjects' have been re-translated, and are here published separate, in a convenient form. The 'Reflections on the Passion' will also be brought out in the same style.

"They were both composed and published together by the saint, when he was in the seventy-eighth year of his age. He was still governing the episcopal see of St. Agatha, in the kingdom of Naples: but, so broken down i

health, and so crippled by most painful infirmities, that it
seemed a miracle that he should still be able, not only to
watch over the affairs of his diocese, but even apply himself
to the composition of several important and learned works.

"Referring to these labors, his learned and pious biog-
rapher, Cardinal Villecourt, remarks: 'In the midst of
all his sufferings of body and mind, St. Alphonsus profited
by every moment of leisure, to contribute by his writings
to the glory of God. Thus, in 1773, he published "Reflections on the Passion of Jesus Christ," and in the same
volume a number of "Devout Reflections on Spiritual
Subjects." Every one saw in this little work a lodestone,
as it were, to attract the hearts of men, and unite them to
that of Jesus Christ.'

"St. Alphonsus himself wrote to one of his penitents:
'As regards the book on the Passion, I myself make use of
it every day. I read likewise, every day, something in the
second book, entitled: "Devout Reflections." I should
wish you to do the same; for I have composed it especially
for those who desire to give themselves entirely to God.'

"To such recommendations nothing could be added.
And we can only hope and pray that this little work, one
of the last written by St. Alphonsus, may be as fruitful of
grace, now, and in this our country, as it was in his native
land, when first it came forth from the pen of the holy
Doctor."

Daily Spiritual Food

Scripture Maxims

A DAILY spiritual bouquet, a sweet little nosegay of devotion, may be gathered from such maxims of the Holy Scripture as those which follow. The Psalms, the Proverbs, the Epistles, and especially the Gospels are replete with beautiful and sublime thoughts, which tend to elevate the soul, to console, encourage, and strengthen us in our daily trials, and to help us onward in the way of salvation.

I

BUT one thing is necessary (*Luke* x. 42).
You can not serve God and Mammon. . . . Lay up to yourselves treasures in heaven; for where thy treasure is there is thy heart also. . . . Be not solicitous for your life, what you shall eat, nor for your body, what you shall put on. Seek ye first the Kingdom of God and His justice, and all these things shall be added unto you (*Matt.* vi).

The fashion of this world passeth away (1 *Cor.* vii. 31).

There is but one step between me and death (1 *Kings* xx. 3).

Eye hath not seen, nor ear heard, neither hath it entered into the heart of man what things God hath prepared for them that love Him (1 *Cor.* ii. 9).

II

WHAT shall it profit a man, if he gain the whole world and suffer the loss of his soul? Or what shall a man give in exchange for his soul?

For he that shall be ashamed of me and of my words in this adulterous and sinful generation: the Son of man also

647

will be ashamed of him, when He shall come in the glory of His Father with the holy angels.

If any man will follow Me, let him deny himself, and take up his cross and follow Me (*Mark* viii.).

III

LET him that thinketh himself to stand, take heed lest he fall (1 *Cor.* x. 12).

But this know ye, that if the householder did know at what hour the thief would come, he would surely watch and would not suffer his house to be broken open.

Be you then also ready; for at what hour you think not, the Son of man will come.

Unto whomsoever much is given, of him much shall be required (*Luke* xii.).

What things a man shall sow, those also shall he reap.

In doing good let us not fail; for in due time we shall reap, not failing (*Gal.* vi. 8, 9).

Those who do not obey the Gospel shall suffer eternal punishment (2 *Thess.* i. 9).

IV

ALL things are naked and open to His eyes (*Heb.* iv. 13).

Walk before Me and be perfect (*Gen.* xvii. 1).

This is the will of God, your sanctification (1 *Thess.* iv. 3).

If you love Me, keep My commandments (*John* xiv. 15).

I meditated on Thy commandments, which I have loved (*Ps.* cxviii. 47).

V

TAKE heed thou never consent to sin, nor transgress the commandments of the Lord our God. Give alms out of thy substance, and turn not away thy face from any poor person: for so it shall come to pass that the face of the Lord shall not be turned away from Thee. According to thy ability be merciful. If thou have much, give abundantly: if thou have little, take care even so to bestow willingly a little. For thus thou storest up to thyself a good reward for the day of necessity. For alms deliver from all sin, and from death, and will not suffer the soul to go into darkness. Alms shall be a great confidence before the most high God, to all them that give it. Take heed to keep thyself, my son, from all fornication. Never suffer pride to reign in thy mind, or in thy words: for from it all perdition took its beginning. If any man hath done any work for thee, immediately pay him his hire, and let not the wages of thy hired servant stay with thee at all. See thou never do to another what thou wouldst hate to have done to thee by another (*Tob.* iv).

VI

JUDGE not that you may not be judged; for with what judgment you judge, you shall be judged, and with what measure you mete, it shall be measured to you again.

And why seest thou the mote that is in thy brother's eye, and seest not the beam that is in thy own eye. Thou hypocrite, cast out first the beam out of thy own eye, and then shalt thou see to cast out the mote out of thy brother's eye (*Matt.* vii. 1–5).

VII

ALL things, therefore, whatsoever you would that men should do to you, do you also to them (*Matt.* vii. 12).

VIII

BEWARE of false prophets: by their fruits you shall know them. Do men gather grapes of thorns or figs of thistles? Even so every good tree bringeth forth good fruit and the evil tree bringeth forth evil fruit.

Not every one that saith to Me, Lord, Lord, shall enter

into the kingdom of heaven, but he that doth the will of my Father Who is in heaven, he shall enter into the kingdom of heaven (*Matt.* vii. 15–21).

II

ACCORDING to Him, that hath called you, Who is holy, be you also in all manner of conversation holy, because it is written: *You shall be holy, for I am holy;* and if you invoke as *Father* Him Who without respect of persons judgeth according to every one's work, converse in fear during the time of your sojourning here. Purifying your souls in the obedience of charity, with a brotherly love, from a sincere heart love one another earnestly (1 *Peter* i. 15–22).

I

MASTER, which is the great commandment in the law? Jesus said to him: Thou shalt love the Lord thy God with thy whole heart, and with thy whole soul, and with thy whole mind.

This is the greatest and the first commandment. And the second is like to this: Thou shalt love thy neighbor as thyself (*Matt.* xxii. 36–39).

II

CHARITY is patient, is kind. Charity envieth not, dealeth not perversely, is not puffed up, is not ambitious, seeketh not her own, is not provoked to anger, thinketh no evil, rejoiceth not in iniquity, but rejoiceth with the truth, beareth all things, believeth all things, hopeth all things, endureth all things. Charity never falleth away (1 *Cor.* xiii. 4–8).

III

I SAY to you: Love your enemies; do good to them that hate you; and pray for them that persecute and calumniate you, that you may be the children of your

Father Who is in heaven, Who maketh His sun to rise upon
the good and bad, and raineth upon the just and unjust
(*Matt.* v. 44, 45).

XLIII

IF YOU will forgive men their offenses, your heavenly
Father will forgive you also your offenses. But if
you will not forgive men, neither will your Father forgive
you your offenses (*Matt.* vi. 14, 15).

If you love them that love you, what reward shall you
have? Do not even the publicans this? And if you
salute your brethren only, what do you more? Do not
also the heathens this? Be you, therefore, perfect, as also
your heavenly Father is perfect (*Matt.* v. 46–48).

XLIV

O HOW have I loved Thy law, O Lord; it is my meditation all the day. By Thy commandments I have
had understanding: therefore have I hated every way of
iniquity.

Thy word is a lamp to my feet, and a light to my paths.

I am Thine; save Thou me, for I have sought Thy
justification. Much peace have they that love Thy law.
Let Thy hand be with me to save me: for I have chosen Thy
precepts (*Ps.* cxviii. 97, 104, 105).

XLV

INSTEAD of a friend become not an enemy to thy neighbor. A sweet word multiplieth friends, and appeaseth
enemies, and a gracious tongue in a good man aboundeth.
Be in peace with many, but let one of a thousand be thy
counsellor. If thou wouldst get a friend, try him before
thou takest him, and do not credit him easily. For there
is a friend for his own occasion, and he will not abide in the
day of thy trouble. And there is a friend that turneth to
enmity: and there is a friend that will disclose hatred

and strife and reproaches; and there is a friend a companion at the table, and he will not abide in the day of distress. A faithful friend is a strong defense: and he that hath found him, hath found a treasure. Nothing can oe compared to a faithful friend, and no weight of gold and silver is able to countervail the goodness of his fidelity. A faithful friend is the medicine of life and immortality: and they that fear the Lord, shall find Him. He that feareth God, shall likewise have good friendship: because according to him shall his friend be (*Ecclus.* vi. 1-17).

XVI

MY SON, do thy works in meekness, and thou shalt be beloved above the glory of men. The greater thou art, the more humble thyself in all things, and thou shalt find grace before God: for great is the power of God alone, and He is honored by the humble (*Ecclus.* iii. 19-21).

Jesus said: You know that the princes of the Gentiles lord it over them; and they that are the greater exercise power upon them. It shall not be so among you; but whosoever will be the greater among you, let him be your minister: And he that will be first among you, shall be your servant. Even as the Son of man is not come to be ministered unto, but to minister, and to give His life a redemption for many (*Matt.* xx. 25-28).

You call me Master and Lord; and you say well, for so I am. If, then, I being your Lord and Master, have washed your feet, you also ought to wash one another's feet. For I have given you an example, that as I have done, so you do also (*John* xiii. 13-15).

XVII

REMEMBER, O man, that thou art dust, "and unto dust thou shalt return" (*Gen.* iii. 19).

We have not here a lasting city; but we seek one that is to come (*Heb.* xiii. 14).

Man, when he shall be dead and stripped and consumed, I pray you, where is he? (*Job* xiv. 10).

We brought nothing into this world, and certainly we can carry nothing out of it (1 *Tim.* vi. 7).

It is appointed unto men once to die (*Heb.* xi. 27).

If the tree fall to the south, or to the north, in what place soever it shall fall, there it shall be (*Eccles.* xi. 3). [Reflection: "Vanity of vanities, and all is vanity" (*Eccles.* i. 2) except to love God and to serve Him alone.] (" Imitation of Christ." Bk. I, c. i, v. 3).

Happy he, who always considers the hour of his death and daily prepares himself to die (*Ibid.* xxiii. 2).

O son, observe the time, and fly from evil (*Ecclus.* iv. 23). [Value it highly, make good use of it.]

Soon, very soon, time shall be no more for you (*Apoc.* x. 6).

Defraud not thyself of the good day, and let not the part of a good gift overpass thee (*Ecclus.* xiv. 14).

Take heed to yourselves, lest perhaps your hearts be overcharged with surfeiting and drunkenness, and the cares of this life, and that day come upon you suddenly (*Luke* xxi. 34).

Wine is a luxurious thing and drunkenness riotous; whosoever is delighted therewith, shall not be wise (*Prov.* xx. i).

The kingdom of God is not meat and drink (*Rom.* xiv. 17).

XVIII

O HOW beautiful is the chaste generation with glory (*Wis.* iv. 1).

Blessed are the undefiled in the way, who walk in the law of the Lord (*Ps.* cxviii. 1).

Blessed are the clean of heart, for they shall see God (*Matt.* v. 8).

Who shall ascend into the mountain of the Lord; or who shall stand in His holy place? The innocent in hands, and clean of heart (*Ps.* xxiii. 3, 4).

Fly fornication. Know you not that your members are the temple of the Holy Ghost, Who is in you, whom you have from God; and you are not your own. For you are bought with a great price. Glorify and bear God in your body (1 *Cor.* vi. 20).

XIX

THE mouth, that belieth, killeth the soul (*Wis.* i. 11). The just shall hate a lying word (*Prov.* xiii. 5).

Jesus said: You are of your father the devil and the desires of your father you will do. Truth is not in him; for he is a liar and the father thereof (*John* viii. 44).

Let your speech be yea, yea: no, no: and that which is over and above these is of evil (*Matt.* v. 37).

A deceitful balance is an abomination before the Lord, and a just weight is His will (*Prov.* xi. 1).

Remove from me the way of iniquity; have mercy on me.

I have chosen the way of truth; I will not forget Thy words (*Ps.* cxviii).

XX

A JOYFUL mind maketh age flourishing; a sorrowful spirit drieth up the bones.

He that is of a perverse heart shall not find good: and he that perverteth his tongue shall fall into evil.

He that setteth bounds to his words is wise. Even a fool, if he will hold his peace, shall be counted wise.

What doth it avail a fool to have riches, seeing he can not buy wisdom?

It is better to meet a bear robbed of her whelps, than a fool trusting in his own folly.

Better is a dry morsel with joy, than a house full of victims with strife.

As silver is tried by fire, and gold in the furnace, so the Lord trieth the hearts.

The evil man obeyeth an unjust tongue, and the deceitful hearkeneth to lying lips.

He that concealeth a transgression seeketh friendships; he, that repeateth it again, separateth friends.

He that maketh his house high seeketh a downfall; and he that refuseth to learn shall fall into evils.

He that is a friend loveth at all times, and a brother is proved in distress (*Prov.* xvii).

XXI

LORD, who shall dwell in Thy tabernacle? Or who shall rest in thy holy hill?

He that walketh without blemish, and worketh justice.

He that speaketh truth in his heart, who hath not used deceit in his tongue; nor hath done evil to his neighbor. He that sweareth to his neighbor and deceiveth not; he that hath not put out his money to usury, nor taken bribes against the innocent. He that doth these things shall not be moved forever (*Ps.* xiv).

XXII

O GOD, incline Thy ear unto me and hear my words. Show forth Thy wonderful mercies, Thou who savest them that trust in Thee.

From them that resist Thy right hand keep me, as the apple of Thy eye.

Protect me under the shadow of Thy wings; from the face of the wicked who have afflicted me (*Ps.* xvi).

In Thee, O Lord, have I hoped, let me never be confounded. Be Thou unto me a God, a protector, and a house of refuge, to save me (*Ps.* xxx).

The Lord ruleth me (The Lord is my Shepherd) and I shall want nothing. He hath set me in a place of pasture. Though I should walk in the midst of the shadow of death, I will fear no evils, for Thou art with me. And Thy mercy will follow me all the days of my life. (*Ps.* xxii).

XXIII

ASK, and it shall be given unto you; seek, and you shall find: knock, and it shall be opened to you (*Matt.* vii. 7). How much more will your Father, Who is in heaven, give good things to them that ask Him? (*Ibid.* vii. 11). For every one that asketh, receiveth; and he that seeketh, findeth (*Ibid.* vii. 8). If you shall ask Me anything in My name, that will I do (*John* xiv. 14). You shall ask whatever you will, and it shall be done unto you (*Ibid* xv. 7). Amen, amen, I say to you, if you ask the Father anything in My name, He will give it you (*Ibid.* xvi. 23). I can do all things in Him Who strengtheneth me (*Phil.* iv. 13). The Lord is nigh unto all them that call upon Him; to all that call upon Him in truth. He will do the will of them that fear Him, and He will hear their prayer and save them (*Ps.* cxliv. 18, 19). "By prayer," says St. Bonaventure, "is obtained the possession of every good, and deliverance from every evil."

He hath regard to the prayer of the humble (*Ps.* ci. 18). God resisteth the proud, and giveth grace to the humble (*Jas.* iv. 6). The prayer of him that humbleth himself shall pierce the clouds; . . . and he will not depart till the Most High behold (*Ecclus.* xxxv. 21). A contrite and humble heart, O God, Thou wilt not despise (*Ps.* l. 19). Thou Who savest them that trust in Thee (*Ibid.* xvi. 7). Because he hath hoped in Me, . . . I will deliver him and I will glorify him (*Ibid.* xc. 14, 15). But they that hope in the Lord, shall renew their strength (*Is.* xl. 31). No one hath hoped in the Lord, and hath been confounded (*Ecclus.* ii. 11). They that trust in the Lord, shall be as Mount Sion (*Ps.* cxxiv. 1). Let Thy mercy, O Lord, be upon us, as we have hoped in Thee (*Ps.* xxxii. 22).

XXIV

LEARN of Me, for I am meek and humble of heart; and you shall find rest for your souls (*Matt.* xi. 29).

Bear ye one another's burdens, and so you shall fulfil the law of Christ (*Gal*. vi. 2).

My son, keep thy soul in meekness (*Ecclus*. x. 31).

In your patience you shall possess your souls (*Luke* xxi. 19).

If doing well you suffer patiently, this is thanksworthy before God; for unto this are you called, because Christ also suffered for us, leaving you an example that you should follow His steps (1 *Peter* ii. 19).

XXV

MAN is born to labor, and the bird to fly (*Job* v. 7). In the sweat of thy face thou shalt eat thy bread (*Gen*. iii. 19).

For whom do I labor and defraud my soul of good things? (*Eccles*. iv. 8).

Whether you eat or drink, or whatsoever else you do; do all things for the glory of God (1 *Cor*. x. 31).

Whatsoever you do in word or in work, do all in the name of the Lord Jesus Christ (*Col*. iii. 17).

He hath done all things well (*Mark* vii. 37).

Not serving to the eye as it were pleasing to men, but as the servants of Christ, doing the will of God (*Eph*. vi. 7).

He that feareth man shall quickly fall (*Prov*. xxix. 25).

Whatsoever thy hand is able to do, do it earnestly (*Eccles*. ix. 10).

XXVI

THE attire of the body, and the laughter of the teeth, and the gait of the man, show what he is (*Eccles*. xix. 27).

The heart of fools is in their mouth, and the mouth of wise men is in their heart (*Eccles*. xxi. 29).

He that uses many words shall hurt his own soul (*Eccles*. xx. 8).

Be not hasty in a feast. Use as a frugal man the things

that are set before thee. Reach not thy hand out first of all; and be not the first to ask for a drink (*Eccles.* xxxi. 17, 21).

Be wise as serpents and simple as doves (*Matt.* x. 16).

Rejoice in the Lord always; again I say, rejoice. Let your modesty be known to all men (*Phil.* iv. 4, 5).

Rejoice with them that rejoice, weep with them that weep (*Rom.* xii. 15).

Let love be without dissimulation, hating that which is evil, cleaving to that which is good (*Rom.* xii. 9).

Be not wise in your own conceit.

If it be possible, as much as is in you, have peace with all men (*Rom.* xii. 16, 18).

XXVII

A GOOD name is better than great riches.

He that soweth iniquity shall reap evils.

He that is inclined to mercy shall be blessed (*Prov.* xxii).

Honor thy father, and forget not the groanings of thy mother.

Remember that thou hadst not been born but through them: and make a return to them as they have done for thee.

With all thy soul fear the Lord, and reverence His priests.

With all thy strength love Him that made thee: and forsake not His ministers.

Honor God with all thy soul, and give honor to the priests, and purify thyself with thy alms.

And stretch out thy hand to the poor, that thy expiation and thy blessing may be perfected.

Be not wanting in comforting them that weep, and walk with them that mourn.

Be not slow to visit the sick: for by these things thou shalt be confirmed in love.

In all thy works remember thy last end, and thou shalt never sin.

Strive not with a man that is full of tongue, and heap not wood upon his fire.

Despise not a man that turneth away from sin, nor reproach him therewith: remember that we are all worthy of reproof.

Despise not a man in his old age: for we also shall become old.

Rejoice not at the death of thine enemy: knowing that we all die, and are not willing that others should rejoice at our death.

Before thou inquire, blame no man: and when thou hast inquired, reprove justly.

Before thou hear, answer not a word, and interrupt not others in the midst of their discourse.

Strive not in a matter which doth not concern thee, and sit not in judgment with sinners.

Praise not a man for his beauty; neither despise a man for his look.

Praise not a man before he speaketh, for this is the trial of men.

Be not surety above thy power, and if thou be surety, think as if thou wert to pay it.

Open not thy heart to every man: lest he repay thee with an evil turn, and speak reproachfully to thee.

Pride is hateful before God and men: and all iniquity of nations is execrable.

For when a man shall die, he shall inherit serpents, and beasts, and worms.

The beginning of the pride of man is to fall off from God.

Because his heart is departed from Him that made him: for pride is the beginning of all sin; he that holdeth it shall be filled with maledictions, and it shall ruin him in the end.

God hath abolished the memory of the proud, and hath preserved the memory of them that are humble in mind.

Pride was not made for men: nor wrath for the race of women.

The fear of God is the glory of the rich, *and* of the honorable, and of the poor.

Despise not a just man that is poor, and do not magnify a sinful man that is rich.

The great man, and the judge, and the mighty is in honor: and there is none greater than he that feareth God.

Believe not every word. There is one that slippeth with the tongue, but not from his heart.

For who is there that hath not offended with his tongue?

Wine and women make wise men fall off.

How sufficient is a little wine for a man well taught (*Ecclus.*).

XXVIII

BETTER is a poor man who is sound, and strong of constitution, than a rich man who is weak and afflicted with evils.

There is no riches above the riches of the health of the body: and there is no pleasure above the joy of the heart.

Give not up thy soul to sadness, and afflict not thyself in thy own counsel.

The joyfulness of the heart is the life of a man, and a neverfailing treasure of holiness: and the joy of a man is length of life.

Have pity on thy own soul, pleasing God, and contain thyself: gather up thy heart in His holiness: and drive away sadness far from thee.

He that loveth gold, shall not be justified: and he that followeth after corruption shall be filled with it.

Many have been brought to fall for gold, and the beauty thereof hath been their ruin.

Gold is a stumbling-block to them that sacrifice to it: woe to them that eagerly follow after it, and every fool shall perish by it.

Blessed is the rich man that is found without blemish: and that hath not gone after gold, nor put his trust in money nor in treasures.

My son, do thou nothing without counsel, and thou shalt not repent when thou hast done.

The hopes of a man that is void of understanding are vain and deceitful: and dreams lift up fools.

Honor the physician for the need thou hast of him: for the Most High hath created him. For all healing is from God, and he shall receive gifts of the king.

The Most High hath created medicines out of the earth, and a wise man will not abhor them.

Was not bitter water made sweet with wood?

The virtue of these things *is come* to the knowledge of men, and the Most High hath given knowledge to men, that he may be honored in his wonders.

By these he shall cure and shall allay their pains, and *of these* the apothecary shall make sweet confections, and shall make up ointments of health, and of his works there shall be no end.

For the peace of God *is* over all the face of the earth.

My son, in thy sickness neglect not thyself, but pray to the Lord, and he shall heal thee.

Turn away from sin, and order thy hands aright, and cleanse thy heart from all offense.

O Death, how bitter is the remembrance of thee to a man that hath peace in his possessions (*Ecclus.*).

XXXX

COME to Me all you that labor and are burdened, and I will refresh you (*Matt.* xi. 28).

The bread that I will give is My flesh, for the life of the world (*John* vi. 52).

Take ye and eat; this is My body, which shall be delivered for you; this do for the commemoration of Me (1 *Cor.* xi. 24).

He that eateth My flesh, and drinketh My blood, abideth in Me, and I in him (*John* vi. 57).

The words that I have spoken to you are spirit and life (*John* vi. 64).

As the Father hath loved Me, I also have loved you. Abide in My love.

He that loveth Me shall be loved of My Father: and I will love him, and will manifest Myself to him.

You are My friends, if you do the things that I command you.

I will not now call you servants: for the servant knoweth not what his lord doth. But I have called you *friends*, because all things whatsoever I have heard of My Father I have made known to you. Greater love than this no man hath, that a man lay down his life for his friends. Peace I leave with you; My peace I give unto you (*John* xiv. 15).

Taste and see that the Lord is sweet (*Ps.* xxxiii. 9).

The Lord is good to them that hope in Him, to the soul that seeketh Him (*Lam.* iii. 25).

Seek ye the Lord, while He may be found; call upon Him while He is near (*Is.* lv. 6).

The Lord waiteth that He may have mercy on you (*Is.* xxx. 18).

My delights are to be with the children of men (*Prov.* viii. 31).

XXX

CHRIST Himself warns us: Watch ye therefore! for you know not when the lord of the house cometh: at even, or at midnight, or at the cockcrowing, or in the morning (*Mark* xiii. 35). Whilst it is day work well; the night cometh when no man can work (*John* ix. 4); *and that night may come sooner than you think.*

He that shall persevere to the end, he shall be saved (*Matt.* xxiv. 13).

We shall all stand before the judgment-seat of Christ (*Rom.* xiv. 10). It is sure and certain that every man must die; and after death comes judgment (*Heb.* ix. 27).

All things that are done, God will bring to judgment (*Eccles.* xii. 14); yea, says Christ, every idle word that men shall speak, they shall render an account for it in the day of judgment (*Matt.* xii. 36).

O Lord, pierce Thou my flesh with Thy fear; for I am afraid of Thy judgments (*Ps.* cxviii. 120).

If we would judge ourselves, we should not be judged (1 *Cor.* xi. 31).

Show, O Lord, Thy ways to me and teach me Thy paths.

The sins of my youth and my ignorances do not remember.

For Thy name's sake, O Lord, Thou wilt pardon my sin: for it is great (*Ps.* xxiv).

In Thee, O Lord, have I hoped, let me never be confounded.

Let me not be confounded, O Lord, for I have called upon Thee.

Make Thy face to shine upon Thy servant: save me in Thy mercy (*Ps.* xxx).

XXXX

THE souls of the just are in the hand of God, and the torment of death shall not touch them. In the sight of the unwise they seemed to die: and their departure was taken for misery: and their going away from us, for utter destruction: but they are in peace, and though in the sight of men they suffered torments, their hope is full of immortality. Afflicted in few things, in many they shall be well rewarded: because God hath tried them, and found them worthy of Himself. As gold in the furnace He hath proved them, and as a victim of a holocaust He hath received them, and in time there shall be respect had to them. They shall judge nations and rule over people, and their Lord shall reign forever. They that trust in Him shall understand the truth: and they that are faithful in love shall rest in Him; for grace and peace are to His elect. For he that rejecteth wisdom and discipline is unhappy: and their hope is vain, and their labors without fruit, and their works unprofitable. For the fruit of good labors is glorious, and the root of wisdom never faileth. The just man, if he be prevented with death, shall be in rest. For venerable old age is not that of long time, nor counted by the number of years; but the understanding of a man is gray hairs, and a spotless life is old age. He pleased God and was beloved, and living among sinners He was translated. He was taken away lest wickedness should alter his understanding, or deceit beguile his soul. For the bewitching of vanity obscureth good things, and the wandering of concupiscence overturneth the innocent mind. Being made perfect in a short space, he fulfilled a long time. For his soul pleased God; therefore He hastened to bring him out of the midst of iniquities; but the people see this, and understand not, nor lay up such things in their hearts; that the grace of God and His mercy is with His saints, and that He hath respect to His chosen. But the just that is dead condemneth the wicked that are living, and youth soon ended, the long life of the unjust. For they shall see the end of the wise man, and shall not understand what God hath designed for him, and why the Lord hath set him in safety. They shall see him, and shall despise him; but the Lord shall laugh them to scorn. Then shall the just stand with great constancy against those that have afflicted them, and taken away their labors. These seeing it shall be troubled with terrible fear, and shall be amazed at the suddenness of their unexpected salvation, saying within themselves repenting, and groaning for anguish of spirit: — These are they whom we had some time in derision, and for a parable of reproach. We fools esteemed their life madness, and their end without honor. Behold how they are numbered among the children of God, and their lot is among the saints (*Wis.*).

Then shall the King say to them, that shall be on His right hand: Come ye blessed of My Father, possess you the kingdom prepared for you from the foundation of the world.

For I was hungry, and you gave Me to eat; I was thirsty, and you gave Me to drink; I was a stranger, and you took Me in; naked, and you covered Me; sick, and you visited Me. I was in prison, and you came to Me.

Then shall the just answer Him, saying: Lord, when did we see Thee hungry, and fed Thee; thirsty, and gave Thee drink? And when did we see Thee a stranger, and took Thee in? or naked, and covered Thee?

Or when did we see Thee sick or in prison, and came to Thee?

And the King answering shall say to them: Amen, I say to you, as long as you did it to one of these my least brethren, you did it to Me (*Matt.* xxv. 34–40).

Meditate upon these things (1 *Tim.* iv. 15).

🕮ittle Office of the Immaculate Conception

AT MATINS

Eia, mea labia, nunc annuntiate	Come, my lips, and wide proclaim
Laudes et præconia Virginis beatæ.	The Blessed Virgin's spotless fame.

V. DOMINA, in adjutorium meum intende.

V. O LADY! make speed to befriend me.

R. Me de manu hostium potenter defende.

R. From the hands of the enemy mightily defend me.

V. Gloria Patri, etc. Alleluia.

V. Glory be to the Father, etc. Alleluia.

From Septuagesima to Easter, instead of Alleluia *is said:*

Laus tibi, Domine, Rex æternæ gloriæ.

Praise be to Thee, O Lord, King of everlasting glory.

Hymn

SALVE, mundi domina,

HAIL, Queen of the heavens!

Coelorum regina:
Salve, virgo virginum.
Stella matutina.

Hail, Mistress of earth!
Hail, Virgin most pure
Of immaculate birth!

Salve plena gratia,
Clara luce divina:
Mundi in auxilium,
Domina, festina.

Clear Star of the morning
In beauty enshrined!
O Lady! make speed
To the help of mankind.

Ab æterno Dominus
Te præordinavit
Matrem unigeniti
Verbi, quo creavit

Thee God in the depth
Of eternity chose;
And formed thee all fair,
As His glorious spouse;

Terram, pontum, æthera.
Te pulchram ornavit
Sibi sponsam, quæ
In Adam non peccavit.
    Amen.

And called thee His Word's
Own Mother to be,
By Whom He created
The earth, sky, and sea.
    Amen.

V. Elegit eam Deus, et præelegit eam.

R. In tabernaculo suo habitare fecit eam.

V. Domina, protege orationem meam.

R. Et clamor meus ad te veniat.

V. God elected her, and pre-elected her.

R. He made her to dwell in His tabernacle.

V. O Lady! aid my prayer.

R. And let my cry come unto thee.

Oremus

Let us pray

SANCTA Maria, regina cœlorum, mater Domini nostri Jesu Christi, et mundi domina, quæ nullum derelinquis, et nullum despicis: respice me, domina, clementer oculo pietatis, et impetra mihi apud tuum dilectum Filium cunctorum veniam peccatorum:

HOLY Mary, Queen of heaven, Mother of Our Lord Jesus Christ, and Mistress of the world, who forsakest no one, and despisest no one, look upon me, O Lady! with an eye of pity, and entreat for me, of thy beloved Son, the forgiveness of all my sins:

ut qui nunc tuam sanctam et immaculatam conceptionem devoto affectu recolo, æternæ in futurum beatitudinis, bravium capiam, ipso, quem virgo peperisti, donante Domino nostro Jesu Christo: qui cum Patre et Sancto Spiritu vivit et regnat, in Trinitate perfecta, Deus, in sæcula sæculorum.

Amen.

that, as I now celebrate, with devout affection, thy holy and immaculate conception, so, hereafter, I may receive the prize of eternal blessedness, by the grace of Him Whom thou, in virginity, didst bring forth, Jesus Christ our Lord: Who, with the Father and the Holy Ghost, liveth and reigneth, in perfect Trinity, God, world without end. Amen.

V. Domina, protege orationem meam.

R. Et clamor meus ad te veniat.

V. Benedicamus Domino.

R. Deo gratias.

V. Fidelium animæ per misericordiam Dei requiescant in pace.

R. Amen.

V. O Lady! aid my prayer.

R. And let my cry come unto thee.

V. Let us bless the Lord.

R. Thanks be to God.

V. May the souls of the faithful, through the mercy of God, rest in peace.

R. Amen.

AT PRIME

V. DOMINA, in adjutorium meum intende.

R. Me de manu hostium potenter defende.

V. Gloria Patri, etc. Alleluia.

V. O LADY! make speed to befriend me.

R. From the hands of the enemy mightily defend me.

V. Glory be to the Father. etc. Alleluia.

Hymn

SALVE, virgo sapiens,
Domus Deo dicata,
Columna septemplici
Mensaque exornata.

Ab omni contagio
Mundi præservata:
Semper sancta in utero
Matris, ex qua nata.

Tu mater viventium,
Et porta es sanctorum:
Nova stella Jacob,
Domina angelorum.

Zabulo terribilis
Acies castrorum;
Porta et refugium
Sis christianorum.
                    Amen.

V. Ipse creavit illam in Spiritu Sancto.

R. Et effudit illam super omnia opera sua;

V. Domina, protege, etc. (*cum oratione ut supra*).

HAIL, Virgin most wise!
Hail, Deity's shrine!
With seven fair pillars,
And table divine!

Preserved from the guilt
Which hath come on us all!
Exempt, in the womb,
From the taint of the fall!

O new Star of Jacob,
Of angels the Queen!
O Gate of the saints!
O Mother of men!

To Zabulon fearful
As th' embattled array!
Be thou of the faithful
The refuge and stay.
                    Amen.

V. The Lord Himself created her in the Holy Ghost.

R. And poured her out over all His works.

V. O Lady, aid, etc. (*with the prayer as above*).

AT TIERCE

V. Domina, in adjutorium, etc.

V. O Lady, make speed, etc.

Hymn

SALVE, arca fœderis,
Thronus Salomonis,
Arcus pulcher ætheris,
Rubus visionis:

Virga frondens germinis:
Vellus Gedeonis:
Porta clausa numinis,

Favusque Samsonis.

Decebat tam nobilem
Natum præcavere
Ab originali

Labe matris Evæ,

Almam, quam elegerat,
Genitricem vere,
Nulli prorsus sinens
Culpæ subjacere.
                    Amen.

V. Ego in altissimis ha-
bito.

R. Et thronus meus in
columna nubis.

V. Domina, protege, etc.
(cum oratione ut supra).

HAIL, Solomon's
        Throne!
Pure Ark of the law
Fair Rainbow and Bush,
Which the patriarch saw!

Hail, Gedeon's Fleece!
Hail, blossoming Rod!
Samson's sweet Honey-
        comb!
Portal of God!

Well-fitting it was
That a Son so divine
Should preserve from all
        touch
Of original sin,

Nor suffer by smallest
Defect to be stained
That Mother, whom He
For Himself had ordained.
                    Amen.

V. I dwell in the highest.

R. And my throne is on
the pillar of the clouds.

V. O Lady, aid, etc.
(with the prayer as above).

AT SEXT

V. Domina, in adju-
torium, etc.

V. O Lady, make speed,
etc.

Hymn

SALVE, virgo puerpera,
    Templum Trinitatis,
Angelorum gaudium,

Cella puritatis:

Solamen mœrentium,
Hortus voluptatis:
Palma patientiæ,
Cedrus castitatis.

Terra es benedicta
Et sacerdotalis,
Sancta et immunis
Culpæ originalis.

Civitas altissimi,
Porta orientalis:
In te est omnis gratia,
Virgo singularis.
                    Amen.

V. Sicut lilium inter spinas.

R. Sic amica mea inter filias Adæ.

V. Domina, protege, etc. (*cum oratione ut supra*).

HAIL, virginal Mother!
    Hail, purity's Cell!
Fair Shrine, where the Trinity
Loveth to dwell!

Hail, Garden of pleasure!
Celestial Balm!
Cedar of chastity!
Martyrdom's Palm!

Thou Land set apart
From uses profane!
And free from the curse
Which in Adam began!

Thou City of God!
Thou Gate of the east
In thee is all grace
O joy of the blest!
                    Amen.

V. As the lily among the thorns.

R. So is my beloved among the daughters of Adam.

V. O Lady, aid, etc. (*with the prayer as above*).

AT NONE

V. Domina, in adjutorium, etc.

V. O Lady, make speed, etc..

Hymn

SALVE, urbs refugii,
  Turrisque munita

David, propugnaculis
Armisque insignita.

In conceptione
Charitate ignita,
Draconis potestas
Est a te contrita.

O mulier fortis,
Et invicta Judith!
Pulchra Abisag virgo
Verum fovens David!

Rachel curatorem
Ægypti gestavit:
Salvatorem mundi

Maria portavit.
                    Amen.
V. Tota pulchra es,
amica mea.

R. Et macula originalis
numquam fuit in te.

V. Domina, protege, etc.
(*cum oratione ut supra*).

HAIL, City of refuge!
  Hail, David's high
    tower,
With battlements crowned
And girded with power!

Filled at thy conception
With love and with light!
The dragon by thee
Was shorn of his might.

O Woman most valiant!
O Judith thrice blest!
As David was nursed
In fair Abisag's breast;

As the saviour of Egypt
Upon Rachel's knee:
So the world's great Re-
    deemer
Was cherished by thee.
                    Amen.
V. Thou art all fair, my
beloved.

R. And the original
stain was never in thee.

V. O Lady, aid, etc.
(*with the prayer as above*).

AT VESPERS

V. Domina, in adju-
torium, etc.

V. O Lady, make speed,
etc.

Hymn

SALVE, horologium,
Quo, retrogadiatur
Sol in decem lineis;
Verbum incarnatur.

Homo ut ab inferis

Ad summa attollatur,
Immensus ab angelis
Paulo minoratur.

Solis hujus radiis
Maria coruscat;
Consurgens aurora
In conceptu micat.

Lilium inter spinas,
Quæ serpentis conterat
Caput: pulchra ut luna
Errantes colustrat.
　　　　　Amen.
V. Ego feci in cœlis, ut
oriretur lumen indeficiens.
R. Et quasi nebula texi
omnem terram.
V. Domina, protege, etc.
(*cum oratione ut supra*).

HAIL, Dial of Achaz!
On thee the true sun
Told backward the course
Which from old he had run!

And, that man might be
　　　raised,
Submitting to shame,
A little more low
Than the angels became.

Thou, rapt in the blaze
Of His infinite light,
Dost shine as the morn
On the confines of night;

As the moon on the lost
Through obscurity dawns;
The serpent's destroyer!
A lily 'mid thorns!
　　　　　Amen.
V. I made an unfailing
light to arise in heaven.
R. And as a mist I over-
spread the whole earth.
V. O Lady, aid, etc.
(*with the prayer as above*).

AT COMPLINE

V. CONVERTAT
nos, Domina,
tuis precibus placatus Jesus
Christus Filius tuus.

V. MAY Jesus Christ,
thy Son, rec-
onciled by thy prayers, O
Lady! convert our hearts.

R. Et avertat iram suam a nobis.

V. Domina, in adjutorium meum intende.

R. Me de manu hostium potenter defende.

V. Gloria Patri, etc.

R. And turn away His anger from us.

V. O Lady! make speed to befriend me.

R. From the hands of the enemy mightily defend me.

V. Glory be to the Father, etc.

Hymn

SALVE, virgo florens,
Mater illibata,
Regina clementiæ,
Stellis coronata.

Super omnes angelos
Pura, immaculata,
Atque ad regis dexteram
Stans veste deaurata.

Per te, mater gratiæ,
Dulcis spes reorum,
Fulgens stella maris,
Portus naufragorum.

Patens cœli janua
Salus infirmorum
Videamus regem
In aula sanctorum.
Amen.

HAIL, Mother most pure!
Hail, Virgin renowned!
Hail, Queen with the stars,
As a diadem, crowned.

Above all the angels
In glory untold,
Standing next to the King
In a vesture of gold.

O Mother of mercy!
O Star of the wave!
O Hope of the guilty!
O Light of the grave!

Through thee may we come
To the haven of rest;
And see heaven's King
In the courts of the blest!
Amen.

V. OLEUM effusum, Maria, nomen tuum.

V. THY name, O Mary! is as oil poured out.

R. Servi tui dilexerunt te nimis.

V. Domina, protege, etc. (*cum oratione ut supra*).

R. Thy servants have loved thee exceedingly.

V. O Lady, aid, etc. (*with the prayers and versicles as above*).

THE COMMENDATION

SUPPLICES offerimus Tibi, virgo pia, Hæc laudum præconia: Fac nos ut in via

Ducas cursu prospero; Et in agonia

Tu nobis assiste, O dulcis Maria.

R. Deo gratias.

Ant. Hæc est virga in qua nec nodus originalis, nec cortex actualis culpæ fuit.

V. In conceptione tua virgo immaculata fuisti.

R. Ora pro nobis Patrem, cujus Filium peperisti.

THESE praises and prayers I lay at thy feet, O Virgin of virgins! O Mary most sweet!

Be thou my true guide Through this pilgrimage here; And stand by my side When death draweth near.

R. Thanks be to God.

Ant. This is the rod in which was neither knot of original sin, nor rind of actual guilt.

V. In thy conception, O Virgin! thou wast immaculate.

R. Pray for us to the Father, Whose Son thou didst bring forth.

Oremus

DEUS qui per immaculatam Virginis conceptionem dignum Filio

Let us pray

O GOD, Who, by the immaculate conception of the Virgin, didst prepare

tuo habitaculum præpa- a worthy habitation for
rasti: quæsumus, ut qui Thy Son: we beseech Thee
ex morte ejusdem Filii tui that, as in view of the death
prævisa eam ab omni labe of that Son, Thou didst
præservasti, nos quoque preserve her from all stain
mundos ejus intercessione of sin, so Thou wouldst
ad te pervenire concedas. enable us, being made pure
Per eumdem Christum Do- by her intercession, to
minum nostrum. come unto Thee. Through
the same Christ our Lord.

R. Amen. *R.* Amen.

Indulgence of 300 days, each time — Pius IX.,
March 31, 1876.

THE THIRTY DAYS' PRAYER TO THE BLESSED VIRGIN MARY,

In Honor of the Passion of Our Lord Jesus Christ.

It is particularly recommended as a proper devotion for
every day in Lent, and on all Fridays throughout the year.

EVER-GLORIOUS and Blessed Virgin, Queen of
virgins, Mother of mercy, hope and comfort of
dejected souls, through that sword of sorrow which
pierced thy tender heart, whilst thine only Son, Jesus
Christ our Lord, suffered death and ignominy on the
cross; through that filial tenderness and pure love He
had for thee, grieving in thy grief, whilst from His cross
He recommended thee to the care and protection of His
beloved disciple, St. John: take pity, we beseech thee,
on our poverty and necessities; have compassion on our
anxieties; assist and comfort us in all our infirmities
and miseries. Thou art the Mother of mercies, the
sweet consolatrix and refuge of the desolate and af-

flicted: look, therefore, with pity on us, miserable children of Eve, and hear our prayer: for since, in just punishment of our sins, we are encompassed by evils, whither can we fly for more secure shelter than to thy maternal protection? Attend, therefore, with an ear of pity, we beseech thee, to our humble and earnest request. We ask it through the mercy of thy dear Son, and through the love and condescension wherewith He embraced our nature, when, in compliance with the divine will, thou gavest thy consent, and Whom, after the expiration of nine months, thou didst bring forth from thy chaste womb to visit this world, and bless it with His presence. We ask it through the anguish of mind wherewith thy beloved Son, our dear Saviour, was overwhelmed on Mount Olivet, when He besought His eternal Father to remove from Him, if possible, the bitter chalice of His future Passion. We ask it through the threefold repetition of His prayer in the garden, from whence afterwards, with mournful tears, thou didst accompany Him to the doleful theater of His sufferings and death. We ask it through the welds and sores of His virginal flesh, occasioned by the cords and whips wherewith He was bound and scourged when stripped of His seamless garment, for which His executioners afterwards cast lots. We ask it through the scoffs and ignominies by which He was insulted, the false accusations and unjust sentence by which He was condemned to death, and which He bore with heavenly patience. We ask it through His bitter tears and sweat of blood, His silence and resignation, His sadness and grief of heart. We ask it through the blood which trickled from His royal and sacred head, when struck with the scepter of a reed and pierced with His crown of thorns. We ask it through the torments

He endured, when His hands and feet were fastened with gross nails to the tree of the cross. We ask it through His vehement thirst and bitter potion of vinegar and gall. We ask it through His dereliction on the cross, when He exclaimed: "My God, My God, why hast Thou forsaken Me?" We ask it through His mercy extended to the good thief, and through His recommending His precious soul into the hands of His eternal Father before He expired, saying: "All is consummated." We ask it through the blood mixed with water which issued from His sacred side when pierced with a lance, and whence a flood of grace and mercy hath flowed to us. We ask it through His immaculate, life, bitter Passion, and ignominious death upon the cross, at which nature itself was thrown into convulsions, by the bursting of rocks, rending of the veil of the Temple, the earthquake, and darkness of the sun and moon. We ask it through His descent into hell, where He comforted the saints of the Old Law, and led captivity captive. We ask it through His glorious victory over death, His triumphant Ascension into heaven, and through the grace of the Holy Ghost, infused into the hearts of the disciples when He descended on them in the form of fiery tongues. We ask it through His awful appearance on the last day, when He shall come to judge the living and the dead, and shall destroy the world by fire. We ask it through the compassion He bore thee, and the ineffable joy thou didst feel at thine assumption into heaven, where thou art absorbed in the sweet contemplation of His divine perfections. O glorious and ever-blessed Virgin, comfort the hearts of thy supplicants, by obtaining for us ——.[1] And as we are persuaded that our divine

---

[1] Here mention your request.

Saviour honors thee as His beloved Mother, to whom He can refuse nothing, so let us experience the efficacy of thy powerful intercession, according to the tenderness of thy maternal affection, and the charity of His amiable Heart, which mercifully granteth the requests, and complieth with the desires of those who love and fear Him. O most Blessed Virgin! besides the object of our present petition, and whatever else we may stand in need of, obtain for us of thy dear Son, Our Lord and Our God, lively faith, firm hope, perfect charity, true contrition, a horror of sin, love of God and our neighbor, contempt of the world, and patience and resignation under the trials and difficulties of this life. Obtain for us, also, O sacred Mother of God! the gift of final perseverance, and the grace to receive the last Sacraments worthily at the hour of death. Lastly, obtain, we beseech thee, for our parents, relatives, our Sisters in Religion, and our benefactors, whether living or dead, life everlasting. Amen.

THE priest, vested in surplice and white stole (or, if the Nuptial Mass is to follow, vested as for Mass, yet without the maniple), in the hearing of the chosen witnesses, asks the man and the woman separately as follows, concerning their consent. First he asks the bridegroom, who should stand at the right hand of the bride:

N., wilt thou take N., here present, for thy lawful wife, according to the rite of our holy Mother the Church?

R. I will.

Then the priest asks the bride:

N., wilt thou take N., here present, for thy lawful husband, according to the rite of our holy Mother the Church?

R. I will.

Having obtained their mutual consent, the priest bids the man and the woman join their right hands. Then they pledge themselves each to the other as follows, repeating the words after the priest.

The man first says:

I N.N., take thee, N.N., for my lawful wife, to have and to hold, from this day forward, for better, for worse, for richer, for poorer, in sickness and in health, until death do us part.

Then the woman says:

I N.N., take thee, N.N., for my lawful husband,
to have and to hold, from this day forward,
for better, for worse, for richer, for poorer, in sickness and in health, until death do us part.

The priest then says:

Ego conjungo vos in matrimonium, in nomine Patris, ✠ et Filii, et Spiritus Sancti.
Amen.

I JOIN you together in marriage, in the name
of the Father, ✠ and of the Son, and of the Holy Ghost.
Amen.

He then sprinkles them with holy water.   This done,
he blesses the ring, saying:

Adjutorium nostrum in nomine Domini.
R. Qui fecit cœlum et terram.
V. Domine, exaudi ora-
tionem meam.
R. Et clamor meus ad Te veniat.
V. Dominus vobis-
cum.
R. Et cum spiritu tuo.

Our help is in the name of the Lord.
R. Who hath made heaven and earth.
V. O Lord, hear my prayer.
R. And let my cry come unto Thee.
V. The Lord be with you.
R. And with thy spirit.

Oremus

Benedic, ✠ Domine, annulum hunc, quem
nos in Tuo nomine benedi-
cimus, ✠ ut quæ eum ges-
taverit, fidelitatem inte-

Let us pray

Bless, ✠ O Lord, this ring, which we
bless ✠ in Thy name,
that she who shall wear
it, keeping true faith

gram suo sponso tenens, in pace et voluntate Tua permaneat, atque in mutua charitate semper vivat. Per Christum Dominum nostrum.

    R. Amen.

unto her spouse, may abide in Thy peace and in obedience to Thy will, and ever live in mutual love. Through Christ our Lord.

    R. Amen.

Then the priest sprinkles the ring with holy water in the form of a cross; and the bridegroom having received the ring from the hand of the priest places it on the third finger of the left hand of the bride, saying:

With this ring I thee wed and I plight unto thee my troth.

    Then the priest says:

IN nomine Patris, ✠ et Filii, et Spiritus Sancti. Amen.

IN the name of the Father ✠ and of the Son and of the Holy Ghost. Amen.

    This done, the priest adds:

    V. Confirma hoc, Deus, quod operatus es in nobis.

    R. A templo sancto Tuo quod est in Jerusalem.

    V. Kyrie eleison.

    R. Christe eleison.

    V. Kyrie eleison.

    Pater noster (*secreto*).

    V. Et ne nos inducas in tentationem.

    R. Sed libera nos a malo.

    V. Confirm, O God, that which Thou hast wrought in us.

    R. From Thy holy temple, which is in Jerusalem.

    V. Lord, have mercy.

    R. Christ, have mercy.

    V. Lord, have mercy.

    Our Father, etc.

    V. And lead us not into temptation.

    R. But deliver us from evil.

V. Salvos fac servos Tuos.

R. Deus meus, sperantes in Te.

V. Mitte eis, Domine, auxilium de sancto.

R. Et de Sion tuere eos.

V. Esto eis, Domine, turris fortitudinis.

R. A facie inimici.

V. Domine, exaudi orationem meam.

R. Et clamor meus ad Te veniat.

V. Dominus vobiscum.

R. Et cum spiritu Tuo.

V. Save Thy servants.

R. Who hope in Thee, O my God.

V. Send them help, O Lord, from Thy holy place.

R. And defend them out of Sion.

V. Be unto them, Lord, a tower of strength.

R. From the face of the enemy.

V. O Lord, hear my prayer.

R. And let my cry come unto Thee.

V. The Lord be with you.

R. And with thy spirit.

Oremus

RESPICE, quæsumus, Domine, super hos famulos Tuos, et institutis Tuis, quibus propagationem humani generis ordinasti, benignus assiste, ut qui Te auctore jungunter, Te auxiliante serventur. Per Christum Dominum nostrum. **Amen.**

Let us pray

LOOK down with favor, O Lord, we beseech Thee, upon these Thy servants, and graciously protect this Thine ordinance, whereby Thou hast provided for the propagation of mankind; that they who are joined together by Thy authority may be preserved by Thy help; through Christ our Lord. **Amen.**

Then, if the Nuptial Blessing is to be given, follows the

Mass for the Bridegroom and Bride

(From "The Roman Missal.")

The Introit

(*Tob.* vii)

MAY the God of Israel join you together; and may He be with you Who was merciful to two only children. And now, O Lord, make them bless Thee more fully. *Ps.* Blessed are all they that fear the Lord, that walk in His ways. *V.* Glory be to the Father, and to the Son, and to the Holy Ghost.

The Collect

GRACIOUSLY hear us, almighty and merciful God, that what is accomplished by our ministry may be perfected by Thy blessing. Through Our Lord Jesus Christ.

The Epistle

(*Eph.* v. 22–33)

BRETHREN: Let women be subject to their husbands, as to the Lord. Because the husband is the head of the wife; as Christ is the Head of the Church; He is the Saviour of His body. Therefore, as the Church is subject to Christ, so also let the wives be to their husbands in all things. Husbands, love your wives, as Christ also loved the Church, and delivered Himself up for it: that He might sanctify it, cleansing it by the laver of water in the word of life: that He might present it to Himself a glorious Church, not having spot or wrinkle, nor any such thing, but that it should be holy and without blemish. So also ought men to love their wives as their own bodies. He that loveth his wife, loveth himself. For no man ever hated his own flesh: but nourisheth and cherisheth it, as also Christ doth the Church: for we are members of His body, of His flesh, and of His bones. "For this cause shall a man leave his father and mother: and shall cleave to his wife, and they shall be two in one flesh." This is a great sacrament: but I speak in Christ and in the Church. Nevertheless, let every one of you in particular love his wife as himself: and let the wife fear her husband.

The Gradual
(*Ps.* cxxvii)

THY wife shall be as a fruitful vine on the sides of thy house. *V.* Thy children as olive-plants around about thy table. *Alleluia, Alleluia. V. Ps.* xix. May the Lord send you help from the sanctuary, and defend you out of Sion. *Alleluia.*

After Septuagesima, instead of Alleluia and V. is said:

The Tract
(*Ps.* cxxvii)

BEHOLD, thus shall the man be blessed that feareth the Lord. May the Lord bless thee out of Sion, and mayest thou see the good things of Jerusalem all the days of thy life. *V.* And mayest thou see thy children's children: peace upon Israel.

In Paschal time, the Gradual is omitted, and the following is said:

Alleluia, Alleluia. May the Lord send you help from the sanctuary, and defend you out of Sion. *Alleluia.* May the Lord out of Sion bless you; He that made heaven and earth. *Alleluia.*

The Gospel

(*Matt.* xix. 3–6)

A**T THAT** time: There came to Jesus the Pharisees, tempting Him, and saying: Is it lawful for a man to put away his wife for every cause? Who answering said to them: Have ye not read, that He who made man from the beginning, made them male and female? And He said: "For this cause shall a man leave father and mother, and shall cleave to his wife, and they two shall be in one flesh." Therefore now they are not two, but one flesh. What, therefore, God hath joined together, let no man put asunder.

The Offertory

(*Ps.* xxx)

I**N** Thee, O Lord, have I put my trust; I said: Thou art my God; my times are in Thy hands.

The Secret Prayer

R**ECEIVE**, we beseech Thee, O Lord, the offering which we make to Thee on behalf of the sacred bond of wedlock, and be Thou the disposer of the work of which Thou art the author. Through Our Lord Jesus Christ.

The Nuptial Blessing

After the Pater Noster, the priest proceeds to the right, or Epistle side of the altar, and turning towards the Bridegroom and Bride, who are kneeling at the altar steps, says over them the following prayers.

Let us pray

MERCIFULLY hear our prayers, O Lord, and graciously protect Thine ordinance, whereby Thou hast provided for the propagation of mankind, that this union made by Thy authority may be preserved by Thy help. Through Our Lord Jesus Christ, etc. Amen.

Let us pray

O GOD, Who by Thy mighty power hast made all things out of nothing; Who, in the beginning having set up the world, didst bestow on man, whom Thou hadst created in Thine own likeness, the inseparable help of woman, fashioning her body from his very flesh, and thereby teaching us that it is never lawful to put asunder what it has pleased Thee to make of one substance; O God, who hast consecrated wedlock by a surpassing mystery, since in the marriage-bond Thou didst foreshow the union of Christ with the Church; O God, by Whom woman is joined to man, and that alliance which Thou didst ordain from the beginning is endowed with a blessing, which alone was not taken away, either in punishment of original sin or by the sentence of the flood, look down in mercy upon this Thy handmaid who, being about to enter upon wedded life, seeks to be strengthened by Thy protection; may the yoke she has to bear be one of love and peace; true and chaste may she marry in Christ, and be a follower of holy women; may she be pleasing to her husband like Rachel; prudent, like Rebecca; long-lived and faithful like Sara; may the author of sin have no share in any of her actions; may she remain firmly attached to the faith and the commandments, and being joined to one man in wedlock, may she fly all unlawful addresses; may she fortify her weakness by strong discipline; may she be respected for her seriousness and venerated for her modesty; may she be well versed in heavenly lore; may she be fruitful in offspring. May her life be pure and blameless; and may she attain to the rest

of the blessed in the kingdom of heaven. May they both
see their children's children even to the third and fourth
generation and arrive at a happy old age; through Our Lord
Jesus Christ Thy Son, Who liveth and reigneth with Thee
in the unity of the Holy Ghost, one God world without end.
Amen.

The Communion

(*Ps.* cxxvii)

BEHOLD, thus shall every man be blessed that feareth
the Lord; and mayest thou see thy children's children:
peace be upon Israel.

The Post-Communion

WE BESEECH Thee, almighty God, in Thy great goodness, to show favor to that order of things which
Thou Thyself hast established, and to keep in abiding peace those whom Thou hast joined together in lawful
bond.

Before giving his blessing to the people, the priest again
turns to the Bridegroom and Bride, and blesses them in
particular, saying:

MAY the God of Abraham, the God of Isaac, and the
God of Jacob, be with you, and may He fulfill His
blessing in you: that you may see your children's
children even to the third and fourth generation, and may
afterwards have life everlasting, by the grace of Our Lord
Jesus Christ, Who, with the Father and the Holy Ghost,
liveth and reigneth God, world without end. Amen.

Then he sprinkles them with holy water, and concludes
the Mass as usual.

Litany of St. Joseph

Approved for public and private recital by His Holiness Pope Pius X, March 18, 1909.

Lord, have mercy on us!
Christ, have mercy on us!
Lord, have mercy on us!
Christ, hear us!
Christ, graciously hear us:
God, the Father of Heaven,[1]
God the Son, Redeemer of the world,
God, the Holy Ghost,
Holy Trinity, one God,
Holy Mary,[2]
Holy Joseph,
Noble scion of David,
Light of the patriarchs.
Spouse of the Mother of God,
Chaste Guardian of the Virgin,
Foster-father of the Son of God,
Sedulous Defender of Christ,
Head of the Holy Family,
Joseph most just,
Joseph most chaste,
Joseph most prudent,
Joseph most valiant,
Joseph most obedient,
Joseph most faithful,
Mirror of patience,
Lover of poverty,
Model of laborers,[3]
Ornament of domestic life,

[1] Have mercy on us!   [2] Pray for us!
[3] Model of artisans.

688

Protector of virgins,[1]
Pillar of families,
Consolation of the afflicted,
Hope of the sick,
Patron of the dying,
Terror of the demons,
Protector of Holy Church,
Lamb of God, who takest away the sins of the world,
   Spare us, O Lord!
Lamb of God, who takest away the sins of the world,
   Graciously hear us, O Lord!
Lamb of God, who takest away the sins of the world,
   Have mercy on us, O Lord!
V.   He made him master of his house:
R.   And ruler of all his possessions.

[1] Pray for us!

Let us pray.

O GOD, who didst deign to elect Blessed Joseph spouse of Thy most holy Mother: grant, we beseech Thee, that we may have him whom we venerate as our protector on earth as our intercessor in heaven. Who livest and reignest world without end.   Amen.

Indulgence.—300 days, once a day, also applicable to the souls in purgatory.—·(Pius X, March 18, 1909.)

Vespers for Sundays

Our Father.—Hail Mary, *in secret.*

DEUS, ✠ in adjutori-
um meum intende.

R. Domine, ad adju-
vandum me festina.

V. Gloria Patri, et
Filio, * et Spiritui Sancto.

R. Sicut erat in princi-
pio, et nunc, et semper, *
et in sæcula sæculorum.
Amen. Alleluia.

O GOD, ✠ come to my
assistance.

R. O Lord, make haste
to help me.

V. Glory be to the
Father, and to the Son,
and to the Holy Ghost.

R. As it was in the
beginning, is now, and
ever shall be, world without end. Amen. Alle-
luia.

From Septuagesima to Maundy Thursday inclusive, instead
of Alleluia, there is said:

Laus tibi, Domine, Rex
æternæ gloriæ.

Praise be to Thee, O
Lord, King of everlasting
glory.

In Advent: The Antiphons are taken from the Lauds of
the current Sunday.

Throughout the year

Ant. Dixit Dominus.

Ant. The Lord said.

In Paschal Time

Ant. Alleluia, * alle-
luia, alleluia.

Ant. Alleluia,* alle-
luia, alleluia.

Under this Antiphon, *Alleluia,* are said all the Psalms up to
the Little Chapter.

Psalmus cix

Dixit Dominus Do-
mino meo:* Sede
a dextris meis:

Donec ponam inimicos
tuos: * scabellum pedum
tuorum.

Virgam virtutis tuæ
emittet Dominus ex Si-
on: * dominare medio
inimicorum tuorum.

Tecum principium in
die virtutis tuæ in splen-
doribus sanctorum: * ex
utero ante luciferum
genui te.

Juravit Dominus, et
non poenitebit eum: * Tu
es sacerdos in æternum
secundum ordinem Mel-
chisedech.

Dominus a dextris tuis,
* confregit in die iræ suæ
reges.

Judicabit in nationi-
bus, implebit ruinas: *
conquassabit capita in
terra multorum.

De torrente in via

Psalm cix

The Lord said to my
Lord: Sit Thou
at My right hand:

Until I make Thine
enemies Thy footstool.

The Lord shall send
forth the scepter of Thy
power out of Sion: rule
Thou in the midst of
Thine enemies.

With Thee is the prin-
cipality in the day of Thy
strength, amid the brightness of the saints: from
the womb before the day-
star have I begotten
Thee.

The Lord hath sworn
and He will not repent:
Thou art a priest forever
according to the order of
Melchisedech.

The Lord at Thy right
hand hath broken kings
in the day of His wrath.

He shall judge among
the nations. He shall
fill ruins: He shall crush
the heads in the land of
many.

He shall drink of the

bibet: * propterea exalta-
bit caput.

Gloria Patri, etc.

Ant. Dixit Dominus
Domino meo: Sede a
dextris meis.
Ant. Magna opera Do-
mini.

Psalmus cx

CONFITEBOR tibi, Do-
mine, in toto corde
meo: * in consilio jus-
torum, et congregatione.

Magna opera Domini:*
exquisita in omnes vol-
untates ejus.
Confessio et magnifi-
centia opus ejus: * et
justitia ejus manet in
sæculum sæculi.
Memoriam fecit mira-
bilium suorum, miseri-
cors et miserator, Domi-
nus: * escam dedit timen-
tibus se.

Memor erit in sæcu-
lum testamenti sui: * vir-

torrent in the way: therefore shall He lift up His
head.
Glory be to the Father,
etc.

Ant. The Lord said
to my Lord: Sit Thou at
My right hand.
Ant. Great are the
works of the Lord.

Psalm cx

I WILL praise Thee, O
Lord, with my whole
heart: in the council of
the just, and in the con-
gregation.
Great are the works of
the Lord: sought out
according to all His wills.
His work is praise and
magnificence: and His
justice continueth for-
ever and ever.
He hath made a re-
membrance of His won-
derful works, being a
merciful and gracious
Lord: He hath given
food to them that fear
Him.
He will be mindful for-
ever of His covenant: He

tutem operum suorum annuntiabit populo suo:

Ut det illis hereditatem gentium: * opera manuum ejus veritas et judicium.

Fidelia omnia mandata ejus: confirmata in sæculum sæculi * facta in veritate et æquitate.

Redemptionem misit populo suo: * mandavit in æternum testamentum suum.

Sanctum et terribile nomen ejus: * initium sapientiæ timor Domini.

Intellectus bonus omnibus facientibus eum: * laudatio ejus manet in sæculum sæculi.

Gloria Patri, etc.

Ant. Magna opera Domini: * exquisita in omnes voluntates ejus.

Ant. Qui timet Dominum.

will show forth to His people the power of His works:

That He may give them the inheritance of the gentiles: the works of His hands are truth and judgment.

All His commandments are faithful: confirmed forever and ever: made in truth and equity.

He hath sent redemption to His people: He hath commanded His covenant forever.

Holy and terrible is His name: the fear of the Lord is the beginning of wisdom.

A good understanding to all that do it: His praise continueth forever and ever.

Glory be to the Father, etc.

Ant. Great are the works of the Lord: sought out according to all His wills.

Ant. He who feareth the Lord.

Psalmus cxi

BEATUS vir qui timet Dominum: * in mandatis ejus volet nimis.

Potens in terra erit semen ejus: * generatio rectorum benedicetur.

Gloria et divitiæ in domo ejus: * et justitia ejus manet in sæculum sæculi.

Exortum est in tenebris lumen rectis: * misericors, et miserator, et justus.

Jucundus homo qui miseretur et commodat, disponet sermones suos in judicio: * quia in æternum non commovebitur.

In memoria æterna erit justus: * ab auditione mala non timebit.

Paratum cor ejus sperare in Domino, confirmatum est cor ejus: * non commovebitur donec despiciat inimicos suos.

Psalm cxi

BLESSED is the man that feareth the Lord: he shall delight exceedingly in His commandments.
His seed shall be mighty upon earth: the generation of the righteous shall be blessed.
Glory and wealth shall be in his house: and his justice remaineth forever and ever.
To the righteous a light is risen up in darkness: he is merciful, and compassionate, and just.
Acceptable is the man that showeth mercy and lendeth; he shall order his words with judgment: because he shall not be moved forever.
The just shall be in everlasting remembrance: he shall not fear the evil hearing.
His heart is ready to hope in the Lord; his heart is strengthened: he shall not be moved until he look over his enemies.

Dispersit, dedit pau-
peribus: justitia ejus
manet in sæculum sæcu-
li, * cornu ejus exaltabi-
tur in gloria.

Peccator videbit, et
irascetur, dentibus suis
fremet et tabescet: * de-
siderium peccatorum pe-
ribit.

Gloria Patri, etc.

Ant. Qui timet Domi-
num, in mandatis ejus
cupit nimis.

Ant. Sit nomen Do-
mini.

Psalmus cxii

LAUDATE, pueri, Do-
minum: * laudate
nomen Domini.

Sit nomen Domini be-
nedictum, * ex hoc nunc,
et usque in sæculum.

A solis ortu usque ad
occasum, * laudabile no-
men Domini.

Excelsus super omnes

He hath distributed, he
hath given to the poor;
his justice remaineth forever and ever: his horn
shall be exalted in glory.

The wicked shall see,
and shall be angry, he
shall gnash with his teeth,
and pine away: the de-
sire of the wicked shall
perish.

Glory be to the Father,
etc.

Ant. He who feareth
the Lord, shall delight exceedingly in His com-
mandments.

Ant. May the name of
the Lord.

Psalm cxii

PRAISE the Lord, ye
children: praise ye
the name of the Lord.

Blessed be the name
of the Lord: from hence-
forth, now and forever.

From the rising of the
sun unto the going down
of the same the name of
the Lord is worthy of
praise.

The Lord is high above

gentes Dominus, * et super cœlos gloria ejus.

Quis sicut Dominus Deus noster, qui in altis habitat, * et humilia respicit in cœlo et in terra?

Suscitans a terra inopem, * et de stercore erigens pauperem:

Ut collocet eum cum principibus, * cum principibus populi sui.

Qui habitare facit sterilem in domo, * matrem filiorum lætantem.

Gloria Patri, etc.

Ant. Sit nomen Domini benedictum in sæcula.

Ant. Deus autem noster.

all nations: and His glory above the heavens.

Who is as the Lord our God, Who dwelleth on high: and looketh down on the lowly things in heaven and in earth?

Raising up the needy from the earth: and lifting up the poor out of the dunghill;

That He may place him with princes: with the princes of His people.

Who maketh a barren woman to dwell in a house: the joyful mother of children.

Glory be, etc.

Ant. May the name of the Lord be blessed forever.

Ant. But our God.

Psalmus cxiii

IN exitu Israel de Ægypto, * domus Jacob de populo barbaro:

Facta est Judæa sanctificatio ejus, * Israel potestas ejus.

Psalm cxiii

WHEN Israel went out of Egypt: the house of Jacob from a barbarous people.

Judea was made His sanctuary: Israel His dominion.

Mare vidit, et fugit, * Jordanis conversus est retrorsum.

The sea saw and fled: Jordan was turned back.

Montes exsultaverunt ut arietes: * et colles sicut agni ovium.

The mountains skipped like rams: and the hills like the lambs of the flock.

Quid est tibi, mare, quod fugisti: * et tu, Jordanis, quia conversus es retrorsum?

What ailed thee, O thou sea, that thou didst flee: and thou, O Jordan, that thou wast turned back?

Montes, exsultastis sicut arietes, * et colles, sicut agni ovium?

Ye mountains, that ye skipped like rams: and ye hills, like lambs of the flock?

A facie Domini mota est terra, * a facie Dei Jacob.

At the presence of the Lord the earth was moved: at the presence of the God of Jacob.

Qui convertit petram in stagna aquarum, * et rupem in fontes aquarum.

Who turned the rock into pools of water: and the stony hill into fountains of waters.

Non nobis, Domine, non nobis: * sed nomini tuo da gloriam.

Not to us, O Lord, not to us: but to Thy name give glory.

Super misericordia tua, et veritate tua * nequando dicant gentes: Ubi est Deus eorum?

For Thy mercy, and for Thy truth's sake: lest the gentiles should say: Where is their God?

Deus autem noster in

But our God is in

cœlo: * omnia quæcumque voluit, fecit.

Simulacra gentium argentum, et aurum, * opera manuum hominum.

Os habent, et non loquentur: * oculos habent, et non videbunt.

Aures habent, et non audient: * nares habent et non odorabunt.

Manus habent, et non palpabunt: pedes habent, et non ambulabunt: * non clamabunt in gutture suo.

Similes illis fiant qui faciunt ea: * et omnes qui confidunt in eis.

Domus Israel speravit in Domino: * adjutor eorum et protector eorum est.

Domus Aaron speravit in Domino: * adjutor eorum et protector eorum est.

Qui timent Dominum, speraverunt in Domino: *

heaven: He hath done all things whatsoever He would.

The idols of the gentiles are silver and gold: the works of the hands of men.

They have mouths, and speak not: they have eyes, and see not.

They have ears, and hear not: they have noses and smell not.

They have hands, and feel not: they have feet, and walk not, neither shall they cry out through their throat.

Let them that make them become like unto them: and all such as trust in them.

The house of Israel hath hoped in the Lord: He is their helper and their protector.

The house of Aaron hath hoped in the Lord: He is their helper and their protector.

They that fear the Lord have hoped in the

adjutor eorum et protector eorum est.

Dominus memor fuit nostri: * et benedixit nobis:

Benedixit domui Israel: * benedixit domui Aaron.

Benedixit omnibus, qui timent Dominum, * pusillis cum majoribus.

Adjiciat Dominus super vos: * super vos, et super filios vestros.

Benedicti vos a Domino, * qui fecit cœlum, et terram.

Cœlum cœli Domino: * terram autem dedit filiis hominum.

Non mortui laudabunt te, Domine: neque omnes, qui descendunt in infernum.

Sed nos qui vivimus, benedicimus Domino, * ex hoc nunc, et usque in sæculum.

Gloria Patri, etc.

Lord: He is their helper and their protector.

The Lord hath been mindful of us: and hath blessed us.

He hath blessed the house of Israel: He hath blessed the house of Aaron.

He hath blessed all that fear the Lord: both little and great.

May the Lord add blessings upon you: upon you, and upon your children.

Blessed be you of the Lord: Who made heaven and earth.

The heaven of heavens is the Lord's: but the earth He has given to the children of men.

The dead shall not praise Thee, O Lord: nor any of them that go down to hell.

But we that live, bless the Lord: from this time now and forever.

Glory be, etc.

Throughout the year

Ant. Deus autem noster in cœlo: omnia quaecumque voluit, fecit.	*Ant.* But our God is in heaven: He hath done all things whatsoever He would.

In Paschal Time

Ant. Alleluia, alleluia, alleluia.

Capitulum	*The Little Chapter*
BENEDICTUS Deus, et Pater Domini nostri *Jesu Christi*, Pater misericordiarum, et Deus totius consolationis, qui consolatur nos in omni tribulatione nostra.	**B**LESSED be the God and Father of Our Lord *Jesus Christ*, the Father of mercies and the God of all consolation, Who comforteth us in all our tribulation.
R. Deo gratias.	*R.* Thanks be to God.

On all Sundays except those presently indicated

Hymnus	*Hymn*
LUCIS Creator optime, Lucem dierum proferens,	**O** BLEST Creator of the light, Who dost the dawn from darkness bring;
Primordiis lucis novæ,	And framing nature's depth and height,
Mundi parans originem.	Didst with the light Thy work begin.
Qui mane junctum ves-	Who gently blending eve

Diem vocari praecipis:

And morn with eve didst call them day:

Illabitur tetrum chaos,

Thick flows the flood of darkness down;

Audi preces cum fletibus.

Oh, hear us as we weep and pray!

Ne mens gravata crimine,

Keep Thou our souls from schemes of crime;

Vitae sit exsul munere,

Nor guilt remorseful let them know;

Dum nil perenne cogitat,

Nor, thinking but on things of time,

Seseque culpis illigat.
Cœleste pulset ostium:

Into eternal darkness go.
Teach us to knock at heaven's high door;

Vitale tollat praemium:

Teach us the prize of life to win:

Vitemus omne noxium:
Purgemus omne pessi-mum.

Teach us all evil to abhor,
And purify ourselves within.

Praesta, Pater piissime

Father of mercies, hear our cry;

Patrique compar Unice,

Hear us, O sole-begotten Son!

Cum Spiritu Paraclito

Who with the Holy Ghost most high,

Regnans per omne saecu-lum. Amen.

Reignest while endless ages run. Amen.

V. Dirigatur, Domine, oratio mea.

V. May my prayer, O Lord, be directed.

R. Sicut incensum in conspectu tuo.

R. As incense in Thy sight.

In Advent, Lent, Passiontide, and Paschal Time, from Low
Sunday to the Fifth Sunday after Easter inclusive, the Hymn
and Versicle as below.

In Advent

Hymnus

CREATOR alme siderum
Æterna lux creden-
tium,

Jesu, Redemptor omni-
um,
Intende votis supplicum.

Qui dæmonis ne fraudi-
bus
Periret orbis, impetu

Amoris actus, languidi

Mundi medela factus es.

Commune qui mundi ne-
fas
Ut expiares, ad crucem

E Virginis sacrario

Intacta prodis Victima.

Cujus potestas gloriæ,

Nomenque cum primum
sonat.

Hymn

DEAR Maker of the
starry skies,
Light of believers ever-
more,
Jesu, Redeemer of man-
kind,
Be near us who Thine
aid implore.

When man was sunk in
sin and death,
Lost in the depth of
Satan's snare,
Love brought Thee down
to cure our ills
By taking of those ills a
share.

Thou, for the sake of
guilty men,
Permitting Thy pure
blood to flow,
Didst issue from Thy
Virgin shrine,
And to the Cross a victim
go.

So great the glory of Thy
might,
If we but chance Thy
name to sound,

Et cœlites et inferi	At once all heaven and hell unite
Tremente curvantur genu.	In bending low with awe profound.
Te deprecamur ultimæ	Great Judge of all! in that last day,
Magnum diei judicem,	When friends shall fail, and foes combine,
Armis supernæ gratiæ	Be present then with us, we pray,
Defende nos ab hostibus.	To guard us with Thy arm divine.
Virtus, honor, laus, gloria	To God the Father, with the Son,
Deo Patri cum Filio,	And Holy Spirit, One and Three,
Sancto simul Paraclito	Be honor, glory, blessing,
In sæculorum sæcula. Amen.	All through the long eternity. Amen.
V. Rorate, cœli, desuper, et nubes pluant justum.	*V.* Drop down, ye heavens, dew from above, and let the clouds rain forth the Just One.
R. Aperiatur terra, et germinet Salvatorem.	*R.* Let the earth be opened, and bring forth the Saviour.

In Lent

Hymnus	*Hymn*
AUDI, benigne Conditor, Nostras preces cum fletibus.	THOU loving Maker of mankind, Before Thy throne we pray and weep;

In hoc sacro jejunio

Oh, strengthen us with grace divine,

Fusas quadragenario.

Duly this sacred Lent to keep.

Scrutator alme cordium,

Searcher of hearts, Thou dost discern

Infirma tu scis virium:

Our ills, and all our weakness know:

Ad te reversis exhibe

Again to Thee with tears we turn;

Remissionis gratiam.

Again to us Thy mercy show.

Multum quidem pecca-vimus,

Much have we sinn'd; but we confess

Sed parce confitentibus:

Our guilt, and all our faults deplore:

Ad nominis laudem tui

Oh, for the praise of Thy great name,

Confer medelam langui-dis.

Our fainting souls to health restore!

Concede nostrum conteri

And grant us, while by fasts we strive

Corpus per abstinentiam;

This mortal body to con-trol,

Culpæ ut relinquant pa-bulum

To fast from all the food of sin,

Jejuna corda criminum.

And so to purify the soul.

Præsta, beata Trinitas,

Hear us, O Trinity thrice blest!

Concede, simplex Unitas;

Sole Unity! to Thee we cry:

Ut fructuosa sint tuis

Vouchsafe us from these fasts below

Jejuniorum munera.
Amen.

V. Angelis suis Deus mandavit de te.

R. Ut custodiant te in omnibus viis tuis.

To reap immortal fruit on high. Amen.

V. God hath given His angels charge over thee.

R. To keep thee in all thy ways.

In Passiontide

Hymnus

VEXILLA Regis prodeunt:

Fulget Crucis mysterium,

Qua vita mortem pertulit,
Et morte vitam protulit.

Quæ, vulnerata lanceæ

Mucrone diro, criminum,

Ut nos lavaret sordibus,

Manavit unda et sanguine.
Impleta sunt quæ concinit
David fideli carmine,

Dicendo nationibus:

Hymn

HORTH comes the standard of the King
All hail, thou Mystery adored!

Hail, Cross! on which the Life Himself
Died, and by death our life restored.

On which the Saviour's holy side,

Rent open with a cruel spear,

Its stream of blood and water pour'd,

To wash us from defilement clear.
O sacred Wood! fulfill'd in thee
Was holy David's truthful lay;

Which told the world, that from a tree

Regnavit a ligno Deus.	The Lord should all the nations sway.
Arbor decora et fulgida,	Most royally empurpled o'er,
Ornata Regis purpura,	How beauteously thy stem doth shine!
Electa digno stipite	How glorious was its lot to touch
Tam sancta membra tangere	Those limbs so holy and divine!
Beata, cujus brachiis	Thrice blest, upon whose arms outstretch'd
Pretium pependit sæculi,	The Saviour of the world reclined;
,Statera facta corporis,	Balance sublime! upon whose beam
Tulitque prædam tartari.	Was weigh'd the ransom of mankind.

The following stanza is said on bended knees.

O Crux, ave, spes unica,	Hail, Cross! thou only hope, of man,
Hoc Passionis tempore	Hail on this holy Passion day!
Piis adauge gratiam,	To saints increase the grace they have;
Reisque dele crimina.	From sinners purge their guilt away.
Te, fons salutis, Trinitas,	Salvation's fount, blest Trinity,
Collaudet omnis spiritus:	Be praise to Thee through earth and skies:

Quibus Crucis victoriam

Largiris, adde præmium.
Amen.
V. Eripe me, Domine,
ab homine malo.
R. A viro iniquo eripe
me.

Thou through the Cross
the victory
Dost give; Oh, give us,
too, the prize! Amen.
V. Deliver me, O Lord,
from the sinful man.
R. And from the evil-
doer save me.

In Paschal Time

Hymnus

AD REGIAS Agni
dapes,
Stolis amicti candidis

Post transitum Maris
Rubri,
Christo canamus Prin-
cipi:
Divina cujus charitas

Sacrum propinat sangui-
nem,
Almique membra cor-
poris
Amor sacerdos immolat.

Sparsum cruorem posti-
bus
Vastator horret angelus:

Fugitque divisum mare:

Hymn

Now at the Lamb's
high royal feast,
In robes of saintly white,
we sing,
Through the Red Sea in
safety brought
By Jesus our immortal
King.
O depth of love! for us
He drains
The chalice of His
agony;
For us a victim on the
cross
He meekly lays Him
down to die.
And as the avenging
angel pass'd
Of old the blood be-
sprinkled door;
As the cleft sea a passage
gave,

Merguntur hostes flucti-
bus.

Then closed to whelm th'
Egyptians o'er;

Jam Pascha nostrum
Christus est,

So Christ, our Paschal
Sacrifice,

Paschalis idem victima,

Has brought us safe all
perils through;

Et pura puris mentibus

While for unleaven'd
bread He asks

Sinceritatis azyma.

But heart sincere and
purpose true.

O vera cœli victima,

Hail, purest victim
Heav'n could find

Subjecta cui sunt tartara,

The powers of hell to
overthrow!

Soluta mortis vincula,

Who didst the bonds of
death unbind;

Recepta vitæ præmia.

Who dost the prize of life
bestow.

Victor, subactis inferis,

Hail, victor Christ! hail,
risen King!

Trophæa Christus ex-
plicat;

To Thee alone belongs
the crown;

Cœloque aperto, subdi-
tum

Who hast the heavenly
gates unbarr'd,

Regem tenebrarum tra-
hit.

And cast the Prince of
darkness down.

Ut sis perenne mentibus

O Jesu! from the death
of sin

Paschale, Jesu, gaudium,

Keep us, we pray; so
shalt Thou be

A morte dira criminum,

The everlasting Paschal
joy

Vitæ renatos libera.	Of all the souls newborn in Thee.
Deo Patri sit gloria,	To God the Father, with the Son,
Et Filio, qui a mortuís	Who from the grave immortal rose,
Surrexit, ac Paraclito,	And Thee, O Paraclete, be praise,
In sempiterna sæcula. Amen.	While age on endlesι ages flows. Amen.

V. M a n e nobiscum, Domine. Alleluia.
R. Quoniam advesperascit. Alleluia.

V. Remain with us, O Lord, Alleluia.
R. For it is now toward evening. Alleluia.

The Versicle and Response having been recited, there follows, with its appointed Antiphon, the

𝕸agnificat, or Canticle of the 𝕭lessed 𝕭irgin 𝕸ary

Luke I. 46-55

ⅯAGNIFICAT * anima mea Dominum:
Et exsultavit spiritus meus * in Deo salutari meo.
Quia respexit humilitatem ancillæ suæ: * ecce enim ex hoc beatam me dicent omnes generationes.

Quia fecit mihi magna

ⅯY soul doth magnify the Lord.
And my spirit hath rejoiced: in God my Saviour.
Because He hath regarded the humility of His handmaid: for behold from henceforth all generations shall call me blessed.

For He that is mighty

qui potens est: * et sanctum nomen ejus.

hath done great things to me: and holy is His Name.

Et misericordia ejus a progenie in progenies * timentibus eum.

And His mercy is from generation to generation: to them that fear Him.

Fecit potentiam in brachio suo: * dispersit superbos mente cordis sui.

He hath showed might in His arm: He hath scattered the proud in the conceit of their heart.

Deposuit potentes de sede,* et exaltavit humiles.

He hath put down the mighty from their seat: and hath exalted the humble.

Esurientes implevit bonis: * et divites dimisit inanes.

He hath filled the hungry with good things: and the rich He hath sent empty away.

Suscepit Israel puerum suum, * recordatus misericordiæ suæ.

He hath received Israel His servant: being mindful of His mercy.

Sicut locutus est ad patres nostros, * Abraham, et semini ejus in sæcula.

As He spoke to our fathers: to Abraham and to his seed forever.

Gloria Patri, et Filio, et Spiritui Sancto.

Glory be to the Father, and to the Son, and to the Holy Ghost.

Sicut erat in principio, et nunc, et semper, et in sæcula sæculorum. Amen.

As it was in the beginning, is now, and ever shall be, world without end. Amen.

The Canticle being completed and the Antiphon repeated, there follows immediately the Versicle:

V. Dominus vobiscum.

V. The Lord be with you.

R. Et cum spiritu tuo.
Oremus.

R. And with thy spirit.
Let us pray.

Then is said the Proper Collect. Then, outside of Paschal Time, on certain Sundays is said the following:

Suffrage of All Saints

Ant. Beata Dei Genitrix Virgo Maria, sanctique omnes intercedant pro nobis ad Dominum.

Ant. May the Blessed Virgin Mary, Mother of God, together with all the saints, intercede for us with the Lord.

V. Mirificavit Dominus sanctos suos.

V. The Lord hath glorified His saints.

R. Et exaudivit eos clamantes ad se.

R. He hath heard their crying unto Him.

Oremus

A CUNCTIS nos, quæsumus, Domine, mentis et corporis defende periculis: et, intercedente beata et gloriosa semper Virgine Dei Genitrice Maria, cum beato Joseph, beatis apostolis tuis Petro et Paulo, atque beato *N.* et omnibus sanctis, salutem nobis tribue benignus et

Let us pray

D EFEND us, we beseech Thee, O Lord, from all dangers of soul and body: and by the intercession of the blessed and glorious Mary, ever a virgin, mother of God, of St. Joseph, of Thy holy apostles Peter and Paul, of blessed *N.* (*the patron saint*), and of all Thy

pacem; ut, destructis adversitatibus et erroribus universis, Ecclesia tua secura tibi serviat libertate. Per eumdem Christum Dominum nostrum.

saints, in Thy loving-kindness grant us safety and peace; that, all adversities and errors being destroyed, Thy Church may serve Thee in freedom and s e c u r i t y. Through the same Christ our Lord.

R. Amen.

R. Amen.

In the preceding prayer, at the indication N. is expressed the name of the Titular Saint, or Patron, of the Church; and the names of the holy Angels or of St. John the Baptist, should such be Titulars, are placed before that of St. Joseph.

In Paschal Time, on certain Sundays, in place of the preceding Suffrage there is made the following:

Commemoration of the Cross

Ant. Crucifixus surrexit a mortuis, et redemit nos, alleluia, alleluia.

Ant. The Crucified hath arisen from the dead, and hath redeemed us, alleluia, alleluia.

V. Dicite in nationibus, alleluia.

R. Quia Dominus regnavit a ligno, alleluia.

V. Tell ye among the nations, alleluia.

R. That the Lord hath reigned from the tree, alleluia.

Oremus

DEUS, qui pro nobis Filium tuum Crucis patibulum subire voluisti, ut inimici a nobis expellere potestatem:

Let us pray

O GOD, Who for our sakes didst will that Thy Son should suffer the death of the cross, and thereby free us from

concede nobis, famulis tuis; ut resurrectionis gratiam consequamur. Per eumdem Christum Dominum nostrum.

R. Amen.

the power of the enemy, grant to us, Thy servants, to have part in the grace of the resurrection:

Through the same Christ our Lord.

R. Amen.

After the last prayer there is added:

V. Dominus vobiscum.

R. Et cum spiritu tuo.
V. Benedicamus Domino.

R. Deo gratias.
V. Fidelium animæ, per misericordiam Dei, requiescant in pace.

R. Amen.

V. The Lord be with you.

R. And with thy spirit.
V. Let us bless the Lord.

R. Thanks be to God.
V. May the souls of the faithful departed, through the mercy of God, rest in peace.

R. Amen.

The Four Great Anthems of the Blessed Virgin Mary

Alma Redemptoris. Ave Regina Cœlorum, Regina Cœli and Salve Regina

They are to be recited in the following order, in the course of the year.

Alma Redemptoris

From the Saturday before the first Sunday of Advent to Candlemas inclusive.

ALMA Redemptoris Matér, quæ pervia cœli porta manes, et stella

MOTHER of Christ! hear thou thy people's cry, star of the

maris, succurre cadenti.

Surgere qui curat, po-
pulo: tu quæ genuisti,
  Natura mirante, tuum
sanctum Genitorem,
  Virgo prius ac pos-
terius Gabrielis ab ore,
  Sumens illud Ave, pec-
catorum miserere.

deep, and portal of the
sky.
  Mother of Him Who
thee from nothing made,
  Sinking we strive and
call to thee for aid.
  Oh, by that joy which
Gabriel brought to thee,
  Pure Virgin, first and
last, look on our misery.

In Advent

V. Angelus   Domini
nuntiavit Mariæ.

R. Et concepit de Spir-
itu Sancto.

V. The angel of the
Lord declared unto Mary.

R. And she conceived
of the Holy Ghost.

Oremus

GRATIAM tuam, quæ-
sumus D o m i n e,
mentibus nostris infunde:
ut qui, angelo nuntiante,
Christi Filii tui incarnationem cognovimus, per
passionem ejus et crucem,
ad resurrectionis gloriam
perducamur. Per eum-
dem Christum Dominum
nostrum.

Let us pray

POUR forth, we be-
seech Thee, O
Lord, Thy grace into our
hearts, that we, to whom
the incarnation of Christ,
Thy Son, was made
known by the message of
an angel, may by His
passion and cross be
brought to the glory of
His r e s u r r e c t i o n.
Through the same Christ
our Lord.

R. Amen.
V. Divinum   auxilium

R. Amen.
V. May the divine as-

maneat semper nobis-
cum.

R. Amen.

V. Post partum, Virgo,
inviolata permansisti.

R. Dei Genitrix, inter-
cede pro nobis.

Oremus

DEUS, qui salutis
æternæ, beatæ
Mariæ Virginitate fœcun-
da, humano generi præ-
mia præstitisti: tribue,
quæsumus; ut ipsam pro
nobis intercedere sentia-
mus; per quam merui-
mus auctorem vitæ sus-
cipere, Dominum nos-
trum Jesum Christum
Filium tuum: qui tecum
vivit et regnat in unitate
Spiritus Sancti Deus, per
omnia sæcula sæculorum.

R. Amen.
V. Divinum auxilium
maneat semper nobis-
cum.

R. Amen.

sistance remain always
with us.

R. Amen.

V. After childbirth, O
Virgin, thou didst remain
inviolate.

R. O Mother of God,
plead for us.

Let us pray

O GOD, Who, by the
fruitful virginity of
blessed Mary, hast be-
stowed upon mankind
the rewards of eternal
salvation, grant, we be-
seech Thee, that we may
evermore experience the
intercession in our be-
half of her through whom
we have been found
worthy to receive the
author of life, our Lord
Jesus Christ, Thy Son,
Who liveth and reigneth
with Thee in the unity
of the Holy Ghost, God,
world without end.

R. Amen.

V. May the divine as-
sistance remain always
with us.

R. Amen.

Ave Regina Cœlorum

From Candlemas until Compline on Holy Saturday exclusively.

Antiphona	*Anthem*

AVE Regina cœlorum,
Ave Domina Angelorum:

Salve radix, salve porta,

Ex qua mundo lux est orta.
Gaude Virgo gloriosa,

Super omnes speciosa:

Vale, O valde decora,
Et pro nobis Christum exora.
V. Dignare me laudare te, Virgo sacrata.

R. Da mihi virtutem contra hostes tuos.

HAIL, O queen of heav'n enthroned!
Hail, by angels mistress owned!

Root of Jesse! Gate of morn,

Whence the world's true Light was born:
Glorious Virgin, joy to thee.

Beautiful surpassingly!
Fairest thou where all are fair!
Plead for us a pitying prayer.
V. Make me worthy to praise thee, O blessed Virgin.
R. Give me strength against thine enemies.

Oremus

CONCEDE, misericors Deus, fragilitati nostræ præsidium, ut qui sanctæ Dei Genitricis memoriam agimus, intercessionis ejus auxilio a

Let us pray

O MOST merciful God, grant succor unto our frailty; that, as we celebrate the memory of the holy Mother of God, so by the help of her in-

nostris iniquitatibus re-
surgamus. Per eumdem
Christum Dominum nos-
trum.

R. Amen.

V. Divinum auxilium
maneat semper nobis-
cum.

R. Amen.

tercession we may rise
again from our sins.
Through the same Christ
our Lord.

R. Amen.

V. May the divine as-
sistance remain always
with us.

R. Amen.

Regina Cœli

From Compline of Holy Saturday until None on the Saturday after Pentecost inclusively.

Antiphona

REGINA cœli, lætare,
Alleluia,
Quia quem meruisti por-
tare, Alleluia,
Resurrexit sicut dixit,
Alleluia.
Ora pro nobis Deum,
Alleluia.

V. Gaude et lætare,
Virgo Maria, Alleluia.

R. Quia surrexit Do-
minus vere, Alleluia.

Anthem

O QUEEN of heaven,
rejoice, Alleluia.
For He Whom thou wast
meet to bear, Alleluia.
Hath risen, as He said,
Alleluia.
Pray for us to God, Al-
leluia.

V. Rejoice and be
glad, O Virgin Mary, Al-
leluia.

R. For the Lord hath
risen indeed. Alleluia.

Oremus

DEUS, qui per resur-
rectionem Filii tui
Domini nostri Jesu
Christi mundum lætifi-

Let us pray

O GOD, Who didst
vouchsafe to give
joy to the world through
the resurrection of Thy

care dignatus es; præsta quæsumus; ut per ejus Genitricem V i r g i n e m Mariam perpetuæ capiamus gaudia vitæ. Per eumdem Christum Dominum nostrum.

R. Amen.
V. Divinum auxilium maneat semper nobiscum.
R. Amen.

Son, Our Lord Jesus Christ; grant, we beseech Thee, that, through His mother, the Virgin Mary, we may obtain the joys of everlasting life. Through the same Christ our Lord.
R. Amen.
V. May the divine assistance remain always with us.
R. Amen.

Salve Regina

From Compline of the Saturday after Pentecost until Advent.

Antiphona

SALVE Regina, Mater misericordiæ, vita, dulcedo, et spes nostra salve.

Ad te clamamus, exsules filii Hevæ;

Ad te suspiramus, gementes et flentes in hac lacrimarum valle.

Eia ergo, advocata nostra, illos tuos misericordes oculos ad nos converte.

Anthem

HAIL, holy queen, mother of mercy! Our life, our sweetness, and our hope.

To thee do we cry, poor banished children of Eve;

To thee do we send up our sighs, mourning and weeping in this vale of tears.

Turn then, most gracious advocate, thine eyes of mercy toward us.

Et Jesum, benedictum fructum ventris tui, nobis post hoc exilium ostende.

O clemens, O pia, O dulcis Virgo Maria.

V. Ora pro nobis sancta Dei Genitrix.

R. Ut digni efficiamur promissionibus Christi.

Oremus

OMNIPOTENS sempiterne Deus, qui gloriosæ Virginis Matris Mariæ corpus et animam ut dignum Filii tui habitaculum effici mereretur, Spiritu Sancto cooperante præparasti: da ut cujus commemoratione lætamur, ejus pia intercessione ab instantibus malis, et a morte perpetua liberemur. Per eumdem Christum Dominum nostrum.

R. Amen.

V. Divinum auxilium maneat semper nobiscum.

R. Amen.

And after this our exile show unto us the blessed fruit of thy womb, Jesus.

O clement, O loving, O sweet Virgin Mary.

V. Pray for us, O holy Mother of God.

R. That we may be made worthy of the promises of Christ.

Let us pray

ALMIGHTY, everlasting God, Who, by the cooperation of the Holy Ghost, didst so make ready the body and soul of the glorious virgin mother, Mary, that she deserved to become a meet dwelling for Thy Son; grant that we, who rejoice in her memory, may by her loving intercession be delivered from the evils that hang over us, and from everlasting death. Through the same Christ our Lord.

R. Amen.

V. May the divine assistance remain always with us.

R. Amen.

INDEX

H

Father Lasance's Prayer-Books

Leather bindings have gold edges
Other bindings have red edges

MY PRAYER-BOOK. Happiness in Goodness.
16mo. 702 pages. Seal grain cloth, stiff covers, square corners
$1.35; imitation leather, limp, $1.50; real leather, $2.25. EXTRA
LARGE TYPE EDITION. Bindings from $1.75 up.

OUR LADY BOOK. A Book of Special Devotion to Our Lady and a Complete Prayer-Book.
24mo. Imitation leather, $1.85; real leather, $3.00; finer
bindings to $4.75.

MY GOD AND MY ALL. A Prayer-Book for Children.
32mo. 4½x3. Black or white cloth bindings, $0.35; imitation
leather, $0.70; real leather, $1.25; celluloid cover with colored
paper, $1.00.

HOLY SOULS BOOK. Reflections on Purgatory.
A Complete Prayer-Book. Imitation leather, round corners, red
edges, $1.75. Gold edges, $2.25; real leather, gold edges, $3.00;
American Morocco, limp, gold edges, $3.00.

REJOICE IN THE LORD. Happiness in Holiness.
Imitation leather, limp, $1.75; real leather, $3.50.

THE YOUNG MAN'S GUIDE.
THE CATHOLIC GIRL'S GUIDE.
} Same bindings and prices as My Prayer-Book

THE PRISONER OF LOVE.
Imitation leather, limp, $2.00; real leather, $3.00.

MANNA OF THE SOUL.
VEST POCKET EDITION. 384 pages. Oblong 32mo. Cloth, $0.85;
imitation leather, $1.25; real leather, $2.00. THIN EDITION, 272
pages. 24mo. Imitation leather, $1.25; real leather, $2.50.
THIN EDITION, with Epistles and Gospels, 363 pages. 24mo.
Imitation leather, $1.50; real leather, $2.75. EXTRA-LARGE-TYPE
EDITION. 544 pages. Imitation leather, $1.75; real leather, $3.25.

THE NEW MISSAL FOR EVERY DAY.
24mo. 1243 pages. Imitation leather, limp, $2.75; leather, $3.75.

THE SUNDAY MISSAL.
32mo. Imitation leather, limp, $1.90; real leather, $3.50.

WITH GOD.
16mo. Imitation leather, limp, red edges, $2.00; real leather, $3.25.

BLESSED SACRAMENT BOOK.
16mo. Imitation leather, limp, $2.25; real leather, $4.00.

VISITS TO JESUS IN THE TABERNACLE.
16mo. Imitation leather, limp, $2.00; real leather, $3.75.

MANUAL OF THE HOLY EUCHARIST.
24mo. Imitation leather, limp, net, $1.75; leather, net, $3.00.

THE SACRED HEART BOOK.
32mo. Imitation leather, net, $1.75; real leather, net, $3.06.

Bless all my relatives, benefactors, and all those who are in distress and for whom I have promised to pray. Bless me that I may become a saint.

I offer all these prayers to Thee, eternal Father, through Our Lord Jesus Christ. Amen.

At the Epistle

EPISTLE. 1 *Peter* iv. 7-9. *Most dearly beloved:* "Be prudent and watch in prayers. But before all things have a constant mutual charity among yourselves: for charity covereth a multitude of sins.

CPSIA information can be obtained
at www.ICGtesting.com
Printed in the USA
LVHW020836221218
600912LV00009B/375/P